REBELLIONS AND CIVIL WARS

This book analyses all relevant questions of State responsibility and attribution arising from the conduct of rebels and governments in the context of civil wars and rebellions aiming at the establishment of a new government or the creation of a new State. Based on a comprehensive analysis of both old and recent State practice, and case law, including investment awards, as well as the works of scholars and the International Law Commission, the book identifies ten basic rules which can be used by States and international tribunals. It explains the history, content and scope of application of the specific solutions adopted in Article 10 of the International Law Commission Articles on State responsibility to address particular problems. The book also critically revisits some of the solutions that have been put forward by tribunals and scholars, and examines a number of questions which have never been addressed by them before.

PATRICK DUMBERRY is Professor in the Faculty of Law (Civil Law Section) at the University of Ottawa. He received his doctorate at the Graduate Institute of International Studies, Geneva, and has many years of experience in law firms involved in international arbitration. He is the author of more than eighty international law publications, including eight books.

CAMBRIDGE STUDIES IN INTERNATIONAL AND COMPARATIVE LAW: 165

Established in 1946, this series produces high quality, reflective and innovative scholarship in the field of public international law. It publishes works on international law that are of a theoretical, historical, cross-disciplinary or doctrinal nature. The series also welcomes books providing insights from private international law, comparative law and transnational studies which inform international legal thought and practice more generally.

The series seeks to publish views from diverse legal traditions and perspectives, and of any geographical origin. In this respect it invites studies offering regional perspectives on core *problématiques* of international law, and in the same vein, it appreciates contrasts and debates between diverging approaches. Accordingly, books offering new or less orthodox perspectives are very much welcome. Works of a generalist character are greatly valued and the series is also open to studies on specific areas, institutions or problems. Translations of the most outstanding works published in other languages are also considered.

After seventy years, Cambridge Studies in International and Comparative Law sets the standard for international legal scholarship and will continue to define the discipline as it evolves in the years to come.

A list of books in the series can be found at the end of this volume.

REBELLIONS AND CIVIL WARS

State Responsibility for the Conduct of Insurgents

PATRICK DUMBERRY

University of Ottawa

CAMBRIDGE
UNIVERSITY PRESS

CAMBRIDGE
UNIVERSITY PRESS

University Printing House, Cambridge CB2 8BS, United Kingdom

One Liberty Plaza, 20th Floor, New York, NY 10006, USA

477 Williamstown Road, Port Melbourne, VIC 3207, Australia

314–321, 3rd Floor, Plot 3, Splendor Forum, Jasola District Centre, New Delhi – 110025, India

103 Penang Road, #05–06/07, Visioncrest Commercial, Singapore 238467

Cambridge University Press is part of the University of Cambridge.

It furthers the University's mission by disseminating knowledge in the pursuit of education, learning, and research at the highest international levels of excellence.

www.cambridge.org
Information on this title: www.cambridge.org/9781316514979
DOI: 10.1017/9781009091503

First published 2022

A catalogue record for this publication is available from the British Library.

Library of Congress Cataloging-in-Publication Data
Names: Dumberry, Patrick, author.
Title: Rebellions and civil wars : state responsibility for the conduct of insurgents / Patrick Dumberry, University of Ottawa.
Description: Cambridge, United Kingdom ; New York, NY : Cambridge University Press, 2022. | Series: Cambridge studies in international and comparative law ; 165 | Includes index.
Identifiers: LCCN 2021027016 (print) | LCCN 2021027017 (ebook) | ISBN 9781316514979 (hardback) | ISBN 9781009091503 (ebook)
Subjects: LCSH: Insurgency – Law and legislation. | Civil war. | War (International law) | State succession. | Government liability. | Non-state actors (International relations)
Classification: LCC KZ6397 .D86 2022 (print) | LCC KZ6397 (ebook) | DDC 341.6/8–dc23
LC record available at https://lccn.loc.gov/2021027016
LC ebook record available at https://lccn.loc.gov/2021027017

ISBN 978-1-316-51497-9 Hardback

CONTENTS

ACKNOWLEDGEMENTS

This book is the result of more than one year of research undertaken in 2020 in the middle of the COVID global pandemic. I would like to thank the Faculty of Law (Civil Law Section) of the University of Ottawa, my colleagues and the members of the administrative staff for their support throughout the years. I am especially indebted to several bright and talented students from the University of Ottawa who have assisted me over the past year with researching and editing. Their assistance was invaluable to the completion of this book. I want to sincerely thank Sofia Radouane, Anas Slim, Gabrielle Rollin, Olga Abimana, Cezar Iliescu and Sophie Bertrand. All of them have done an amazing job. I would furthermore like to thank all the people at Cambridge University Press (and especially Tom Randall, Laura Blake, Gayathri Tamilselvan and Helen Kitto) for their patience and support during the process of creating this book. More particularly, I would like to express my gratitude to Professors Larissa van den Herik (Leiden University) and Jean d'Aspremont (University of Manchester and Sciences Po Law School), General Editors of the *Cambridge Studies in International and Comparative Law*, for agreeing to publish my book in this prestigious series.

Most importantly, I would like to dedicate this book to my mother and my beautiful, funny and bright children, Ophélie and Florent. Your love and affection have given me the strength to write this book. I hope that one day you will read this book and fully understand the extent to which this whole odyssey would have simply been impossible (and really pointless) without your constant love and support. The 2020–1 COVID global pandemic has been a terrible period for everyone. I consider myself very lucky to have kept my job and stayed healthy. The daily burden of bad news, social distancing and other (seemingly endless) restrictions would have been simply overwhelming without the love and care of my mom, my kids and my friends. The period was also an opportunity to rediscover the simple joy of long walks in the city, playing soccer and hockey outside with my kids, having drinks with friends at the park, etc. While this period was overall (let's be honest) very boring, it also gave me the opportunity to read again great classics (*1984* by Orwell, *The Trial* by Kafka and the entire work of Michel Houellebecq), to watch amazing movies and to confirm that the greatest rock band in the world is Radiohead (Montreal-based Patrick Watson finished second)! A couple of years ago my daughter Ophélie (who is now twelve years old) told me 'Daddy, I personally don't really care what your books are all about, what I am happy about is that you like to write them so much.' She was right back then, and she still is to this day. I truly enjoy writing books. This was especially true in 2020–1 as there was honestly not much else to do. Florent (now ten years old), I promised you a couple of years ago that one day I would write an international law book involving 'Pirates' (and Ninja Turtles . . .). Well, consider it done ;)

Merci à vous deux mes amours!

TABLE OF CASES

Investor-State Arbitration Arbitral Awards

ICJ and PCIJ Cases

Other Arbitral Awards

Domestic Court Decisions

Irish Free State v. Guaranty Safe Deposit Co., United States, 215 N.Y.S. 255 (1927). 337–339

Kaddour case, France, Conseil d'Etat, case no. 04642, 10 May 1968, in Recueil Lebon. 371

Minister of Defence, Namibia v. Mwandinghi, Namibia, 25 October 1991, 1992 (2) SA 355 (NmS), in *ILR* 91. 52, 324, 379

Mutua et al. v. The Foreign and Commonwealth Office, United Kingdom, 21 July 2011, [2011] EWHC 1913 (QB) and of 5 October 2012, [2012] EWHC 2678 (QB), Judgment. 372–375

Mwandinghi v. Minister of Defence, Namibia, Namibia, High Court, 14 December 1990, in 1991 (1) SA 851 (Nm); ILR 91. 52, 324, 379

Perriquet, France, Conseil d'État, case no. 119737, 15 March 1995, in Recueil Lebon. 345

Poldermans v. State of the Netherlands, Netherlands, Court of Appeal of The Hague (First Chamber), 8 December 1955, in N.J. (1959), no. 7 (with an analysis by Boltjes); ILR (1957), p. 69. 382

Poldermans v. State of the Netherlands, Netherlands, Supreme Court, 15 June 1956, in N.J. (1959), no. 7 (with an analysis by Boltjes); ILR (1957). 382

Popp Claim, United States, US International Claims Commission, in Settlements of Claims, 1949–1955, p. 76; ILR (1954), p. 63. 394

Rainoldi *v.* Ministero della Guerra, Italy, Court of First Instance of Brescia, 20 February 1946, in Foro Italiano (1947) I, 151, in Annual Digest (1946). 157

Socony Vacuum Oil Co. Claim, United States, US Foreign Claims Settlement Commission, Award, 1954, in Settlements of Claims, 1949–1955, p. 77; ILR (1954). 176, 336, 372, 386, 387, 393, 401, 402

Thorington v. Smith, United States, 75 U.S. 1, 8 (1868). 103, 171

Union régionale d'Algérie de la C.F.T.C., France, Conseil d'Etat, 5 March 1965, in Ch. Rousseau, 'Jurisprudence française en matière de droit international public', RGDIP (1965). 371

United States v. Rice, United States, Supreme Court, 17 U.S. (4 Wheat.) 246 (1819). Van der Have v. State of the Netherlands, Netherlands, District Court of The Hague, 12 January 1953, in N.J., 1953, no. 133; ILR (1953), p. 80. 176

Versic Claim, United States, US International Claims Commission, in Settlements of Claims, 1949–1955, p. 58; ILR (1954), p. 63. 394

Williams v. Bruffy, United States, 96 U.S. Sup. Ct., 176 (1877). 94, 95, 333, 334, 337, 338

Others

Prosecutor v. Tadić, ICTY, Case No IT-94-1-T, Judgment, Trial Chamber, 7 May 1997, in ILR 112, p. 1, 220–2. 204

Prosecutor v. Haradinaj et al., ICTY, Case No. IT-04-84-T, Trial Chamber I, Judgment, 3 April 2008. 20

ABBREVIATIONS

AAPL case, 1990	Asian Agricultural Products ltd. *v.* Sri Lanka, ICSID Case No ARB/87/3, Final Award, 27 June 1990.
AFDI	Annuaire français de droit international
Affaire des biens britanniques au Maroc espagnol, 1925	Affaire des biens britanniques au Maroc espagnol (Espagne *v.* Royaume-Uni), 1 May 1925, UNRIAA 2.
AJIL	American Journal of International Law
Akehurst, 'State Responsibility'	Akehurst, M., 'State Responsibility for the Wrongful Acts of Rebels – An Aspect of the Southern Rhodesian Problem', *British YIL* 43 (1968–1969).
Al-Ganzory, 'International Claims and Insurgence'	Al-Ganzory, A. A., 'International Claims and Insurgence', *REDI* 33 (1977).
Al-Rashid et al., 'Investment Claims'	Al-Rashid, M., U. Bardyn, and L. Golendukhin, 'Investment Claims amid Civil Unrest: Questions of Attribution and Responsibility', *BCDR International Arbitration Review* 3(2) (2016).
Am. J. Comp. L.	American Journal of Comparative Law
Annuaire IDI	Yearbook of Institute of International Law
Annual Digest	Annual Digest of Public International Law Cases
APSR	American Political Science Review
Arb. Int.	Arbitration International
ASIL Proc.	American Society of International Law Proceedings
Atlam, *Succession d'États*	Atlam, H. M., *Succession d'États et continuité en matière de responsabilité internationale,*

	Doctoral Thesis, Université de droit, d'économie et des sciences d'Aix-Marseille (France) (1986).
Atlam, 'National Liberation Movements'	Atlam, H. M., 'National Liberation Movements and International Responsibility', in M. Spinedi and B. Simma (eds.), *United Nations Codification of State Responsibility* (New York, Oceana, 1987).
Baltic YIL	Baltic Yearbook of International Law
BCDR Int. Arb. Rev.	Bahrain Chamber for Dispute Resolution International Arbitration Review
BITs	Bilateral investment treaties
BIICL	British Institute of International and Comparative Law
Borchard, *The Diplomatic Protection of Citizens Abroad*	Borchard, E. M., *The Diplomatic Protection of Citizens Abroad (or the Law of International Claims)* (New York: The Banks Law Publ., 1915).
Borchard, 'International Pecuniary Claims against Mexico'	Borchard, E. M., 'International Pecuniary Claims against Mexico', *Yale LJ* 26 (1917).
British YIL	British Yearbook of International Law
Cahin, 'Attribution of Conduct to the State'	Cahin, G., 'Attribution of Conduct to the State: Insurrectional Movements', in J. Crawford, A. Pellet, S. Olleson and K. Parlett (eds.), *The Law of International Responsibility* (Oxford University Press, 2010).
Cambridge JICL	Cambridge Journal of International and Comparative Law
Canadian YIL	Canadian Yearbook of International Law
Cengiz case, 2018	Cengiz In$Aat Sanayi VeTicaret A.$. *v.* Libya, International Court of Arbitration of the ICC, Case No. 21537/ZF/AYZ, Final Award, 7 November 2018.
Chinese JIL	Chinese Journal of International Law
CIS	Commonwealth of Independent States
Colum J. Transnat'l L	Columbia Journal of Transnational Law

Columbia JEL	Columbia Journal of European Law
Colum L. Rev.	Colombia Law Review
Comp. & Int'l L.J. S. Afr.	Comparative & International Law Journal of Southern Africa
Conn. L. Rev.	Connecticut Law Review
Corten, *La rébellion et le droit international*	Corten, O., *La rébellion et le droit international: le principe de neutralité en tension* (Pocket Books of The Hague Academy of International Law, Leiden, Brill, 2016).
Crawford, *Brownlie's Principles of Public International Law*	Crawford, J., *Brownlie's Principles of Public International Law* (8th ed., Oxford University Press, 2012).
Crawford, *State Responsibility*	Crawford, J., *State Responsibility: The General Part* (Cambridge University Press, 2013).
Crawford, *The Creation of States in International Law*	Crawford, J., *The Creation of States in International Law* (2nd ed., Oxford University Press, 2006).
Crawford, 'Insurgency'	Crawford, E., 'Insurgency', in *Max Planck Encyclopedia of Public International Law* (Oxford University Press, 2012).
Czaplinski, 'State Succession and State Responsibility'	Czaplinski, W., 'State Succession and State Responsibility', *Canadian YIL* 28 (1990).
d'Aspremont, 'Rebellion and State Responsibility'	d'Aspremont, J., 'Rebellion and State Responsibility: Wrongdoing by Democratically Elected Insurgents', *ICLQ* 58 (2009).
de Beus, *The Jurisprudence of the General Claims Commission*	de Beus, G., *The Jurisprudence of the General Claims Commission United States and Mexico under the Convention of September 8, 1923* (Dordrecht, Nijhoff, 1938).
de Brabandere, 'Host States' Due Diligence Obligations'	de Brabandere, E., 'Host States' Due Diligence Obligations in International

Investment Law', *Syracuse JIL & Commerce* 42(2) (2015).

De Visscher, *Théories et réalités* — De Visscher, C., *Théories et réalités en droit international public* (2nd ed., Paris, Pedone, 1955).

Degan, 'Création et disparition de l'État' — Degan, V. D., 'Création et disparition de l'État (à la lumière du démembrement de trois fédérations multiethniques en Europe)', *Rec des cours* 279 (1999).

Dumberry, 'New State Responsibility' — Dumberry, P., 'New State Responsibility for Internationally Wrongful Acts by an Insurrectional Movement', *EJIL* 17 (2006).

Dumberry, *State Succession to International Responsibility* — Dumberry, P., *State Succession to International Responsibility* (Dordrecht, Martinus Nijhoff, 2007).

Dumberry, *A Guide to State Succession in International Investment Law* — Dumberry, P., *A Guide to State Succession in International Investment Law* (Cheltenham, Edward Elgar Publishing, 2018).

Eagleton, *The Responsibility of States* — Eagleton, C., *The Responsibility of States in International Law* (New York University Press, 1928).

Eatwell, 'State Responsibility, Successful, Insurrectional Movements', — Eatwell, T. J., 'State Responsibility, Successful, Insurrectional Movements and Governments of National Reconciliation', in J. Summers and A. Gough (eds.), *Non-State Actors and International Obligations* (Leiden, Brill, 2018).

Eatwell, *State Responsibility* — Eatwell, T. J., *State Responsibility for the Unlawful Conduct of Armed Groups*, Doctoral Thesis, University of Cambridge (2019), two chapters on file with author.

EJIL	European Journal of International Law
EJIL Talks!	European Journal of International Law: Talks!
Fortin, 'The Relevance of Article 9'	Fortin, K., 'The Relevance of Article 9 of the Articles on State Responsibility for the Internationally Wrongful Acts of Armed Groups', in J. Summers and A. Gough (eds.), *Non-State Actors and International Obligations* (Leiden, Brill Nijhoff, 2018).
FPS	Full protection and security
FTA	Free Trade Agreement
FRY	Federal Republic of Yugoslavia
Garner, 'Responsibility of States'	Garner, J. W., 'Responsibility of States for Injuries Suffered by Foreigners within Their Territories on Account of Mob Violence, Riots and Insurrection', *ASIL Proc.*, 21 (1927).
Geo. Wash. Int'l L. Rev.	George Washington International Law Review
German YIL	German Yearbook of International Law
GPO	Government publication office
Greenman, 'Aliens in Latin America'	Greenman, Kathryn, 'Aliens in Latin America: Intervention, Arbitration and State Responsibility for Rebels', *Leiden JIL* 31 (2018).
Greenman, 'The Secret History'	Greenman, K., 'The Secret History of Successful Rebellions in the Law of State Responsibility', *ESIL Reflections* 6(9) (2017).
Hanse LR	Hanse Law Review
Harvard Draft Convention, 1929	Harvard Draft Convention on the International Responsibility of States for Injuries to Aliens, *AJIL* Spec. Supp. 23 (1929).
Hopkins case, 1926	George W. Hopkins *v.* United Mexican States, US–Mexico Claims Commission, Award of 31 March 1926, UNRIAA 5.
Houghton, 'The Responsibility of the State'	Houghton, N. D., 'The Responsibility of the State for the Acts and Obligations of Local De Facto Governments and

	Revolutionists', *Minnesota LR* 14(3) (1930).
ICC	International Chamber of Commerce
ICJ	International Court of Justice
ICJ, Genocide case, 2015	Application of the Convention on the Prevention and Punishment of the Crime of Genocide (Croatia *v.* Serbia), Judgment of 3 February 2015, ICJ Rep. 2015.
ICJ Rep.	International Court of Justice Reports of Judgments, Advisory Opinions and Orders
ICJ Statute	Statute of the International Court of Justice
ICLQ	International and Comparative Law Quarterly
ICSID Rev	International Centre for Settlement of Investment Disputes Review – Foreign Investment Law Journal
ICSID	International Centre for Settlement of Investment Disputes
IIL	Institute of International Law
IIL, 'Responsabilité internationale des États', 1927	'Responsabilité internationale des États à raison des dommages causés sur leur territoire à la personne et aux biens des étrangers', Resolution of 1927, in *Annuaire IDI* 18(1).
IIL, 'State Succession in Matters of State Responsibility', 2015	'State Succession in Matters of State Responsibility', Rap. M.G. Kohen, 2015, in *Annuaire IDI* 76 (2015), p. 703.
IIL, 'Final Report', 2015	'State Succession in Matters of State Responsibility', Final Report' by Rapporteur M. G. Kohen, 28 June 2015, in: *Annuaire IDI* 76 (2015), p. 511 ff.
ILA	International Law Association
ILA, 'Non State Actors'	'Non State Actors', 3rd Report prepared by Co-Rapporteurs, C. Ryngaert and J. d'Aspremont, Washington Conference (2014).
ILA, 'Study Group on Due Diligence', First Report	'Study Group on Due Diligence in International Law', First Report by

Rapporteur D. French (Chair) and T. Stephens (Rapporteur), 7 March 2014.

ILA, 'Study Group on Due Diligence', Second Report
: 'Study Group on Due Diligence in International Law', Second Report by D. French (Chair) and T. Stephens (Rapporteur), July 2016.

ILC
: International Law Commission

ILC Articles on State Responsibility
: Titles and Texts of the Draft Articles on Responsibility of States for Internationally Wrongful Acts Adopted by the Drafting Committee on Second Reading, fifty-third session, 26 July 2001 (A/56/10).

ILC, Ago Report, 1972
: 'Fourth Report on State Responsibility, by Mr Roberto Ago, Special Rapporteur – The Internationally Wrongful Act of the State, Source of International Responsibility', 30 June 1972 and 9 April 1973, UN Doc. A/CN.4/264 and Add.l, *ILC Yearbook* vol. II (1972)

ILC Commentaries, 2001
: Commentaries to the Draft Articles on Responsibility of States for Internationally Wrongful Acts Adopted by the ILC at its Fifty-Third Session (2001), November 2001

ILC, Crawford First Report, 1998
: 'First Report on State Responsibility, by Mr James Crawford, Special Rapporteur', 24 April, 1, 5, 11 and 26 May, 22 and 24 July, 12 August 1998, UN Doc. A/CN.4/490 and Add. 1–7*, *ILC Yearbook* vol. II (1) (1998)

ILC, First Report Šturma, 2017
: 'First Report on Succession of States in Respect of State Responsibility', by P. Šturma, Special Rapporteur, 69th session, 2017, UN Doc. A/CN.4/708, 31 May 2017

ILC, 'Force majeure and Fortuitous event', 1978
: 'Force majeure and Fortuitous event as Circumstances Precluding Wrongfulness: Survey of State Practice, International Judicial Decisions and Doctrine', Study

	Prepared by the Secretariat, 1978, UN Doc. A/CN.4/315, in *ILC Yearbook* vol. II (1) (1978)
ILC, Garcia Amador Report, 1957	'International Responsibility', Second Report by F.V. Garcia Amador, Special Rapporteur, 15 February 1957, UN Doc. A/CN.4/106, *ILC Yearbook* vol. II (1957), p. 122
ILC, Ninth Report Bedjaoui, 1977	'Ninth Report on Succession of States in Respect of Matters Other than Treaties', by Mr M. Bedjaoui, Special Rapporteur, 1977, UN Doc. A/CN.4/301 and Add.1, *ILC Yearbook* vol. II (1) (1977)
ILC, Second Report Šturma, 2018	'Second Report on Succession of States in Respect of State Responsibility', by P. Šturma, Special Rapporteur, 70th session, A/CN.4/719, 6 April 2018
ILC, Report, 1975	'Report of the International Law Commission on the work of its twenty-seventh session', 5 May–25 July 1975, UN Doc. A/10010/Rev.l, *ILC Yearbook* vol. II (1975)
ILM	International Legal Materials
ILR	International Legal Reports
Int. J. Arab Arb.	International Journal of Arab Arbitration
Iran-US CTR	Iran–United States Claims Tribunal
Italian YIL	Italian Yearbook of International Law
J. Conflict & Security L.	Journal of Conflict & Security Law
J. Int. Arb.	Journal of International Arbitration
J. Int. Criminal Justice	Journal of International Criminal Justice
J. Int. Disp. Settl.	Journal of International Dispute Settlement
J. Int. Humanitarian Legal Stud.	Journal of International Humanitarian Legal Studies
J. World Invest. & Trade	Journal of World Investment & Trade
Kohen and Dumberry, *The Institute of International Law's Resolution*	Kohen, M.G. and P. Dumberry, *The Institute of International Law's Resolution on State Succession and State Responsibility: Introduction, Text and Commentaries* (Cambridge University Press, 2019).

Kolb, *The International Law of State Responsibility*
Kolb, R., *The International Law of State Responsibility: An Introduction* (Cheltenham, Edward Elgar Publishing, 2018).

League of Nations, 1929, 'Basis of Discussion'
League of Nations publication, V. Legal, 1929.V.3, Doc. C.75.M.69.1929.V, p. 107, Preparatory Committee of the Hague Conference for the Codification of International Law, 'Basis of Discussion'.

Leiden JIL — Leiden Journal of International Law

LGDJ — *Librairie générale de droit et de jurisprudence*

LPICT — Law and Practice of International Courts and Tribunals

Magnússon, *Full Protection and Security*
Magnússon, F., *Full Protection and Security in International Law*, PhD Thesis, Vienna University (2012).

Mantilla Blanco, *Full Protection and Security*
Mantilla Blanco, S. *Full Protection and Security in International Investment Law* (Cham, Springer, 2019).

Max Planck UNYB — Max Planck Institute for Comparative Public Law

McNair, *International Law Opinions* — McNair, Lord, *International Law Opinions* (Cambridge University Press, 1956).

Michigan LR — Michigan Law Review

Minnesota LR — Minnesota Law Review

Mohtashami, 'Protecting the Legitimacy of the Arbitral Process'
Mohtashami, R., 'Protecting the Legitimacy of the Arbitral Process: Jurisdictional and Procedural Challenges in Public-Private Disputes', in J. Kalicki and M. A. Raouf (eds.), *Evolution and Adaptation: The Future of International Arbitration* (ICCA Congress Series, Leiden, Kluwer Law International, 2019).

Moore, *Digest of International Law*	Moore, J.B., *Digest of International Law* (Washington DC, GPO, 1906).
Moore, *History and Digest of the International Arbitrations*	Moore, J.B., *History and Digest of the International Arbitrations to which the United States Has Been a Party* (Washington DC, GPO, 1898).
Morris, 'Revolutionary Movements'	Morris, D., 'Revolutionary Movements and De Facto Governments – Implications of the "Arab Spring" for International Investors', *Arbitration International* 28(4) (2012)
MST	Minimum standard of treatment
Nordic JIL	Nordic Journal of International Law
Netherlands ILR	Netherlands International Law Review
O'Connell, *International Law*	O'Connell, D. P., *International Law* (2nd ed., London, Stevens & Sons, vol. II, 1970).
OECD	Organisation for Economic Co-operation and Development
Pace ILR	Pace International Law Review
Pantechniki case, 2009	Pantechniki S.A. Contractors & Engineers *v.* Albania, ICSID Case No. ARB/07/21, Award, 30 July 2009.
PCA	Permanent Court of Arbitration
PCIJ	Permanent Court of International Justice
Piguet, *La Guerre civile en droit international*	Piguet, C., *La Guerre civile en droit international. Contribution à l'étude de la responsabilité internationale de l'Etat à raison des dommages éprouvés sur son territoire par des étrangers, du fait du mouvement insurrectionnel*, Doctoral Thesis, Université de Lausanne (1982).
Pinson case, 1928	Georges Pinson (France) *v.* United Mexican States (Decision No 1), French–Mexican Claims Commission, 10 October 1928, UNRIAA 5
Pisillo-Mazzeschi, 'The Due Diligence Rule'	Pisillo-Mazzeschi, R., 'The Due Diligence Rule and the Nature of the International

	Responsibility of States', *German YIL* 35 (1992)
Prats case, 1868	Salvador Prats *v.* United States, United States–Mexico Mixed Commission, case no. 748, Opinions of Commissioners, 4 July 1868, UNRIAA 29.
RBDI	Revue belge de droit international
Rec. des cours	Collected Courses of the Hague Academy of International Law
REDI	Revue égyptienne de droit international
RGDIP	Revue générale de droit international public
Ryngaert, 'State Responsibility and Non-State Actors'	Ryngaert, C., 'State Responsibility and Non-State Actors', in Math Noortmann, August Reinisch and Cedric Ryngaert (eds.), *Non-State Actors in International Law* (Oxford, Hart Publishing, 2015).
Sambiaggio case, 1903	Sambiaggio case, Italian–Venezuelan Mixed Claims Commission, 1903, UNRIAA 10
Schwarzenberger, *International Law*	Schwarzenberger, Georg, *International Law* (3rd ed., London, Stevens & Sons, vol. I, 1957).
SFRY	Socialist Federal Republic of Yugoslavia
Silvanie, *Responsibility of States*	Silvanie, H., *Responsibility of States for Acts of Unsuccessful Insurgent Governments* (Columbia University Press, 1939).
Silvanie, 'Responsibility of States for Acts of Insurgent Governments'	Silvanie, H., 'Responsibility of States for Acts of Insurgent Governments', *AJIL* 33(1) (1939).
South African YIL	South African Yearbook of International Law
SSRN	Social Science Research Network
Stern, 'Responsabilité internationale'	Stern, B., 'Responsabilité internationale et succession d'Etats', in L. Boisson de Chazournes and V. Gowlland-Debbas (eds.), *The International Legal System in Quest of Equity and Universality / L'ordre juridique international, un système enquête d'équité et d'universalité. Liber*

	amicorum Georges Abi-Saab (Dordrecht, Martinus Nijhoff, 2001).
Strabag case, 2020	Strabag SE *v.* Libya, ICSID Case No. ARB(AF)/15/1, Award, 29 June 2020.
Syracuse JIL & Commerce	Syracuse Journal of International Law & Commerce
Talmon, 'Recognition of Opposition Groups'	Talmon, S., 'Recognition of Opposition Groups as the Legitimate Representative of a People', *Chinese JIL* 12 (2013).
TDM	Transnational Dispute Management Journal
U.C. Davis L. Rev.	University of California (CA) at Davis Law Review
Udina, 'La succession des États'	Udina, M., 'La succession des États quant aux obligations internationales autres que les dettes publiques', *Rec. des cours* 44 (1933-II)
UN	United Nations
UNCITRAL	United Nations Commission on International Trade Law
UNCTAD	United Nations Conference on Trade and Development
UNTS	United Nations Treaty Series
UNRIAA	United Nations Reports of International Arbitral Awards
UKTS	United Kingdom Treaty Series
USSR	Union of Soviet Socialist Republics
US	United States
VCLT	Vienna Convention on the Law of Treaties
VCST	Vienna Convention on Succession of States in Respect of Treaties
Verhoeven, 'International Responsibility'	Verhoeven, S.I., 'International Responsibility of Armed Opposition Groups. Lessons from State Responsibility for Actions of Armed Opposition Groups', in N. Gal-Or, C. Ryngaert and M. Noortmann (eds.), *Responsibilities of the Non-State Actor in Armed Conflict and the Market Place. Theoretical Considerations and*

	Empirical Findings (Leiden, Brill Nijhoff, 2015).
Virginia JIL	Virginia Journal of International Law
Volkovitsch, 'Righting Wrongs'	Volkovitsch, M. J., 'Righting Wrongs: Toward a New Theory of State Succession to Responsibility for International Delicts', *Colum. L. Rev.* 92(8) (1992).
Whiteman, *Digest of International Law*	Whiteman, M. M., *Digest of International Law* (Washington DC, Dept. of State, vol. II, 1973).
Yale Human Rights and Dev. Law J.	Yale Human Rights and Development Law Journal
Yale LJ	Yale Law Journal
Yearbook ILC	Yearbook of the International Law Commission

1

Introduction

1.1 Scope of This Book

1.1.1 What This Book Is About

This book examines the scope and content of Article 10 of the Articles on Responsibility of States for Internationally Wrongful Acts adopted by the International Law Commission in 2001 ('ILC Articles').[1] It analyses all of the relevant questions of State responsibility and attribution arising from the 'conduct' of 'an insurrectional movement' (or 'other movements') in the context of a rebellion or a civil war which results in either the establishment of a new government or the creation of a new State. The aim of the book is to identify the basic rules and principles that have been applied by States in their practice with other States and foreigners in relation to acts committed by insurrectional movements and governments during insurrections. The book will provide an analysis of numerous court decisions which have dealt with matters of responsibility and attribution in the context of rebellions and civil wars. The work of the ILC on Article 10 and the reports of both Special Rapporteurs Ago and Crawford will be analysed in detail. Special attention will also be given to scholarly books and articles which have comprehensively examined the issue.

A few words should be said about what this book does *not* intend to cover.

First, one aspect that this book will not focus on is whether rebels (or other non-State actors) can actually commit internationally wrongful

[1] Draft Articles on Responsibility of States for Internationally Wrongful Acts, Text adopted by the International Law Commission at its fifty-third session, in 2001, and submitted to the General Assembly as a part of the Commission's report covering the work of that session (A/56/10).

acts under international law. I take for granted, like the vast majority of writers, that rebels do have obligations under international law and that, quite logically, they are internationally responsible for any breach of such obligations.[2] As noted by one writer, 'the ILC has clearly accepted the existence of a principle of international responsibility of insurrectional movements, albeit without expressly including it in the text of the Articles'.[3] Crawford also noted that 'international law now apparently contemplates that the insurrectional movement may itself be held internationally responsible for its acts'.[4] This is a matter that I will briefly touch on when examining the consequences arising from the rebels' failed attempt to establish a new government. I will explain that, as a matter of principle, the rebels are responsible for *their own* wrongful acts committed during the insurgency (hereinafter referred to as Rule no. 5).[5] In this context, I will examine the question of whether or not insurgents have any obligations under international law. It should be added that this book is only concerned with the 'collective' responsibility of insurrectional movements *as a group*; it does not address the other question of the *personal individual* responsibility of members of such groups under international criminal law or international human rights law.[6]

Second, the aim of this book is clearly not to provide an assessment of the different types of wrongful acts which rebels can commit during an insurrection. Therefore, I am not going to examine what the different obligations of rebels are in the context of civil wars and rebellions, including in the fields of humanitarian law, international human rights law, etc. While some of the examples of wrongs examined in this book are indeed violations of human rights or the laws of war, this is not a book intended to provide a detailed classification of such wrongs. I am

[2] International Law Commission, 'Report of the International Law Commission on the work of its twenty-seventh session', 5 May–25 July 1975, UN Doc. A/10010/Rev.l, *ILC Yearbook* vol. II (1975) [hereinafter referred to as ILC, Report, 1975], p. 92, para. 4: 'as soon as they begin their separate existence on the international scene, such movements may be capable within certain limits of committing internationally wrongful acts of their own'.

[3] Gérard Cahin, 'The Responsibility of Other Entities: Armed Bands and Criminal Groups', in James Crawford, Alain Pellet, Simon Olleson and Kate Parlett (eds.), *The Law of International Responsibility* (Oxford University Press, 2010), p. 339.

[4] James Crawford, *State Responsibility: The General Part* (Cambridge University Press, 2013), p. 180.

[5] See analysis in Part I, Section 3.2.1.

[6] This question is relevant in the context of a government granting an amnesty to individuals who were former members of an insurgent group. It will be examined in Part I, Section 3.3.3.4.1.

generally interested in *all types* of wrongful acts occurring during civil wars, including pillage, destruction, expropriation and confiscation of property, etc.

Third, while the question of whether rebel groups can be held *directly* responsible under international law for violations they have committed remains controversial,[7] it does not need to be definitely answered in this book. This is because the aim of this book is not to address in great detail the (undeniable) possibility for the victims of wrongful acts committed by rebels to make claims against them *during* the insurgency.[8] Thus, my book focuses on what happens *after* the civil war. As noted by one author, when the rebellion is over 'the movement either wins and then its international responsibility is absorbed into that of a state, or is defeated and then its international responsibility can hardly yield any results since the movement ceases its existence'.[9] I am therefore interested in what happens to the responsibility of rebel groups *after* they have won or lost their struggle.

This book examines a fundamental question: what happens after the end of a civil war in terms of responsibility and attribution of acts (including wrongful acts) committed *by the rebels* during this period of insurgency? The same question will be asked regarding the acts committed *by the government* during the fight against a rebellion. At the heart of this enquiry is the assessment of who is 'responsible' for the consequences

[7] ILA, 'Non State Actors', 3rd Report prepared by Co-Rapporteurs, Cedric Ryngaert and Jean d'Aspremont, Washington Conference (2014), p. 9–10, speaking of the issue 'as very much a question of progressive development of international law' and adding that 'If it were someday established that [rebel groups] can incur direct responsibility under international law – which remains hypothetical in the present state of international law.' See also: S. Verhoeven, 'International Responsibility of Armed Opposition Groups', in N. Gal-Or, C. Ryngaert and M. Noortmann (eds.), *Responsibilities of the Non-State Actor in Armed Conflict and the Market Place* (Leiden, Brill Nijhoff, 2015), p. 297: 'it is unclear that international law recognizes international accountability of insurrectional movements through the invocation of international responsibility of the movement, although there is some limited state practice in this respect, involving insurgents who have control over part of the State's territory'. On this question, see also: A. Bellal, 'Establishing the Direct Responsibility of Non-State Armed Groups for Violations of International Norms: Issues of Attribution', in Gal-Or *et al.*, ibid.; Veronika Bílková, 'Establishing Direct Responsibility of Armed Opposition Groups for Violations of International Humanitarian Law?', in Gal-Or *et al.*, ibid.; A. Clapham, 'Extending International Criminal Responsibility beyond the Individual to Corporations and Armed Opposition Groups', *J. Int. Criminal Justice* 6 (2008), p. 899–926.

[8] The question is examined in Part I, Section 3.2 (Rule no. 5).

[9] E. David, *Principes de droit des conflits armés* (3rd ed., Brussels, Bruylant, 2002), p. 643, quoted (and translated) in ILA, 'Non State Actors', p. 9.

arising from the commission of these acts. This book also addresses the question of whether acts perpetrated by the rebels can be 'attributable' to a State.[10] There is no general answer to this question. Different set of answers and solutions can be contemplated depending on two essential factors:

- Whether the goal of the rebellion was the establishment of a new government or the creation of a new State; and
- Whether the rebels' struggle has actually been successful or not.

This book will therefore examine four different scenarios which can be summarized as follows:

- The aim of the insurrection was the establishment of a new government:
  - The rebels' struggle has been successful; or
  - Their struggle has not been successful.
- The aim of the insurrection was the creation of a new State:
  - The rebels' struggle has been successful; or
  - Their struggle has not been successful.

The book will identify ten basic rules reflecting State practice, case law, the impressive work of the ILC (including the reports of ILC Special Rapporteurs Ago and Crawford) and the work of scholars on all relevant matters of attribution and responsibility arising from the conduct of the rebels and the governments fighting each other during civil wars.

It should be added that I have only found limited existing State practice and case law regarding a number of specific issues. In fact, one of the surprising findings of my research is that many relevant questions have simply never been addressed by scholars in the past.[11] Whenever it is the case, I will explain the rationale and the reasons for adopting my own solution to address these problems. The different solutions adopted in this book are not only based on solid legal precedents, but also on an assessment of what would be the most logical, appropriate, fair and reasonable outcome given the specific circumstances and relevant factors

[10] The difference between 'attribution' and 'responsibility' is further examined in Section 1.1.3.5.

[11] One example concerns the principle whereby whenever a rebel group is successful at creating a new State, the acts committed by the rebels during the insurgency are attributable to the new State (Rule no. 7). The question as to how Rule no. 7 should find application for different types of State succession has never been systematically addressed by scholars. See Part II, Section 4.2.5.

of each situation. Furthermore, my analysis will be guided by the following principles.

First, one important concern which is at the heart of this book is to ensure that the different rules put forward take into account the interests of all the actors involved, that is, not only the rebels and the government which were fighting each other, but also the victims of any wrongful act. This is important given that some of the principles which have been applied by tribunals in the past (and supported by scholars) did not take into account the interests of the victims of wrongs (third States, foreigners). For instance, they often did not provide them with the possibility to seek reparation for the damages suffered. Whenever this is the case, I have examined whether any other alternative solutions could not be more appropriate.[12]

Second, one of the fundamental goals of the rules put forward in this book is to avoid situations where an internationally wrongful act committed during an insurrection would remain unpunished after a government has successfully suppressed a rebellion. I will explain that under international law, a State is responsible for its own failure to exercise its due diligence obligation to protect foreigners and third States in relation to the conduct of the rebels during the insurgency (Rule no. 6).[13] This due diligence obligation requires a State, after the (unsuccessful) insurrection, to adequately punish the perpetrators (individuals, former members of insurgent groups) for the injurious acts committed during the civil war.[14] With this in mind, I will examine whether a State should be considered to have breached its due diligence obligation by granting an amnesty to former rebels.[15] I will also clarify that the grant of an amnesty should only be allowed in a limited number of circumstances. The aim is to avoid, to the extent possible, that wrongs remain unpunished.

[12] One example concerns Rule no. 2 (applicable when the rebels are successful at establishing a new government) whereby the acts committed by the rebels during the insurgency are attributable to the State. According to ILC Special Rapporteur Crawford, there should be an *exception* to Rule no. 2 in the specific context of national reconciliation governments (see Part I, Section 2.2.4.4). In my view, while Crawford's modification proposal should be praised insofar as it provides an 'incentive' for the parties to reach a peace settlement (Section 2.2.4.4.2), it remains problematic given that the modification results in an unsatisfactory outcome for the injured party (Section 2.2.4.4.3). For that reason, I have put forward an alternative solution which would better protect the interests of the victims of wrongs (Section 2.2.4.4.4).

[13] The question is examined in Part I, Section 3.3.

[14] The question is examined in Part I, Section 3.3.3.2.3.

[15] The question is examined in Part I, Section 3.3.3.4.1.

Third, another important concern was to avoid situations where the government, after having successfully defeated a rebellion, would somehow subsequently 'benefit' from some of the actions undertaken by the rebels during this period. The goal is to avoid situations of 'unjust enrichment', a well-known 'general principle of law'.[16] One of the basic rules put forward in this book is that a government that has successfully crushed a rebellion should *not*, as a matter of principle, be 'responsible' for acts committed by rebels during an insurgency (Rule no. 3). These acts are *not attributable* to the State. Yet, I also explain that there should also be some 'exceptions' to this Rule. Thus, a State should be bound by *lawful* 'governmental' 'routine activities' performed by rebels when they have established a local de facto government in a portion of the territory during an insurgency (Rule no. 4A).[17] A State should also provide proper reparation to a foreign investor to compensate any damage suffered as a result of an act of expropriation committed by the rebels whenever it has resulted in some *benefits* for *the State* (Rule no. 4B).[18]

Fourth, another preoccupation was to avoid situations where the normal application of Article 10(1) of the ILC Articles would lead to consequences that could be considered as unfair or unreasonable for the new government established by successful rebels. Thus, one of the most well-established rules is that when the rebels are successful at establishing a new government, that new government remains responsible for the acts committed by the *previous* government in fighting the rebellion (Rule no. 1). I believe that there should be an exception to Rule no. 1: it should not apply to the particular situation of a rebellion overthrowing a racist colonial regime.[19] To take a simple illustration, it would simply be unfair if the wrongful acts committed by the racist regime of South Africa against third parties while fighting the ANC were subsequently attributed to the new government established after the end of Apartheid.

Some of the solutions I have proposed in this book differ from those traditionally supported by scholars. In that sense, some of the findings contained in this book should be seen as a 'progressive development' of the law rather than a codification of existing practices. This is particularly the case in a number of instances where the issue has simply never been addressed by

[16] For an analysis showing that the principle of unjust enrichment is a 'general principle of law', see: Patrick Dumberry, *A Guide to General Principles of Law in International Investment Law* (Oxford University Press, 2020), p. 232.

[17] The question is examined in Part I, Section 3.1.5.

[18] The question is examined in Part I, Section 3.1.6.

[19] The question is examined in Part I, Section 2.1.4.

tribunals. The book is therefore much more than a simple compilation (or a 'recapitulation') of what others have said in the past. It offers a fresh and innovative perspective regarding an old topic.

1.1.2 *The Book Fills a Gap in the Literature*

I believe that this book fills a gap in the literature. While scholars have addressed in great detail numerous theoretical aspects dealing with matters of State responsibility and attribution, they have rarely examined the scope and content of Article 10 of the ILC Articles. Apart from some earlier works published a century ago,[20] very few scholars have examined this question. In fact, the only truly comprehensive studies were published a long time ago. The first book, entirely devoted to the topic, was published by Silvanie in 1939.[21] However, its scope is limited to evaluating situations where the rebels were not successful in their attempts to establish a new government or creating a new State.[22] The second major study is Piguet's PhD thesis published in 1982.[23] My analysis will often rely on these important books. Since then only a few scholars (including myself)[24] have written articles dealing specifically with the issue.[25]

[20] See for instance the following works: Edwin M. Borchard, *The Diplomatic Protection of Citizens Abroad (or the Law of International Claims)* (New York, The Banks Law Publishing Co., 1915); James W. Garner, 'Responsibility of States for Injuries Suffered by Foreigners within Their Territories on Account of Mob Violence, Riots and Insurrection', *ASIL Proc.* 21 (1927); C. Eagleton, *The Responsibility of States in International Law* (New York University Press, 1928).

[21] Haig Silvanie, *Responsibility of States for Acts of Unsuccessful Insurgent Governments* (New York, Columbia University Press, 1939).

[22] See also his article dealing with the question of successful rebellions: Haig Silvanie, 'Responsibility of States for Acts of Insurgent Governments', *AJIL* 33(1) (1939).

[23] Christophe Piguet, *La Guerre civile en droit international. Contribution à l'étude de la responsabilité internationale de l'État à raison des dommages éprouvés sur son territoire par des étrangers, du fait du mouvement insurrectionnel*, Doctoral Thesis, Université de Lausanne, (1982).

[24] P. Dumberry, 'New State Responsibility for Internationally Wrongful Acts by an Insurrectional Movement', *EJIL* 17 (2006), and one chapter in Dumberry, *State Succession to International Responsibility*, p. 224–250.

[25] The most important works include the following: Hazem M. Atlam, 'National Liberation Movements and International Responsibility', in M. Spinedi and B. Simma (eds.), *United Nations Codification of State Responsibility* (New York, Oceana, 1987); Abdel-Azzeem Al-Ganzory, 'International Claims and Insurgence', *REDI* 33 (1977); Michael Akehurst, 'State Responsibility for the Wrongful Acts of Rebels – An Aspect of the Southern Rhodesian Problem', *British YIL* 43 (1968–9); Jean d'Aspremont, 'Rebellion and State Responsibility: Wrongdoing by Democratically Elected Insurgents', *ICLQ* 58 (2009); Gérard Cahin, 'Attribution of Conduct to the State: Insurrectional Movements', in

In this respect, reference should be made to the important work of the ILC on the question,[26] including the 1975 Report[27] and the ILC Commentaries on the final 2001 Articles.[28] The most detailed analysis of the question was undertaken by ILC Special Rapporteur Ago in his 1972 Report.[29] While the ILC 1975 Report heavily relied on the work of Ago, it also differed on a number of accounts.[30] Crawford's analysis, both in his reports as ILC Special Rapporteur[31] and in his subsequent book on State responsibility,[32] also made very important contributions. It should be added that private international law organizations have also examined questions of attribution and responsibility in relation to conduct of rebels. This is indeed the case of the 1929 Harvard 'Draft Convention on the International Responsibility of States for Injuries to Aliens'[33] and its subsequent 1961 draft.[34] The Institute of International law has also examined several aspects relevant to the present discussion in its resolutions adopted in 1927,[35] 1975[36] and 2015.[37] The work

James Crawford, Alain Pellet, Simon Olleson and Kate Parlett (eds.), *The Law of International Responsibility* (Oxford University Press, 2010); Kathryn Greenman, 'The Secret History of Successful Rebellions in the Law of State Responsibility', *ESIL Reflections* 6(9) (2017); Verhoeven, 'International Responsibility of Armed Opposition Groups'.

26 The ILC is a body of experts, elected by the United Nations General Assembly, who are responsible for helping develop and codify international law.

27 ILC, Report, 1975.

28 International Law Commission, 'Commentaries to the Draft Articles on Responsibility of States for Internationally Wrongful Acts Adopted by the ILC at its Fifty-Third Session', November 2001, UN Doc. A/56/10, *ILC Yearbook* vol. II (2) (2001) [hereinafter referred to as ILC, Commentaries, 2001].

29 International Law Commission, 'Fourth Report on State Responsibility, by Mr. Roberto Ago, Special Rapporteur – The Internationally Wrongful Act of the State, Source of International Responsibility', 30 June 1972 and 9 April 1973, UN Doc. A/CN.4/264 and Add.l, *ILC Yearbook*, vol. II (1972) [hereinafter referred to as ILC, Ago Report, 1972].

30 ILC, Report, 1975.

31 See International Law Commission, 'First Report on State Responsibility, by Mr. James Crawford, Special Rapporteur', 24 April, 1, 5, 11 and 26 May, 22 and 24 July, 12 August 1998, UN Doc. A/CN.4/490 and Add. 1–7*, *ILC Yearbook* vol. II(1) (1998), [hereinafter referred to as ILC, Crawford First Report, 1998]; ILC, Commentaries, 2001.

32 Crawford, *State Responsibility*.

33 Harvard Draft Convention on the International Responsibility of States for Injuries to Aliens, *AJIL* Spec. Supp. 23 (1929) also in *ILC Yearbook* vol. II (1956), p. 229.

34 1961 Harvard Draft, in *ILC Yearbook* vol. II (1969).

35 Institute of International Law, 'Responsabilité internationale des États à raison des dommages causés sur leur territoire à la personne et aux biens des étrangers', Resolution of 1927, in *Annuaire IDI* 18(1).

36 Institute of International Law, 'The Principle of Non-Intervention in Civil Wars', Session of Wiesbaden, 1975.

37 Institute of International Law, 'State Succession in Matters of State Responsibility', Rap. M.G. Kohen, 2015, in *Annuaire IDI* 76 (2015), p. 703.

of these organizations is important as they codified existing State practice and case law at the time. They also represent the views of some of the most important international law scholars and experts. The ILC has subsequently relied on these codification efforts when it started examining the matter in the 1970s. I will systematically refer to the works of these organizations throughout the book.

In the past, writers have examined in great detail the rights and obligations of rebels in the specific context of the application of the laws of war, international human rights law and international criminal law. It seems that writers have only focused their attention on the rules prevailing *during* a conflict while leaving aside what happens *after* the uprising ends. Scholars have indeed rarely addressed (with a few exceptions)[38] the more general (and basic) question of who should be held 'responsible' for the acts committed by the rebels when they succeed (or do not succeed) in their struggle to gain power.

One of the reasons often mentioned to explain this general lack of interest regarding the scope and content of Article 10 of the ILC Articles is the near absence of recent practice and case law dealing specifically with this question. Thus, as noted by Eatwell, in recent conflicts 'questions of State responsibility, other than the duty to prosecute and to provide reparation to victims, have been largely ignored'.[39] However, it is no longer the case in the wake of ongoing (or very recent) civil wars in Syria, Libya and Yemen. A number of papers have recently been published following several arbitration claims filed by foreign investors against Libya alleging breaches of BITs committed in the context of the

[38] To the list of writers just mentioned should be added the recent PhD thesis of Eatwell dealing, more generally, with the question of 'State Responsibility for the Unlawful Conduct of Armed Groups', but which contains two chapters devoted to questions examined in this book: T. J. Eatwell, *State Responsibility for the Unlawful Conduct of Armed Groups*, Doctoral Thesis, University of Cambridge (2019), two chapters on file with author. See also: T. J. Eatwell, 'State Responsibility, Successful, Insurrectional Movements and Governments of National Reconciliation', in J. Summers and A. Gough (eds.), *Non-State Actors and International Obligations* (Leiden, Brill, 2018), p. 388. Greenman has also recently addressed the question of the historical developments which led to the emergence of the principles now embodied in Article 10: Kathryn Greenman, *The History and Legacy of State Responsibility for Rebels 1839–1930: Protecting Trade and Investment against Revolution in the Decolonised World*, PhD Thesis, Amsterdam University (2019), which has been published: K. Greenman, *State Responsibility and Rebel: The History and Legacy of Protecting Investment Against Revolution* (Cambridge University Press, 2021). At the time of writing this book, her book had not yet been published. See also: Greenman, 'The Secret History of Successful Rebellions'.

[39] Eatwell, 'State Responsibility, Successful, Insurrectional Movements', p. 398.

civil war in Libya.[40] According to one source, more than twenty cases have been filed against Libya.[41] At the time of writing (end of 2020), a number of awards in these cases had already been rendered (some of them are, however, not publicly available). These awards will be critically examined in this book.[42] These cases are important to the present analysis because they involve several questions at the heart of this book.

This book will provide guidance to States and adjudicators on how to solve State responsibility and attribution issues arising from the conduct of the rebels and the governments fighting each other during civil wars. The goal is also to provide parties to ongoing (and future) arbitration cases involving civil wars, rebellions and revolutions with a comprehensive analysis of all issues relevant to the application of Article 10 of the ILC Articles. It will provide States, foreign investors and arbitrators with indispensable (yet currently scarcely available) tools to enhance their ability to solve disputes between States and foreign investors dealing with this question.[43] Using both classic

[40] Danielle Morris, 'Revolutionary Movements and De Facto Governments – Implications of the "Arab Spring" for International Investors', *Arb. Int.* 28(4) (2012); Finnur Magnusson, 'Investment Protection and Revolutionary Movements', *Scandinavian Studies in Law*, 63 (2017), p. 219–44; Meriam Al-Rashid, Ulyana Bardyn and Levon Golendukhin, 'Investment Claims amid Civil Unrest: Questions of Attribution and Responsibility', *BCDR Int. Arb. Rev.* 3(2) (2016); Noradèle Radjai, Laura Halonen and Panagiotis A. Kyriakou, 'An Analysis of the Compensation Regime Applicable to Claims Arising from Armed Conflicts Affecting Investments in MENA', *BCDR International Arbitration Review* 3(2) (2016). See also: Sebastián Mantilla Blanco, *Full Protection and Security in International Investment Law* (Cham, Springer, 2019), examining these questions in the context of the due diligence obligation embodied in FPS clauses which are typically contained in BITs.

[41] Leonardo Carpentieri, 'The Invocation of State Defenses in Times of Conflict: Force Majeure, Necessity and the Libyan Example', *Int. J. Arab Arb.* 11(2) (2019).

[42] For instance, *Cengiz In$Aat Sanayi VeTicaret A.Ş.* v. *Libya*, International Court of Arbitration of the ICC, Case No. 21537/ZF/AYZ, Final Award, 7 November 2018; *Strabag SE* v. *Libya*, ICSID Case No. ARB(AF)/15/1, Award, 29 June 2020.

[43] Matters of State responsibility and attribution arising in investor-State investment arbitrations are governed by the ILC Articles, including Article 10. As noted by James Crawford, 'Investment Arbitration and the ILC Articles on State Responsibility', *ICSID Rev.* 25(1) (2010), p. 132:

> [q]uestions surrounding attribution are the primary subject area in which arbitral tribunals have referred to the ILC Articles. This is, in principle, a justifiable use of the Articles. In the absence of a lex specialis – such as that found by the Tribunal in UPS v. Canada – the ILC Articles dealing with attribution are regarded by international lawyers and by the International Court of Justice as reflecting customary international law.

BITs are silent on matters of responsibility and attribution arising in the context of rebellions and civil wars. Investment tribunals must therefore refer to Article 10 of the

material[44] and new research tools,[45] I will reassess old (and often almost forgotten) examples of State practice and case law which had been discussed by scholars in the past. This book will show that the findings of these ancient precedents are perfectly applicable to modern international investment law situations where the rebels' struggle is successful (or not) at establishing a new government or creating a new State. The same goes for the analysis of great scholars who have examined these issues for the last 100 years. Their impressive works should not be forgotten during a time when they are most needed by arbitrators. Yet, investment tribunals have so far made almost no reference to these important precedents. I hope the identification of ten basic rules will provide easily accessible guidelines which can be used by all parties involved in arbitration proceedings and State-to-State disputes.

1.1.3 *Essential Definitions*

This section examines the definitions of the following terms and concepts which are relevant to the analysis of Article 10:

- Rebellions and civil wars (Section 1.1.3.1);
- Insurrectional movements and rebels (Section 1.1.3.2);
- The conduct (including wrongful acts) of rebels and governments (Section 1.1.3.3); and
- The establishment of a new government or the creation of a new State (Section 1.1.3.4).

Finally, I will also examine the important difference between matters of 'attribution' and 'responsibility' (Section 1.1.3.5).

ILC Articles to deal with such issues. The ten rules set out in this book will be relevant for tribunals whenever they are examining the scope and content of several clauses found in BITs, including Full Protection and Security, expropriation and 'war losses' clauses. See *Asian Agricultural Products ltd.* v. *Sri Lanka*, ICSID Case No ARB/87/3, Final Award, 27 June 1990, paras. 67 ff.; *Cengiz İnşaat Sanayi veTicaret A.S* v. *Libya*, ICC Case No. 21537/ZF/AYZ, Final Award, 7 Nov. 2018, paras. 410 ff.

[44] I have systematically examined all cases dealing with rebellion and civil war published in law digests, including: Annual Digest of Public International Law Cases, United Nations Reports of International Arbitral Awards (UNRIAA), International Legal Materials (ILM), and International Legal Reports (ILR).

[45] I have examined all cases dealing with rebellion and civil war mentioned in databases, including: Oxford Public International Law, Oxford Reports on International Law in Domestic Courts, Kluwer Arbitration Law, ITAlaw, Investor-State Law Guide, Investment Claims, etc.

1.1.3.1 The Context: Rebellions and Civil Wars

At the outset, it should be highlighted that this book only deals with *internal conflicts* within a State. It does not address conflicts or wars *between* States (i.e. international conflicts). Further, it also does not cover the complex question of interventions by other States in internal civil wars, nor does it address the principle of neutrality which they must observe in such conflicts.[46]

The terms 'insurgency' or 'rebellion' are not clearly defined under international law. According to one writer, an insurgency 'is an uprising or rebellion by an organized group against their government or governing authority', adding that other terms are often used to describe situations of insurgency, such as 'uprising, rebellion, and insurrection'.[47] In fact, the use of certain terms often depends on the scale and intensity of the troubles.[48] From the lowest to the highest scale of the spectrum in terms of intensity, are riots which are followed by rebellions and insurrections leading to full scale revolutions.[49] As a result, rebellions and insurgencies (or insurrections), which are typically used as synonymous, have been described as situations 'when persistent, extensive internal armed violence [are] taking place'.[50] Another relevant concept is 'belligerency'. In a recent book, Rodenhäuser explained (in the context of the development of the laws of war) that rebellions and insurrections were both successive stages which were below the threshold of violence necessary for a conflict to qualify as 'belligerency'.[51] Thus, 'only if the insurgents fulfilled certain criteria, could they be officially, legally recognized as belligerents and be given the protections and rights granted to States under the law of armed conflict'.[52] The classic list of cumulative requirements necessary for recognizing 'belligerency' has been enumerated by Lauterpacht.[53]

46 For a recent and comprehensive analysis of this question, see: O. Corten, *La rébellion et le droit international: le principe de neutralité en tension* (The Pocket Books of The Hague Academy of International Law, Leiden, Brill, 2016).

47 Emily Crawford, 'Insurgency', in *Max Planck Encyclopedia of Public International Law* (Oxford University Press, 2012), para. 1.

48 Piguet, *La Guerre civile en droit international*, p. 15 ff.

49 Ibid.

50 Crawford, 'Insurgency', para. 3.

51 Tilman Rodenhäuser, *Organizing Rebellion: Non-State Armed Groups under International Humanitarian Law, Human Rights Law, and International Criminal Law* (Oxford University Press, 2018), p. 30.

52 Crawford, 'Insurgency', para. 3.

53 Hersch Lauterpacht, *Recognition in International Law* (Cambridge University Press, 1947), p. 176:

As further explained below,[54] the concept of the recognition of 'belligerency' is no longer considered to be an important feature in modern international law. Suffice it to note that in the past recognition of belligerency could have two effects:

- '[W]hen the territorial state recognized the non-state party as a belligerent against which it is engaged in war, the laws of war became applicable between the warring parties'; and
- '[W]hen third parties recognized belligerency between a state and a non-state party, the laws of neutrality became pertinent in the relationship between the recognizing state and the parties to the conflict'.[55]

The concept of 'revolution' has been described as being at the highest scale of the spectrum in terms of intensity. Yet, as noted by the Commission in the *Pinson* case, this term does not have any precise meaning under international law[56] and can hardly be distinguished from the concept of 'insurrection'.[57] In fact, the Commission also explained in the *Pinson* case that international law does not clearly differentiate between the different terms typically used to define such troubles.[58]

The best term to define all these situations of internal troubles is probably 'civil war'. Piguet defined the concept as 'tout conflit armé mettant aux prises le gouvernement établi avec un ou plusieurs mouvements insurrectionnels dont les buts tendent soit à renverser le gouvernement ou le régime de l'État, soit à obtenir la sécession d'une partie de cet

> [F]irst, there must exist within the State an armed conflict of a general (as distinguished from a purely local) character; secondly, the insurgents must occupy and administer a substantial portion of national territory; thirdly, they must conduct the hostilities in accordance with the rules of war and through organized armed forces acting under a responsible authority; fourthly, there must exist circumstances which make it necessary for outside States to define their attitude by means of recognition of belligerency.

[54] See Part I, Section 2.2.4.1.

[55] Rodenhäuser, *Organizing Rebellion*, p. 24.

[56] *Georges Pinson (France)* v. *United Mexican States* (Decision No 1), French–Mexican Claims Commission, 10 October 1928, UNRIAA 5, p. 424.

[57] Ibid., indicating that 'la thèse, suivant la quelle le mot "révolution" aurait, en droit international, un sens bien déterminé, nettement distinct de tous les autres termes en circulation, notamment de "insurrection", est sans fondement' ('the thesis, according to which the word "revolution" would have, in international law, a definite meaning, clearly distinct from all the other terms used, in particular of "insurrection", is without foundation').

[58] Ibid., p. 426.

État'.[59] The expression 'civil war' has been defined by the Institute of International Law in Article 1 of its 1975 resolution on 'The Principle of Non-Intervention in Civil Wars' as follows:

1. For the purposes of this Resolution, the term 'civil war' shall apply to any armed conflict, not of an international character, which breaks out in the territory of a State and in which there is opposition between:
   a) the established government and one or more insurgent movements whose aim is to overthrow the government or the political, economic or social order of the State, or to achieve secession or self-government for any part of that State, or
   b) two or more groups which in the absence of any established government contend with one another for the control of the State.
2. Within the meaning of this Resolution, the term 'civil war' shall not cover:
   a) local disorders or riots;
   b) armed conflicts between political entities which are separated by an international demarcation line or which have existed de facto as States over a prolonged period of time, or conflicts between any such entity and a State;
   c) conflicts arising from decolonization.[60]

It is noteworthy that the expression 'civil war', as defined in that Resolution, does not cover riots or other troubles which are considered to be lower on the intensity scale. It also does not cover 'national liberation' wars in the specific context of decolonization given that they are considered to be *international* conflicts.[61] A number of examples involving Newly Independent States will nevertheless be examined in this book.

In sum, the terms insurgency (or insurrection), rebellion and civil war will be used as synonyms in this book.[62] What really matters is not so

[59] Piguet, *La Guerre civile en droit international*, p. 18 ('any armed conflict between the established government and one or more insurrectionary movements whose aims are either to overthrow the government or the regime of the state, or to obtain the secession of part of that state').

[60] Institute of International Law, 'The Principle of Non-Intervention in Civil Wars', Session of Wiesbaden – 1975, Art. 1.

[61] The question is examined in Piguet, *La Guerre civile en droit international*, p. 19 ff.

[62] A.C. Bundu, 'Recognition of Revolutionary Authorities: Law and Practice of States', *ICLQ* 27(1) (1978), p. 20–21, noting that 'a variety of terminology is often used to describe revolutionary change of government' (referring to these terms: insurrection, rebellion, military coup d'État, civil war, civil strife, revolution, revolt, war of national liberation) and concluding that 'in international law, it is doubtful whether any useful purpose can be achieved by attempting precise distinctions of legal meaning between these term'. See

much how to qualify the conflict, but rather to examine whether the main actors involved in it fulfil the basic conditions for the events to be considered as something more than mere troubles or riots and, therefore, be covered by Article 10 of the ILC Articles. This question is further examined in the next section.

1.1.3.2 The Actors: 'Insurrectional Movements', Rebels and Insurgents

A civil war involves an armed conflict which opposes two adversaries. On the one hand, there is the established government fighting to stay in power. Different terms have been used to describe this entity: central government, legitimate government,[63] government in charge, etc. I will simply use the term 'government' in this book. On the other hand, a non-State actor is fighting to get into power and defeat the government. Many terms have been used to describe this group: insurgents, rebels, insurrectional movements, etc. For reasons explained in the next paragraphs, all these expressions will be used as synonyms in this book.

The term 'insurrectional movement' has been used by both ILC Special Rapporteurs Ago and Crawford throughout their works on Article 10. While some ILC members contested the use of the term (for being somewhat 'outdated' and no longer relevant today,[64] or for having a 'negative connotation'),[65] the Drafting Committee nevertheless decided in 2001 to keep this expression in the final text.

also, p. 24 ('not only is there no generally agreed legal definition of the terms "insurrection", "rebellion" and "civil war", etc., but that it is irrelevant in international law which term is chosen to describe a particular situation of civil strife').

63 The expression is sometimes used by Ago. See for instance: ILC, Ago Report, 1972, p. 130, para. 155; ibid., p. 151, para. 213.

64 See the comment made by Dugard in 'Summary Records of the Meetings of the Fiftieth Session', 2556th meeting, 5 August 1998, UN Doc. A/CN.4/SER.A/1998, *ILC Yearbook* vol. I (1998), p. 249, at p. 251 (para. 9). The same position was adopted by Mikulka (ibid., para. 25: '[t]he draft articles were 20 years old, and their terminology was a little dated. The new situations which had emerged in the meantime justified new approaches to the legal concept of insurrectional movement and the adaptation of the draft articles, to bring them up to date, as it were'). On this point, another member (Simma) responded (ibid., para. 16) that the term 'insurrectional movement' 'was already an old term but that "national liberation movement" was scarcely less old'.

65 See the comment made by Pellet, in ibid., p. 255 (para. 52), indicating that 'insurrectional movement' had a negative connotation, whereas 'national liberation movement' had 'a rather positive one' and therefore proposing 'that the language of the new article 15 should be amended by inserting "of a national liberation movement or" before "an insurrectional movement"'.

In order to avoid this contentious issue, the 1975 ILC Report indicates that the question of defining 'insurrectional movement' was beyond the scope of its report.[66] This lack of definition has been mentioned by d'Aspremont as a main 'uncertainty pertaining to [the] precise scope of application [of Article 10(1) which] constitutes a more serious impediment to its application as well as its crystallization into a rule of customary international law'.[67] The ILC only went so far as to indicate that, in the context of Article 10, no distinction should be made between insurrectional movements which may be considered to be 'legitimate' and those which may not.[68] As further discussed below,[69] the provision covers both situations. The ILC Commentaries explained that the term 'insurrectional movement' was meant to be neutral and aimed at encompassing different situations.[70]

The wide scope of application of the provision is even more evident at paragraph 2 of Article 10 (dealing with insurrections leading to the creation of new States) given that the provision speaks of insurrectional movements as well as 'other' movements. This was meant to include national liberation movements fighting for independence in the context of decolonization.

Yet, the scope of the expression 'insurrectional movement' is not unlimited either. The Commentaries of the ILC explain that Article 10 does *not* cover 'situations of internal disturbances and tensions, such as riots, isolated and sporadic acts of violence and other acts of a similar nature'.[71] The Commentaries also indicate that Article 10 does not 'extend to encompass the actions of a group of citizens advocating separation or revolution'.[72] In

66 ILC, Report, 1975, p. 92, paras. 5–6.

67 d'Aspremont, 'Rebellion and State Responsibility', p. 433.

68 ILC, Commentaries, 2001, p. 51, para. 11.

69 See Part II, Sections 4.2.3.2.2 and 4.2.5.2.1.

70 ILC, Commentaries, 2001, p. 51, para. 9:

> A comprehensive definition of the types of groups encompassed by the term 'insurrectional movement' as used in article 10 is made difficult by the wide variety of forms which insurrectional movements may take in practice, according to whether there is relatively limited internal unrest, a genuine civil war situation, an anti-colonial struggle, the action of a national liberation front, revolutionary or counter-revolutionary movements and so on.

71 Ibid., p. 51, para. 10, referring to the language used in the Protocol Additional to the Geneva Conventions of 12 August 1949, and relating to the protection of victims of non-international armed conflicts (Protocol II), Art. 1(1).

72 ILC, Commentaries, 2001, p. 51, para. 10.

other words, the term 'insurrectional movement' does not cover groups and political parties which are merely advocating political changes or secession by non-violent means. Something more is required (a point further examined in the next paragraphs).

Scholars have long explained the different nature of mob or riot violence as compared to actions of insurgents.[73] This distinction is essential in terms of State responsibility and matters of attribution under international law. As a matter of principle, a State is not responsible for the acts of individuals (such as rioters) that are not organs of the State.[74] However, at the same time, a government must always exercise its due diligence duty to protect foreigners. A government's failure to prevent and/or suppress mob or riot violence may, depending on the circumstances, be considered as a breach of its due diligence obligation[75] Whenever this is the case, the government will be responsible for the consequences arising from the acts of mobsters committed against foreigners or third States.[76] The situation is somewhat different once a group is *organized enough* to be considered as an 'insurrectional

[73] Garner, 'Responsibility of States', p. 55:

> [t]hose committed by mobs differ also from those committed by insurgents in that the former are the acts usually of a relatively small number of persons excited and inflamed by some act or conduct on the part of the victim or victims and are often directed exclusively against such persons mainly because they are foreigners. The injuries committed by insurgents, on the other hand, are the acts of larger numbers of persons who are in revolt against the established authority; they are not necessarily assimilable to the acts of murderers; they are usually not committed by men in disguise; their object is not private vengeance, but the overthrow of the government; and they are not ordinarily directed against foreigners as such but are usually the incidental result of the military operations of the insurgent forces against the government.

[74] This question is further examined in Section 1.1.3.5.

[75] Charles De Visscher, *Théories et réalités en droit international public* (2nd ed., Paris, Pedone, 1955), p. 349.

[76] D.P. O'Connell, *International Law* (2nd ed., London, Stevens and Sons, vol. II, 1970), p. 968. See Garner, 'Responsibility of States', p. 57:

> [a]s to the responsibility for injuries suffered by aliens on account of acts committed by mobs, the now generally accepted rule is that the state is liable to make reparation where it can be held to have been at fault, as where there has been lack of due diligence on the part of the proper authorities to prevent the injury, and when they themselves have been accomplices directly or indirectly the liability is of course all the greater.

movement'. This organizational 'transformation' has been well-described by the ILC in its 1975 Report.[77]

What is the impact of this organizational development in terms of State responsibility? As noted by O'Connell, 'when the group acquires such cohesion and relative independence of control as to be designated insurgents the State *ceases to be responsible* for their wrongful actions, unless they successfully substitute themselves in the government of the country'.[78] Thus, the more organized and structured the rebels become while the insurrection increases in terms of strength and magnitude, the more likely the government is to have lost control over parts of its territory. Whenever this is the case, the government will be unable to exercise its due diligence obligation towards foreigners and third States. In the words of De Visscher, an insurrection 'aggravent les charges des autorités et restreignent les moyens d'actions' ('increases the burden on the governmental authorities and restrict its means of action').[79] This loss of control has a direct impact on State responsibility. In the *Prats* case, decided by the United States-Mexico Mixed Commission, Mexican Commissioner, Mr Palacio, explained that 'the duty of the government must be measured in accordance with' a new situation of a 'state of war' and that 'its responsibility must be determined without losing sight of that important fact'.[80] As noted by Huber in the *Spanish Zone of Morocco Claims*, in the context of a rebellion 'la responsabilité est limitée parce que la puissance publique se trouve en présence d'une résistance exceptionnelle' ('the liability is limited because the public

[77] ILC, Report, 1975, p. 91, para. 3:

> It is true that, at the beginning of the insurrection, the conduct of persons or groups of persons who thereafter become organs of an insurrectional movement presents itself as the conduct of private individuals. For the purposes of attribution of an act to the State as a possible source of international responsibility, such conduct can in fact be placed on the same footing as that of persons or groups of persons who participate in a riot or mass demonstration and, like the conduct of such persons . . .. But the situation changes as soon as an insurrectional movement, in the sense which this term has in international law, takes shape. From this time on there is in existence, side by side with the State, an organization which has its own machinery and whose organs may act on behalf of the insurrectional movement itself in a portion of the territory under the sovereignty or administration of the State.

[78] O'Connell, *International Law*, p. 969, emphasis added.

[79] De Visscher, *Théories et réalités*, p. 350.

[80] *Salvador Prats* v. *United States*, United States-Mexico Mixed Commission, Case no. 748, UNRIAA 29, Mexican Commissioner, Mr. Palacio, p. 197–8.

authorities find themselves in the presence of exceptional resistance').[81] This point has also been well-explained by Eagleton.[82]

The qualification of a group as an 'insurrectional movement' therefore becomes essential, precisely because of the impact it has on matters of State responsibility. Cahin accurately noted that Article 10 'leaves open the question of the moment at which an opposition group may be characterized as an insurrectional movement'.[83] In his First Report, Crawford also mentioned that the provision does *not* 'define the point at which an opposition group within a State qualifies as an "insurrectional movement"', adding that 'this is a matter which can only be determined on the basis of the facts in each case'.[84] This is obviously correct.[85]

While Article 10 is silent on this important point, there is no doubt that a certain threshold (or a 'minimum' level)[86] of *intensity of combats* is required. Ago speaks of a 'quantitative difference – determined by the intensity of the disruption' between an insurrection and a riot.[87] Thus, as noted by one writer, 'the intensity of armed resistance has to amount to a non-international armed conflict' which means that 'riots, violent demonstrations, civil disturbances and short-lived revolutions' are not covered by the provision.[88]

It is also clear that a certain threshold of organization and structure needs to be reached by a movement in order for its actions to be deemed covered by Article 10. The ILC Commentaries indicated what that

[81] *Affaire des biens britanniques au Maroc espagnol (Espagne* v. *Royaume-Uni),* 1 May 1925, UNRIAA 2, p. 644.

[82] Eagleton, *The Responsibility of States*, p. 138:

> But while in the case of mob injuries the result is almost always to fix responsibility upon the state, the operation of the same rules, due to quite different factors, produces very nearly the opposite results in the case of civil war injuries. Belligerent action represents the extreme extent of injury which can be occasioned within a state; but it also necessarily calls into play the utmost energies of the state, with the result that lack of due diligence can rarely be imputed to the state.

[83] Cahin, 'Attribution of Conduct to the State', p. 248.

[84] ILC, Crawford First Report, 1998, note no. 3 to new Draft Article 15, p. 57.

[85] Cahin, 'Attribution of Conduct to the State', p. 252: 'the determination of the moment in which an opposition group may be characterized as an insurrectional movement for the purposes of attribution of conduct depends less on a categorical determination than on a case-by-case pragmatic approach'.

[86] Eatwell, *State Responsibility*, p. 178.

[87] ILC, Ago Report, 1972, p. 129, para. 153.

[88] Verhoeven, 'International Responsibility', p. 289.

threshold is. It mentions that the definition of 'dissident armed forces' contained in the Protocol Additional to the Geneva Conventions of 12 August 1949, and relating to the protection of victims of non-international armed conflicts (Protocol II)[89] 'may be taken as a guide' for the application of Article 10 since it reflects the 'essential idea of an insurrectional movement'.[90] Article 1(2) of the Protocol defines 'dissident armed forces or other organized armed groups' as those 'which, under responsible command, exercise such control over a part of [the relevant State's] territory as to enable them to carry out sustained and concerted military operations and to implement this Protocol'.[91] The ILC Commentaries' *renvoi* to this definition means, in practical terms, that the essential characteristics of an insurrectional movement are the following:

- An armed forces or group;
- Which is 'sufficiently organized' to be able to confront the government by military means;[92]

[89] Protocol Additional to the Geneva Conventions of 12 August 1949, and relating to the protection of victims of non-international armed conflicts (Protocol II).

[90] ILC, Commentaries, 2001, p. 51, para. 9. See also: R. Kolb, *The International Law of State Responsibility: An Introduction* (Cheltenham, Edward Elgar, 2018), p. 95; Eatwell, *State Responsibility for the Unlawful Conduct of Armed Groups*, p. 178.

[91] Protocol Additional to the Geneva Conventions of 12 August 1949, and relating to the protection of victims of non-international armed conflicts (Protocol II).

[92] What that means has been well-explained by the International Criminal Tribunal for the former Yugoslavia (ICTY) in *Prosecutor* v. *Haradinaj et al.*, Case No. IT-04–84-T, Trial Chamber I, Judgment, 3 April 2008, para. 60:

> [t]hese cases highlight the principle that an armed conflict can exist only between parties that are sufficiently organized to confront each other with military means. State governmental authorities have been presumed to dispose of armed forces that satisfy this criterion. As for armed groups, Trial Chambers have relied on several indicative factors, none of which are, in themselves, essential to establish whether the 'organization' criterion is fulfilled. Such indicative factors include the existence of a command structure and disciplinary rules and mechanisms within the group; the existence of a headquarters; the fact that the group controls a certain territory; the ability of the group to gain access to weapons, other military equipment, recruits and military training; its ability to plan, coordinate and carry out military operations, including troop movements and logistics; its ability to define a unified military strategy and use military tactics; and its ability to speak with one voice and negotiate and conclude agreements such as cease-fire or peace accords.

On this point, see: Verhoeven, 'International Responsibility of Armed Opposition Groups', p. 289.

- Which exercises control over a part of the State's territory[93] as to enable it to carry out sustained and concerted military operations;[94] and
- Which is able to implement the application of the laws of armed conflict contained in the Protocol Additional to the Geneva Conventions.

This *renvoi* provides useful guidance to define the concept of insurrectional movement for the purposes of the application of Article 10.[95] For instance, it helps to clarify that the participants in the recent uprisings during the 'Arab Spring' (2010–11) would probably not fit the definition of an 'insurrectional movement'.[96] Similarly, a coup d'État conducted by members of the armed forces or by government officials would not be covered by Article 10.[97] However, it has been argued by

[93] It should be added that the scope of Article 10 is actually broader. Thus, the 1975 ILC Report (p. 92, para. 7; p. 99, para. 29) mentioned that the provision also covers the situation where an 'insurrectional movement operates in, or from within, a third State' and is fighting the government of another State where it wants to gain power. See also, ILC, Crawford First Report, 1998, p. 52, para. 269: 'insurrectional movements are intended to be covered whether they are based on the territory of the "target" State or on the territory of a third State'.

[94] O'Connell, *International Law*, p. 969, referring to the 'formidable character of the uprising, the rapidity of the movement, the immobilising of government forces, and the exclusion of governmental control from the area in question'.

[95] Cahin, 'Attribution of Conduct to the State', p. 252, noting that 'the International Criminal Tribunal for Rwanda considered that the Rwandese Patriotic Front (RPF) met these conditions, and the competent organs of the UN and the OAS considered that the Sudanese People's Liberation Movement, the FMLN in Salvador, and the armed opposition groups in Colombia also did so'.

[96] Eatwell, *State Responsibility*, p. 178–9:

> [i]t would appear from the [ILC] Commentary that the conduct of political opposition groups in Tunisia, Egypt and Yemen that successfully deposed the former governments through mass demonstrations in 2010 and 2011 in circumstances that did not cross the threshold of armed conflict would not be attributable to the state. In each of these cases, an identifiable political group took over government. However, that group's success rode on the wave of the masses. This gives rise to the question whether the organisation that succeeds to government as a result of revolution, whatever the form that revolution may take, should fall within the definition of insurrectional movement. The reliance by the [ILC] Commentary on [the Protocol] as a guide would appear to exclude the possibility that mass demonstrations, even ones that entail the commission acts of violence or damage to property by participants in those demonstrations will fall within the definition of 'insurrectional movement'.

[97] d'Aspremont, 'Rebellion and State Responsibility', 435; Verhoeven, 'International Responsibility', p. 289.

one writer that the definition seems 'to limit the envisaged situations to those of a large-scale civil war',[98] and, by another one, that the provision should also apply to situations where the rebels succeed 'in taking over a government by a short, sharp insurrection, rather than an enduring civil war'.[99]

One fundamental characteristic of an insurrectional movement, which appears implicitly in the elements listed above, is the identification of the *goal* of the uprising. This book only focuses on armed groups with the objective of taking power by force to either replace the government or create a new State.[100] As noted by Schwarzenberger, 'this purpose distinguishes them from mere bandits and robbers'.[101] While this distinction is not always easy to make in practice,[102] focusing on this purpose remains essential to define insurrectional movements as illustrated by the *Pinson*

[98] Cahin, 'Attribution of Conduct to the State', p. 252.

[99] Eatwell, *State Responsibility*, p. 174, noting that the February 1917 Revolution in Russia lasted only one week.

[100] Verhoeven, 'International Responsibility', p. 289, 295, noting that 'not all insurrectional movements have the objective to replace the government or to create a new State', and that some may 'fight for more autonomy, better minority protection, or for a better redistribution of national resources'. On the importance of this element, see: Piguet, *La Guerre civile en droit international*, p. 23; Silvanie, 'Responsibility of States for Acts of Insurgent Governments', p. 78. One US domestic court decision involving the scope of an insurance policy covering buildings destroyed by fire mentioned: '[We] think the district [Court] judge correctly told the jury that, to constitute an insurrection or rebellion within the meaning of these policies, there must have been a movement accompanying actions specifically *intended to overthrow the constituted Government and take possession of the inherent powers thereof*. (*Home Insurance Company of New York* v. *Davila*, 212 F.2d 731 (1st Cir. 1954), p. 736, emphasis added).

[101] Georg Schwarzenberger, *International Law* (3rd ed., London, Stevens and Sons, vol. I, 1957), p. 627. The latter group is examined in Cahin, 'The Responsibility of Other Entities: Armed Bands and Criminal Groups'.

[102] Cahin, ibid., p. 334:

> [t]he characteristics of modern armed conflict put this distinction, which is a priori clear cut, into perspective. Numerous insurrectional movements turn to criminal activities in order to finance the war they are waging against established authority, including by trafficking of diamonds, as practiced by UNITA in Angola and the RUF in Sierra Leone, or trafficking of drugs as practised by the Shining Path in Peru, FARC in Colombia, or the UCK in Kosovo.

The *Santa Isabel* case (*Cornelia J. Pringle, et al., (Santa Isabel Claims) (U.S.A.)* v. *United Mexican States*, UNRIAA 4, 83 ff.) is a good example where the Commission distinguished the two groups. The case is examined in Silvanie, *Responsibility of States*, p. 206.

case,[103] and the above-mentioned definition of 'civil war' adopted by the Institute in 1975.[104]

Finally, reference should be made to Ago's theory according to which an insurrectional movement is a separate *subject* of international law.[105] He believes that their actions 'are different from those committed by individuals or groups of individuals during a riot or demonstrations by a rebellious mob';[106] rather they are those of 'organs of a subject of international law other than the State'.[107] Consequently, 'to the extent allowed by its limited international capacity, this subject is perfectly capable of committing internationally wrongful acts'.[108] This theory was later abandoned by the ILC in its 1975 Draft Articles. As further discussed below, Crawford did not use the concept of international legal personality.[109] It follows that an insurrectional movement does not need to be recognized as such by the government against which it is fighting (or by other States) for Article 10 to apply.[110]

1.1.3.3 The Action: Conduct (Including Wrongful Acts) of Rebels and Governments

This book focuses on *wrongful* acts committed by both the rebels and the government when fighting for power. Two remarks should be made at this juncture.

First, I will specifically examine the fate of wrongs that affect a *third* party (i.e. neither the rebels nor the government). In other words, this book focuses on wrongs committed by the rebels or the government that have caused damages to *another* State (not involved in the conflict) or to

103 *Georges Pinson (France)* v. *United Mexican States* (Decision No 1), French-Mexican Claims Commission, 10 October 1928, UNRIAA 5, p. 424.

104 Institute of International Law, 'The Principle of Non-Intervention in Civil Wars', Article 1, defining civil war as an armed conflict between the government and an insurgent movement whose 'aim is to overthrow the government or the political, economic or social order of the State, or to achieve secession or self-government for any part of that State'.

105 He speaks of the 'very existence, parallel with the State and in a portion of the territory under its sovereignty of a *separate subject of international law*' (ILC, Ago Report, 1972, p. 129, para. 153, emphasis added).

106 Ibid., p. 139, para. 180.

107 Ibid., p. 139, para. 180.

108 Ibid., p. 129, para. 153.

109 ILC, Crawford First Report, 1998, p. 52, para. 270, noting that 'even a movement which clearly possessed all the characteristics listed in article 1, paragraph 2 [of the Protocol], would not necessarily be regarded as having international legal personality'.

110 Eatwell, *State Responsibility*, p. 177, noting that the 'recognition of the international legal personality of insurrectional movements appears to have fallen into disuse'.

foreigners (including foreign investors). This book does not intend to examine wrongful acts that have been committed by either the rebels or the government against the *local population* of the territory where the insurgency is taking place. While some of the cases examined in this book do involve such wrongs (for instance, in the context of the rebellion of the FLN fighting for the independence of Algeria), my intention is not to specifically analyse human rights abuses committed by either parties to the conflict.

Second, I do not intend to examine wrongs that are committed by one party and that directly affect its adversaries in the conflict. Thus, I will not examine the outcome of wrongs committed by the government that result in a direct damage to the rebels themselves (or vice versa).[111] While some of the examples of State practice analysed in this book involve such 'war damages', the focus of my book is not on them. I am also not going to examine breach of agreements (armistice, cease fire, etc.) concluded by insurgents with States.

At the outset, it must be highlighted that my analysis will not be limited only to *wrongful* acts. I will show that the term 'conduct' used in Article 10 of the ILC Articles was meant to include all acts performed or done by an insurrectional movement during a rebellion. I will show that even when an insurrection by rebels to overthrow the government is ultimately unsuccessful, the State should still be bound by the 'governmental' lawful 'routine activities' performed by rebels in situations where they have established a local de facto government in part of the territory.[112] In this context, I will discuss whether the concept of 'routine activities' includes taxes, customs duties, debts and loans, as well as contracts and concession agreements.

Finally, the term 'conduct' used in Article 10 of the ILC Articles not only covers actions by either the rebels or the government, but also 'omissions'. This category will be particularly relevant when assessing

[111] What this book does (and does not) cover can be illustrated by using the simple illustration of the rebellion of the FLN insurgent group fighting for the independence of Algeria. I am interested in matters of State responsibility and attribution arising from the commission of wrongs by the FLN in the context of its armed struggle against France, which caused damages to other States (say, the destruction of the German consulate) or to foreigners (say, the pillage or the expropriation of a factory belonging to a German investor). I will also examine the reverse situation of wrongs committed by France while fighting the rebels which caused damages to third parties. I will not, however, examine wrongs committed by France which have directly affected the FLN (such as the killing of rebel members, the destruction of property belonging to the FLN, etc.) (or vice versa).

[112] See Part I, Section 3.1.5 (Rule no. 4A).

whether a State has failed to discharge its due diligence duty of vigilance, prevention and punishment towards foreigners and third States in relation to the conduct of rebels. I will show that in some circumstances, doing nothing can be considered as a violation of international law.

1.1.3.4 The Outcome: The Establishment of a New Government or the Creation of a New State

The present book deals with two distinct phenomena resulting from a successful rebellion undertaken by insurgents. The rebels' victory may lead to the establishment of a new *government* (Part I) or result in the creation of a new *State* (Part II). These two different outcomes must be clearly distinguished.

The term 'State succession' refers to 'the replacement of one State by another in the responsibility for the international relations of territory'. This definition of 'succession of States' was coined by the ILC in different instruments dealing with the issue.[113] The same definition was adopted by the Institute in its Resolutions in 2001[114] and in 2015.[115] The creation of a new State (such as in the case of secession) is a typical situation of State succession.[116] This situation (examined in Part II) needs to be clearly distinguished from other cases where there is, on the contrary, *continuity* of State.[117] Thus, a State may be affected by important changes, but its legal identity can nevertheless remain intact.[118] One

[113] Article 2(1)b), *Vienna Convention on Succession of States in Respect of Treaties*, signed on 23 August 1978 and entered into force on 6 November 1996, 1946 UNTS 3, in *ILM* 17 (1978), p. 1488; Article 2(1)a) of the 1983 *Vienna Convention on Succession of States in Respect of State Properties, Archives and Debts*, in *ILM* 22 (1983), p. 306. The same definition can also be found in Article 2 of the *Draft Articles on Nationality of Natural Persons in Relation to the Succession of States*, adopted by the ILC on second reading in 1999, ILC Report, UN Doc. A/54/10, 1999, ch. IV, in *ILC Yearbook* vol. II (1997). See also: ILC, 'First Report on Succession of States in respect of State Responsibility', by Special Rapporteur Pavel Šturma, 69th session, 2017, UN Doc. A/CN.4/708, 31 May 2017.

[114] Institute of International Law, 'State Succession in Matters of Property and Debts', Session of Vancouver, 2001, in *Annuaire IDI* 69 (2000–2001), p. 713 ff.

[115] Institute of International Law 'State Succession in Matters of State Responsibility', Rap. M. G. Kohen, 2015, in *Annuaire IDI* 76 (2015), p. 703. Art. 1.

[116] As further examined below, not all types of State succession involve the creation of a new State. Transfer of territory and incorporation of States are good examples.

[117] A. Zimmermann, 'Continuity of States', *Max Planck Encyclopedia of Public International Law* (Oxford University Press, online ed., 2006), para. 6 ('As a matter of principle, State continuity and State succession are mutually exclusive concepts').

[118] On the concept of 'identity' of States, see: Krystyna Marek, *Identity and Continuity of States in Public International Law* (Geneva, Librairie Droz, 1968).

example is a change of government, which does not result in the creation of a new State. This situation is examined in Part I.

To assess any question relating to State identity, one must examine the characteristics of an entity at two different moments in time: before and after the events taking place at a certain date. In other words, one must analyse whether the State can be considered as the *same* State before and after the events that led to the territorial transformation.[119] When the two entities, examined at two different moments, are considered to be 'identical', this means that there is a 'continuing' international legal personality. In other words, because there is an 'identity' of State (i.e., that it is the same State), it follows that there is a 'continuity' of that State's international personality.[120] When this is the case, no issue of succession arises. In practical terms, State identity means that this entity continues having the same rights and obligations.[121] Yet, it should be added that qualifying two entities as 'identical' at two different points in time is, of course, a legal fiction.[122] I have examined elsewhere the most important criteria which have been put forward by scholars to distinguish between cases of continuity and those of discontinuity.[123] They include changes

[119] W. Czaplinski, 'La continuité, l'identité et la succession d'États: évaluation de cas récents', *RBDI* 26 (1993), p. 374.

[120] Marek, *Identity and Continuity of States*, p. 6 ('there can obviously be no continuity without identity').

[121] Zimmermann, 'Continuity of States', para. 6.

[122] Brigitte Stern, 'La succession d'États', *Rec des cours*, t. 262 (1996), p. 40; Czaplinski, 'La continuité', p. 374. The State that exists after the events is necessarily not perfectly 'identical' to the one that existed prior to the territorial changes. Thus, the very question of continuity arises because some doubt may exist as to whether two entities are in fact truly identical. In other words, no question of continuity arises when a State's borders have not been altered in the slightest. For example, no one is doubting or questioning whether there is State identity between France in 2010 and France in 2012: it is clearly the same State. The relevant question to be asked is therefore not whether two entities are 'identical' per se, but rather whether they can be considered as the 'same' State (having the same international legal personality) *despite* substantial changes to its territory and government. As explained by Stern, 'Cette situation évoque irrésistiblement deux amis d'enfance qui se revoient après cinquante ans de séparation et déclarent: "Tu n'as pas changé, tu es toujours le même!" Identité essentielle, au-delà des changements existentiels' ('This situation irresistibly evokes two childhood friends who meet again after fifty years of separation and declare: "You haven't changed, you're still the same!" Essential identity, beyond existential changes') (Stern, ibid., p. 40). In other words, a State may very well remain the same in its 'essence' while at the same time having also changed in terms of its secondary characteristics.

[123] P. Dumberry, *A Guide to State Succession in International Investment Law* (Cheltenham, Edward Elgar, 2018), p. 14 ff; P. Dumberry, 'Is Turkey the "Continuing" State of the Ottoman Empire under International Law?', *Netherlands ILR* 59(2) (2012), p. 235–62.

related to territory, government, population as well as the concept of the 'essential portion of a State', and recognition by other States.

1.1.3.5 The Important Distinction between Matters of 'Attribution' and 'Responsibility'

Article 1 of the ILC's Articles provides that 'every internationally wrongful act of a State entails the international responsibility of that State'.[124] According to ILC Special Rapporteur Crawford, this provision 'affirms the basic principle that each State is responsible for its own wrongful conduct'.[125] Article 2 of the ILC articles sets out the conditions required to establish the existence of an 'internationally wrongful act'. It is the case when a conduct consisting of an action or an omission:

(a) is attributable to that State under international law; and
(b) constitutes a breach of an international obligation of that State.

For a conduct to be characterized as an 'internationally wrongful act', it must therefore be 'attributable' to the State. The State is an 'organised entity' which 'cannot act in itself' but only through its agents and representatives, that is, human beings.[126] The question of attribution that must be asked is 'which persons should be considered as acting on behalf of the State' 'for the purposes of State responsibility'.[127] In other words, the term 'attribution' is used in the ILC Articles 'to denote the operation of attaching a given action or omission to a State'.[128]

Part II of the ILC Articles defines the circumstances in which such an attribution is 'justified', that is, 'when conduct consisting of an act or omission . . . is to be considered as the conduct of the State'.[129] As a general rule, a State is not responsible for the acts of private individuals or other non-State entities (such as, for instance, corporations, NGOs, etc.). The only conduct that is attributable to the State is that of its organs. Article 4 establishes the basic principle that the conduct of a State organ is considered as an act of that State under international

[124] *Titles and Texts of the Draft Articles on Responsibility of States for Internationally Wrongful Acts Adopted by the Drafting Committee on Second Reading*, 26 July 2001, UN Doc. A/CN.4/L.602/Rev.1.

[125] ILC, 'First Report on State Responsibility (addendum no. 4)', by Mr James Crawford, Special Rapporteur, 26 May 1998, U.N. Doc. A/CN.4/490/Add.4, at para. 110.

[126] ILC, Commentaries, 2001, p. 35, para. 5.

[127] Ibid.

[128] Ibid., p. 36, para. 12.

[129] Ibid., p. 38, para. 1.

law.[130] Under the ILC Articles there are a number of exceptions to this general principle, including when a person or an entity is empowered to exercise elements of governmental authority (Article 5)[131] or to act under the instruction, or the control of the State (Article 8). The conduct of individuals can be attributable to the State only if they 'have acted under the direction, instigation or control of those organs, i.e. as agents of the State'.[132]

This book only focuses on Article 10 of the ILC Articles dealing with matters of attribution in relation to the conduct of insurrectional movements during civil wars. The conduct of the members of such a movement is that of private individuals.[133] These individuals are not an organ of the State. The movement is also not an organ of the State. As such, their conduct is not attributable to the State. As noted by Kolb, 'the acts and omissions engage the responsibility of that movement alone'.[134] Article 10 indicates that there are 'exceptional circumstances' under which the ILC Articles provide 'for the attribution of the conduct of the successful insurrectional or other movement to the State'.[135] In his book, Crawford explained that Article 10 concerns an 'exceptional category' of attribution 'in which the actions of non-state entities may be considered attributable to the State without any prior intervention, delegation or instructions from an Article 4 organ'.[136] This is indeed a unique situation where a non-State entity is 'not acting under the direction or control of State organs', but its actions 'may nonetheless be attributed to the State'.[137] Under Article 10(1), the acts committed by the rebels during the insurgency, which is ultimately successful and establishes a new

[130] James Crawford, *Brownlie's Principles of Public International Law* (8th ed., Oxford University Press, 2012), p. 542 ff., identifying the 'organs' as the executive, administration, armed forces, federal units, provinces and other internal divisions, the legislature and the judiciary.

[131] Article 7 explains that the conduct of organs or entities empowered to exercise governmental authority (as set out in Articles 5 and 6) is attributable to the State even in situations where it was carried out outside the authority of the organ or person concerned or when it was contrary to instructions. Article 9 concerns the conduct of a person (or a group of persons) involving elements of governmental authority, carried out in the absence of the official authorities.

[132] ILC, Commentaries, 2001, p. 38, para. 2. It should be added that Article 11 deals with conduct not attributable to the State under Articles 5 to 10 which is nonetheless adopted by the State, expressly or by conduct, as its own.

[133] Ibid., p. 50, para. 2.

[134] Kolb, *The International Law of State Responsibility*, p. 94.

[135] ILC, Commentaries, 2001, p. 50, para. 4.

[136] Crawford, *State Responsibility*, p. 116.

[137] Ibid., p. 166.

government, are attributable to the State (Rule no 2). As further examined in Part I,[138] according to the ILC, the attribution to the State is based on the 'continuity' which is said to exist 'between the new organization of the State and that of the insurrectional movement'.[139] Yet, as noted by d'Aspremont (and further discussed below in Part I, Section 2.2.2.2.4), the principle underlying Article 10(1) could have been based on a rule of 'attribution of responsibility', rather than a rule of attribution of conduct.[140]

Another important point to highlight is that the issue of *attribution* of conduct to the State is different from the question of whether such a conduct is a wrongful act. Thus, as stated in the Commentary of the ILC Articles, 'to show that conduct is attributable to the State says nothing, as such, about the legality or otherwise of that conduct'.[141] In other words, once a certain conduct of rebels is attributable to the State, it does not follow automatically that there is an international responsibility for that State. Responsibility arises only if the rebels have breached an international law obligation.[142] As explained by Kolb, 'the conduct of the insurrectional movement attributable to the State – in the case of success as envisaged by article 10 ASR – is that of the group itself', adding that 'this conduct represents an IWA only if at the time it was committed it breached some obligations of international law applicable to the armed group'.[143] As mentioned above, the basic assumption underlying this book is that rebels have such obligations under international law.[144]

Article 10 of the ILC Articles only covers the question of attribution of conduct. This book is much broader in scope than the contours of this provision since it deals with matters of international *responsibility* arising from the breach of an international obligation. Thus, I will examine many examples where (1) the actions of an insurrectional movement *are attributable* to the State under Article 10, and (2) such actions are in

138 Part I, Section 2.2.2.2.4.

139 ILC, Commentaries, 2001, p. 50, para. 5.

140 d'Aspremont, 'Rebellion and State Responsibility', p. 431.

141 ILC, Commentaries, 2001, p. 39, para. 4.

142 ILC, Report, 1975, p. 91, para. 3: '[a]s organs of an insurrectional movement they may engage in conduct liable to bring an international responsibility upon the insurrectional movement itself if that conduct should constitute a breach of an international obligation recognized as incumbent on the insurrectional movement'. The question is examined in Part I, Section 2.2.4.2.

143 Kolb, *The International Law of State Responsibility*, p. 98.

144 See analysis in Part I, Section 3.2.1.

breach of an international law obligation. As mentioned above, these are the two elements of an 'internationally wrongful act' (Article 2), which entails the international *responsibility* of that State (Article 1).

In fact, some of the 'rules' set out in this book do not involve any matters of attribution of conduct *involving rebels*. They only concern the commission of a wrongful act by a State in breach of an international obligation which entails the international responsibility of that State. A good example is Rule no. 1, applicable when the rebels are successful at establishing a new government. Under that rule, the new government remains responsible for the acts committed by the previous government while fighting the rebels. In this case, responsibility arises as a result of the commission by the organ of that State of *its own* wrongful act. This is therefore not a matter of attribution involving an entity *other* than the organ of a State. Another example is Rule no. 6, applicable when the rebels are *not* successful at establishing a new government. Under this well-established rule, the State is responsible for its own failure to exercise its due diligence obligation to protect foreigners and third States. In this case, responsibility arises as a result of a State's *own failure* to discharge its due diligence duty of vigilance, prevention and punishment in relation to the conduct of rebels. The wrongful act here is committed *by an organ of that State*; it involves no other entity.

I will explain for each rule set out below whether it involves a matter of attribution or responsibility.

1.2 The Structure of This Book

This book contains two Parts:

- Acts committed in the context of the establishment of a new *government* (Part I); and
- Acts committed in the context of the creation of a new *State* (Part II).

Part I focuses on the first situation where acts by the rebels or the government are committed in the context of the insurgent's struggle for the establishment of a new *government*. In this context, two entirely distinct situations must be distinguished. First, what happens when the rebels are *successful* at establishing a new government? I will show that two basic principles should find application:

- The new government (set up by former rebels) remains responsible for the acts committed by the previous government while fighting the rebels (Rule no. 1); and

- The acts committed by the rebels during the insurgency are attributable to the State after their victory (Rule no. 2).

Second, what happens when the rebels are *not successful* in their attempt to establish a new government? As a matter of principle, the acts committed by the rebels during the insurgency are not attributable to the State once the insurgency has failed (Rule no. 3). Yet, in my view, there are two 'exceptions' to this general principle. Even when the insurgency is ultimately unsuccessful, a State should nevertheless be bound by the 'governmental' lawful 'routine activities' performed by the rebels in situations where they have established a local de facto government in part of the territory (Rule no. 4A). In my view, the State should also be responsible for the consequences arising from an expropriation act committed by rebels if it results in some benefits for the State (Rule no. 4B). The fact that, in general, the acts of *unsuccessful* rebels are not attributable to the State does not necessarily mean that such wrongs will go unpunished. Thus, the rebels are always responsible for their own wrongful acts (Rule no. 5). In any event, I will show that a State is not responsible for damages resulting from its use of military force while fighting an insurgency unless its conduct breaches its international law obligations. Yet, the State will always be responsible for *its own* failure to exercise its due diligence obligation to protect third States and foreigners during the (ultimately unsuccessful) insurgency (Rule no. 6). Thus, responsibility arises as a result of a State's failure to discharge its due diligence obligation of vigilance, prevention and punishment in relation to the conduct of rebels. I will examine the scope and content of this due diligence obligation as well as the applicable test to determine whether any breach of the obligation has been committed.

Part II focuses on the situation where the acts by rebels or the government were committed in the context of the insurgents' struggle to create a *new State*. As highlighted previously, there are two situations that must be distinguished. First, what happens when the rebels are *successful* in creating a new State? I will show that two basic principles should find application:

- The acts committed by the rebels during the insurgency are attributable to the new State (Rule no. 7); and
- A new State is not responsible for the acts committed by the predecessor State while fighting the rebels during the insurgency (Rule no. 8).

The predecessor State (if it continues to exists) remains responsible for its own wrongs.

Second, what happens when the rebels are *not successful* in creating a new State? I will show that two basic principles should apply:

- The acts committed by the rebels during the insurgency are not attributable to the State (Rule no. 9); and
- The State is responsible for its own failure to exercise its due diligence obligation to protect foreigners and third States in relation to the conduct of rebels (Rule no. 10).

Finally, in a last conclusion chapter, I will provide a summary of my findings.

PART I

Acts Committed in the Context of the Establishment of a New Government

The situation that is contemplated in this Part does *not* involve the creation of a *new State* (this other question is examined in Part II). As noted by ILC Special Rapporteur Ago, the scenario laid out in this Part is when the victory of an insurrection 'result[s] in a change of government without any interruption in the continuity of the State'.[1] Elsewhere, Ago described the situation as one involving 'changes, sometimes radical changes, particularly at the summit of the organization of the State, without the entire State organization collapsing and, above all, without the continuity of the State being affected'.[2] In other words, the successful revolt leads to the establishment of a new government.

This Part is divided into two Chapters. First, I will examine the situation where the rebels *are successful* at establishing a new government (Chapter 2), which will then be followed by an analysis of the different case where the rebels are *not successful* at establishing a new government (Chapter 3).

[1] International Law Commission, 'Fourth Report on State Responsibility, by Mr. Roberto Ago, Special Rapporteur – The Internationally Wrongful Act of the State, Source of International Responsibility', 30 June 1972 and 9 April 1973, UN Doc. A/CN.4/264 and Add.l, *ILC Yearbook*, vol. II (1972) [hereinafter referred to as ILC, Ago Report, 1972], p. 72, at p. 131, para. 158.

[2] Ibid., p. 145, para. 196. He further explains that 'the leadership organization of the insurrectional movement installs itself in power, certain institutions are replaced, others are added, still others are reformed or reorganized, but the State remains the same, both at the internal level and at the international level' (ibid.). See also, ibid., p. 131, para. 158, referring to 'the State as a subject of international law remains unchanged'.

2

When the Rebels Are Successful at Establishing a New Government

This chapter deals with the situation where the rebels *are successful* at establishing a new government. I will examine the following two basic principles:

- The new government remains responsible for the acts committed by the previous government while fighting the rebels (Rule no. 1) (Section 2.1); and
- The acts committed by the rebels during the insurgency are attributable to the State (Rule no. 2) (Section 2.2).

2.1 Rule No. 1: The New Government Remains Responsible for the Acts Committed by the Previous Government while Fighting the Rebels

As further discussed in the next section,[3] whenever the rebels are *successful* in their insurgency and ultimately manage to install a new government, the general principle is set out in Article 10(1) of the ILC Articles. It provides that the conduct *of an insurrectional movement* during the insurgency is attributable to the State (this general principle will hereinafter be referred to as 'Rule no. 2'). The 2001 ILC Commentary explained that the State was the 'only subject of international law to which responsibility can be attributed'.[4] It added that such a 'situation requires that acts committed during the struggle for power by the apparatus of the insurrectional movement should be attributable to the State, *alongside acts of the then established Government*'.[5] The last words indicate that the

[3] See Section 2.2.

[4] International Law Commission, 'Commentaries to the Draft Articles on Responsibility of States for Internationally Wrongful Acts Adopted by the ILC at its Fifty-Third Session', November 2001, UN Doc. A/56/10, *ILC Yearbook* vol. II (2) (2001) [hereinafter referred to as ILC, Commentaries, 2001], p. 50, para. 5.

[5] Ibid., emphasis added.

State should, as matter of principle, *also continue* to be held responsible for the acts committed by the previous government during the insurgency right before the change of government (this general principle will hereinafter be referred to as 'Rule no. 1'). The present section deals with Rule no. 1.

In the following sections, I will first examine the drafting history of Article 10 of the ILC Articles (Section 2.1.1), which will then be followed by an analysis of the main reason behind the existence of Rule no. 1: a State remains responsible for its own acts because its identify is not affected by a change of government (Section 2.1.2). While Rule no. 1 is well-established and generally just and fair, I will nevertheless show that its concrete application can lead to some curious results (Section 2.1.3). Finally, I will investigate the specific question as to whether Rule no. 1 should apply to the particular case of a rebellion overthrowing a racist regime (Section 2.1.4).

2.1.1 Drafting History

The general drafting history of Article 10 of the ILC Articles can be broadly summarized as follows:

- ILC Special Rapporteur Ago submitted his Fourth Report on State Responsibility in 1972, which included a number of proposed articles, including two provisions dealing with the issues concerning insurrectional movements: Articles 12 and 13.[6] The 1972 report by Ago was the first comprehensive analysis of the question to be undertaken by the ILC. It contained numerous examples of case law and State practice. It provided indispensable guidelines for the future work of the ILC.
- At its 1345th meeting, the Commission examined the texts of Articles 10 to 15 as proposed by the Drafting Committee, and adopted the text of those articles on first reading. The relevant articles concerning insurrectional movements (now Articles 14 and 15) were examined by the ILC in its 1975 'Report of the International Law Commission on the work of its twenty-seventh session'.[7] The 1975 ILC Report relied heavily on the work initially undertaken by ILC Special Rapporteur

6 ILC, Ago Report, 1972, p. 126 ff.

7 The provisions and commentaries are found in International Law Commission, 'Report of the International Law Commission on the work of its twenty-seventh session', 5 May–25 July 1975, UN Doc. A/10010/Rev. l, *ILC Yearbook* vol. II (1975) [hereinafter referred to as ILC, Report, 1975], p. 47, at p. 91 ff.

Ago in his 1972 Report. The ILC nevertheless adopted a different position on a number of specific aspects (further examined throughout this book).

- When appointed as Special Rapporteur, Crawford reassessed the work of the ILC on issues concerning insurrectional movements. Articles 14 and 15 were examined by him in his First Report on State Responsibility in 1998.[8] He suggested many changes, such as striking out Article 14 with some of its substance to be conserved and later included in a new Article 15.[9] Crawford's report also contained several examples of case law and State practice. He adopted a different position than that of Ago on a number of issues (further examined throughout this book).
- In 1998, in the Draft Articles Proposed by the Drafting Committee on Second Reading, it was agreed to delete Article 14. Some other modifications were also made to the content of Article 15.[10]
- In the Draft articles provisionally adopted by the Drafting Committee on second reading in 2000,[11] the text of Article 15 remained unchanged; it ultimately became Article 10 in the final 2001 version of the ILC Draft Articles. The final product is a collective effort by all ILC members since the 1970s under the leadership of both Ago and Crawford.

The basic principle behind Rule no. 1 can be found in the last sentence of Article 13(2) (titled 'Retroactive attribution to a State of the acts of organs

[8] International Law Commission, 'First Report on State Responsibility, by Mr. James Crawford, Special Rapporteur', 24 April, 1, 5, 11 and 26 May, 22 and 24 July, 12 August 1998, UN Doc. A/CN.4/490 and Add. 1-7*, *ILC Yearbook* vol. II(1) (1998) [hereinafter referred to as ILC, Crawford First Report, 1998], at p. 51.

[9] ILC, Crawford First Report, 1998, was discussed by the ILC in meetings in 1998. See International Law Commission, 'Summary Records of the Meetings of the Fiftieth Session 20 April–12 June 1998, 27 July–14 August 1998', UN Doc. A/CN.4/SER.A/1998, *ILC Yearbook* vol. I (1998), at p. 247 ff.; International Law Commission, 'Report of the Commission to the General Assembly on the work of its fiftieth session', UN Doc. A/CN.4/SER.A/1998/Add.l, *ILC Yearbook* vol. II(2) (1998), p. 85 ff.

[10] Draft Articles Proposed by the Drafting Committee on Second Reading, in International Law Commission, 'Summary Records of the Meetings of the Fiftieth Session 20 April–12 June 1998, 27 July–14 August 1998', UN Doc. A/CN.4/SER.A/1998, *ILC Yearbook* vol. I (1998), p. 287–8.

[11] International Law Commission, 'Texts of Draft Articles on State responsibility Provisionally Adopted by the Drafting Committee on Second Reading', Fifty-second session Geneva, 1 May–9 June and 10 July–18 August 2000, 21 August 2000, UN Doc. A/CN.4/L.600*, 21 August 2000.

of a successful insurrectional movement') of the 1972 draft presented by Ago:

> The conduct of a person or group of persons who, at the time when such conduct was engaged in, were organs of an insurrectional movement whose structures have subsequently been integrated, in whole or in part, with those of the pre-existing State is retroactively considered to be an act of that State. However, such attribution *does not preclude the parallel attribution to the said State of the conduct* of a person or group of persons who, at the aforementioned time, were *organs of the government which was at that time considered to be legitimate.*[12]

As explained by Ago,

> this provision emphasizes that the attribution to the State of the behaviour of the organs of the insurrectional movement [i.e. Rule no. 2] in no way excludes the *parallel attribution* to that State of the actions carried out, during the conflict, by the *organs of the government then established*, since it is important to maintain the possible responsibility of the State for the acts of the government which had been in power until the moment of its replacement by that of the insurrectional movement.[13]

This passage makes it clear that Rule no. 1 has nothing to do with the issue of attribution of conduct of a *non-State* entity. It only involves the attribution to the State of acts committed by its organs. The same general idea was also provided in the last sentence of Article 15(1) of the 1975 Draft:

> The act of an insurrectional movement which becomes the new government of a State shall be considered as an act of that State. *However, such attribution shall be without prejudice to the attribution to that State of conduct which would have been previously considered as an act of the State by virtue of articles 5 to 10.*[14]

It is noteworthy that the 1975 version is less explicit than the 1972 draft about the basic principle embodied in Rule no. 1. It simply makes a general *renvoi* to other provisions of the Draft Articles whereby a State is responsible for the acts committed by its organs.

The same language was finally adopted in Article 10(3) of the 2001 Draft Articles, which applies to both situations where the rebels establish a new government and when the rebellion leads to the creation of a new State:

[12] ILC, Ago Report, 1972, p. 151, para. 214, emphasis added.

[13] ILC, Report, 1975, p. 105, para. 21, emphasis added. See also: ILC, Ago Report, 1972, p. 151, para. 213.

[14] ILC, Report, 1975, emphasis added.

> This article is without prejudice to the attribution to a State of any conduct, however related to that of the movement concerned, which is to be considered an act of that State by virtue of articles 4 to 9.[15]

The next section examines the main reason behind the existence of Rule no. 1.

2.1.2 A State Remains Responsible for Its Own Acts Because Its Identify Is Not Affected by a Change of Government

Rule no. 1 is based on one of the most established principles of international law: a change of government does not affect the identity of a State. Thus, such a change does not, in itself, amount to the creation of a new State.[16] The identity of a State is not affected by a change of government even when it arises as a result of a revolution or a *coup d'État*.[17] A classic example is that of France which radically changed regimes many times over the course of the last three centuries.[18] Another example is the 1979 Revolution in Iran which, however radical its effect may have been on all levels of Iranian society, did *not* alter Iran's continuous international legal personality as a State. Similarly, the 1917 Bolshevik Revolution in Russia was considered as a mere change in government, not the creation of a new State.

The consequences of such State continuity are twofold:

- Generally, the new government should continue to be responsible for the State's international obligations, including those undertaken by the previous government (Section 2.1.2.1); and

[15] ILC, Commentaries, 2001, Article 10(3).

[16] Krystyna Marek, *Identity and Continuity of States in Public International Law* (Geneva, Librairie Droz, 1968), p. 24 ff.

[17] Josef L. Kunz, 'Identity of States Under International Law', *AJIL* 49 (1955), p. 73; W. Czaplinski, 'La continuité, l'identité et la succession d'États-évaluation de cas récents', *RBDI* 26 (1993), p. 378; Marek, ibid., p. 25.

[18] Sir Robert Jenning and Sir Arthur Watts, *Oppenheim's International Law* (Peace: Introduction and Part 1) (9th ed., Longman, vol. I, 1996), p. 204–5:

> [t]he continuity of a State as an international person notwithstanding changes of the kind mentioned may be illustrated by the history of France, which has over the centuries retained its identity although it acquired, lost and regained parts of its territory, changed its dynasty, was a kingdom, a republic, an empire, again a kingdom, again a republic, again an empire, and is now once more a republic. All its international rights and duties as an international person continued in spite of these important changes. Even such loss of territory as occasions the reduction of a major power to a lesser status does not affect the state as an international person.

- The new government should also, more specifically, continue to be responsible for the wrongful acts committed by the previous government while fighting the rebels (Section 2.1.2.2).

2.1.2.1 The New Government Is Responsible for the International Obligations Undertaken by the Previous Government

All writers support the general principle that 'if the State remains the same, no change in its obligations, responsibilities, and rights takes place'.[19] There is no reason why the outcome should be any different given that the State's identity has not been affected by a change of government.[20] A new government is bound to respect the international obligations undertaken by the previous government it has effectively and successfully replaced.[21] This principle is well-established in State practice, as illustrated by the position adopted by States in the context of the 1917 Russian Revolution. The new revolutionary regime initially argued that it could not be bound by any of the previous obligations undertaken by the Monarchist government.[22] This position was strongly rejected by all other States and was subsequently abandoned by the Soviet Union.[23] It

[19] Hans Kelsen, *Principles of International Law* (2nd ed. rev. and ed. by Robert W. Tucker, New York, Holt, Rinehart and Winston Inc, 1966), p. 383. See also, inter alia: Ian Brownlie, *Principles of Public International Law* (6th ed., Oxford, Clarendon Press, 2003), p. 80 ('legal rights and responsibility of States are not affected by changes in the head of State or the internal form of government').

[20] In fact, Marek, *Identity and Continuity*, p. 5, defines the legal identity of a State as 'the identity of the sum total of its rights and obligations under both customary and conventional International Law'.

[21] Louis Cavaré, *Le droit international positif* (2nd ed., Paris, Pedone, vol. I, 1961), p. 372 ('les actes juridiques accomplis par un État subsistent, même si le gouvernement change'); Nguyen Quoc Dinh, Patrick Daillier and Alain Pellet, *Droit international public* (6th ed., Paris, LGDJ, 1999), p. 534) Meriam Al-Rashid, Ulyana Bardyn and Levon Golendukhin, 'Investment Claims amid Civil Unrest: Questions of Attribution and Responsibility', *BCDR Int. Arb. Rev.* 3(2) (2016), p. 184.

[22] This example is well-documented in Marek, *Identity and Continuity*, p. 34 ff.

[23] The firm position adopted by Western States is shown in this 1921 official communication from the British Government to Mr Krassin, the agent of the Soviet Union in London: '[t]he first [question] is that of the acceptance by the Soviet Government of the obligations which had been entered into and were binding upon previous Government in Russia. The accepted rule among civilized States is that contracts made by and debts incurred by a Government are to be regarded as the obligations of the nation it represented and not as the personal engagements of the ruler. Although the form of Government may change, the people remain bound' (in Lord McNair, *International Law Opinions* (Cambridge University Press, vol. I, 1956), p. 9). See also, the joint declaration of 28 March 1918 adopted by Great Britain and France: 'aucun principe n'est mieux établi

is relevant to mention that the rule is applicable regardless of whether or not the change of government occurs in conformity with the internal constitutional order.[24] This notion was clearly expressed by the Sole Arbitrator in the *Tinoco* case[25] and by other arbitral tribunals in the *Dreyfus* case[26] and the *Hopkins* case.[27] Therefore, even in cases of a revolution, the new government is bound to respect the international obligations undertaken by the previous government.[28] The principle has even been applied in cases where the acts were committed by a government that had not been recognized by other States.[29]

que celui d'après lequel une nation est responsable des actes de son gouvernement sans qu'un changement d'autorité affecte les obligations encourues: ces engagements ne peuvent être répudiés par aucune autorité, quelle qu'elle soit, sans quoi la base même du droit international se trouverait ébranlée' ('no principle is better established than that according to which a nation is responsible for the acts of its government without a change of authority affecting the obligations incurred: these commitments cannot be repudiated by any authority whatsoever, otherwise the very basis of international law would be shaken') (in Paul Fauchille, *Traité de droit international public* (8th ed., Paris, Librairie A. Rousseau, vol. I (1), 1922), p. 342).

[24] Edwin M. Borchard, *The Diplomatic Protection of Citizens Abroad (or the Law of International Claims)* (New York, The Banks Law Publishing Co., 1915). This is also the position of Fauchille, *Traité de droit international public*, p. 339. See also: Czaplinski, 'La continuité, l'identité et la succession d'États', p. 378.

[25] *Aguilar-Amory and Royal Bank of Canada claims (Tinoco case)* (Great Britain v. Costa Rica), Award of 18 October 1923, UNRIAA 1, p. 375, p. 381.

[26] *Dreyfus case (France* v. *Chile)*, Award of 7 July 1901, in Deschamps and Renault, *Recueil international des traités du XXe siècle* (1901), p. 398.

[27] *George W. Hopkins* v. *United Mexican States*, US–Mexico Claims Commission, Award of 31 March 1926, UNRIAA 5 [hereinafter referred to as '*Hopkins* case, 1926'], p. 45: '[t]he binding force of such acts of the Huerta administration as partook of the personal character as contradistinguish from the Government itself will depend upon its real control and paramountcy at the time of the act over a major portion of the territory and a majority of the people of Mexico. As long as the Huerta régime was in fact the master in the administration of the affairs of the Government of Mexico its illegal origin did not defeat the binding force of its executive acts'.

[28] D. Anzilotti, *Cours de droit international public* (Paris, Sirey, 1929), p. 178 ('Les changements constitutionnels, qu'ils soient pacifiques ou qu'ils soient révolutionnaires, n'exercent pas d'influence sur les obligations internationales de l'État').

[29] Danielle Morris, 'Revolutionary Movements and De Facto Governments – Implications of the "Arab Spring" for International Investors', *Arb. Int.* 28(4) (2012), p. 724–5, quoting: Jennings and Watts, *Oppenheim's International Law*, § 44 ('[T]he effect of a revolution resulting in a government which for a time fails to secure any recognition from foreign states, does not destroy the international personality of the state or free it, permanently at any rate, from existing treaty obligations; though it involves an interruption in that state's ability to exercise its legal capacity for international purposes').

In practical terms, a new government must respect treaties entered into by the previous government.[30] The ICJ[31] and the Iran–US Claims Tribunal[32] have both held the opinion that post-revolutionary Iran remained bound by international agreements, such as the 1955 Treaty of Amity, Economic Relations and Consular Rights between the United States and Iran, which the previous government had entered into before the 1979 Revolution.

In several international arbitration cases, arbitral tribunals have ruled that a new government is compelled to respect the *contractual commitments* that the previous government had undertaken with foreign companies. One classic example is the *Tinoco* case, where the Sole Arbitrator concluded that, as matter of principle, the new Government of Costa Rica was bound by previous engagements and obligations (concessions rights and a banknote) given by the former government to foreign investors.[33] This rule applies regardless of whether the government has been recognized by other States. The principle has also been recognized, inter alia, by the Iran–US Claims Tribunal.[34] Writers have also recognized that some exceptions may

[30] John Bassett Moore, *Digest of International Law* (Washington DC, GPO, vol. I, 1906), p. 249 ('the State is bound by engagements entered into by governments that have ceased to exist').

[31] *United States Diplomatic and Consular Staff in Tehran*, Judgment, ICJ Rep. 1980, p. 28, para. 54.

[32] See inter alia: *Amoco Int'l Finance Corporation ('AIFC')* v. *Government of the Islamic Republic of Iran, National Iranian Oil Company ('NIOC'), National Petrochemical Company ('NPC') and Kharg Chemical Company ('Khemco')*, Iran–US Claims Tribunal, Award No. 310-56-3, 14 July 1987, 15 *Iran-US CTR*, p. 189, para. 94; *INA Corporation* v. *The Government of the Islamic Republic of Iran*, Iran–US Claims Tribunal, Award No. 184-161-1, 13 August 1985, 8 *Iran-US CTR*, p. 373; *Phelps Dodge Corp., et al.* v. *The Islamic Republic of Iran*, Iran–US Claims Tribunal, Award No. 217-99-2, 19 March 1986, 10 *Iran-US CTR*, p. 121; *Sedco, Inc.* v. *National Iranian Oil Company, et al.*, Iran–US Claims Tribunal, Interlocutory Award No. ITL 59-129-3, 27 March 1986, 10 *Iran-US CTR*, p. 180.

[33] *Aguilar-Amory and Royal Bank of Canada claims (Tinoco case)* (Great Britain v. Costa Rica), Award of 18 October 1923, UNRIAA 1, p. 375. However, the Sole Arbitrator concluded that in the present case the concession contract was invalid under the Constitution of Costa Rica.

[34] *Phillips Petroleum Company Iran* v. *The Islamic Republic of Iran, et al.*, Iran–US Claims Tribunal, Award No. 425-39-2, 29 June 1989, 21 *Iran-US CTR*, p. 79, p. 111 ('[A] revolutionary regime may not simply excuse itself from legal obligations by changing governmental policies, nor take for the public benefit businesses operated by foreign private persons under the previous regime'); *Rockwell International Systems, Inc. and The Government of the Islamic Republic of Iran (The Ministry of National Defence)*, Iran–US Claims Tribunal, Award No. 438-430-1, 5 September 1989, 23 *Iran-US CTR*, p. 150, p. 171, para. 92 ('The Tribunal

apply to this general principle. For instance, a new government arising from a rebellion is not responsible for contractual commitments when the obligations are related to the personal benefit of officials of the previous government.[35] Another exception (identified, inter alia, by the Iran–US Claims Tribunal)[36] is regarding the so-called 'odious debts' contracted by a government 'with a view to attaining objectives contrary to the major interests' of the State or contracted 'with an aim and for a purpose not in conformity with international law'.[37] The concept of 'odious debts' will be further discussed below.[38]

does not find, however, that the victory of the Islamic Revolution, as such, automatically, that is, without additional actions by either party, resulted in a cancellation of all contractual obligations').

35 Morris, 'Revolutionary Movements', p. 749: 'when the government is on the verge of falling and enters into obligations for the personal benefit of outgoing officials or otherwise in prejudice of a future government's rights' (referring to the *Tinoco* case, p. 734). See also, p. 750: '[a]ny contract entered into or renegotiated in the period shortly before the fall of the government could be subject to examination by an arbitral tribunal should the post-revolutionary government refuse to honour the agreement. ... Arbitral jurisprudence suggests that an investor's ability to demonstrate that die contract was part of a normal course of business and did not personally benefit any officials of the prior regime may be essential to the tribunal's determination.'

36 *United States of America* v. *The Islamic Republic of Iran (Case B-36)*, Iran–US Claims Tribunal, Award No. 574–B36–2, 3 December 1996, 32 *Iran-US CTR*, p. 162. Iran argued that a 1948 contract between the United States and pre-revolution Iran was actually imposed by the former on the latter. The Tribunal rejected this argument and indicated (at para. 51) that: '[t]he Tribunal is of the opinion that the debt under the 1948 Contract cannot be classified under the notion of "odious debts" as understood in international law. They were not contracted with a view to attaining objectives contrary to the legitimate interests of Iran nor were they contracted with an aim and for a purpose not in conformity with international law.' It should be noted that the Tribunal also indicated (at para. 49) that there was no evidence that these were 'subjugation debts', since the debts had not been 'incurred by Iran for the purpose of suppressing any such war or revolution'.

37 This is the definition given by ILC Special Rapporteur Bedjaoui in the context of State succession: ILC, 'Ninth Report on Succession of States in Respect of Matters Other than Treaties', by Mr M. Bedjaoui, Special Rapporteur, 1977, UN Doc. A/CN.4/301 and Add.1, *ILC Yearbook* vol. II(1) (1977) [hereinafter referred to as ILC, Ninth Report Bedjaoui, 1977], p. 45, p. 70. For a recent examination of this concept: James Gallen, 'Odious Debt and Jus Post Bellum', *J. World Investment & Trade* 16 (2015), p. 666.

38 See Section 2.1.4.

2.1.2.2 The New Government Is Responsible for Wrongful Acts Committed by the Previous Government

As a matter of principle, a new government should also be held responsible for the *illegal acts* committed by the previous government in its attempt to maintain control. As mentioned by Schwarzenberger, 'acts of the former legitimate government are imputable to a State because, at the time of the illegal act, it was the real government'.[39] This is the situation that generally prevails in *all cases* where a change of government occurs, whether through an election or by non-democratic means. There is no reason why this well-established principle should not find application when a change of government is the result of a successful rebellion by insurgents.

In the next sections, I will examine the following points:

- The rationale behind the principle (Section 2.1.2.2.1);
- Different types of wrongs covered by Rule no. 1 (Section 2.1.2.2.2); and
- The principle is supported by case law (Section 2.1.2.2.3).

2.1.2.2.1 The Rationale behind the Principle The reason why a new government should be held responsible for the *illegal acts* committed by the previous government in the context of revolution was clearly explained by Ago as follows: 'the State does not cease to exist and its organization persists, even if it undergoes some alterations, with the result that, after the success of the insurrectional movement, the previous acts or omissions of members of that organization will continue to be attributed to the State'.[40] The same idea is mentioned in the 1975 ILC Report.[41] As further

[39] Georg Schwarzenberger, *International Law* (3rd ed., London, Stevens and Sons, vol. I, 1957), p. 628.

[40] ILC, Ago Report, 1972, p. 145, para. 197. See also, para. 199.

[41] ILC, Report, 1975, p. 100, para. 5:

> The State does not cease to exist as a subject of international law. Its identity remains the same, without any break in continuity, despite the changes, reorganizations and adaptations which occur in the institutions of the State. That means that it is necessary to continue to attribute to the State, after the success of the insurrectional movement, the conduct previously engaged in by the organs of the pre-existing State apparatus. Consequently, the situation requires that the State should be responsible for acts committed during the struggle for power both by the apparatus of the insurrectional movement and by the apparatus of the legitimate government.

examined in Part II,[42] the situation is obviously different when the rebels are successful in their attempt to create a *new State*, rather than establishing a new government.[43]

In practical terms, the meaning behind Rule no. 1 is that, after the successful rebellions and the establishment of a new government, the State can be 'called upon to answer at the same time for acts emanating from *two different organisations*', that is, the rebels and the previous government.[44] In fact, as further explained below in Part I, Section 2.2.2.2.2, Ago speaks of the '*parallel attribution* to that State of the conduct engaged in during the same period by organs of the government which was then regarded as "legitimate"' as well as the conduct of rebels.[45] He, however, identified this particular situation as one of the 'difficulties' which he said 'arise in connexion with the attribution to the State of the acts of agents of a successful insurrectional movement'.[46] But for him, 'there is nothing surprising in this':[47]

> During the insurrectional struggle, two organizations are opposed to each other and are fighting for final victory. Each of the two wishes to be the organization of the State; at the outset, one is so in fact and the other potentially. In the case where the insurgents triumph and install themselves in the government of the pre-existing State, the organization of the insurrectional movement is integrated within the framework of the State organization.[48]

[42] See Part II, Section 4.3.

[43] ILC, Report, 1975, p. 101, para. 6: '[t]he acts of the organs of the pre-existing State are in no way attributable to the new State, which has separated from the pre-existing State by secession or decolonization. These are and remain exclusively the acts of the pre-existing State, which as a general rule, moreover, will continue to exist after the constitution of the new State by the insurrectional movement'. This basic principle will be referred to as Rule. No. 8 (further examined in Part II, Section 4.3).

[44] ILC, Ago Report, 1972, p. 145, para. 197.

[45] Ibid., p. 151, para. 213:

> it appears essential to indicate explicitly that, where a subversive movement only achieves the installation of a new government of a State, whose identity does not in itself change, the retroactive attribution to that State of the conduct of organs of the movement in question in no way precludes the parallel attribution to that State of the conduct engaged in during the same period by organs of the government which was then regarded as 'legitimate'.

[46] ILC, Ago Report, 1972, p. 145, para. 197.

[47] Ibid., p. 100, para. 5.

[48] Ibid., p. 100, para. 5.

In the event that the rebels win and establish a new government, 'the resulting State apparatus is in reality the *continuation of both the organizations* which confronted each other during the struggle'.[49] Thus, on one hand, there is an 'organic' or 'structural' continuity between the insurgents and the new government they have established (a point further explained below).[50] On the other hand, the element of continuity is undeniably present regarding the State: it is the same State with the same international legal personality before and after the rebellion leading to the creation of a new government. This is therefore not a matter of attribution of conduct of a non-State entity. In this context, Ago considers it 'logical' that the acts of *both organizations* are attributable to the State: '[i]t is therefore logical to attribute to the State the acts of organs of its preceding organization and the acts of organs of the organization which grew up during the insurrection and then became the organization of the State itself'.[51]

2.1.2.2.2 Different Types of Wrongs Covered by Rule No. 1 Rule no. 1 covers different factual situations regarding wrongs committed by governments.[52]

The first situation covered by Rule no. 1 is where a wrong is *directly* committed by the government against a third State or a foreigner in the context of fighting an insurgency. One example could involve the army or police forces committing acts of expropriation, destruction or pillage of property belonging to foreign investors. Another example would be for the government forces to take over a third State's embassy and causing damage to either its property or its personnel. These are the typical acts that are covered under Rule no. 1.

Yet, as further explained in the next Chapter dealing with *unsuccessful* insurgencies,[53] a State is not responsible for damages

[49] Ibid., p. 100, para. 5, emphasis added.

[50] See Section 2.2.2.2.4.

[51] ILC, Ago Report, 1972, p. 100, para. 5.

[52] It should be mentioned that this section does not deal with the situation when a wrongful act committed by the government caused damages directly *to the rebels themselves*. Whenever that is the case, the State is theoretically responsible for such acts during the insurgency as well as after. Yet, after their victory the rebels will now be forming the new government. Whether or not the new government may request any reparation against members of the previous government is a matter of domestic law. This question is beyond the scope of this book.

[53] See Section 3.3.2.

resulting from its use of military force while fighting an insurgency unless its conduct breaches its international law obligations. In other words, the fact that the use of force by the army may have caused damages to third States or to foreigners does not *necessarily* mean that the State should be legally held responsible for such damages. Something more is required. It has to be shown that a breach of international law was committed.[54] This was the conclusion reached by the Umpire in the *French Company of Venezuelan Railroads* case which involved wrongs committed by both rebels and governmental forces.[55]

I have found another relevant example of State practice illustrating this distinction between legal and illegal acts in the context of the successful revolution led by Fidel Castro and his revolutionary forces in establishing a new government in Cuba. Instructions from the US Department of State expressed its position on the liability of the new government for damages caused during the

[54] League of Nations publication, V. Legal, 1929.V.3, Doc. C.75.M.69.1929.V, p. 107, Preparatory Committee of the Hague Conference for the Codification of International Law, 'Basis of Discussion' [hereinafter referred to as League of Nations, 1929, 'Basis of Discussion'], no. 21: '[a] State is not responsible for damage caused to the person or property of a foreigner by its armed forces or authorities in the suppression of an insurrection, riot or other disturbance'. Yet, the Preparatory Committee also recognized a number of *specific obligations* under international law towards foreigners: 'The State must, however:

(1) Make good damage caused to foreigners by the requisitioning or occupation of their property by its armed forces or authorities;
(2) Make good damage caused to foreigners by destruction of property by its armed forces or authorities, or by their orders, unless such destruction is the direct consequence of combatant acts;
(3) Make good damage caused to foreigners by acts of its armed forces or authorities where such acts manifestly went beyond the requirements of the situation or where its armed forces or authorities behaved in a manner manifestly incompatible with the rules generally observed by civilized States;
(4) Accord to foreigners, to whom damage has been caused by its armed forces or authorities in the suppression of an insurrection, riot or other disturbance, the same indemnities as it accords to its own nationals in similar circumstances'.

[55] *French Company of Venezuelan Railroads* case, French–Venezuelan Mixed Claims Commission, 31 July 1905, UNRIAA 10, p. 354:

> When revolution laid waste both country and village, or seized the railroad and its material, or placed its hands upon the boats and wrought serious injury to all, it is regrettable, deplorable, but it is not chargeable upon the respondent Government, *unless the revolution was successful* and *unless* the acts were such as to *charge responsibility under the well-recognized rules of public law*. (emphasis added).

revolutionary disturbances by the rebels (a point further examined below in Section 2.2.3.1), but also by governmental forces. The document clearly made a distinction between damages resulting from the 'legitimate military operations of forces' by the government and those that were not. It stated that only those acts that were *not* legitimate or legal could be attributable to Cuba after the Revolution.[56]

The second situation covered (at least theoretically) by Rule no. 1 concerns those wrongs *not* committed *directly* by the government, but rather by the rebels themselves. The 2001 ILC Commentary made the following comment on the issue: 'exceptional cases may occur where the State was in a position to adopt measures of vigilance, prevention or punishment in respect of the movement's conduct but improperly failed to do so'.[57] This is a situation where the government in charge failed to fulfil its due diligence obligations towards foreigners in relation to wrongs committed by rebels. One example could be the failure of a government to

[56] M. M. Whiteman, *Digest of International Law* (Washington, Dept. of State, vol. 8, 1973), p. 819–20, referring to a document sent by the US Department of State to the American Embassy, Habana, instruction, No. A-180, 26 January 1959, MS. Department of State, file 237.1141/12–1958:

> There is first, of course, the basic question of whether the losses resulted from acts for which the present Government of Cuba is responsible from an international legal standpoint. As a general rule, a government which becomes the legitimate government of a state by a successful revolution, such as the present Government of Cuba, is *not internationally liable* for damages resulting from *legitimate military operations of forces* or authorities of *either the former government* or of the successful revolutionists. On the other hand, it is internationally responsible as a general rule for damages caused by acts of forces or authorities of both *the former government* and the revolutionists which were *not legitimate from a military standpoint or sanctioned by the rules of warfare, such as wanton or unnecessary injury to persons or property and pillage*. The government of the successful revolutionists is also internationally obligated to pay for property which was requisitioned by either the former government or the revolutionists. (The anomalous rule that a successful revolutionary government is liable for wrongful acts of forces and authorities of the former government rests on the broader principle that a successor government is liable for all of the international obligations of prior governments.) In the circumstances, it would not appear to be possible to determine whether a claimant has a valid legal basis for a claim until all of the facts with respect to the circumstances under which the losses occurred are known. (emphasis added).

[57] ILC, Commentaries, 2001, p. 50, para. 5.

take all possible and reasonable measures within its capacity to prevent attacks by rebels which ultimately caused destruction to property belonging to foreigners. Another example may be 'the failure by a State to take available steps to protect the premises of diplomatic missions, threatened from attack by an insurrectional movement'.[58] The scope and content of this due diligence obligation will be examined in detail below in Chapter 3 dealing with *unsuccessful* insurgency.[59] I will show that, as a matter of principle, the acts committed by the rebels during an unsuccessful insurgency are *not* attributable to the State once their struggle has failed (Rule no. 3). Yet, even when an insurgency ends up being unsuccessful, the State will still be held responsible for *its own* failure to exercise its due diligence obligation to protect third States and foreigners during the insurgency (Rule no. 6). While this due diligence obligation is of great relevance in the context of an *unsuccessful* insurgency, it plays a limited role when the rebels achieve their goal and establish a new government. Indeed, the basic principle applicable under this scenario is that the acts committed by the rebels during the insurgency are attributable to the State (Rule no. 2). After the civil war, the State will therefore have to provide appropriate compensation to foreign investors for any acts of expropriation, destruction or damage to property caused by the rebels during the insurgency. In other words, a foreign investor does not need to rely on the due diligence principle in order to be provided with adequate reparation regarding the damages suffered.

2.1.2.2.3 The Principle Is Supported by Case Law Ago mentioned that Rule no. 1 is supported by scholars.[60] This is indeed the case. All scholars (with the exception of Piguet)[61] support the principle set out in Article 10(3) of the 2001 Articles, in the context of rebels establishing

58 Ibid., p. 50, para. 5.

59 See Section 3.3 examining Rule no. 6.

60 ILC, Ago Report, 1972, p. 150, para. 210: '[t]he international scholars are also generally agreed in affirming that in the former situation the fact that the State is held responsible for wrongful acts committed by insurgents during the revolution in no way precludes the possibility of attributing to it, at the same time, responsibility for the acts or omissions of organs of the preceding government'.

61 Christophe Piguet, *La Guerre civile en droit international. Contribution à l'étude de la responsabilité internationale de l'État à raison des dommages éprouvés sur son territoire par des étrangers, du fait du mouvement insurrectionnel*, Doctoral Thesis, Université de Lausanne (1982), p. 144, for whom this principle is less well established by State practice and is not part of positive law.

a new government.[62] It is perhaps surprising that scholars generally do not mention any example of State practice supporting this principle in the context of successful rebellions.[63] In the following sections, I will first examine older cases, which will then be followed by an analysis of the recent *Strabag* case.

2.1.2.2.3.1 Older Cases The first relevant example has already been mentioned in the context of the 1959 Cuban revolution. The US government explained that the new government of Cuba (made up of former rebels) was 'internationally responsible as a general rule for damages caused by acts of forces or authorities of both *the former government* and the revolutionists which were *not legitimate from a military standpoint or sanctioned by the rules of warfare, such as wanton or unnecessary injury to*

[62] Patrick Daillier, Mathias Forteau and Alain Pellet, *Droit international public* (8th ed., Paris, LGDJ, 2009), p. 870, James Crawford, *Brownlie's Principles of Public International Law* (8th ed., Oxford University Press, 2012), p. 553; James Crawford, *State Responsibility: The General Part* (Cambridge University Press, 2013), p. 175; Gérard Cahin, 'Attribution of Conduct to the State: Insurrectional Movements', in James Crawford, Alain Pellet, Simon Olleson and Kate Parlett (eds.), *The Law of International Responsibility* (Oxford University Press, 2010), p. 249 ('In the first hypothesis, that of seizure of power within a State, the insurrectional movement integrates itself into the pre-existing State structures, so that the pre-existing State continues to be responsible even for the conduct of its organs which were engaged in the conflict against the movement before being replaced by the movement itself'); Abdel-Azzeem Al-Ganzory, 'International Claims and Insurgence', *REDI* 33 (1977), p. 93; Morris, 'Revolutionary Movements', p. 754 ('If, on the other hand, the revolutionary movement succeeds in establishing a general *de facto* government, it will be liable under international law for all of the acts of the revolution from its inception *and for the acts of the prior established government.* As such, the post-revolutionary governments of Egypt or Libya could be held liable under relevant investment treaties for any breaches committed by the prior regimes or by revolutionary forces, even if such a breach occurred before the rebels succeeded in establishing a *de facto* government, whether (initially) local or (ultimately) general', emphasis added); Edwin M. Borchard, 'International Responsibility of the State for Injuries Sustained by Aliens during Civil War', *APSR* 8(1) (1914), p. 122; Borchard, *The Diplomatic Protection of Citizens Abroad*, p. 241 ('A successful revolution stands on an entirely different basis. The government created through its efforts is liable for the acts of the revolutionists as well as for those of the titular government it has replaced').

[63] For instance, the examples mentioned in Piguet, *La Guerre civile en droit international*, p. 57 ff. involve situations where the rebellion was *not* successful. It should be added that another relevant case (mentioned by Piguet, ibid., p. 49–50) involves the bombardment of the city of Antwerp in the context of the secession of Belgium from the Kingdom of the Netherlands (1830). This case is however involving the creation of a new State and will therefore be examined in Part II, Section 4.3.2.2.3.

persons or property and pillage'.[64] Another relevant example is the *French Company of Venezuelan Railroads* case decided by the French–Venezuelan Mixed Claims Commission. It involved a claim for damages arising from the use by successful insurgents of railroad property. Umpire Plumley held that the State was to be held responsible for the damages resulting from *both* acts of the former government and the rebels.[65]

Another relevant example is the *Pinson* case decided in 1924 by the French–Mexican Claims Commission. The award dealt with a situation where the rebels were not even successful in their attempt to overthrow the Zapata government at the time. Yet, the award nevertheless mentioned a hypothetical number of examples where a State should be held responsible for acts committed by the governmental armed forces (and by the rebels, a point further examined below, Section 2.2.3.2) in the context of a successful revolution.[66]

[64] M. M. Whiteman, *Digest of International Law* (Washington, Dept. of State, vol. 8, 1973), p. 819–20, referring to a document sent by the US Department of State to the American Embassy, Habana, instruction, No. A-180, 26 January 1959, MS. Department of State, file 237.1141/12–1958, emphasis added.

[65] *French Company of Venezuelan Railroads* case, French–Venezuelan Mixed Claims Commission, 31 July 1905, UNRIAA 10, p. 354:

> The injuries done the railroad, the buildings and the material, by use in war, must have been considerable, and since the revolution was successful, the respondent Government is properly chargeable for its use and for the injuries and damages which resulted. There is no question as to the *liability of the respondent Government* for the natural and consequential damages which resulted to the railroad properties *while they were in the use and control of the titular Government*. Hence there is unquestioned and complete responsibility on the part of the respondent Government for all the necessary, natural, and consequential injuries which resulted to the railroad and its properties when used by *either the revolutionary or the governmental forces*. (emphasis added).

[66] *Georges Pinson (France)* v. *United Mexican States* (Decision No 1), French–Mexican Claims Commission, 10 October 1928, UNRIAA 5 [hereinafter referred to as '*Pinson* case, 1928'], p. 353: 'La thèse de l'irresponsabilité [supported by the Mexican government] est inacceptable, car il est incontestable qu'il peut se présenter bien des dommages révolutionnaires, dont l'État est sans aucun doute obligé d'assumer la responsabilité. . . . Par contre, si les dommages trouvent leur origine, par exemple dans des *réquisitions ou contributions forcées réclamées par le Gouvernement légitime* pendant sa lutte contre les insurgés, ou par les révolutionnaires avant leur triomphe final, ou qu'ils aient été causés par des *actes délictueux du Gouvernement légitime ou de ses forces militaires*, ou par des délits commis par les forces révolutionnaires victorieuses, la responsabilité de l'État ne saurait, à mon avis, être niée' ('The irresponsibility thesis [supported by the Mexican government] is unacceptable, for it is indisputable that there may well be revolutionary damage, for which the state is undoubtedly obliged to assume responsibility. . . . On the

Finally, another case (the *Shrigley* case) may to some extent be considered as supporting Rule no. 1, given that the principle may have been applied by the US–Chile Claims Commission.[67] In his First Report,[68] ILC Special Rapporteur Crawford referred to the case of *Minister of Defence, Namibia* v. *Mwandinghi*, where the Supreme Court of Namibia stated that, under Article 10 of the ILC Articles, 'the new government inherits responsibility for the acts committed by the previous organs of the State'.[69] Crawford rightly pointed out, however, that this case is not relevant for the analysis of Rule no. 1 since it did not involve the establishment of a new government, but rather the creation of a new State. The example will be examined in Part II.[70]

2.1.2.2.3.2 The Strabag *v.* Libya *Case* The 2020 *Strabag* award, decided under the Austria-Libya BIT, is a good illustration of the concrete application of Rule no. 1. The dispute involved an investment made in Libya by Strabag SE (an Austrian company) through a wholly owned German subsidiary, Strabag International (SI). In 2007, SI signed a joint venture contract with a Libyan State-owned company (LIDCO) which led to the creation of a local company, Al Hani (in which Strabag SE owned an indirect 60 per cent interest). Al Hani signed several road and infrastructure construction contracts with a number of Libyan State-owned entities.

other hand, if the damage originates, for example in requisitions or forced contributions demanded by the legitimate Government during its struggle against the insurgents, or by the revolutionaries before their final triumph, or whether they were caused by criminal acts of the legitimate Government or its military forces, or by offenses committed by victorious revolutionary forces, the responsibility of the State cannot, in my opinion, be denied') (emphasis added).

[67] *William S. Shrigley* v. *Chile*, in V. Coussirat-Coustère and P. M. Eisemann, *Répertoire de la Jurisprudence Arbitrale Internationale* (Nijhoff, Dordrecht, vol. I, 1989), p. 307(also in J. B. Moore, *History and Digest of the International Arbitrations to Which the United States Has Been a Party* (Washington, GPO, vol. 4, 1898), p. 3711–12). The case dealt with the destruction of property belonging to an US national by the Chilean army during the civil war of 1891 in Chile, which resulted in the defeat of the Balmaceda government. The Commission concluded: '[n]eutral property taken for the use of service of armies or functionaries thereunto authorized gives a right to the owner to demand compensation from the government exercising such authority'. The Commission did not however seem to have based its conclusion on the rationale behind Rule no. 1.

[68] ILC, Crawford First Report, 1998, p. 53, para. 274.

[69] *Minister of Defence, Namibia* v. *Mwandinghi*, 25 October 1991, 1992 (2) *SA* 355 (NmS), in *ILR* 91, p. 358, p. 361.

[70] See Part II, Section 4.3.2.2.4.

The award dealt with damages suffered by the company Al Hani during the civil war which occurred in Libya in 2011 as well as with events that took place after the establishment of the new government (at the end of 2011) following the victory of the rebels.[71]

The award explained that in early 2011 'the mounting conflict between rebel forces and troops loyal to the regime and other supporters was accompanied by a widespread breakdown of law and order'.[72] The Tribunal referred specifically to the commission of a number of wrongful acts by the troops loyal to the Gaddafi government against Al Hani facilities at the Tweisha facility.[73] The Tribunal also mentioned that the violence has continued *after* the rebels (the Libyan National Transitional Council, 'NTC') were successful in overthrowing the Gaddafi regime: '[f]ollowing the end of active hostilities in the fall of 2011, the evidence indicates that widespread violence and breakdown of law occurred in the areas of Al Hani's camps'.[74]

The case involved a number of claims alleging BIT and contract violations. The treaty claims (the only relevant claims for the purpose of this book) were divided by the Claimant in two categories, which were followed by the Tribunal:

- Claim no. 1 (including four items: 1.A to 1.D) alleging breaches of the war loss clause (Article 5 of the Treaty) resulting from wrongful acts committed in 2011 by the government troops *during* the civil war; and
- Claim no. 2 alleging breaches of the full protection and security (FPS) clause (Article 3(1) of the Treaty) and involving actions (and omissions) committed by the *new* government *after* the successful revolution (end of 2011).

[71] The history of the different phases of the civil war are further discussed in Section 3.1.4.2.2 dealing with the *Cengiz* v. *Libya* case.

[72] *Strabag SE* v. *Libya*, ICSID Case No. ARB(AF)/15/1, Award, 29 June 2020 [hereinafter referred to as '*Strabag* case, 2020'], para. 77.

[73] Ibid., para. 79: 'Beginning in March and April of 2011, and continuing for several months thereafter, some Al Hani sites were occupied for varying lengths of time by organized military units loyal to the regime. Al Hani's major facility at Tweisha was occupied for substantial periods by soldiers of the 32nd Reinforced Brigade, who requisitioned numerous vehicles and a great deal of equipment, some of it against receipts. Military forces occupying the camps are said to have stolen other equipment, and looted and damaged structures and equipment.' See also, para. 82: 'In about August 2011, as the regime neared collapse, the elements of the 32nd Brigade that had occupied the Tweisha camp withdrew. Before doing so, they are said to have extensively vandalized the premises and remaining equipment.'

[74] Ibid., para. 84. See also, paras. 85 ff.

Claim no. 1, involving the war loss clause, will be first examined. One important aspect of this clause applicable in the context of, inter alia, 'revolution, insurrection, civil disturbance' is that it requires the host State to provide compensation to an investor who has suffered a loss resulting from the 'requisitioning' or the 'destruction' ('not required by the necessity of the situation') of its investment by 'the forces or authorities' of Libya. The clause does *not* cover wrongful acts committed by the rebels during the insurrection.[75]

With respect to Claim 1.A, the Tribunal mentioned that 'numerous vehicles, generators, fuel tanks and other valuable Al Hani equipment was requisitioned by personnel of Libya's 32nd Reinforced Brigade, an elite security unit commanded by Col. Gaddafi's youngest son, Khamis Gaddafi'.[76] Under the war loss clause, Libya was responsible for such damages.[77]

Claim 1.B dealt with the allegation that 'Libyan armed forces also damaged and destroyed property which constituted part of Strabag's investment in Libya'.[78] The Tribunal mentioned that 'responsibility for particular damage is often not clear' and that 'in the chaotic conditions of the Revolution, Al Hani's vehicles and equipment were taken, destroyed, or damaged by multiple actors'.[79] Most importantly, the Tribunal noted that 'losses sometimes involved Government forces in non-combat situations in circumstances that fell under Article 5(2) of the Treaty, but there were also losses attributable to looters, rebels, and NATO bombing'.[80] In fact, the Tribunal acknowledged that 'the difficulty lies in determining how much of the claimed damage is attributable to Government forces, as opposed to rebels, looters, NATO bombing, or other possible causes'.[81]

[75] It should be added that in one recent (unpublished) award, the majority of the Tribunal considered that under the war loss clause contained in the BIT, any war losses suffered by the investor must be compensated under this provision, and not only those losses caused by acts attributable to the host State. See: (unnamed) *Turkish investors* v. *Syria*, ICC Case No. 21845/ZF/AYZ, Award, 31 August 2020, discussed in IAReporter, 'Analysis: in previously unseen Turkey-Syria BIT award, majority imports a more favourable war-losses clause; in dissent Ziade warns of "exorbitant" implications of majority reading', 13 Nov. 2020.

[76] *Strabag* case, 2020, para. 249. See also, para. 257.

[77] It determined that close to €6 million should be awarded to the Claimant in compensation (ibid., para. 263). Given the Claimant's ownership interest in Al Hani, this entitled it to be compensated for 60 per cent of that amount.

[78] Ibid., para. 266.

[79] Ibid., para. 287.

[80] Ibid., para. 287.

[81] Ibid., para. 289. See also, para. 292.

The Tribunal finally decided that 'one-third of the claimed losses are attributable to the actions by State forces not involving military necessity, actions for which Respondent is liable pursuant to Article 5(2)(b) of the Treaty'.[82]

Finally, Claim 1.D dealt with alleged 'damage to or destruction of Al Hani's construction sites, vehicles, equipment and material by Libyan Government forces'.[83] The Tribunal concluded that while 'there clearly was relevant loss and damage caused by members of Libya's armed forces occupying Al Hani's sites in non-combat situations',[84] the company's property and facilities 'were also damaged or looted by others – including rebels, NATO, looters, and Al Hani's own employees' for which the Respondent could not be held legally responsible under Article 5.[85] The Tribunal's 'best assessment of how much damage is attributable to actions by Libya's armed forces' was estimated to be at one-third of the actual damage done to Al Hani's property.[86]

Two observations should be made regarding the three claims involving wrongful acts committed by the troops loyal to the Gaddafi regime in 2011 *before their defeat*.[87]

First, the Tribunal simply applied the war loss provision to these claims. There was indeed no doubt that when the wrongful acts were committed for the better part of 2011, they were done by the 'forces or authorities of the other Contracting Party' (i.e. by the army forces who were loyal to the Gaddafi regime). Under the war loss clause, the State was clearly responsible for such damages.

Yet, it is worth highlighting that between the time the wrong took place and the moment the award was rendered (in 2020), the 'forces or authorities of the other Contracting Party' were clearly not the same actors. The Gaddafi regime forces had been defeated at the end of 2011

[82] Ibid., para. 298. The Tribunal awarded some €3.5 million for such losses. Given the Claimant's ownership interest in Al Hani, this entitled it to be compensated for 60 per cent of that amount. The other two-thirds of losses were not covered by Article 5(2)(b) because 'a portion of the loss at issue in this claim was inflicted by rebel or NATO forces; another portion involved losses due to looting by civilians and thefts by Al Hani's own employees'.

[83] Ibid., para. 305.

[84] Ibid., para. 309. See also, para. 315.

[85] Ibid., para. 320.

[86] Given the Claimant's ownership interest in Al Hani, this entitled it to be compensated for 60 per cent of the amount of € 900,000. It should be added that Claim 1.C was rejected by the Tribunal.

[87] Other claims (such as Claim 2, examined in the next paragraphs) dealt with damages arising from events which took place *after* the rebels had established themselves as the new government.

and the former rebels (the NTC) were now the force in power. In other words, when the award was rendered the 'forces or authorities' of Libya were not those who had actually committed the wrongs. The Tribunal never quite explained why the *new government* should be held responsible for the wrongs committed by the *previous* government in the course of the civil war. In reaching its conclusion, the Tribunal did not refer to Article 10 of the ILC Articles, nor to any other principles of international law on the matter. This omission is surprising given that Article 10(3) of the ILC Articles clearly supports the general conclusion reached by the Tribunal on this issue of responsibility. At the end of the day, the reasoning of the Tribunal supports Rule no. 1 whereby when the rebels are successful at establishing a new government (as they did at the end of 2011), that government remains responsible for the acts committed by the previous government while fighting the rebels. It seems that the Tribunal has simply applied Rule no. 1 without giving any further explanation.

Second, it is also noteworthy to observe that the Tribunal awarded no compensation for the damages which were caused *during* the revolution *by the rebels* before they successfully overthrew the Gaddafi regime at the end of 2011 and established themselves as the new government.[88] This is rather surprising given that the award specifically mentioned that such wrongful acts were committed by the rebels. In fact, the reasoning of the Tribunal suggests that one-third of the damages claimed under Claim 1.B were 'inflicted by rebel or NATO forces'.[89] The same quantification logic also seems to have been applied to Claim 1.D.[90] The Tribunal could have therefore applied Article 10 of the ILC Articles whereby the acts committed by the rebels during the insurgency are attributable to the State when the rebels are finally successful at establishing a new government (Rule no. 2).

It is true that such acts were not covered by the war loss clause. But this clause did not have the effect of preventing the Tribunal from applying other BIT clauses: 'the Tribunal finds that Article 5 of the Treaty does not preclude the possibility of claims based on other provisions of the treaty with respect to the matters that also fall under Article 5 of the Treaty'.[91] The same logic goes for other principles of international law. Nothing

[88] The Tribunal also did not examine whether the government in charge at the time (the Gaddafi regime) had failed to take all reasonable measures to prevent injurious conduct by rebels and damages from occurring.

[89] *Strabag* case, 2020, para. 298.

[90] Ibid., paras. 320, 321.

[91] Ibid., para. 228.

prevented the Tribunal from applying Article 10 of the ILC Articles. The award does not contain any reference to this important legal point. This silence can probably be explained by the simple fact that (according to the information at hand) the Claimant did not request compensation for such wrongs. It probably decided not to do so because of the difficulty in actually quantifying the damages that were specifically the result of rebels' actions (as opposed to those of rioters, looters, NATO forces, etc.). Yet, this is an important legal point which could have been, at least briefly, mentioned by the Tribunal.

Finally, the Tribunal also dealt with a number of other claims regarding the damages arising from events that took place *after* the revolution. Thus, Claim 2 concerned damages regarding 'a large amount of Al Hani's vehicles and heavy equipment removed from the Tweisha yard by unidentified persons at some time after October 2013 but before July 2014'.[92] Interestingly, the Tribunal did not apply the war loss clause to this claim. Instead, it applied the FPS clause. This outcome was probably dictated by the Claimant's own choice to argue its case in such a fashion. FPS clauses (which are contained in most BITs) apply to acts committed by both the governments and the rebels.[93] This basic point has been recognized by the *Cengiz* Tribunal.[94]

In any event, the Tribunal applied the FPS clause to damages arising from events which took place in 2013–14, that is, long *after* the rebels had successfully established a new government. At the time (in 2014), the new government was itself now fighting other insurgent groups in the context of a new civil war.[95] The Tribunal therefore correctly assessed this

92 Ibid., para. 322.

93 Christoph Schreuer, 'War and Peace in International Investment Law', in K. Fach Gómez, A. Gourgourinis and C. Titi (eds.), *International Investment Law and the Law of Armed Conflict* (European Yearbook of International Economic Law, Cham, Springer, 2019), p. 12 ('The duty to protect involves the obligation to defend the investment against violence by non-State actors. . . . These non-State actors may be rebels or insurgents engaged in a struggle against the government or private groups engaged in violent action against the investment'). See also: Sebastián Mantilla Blanco, *Full Protection and Security in International Investment Law* (Cham, Springer, 2019), p. 206 ff., citing several investment cases.

94 *Cengiz İnşaat Sanayi veTicaret A.S* v. *Libya*, ICC Case No. 21537/ZF/AYZ, Final Award, 7 Nov. 2018 [hereinafter referred to as '*Cengiz* case, 2018'], para. 403: '[i]n the most basic formulation, the purpose of the FPS standard is to protect the physical integrity of an investment against interference by use of force. The perpetrator of such interference is irrelevant: it could be the State itself, (including agencies, groups, entities or other organs whose actions can be attributed to the State), or any other third party'.

95 *Strabag* case, 2020, paras. 334, 345.

specific claim (Claim 2) as one involving a situation where (at the time the award was rendered in June 2020) the insurgents had *not* been successful in their attempt to establish a new government. Yet, this is an important point which is not addressed at all in the award. As further explained below,[96] the Tribunal concluded that the government was not responsible for any failure to exercise its due diligence obligation towards the investor 'with respect to the unexplained disappearance of Al Hani's property'.[97]

2.1.3 *The Rule Is Just and Fair Even If Its Application May Lead to Curious Results*

While Rule no. 1 is well-established (at least by scholars and it has also been endorsed by ILC Special Rapporteurs Ago and Crawford), it remains that its concrete application leads to some rather curious results. Perhaps surprisingly, this aspect has not been explored by scholars. Generally, they simply mention the rule without much analysis. A good example is Eagleton for whom 'It [i.e., the new government formed by successful rebels] is accountable also, of course, for the illegal acts of the preceding government. *Forma regiminis mutata, non mutatur civitas*.'[98] Yet, the rule states that the rebels now forming the new government should be held responsible for the wrongful acts committed by the previous government while *fighting against them*. Blanco believes that the effect of this rule is 'not self evident and could even appear to be counterintuitive', but without explaining why this appears to be so.[99] In fact, some members of the ILC have been critical about this aspect[100] and the rule has been contested by some writers on this ground.[101]

96 See Section 3.3.3.2.2.

97 *Strabag* case, 2020, para. 345.

98 C. Eagleton, *The Responsibility of States in International Law* (New York University Press, 1928), p. 148.

99 Mantilla Blanco, *Full Protection and Security*, p. 229–30. See also: Kathryn Greenman, 'The Secret History of Successful Rebellions in the Law of State Responsibility', *ESIL Reflections* 6(9) (2017), p. 8, explaining that 'the state will potentially be responsible for the acts of both the rebels and the government they are seeking to overthrow' and that 'there is very little effort to address why this should be or how there can be two authorities legitimate to represent the state internationally at the same time'.

100 Piguet, *La Guerre civile en droit international*, p. 141, citing the position of Ouchakov.

101 Ibid., p. 144 for whom this principle is less well established by State practice and is not part of positive law. He also (p. 141) refers to the work of Graefrath.

The curious aspect of the rule is that, had the government been *successful* at repressing the rebellion, the acts committed by the rebels during the insurgency would *not* have been attributable to that government (Rule no. 3).[102] This is because the government was in fact fighting *against* the rebels. Thus, as noted by Crawford, 'by definition, such a [rebel] movement cannot be considered to be aligned to the interests of the state against which it is fighting'.[103] Umpire Ralston in the *Sambiaggio* case stated that the acts of insurgents 'are committed to destroy the government, and no one should be held responsible for the acts of an enemy attempting his life'.[104] But the same remark also logically applies to the reserve situation of governmental acts committed against the rebels. To paraphrase Umpire Ralston, the government is certainly committed to destroy the rebels and, logically, the rebels should, therefore, not be held responsible for the acts 'of an enemy attempting' their lives. As Piguet rightly noted, 'comment admettre que les insurgés une fois vainqueur, soient liés par les agissements antérieurs des forces gouvernementales qui, si elles avaient vaincu, n'auraient pas encouru de responsabilité pour les préjudices causés par les révolutionnaires?'.[105] There is indeed something asymmetrical about this outcome: if the rebels win they *are* 'responsible' for actions of the previous government in its fight against them (Rule no. 1), but if the government wins it is *not* 'responsible' for the acts committed by the rebels while fighting against it (Rule no. 3). The situation seems to be 'unbalanced', at least from the perspective of the rebels. Then again, the rules of international law are made *by States*, not rebels. As previously mentioned, rebels are considered under domestic law as outlaws fighting illegally to overthrow the government. There is nothing surprising in the reaction of States creating rules which are more favourable to governments and detrimental to rebels. In any event, by definition, once in power, former rebels will also adopt a position not favourable to present or future rebels. This is because they are now in power and, quite logically, they themselves now want to avoid being overthrown by others.

102 See Section 2.2.

103 Crawford, *State Responsibility*, p. 170.

104 *Sambiaggio* case, Italian–Venezuelan Mixed Claims Commission, 1903, UNRIAA 10 [hereinafter referred to as '*Sambiaggio* case, 1903'], p. 512–13.

105 Piguet, *La Guerre civile en droit international*, p. 141 ('how to accept that the insurgents, once victorious, are bound by the previous actions of the government forces which, if they had won, would not have incurred responsibility for the damage caused by the revolutionaries').

While Rule no. 1 may lead to some curious results, one needs to consider what would be the possible outcome if the rule *did not* apply. In other words, what would happen if the wrongful acts committed by the previous government in its fight against the rebels would *not* be attributable to the new government (now formed by the rebels)? In practical terms, it would mean that only the acts committed by the rebels during the insurgency could be attributable to the new government (Rule no. 2). The wrongful acts committed by the previous government against other States or foreigners would go unpunished. A foreign investor or a third State which has suffered a damage during the insurgency as a result of a wrongful act committed by the previous government would have no possible remedy and would therefore get no reparation. Such an outcome would certainly be unfair from the perspective of the victim. Under this scenario, the victim would have a clear advantage in seeing the government ultimately prevailing in its fight against the rebels. Thus, if the government ultimately wins, the foreign investor or the injured third State will get some reparation. This is because a State remains responsible for its own wrongful acts during an unsuccessful insurgency.[106]

In the end, there is at least one reason that justifies the existence of Rule no. 1. The meaning behind the concrete application of the rule is that, regardless of the outcome of the fighting between the rebels and the government, those which have suffered damages as a result of wrongful acts committed *by the government* during the insurgency will get some reparation.[107] The rule is therefore fair. International law should aim to protect the interests of the victims of wrongful acts.[108] Another benefit resulting from the application of the rule is that foreign investors and third States are likely to remain *neutral* regarding the internal conflict. The main reason that explains such behaviour is because regardless of the outcome (i.e., whether or not the rebels ultimately win), they are aware that their interests will be protected. This concern is in line with the principle of non-intervention in civil wars. Article 2 of the resolution on 'The Principle of Non-Intervention in Civil Wars' adopted by the

[106] This question is examined in Section 3.3.2.

[107] The different question of wrongful acts committed *by the rebels* during the insurgency will be discussed below, see Section 2.2.

[108] For the application of this basic principle in the specific context of State succession to international responsibility, see: Marcelo G. Kohen and Patrick Dumberry, *The Institute of International Law's Resolution on State Succession and State Responsibility: Introduction, Text and Commentaries* (Cambridge University Press, 2019), p. 10 ff.

Institute in 1975 provides that 'Third States shall refrain from giving assistance to parties to a civil war which is being fought in the territory of another State'.[109]

2.1.4 *Should the Rule Apply to the Particular Case of Rebellions Overthrowing Racist Regimes?*

Finally, it is worth mentioning the position of Atlam that examines one specific aspect of this question regarding national liberation movements in the special context of decolonization. As mentioned above,[110] insurrections led by national liberation movements are beyond the scope of this book because such conflicts are considered to be *international* conflicts. The focus of this book is on internal (or civil) wars. Another important point is that the aim of wars involving national liberation movements is to achieve self-determination, which will typically result in the creation of a *new State*, rather than the establishment of a new government.[111] Yet, this may not always be the case. In his 1987 article, Atlam mentioned the possibility that the victory of a national liberation movement could be resulting in 'the defeat of a racist government and its replacement in the entire territory of the State by a new governments which represents the majority of the population instead of a minority'.[112] This is indeed the scenario which prevailed in South Africa. The national liberation movement's objective was to fight a racist power; it was not for the creation of a new State, but for the establishment of a radically new government representing the oppressed majority of the population.

The question examined in this section is whether or not Rule no. 1 should apply to such a special situation of a rebellion overthrowing

109 Institute of International Law, 'The Principle of Non-Intervention in Civil Wars', Session of Wiesbaden, 1975.

110 See Introduction, Section 1.1.3.1.

111 I will provide in Part II several examples involving insurgents in the context of decolonization leading to the creation of new States.

112 Hazem M. Atlam, 'National Liberation Movements and International Responsibility', in M. Spinedi and B. Simma (eds.), *United Nations Codification of State Responsibility* (New York, Oceana, 1987), p. 51. Interestingly, in his doctoral thesis (Hazem M. Atlam, *Succession d'États et continuité en matière de responsabilité internationale*, Doctoral Thesis, Université de droit, d'économie et des sciences d'Aix-Marseille (France) (1986), p. 79–103, 258–67, 275–81, 289–93) he dealt with the same scenario but from the different angle of the creation of a 'new State' on the entire territory of the predecessor State. This very exceptional hypothesis was also envisaged by Ago at some point (it will be examined later in Part II, Section 4.1).

a racist regime.[113] It should be recalled that under the 'normal' application of this rule, the acts committed by a racist regime while fighting the rebels which caused damages to third States or foreigners would be attributable to the new government after the successful revolution.[114] In order to illustrate this point, Atlam refers to the 'unacceptable solution' whereby the national liberation movement struggling against the racist regime in South Rhodesia could be held accountable (once in power after its successful insurgency) for the illegal acts committed by the government of Ian Smith while fighting the rebels. While Atlam does not refute that the acts of the rebels could be attributable to the new government since there exists a *continuity* between them, he does point out that there is clearly no such 'continuity' between the predecessor racist regime and the new government established by the rebels fighting discrimination.[115] For him, 'by minimizing the importance of the international legality of wars of liberation and by having recourse to the fiction of continuity between pre-existing racist government and the government created after the war of liberation, the ILC has endorsed an unacceptable solution'.[116] This is the reason why he believes that, in these circumstances, the new government should *not* be responsible for acts committed by the predecessor racist regime which have caused injuries to third States or foreigners.

The solution put forward by Atlam is undoubtedly appealing.[117] It seems hardly justifiable that the wrongful acts committed by the racist regime of South Africa while fighting the ANC may be attributable to the government after the end of Apartheid.[118] A third State injured by

[113] The ILC makes no difference between rebels and national liberation movements and, as a matter of principle, Rule no. 1 embodied in Article 10 applies to both situations. This question is further examined in Part II, Section 4.2.5.2.1.

[114] Atlam, 'National Liberation Movements', p. 51.

[115] Ibid., p. 51.

[116] Ibid., p. 52. See also, p. 55–6.

[117] In support: Cahin, 'Attribution of Conduct to the State', p. 250–1.

[118] Z. Matala, 'Under International Law, Does The New Order in South Africa Assume The Obligations And Responsibilities of The Apartheid Order: An Argument For Realism Over Formalism', *Comp. & Int'l L.J. S. Afr.* 30 (1997), p. 287–303, examining the question and concluding that while the changes are not involving a matter of State succession per se, it should be not considered either as a mere example of a change of government. According to the author, the change in South Africa 'reflects a change (both from an international law perspective and in reality) to a new state free from a situation approximating colonial rule' (p. 301). For this reason, he believes that:

> [t]he 1994 elections marked the first exercise of self-determination on the part of the entire South African population. Therefore, the new order

a wrong that was committed by the former government of South Africa may indeed appreciate such a reality. There would be very good moral, political and economic justifications not to pursue a claim against the new post-Apartheid government under these circumstances.

In fact, this is a situation where the concept of 'odious debts' (mentioned above) could be useful. One aspect of 'odious debts' are those debts contracted by a government 'for purposes that are not in conformity with contemporary international law and, in particular, the principles of international law embodied in the Charter of the United Nations'.[119] Any government upholding a racist colonial regime against the will of the majority of its people while preventing them from freely exercising their right of self-determination is clearly not acting 'in conformity with contemporary international law'. Needless to mention that the use of military forces by such a regime against a national liberation movement in its legitimate struggle for self-determination is also in violation of international law. In his Report, Bedjaoui provides two examples of debts contracted in violation of international law which are very relevant for the present purposes.[120] Another variation of such 'odious debt' is the so-called 'subjugation' debt (or 'hostile debt')[121] which has been defined as that 'contracted by a State with a view to attempting to repress an

should not be responsible for the wrongs committed under the apartheid order. Moreover, the new order has the option of approaching international treaties entered into by the apartheid order in terms of a clean slate or pick and choose approach.

119 ILC, Ninth Report Bedjaoui, 1977, p. 68, para. 129.

120 Ibid., p. 69, para. 134–5:

> If, for example, the predecessor State contracted a debt in order to purchase arms that were used to flout human rights through genocide, racial discrimination or apartheid, the successor State must consider this debt as odious even if its own population or that of the territory ceded to it did not directly suffer from those policies. The successor State should not assume any part of the general debt of the predecessor State corresponding to such arms purchases. Similarly, if the predecessor State contracted debts intended to finance a policy of subjugating a people and colonizing its territory or, in general, any policy contrary to the right of peoples to self-determination, such debts will be odious in the eyes of the international community. If there is subsequently a succession of States – for example a transfer of a part of a territory from one State to another – the successor State, even if it was not a victim of that policy, will not have to accept any part of these specific debts in the general debt of the predecessor State. The same holds true, for even greater reason, if the successor State or the territory transferred to it have themselves suffered from such a policy on the part of the predecessor State.

121 Gallen, 'Odious Debt and Jus Post Bellum', p. 671.

insurrectionary movement or war of liberation in a territory that it dominates or seeks to dominate, or to strengthen its economic colonization of that territory'.[122] The military effort of a government against the will of the majority of its people to maintain a racist or colonial regime would seem to perfectly fit this definition. As further discussed below,[123] it is generally recognized that a *new State* is not considered 'responsible' for such 'odious debts' contracted by the predecessor State.[124]

The other question as to whether the same solution should apply to *wrongful acts* (not 'debts' per se) is controversial.[125] In his Report, Bedjaoui noted that 'if the [odious] debt was contracted by a State for the purpose of committing a wrongful act against another State, the position is clear: the other State, if it becomes a successor State, will not acknowledge the debt'.[126] It would be logical that the same solution applies to the wrongful act *itself*. It should be the case whenever the act has an 'odious' character, such as the repression of the legitimate struggle of a national liberation movement fighting to end a racist or colonial oppression against the majority of the population. There is support in favour of the principle of non-succession to responsibility for the consequences arising from the commission of a wrongful act (having an 'odious' character) in a situation involving claims *between* the predecessor State and its successor for acts committed *against each other*.[127] Thus, it seems logical that East Timor, as a new State, should *not* be held responsible for the consequences arising from the perpetration of 'odious' wrongful acts which were committed by Indonesia (the predecessor colonial State) *against the Timorese people* and its national liberation movement in its effort to defeat its legitimate struggle for independence. The other question, which happens to be much more controversial, is whether the same solution should apply when the wrong affects *a third party* (a third State or a foreign investor).[128] In any event, it is generally recognized that the obligations arising from an internationally wrongful act committed by the

[122] ILC, Ninth Report Bedjaoui, 1977, p. 67, para. 118.

[123] See Part II.

[124] ILC, Ninth Report Bedjaoui, 1977, p. 67, paras. 115 ff., see para. 173, Article D ('Non-transferability of odious debts'), providing that 'odious debts contracted by the predecessor State are not transferable to the successor State'.

[125] See Patrick Dumberry, *State Succession to International Responsibility* (Leiden, Martinus Nijhoff Publ., 2007), p. 294–7.

[126] ILC, Ninth Report Bedjaoui, 1977, p. 68, para. 130.

[127] See Dumberry, *State Succession to International Responsibility*, p. 295.

[128] Ibid., p. 294–7. I have explained that while some scholars tend to support the non-responsibility approach in that specific context, there is no State practice and case law in favour of this proposition.

(colonial) predecessor State against a third party do not pass to the Newly independent State.[129] But this is a situation involving the creation of a *new State*, not one dealing with the establishment of a new government.

There are good reasons to extend the findings mentioned above about 'odious' or 'subjugation' debts to the different context of *wrongful acts* committed by a racist regime in its effort to suppress a national liberation movement which eventually succeed in establishing a *new government*. It would indeed seem logical that the new government should *not* have the burden to provide reparation for wrongs which were committed by the previous racist government during its illegal attempts to crash the legitimate struggle for (internal) self-determination of an oppressed people. Yet, while this solution is undoubtedly as morally satisfying as it is fair, it also has a downside. Thus, recognizing the existence of an exception to Rule no. 1 in the specific context of rebellions overthrowing racist regimes may lead to some unsatisfactory consequences. The injured party would have no possible remedy for the damage it suffered as a result of acts committed by the government. Such an outcome may be considered as unfair from the perspective of the victim.[130] Another negative effect is that under this scenario, the victim would have a clear advantage in seeing the government ultimately prevailing in its fight against the rebels in order to get any reparation. While these negative aspects are significant, I believe that, on balance, there should exist an exception to Rule no. 1 in the special context of rebels overthrowing racist regimes.

2.2 Rule No. 2: The Acts Committed by the Rebels during the Insurgency Are Attributable to the State

The principle set out in Article 10(1) of the ILC Articles is straightforward: the acts committed by the rebels during the (ultimately successful)

129 See Article 16(1) of the Resolution adopted by Institute of International Law, 'State Succession in Matters of State Responsibility', Rap. M.G. Kohen, 2015, in *Annuaire IDI* 76 (2015), p. 703. On this provision, see: Kohen and Dumberry, *The Institute of International Law's Resolution*, p. 128 ff.

130 Yet, it could be argued that a foreign investor should not be investing in the first place in a country where the government is imposing by force systematic and institutional racist policies against the majority of the population. An investor should know that doing business in such an environment where a civil war is ongoing is, by definition, very risky and that the potential of being cut in crossfire between rebels and the government is high. This remark does not apply, however, to the other situation of a third State who's embassy, properties or its personnel may suffer damages as a result of actions taken by a racist government during a civil war.

insurgency are attributable to the State (Rule no. 2). The provision reads as follows: 'The conduct of an insurrectional movement which becomes the new Government of a State shall be considered an act of that State under international law'. In the next sections, I will examine the following issues:

- The drafting history of Article 10(1) of the ILC Articles (Section 2.2.1);
- The rationale behind Rule no. 2 (Section 2.2.2);
- Case law and State practice supporting this principle (Section 2.2.3); and
- An analysis of a number of other related questions (Section 2.2.4).

2.2.1 *Drafting History*

The first sentence of Article 15(1) of the 1975 Draft contained almost the same language as Article 10(1) of the 2001 ILC Articles (but it referred to the 'act' rather than the 'conduct' of an insurrectional movement). In contrast, Article 13(2) of the 1972 draft presented by Ago contained the same elements but used slightly more complicated language.[131] One noticeable change is that the straightforward formula an 'insurrectional movement which becomes the new Government of a State' replaced in the 1975 draft the rather complicated reference to the organs of an insurrectional movement whose structures have 'subsequently been integrated, in whole or in part, with those of the pre-existing State'. This was a most welcome change. What really matters is that the rebels have established a new government. The phrase 'the conduct of an insurrectional movement' is also preferable to the earlier convoluted language ('The conduct of a person or group of persons who, at the time when such conduct was engaged in, were organs of an insurrectional movement'). It may be complicated to determine in some cases what the 'organs' of a rebel group are.[132] Another interesting aspect is that the notion of 'retroactivity' is no longer present.[133] Ago explained in his 1972 Report

[131] ILC, Ago Report, 1972, p. 151, para. 214: 'The conduct of a person or group of persons who, at the time when such conduct was engaged in, were organs of an insurrectional movement whose structures have subsequently been integrated, in whole or in part, with those of the pre-existing State is retroactively considered to be an act of that State.'

[132] On this question, see S. I. Verhoeven, 'International Responsibility of Armed Opposition Groups. Lessons from State Responsibility for Actions of Armed Opposition Groups', in N. Gal-Or, C. Ryngaert and M. Noortmann (eds.), *Responsibilities of the Non-State Actor in Armed Conflict and the Market Place. Theoretical Considerations and Empirical Findings* (Leiden, Brill, 2015), p. 299 ff.

[133] Article 13(2) of the 1972 draft was indeed entitled 'Retroactive attribution to a State of the acts of organs of a successful insurrectional movement'.

that the acts initially committed by the rebels during the insurgency 'are to be regarded, retroactively' once the rebels have established a new government 'as "acts of the State"'.[134]

In his First Report in 1998, Crawford proposed the following version of Article 15 (entitled 'Conduct of organs of an insurrectional movement'):

1. The conduct of an organ of an insurrectional movement, established in opposition to a State or to its government, shall not be considered an act of that State under international law unless:
   (a) The insurrectional movement succeeds in becoming the new Government of that State; or
   (b) The conduct is otherwise considered to be an act of that State under articles 5, 7, 8, 9 or 15 bis.

Crawford explained that the provision used a negative form as a means 'to meet concerns expressed about the attribution to the State of unsuccessful insurrectional movements'.[135] He left it to the Drafting Committee to decide whether the provision should be formulated in a 'negative' or a positive form.[136] The Drafting Committee decided not to include such a 'negative attribution' clause and therefore deleted the first paragraph.[137] The draft provision put forward by Crawford also referred to insurrectional movements which were 'established in opposition to a State or to its government'. The word 'established' had been added by Crawford to highlight the existence of a certain 'threshold at which movements acquired a certain international status'.[138] The Drafting Committee decided that 'it was preferable not to qualify the term "insurrectional movement" by the insertion of such a phrase as "established in opposition to a State or Government", taking into account the wide variety of insurrectional movements existing in practice which should be covered by paragraph 1'.[139] Crawford also explained that the term 'organ' of an insurrectional movement was used so that 'a distinction must be drawn between the more or less uncoordinated conduct of the supporters of such a movement and

[134] ILC, Ago Report, 1972, p. 150, para. 211.

[135] ILC, Crawford First Report, 1998, note no. 4 to new Draft Article 15 (ibid., p. 57).

[136] See Comment by Crawford in ILC, 'Summary records of the meetings of the fiftieth session', 2558th meeting 7 August 1998, UN Doc. A/CN.4/SER.A/1998, *ILC Yearbook* vol. I (1998), p. 249, p. 269, para. 52.

[137] Ibid., p. 287, p. 290, para. 86.

[138] Ibid., p. 269, para. 53.

[139] Ibid., p. 287, p. 290, para. 87.

conduct which for whatever reason is attributable to an "organ" of that movement'.[140] The Drafting Committee debated whether to keep the word 'organ' in the final draft, but ultimately decided not to, 'given the fact that some movements which should have been covered by the article might not be sufficiently structured so as to have "organs"'.[141] The purpose of deleting the words 'established' and 'organ' was to give Article 10(1) a wide scope of application and to cover as many rebel groups as possible.

Yet, it is noteworthy that Article 10(1) only refers to the conduct of 'an insurrectional movement', while Article 10(2) refers in addition to the conduct of 'other' movements. As further discussed in Part II, the addition of the term 'other' in the context of rebels struggling to create a new State was meant to broaden the scope of the provision and to encompass national liberation movements fighting in the specific context of decolonization.[142] It has been argued by one writer that 'the omission of other movements in the first paragraph of the provision appears to be an oversight, since national liberation movements include groups that fight against racist regimes as established governments of a State'.[143] As mentioned above,[144] national liberation movements fighting for the establishment of a radically new government (rather than creating a new State) is a rare but possible scenario. In fact, the examples of South Africa and South Rhodesia are a good illustration that such a scenario occurred in the past. Yet, given that

140 ILC, Crawford First Report, 1998, note no. 3 to new Draft Article 15 (ibid., p. 57). See also, comment by Crawford, ILC, 'Summary records of the meetings of the fiftieth session', 2555th meeting 4 August 1998, UN Doc. A/CN.4/SER.A/1998, *ILC Yearbook* vol. I (1998), p. 249, p. 248, para. 54, indicating that he

> had tried to convey that nuance by using the term 'the conduct of an organ of an insurrectional movement' and to take into account at least the general terms of the principle contained in Protocols I and II to the Geneva Conventions of 12 August 1949 and in the jurisprudence as to the threshold beyond which an insurrectional movement became an organization and up to which its activities were limited to local rioting or disturbances which fell within the scope of other rules.

141 ILC, 'Summary records of the meetings of the fiftieth session', UN Doc. A/CN.4/SER.A/1998, *ILC Yearbook* vol. I (1998), p. 287, p. 290, para. 86.

142 See Part II, Section 4.2.5.2.1.

143 Verhoeven, 'International Responsibility', p. 289, referring to: E. Roucounas, 'Non-State Actors: Areas of International Responsibility in Need of Further Exploration', in M. Ragazzi (ed.), *International Responsibility Today: Essays in Memory of Oscar Schachter* (Leiden, Nijhoff, 2005), p. 393.

144 See Section 2.1.4.

such cases are truly exceptional, one can understand why Article 10(1) does not refer to the conduct of 'other' movements.

The next section examines the rationale behind Rule no. 2.

2.2.2 *The Rationale behind the Principle*

In this section, I will examine the reasons why the ILC adopted the principle set out in Article 10(1) and the rationale which has been mentioned by scholars and ILC Special Rapporteurs in support of such a rule. I will first examine, in the words of Ago, the 'special case of attribution' of the conduct of rebels to the State (Section 2.2.2.1). I will then explain that the foundation of this special rule is the existence of an 'organic' or 'structural' continuity between the insurgents and the new government (Section 2.2.2.2).

2.2.2.1 A 'Special Case of Attribution' of the Conduct of Rebels to the State

While some writers have argued otherwise in the past,[145] the starting point of the analysis is to acknowledge the basic point that the acts of *individuals* participating in riots or any other kinds of internal troubles are clearly *not* attributable to the State.[146] Thus, these individuals are *not* organs of the State. The situation is no different 'once an organized movement comes into existence as a matter of fact'.[147] Even if individuals participating in riots may become better organized over time and may develop some sort of structure, that does not alter the basic fact that they are *not* organs of the State. In fact, as noted in the 2001 ILC Commentary, 'once an organized movement comes into existence as a matter of fact, it will be *even less possible* to attribute its conduct to the State, which will not be in a position to exert effective control over its activities'.[148] The 2001 ILC Commentary makes it clear that 'the conduct of the members of the movement presents itself purely as the conduct of private individuals' and that 'it can be placed on the same footing as that of persons or groups who participate in a riot or mass demonstration'.[149] Thus, the basic

[145] See writers mentioned in Piguet, *La Guerre civile en droit international,* p. 134, and in particular the work of J. H. Ralston, *The Law and Procedure of International Tribunals* (Stanford University Press, 1926), p. 343.

[146] ILC, Commentaries, 2001, p. 50, para. 2.

[147] Ibid.

[148] Ibid., emphasis added.

[149] Ibid.

'general principle' remains that the 'conduct of an insurrectional or other movement is not attributable to the State'.[150] While the 1961 Harvard Draft adopted a different view in the past,[151] no one can deny this basic principle today. This is simply because the 'structures and organization of the movement are and remain independent of those of the State'.[152] In other words, they are different entities.

In any event, the ILC in its Commentaries adds that 'this will be the case where the State successfully puts down the revolt'.[153] Thus, as further explained in Section 3.1, when the rebels are *not successful* at establishing a new government, the wrongful acts committed by them during the uprising will *not* be attributable to the State (Rule no. 3). As explained by Ago,[154] at the end of an *unsuccessful* insurgency, the government in charge will *only* be responsible for *its own acts* committed during the fighting (Rule no. 6).[155]

However, what happens when the rebels *win* and eventually establish a new government? As a matter of principle, the situation is, quite logically, the same. Thus, the acts of one entity (the rebels) committed during the insurgency still cannot, in any way, be attributable to another entity (the State). Ago emphasized on the fact that they are *different organizations*: 'at the time when the acts complained of occurred, those who committed them belonged to an organization which was not to be integrated with that of the State until later and which, at the time in question, was opposed to the organization that was termed legitimate'.[156] Thus, not only the rebels and the government are different organizations,

150 Ibid., p. 50, para. 4.

151 Article 18(1), 1961 Harvard Draft (in *ILC Yearbook* vol. II (1969), p. 146): '[i]n the event of a revolution or insurrection which brings about a change in the government of a State . . ., an act or omission of an organ, agency, official, or employee of a revolution or insurrectionary group is, for the purposes of this Convention, *attributable to the State* in which the group established itself as the government' (emphasis added).

152 ILC, Commentaries, 2001, p. 50, para. 4.

153 Ibid.

154 ILC, Ago Report, 1972, p. 145, para. 199:

> In the event of the struggle's ending in victory for the pre-existing power, the insurrectional organization is dissolved and only the established apparatus remains. It is logical that one should attribute to the State only the acts or omissions of the members of that apparatus, which continues, and not the acts of members of the organization which has ceased to exist without ever having succeeded in being the actual organization of the State or at least participating in it.

155 See Section 3.3.

156 ILC, Ago Report, 1972, p. 145, para. 197.

but they were, moreover, *fighting each other* for power: '[d]uring a civil war, two organizations are opposed to each other and are fighting for final victory. Each of the two wishes to be the organization of the State; at the outset, one is so in fact and the other potentially.'[157]

No one denies the logic and soundness of the basic principle that the acts of a rebellion movement cannot, as a matter of principle, be attributable to the State (because they are different entities and organizations). But, the interesting question is how would this principle apply in practice if the rebels *succeed* in establishing a new government? The application of the principle would lead to, in the words of Crawford, an 'anomalous' outcome.[158] Thus, since the rebels have gained power and are now forming the new government they simply no longer exist as an independent organization. The acts committed by the rebels during the uprising are still attributable to them, and only to them. But since they no longer exist as an entity, it means that no one could be responsible for such acts committed during the uprising. Ultimately, the 'normal' application of the basic rules of attribution would lead to an extraordinary outcome in the event that the rebels are successful at establishing a new government. Thus, *no one* would be responsible for the acts of the rebels. The victims of such acts (third States, foreigners) would have no remedy for the damages they have suffered. Such an outcome would be particularly unfair for the victims given that this is *not* a situation where the entire State has collapsed.[159]

Faced with such an extraordinary outcome, the ILC Commentaries stated that 'it would be anomalous if the new regime ... could avoid responsibility for conduct earlier committed *by it*'.[160] Thus (as further examined in detail in the next section), the last words of this quote ('by it') make it clear that the acts committed by the rebels during the insurgency are considered by the ILC as those of the 'new regime' (i.e. the new government). In fact, the ILC Commentaries explained that 'in these exceptional circumstances, Article 10 provides for the attribution of the conduct of the successful insurrectional or other movement to the State'.[161] One important point highlighted by Ago is that Rule no. 2 does *not* involve

[157] Ibid., para. 199.
[158] ILC, Commentaries, 2001, p. 50, para. 4.
[159] This is not a case of State succession. This is a situation involving merely a change of government. The identity of the State, as a subject of international law, has not been altered as a result of such a change of government.
[160] ILC, Commentaries, 2001, p. 50, para. 4, emphasis added.
[161] Ibid.

a State being actually *responsible* for the acts of the rebels. It is a question of *attribution* and nothing else: 'It should be noted, in this connexion, that references are often made to international responsibility of the State for the wrongful acts of a successful insurrectional movement, whereas what is in fact involved is the attribution of those acts to the State, as a source of the latter's responsibility.'[162] The ILC Commentaries indeed refer to these exceptional circumstances as a '*special case* of attribution to a State'.[163] For the ILC, 'this situation *requires* that acts committed during the struggle for power by the apparatus of the insurrectional movement should be attributable to the State, alongside acts of the then established government'.[164] This point was also emphasized in the past by Brownlie who stated that the principle was not based on 'an actual assumption of responsibility', but rather as 'a *categorical imposition* of responsibility for all acts of the insurgents forces'.[165] The same idea was also mentioned by Crawford in his subsequent writing.[166]

Two observations should be made at this juncture. First, it is clear that Rule no. 2 was designed to fill an accountability gap. While d'Aspremont is very critical about the logical foundation of Rule no. 2, he nevertheless believes that it serves 'a very useful as well as lofty purpose which makes it worthy'.[167] For him, 'the rule of attribution of acts of victorious rebels'

162 ILC, Ago Report, 1972, p. 145, para. 196.

163 ILC, Commentaries, 2001, p. 50, para. 1, emphasis added.

164 Ibid., p. 50, para. 5, emphasis added.

165 Ian Brownlie, *State Responsibility, Part I* (Oxford, Clarendon Press, 1983), p. 178, emphasis added.

166 Crawford, *State Responsibility*, p. 171: 'Article 10 is in effect a negative attribution clause to which is attached a curious form of secondary, contingent responsibility based on the successful outcome of the insurgency. It is as if the state represented by the successful insurgents is *precluded from denying the attribution to it* of their conduct in the course of the insurgency' (emphasis added). See also, the comment made by Crawford, in ILC, 'Summary records of the meetings of the fiftieth session', 2556th meeting 5 August 1998, UN Doc. A/CN.4/SER.A/1998, *ILC Yearbook* vol. I (1998), p. 249, at p. 254, para. 39: '[t]he article provided in fact that acts which were not attributable to the State at the time when they were committed might be attributable to it a posteriori as a result of a subsequent event, for example the success of an insurrectional movement'.

167 Jean d'Aspremont, 'Rebellion and State Responsibility: Wrongdoing by Democratically Elected Insurgents', *ICLQ* 58 (2009), p. 432. See also: Verhoeven, 'International Responsibility', p. 294: '[t]he attribution of conduct of successful insurrectional movements to the (new) State undoubtedly contributes to the reducing of the accountability gap for violations of international law by such movements'. But he also noted that 'The attribution of conduct of insurrectional movements to a State is . . . not adequate to hold armed opposition groups accountable for their conduct in all situations' (p. 296) and that any such accountability gap 'will be reduced by the introduction of an international legal responsibility of insurrectional movements' (p. 303).

under Article 10(1) 'is not inherent to the "logic" of the mechanism of State responsibility and is rather an exception carved with a view to fighting impunity'.[168] Thus, 'the attribution of the acts of the rebels to the State following their triumph undoubtedly was primarily designed to fill an accountability gap', adding that 'the idea of "justice" that seems to underlie this exceptional rule of attribution is not expressly invoked by the ILC'.[169] He believes that 'this is a righteous purpose which suffices to justify the rule' and that 'one may accordingly find it bewildering that the ILC has balked at expressly stating this underlying political motive when devising that rule and preferred to cloak its desire to curb impunity in a flimsy argument based on continuity'.[170]

Second, the ILC Commentary has indeed taken the position that 'the basis for the attribution of conduct of a successful insurrectional or other movement *to the State* under international law lies in the continuity between the movement and the eventual Government'.[171] The specific question of this 'continuity' between the movement and the new government will be examined in the next section. The important point that has to be highlighted here is that the acts committed by the rebels are attributable *to the State itself*. It is *not* a question of the attribution of acts committed by the rebels *to the new government*. While some writers have supported this position in the past[172] (notably Eagleton),[173] the ILC did not follow this path. The ILC further explained why the conduct of a successful insurrectional movement should be attributable *to the State*:

168 d'Aspremont, 'Rebellion and State Responsibility', p. 435.

169 Ibid., p. 432. See also, p. 438:

> [i]ndeed, the ILC saw the responsibility of the State for acts of victorious rebels as a means to fill a gap of accountability in the case of violations of international law by non-State actors. It has been shown that filling the accountability gap was the only serious underpinning for Article 10 as no systemic reasons or precedents buttress this exception to the principle that only acts of organs become acts of the State.

170 Ibid., p. 433.

171 ILC, Commentaries, 2001, p. 50, para. 4, emphasis added.

172 See Schwarzenberger, *International Law*, p. 628, indicating that 'the real ground of the retroactivity of tortious liability is estoppel'. See also, p. 629: 'acts of the successful revolutionaries can be equated retrospectively with such acts because the revolutionary government is estopped from asserting the true position'.

173 Eagleton, *The Responsibility of States*, p. 147: '[t]he rule is also well established that the government set up by successful revolutionists must accept responsibility for their acts as insurgents from the beginning, a conclusion logically deducible from the fact that the *acts of the insurgents have now become the acts of the government*, for which it must accept responsibility', emphasis added.

'In such a case, the State does not cease to exist as a subject of international law. It remains the same State, despite the changes, reorganizations and adaptations which occur in its institutions. Moreover, it is the only subject of international law to which responsibility can be attributed'.[174]

The next section examines the main reason which the ILC identified as 'lead[ing] naturally to the attribution to the State of conduct which the insurrectional movement may have committed during the struggle': the *continuity* which exists between the 'new organization of the State and that of the insurrectional movement'.[175]

2.2.2.2 The Continuity between the Insurgents and the New Government

In this section, I will first examine two 'justifications' which have been put forward by scholars in the past to explain the 'special' rule of attribution mentioned in Article 10(1) (Section 2.2.2.2.1). I will then expose Ago's idea of the State representing the 'dual continuation' of both the rebels and the previous government (Section 2.2.2.2.2). I will then show that the ILC did not consider the question, as to whether or not an insurrectional movement has an international legal personality, to be relevant (Section 2.2.2.2.3). Finally, I will explain that Crawford has endorsed the idea of the existence of an 'organic' or 'structural' continuity between an insurrectional movement and the new government (Section 2.2.2.2.4).

2.2.2.2.1 Other Less Convincing 'Justifications' Explaining the 'Special' Rule of Attribution in Article 10(1) In his 1972 Report, Ago examined a number of 'justifications' which have been put forward to explain the 'special' rule of attribution mentioned in Article 10(1).

He first mentioned the position of some writers for whom attribution should be based on the fact that the 'insurgents were exercising their authority as a "*de facto* government" in at least part of the territory of the State' when the wrong was committed by them.[176] There is some support for this position.[177] The *Dix* case, decided by the US–Venezuela Mixed Claims Commission, stated that the revolution 'proved successful, and its acts, under a well-established rule of international law, are to be regarded

[174] ILC, Commentaries, 2001, p. 50, para. 5.
[175] Ibid.
[176] The theory will be further addressed below when examining situations where rebellions lead to the creation of new States. See Part II, Section 4.2.3.2.1.
[177] I will examine in Section 2.2.3.2 below several awards which support this position.

as the acts of a *de facto* government'.[178] Ago analysed a number of other cases supporting the proposition that 'acts of an insurrectional movement that is subsequently successful should be attributable to the State, since at the time when the injuries were caused by its agents it was already exercising the authority of a *de facto* government'.[179] He explained, however, that this de facto government justification is not actually followed in practice: 'in practice a distinction is not made, for the purpose of attributing acts to the State, according as the acts of the insurgents precede or follow their acquisition of effective power over a given region'.[180]

Ago also explained another reason why the attribution of insurgent actions to the State 'is quite independent of the exercise of *de facto* power by the insurgents in question'.[181] This is because 'the acts committed by insurgents are not considered to be acts of the State when the final outcome of the civil war is unfavourable to them, even if they were able to exercise *de facto* authority over some portion of the territory of the State'.[182] Ago therefore suggests that if the exercise of de facto power by the insurgents was the relevant criterion during the insurgency, this important fact should, logically, have some impact at the end of the rebellion, *even if* the rebels are not successful. This is because the rebels were acting as the de facto government at the time when the wrong was committed. Logically, these acts should be attributable to the government after the conflict. According to Ago, the fact that the acts of insurgents are not considered as those of the State at the end of their unsuccessful rebellion (Rule no. 3) shows that the criterion as to whether or not they were able to exercise de facto authority is not relevant. Ago is right to say that the importance of this criterion is rather doubtful given that it depends entirely on the outcome of the conflict.[183] The criterion would

[178] *Dix (U.S.* v. *Venezuela)*, US–Venezuela Mixed Claims Commission, 1903, UNRIAA 9, p. 120.

[179] ILC, Ago Report, 1972, p. 146, para. 202.

[180] Ibid., p. 145, para. 198. See also: ILC, Report, 1975, p. 100, para. 2.

[181] ILC, Ago Report, 1972, p. 145, para. 198. See also: ILC, Report, 1975, p. 100, para. 2.

[182] Ibid.

[183] The point is made clear by N. D. Houghton, 'The Responsibility of the State for the Acts and Obligations of Local De Facto Governments and Revolutionists', *Minnesota LR* 14 (3) (1930), p. 255:

> the capacity of a local *de facto* government to bind the state, and therefore, succeeding governments, depends largely upon its ultimate success. If it finally becomes the *de jure* government of the state, or if the region over which it exercises control becomes an independent state, then its acts, from its inception, are binding, upon the old state or the new state, as the case

thus be relevant in cases of successful rebellions, but not at all when such an uprising fails. Yet, it should be added that Ago's statement is partially misleading. As mentioned below, there are situations where the fact that certain acts were committed by rebels exercising de facto authority is highly relevant in the context of unsuccessful rebellions.[184]

Another justification[185] which has been advanced in support of the 'special' rule of attribution in Article 10(1) is the one given by Umpire Plumley in the 1903 *Bolivar Railway* case decided by the Venezuelan–British Mixed Claims Commission.[186] He stated that a successful revolution represents 'a changing national will, crystallizing in the finally successful result'. The following quote illustrates his reasoning:

> Responsibility comes because it is the same nation. Nations do not die when there is a change of their rulers or in their forms of government. These are but expressions of a change of national will. 'The king is dead; long live the king!' has typified this thought for ages. The nation is responsible for the debts contracted by its titular government, and that responsibility continues through all changing forms of government until the obligation is discharged. The nation is responsible for the obligations of a successful revolution from its beginning, because in theory, it represented ab initio a changing national will, crystallizing in the finally successful result.[187]

Ago described the above argument as follows: 'where the action of the insurgents was successful, the insurgents would be regarded as having represented the true national will ever since their uprising against the constituted power'.[188] Some writers have indeed supported this position in the past.[189] Thus, for Rousseau, 'il y a là comme une sorte de

> may be. But if it fails, the succeeding *de jure* government may refuse to consider many of its acts and obligations as binding upon the state.

See also, p. 268.

[184] I will explain in Section 3.1.5 that even when the insurgency is ultimately unsuccessful, it remains that the State should nevertheless be bound by the governmental lawful 'routine activities' performed by rebels in situations where they have established a local de facto government in part of the territory (Rule no. 4A).

[185] The theory will be further examined below when examining situations where rebellions lead to the creation of new States. See Part II, Section 4.2.3.2.2.

[186] *Bolivar Railway Co.* Case, UK–Venezuela Claims Commission, Opinion of the Umpire, 1903, UNRIAA 9, p. 445, 452–3.

[187] Ibid., p. 452–3.

[188] ILC, Ago Report, 1972, p. 145, para. 198.

[189] G. Berlia, 'La guerre civile et la responsabilité internationale de l'État', *RGDIP* 11(1) (1937), p. 59; Ganzory, 'International Claims and Insurgence', p. 92–3; Reza Mohtashami, 'Protecting the Legitimacy of the Arbitral Process: Jurisdictional and Procedural Challenges in Public-Private Disputes', in Jean Kalicki and Mohamed

confirmation rétroactive de l'action des insurgés, fondée sur ce succès final' ('there is a sort of retroactive confirmation of the action of the insurgents, based on this ultimate success').[190] Borchard also endorsed this position.[191] More recently, the 'national will' argument seems to have been endorsed by Judge *ad hoc* Kreća in his separate opinion in the 2015 *Genocide* case.[192] Based on the above-mentioned dictum of the *Bolivar Railway* case, Kreća considered the situation as one of a 'change of government' where the identity of the State remains intact.[193]

Ago has well-explained why one needs to be cautious about the concept of 'national will'.[194] He also pointed out another reason why this 'national will' theory should be rejected. Thus, if the theory were to be applied it

Abdel Raouf (eds.), *Evolution and Adaptation: The Future of International Arbitration* (Leiden, ICCA Congress Series, Kluwer Law International, 2019), p. 622.

190 C. Rousseau, *Droit international public* (Paris, Sirey, vol. V, 1977), p. 85–86.

191 Borchard, *The Diplomatic Protection of Citizens Abroad*, p. 241:

> A successful revolution stands on an entirely different basis. The government created through its efforts is liable for the acts of the revolutionists as well as for those of the titular government it has replaced. Its acts are considered as at least those of a general *de facto* government, for which the state is liable from the beginning of the revolution, *on the theory that the revolution represented ab initio a changing national will, crystallizing in the final successful result.* Thus the government created through a successful revolution becomes liable for all services rendered to the revolutionists. The unlawful acts of successful revolutionists render the government equally liable. The successful revolutionists appear to be bound from the beginning of the revolution by the stipulations of national treaties, for the violation of which they will be held liable as successors to the titular government. (emphasis added).

See also: Borchard, 'International Responsibility of the State for Injuries', p. 122.

192 *Application of the Convention on the Prevention and Punishment of the Crime of Genocide (Croatia v. Serbia)*, Judgment of 3 February 2015, ICJ Rep. 2015 [hereinafter referred to as 'ICJ, *Genocide* case, 2015'], Separate Opinion of Judge Kreća, para. 66.1.

193 Ibid., para. 66.1: 'In case of revolutionary change of Government, the State remains the identical subject of international law, responsible on the basis of the fact that "it represented ab initio a changing national will, crystallizing in the fully successful result" (Bolivar Railway Company, United Nations, RIAA, 1903, Vol. IX, p. 445).'

194 ILC, Ago Report, 1972, p. 145, para. 198:

> But the very concept of 'national will' is to be treated with caution, quite apart from the fact that, in general, international law is not greatly concerned with whether a given government is or is not the representative of the 'true' national will. Even leaving that aside, it is difficult to maintain that the outcome of the fighting in a civil war should, like a judgement of God, establish retrospectively that those who triumphed were, from the outset of the civil war, more representative of the true national will than those who lost.

would mean that '*only* the acts of organs of that movement could be considered retroactively to be acts of the State'.[195] This is because *only the rebels* would be deemed to be representing the 'national will'. As a result, a State should *not*, quite logically, be responsible for the acts committed by the previous government while fighting the rebels. This is simply because the previous government would not be considered to represent the 'national will'. Indeed, the rebels and the previous government cannot be *both* representing the 'national will' at the same time while they are in fact *fighting each other* for power. Schwarzenberger rightly rejects the possibility that the 'national will' can be 'represented simultaneously by two governments'.[196] In any event, such an outcome would be contrary to State practice 'which holds the State responsible also for acts committed during the struggle by the "legitimate" government which is subsequently overthrown'.[197] This is indeed a well-established principle (examined above):[198] when the rebels are successful at establishing a new government, the State remains responsible for the acts committed by the previous government while fighting the rebels (Rule no. 1). The very existence of this rule is simply incompatible with the theory of the 'national will'.

In his book, Crawford is also particularly critical of the theory that the success of the insurgents reflects the 'national will' of the people.[199] He believes (like others)[200] that the thesis is 'unsatisfactory for a number of reasons', referring to the reasoning of Ago (mentioned above)[201] and quoting the work of Schwarzenberger (who described the 'national will' theory as 'no more than an empty fiction in the verbiage of political philosophy').[202] Schwarzenberger noted that, in fact, at the time when the

[195] Ibid., emphasis added. See also: ILC, Report, 1975, p. 100, para. 2.

[196] Schwarzenberger, *International Law*, p. 628.

[197] ILC, Report, 1975, p. 145, para. 198.

[198] See Section 2.1.

[199] Crawford, *State Responsibility*, p. 175.

[200] Cahin, 'Attribution of Conduct to the State', p. 249:

> Arbitrators and authors have advanced different justifications for this rule, assimilating the successful insurrectional movement to a *de facto* government or seeing the movement as the *ab initio* incarnation of a genuine national will. But the attribution of the movement's conduct to the State is in practice independent from the former's effective authority over a portion of the territory, and the outcome of the conflict is an inadequate means to retrospectively designate the authentic representative of the national will.

[201] Crawford, *State Responsibility*, p. 175, referring to ILC, Ago Report, 1972, p. 145. See also: ILC, Report, 1975, p. 100.

[202] Crawford, *State Responsibility*, p. 176, referring to Schwarzenberger, *International Law*, p. 628.

acts were committed, the perpetrators were 'merely private individuals and, by their own municipal law, criminal at large'.[203] He is right. Rebels are considered as outlaws and criminals under domestic laws. There is something very artificial in 'magically' considering them, after the facts, as representing the 'national will' for the simple reason that they won their struggle.[204]

Ago concluded his analysis by stating that 'the point is not so much to find a justification for the possible attribution to the State' of acts by the rebels.[205] For him, 'what is important is to determine whether that attribution is or not made in the real world of international relations'.[206] This is a curious statement. It suggests that, at this stage, Ago was somehow no longer looking for a probable 'justification' for the 'special' rule of attribution set out in Article 10(1). He simply looked at what States were doing 'in real life'. Ago then made this interesting statement: 'If we do wish to find a justification of principle for such an attribution, we must seek it, once again, in the idea of continuity which appears, indeed, to be the determining criterion for the solution of the various problems envisaged here.'[207] This passage (and the use of the word 'appears') suggests that Ago considered 'the idea of continuity' to be possibly relevant here. A similar reference is also found in the 1975 ILC Report: '[b]ut if we do wish, nevertheless, to find a justification of principle for such an attribution, we ought perhaps to seek it in the fact that there is continuity'.[208] Thus, Ago does not seem to be convinced at all that this 'idea of continuity' is the proper justification for the 'special' rule of attribution. This question is fully examined in the next sections.

2.2.2.2.2 Ago's Idea of the State Representing the 'Dual Continuation' of Both the Rebels and the Previous Government In his 1972 Report, Ago suggests the existence of a 'dual' continuation. Thus, if the rebels win, 'the revolutionary structures' of the insurgents are 'integrated within the framework of the previous organization', that

203 Schwarzenberger, *International Law*, p. 628.

204 Accepting this theory leads to the rather absurd consequence that 'la représentativité du mouvement devrait être déterminée uniquement d'après le sort des armes' ('the representativeness of the movement should be determined only after the fate of arms'): Atlam, *Succession d'États*, p. 462. See also: Greenman, 'The Secret History', p. 8 ('it is not necessarily the case that the success or otherwise of a revolution reflects the national will, there may be all sorts of determining factors').

205 ILC, Ago Report, 1972, p. 145, para. 199.

206 Ibid.

207 Ibid.

208 ILC, Report, 1975, p. 100, para. 3.

is, the government in charge.[209] This idea was reflected in Article 13(2) of the 1972 Draft presented by Ago which referred to 'organs of an insurrectional movement whose structures have subsequently been integrated, in whole or in part, with those of the pre-existing State'.[210] The 1975 ILC Report referred to two elements of continuity. The *first* element of continuity, between one organization (the insurrectional movement) and another (the new government) is explained in these two extracts of the Report:

> there is continuity between the organization with which the insurrectional movement had provided itself before taking power and the organization with which, as the result of its success, it has endowed the government of the pre-existing State .... It is indeed the existence of this continuity which justifies wondering whether or not it is possible to attribute to the State in question, as a possible source of international responsibility for that State, conduct engaged in by the organs of the insurrectional movement before the victory of the movement in the civil war.[211]
>
> the insurrectional movement, as a new government or new regime, replaces the previous government or regime of the State. The ruling organization of the insurrectional movement takes power in the State and becomes the ruling organization of that State or is at least integrated, in one way or another, into the previous organization of the State. The continuity which thus exists between the new organization of the State and that of the insurrectional movement therefore naturally leads to the attribution to the State of the acts which the organs of the insurrectional movement may have committed during the struggle; this is without derogation from the principles habitually applied.[212]

The *second* element of continuity concerns the State itself whose international legal personality is not altered by a change of government: 'The State does not cease to exist as a subject of international law. Its identity remains the same, without any break in continuity, despite the changes, reorganizations and adaptations which occur in the institutions of the State.'[213] As a result, 'it is necessary to continue to attribute to the State, after the success of the insurrectional movement, the conduct previously engaged in by the organs of the pre-existing State apparatus'.[214]

209 ILC, Ago Report, 1972, p. 146, para. 199.
210 Ibid., p. 151, para. 214.
211 ILC, Report, 1975, p. 100, para. 3.
212 Ibid., p. 100, para. 4.
213 Ibid., p. 100, para. 5.
214 Ibid.

For Ago, 'the State apparatus which results' from the successful attempt by the rebels to take power 'is in reality the *continuation of both the organizations* which confronted each other during the civil war'.[215] Thus, during the first phase of the 'insurrectional struggle, two organizations are opposed to each other and are fighting for final victory'; 'each of the two wishes to be the organization of the State; at the outset, one is so in fact and the other potentially'.[216] The second and final phase is marked by the victory of the rebels, who take over and establish the new government. In fact, the existence of this 'dual continuation' explains why the acts of *both* the rebels and the previous government are 'attributable' to the State: 'In that case, there is therefore nothing surprising in the attribution to the State of the acts not only of members of its preceding organization but also of members of the organization that grew up during the insurrection and is subsequently united with the preceding organization, which is thereby transformed to a greater or lesser extent.'[217]

2.2.2.2.3 The Irrelevance of the Question As to Whether or Not an Insurrectional Movement Has an International Legal Personality The 1972 Report explained that there is 'no other condition for attribution to the State, as a potential source of international responsibility, of the conduct of organs of the insurrectional movement than the *mere existence* of that movement'.[218] Thus, 'it is in no way required, although such is frequently the case, that the movement in question should possess international personality'.[219] In other words, the 'special' attribution of acts of the successful rebels to the State is not the result of the recognition of the movement as a subject of international law possessing an international legal personality. It should be added that Ago nevertheless believed that insurrectional movements indeed had such personality. Thus, as further discussed below,[220] Ago's refusal to attribute actions committed by (ultimately) unsuccessful rebels to the government in charge is based on the grounds that the rebels are a *different subject* of

215 ILC, Ago Report, 1972, p. 146, para. 199, emphasis added. See also: ibid., p. 100, para. 5.
216 ILC, Report, 1975, p. 100, para. 5.
217 ILC, Ago Report, 1972, p. 146, para. 199. See also: ibid., p. 100, para. 5: '[i]t is therefore logical to attribute to the State the acts of organs of its preceding organization and the acts of organs of the organization which grew up during the insurrection and then became the organization of the State itself'.
218 ILC, Ago Report, 1972, p. 151, para. 213, emphasis added.
219 Ibid., p. 151 para. 213.
220 See Section 3.1.2.

international law.[221] In the same vein, the ILC 1975 Report emphasized that the 'special' rule of attribution set out in Article 10(1) is not a question of State succession.[222] Put simply, Rule no. 2 exists independently of the question as to whether the rebels are a subject of international law or not. What matters is that there is a 'continuity between the apparatus of the insurrectional movement and the new governmental apparatus of the State'.[223]

In his First Report as ILC Special Rapporteur, Crawford made it clear that the concept of subject of international law was not relevant regarding the 'special' rule of attribution in Article 10(1):

> if the rationale for the rule of attribution in article 15 [which later became Article 10] is one of institutional continuity and of the continuing responsibility of the entities concerned for their own acts while they were in armed opposition, there is no reason why it should be limited to situations where the insurrectional movement is recognized as having legal personality.[224]

In his subsequent book, Crawford similarly concluded that 'it is doubtful that tying responsibility to the legal personality of the insurgents as such is helpful, since their disappearance is eventually ensured, either because the insurrection fails or because it succeeds'.[225] In fact, it has been argued

221 ILC, Ago Report, 1972, p. 132, para. 160. See also, para. 193: '[o]ur conclusion was that the conduct of a person or group of persons acting in the territory of a State as organs of another State, or of an international organization, or of an insurrectional movement *possessing separate international personality*, is not considered to be an act of that State in international law' (emphasis added).

222 ILC, Report, 1975, p. 101, para. 8, indicating that it has nothing to do with the 'succession of the State as one subject of international law to the insurrectional movement as another'. This point is also highlighted by d'Aspremont, 'Rebellion and State Responsibility', p. 430.

223 ILC, Report, 1975, p. 101, para. 8:

> it is obvious that, whenever the identity of the State and the continuity of its existence have not been called into question because of the ultimate success of the insurrectional movement, no question of succession as between different subjects of international law arises. As we have shown, acts committed by agents of the insurrectional movement before the movement takes power are attributed to the State because there is continuity between the apparatus of the insurrectional movement and the new governmental apparatus of the State, not a succession of the State as one subject of international law to the insurrectional movement as another.

224 ILC, Crawford First Report, 1998, p. 53, para. 270. He added that 'it should be irrelevant to the application of the rules stated in articles 14 and 15 whether and to what extent the insurrectional movement has international legal personality' (ibid., para. 271).

225 Crawford, *State Responsibility*, p. 171.

that one of the advantages of the principle embodied in Article 10(1) is precisely the fact that it avoids any discussion on whether or not insurgent groups have such a personality.[226]

2.2.2.2.4 Crawford's Endorsement of the Idea of 'Organic' or 'Structural' Continuity In his First Report, Crawford noted that the 1975 Commentary explained the rule set out in Article 15(1) (which later became Article 10) 'on the basis of the organizational continuity of an insurrectional movement which succeeds in displacing the previous government of the State'.[227] Yet, Crawford did not seem convinced at the time by the theory advanced by Ago in support of the principle. Thus, he stated that 'it is not clear what the systematic or structural basis for responsibility is, but the earlier jurisprudence and doctrine, at least, firmly support' the rule set out in Article 15(1).[228] He also noted that 'there [were] continuing difficulties of rationalization' in favour of the principle set out in Article 15(1), but that the attribution rule 'seem[s] to be accepted, and to strike a fair balance *at the level of attribution* in terms of the conflicting interests involved'.[229] He added that 'there ha[d] so far been no suggestion in government comments or in the literature that the substantive rules should be deleted'.[230] It is interesting to note that these hesitations are no longer present in the 2001 ILC Commentaries. Crawford explained the rationale for this 'special' rule of attribution as 'the continuity between the movement and the eventual Government'.[231]

226 Cahin, 'Attribution of Conduct to the State', p. 251. See also, Verhoeven, 'International Responsibility', p. 294, adding that 'It also avoids the danger that States would be considered to intervene in the internal affairs of other states by directly invoking the responsibility of the armed opposition movements and thereby creating the impression that the armed opposition group is considered the legitimate government of the state.'

227 ILC, Crawford First Report, 1998, p. 51, para. 264.

228 Ibid.

229 Ibid., p. 53, para. 276, emphasis in the original.

230 Ibid.

231 ILC, Commentaries, 2001, p. 50, para. 4:

> Where the insurrectional movement, as a new Government, replaces the previous Government of the State, the ruling organization of the insurrectional movement becomes the ruling organization of that State. The continuity which thus exists between the new organization of the State and that of the insurrectional movement leads naturally to the attribution to the State of conduct which the insurrectional movement may have committed during the struggle.

In subsequent writing, Crawford refers to this position as being 'reflective of the thesis' of 'organic' or 'structural' continuity.[232] He described this theory as involving a situation where 'the factual links connecting a former insurrection movement with a current government are sufficient to generate state responsibility not only for the acts of the insurgency prior to its success, but also for the acts of the former government in attempting to suppress the insurgency'.[233] Interestingly, the concept of 'organic' or 'structural' continuity does not appear at all in the work of the ILC. The ILC refers only to the general idea of 'continuity'. One passage goes further and mentions the 'real and substantial continuity'.[234] Another passage refers to a successful movement which 'has substituted its *structures* to those of the previous government'.[235] The concept of 'organic' or 'structural' continuity per se only seems to have been introduced by Crawford in his subsequent book. In his book, Crawford refers, in a footnote, to my earlier work[236] where I have used this terminology. It should be added that in my book, I used this terminology (relying on the work of Atlam)[237] in the different context of a rebellion leading to the creation of a *new State* (rather than a change of government).[238]

In any event, Crawford endorsed the concept of 'organic' or 'structural' continuity and explained in his book that this theory had 'largely replaced earlier justifications for the rule'.[239] Crawford also referred to the concept in the context of his pleading as counsel for Croatia in the *Genocide* case (dealing with the different question of the creation of a new State).[240] Other

[232] Crawford, *State Responsibility*, p. 175, referring to Patrick Dumberry, 'New State Responsibility for Internationally Wrongful Acts by an Insurrectional Movement', *EJIL* 17 (2006), p. 611–12.

[233] Crawford, *State Responsibility*, p. 175.

[234] ILC, Commentaries, 2001, p. 51, para. 7: 'the criterion of application of paragraph 1 is that of a real and substantial continuity between the former insurrectional movement and the new Government it has succeeded in forming'.

[235] Ibid., p. 51, para. 7, emphasis added.

[236] Dumberry, 'New State Responsibility', p. 611–12. See also, Dumberry, *State Succession to International Responsibility*, p. 245–6.

[237] Atlam, 'National Liberation Movements', p. 468 ff.

[238] This specific question is further examined in Part II, Section 4.2.3.2.2.

[239] Crawford, *State Responsibility*, p. 175.

[240] ICJ, *Genocide* case, 2015, Verbatim Record, 21 March 2014, CR 2014/21, 21, para. 55 (Crawford):

> As Patrick Dumberry, who studied this subject in some detail, says '[t]he new state should remain responsible for acts which took place before its independence because there is a "structural" and "organic" continuity of the legal personality of what was then a rebel movement' – or, in this case, an 'other' movement with all the relevant characteristics – that 'has since

writers have since then adopted the same terminology of 'organic' or 'structural' continuity,[241] or, more generally, endorsed the idea of continuity.[242] One notable exception is d'Aspremont, for whom 'it is far from certain that the idea of continuity suffices to justify such an exception' to the general rule of attribution whereby a State is only responsible for the acts committed by its organs.[243] Thus, given that 'State responsibility always presupposes continuity,' he believes that 'continuity alone fails to justify that rule of attribution of triumphant insurgents'.[244] In his view, 'it would have been conceivable to devise the principle whereby the State is responsible for acts of victorious insurgents not as a rule of *attribution of conduct* but as a rule of *attribution of responsibility*'.[245]

> successfully become a new independent state'. In our case the 'structural' and 'organic' continuity between the Serbian military and political leadership and the FRY was complete.

241 Cahin, 'Attribution of Conduct to the State', p. 249: '[t]he only pertinent explanation can be found in the principle of the continuity of the State, since from the moment of victory the movement maintains a close organic link with the State's structures'.

242 See: R. Kolb, *The International Law of State Responsibility: An Introduction* (Elgar, 2018), p. 95 ('The exceptional attribution rule in the event of success of the insurrection (provoking an ex post facto attribution) is based on equitable considerations. The point is to satisfy the need for legal continuity and to allow other States to claim for losses which the persons now forming the State have caused'); Cedric Ryngaert, 'State Responsibility and Non-State Actors', in Math Noortmann, August Reinisch and Cedric Ryngaert (eds.), *Non-State Actors in International Law* (Oxford, Hart Publishing, 2015), p. 175 ('the movement and the eventual (new) Government of the (possibly new) state are seen as continuous, and thus, the movement's acts will post factum be attributed to the state'); Greenman, 'The Secret History', p. 9 ('the fact of the continuity between the rebels and the government they end up forming has some purchase as an argument').

243 d'Aspremont, 'Rebellion and State Responsibility', p. 430.

244 Ibid., p. 430.

245 Ibid., p. 431, emphasis in the original. He explained the two concepts as follows:

> [i]f continuity were to underpin any rule of attribution, the rule of attribution of acts of triumphant insurgents should have been construed, not in terms of attribution of conduct, but rather as a principle of attribution of responsibility. Attribution of responsibility – also called responsabilité derivée ('derived responsibility') – is commonly interpreted as an exception to the principle of independent responsibility in that a State is held responsible for an act factually committed by another legal subject.

He also explained that the ILC 'decided to devise the principle of the responsibility of victorious rebels as a rule of attribution of conduct and not as a rule of attribution of responsibility to bypass the difficult question of the legal personality of insurgent movements which the ILC probably wanted to dodge'.

As further discussed in detail below,[246] the concept of continuity has surprisingly been explicitly recognized by only a few tribunals. One example is the Iran–US Claims Tribunal in *Alfred L.W. Short* v. *Iran*. The award states that in cases of revolution, 'the successor government is also held responsible for the acts imputable to the revolutionary movement which established it, even if those acts occurred prior to its establishment, as a consequence of the continuity existing between the new organization of the State and the organization of the revolutionary movement'.[247] In the *Yeager* case, the Iran–US Claims Tribunal mentioned that 'acts of a revolutionary movement which becomes the new government can be attributable to the State under certain circumstances'.[248] One such 'circumstance' was the continuity in the person of the leader of the revolutionaries who later became the leader of the new government: '[t]he Tribunal is convinced that statements and acts of Ayatollah Khomeini are attributable to the new Government, as it is beyond doubt that he was the leading organ of the revolutionary movement which became the new Government'.[249]

2.2.3 *Case Law and State Practice Support This Principle*

In his report, Ago refers to many authorities supporting Rule no. 2 set out in Article 10(1) of the ILC Articles.[250] The 1975 ILC Report even goes as far as to say that 'there can be no exceptions to this general principle'.[251] In the 2001 ILC Commentaries, Crawford indicated that 'arbitral decisions, together with State practice and the literature, indicate a general acceptance of the two positive attribution rules in article 10'.[252] Thus, the content of Rule no. 2 does not seem to have been opposed by States.[253] Rule no. 2

[246] See Section 2.2.3.2.

[247] *Alfred L.W. Short* v. *The Islamic Republic of Iran*, Iran–US Claims Tribunal, Case No. 11135, Award of 14 July 1987, para. 33.

[248] *Kenneth P. Yeager, a claim of less than US$250,000 presented by the United States of America* v. *The Islamic Republic of Iran*, Iran–US Claims Tribunal, Case No. 10199 (324–10199-1), Partial Award, 2 November 1987, para. 35.

[249] Ibid. The Tribunal added that 'it cannot make a finding, however, whether statements and acts of other persons are attributable to the new Government as well, as the Claimant has not presented sufficient evidence as to the statements and acts by others'.

[250] ILC, Ago Report, 1972, p. 149, paras. 210–11.

[251] ILC, Report, 1975, p. 105, para. 21.

[252] ILC, Commentaries, 2001, p. 51, para. 12.

[253] Cahin, 'Attribution of Conduct to the State', p. 248. See ILC, 'Comments and observations received from Government', 53rd Session, UN Doc A/CN.4/515, 19 March 2001, p. 50, citing only one observation by the Netherlands (which appears to have misinterpreted the provision).

has indeed been accepted by (almost) all writers.[254] It has even been considered by some as a rule of customary international law.[255] To the best of my knowledge, only a few writers have contested the validity of this well-established principle. D'Aspremont is certainly the most prominent writer who has been critical of the provision:

> This paper argues that the rule enshrined in Article 10 of the International Law Commission's articles on State responsibility, according to which violations of international law by rebels that subsequently seize power are attributable to the State, rests neither on sound precedential nor systemic grounds. It seeks to demonstrate that this provision rather constitutes the outcome of a political choice to lessen impunity and promote accountability in case of violation of international law by non-State actors. Since the rule is not based on any precise precedent nor systemic logic but only on political motives, there is no reason why one could not resort to similar motives to attempt to refine the currently hazy scope of application of that rule.[256]

According to d'Aspremont, 'the actual scope of application [of Article 10(1)] remains largely hazy and vague' as 'the rule fails to define what an insurgent is and, correlatively, the moment from which the acts of the insurgency can be retroactively attributable to the State', adding that it is 'silent on the manner in which the insurgents must seize power for

[254] Morris, 'Revolutionary Movements', p. 723; Cahin, 'Attribution of Conduct to the State', p. 248; Crawford, *Brownlie's Principles of Public International Law*, p. 553; Crawford, *State Responsibility*, p. 174–5; Edwin M. Borchard, 'International Pecuniary Claims against Mexico', *Yale LJ* 26 (1917), p. 339 ('While it is a general principle that a state or nation is not responsible for the acts of unsuccessful revolutionists beyond its control, the rule in the case of successful revolutionists is quite different. The government created through its efforts is liable for the acts of the revolutionists as well as for those of the titular government it has displaced'); Ganzory, 'International Claims and Insurgence', p. 92; G. de Beus, *The Jurisprudence of the General Claims Commission United States and Mexico under the Convention of September 8, 1923* (The Hague, Nijhoff, 1938), p. 108; Al-Rashid *et al.*, 'Investment Claims', p. 186–7. See many writers cited in Mantilla Blanco, *Full Protection and Security*, p. 226, 228; Piguet, *La Guerre civile en droit international*, p. 133.

[255] Mantilla Blanco, *Full Protection and Security*, p. 227; Cahin, 'Attribution of Conduct to the State', p. 249; Gérard Cahin, 'The Responsibility of Other Entities: Armed Bands and Criminal Groups', in James Crawford, Alain Pellet, Simon Olleson and Kate Parlett (eds.), *The Law of International Responsibility* (Oxford University Press, 2010), p. 334. *Contra*: d'Aspremont, 'Rebellion and State Responsibility', p. 433: 'the uncertainty pertaining to its precise scope of application constitutes a more serious impediment to its application as well as its crystallization into a rule of customary international law'. See also: Verhoeven, 'International Responsibility', p. 286, speaking of 'doubt whether this rule belongs to customary international law'.

[256] d'Aspremont, 'Rebellion and State Responsibility', p. 427.

the rule to apply, thereby implying that it automatically applies to any sort of victorious rebellion'.[257] His position on this last point will be further examined below.[258] Suffice it to note here that he believes that Rule no. 2 embodied in Article 10 is 'not only barely supported by any systemic logic but is also hardly buttressed by practice'.[259] Yet, and importantly, for him 'this should however not lead to a rejection of the rule' since it 'may well serve a very useful as well as lofty purpose which makes it worthy'.[260]

Another critical author is Greenman, for whom the rule 'arose not as a matter of logic or policy, but out of confusion', adding that 'Article 10(1) is both practically irrelevant and intellectually unstable.'[261] She argued that the practice of Latin America States shows that at the time there was a 'general rule of non-responsibility' applicable in all cases (whether or not the rebellion was successful). This 'general rule of non-responsibility' was however 'conditional upon the state exercising due diligence in protecting against rebels and duly administering justice in respect of any harm caused by them'.[262] Thus, 'retroactive responsibility for successful rebels was a particular rule carved out from this general principle, to which it was secondary'.[263] She is very critical of the earlier authorities supporting this principle.[264] Her work will be further discussed below in Section 3.3.3.1.

2.2.3.1 State Practice

There is a long history behind Rule no. 2. It was recognized in the Harvard Draft of 1929 in Article 13(b): '[i]n the event of a successful revolution, the state whose government is established thereby is responsible under article 7, if an injury to an alien has resulted from a wrongful act or omission of the revolutionists committed at any time after the

[257] Ibid., p. 428.
[258] See Section 2.2.4.4.3.
[259] D'Aspremont, p. 432.
[260] Ibid.
[261] Greenman, 'The Secret History', p. 2.
[262] Ibid., p. 3.
[263] Ibid., p. 3. See also: Kathryn Greenman, 'Aliens in Latin America: Intervention, Arbitration and State Responsibility for Rebels', *Leiden JIL* 31 (2018), p. 631–2.
[264] Ibid., p. 4 ff., for instance, indicating that the single case (the *Hughes* case, decided by the Mexican–US Mixed Claims Commission) cited by Moore in his book *History and Digest of the International Arbitrations to Which the United States Has Been a Party* (1898) 'in support of the rule of responsibility for successful rebels is not a convincing authority'.

inception of the revolution'.[265] The same principle was set out more clearly in the 1961 Harvard Draft in Article 18(1).[266]

In his report, Ago explained that the principle is supported by State practice and provides numerous examples supporting that claim.[267] One example of older State practice is the comments sent by governments to the Preparatory Committee of the 1930 Hague Conference. Ago considered this practice as 'the main source for ascertaining the views of Governments' which was to the effect that 'where an insurrection is successful and the insurrectionist party, having taken power, has become the Government of the State, the latter must be liable for injuries caused by the insurgents during the civil war to the person or property of foreigners'.[268] Having received these comments from governments, the Preparatory Committee came up with the following 'Basis of Discussion' no. 22 (c): '[a] State is responsible for damage caused to foreigners by an insurrectionist party which has been successful and has become the Government to the same degree as it is responsible for damage caused by acts of the Government *de jure* or its officials or troops'.[269] While the Hague Conference ultimately failed to adopt any resolution, there is no indication that governments rejected the basic principle embodied in 'Basis of Discussion' no. 22 (c).

In his article, d'Aspremont noted that 'the commentary of Article 10 and that of former Article 15 allude to dated arbitral decisions of 1920–1930 but fail to refer to any post–WWII practice, especially practice pertaining to decolonization or wars of national liberation'.[270] He rightfully points out

265 Harvard Draft Convention on the International Responsibility of States for Injuries to Aliens, *AJIL* Spec. Supp. 23 (1929) [hereinafter referred to as 'Harvard Draft Convention, 1929'], also in *ILC Yearbook* vol. II (1956), p. 229.

266 The document is quoted in *ILC Yearbook* vol. II (1969), p. 146: 'In the event of a revolution or insurrection which brings about a change in the government of a State . . ., an act or omission of an organ, agency, official, or employee of a revolution or insurrectionary group is, for the purposes of this Convention, attributable to the State in which the group established itself as the government'.

267 ILC, Ago Report, 1972, p. 147, paras. 204 ff.

268 Ibid., p. 148, para. 207. See also: ibid.: 'the replies sent by Governments to the Preparatory Committee's questionnaire seem to be sufficient to confirm the widely recognized existence of a general principle of international law: a principle providing precisely for attribution to the State resulting from a successful revolution of acts committed by the insurgents during their struggle to take power, as a source of responsibility'.

269 League of Nations publication, V. Legal, 1929.V.3, Doc. C.75.M.69.1929.V, p. 107, Preparatory Committee of the Hague Conference for the Codification of International Law, p. 108, 116, in *ILC Yearbook* vol. II (1956), p. 224.

270 d'Aspremont, 'Rebellion and State Responsibility', p. 432.

the rarity of recent examples of State practice. One example of post–World War II State practice (already mentioned above)[271] supporting Rule no. 2 is the instructions from the US Department of State expressing its position on the liability of the new government of Cuba for damages caused during the revolutionary disturbances by the rebels and governmental forces.[272] The distinction that the document highlights between damages resulting from the 'legitimate' and 'non legitimate' military operations will be further dealt with later.[273] Suffice it to note here that, generally speaking, the document endorsed Rule no. 2.[274] Cahin refers to another recent example of State practice which he believes supports the principle set out in Article 10(1): '[t]he commitment of the Russian Government [after the break-up of the USSR in 1990] to honour the debt contracted by the Bolshevik government with French bondholders that it had dispossessed confirmed the authority recognized to the rule establishing the attribution to the State of conduct of revolutionary movements'.[275] In my view, this is not the case. The wrongful acts were committed by the Bolshevik government only *after* they had successfully gained power in 1917.[276] In other words, the actions were taken by the new government, not by the rebels during the insurrection. The example is therefore not relevant for the analysis of Article 10(1).[277]

One relevant recent example of State practice concerns a successful rebellion in the Central African Republic.[278] In December 2012, the

[271] See Section 2.1.2.2.3.1.

[272] M. M. Whiteman, *Digest of International Law* (Washington, Dept. of State, vol. 8, 1973), p. 819–20, referring to a document sent by the US Department of State to the American Embassy, Habana, instruction, No. A-180, 26 January 1959, MS. Department of State, file 237.1141/12–1958.

[273] See Section 3.3.2.

[274] The document indicates that the new government of Cuba 'is internationally responsible as a general rule for damages caused by acts of forces or authorities of both the former government and *the revolutionists* which were not legitimate from a military standpoint or sanctioned by the rules of warfare, such as wanton or unnecessary injury to persons or property and pillage', emphasis added.

[275] Cahin, 'Attribution of Conduct to the State', p. 249.

[276] Sandra Szurek, 'Epilogue d'un contentieux historique. L'accord sur le règlement des créances réciproques entre la France et la Russie', *AFDI* (1998), p. 146.

[277] The example is relevant for matters of State succession in the context of a continuing State (Russia) taking over the consequences arising from the commission of a wrongful acts committed by the predecessor State (USSR). This example is discussed in Dumberry, *State Succession to International Responsibility*, p. 154.

[278] The example is mentioned in Tatyana Eatwell, 'State Responsibility for Human Rights Violations Committed in the State's Territory by Armed Non-State Actors', *Geneva Academy Briefing* 13 (2019), p. 31.

Séléka, a coalition of rebel groups, launched an offensive in the Central African Republic which overthrown, in March 2013, the government of President François Bozizé. In a 2013 Report by the HCHR on the 'Situation of Human Rights in the Central African Republic', it was noted that 'following the beginning of the Séléka offensive and the subsequent fall of Bangui [the capital], the Central African Republic witnessed a rapid breakdown in law and order resulting from the absence of civilian administration and of defence and police forces across the country'.[279] The Report concluded to the 'existence of a non-international armed conflict during the initial period', adding that 'this implies that international humanitarian law was applicable from 10 December 2012 until the takeover by the Séléka of Bangui, on 24 March 2013'.[280] The Report also explained that the government had a 'clear obligation to respect international human rights law'[281] during that period and added: '[m]oreover, it is increasingly accepted that a non-State armed group, such as the Séléka before taking power in the Central African Republic, must respect and ensure respect for human rights in the territory it controls'.[282] The conclusion of the Report is as follows: 'both the forces of the former Government and the non State armed group Séléka committed serious violations of international humanitarian law and international human rights law during the conflict, from 10 December 2012 to 23 March 2013, with the majority of violations and abuses committed by Séléka members'.[283] Most importantly, the Report also referred to Article 10(1) of the ILC Articles and explained that the State was responsible for the acts committed during the insurrection by the successful rebels:

[279] HCHR, 'Situation of Human Rights in the Central African Republic, Report of the United Nations High Commissioner for Human Rights', UN Doc. A/HRC/24/59, 12 September 2013, para. 13.

[280] Ibid., para. 20.

[281] Ibid., para. 21.

[282] Ibid., para. 22.

[283] Ibid., para. 91. The violations were described as follows:

> [t]he violations committed during the conflict included summary executions and extrajudicial killings, enforced disappearances, attacks on civilians, sexual and gender-based violence, and grave violations against children, which constitute war crimes notably under the Rome Statute, in addition to being gross human rights violations. Other serious violations of international human rights law included arbitrary arrests and detention, retaliation and intimidation measures against all those identified or considered supporters of the opposition, and widespread looting of property, including hospitals, schools and places of worship. (para. 92)

'in accordance with article 10 of the draft articles on Responsibility of States for Internationally Wrongful Acts, the Séléka, after it seized power, engaged the State responsibility of the Central African Republic for all violations committed by Séléka members in the country during the armed conflict'.[284]

As noted by one writer, this is a rare example of State practice where Article 10(1) of the ILC Articles is mentioned in the context of recent situations of civil wars involving human rights violations.[285]

2.2.3.2 Case Law

In his 1972 Report, Ago indicates that 'some instances can be found' of 'international arbitral cases' 'where the international responsibility of the State for acts committed during a civil war by agents of an insurrectional movement which was subsequently successful is recognized in principle'.[286] He, however, admits that 'such declarations are less numerous than those which could be cited in connexion with' cases where the rebels are *not* successful in establishing a new government.[287] Ago provides the following explanation for the existence of only a few cases supporting Rule no. 2: 'this can be explained precisely by the fact that there is no divergence of views, no doubt whatsoever, as to the validity of the principle in question'.[288] This is a curious statement.[289] Thus, the few

[284] Ibid., para. 25.

[285] T.J. Eatwell, *State Responsibility for the Unlawful Conduct of Armed Groups*, Doctoral Thesis, University of Cambridge (2019), two chapters on file with author, p. 171:

> the question of Article 10's applicability to these situations has been notably absent from discussions of these conflicts and of state responsibility for human rights violations and war crimes committed by armed groups that have successfully overthrown the preexisting government. The lack of discussion or application of Article 10 may be due to a prevailing focus on individual criminal responsibility for violations of international law by human rights advocates and the Security Council. In the cases of Nepal and of Libya serious violations of IHL and IHRL were documented by the OHCHR and the International Commission of Inquiry into Libya. These included unlawful killings, arbitrary detention and enforced disappearances, torture and attacks on civilians (in the case of Libya on both Libyan and foreign citizens). The emphasis of both reports is on individual criminal responsibility and the state's responsibility to ensure the appropriate mechanisms are in place to ensure individual accountability for crimes and human rights violations. Neither report refers to Article 10 ARS. Yet, these situations are precisely those that Article 10 ARS seeks to address.

[286] ILC, Ago Report, 1972, p. 146, para. 200.

[287] Ibid.

[288] Ibid.

[289] On this point, see: d'Aspremont, 'Rebellion and State Responsibility', p. 432.

cases in support of a given principle cannot be explained by the simple fact that everyone agrees with the existence of such a principle. They are two different things which are not necessarily connected. In any event, this apparent unanimity of views in support of the principle led Ago to focus only on 'arbitral awards made during the twentieth century'.[290] In his First Report, Crawford also mentioned that 'earlier jurisprudence' 'firmly support' Rule no. 2 embodied in Article 10(1).[291] There are indeed many cases supporting this principle. Yet, as further examined in the next paragraphs, some of these cases can hardly qualify as solid precedents. The justifications mentioned in some other cases in support of Rule no. 2 are also often not persuasive.

The classic case usually invoked in support of Rule no. 2 is the reasoning of Umpire Plumley in the 1903 *Bolivar Railway* case, decided by the Venezuelan–British Mixed Claims Commission:

> Such, however, is not the ground on which successful revolutions are charged, through the government, with responsibility. Responsibility comes because it is the same nation. Nations do not die when there is a change of their rulers or in their forms of government. These are but expressions of a change of national will. 'The king is dead; long live the king!' has typified this thought for ages. The nation is responsible for the debts contracted by its titular government, and that responsibility continues through all changing forms of government until the obligation is discharged. The nation is responsible for the obligations of a successful revolution from its beginning, because in theory, it represented ab initio a changing national will, crystallizing in the finally successful result.[292]

As mentioned above,[293] Plumley's statement that a successful revolution represents 'a changing national will, crystallizing in the finally successful result' is unconvincing. Ago mentioned that the award is 'the best known declaration of principle, to the authority of which many authors have referred'.[294] That may be so, but it is clearly not the most persuasive authority supporting Rule no. 2. As noted by Ago himself, the case dealt with a lawful act, a debt contracted by the insurgents, and not with any wrongful act. It is also noteworthy that the award cites only a single case in support of its proposition:

[290] ILC, Ago Report, 1972, p. 146, para. 200.

[291] ILC, Crawford First Report, 1998, para. 264.

[292] *Bolivar Railway Co.* case, UK–Venezuela Claims Commission, Opinion of the Umpire, 1903, UNRIAA 9, p. 445, 452–3.

[293] See Section 2.2.2.2.1.

[294] ILC, Ago Report, 1972, p. 146, para. 201.

Williams v. *Bruffy*.[295] As noted by Greenman, that case is clearly not the most convincing source in this respect.[296] The following paragraphs explain the reasons why.

The passage that Umpire Plumley actually quoted only concerns the rule of attribution in the *different* context of secession (Rule no. 7, whereby the acts committed by the rebels during the insurgency are attributable to the new State).[297] The passage does not support Rule no. 2 in the different context of the establishment of a new government by successful rebels. Thus, the US Supreme Court in *Williams* v. *Bruffy* discussed *two types* of de facto governments, a distinction which was obviously overlooked by Umpire Plumley.[298] One type involved secession and the other was related to rebels establishing a de facto government replacing *only temporarily* the legitimate government. The Court defined this last type as one which exists after the rebels have 'expelled the regularly constituted authorities from the seats of power and the public offices, and established its own functionaries in their places, so as to represent in fact the sovereignty of the nation'.[299] In such a case, the Court stated that the rule of continuity would apply and that other States generally recognize the acts of such a de facto authority as those of the government.[300] Yet, and importantly, the situation that the Court

[295] *Bolivar Railway Co.* case, UK–Venezuela Claims Commission, Opinion of the Umpire, 1903, UNRIAA 9, p. 453, indicating that 'This rule was laid down in *Williams* v. *Bruffy*, 96 U.S. Sup. Ct., 176, wherein the court say, speaking of a similar condition'. The award then refers to this passage from the judgement:

> such as exists where a portion of the inhabitants of a country have separated themselves from the parent state and established an independent government. The validity of its acts, both against the parent state and its citizens or subjects, depends entirely upon its ultimate success. If it fails to establish itself permanently, all such acts perish with it. If it succeed and become recognized, its acts from the commencement of its existence are upheld as those of an independent nation.

[296] Greenman, 'The Secret History', p. 6–7.

[297] This Rule is discussed below in Part II, Section 4.2.

[298] Greenman, 'The Secret History', p. 7.

[299] *Williams* v. *Bruffy*, 96 U.S. Sup. Ct., 176.

[300] In any event, the Court made it clear that the Confederate States did not fulfil the conditions for this type of de facto government:

> [b]ut the Confederate government was not of this kind. It never represented the nation, it never expelled the public authorities from the country, it never entered into any treaties, nor was it ever recognized as that of an independent power. It collected an immense military force, and temporarily expelled the authorities of the United States from the territory over which it exercised an usurped dominion: but in that expulsion the United

described is *not* one where the rebels are actually successful, but rather one where they de facto control part of a territory for a while but are soon after *defeated* by the legitimate government.[301] In other words, the situation envisaged in that case is not the one dealt with under Rule no. 2. The *Williams* v. *Bruffy* case can hardly be considered as supporting Rule no. 2. The fact that the *Bolivar Railway* award only cites this source in support of its finding undermines its authority as a solid precedent in favour of Rule no. 2. It is therefore surprising that the case was quoted by many subsequent awards, including the *Puerto Cabello and Valencia Railway Company* case decided by the Venezuelan–British Mixed Claims Commission, as an authority in support of Rule no. 2.[302]

A number of other tribunals seem to have based their decisions in support of Rule no. 2 on the fact that the rebels were acting as a de facto government during the time the acts were committed. Yet, as mentioned above,[303] the de facto justification has been rejected by Ago for not being a valid reason behind the principle set out in Article 10(1) of the ILC Articles. One clear example is the *Dix* case, decided by the US–Venezuela Mixed Claims Commission, which held Venezuela liable for the taking of the property of an American citizen by the successful revolutionary armies of General Castro in 1899. The Commission mentioned the 'well-established rule of international law' that the acts of successful rebels should be 'regarded as the acts of a *de facto* government'.[304]

> States never acquiesced; on the contrary, they immediately resorted to similar force to regain possession of that territory and re-establish their authority, and they continued to use such force until they succeeded. It would be useless to comment upon the striking contrast between a government of this nature, which, with all its military strength, never had undisputed possession of power for a single day, and a government like that of the Commonwealth of England under Parliament or Cromwell.

301 This is clear from this extract: '[a]s far as other nations are concerned, such a government is treated as in most respects possessing rightful authority; its contracts and treaties are usually enforced; its acquisitions are retained; its legislation is in general recognized; and the rights acquired under it are, with few exceptions, *respected after the restoration of the authorities which were expelled*', emphasis added.

302 *Puerto Cabello and Valencia Railroad Company*, British–Venezuelan Commission, 1903, UNRIAA 9, p. 513: '[i]t was settled for this Commission by the opinion of the umpire in the claim of the Bolivar Company that the respondent Government, subject to certain exceptions, was liable for the acts of successful revolutionists'.

303 See Section 2.2.2.2.1.

304 *Dix (U.S.* v. *Venezuela)*, US–Venezuela Mixed Claims Commission, 1903, UNRIAA 9, p. 120:

Another example where the tribunal based its decision on this de facto government justification is the *Heny* case decided by the US–Venezuela Mixed Claims Commission. The case involved the forcible taking of horses, cattle, lumber, tools, and money of an American citizen by successful insurgents during the 'Legalista' revolution in Venezuela in 1892.[305] Umpire Barge of the Commission held that Venezuela was liable on the grounds that 'the revolution proved ultimately successful in establishing itself as the *de facto* Government so that the liability of the Venezuelan Government for these acts can not be denied'.[306] Similarly, in the *Hopkins* case[307] (dealing with an unsuccessful rebellion) the US–Mexico General Claims Commission relied on the notion of 'control'.[308] It stated that the extent to which 'an administration which seizes the reins of government by force and is illegal in its inception' can bind the nation 'will depend upon its real control and paramountcy at the time of the act over a major portion of the territory and a majority of the people' of the State.[309] Thus, acts of such an insurgent administration 'become binding on the nation as of the date [the] territory comes under its domination and control *conditioned* upon its ultimate success'.[310] In other words, the acts of successful rebels should be attributable to the State because they were *in control* of parts of the territory and were acting as a de facto government. Another award mentioning the importance of 'control' is the *Short* case decided by the Iran–US Claims Tribunal:

> The Revolution of 1899, led by General Cipriano Castro, proved successful, and its acts, under a well-established rule of international law, are to be regarded as the acts of a *de facto* government. Its administrative and military officers were engaged in carrying out the policy of that Government under the control of its executive. The same liability attaches for encroachments upon the rights of neutrals in the case of a successful revolutionary government, as in the case of any other *de facto* government.

It should be noted that the Commission nevertheless rejected the claim. Thus, it concluded that in the circumstances of the case, the losses complained were too remote to entitle Mr Dix to compensation and, in any event, that the rebels had no deliberate intention to injure him.

305 *Heny* case, US–Venezuela Mixed Claims Commission, 17 February 1903, UNRIAA 9, p. 134, indicating that the claim is for 'the partial destruction of the plantations, the confiscation of horses, cattle, and other valuables, and the imposing of loans upon the estate "La Fundaciôn" during the "Legalista" revolution in 1892'.

306 Ibid., p. 133.

307 The case is further discussed in Section 3.1.5.3.

308 *Hopkins* case, 1926, p. 41 ff.

309 Ibid., p. 45.

310 Ibid., p. 45, emphasis in the original.

> Where a revolution leads to the establishment of a new government the State is held responsible for the acts of the overthrown government insofar as the latter *maintained control* of the situation. The successor government is also held responsible for the acts imputable to the revolutionary movement which established it, even if those acts occurred prior to its establishment, as a consequence of the *continuity* existing between the new organization of the State and the organization of the revolutionary movement.[311]

It is noteworthy that the *Short* case is one of a handful of cases which have explained their decisions to apply Rule no. 2 based on the idea of the 'continuity' existing between the 'new organization of the State and the organization of the revolutionary movement'.[312] Thus, none of the awards examined so far in this section refer to 'continuity' as the reason for applying Rule no. 2. This is surprising given that the 'continuity' justification has been put forward by both ILC Special Rapporteurs (especially Crawford) as the main explanation behind Rule no. 2.

In fact, several other tribunals seem to have based their decisions on the simple fact that the revolution was ultimately successful, without mentioning any other justification. In the *French Company of Venezuelan Railroads* case, the French–Venezuelan Mixed Claims Commission was concerned with a claim for damages for injuries to French railroad property resulting from its use by successful insurgents and governmental forces. Umpire Plumley held that the State was responsible for the damages resulting from *both* acts of the former government and the rebels.[313] The only reason mentioned in

[311] *Alfred L.W. Short* v. *The Islamic Republic of Iran*, Iran–US Claims Tribunal, Case No. 11135, 14 July 1987, para. 33, emphasis added. See also, dissenting opinion of Judge Brower, paras. 28–9.

[312] Another one is *Kenneth P. Yeager, a claim of less than US$250,000 presented by the United States of America* v. *The Islamic Republic of Iran*, Partial Award, Case No. 10199 (324–10199-l), 2 November 1987, para. 35.

[313] *French Company of Venezuelan Railroads* case, French–Venezuelan Mixed Claims Commission, 31 July 1905, UNRIAA 10, p. 285, p. 354 (1902):

> [t]he injuries done the railroad, the buildings and the material, by use in war, must have been considerable, and *since the revolution was successful, the respondent Government is properly chargeable for its use and for the injuries and damages which resulted.* There is no question as to the liability of the respondent Government for the natural and consequential damages which resulted to the railroad properties while they were in the use and control of the titular Government. Hence there is unquestioned and complete responsibility on the part of the respondent Government for all the necessary, natural, and consequential injuries which resulted to the railroad and its properties when used by either the revolutionary or the governmental forces. (emphasis added).

the award to arrive at this conclusion was the success of the revolution. Another relevant example where the same lack of reasoning is notable is the *Pinson* case decided by the French–Mexican Claims Commission. The President of the Commission, Verzijl, stated that 'en général, un État qui a traversé l'épreuve d'un mouvement révolutionnaire, ne peut être réputé responsable des actes juridiques et des actes illégaux des révolutionnaires que si ledit mouvement a fini par avoir le dessus'.[314] While the award dealt with a case where the rebels were not successful, it nevertheless hypothetically mentioned a number of situations where a State should be held responsible for acts committed by the rebels (and by the governmental armed forces).[315] Yet, the award never quite explains *why* the new government should take over the wrongs committed by the rebels. Rule no. 2 was also applied in a number of other arbitration cases,[316] including *Puerto Cabello and Valencia Railroad Company*,[317] *Pomeroy's El Paso Transfer Company*,[318] *Russel*,[319] *Hill*[320] and *Venezuelan Steam Transportation*

[314] *Pinson* case, 1928, p. 430 ('in general, a state which has gone through the ordeal of a revolutionary movement can only be held responsible for legal acts and illegal acts of revolutionaries if said movement has finally gained the upper hand').

[315] Ibid., p. 353: 'La thèse de l'irresponsabilité [supported by the Mexican government] est inacceptable, car il est incontestable qu'il peut se présenter bien des *dommages révolutionnaires*, dont l'État est sans aucun doute obligé *d'assumer la responsabilité*. . . . Par contre, si les dommages trouvent leur origine, par exemple dans des *réquisitions ou contributions forcées* réclamées par le Gouvernement légitime pendant sa lutte contre les insurgés, ou *par les révolutionnaires avant leur triomphe final*, ou qu'ils aient été causés par des actes délictueux du Gouvernement légitime ou de ses forces militaires, ou par des *délits commis par les forces révolutionnaires* victorieuses, la responsabilité de l'État ne saurait, à mon avis, être niée'. emphasis added.

[316] See analysis in Haig Silvanie, 'Responsibility of States for Acts of Insurgent Governments', *AJIL* 33(1) (1939), p. 83 ff.

[317] *Puerto Cabello and Valencia Railroad Company*, British–Venezuelan Commission, 1903, UNRIAA 9, p. 513: '[i]t was settled for this Commission by the opinion of the umpire in the claim of the Bolivar Railway Company that the respondent Government, subject to certain exceptions, was liable for the acts of successful revolutionists and for the acts of the titular government as well, the liability in either case being predicated upon the same state of evidential facts'.

[318] *Pomeroy's El Paso Transfer Company* case, Mexico–United States General Claims Commission, 8 October 1930, dissenting opinion of Nielsen, UNRIAA 4, p. 563: '[i]nternational tribunals have repeatedly held a government responsible for acts of successful revolutionist'.

[319] *Naomi Russell, In Her Own Right and As Administratrix and Guardian (U.S.A.)* v. *United Mexican States*, Mexico–US Special Claims Commission, Decision no. 5, 24 April 1931, opinion of Umpire Nielsen, UNRIAA 4, p. 824, stating that according to general international law 'a government is responsible for the acts of successful revolutionists'.

[320] *George Hill* case, US–Peru Claims Commission, in Moore, *History and Digest of the International Arbitrations* (vol. II), p. 1655–6. The case dealt with the imprisonment and

Company.[321] The Iran–US Claims Tribunal also came to the same conclusion in a few cases, including *Starrett Housing*[322] and *Rankin*.[323] Yet, in all of these decisions, the Iran–US Claims Tribunal came to this conclusion without much analysis.

One recent investment arbitration case where the principle was mentioned is *Cengiz*. After having cited Article 10 of the ILC Articles, the Tribunal noted that 'the rule implies that acts committed by members of an insurrectional movement are attributable to the State, if such movement eventually is successful and takes over the Government of such State'.[324] Applying the rule to the facts of the case, the Tribunal held that 'the Libyan State must be deemed responsible for acts and omissions committed by both its regular army (without taking into consideration which Government the army was defending) and by all insurrectional groups and militias, which defended the NTC Government and fought the Gaddafi regime, and which ultimately were successful'.[325] Whether or not the Tribunal actually applied correctly Article 10 of the ILC Articles to the specific facts of the case is very much questionable (this question will be examined below).[326]

In sum, while there is no doubt that case law supports Rule no. 2, what is rather surprising is the general lack of explanation as to why this principle should be applied. The few awards which have discussed the

improper personal ill-treatment of Mr Hill by revolutionaries which subsequently became the government in Peru.

321 *Venezuelan Steam Transportation Company* case, United States–Venezuelan Claims Commission, in Moore, ibid., p. 1693–732. The Commission held Venezuela liable for injuries, losses and damages arising from the wrongful seizure, detention, and employment of three American vessels by successful insurgents under General Blanco during the civil war of 1871–2.

322 *Starrett Housing Corporation, Starrett Systems, Inc. and others* v. *The Government of the Islamic Republic of Iran, Bank Omran and others*, Iran–US Claims Tribunal, Case No. 24 (ITL 32-24-1), Interlocutory Award, 19 December 1983, text attached to fn. 4; 'It seems clear that these events did create a force majeure situation for Starett. They may also have constituted a taking, since under international law the Islamic Republic of Iran is responsible for the acts of the successful group which brought about the victory of the Revolution'.

323 *Jack Rankin, A Claim of Less than U.S.$ 250,000 Presented by the United States of America* v. *The Islamic Republic of Iran*, Iran–US Claims Tribunal, Case No. 10913 (326-10913-2), Award, 3 November 1987, para. 25: '[f]or example, several problems remain even though it is an accepted principle of international law that acts of an insurrectional or revolutionary movement which becomes the new government of a State are attributable to the State'.

324 *Cengiz* case, 2018, para. 430.

325 Ibid., para. 431. See also, para. 435.

326 See Section 3.1.4.2.2.

matter typically offer reasons other than 'continuity' between the rebels and the new government. The idea of 'continuity', which has been supported by both ILC Special Rapporteurs and by many scholars (including myself), has generally not been explicitly endorsed by tribunals.

2.2.4 *Other Related Questions*

This last section examines a number of questions which have been analysed by tribunals and discussed by scholars in relation to the concrete application of Article 10(1) of the ILC Articles. These issues will be examined in the following sections:

- What are the relevant criteria to determine when a new government can be considered to be established? (Section 2.2.4.1);
- Which types of acts committed by the rebels are attributable to the State? (Section 2.2.4.2);
- How far back should retroactivity apply under Article 10(1)? (Section 2.2.4.3); and
- Should Rule no. 2 apply to cases of governments of national reconciliation? (Section 2.2.4.4).

2.2.4.1 Relevant Criteria to Determine When a New Government Can Be Considered to Be Established

One critical question that has been discussed by tribunals and writers is the determination of the moment at which the insurgency can be considered to have been successful in a context of a revolution or a civil war. In other words, during a rebellion, when can it be said that the insurgents have 'triumphed'?[327] To use the language adopted by ILC Special Rapporteur Crawford in the 1998 Report, when can it be considered that the 'opposition movement actually *defeated and replaced* the Government of the State concerned'?[328] Article 10 and the ILC Commentaries are 'vague as to when a movement has successfully become the new government'.[329] A number of criteria have been put forward by writers to assess this question.

[327] ILC, Commentaries, 2001, p. 51, para. 7.

[328] ILC, 'Report of the Commission to the General Assembly on the work of its fiftieth session', UN Doc. A/CN.4/SER.A/1998/Add.l, *ILC Yearbook* vol. II(2) (1998), p. 85, para. 416, emphasis added.

[329] Verhoeven, 'International Responsibility', p. 288.

The most important criterion is that the revolutionary movement 'be in actual control of the territory and in possession of the machinery of State'.[330] De Beus speaks of the situation when a 'revolutionary movement seizes the reins of government at the latter's very seat, thus establishing itself as the central authority of the country, even though part of the territory may not be under its control'.[331] For Silvanie, it needs to be shown that 'the titular government was destroyed and dispersed', that 'the whole country became under the control of the insurgent government' and that 'the success of the insurgents movement was a matter of public notoriety'.[332] The principle of effectiveness is indeed at the core of the question relating to when a new government can be deemed to have been established.[333] This is a question of facts.[334] The relevant elements, or factors, which need to be assessed to determine whether effective control has been established by a government are listed by Morris:

> [T]hese factors include the ability of the regime to control the State's territory (whether a portion of that territory in the case of a local *de facto* government or all or virtually all of the territory in the case of a general *de facto* government); the lack of significant resistance to the regime; the ability of the regime to govern effectively without the support or intervention of other States; whether the regime has succeeded in reviving the

330 Morris, 'Revolutionary Movements', p. 727.

331 de Beus, *The Jurisprudence of the General Claims Commission*, p. 107. According to him, in such a situation 'the acts of such government are held to be binding upon the State, because they could be considered as acts of the country'. He distinguished this case with the other situation where 'a revolution starts somewhere in the province, gradually spreading over other regions, until it brings the capital within its power', in which case the 'obligations undertaken by its representatives can not be considered as having been undertaken by the country'.

332 Haig Silvanie, *Responsibility of States for Acts of Unsuccessful Insurgent Governments* (New York, Columbia University Press, 1939), p. 50.

333 Stefan Talmon, 'Recognition of Opposition Groups as the Legitimate Representative of a People', *Chinese JIL* 12 (2013), p. 231:

> The main criterion in international law for government status is that the individual or group of individuals claiming to be the government of a State exercise effective control over the State's territory. A claimant to government status must be able to exercise effective control over the entire or, at least, a large majority of the territory of the State concerned, and must be likely to continue to do so. For a claimant to be in effective control of the State's territory, it must be in possession of the machinery of State which, as a rule, requires control of the State's capital.

334 *Jarvis* case, US–Venezuela Claims Commission, in Jackson H. Ralston, *Venezuelan Arbitrations of 1903* (Washington, GPO, 1904), p. 150: '[i]t is doubtless true that the question whether the Paez government was or was not the *de facto* government of Venezuela at the time the bonds were issued is one of fact'.

> machinery of State or put in place a new structure, such as by appointing ministers and providing basic services for the populace; and whether the regime generally appears to be stable, with a reasonable prospect of remaining in control of the State.[335]

One criterion not listed above that has been used by some tribunals to consider whether an attempt to create a new government was successful is the popular support for the rebels.[336] A clear example is the *Jansen* case, decided by the US–Mexico Mixed Claims Commission of 1868, dealing with the confiscation of an American bark by the 'Maximillian' government. The Commission agreed with Mexico's argument that the rebels never established a new government based, inter alia, on the grounds of lack of popular support.[337] The relevance of this factor has, however, been contested by writers.[338]

The expression 'general de facto government' is often used to describe cases where insurgents have an effective control over all (or almost all) the territory of the State.[339] This situation must be distinguished from the one where a government exercises effective control only over a limited portion of a State's territory, which can be referred to by the term 'local' de facto government.[340] The situation of a *general*

335 Morris, 'Revolutionary Movements', p. 736.

336 *McKenny* case, in Moore, *History and Digest of the International Arbitrations* (vol. III), p. 2881, p. 2885: 'the great mass of the people of Mexico continued to adhere to and obey the government of President Juarez from the start, and continued to resist the attempt to set up another government'.

337 *Jansen* case, in Moore, *History and Digest of the International Arbitrations* (vol. III), p. 2902, p. 2930:

> the so-called empire was not a government *de facto*; because, lacking the element of popular support or of habitual obedience from the mass of the people, it rested alone on the assistance of foreign force, which contemplated and extended only a temporary interference, and because another government, disputing successfully its pretensions, bore rule in Mexico as a fact, in possession of much the largest part of the territory, and sustained by the mass of the people.

338 A.C. Bundu, 'Recognition of Revolutionary Authorities: Law and Practice of States', *ICLQ* 27(1) (1978), p. 40: '[t]he preponderance of the practice of States nowadays considers the principle of effectiveness as controlling; any manifestation of popular consent being treated merely as an affirmation of that principle. The absence of popular consent is therefore not a conclusive factor militating against the issue of effectiveness'.

339 See Al-Rashid *et al.*, 'Investment Claims', 185 ff.

340 See M. J. Peterson, 'Recognition of Governments', in Gëzim Visoka, John Doyle and Edward Newman (eds.), *Routledge Handbook of State Recognition* (Abingdon, Routledge, 2020), p. 209, defining 'local' de facto government as situations where the 'rebel movement has sufficiently organized and disciplined armed forces to wage effective war against rival forces and sufficiently secure control over some portion of the state's

de facto government has been described in *Thorington* v. *Smith* as one involving a government which 'expels the regular authorities from their customary seats and functions, and establishes itself in their place, and so becomes the actual government of a country'.[341] As a result, it has been argued that 'a general *de facto* government assumes the role of the prior *de jure* government' and 'the responsibility of representing the state in international affairs and, accordingly, its actions become generally binding on the nation (and, accordingly, successor governments)'.[342] The question of the 'legitimacy' of such a de facto government is not relevant in this context, as recognized by Arbitrator Taft in the *Tinoco* case.[343]

It is interesting to note that in the *Cengiz* case, the Tribunal did refer to this notion of 'legitimacy'. Thus, the Tribunal noted that it was necessary to establish who was 'the legitimate Government of Libya at a certain time', that is, when the attacks on a foreign investor's property took place.[344] The Tribunal held that when the 'first incidents occurred – end of August 2011 – the legitimate Government of Libya was that of the NTC'.[345] It came to this conclusion based on the fact that a number of States had already formally recognized the NTC 'as the country's "legitimate authority"' and therefore that the 'evidence shows that by the end of August, international legitimacy had passed from the Gaddafi Government to the NTC Government, which had arisen out of the Libyan Revolution'.[346] The Tribunal also added that 'by that date, the NTC was also in control of the major part of Libyan territory'.[347] It may be that the Tribunal simply referred to the NTC as the 'legitimate' government of Libya because this was the language actually used by several States in their recognition statements. As further examined below, it has been argued that such declarations (as of June 2011) were mainly

territory to have a stable base of operations', adding that a rebel group is then 'capable of taking administrative action within the territory it controls and developing limited relations with the governments of other states'. The question as to whether or not the acts of a 'local' de facto government can bind the government is examined below. See Section 3.1.5.

341 *Thorington* v. *Smith*, 75 U.S. 1, 8 (1868), quoted in Al-Rashid *et al.*, 'Investment Claims', p. 185.

342 Al-Rashid *et al.*, ibid., p. 185.

343 *Aguilar-Amory and Royal Bank of Canada Claims (Great Britain* v. *Costa Rica)*, 1923, UNRIAA 1, p. 369, p. 381–2.

344 *Cengiz* case, 2018, para. 413.

345 Ibid., para. 414.

346 Ibid., para. 416.

347 Ibid., para. 417.

political in nature and did not have the effect of recognizing the NTC as the *new government.*[348] As noted by Talmon, 'international law does not distinguish between illegitimate regimes and lawful governments', adding that legitimacy 'is a political concept and not a legal term of art'.[349] Thus, the fact that by the end of August 'international legitimacy had passed from the Gaddafi Government to the NTC Government'[350] does not say anything about who was really the 'government' of Libya at the time of the attacks.[351] This question will be further examined below.[352]

The term de jure government is used to describe governments that have been formally recognized by other States. Such recognition is usually based on the principle of effectiveness.[353] It has been argued that if a State recognizes prematurely the formation of a de jure new government when the insurgents do not have effective control, it can be considered as a breach of international law and as an interference in the internal affairs of that State.[354] The main takeaway is that whether or not

348 Dapo Akande, 'Which Entity Is the Government of Libya and Why Does It Matter?', *EJIL Talk!*, 16 June 2011.

349 Stefan Talmon, 'The Difference between Rhetoric and Reality: Why an Illegitimate Regime May Still be a Government in the Eyes of International Law', *EJIL Talk!*, 3 March 2011, adding: '[i]n fact, international law does not provide any criteria for defining and determining legitimacy. If consent of the people or a democratic mandate were indeed such criteria, many governments in the world would have to be "downgraded" to illegitimate regimes.' He further examined this last point in Talmon, 'Recognition of Opposition Groups'.

350 *Cengiz* case, 2018, para. 416.

351 Talmon, 'Recognition of Opposition Groups', p. 239:

> [w]ith the government of the State having lost legitimacy, there is room for another legitimate representative of the State's people. But, legitimacy is not to be confused with legality in the sense of enjoying a certain legal status or representative capacity under international law. The fact that a government loses its legitimacy does not mean that it also automatically loses its government status.

352 See Section 3.1.4.2.2.1.

353 Bundu, 'Recognition of Revolutionary Authorities', p. 36–7, indicating that 'a revolutionary government must be in effective control with a reasonable prospect of permanence and stability over the whole-or practically the whole-territory of the State'. See also: Morris, 'Revolutionary Movements', p. 727, referring to many authorities, and indicating that 'some States have added requirements beyond effective control alone before recognizing a revolutionary movement as the new government, such as a willingness to comply with international law obligations or a demonstration of the consent of the populace in the change of regime'.

354 Morris, 'Revolutionary Movements', p. 726, referring to many authorities including *Restatement (Third), Foreign Relations Law of the United States*, Vol. I, St. Paul, American Law Institute Publ., 1987, § 203, comment (g), p. 86 ('recognizing or treating a rebellious regime as the successor government while the previously recognized government is still in control constitutes unlawful interference in the internal affairs of that state').

the insurgents have been recognized by other States as the de facto government is not per se a determinant factor to assess whether the group should be considered as the new government having replaced the previous one.[355] In the same way, Morris noted that 'recognition alone is *neither necessary nor sufficient*'.[356] One clear example is the *Tinoco* case where the non-recognition by Great Britain of a general interim government was considered by the arbitrator as 'neither determinative of the question of whether that administration constituted a *de facto* government nor served to estop a claim by Great Britain on behalf of its citizens'.[357] Nonetheless, it does not mean that States' recognition of revolutionaries as forming a new government is altogether irrelevant. Any such recognition can be considered as evidence of rebels having effective control.[358] In other words, recognition is a relevant indicia to assess whether the rebels have been ultimately successful in establishing a new government.[359] Many arbitration cases support that position.[360]

355 Verhoeven, 'International Responsibility', p. 290.

356 Morris, 'Revolutionary Movements', p. 724, emphasis added. See also: Al-Rashid *et al.*, 'Investment Claims', p. 195; Houghton, 'The Responsibility of the State', p. 253 ('it appears that it has not been deemed essential that such a *de facto* government shall have been recognized at the time of the acts in question by the government of the claimant, in order that the state be held responsible for such acts'); Mohtashami, 'Protecting the Legitimacy of the Arbitral Process', p. 624.

357 Morris, 'Revolutionary Movements', p. 724.

358 Ibid., p. 736: 'recognition by other States is not determinative, but inasmuch as recognition represents those States' considered opinion regarding the effectiveness and stability of the revolutionary regime, it can be a helpful indicator that a local or general *de facto* government has succeeded in establishing itself'.

359 Al-Rashid *et al.*, 'Investment Claims', p. 195: '[a]s far as responsibility of *de facto* governments is concerned, recognition – in and of itself – has not been regarded as a condition either necessary or sufficient. That said, recognition (or non-recognition) may nevertheless serve as important evidence of the existence of a *de facto* government'. See also: Borchard, 'International Pecuniary Claims against Mexico', p. 346.

360 *Jarvis* case, US–Venezuela Claims Commission, in Jackson H. Ralston, *Venezuelan Arbitrations of 1903* (Washington, GPO, 1904), p. 150:

> [i]t is doubtless true that the question whether the Paez government was or was not the *de facto* government of Venezuela at the time the bonds were issued is one of fact. But the decision of the political department of the United States Government on November 19, 1862, that there was no such conclusive evidence that the Paez government was fully accepted and peacefully maintained by the people of Venezuela as to entitle it to recognition must be accorded great weight as to the fact, and is in any event conclusive upon its own citizens.

See also, Al-Rashid *et al.*, 'Investment Claims', p. 195, citing a few cases.

Finally, it should be added that a different question arises in the context of a government's standing before an international tribunal when it is in the middle of a civil war.[361] As noted by one writer, arbitral tribunals 'have relied on the regime's international recognition – rather than examining the nature and extent of control of the regime over the nation's territory – as the means to resolve the question of whether a political faction claiming to be the legitimate government of a state is entitled to represent that state'.[362] Thus, in *BUCG* v. *Yemen*, the Tribunal was faced by competing claims from two opposing regimes (the so-called 'Hadi' Government and the 'Sana'a' Government) each of whom claimed legitimacy in representing Yemen in the arbitration proceedings. The Tribunal acknowledged that the 'Revolutionary Leadership' of the Sana'a Government 'controls the capital, Sana'a, in which the subject airport is located, and that the government of the "resigned" President Hadi is no longer in control'. Yet, the Tribunal focused instead on the fact that the 'Hadi' Government was recognized by the international community as the legitimate government.[363]

361 For an analysis of State succession issues affecting a respondent State during arbitration proceedings under BITs, see: Dumberry, *A Guide to State Succession in International Investment Law*, p. 403 ff. The question of who should be considered as the representative of the government arose in several cases in the context of the recent events in Venezuela. See Iareporter, 'ICSID Declines Disqualification Proposal Arising out of "Solomonic Solution" to the Problem of Venezuela's Representation', 28 July 2020; Iareporter, 'In Now-Public Decision, an ICSID Ad Hoc Committee Finds That it has the Power to Decide the Question of Venezuela's Representation, and Rules in Favor of the Maduro Government', 2 April 2020, discussing these two cases: *Conocophillips* v. *Venezuela*, ICSID Case No. ARB/07/30; *Valores Mundiales and Consorcio Andino* v. *Venezuela*, ICSID Case No. ARB/13/11.

362 Mohtashami, 'Protecting the Legitimacy of the Arbitral Process', p. 624 ff. See also, p. 627:

> [t]he reference to international recognition as a means to determine the standing of a regime to represent the state in an international proceeding departs from the practice under international law in relation to determining the attribution to the state of acts committed by a governing regime. In the latter analysis, as discussed above, the international recognition (or lack thereof) of a *de facto* government or revolutionary movement has not been a determining factor.

363 *Beijing Urban Construction Group Co Ltd* v. *Republic of Yemen*, ICSID Case No. ARB/14/30, Procedural Order No. 2, 8 November 2016, paras. 5–6:

> The Tribunal notes that as recently as 23 September 2016 the UN General Assembly invited President Hadi to address it as the internationally recognized representative of the Republic of Yemen, which followed the 'affirmation' by the UN Security Council by Resolution No 2216 (dated 14 April 2015) of the 'legitimacy of the President of Yemen, Abdo Rabbo Mansour Hadi'. Although a lot has happened on the ground in the

The same situation arose in the *Mobile Telephony-Sabafon* case. The Tribunal held that if Yemeni law were to apply, the 'Hadi' Government was the legitimate government of Yemen. It also noted that under international law, 'the Hadi Government has consistently been recognized by the international community and by third States as the *de jure* government of Yemen' and that 'at the same time, the Houthis have consistently been condemned for consolidating their *de facto* power over the capital Sana'a and surrounding provinces'.[364] It concluded its analysis as follows:

> [T]here can be no question that the Houthis exercise effective control over the entire territory of Yemen. Accordingly, the Tribunal finds that the facts on the ground do not support the application of the effective control doctrine, or, in other terms, the facts on the ground are not sufficient to disregard the recognition by the international community of the Hadi Government. The Tribunal therefore concludes that the Hadi Government is the legitimate government both as a matter of Yemeni law and international law. The Tribunal is bound to take note of this state of affairs and to draw the necessary conclusions for the present case.[365]

These two cases are interesting as they illustrate that the de jure recognition is what matters to determine which entity should be considered as the 'government' of the respondent State in the specific context of ongoing arbitration proceedings. There is indeed a very practical reason for adopting such a position. Relying on effective control in this context may not be realistic and could create uncertainty given that the answer to the question as to who actually controls what part of the territory may change during the proceedings. In other words, there may be good reasons not to rely on effectiveness in this specific and unique context.

2.2.4.2 Which Types of Acts Committed by the Rebels Are Attributable to the State?

One question, which has surprisingly not been addressed by scholars, is the types of rebels' acts that can be attributable to the State. Article 10(1)

> last year, ..., the legal status of the Hadi government appears to be unchanged.

The award is not publicly available but is cited in Mohtashami, 'Protecting the Legitimacy of the Arbitral Process', p. 25–6.

364 *Yemen Company for Mobile Telephony-Sabafon* v. *The Government of the Republic of Yemen*, PCA Case No. 2010-03, Procedural Order No. 11, 2 May 2018, para. 80, cited in Mohtashami, 'Protecting the Legitimacy of the Arbitral Process', p. 625–6.

365 Ibid., paras. 88 and 89.

of the ILC Articles speaks generally of 'conduct' by rebels, which suggests that it includes *all acts* committed by the rebels during an insurrection that caused some damages to a third party. According to Piguet, 'conduct' would cover *both* illegal acts and those which could be considered as 'legitimate' from the standpoint of the laws of war.[366] There is no doubt that the provision covers *wrongful* acts. But what about acts which are not considered as wrongful? The 1975 ILC Report mentioned that 'organs of an insurrectional movement . . . may engage in conduct liable to bring an international responsibility upon the insurrectional movement itself if that conduct should constitute a *breach of an international obligation* recognized as incumbent on the insurrectional movement'.[367] This passage suggests that Rule no. 2 only covers *wrongful* acts. This is also the position adopted by Kolb.[368] As further explained below in Part II, this is also the position which was adopted by Serbia in its pleadings in the *Genocide* case before the ICJ.[369] I have found a few examples of State practice and case law which support this position. They will be examined in the next paragraphs.

One example, which has already been mentioned above, involves instructions given by the US Department of State expressing its position on the liability of the new government of Cuba following the successful revolution of Castro's troops. The document dealt with the acts committed by governmental forces (a point already examined above)[370] and by the rebels. The document makes an important distinction between damages resulting from the 'legitimate military operations of forces' and those which are not. It stated that not all acts committed by the rebels could be attributable to Cuba. The State would only be responsible for those military operations which were not 'legitimate' or those which were illegal under the laws of war.[371]

366 Piguet, *La Guerre civile en droit international*, p. 133 ('par agissements, il faut entendre tant les mesures de droit public que les actes illicites' ('by acts, we must understand both measures of public law and unlawful acts').

367 ILC, Report, 1975, p. 91, para. 3.

368 Kolb, *The International Law of State Responsibility*, p. 95, p. 98: 'the conduct of the insurrectional movement attributable to the State – in the case of success as envisaged by article 10 ASR – is that of the group itself. This conduct represents an IWA only if at the time it was committed it breached some obligations of international law applicable to the armed group, e.g. under the law of armed conflicts or under agreements, armistice or other'.

369 The question is examined in Part II, Section 4.2.2.

370 See Section 2.1.2.2.3.1.

371 M. M. Whiteman, *Digest of International Law* (Washington, Dept. of State, vol. 8, 1973), p. 819–20, referring to a document sent by the US Department of State to the American

Another relevant example is the *Pinson* case decided by the French–Mexican Claims Commission. The award dealt with a situation where the rebels were not successful, but nevertheless, it hypothetically mentioned a number of examples where a State should be held responsible for acts committed by the rebels (and governmental forces) in the context of a successful revolution. The award mentioned that the State should be held 'responsible' for the 'delictual' acts and forced requisition acts committed by the rebels; it did not refer to all types of conduct by them.[372]

Finally, reference should be made to the *Rankin* case decided by the Iran-US Claims Tribunal.[373] The Tribunal recognized the 'accepted principle of international law that acts of an insurrectional or revolutionary movement which becomes the new government of a State are attributable to the State'.[374] However, it also noted that 'several problems remain' with this principle.[375] The reasoning of the award suggests that only *some* acts of the revolutionary movement could be attributable to Iran. Thus, Article 10(1) would cover only those acts which were 'directed by revolutionaries against the alien because of his nationality', and not those 'incidental or collateral damage' arising, more generally, from the climate of violence prevailing during the revolution.

Embassy, Habana, instruction, No. A-180, 26 January 1959, MS. Department of State, file 237.1141/12-1958. The relevant part of the quote was mentioned above in Section 2.1.2.2.2.

372 *Pinson* case, 1928, p. 353.

373 *Jack Rankin, A Claim of Less than U.S. $250,000 Presented by the United States of America* v. *The Islamic Republic of Iran*, Iran–US Claims Tribunal, Case No. 10913 (326–10913–2), Award, 3 November 1987, para. 25.

374 Ibid.

375 Ibid.:

> First, when property losses are suffered by an alien during a revolution, there may be a question whether the damage resulted from violence which was directed at the alien or his property per se or was merely incidental or collateral damage resulting from the presence of the alien's property or property interests during the period of revolutionary unrest. Second, even with respect to some property losses that are not the result of incidental or collateral damage – for example, losses resulting from acts directed by revolutionaries against the alien because of his nationality – a further question of attribution remains, that is, whether those acts are acts of the revolutionary movement itself, rather than acts of unorganized mobs or of individuals that are not attributable to the movement.

Another question is whether or not Rule no. 2 covers *contracts* signed by rebels during the insurrection. For Silvanie, a State is 'bound by acts *and contracts* of successful insurgents'.[376] This is indeed true. Some awards have applied Rule no. 2 to *contractual* obligations undertaken by foreigners with rebels forming a de facto government during the insurgency.[377] A few cases will be examined in the following paragraphs.

The *United Dredging Company* case decided by the US–Mexico General Claims Commission involved a US company undertaking (without a written contract) salvaging work on a boat at the request of the rebels (General Carranza and the 'Constitutionalist' army) during the insurgency. The work was later suspended, and the company was not fully paid. The 'Constitutionalists' were successful in their rebellion and subsequently formed the new government. The United States argued that Mexico was 'responsible for obligations of the so-called "Constitutionalists" headed by General Carranza who as successful revolutionists established themselves in power in Mexico'.[378] Mexico apparently did not object to this argument.[379] The Commission held that Mexico was liable for the failure by the rebels to fulfil contractual obligations undertaken during the insurgency.

[376] Silvanie, 'Responsibility of States for Acts of Insurgent Governments', p. 80, emphasis added.

[377] Ibid.:

> Beginning in about the second half of the nineteenth century the question whether the state is bound by acts *and contracts* of successful insurgents appears to have been regarded primarily as a judicial question and was almost uniformly referred to international tribunals for adjudication. The recorded decisions of international courts of arbitration on this point are, without exception, in conformity with the view adopted by the United States during the controversy with France and the Two Sicilies, that is, they affirm the principle that the state is bound by acts of successful insurgent governments. (emphasis added).

See also, p. 83: '[t]he principle that the state is bound by acts *and contracts* of successful insurgents has been applied by other international tribunals in a variety of situations since about the middle of the nineteenth century', emphasis added. He examined several cases.

[378] *United Dredging Company (US)* v. *Mexico*, US–Mexico General Claims Commission, 1927, UNRIAA 4, p. 264.

[379] Ibid. The award thus mentioned that 'No question being raised as to responsibility for obligations incurred by General Carranza, or as to the performance of the services for which compensation is sought, or as to the propriety of the amount claimed for those services, an award should be rendered in favor of the claimant in that amount'.

Another interesting case is the *Central and South American Telegraph Company* award.[380] The Claimant requested damages to Chile for breach of a concession contract under which 'the Government reserves the right of suspending the service or use of the cable in case of danger to the security of the state'. The company alleged that during the civil war, it was prevented by the rebels (the Congressionalists) from using its cable within the territory under the control of the insurgents. The company argued that under the contract only the regular government of President Balmaceda had the right to suspend the service, and that the suspension by the Congressionalists was therefore in violation of its contractual rights. The Congressionalists ultimately defeated President Balmaceda and established a new government. The majority of the Commission held that the rebels had the right under the contract to suspend the service of the cable without incurring liability. The term 'the government' in the contract was interpreted by the majority of the Commission to apply not only to the legitimate government in power, but also to the rebels which were exercising de facto authority in the region (and were ultimately successful).[381] Thus, the insurgents 'had the character of a *de facto* government, possessing in the territory subject to its dominion the right to exercise jurisdiction according to the laws enacted and engagements accepted by and for the country'.[382] The reasoning of the majority of the Commission suggests that it would have supported the proposition whereby contractual obligations undertaken by the rebels during an insurgency are attributable to the State in the event that the rebellion is successful.

Finally, reference should be made to the decision of the High Court of Uganda in *44123 Ontario Ltd* v. *Crispus Kiyonga and Others*.[383] The case involved a contract signed by a Canadian company with the National Resistance Movement, an insurrectional movement which was fighting the government at the time.[384] The rebels won their struggle and later became the new Government. The government

[380] *Central and South American Telegraph Company* case, in Moore, *History and Digest of the International Arbitrations* (vol. III), p. 2933–44.

[381] Silvanie, 'Responsibility of States for Acts of Insurgent Governments', p. 84.

[382] *Central and South American Telegraph Company* case, in Moore, *History and Digest of the International Arbitrations* (vol. III), p. 2942.

[383] *44123 Ontario Ltd.* v. *Crispus Kiyonga and Others*, High Court, Uganda, in 11 *Kampala LR* (1992), p. 14, p. 20–1; *ILR* 103, p. 259, p. 266.

[384] The case is mentioned in ILC, Crawford First Report, 1998, p. 53, para. 275.

(i.e., the former rebels) however denied its liability to perform the remainder of the contract. The High Court of Uganda rejected the claim by the company on the ground, inter alia, that 'at the time of the contract the Republic of Uganda had a well established government and therefore there cannot have been two governments contending for power whose acts must be recognized as valid'.[385] The Court considered the contract to be illegal under Ugandan law because to be 'binding it must be between persons existing at the time the contract is made'. The Court considered that the National Resistance Movement did not have a legal personality at the time of the insurgency. The relevance of this decision has been rightly questioned by Crawford on the grounds that it was made 'without any reference to international law or to Article 15' (now Article 10) of the ILC Articles.[386] The same conclusion was reached by Judge Kreća in his separate opinion in the ICJ 2015 *Genocide* case.[387]

2.2.4.3 How Far Back Should Retroactivity Apply under Article 10(1)?

The general principle set out in Article 10(1) of the ILC Articles is that the conduct of an (ultimately successful) insurrectional movement during the rebellion is attributable to the State (Rule no. 2). Ago speaks of a 'retroactive' attribution to the State of the acts committed by the rebels.[388] But, as pointed out by d'Aspremont, 'as it stands today, the rule fails to define . . . the moment from which the acts of the insurgency can be retroactively attributed to the State'.[389] The 2001 ILC Commentaries are indeed silent on this important point. At least three different solutions have been put forward by scholars.

First, the writing of some authors suggests that attribution should go back to all illegal acts committed by the rebels from the *inception* of

[385] Ibid.

[386] Ibid.

[387] ICJ, *Genocide* case, 2015, Separate Opinion of Judge Kreća, para. 66.2: '[t]he decision in Ontario Ltd. v. Crispus Kiyonga and Others is also of little, if any relevance, to the issue at hand. . . . The Judgment is based entirely on municipal contract law and does not refer to international law.'

[388] ILC, Ago Report, 1972, p. 145, para. 196, identifying the question as being: 'whether or not it is possible to attribute retroactively to the State, as a source of State responsibility, the acts or omissions of agents of the revolutionary movement before the organization of that movement was integrated with the State organization and thus became identified with it'. See also, ibid., p. 149, paras. 210–11.

[389] d'Aspremont, 'Rebellion and State Responsibility', p. 428.

a revolution.[390] This approach was adopted by the Harvard Draft of 1929 in Article 13(b) which refers to an injury to an alien which has resulted from 'an act or omission of the revolutionists committed at any time after the inception of the revolution'.[391] The same point was mentioned by Umpire Plumley in the *Bolivar Railways* case: 'the nation is responsible for the obligations of a successful revolution *from its beginning*, because, in theory, it represents *ab initio* a changing national will, crystallising in the finally successful results'.[392] While this solution has the undeniable merit of being simple and straightforward, its concrete application is far from obvious. It is never quite clear when a revolution can truly be said to have 'started'. The events which have eventually led to a successful taking over of power may have started as troubles or riots. Yet, as mentioned above,[393] the government *is* responsible for the acts of individuals and mobs committed against foreigners.[394] As noted by O'Connell, 'when the group acquires such cohesion and relative independence of control as to be designated insurgents the State *ceases to be responsible* for their wrongful actions, unless they successfully substitute themselves in the government of the country'.[395] It is when a group becomes better

[390] Morris, 'Revolutionary Movements', p. 754; Al-Rashid *et al.*, 'Investment Claims', p. 184; Rousseau, *Droit international public*, p. 86; D.P. O'Connell, *International Law* (2nd ed., London, Stevens and Sons, vol. II, 1970), p. 958 ('states are liable for . . . all acts [of successful revolutionaries] committed when they were merely mobs as well as when they became *de facto* governments'); L. B. Sohn and R. Baxter, Convention on the International Responsibility of States for Injuries to Aliens, Final Draft, comments to Article 18, in F.V. García Amador, Louis B. Sohn and Richard Baxter (eds.), *Recent Codification of the Law of State Responsibility for Injuries to Aliens* (Leiden, Brill, 1974) (liability 'should attach as early as possible, even before a group of insurgents has achieved the status of a full-fledged revolution'); Borchard, 'International Responsibility of the State for Injuries', p. 122; Houghton, 'The Responsibility of the State', p. 252; Kolb, *The International Law of State Responsibility*, p. 95 ('The attribution is retroactive to the moment when the insurrection began, or, more precisely, to the first IWA committed by the insurgents'); Chittharanjan F. Amerasinghe, *State Responsibility for Injuries to Aliens* (Clarendon, 1967), p. 54 (indicating that attribution should go 'as from the beginning of the revolution'); Borchard, *The Diplomatic Protection of Citizens Abroad*, p. 241 ('The government created through its efforts is liable for the acts of the revolutionists as well as for those of the titular government it has replaced. Its acts are considered as at least those of a general *de facto* government, for which the state is liable from the beginning of the revolution').

[391] Article 13(b), Harvard Draft Convention, 1929.

[392] *Bolivar Railway Co.* case, UK–Venezuela Claims Commission, Opinion of the Umpire, 1903, UNRIAA 9, p. 452–3, emphasis added.

[393] See Introduction, Section 1.1.3.2.

[394] O'Connell, *International Law*, p. 968.

[395] Ibid., p. 969, emphasis added.

organized that it can truly be characterized as an insurrectional movement. Yet, as the next paragraph will highlight, this degree of organization may not be present in the early stages of a revolution.

Second, it has been argued that attribution should go back to all acts committed by the rebels only once they can be considered organized enough to be characterized as an insurrectional movement. This is the position of Ago.[396] For him, 'attribution to the State is retroactive to the very first moment of the movement's existence'.[397] In my view, this is indeed the better approach.[398] It is generally agreed by writers that the question 'is independent of the recognition of the international personality of the insurrectional movement'.[399]

Third, other writers have argued that responsibility should be limited to situations where the insurgents actually exercised a minimum of control over the territory when the wrong was committed.[400] One example is the *Alfred L.W. Short* v. *Iran* case decided by the Iran–US Claims Tribunal. The award stated that 'where a revolution leads to the establishment of a new government the State is held responsible for the acts of the overthrown government

[396] It should be noted that there are some passages from the 1972 Report which tend to suggest that he rather favoured the first position mentioned above: ILC, Ago Report, 1972, p. 131, para. 158: '[t]he question arises in such a case whether or not it is possible to attribute to the State the acts committed by the organs of the insurrectional movement during the period between *the beginning of the revolutionary uprising* and the final seizure of power', (emphasis added).

[397] ILC, Ago Report, 1972, p. 151, para. 213. See also: ibid., p. 150, para. 210. See also: ILC, Report, 1975, p. 92, para. 4: 'as soon as they begin their separate existence on the international scene, such movements may be capable within certain limits of committing internationally wrongful acts of their own'.

[398] See also: Eatwell, *State Responsibility*, p. 176: '[t]his approach [referring to the position of Ago] suggests that conduct will only be attributable to the state from the point at which the insurrectional movement is sufficiently organised such that its organs are identifiable'.

[399] Cahin, 'Attribution of Conduct to the State', p. 248. See also: Crawford, *State Responsibility*, p. 173–4. See also: ILC, Ago Report, 1972, p. 151, para. 213.

[400] It may be argued that this is the position (at least implicitly) supported by Crawford, *State Responsibility*, p. 173–4, referring to Article 1(1) of the Protocol II to the Geneva Conventions which does mention the notions of 'control' ('dissident armed forces or other organized groups which, under responsible command, exercise such control over a part of [the relevant State's] territory as to enable them to carry out sustained and concerted military operations and to implement this Protocol'). See also: Tom Grant, 'Secession and State Succession', in Peter Radan and Aleksandar Pavkovic (eds.), *The Ashgate Research Companion to Secession* (Abingdon, Routledge, 2013), p. 368: '[t]he result is the back-dating of the responsibility of the new state: the conduct of the liberation movement, from the inception of its effective control over at least some of the territory it claims, is "considered an act of the new State"'.

insofar as the latter *maintained control* of the situation'.[401] The Tribunal also noted that when the Claimant departed from Iran (a few days before the proclamation on 11 February 1979 of the Islamic Revolutionary Government), 'the revolutionary movement *had not yet been able to establish control* over any part of Iranian territory, and the Government had demonstrated its loss of control'.[402] In this context, the Tribunal concluded that the Claimant was unable 'to identify any agent of the revolutionary movement, the actions of which compelled him to leave Iran'[403] and, therefore, that his departure could not be the result of actions of the new government that was established following the success of the Revolution.

One related question is the distinction between the 'organs' of an insurrectional movement and its simple 'supporters'. While it is true that, as a matter of principle, 'a movement will be responsible for breaches of international law committed by its organs', it is not always easy to identify the organs of rebel groups.[404] This question arose in the case of *Arthur Young & Co*, decided by the Iran–US Claims Tribunal, which dealt with a claim of wrongful expulsion by agents of the Iranian government.[405] The Tribunal denied the claim on the grounds that the Claimant had failed to prove 'who these "agents" were and how they were associated with the Government of Iran'.[406] The Tribunal held that 'attribution of acts to the State is justified only when the identity of acting persons and their association with the State is established with reasonable certainty'.[407] In other words, the new revolutionary government is not responsible for the acts committed by supporters of the Revolution more broadly. This is because one cannot establish 'with reasonable certainty' the 'identity' of these people and their 'association' with the new government.

A similar finding was made by the Iran–US Claims Tribunal in *Alfred L.W. Short* v. *Iran*, where the Claimant was unable to prove that his wrongful expulsion was due to the acts of the 'Revolutionary Guard'

[401] *Alfred L.W. Short* v. *The Islamic Republic of Iran*, Iran–US Claims Tribunal, Case No. 11135, Award of 14 July 1987, para. 33.

[402] Ibid., (emphasis added).

[403] Ibid., para. 34.

[404] Verhoeven, 'International Responsibility', p. 299, examining this question in some detail.

[405] *Arthur Young & Company* v. *The Islamic Republic of Iran, Telecommunications Company of Iran, Social Security Organization of Iran*, Iran–US Claims Tribunal, Case No. 484, Award No. 338–484–1, para. 48.

[406] Ibid.

[407] Ibid.

rather than those of supporters of the Revolution. The majority of the Tribunal made this distinction very clearly.[408] The acts of the supporters of the Revolution could not be attributable to the new revolutionary government once in power. The same remark was made in other awards.[409] In his dissenting opinion, Judge Brower is critical of the approach adopted by the majority in the *Short* case.[410] For Brower, the 'test' mentioned by the majority is *too narrow* insofar as Article 10(1) of the ILC Articles would then only find application in cases where the perpetrators of wrongs were an 'identifiable organized units, visibly controlling specified territory'. For him, it was 'unrealistic' to apply this narrow test in the context of the Revolution in Iran given the breadth of support amongst the population. In his view, since the Revolution was so popular and widely supported, Article 10 should therefore be applied more loosely. In this context, he believes that acts committed by 'unorganized or loosely organized adherents of the successful Revolution' should also be attributable to the new government.[411]

As noted by Eatwell, it is not always easy to distinguish between members of an insurrectional movement and mere supporters, especially at the early

[408] *Alfred L.W. Short* v. *The Islamic Republic of Iran*, Iran–US Claims Tribunal, Case No. 11135, Award of 14 July 1987, para. 34:

> The Claimant relies on acts committed by revolutionaries and seeks to attribute responsibility for their acts to the government that was established following the success of the Revolution. He is unable, however, to identify any agent of the revolutionary movement, the actions of which compelled him to leave Iran. The acts of supporters of a revolution cannot be attributed to the government following the success of the revolution just as the acts of supporters of an existing government are not attributable to the government.

[409] *Jack Rankin, A Claim of Less than U.S. $250,000 Presented by the United States of America* v. *The Islamic Republic of Iran*, Iran–US Claims Tribunal, Case No. 10913 (326–10913–2), Award, 3 November 1987, para. 25 stating that 'several problems remain even though it is an accepted principle of international law that acts of an insurrectional or revolutionary movement which becomes the new government of a State are attributable to the State'. The Tribunal identified one such 'problem' as follows: 'a further question of attribution remains, that is, whether those acts are acts of the revolutionary movement itself, rather than acts of unorganized mobs or of individuals that are not attributable to the movement'.

[410] *Alfred L.W. Short* v. *The Islamic Republic of Iran*, Iran–US Claims Tribunal, Case No. 11135, Award of 14 July 1987, dissenting opinion of Judge Brower, paras. 26–9.

[411] Ibid., para. 30: '[i]n short, something less than what the Award here posits as necessary is sufficient to establish the nexus between the injury to the alien and the successful revolutionary government making the latter responsible for the former. It is the Award's failure thus to adapt traditional concepts to unique events that is especially disappointing.'

stages of an insurrection.[412] Despite this distinction being sometimes difficult to draw in practice, it is an essential one that should be maintained. Otherwise, as Eatwell rightly stated, 'if any or all acts of any or all persons during a revolution were attributable to the state', there would be a 'risk that the exceptional status of Article 10 would be diluted and the importance of the notion that the conduct is carried out on behalf of the movement would be lost'.[413] ILC Special Rapporteur Crawford also emphasized in the 1998 Report that the rule in Article 10(1) 'should only be limited to "the conduct of an organ of an insurrectional movement" which was "established"; it should not apply to the uncoordinated conduct of its supporters'.[414]

2.2.4.4 Should Rule No. 2 Apply to Cases of Governments of National Reconciliation?

D'Aspremont has noted that the most important 'lingering question mark hanging over Article 10' is the fact that 'the rule of attribution of acts of victorious rebels to the State is silent as to the manner in which the rebels "triumph"'.[415] This is indeed true. The 2001 ILC Commentaries refer rather vaguely to an 'insurrectional movement, having triumphed' which 'has substituted its structures for those of the previous Government of the State in question'.[416] That does not say anything about the way the rebels came to power and are now forming the new government. Article 10(1) only deals with the *consequences* of the rebels' victory: their acts committed during the (ultimately successful) insurgency are attributable to the State (Rule no. 2). What is clear is that

[412] Eatwell, *State Responsibility*, p. 180: '[t]here is no clear answer to the question how members of an insurrectional movement should be identified, particularly in the embryonic stages of revolution'. She also noted that

> the requirement that the claimant should prove that the perpetrators of their injury were acting under the direction and control of the insurrectional movement sits uneasily with idea that a revolution can be the sum of acts of individual supporters of a charismatic figure, a movement or an opposition party who respond to a call to arms but are not instructed to carry out a specific task and do not act under the control of the figure, movement or party. (p. 183)

[413] Ibid., p. 183.

[414] ILC, 'Report of the Commission to the General Assembly on the work of its fiftieth session', UN Doc. A/CN.4/SER.A/1998/Add.l, *ILC Yearbook* vol. II(2) (1998), p. 85, para. 417. See also, ILC, Crawford First Report, 1998, note no. 3 to new Draft Article 15 (ibid., p. 57).

[415] d'Aspremont, 'Rebellion and State Responsibility', p. 434.

[416] ILC, Commentaries, 2001, p. 51, para. 7.

Article 10(1) covers situations where the insurgents have gained access to power through an armed conflict or violence. The provision would therefore not cover cases where the rebels have stopped fighting, and subsequently became the new government after winning an election. The question addressed in this section is whether Rule no. 2 set out in Article 10(1) applies to situations where the rebels come to power via a government of national reconciliation following an agreement with the government.[417]

The next sections will address the following issues:

- An analysis of Crawford's different solution than the one followed by Ago (Section 2.2.4.4.1);
- Crawford's modification proposal providing an 'incentive' for the parties to reach a peace settlement (Section 2.2.4.4.2);
- How the proposed modification results in an unsatisfactory outcome for the injured party (Section 2.2.4.4.3); and
- Whether an alternative solution can be envisaged (Section 2.2.4.4.4).

2.2.4.4.1 Crawford Adopted a Different Solution than the One Followed by Ago In his 1972 Report, Ago envisaged that Rule no. 2 could cover situations where a movement would become the new government by means others than revolutions and civil war. Thus, he mentioned that Article 10(1) would apply the same way for *all cases*, even in situations where the new government is one of national reconciliation including former rebels.[418] The same comment is found in the

[417] On this question, Eatwell, *State Responsibility*; T. J. Eatwell, 'State Responsibility, Successful, Insurrectional Movements and Governments of National Reconciliation', in J. Summers and A. Gough (eds.), *Non-State Actors and International Obligations* (Leiden, Brill, 2018), p. 388.

[418] ILC, Ago Report, 1972, p. 149, para. 209: 'the principle that it is legitimate to attribute to a government resulting from a successful revolution the injurious acts committed earlier by the revolutionaries must also apply to the case of a coalition government formed following an agreement between the "legitimate" authorities and the leaders of the revolutionary movement'. See also: ibid., p. 146, para. 199:

> [l]astly, if the insurgents triumph but this does not lead to the total collapse of the pre-existing State organization – if, in other words, the revolutionary structures are integrated within the framework of the previous organization – the State apparatus which results is in reality the continuation of both the organizations which confronted each other during the civil war. In that case, there is therefore nothing surprising in the attribution to the State of the acts not only of members of its preceding organization but also of members of the

ILC 1975 Report.[419] Ago also mentioned that the 'situation has occurred very rarely', referring to two examples of State practice.[420] The position of Ago has also been supported by other writers in the past.[421] In his book, Silvanie refers to the situation of an 'agreement' between the rebels and the government[422] as one of the few 'exceptions' to the 'general rule that the State is not liable for damages caused to foreign persons and property by wrongful acts of unsuccessful insurgents'.[423] He refers to the *McCord* case in support of his position.[424]

ILC Special Rapporteur Crawford took a different position. In the 1998 Report, he mentioned that Article 10(1) 'should *only* apply in the narrow case where the opposition movement actually *defeated and replaced* the Government of the State concerned'.[425] This comment suggests that Article 10(1) does not apply to governments of national reconciliation. In the 2001 ILC Commentaries, Crawford also mentioned that Rule no. 2 'should not be pressed too far' in situations of 'governments of national reconciliation, formed following an agreement between the existing authorities and the leaders of an insurrectional movement'.[426] For the

organization that grew up during the insurrection and is subsequently united with the preceding organization, which is thereby transformed to a greater or lesser extent. It should be added that this conclusion appears to be justified both in the case of total victory for the insurrectional movement, which then modifies the structures of the State apparatus to its liking, and *in the case of an agreement between the legitimate government and the insurrectional government* under which members of the insurrection are called upon to participate in the government of the State. (emphasis added).

[419] ILC, Report, 1975, para. 5: 'in the case of an *agreement* between the legitimate government and the insurrectional government under which members of the insurrection are called upon to participate in the government of the State' (emphasis added).

[420] ILC, Ago Report, 1972, p. 149, para. 209.

[421] Charles Cheney Hyde, *International Law Chiefly as Interpreted and Applied by the United States* (Boston, Little, Brown & Co., vol. I, 1922), p. 543, referred to in Silvanie, *Responsibility of States*, p. 209–10. See also: Michael Akehurst, 'State Responsibility for the Wrongful Acts of Rebels – An Aspect of the Southern Rhodesian Problem', *British YIL* 43 (1968–9), p. 58: '[s]ince a State is liable for the acts of successful revolutionaries, it is only logical that it should be liable if the rebels and the *de jure* government get together to form a coalition government'.

[422] Silvanie, *Responsibility of States*, p. 208–10.

[423] Ibid., p. 159.

[424] *McCord* case, in Moore, *Digest of International Law* (vol. IV), p. 987. The case is also examined in ILC, Ago Report, 1972, p. 149, para. 209.

[425] ILC, 'Report of the Commission to the General Assembly on the work of its fiftieth session', UN Doc. A/CN.4/SER.A/1998/Add.l, *ILC Yearbook* vol. II(2) (1998), p. 85, para. 416, emphasis added.

[426] ILC, Commentaries, 2001, p. 51, para. 7.

ILC, this is a situation where the acts of the rebels should *not* be attributable to the State:

> The State should not be made responsible for the conduct of a violent opposition movement merely because, in the interests of an overall peace settlement, elements of the opposition are drawn into a reconstructed government. Thus, the criterion of application of paragraph 1 is that of a *real and substantial continuity* between the former insurrectional movement and the new Government it has succeeded in forming.[427]

This comment suggests that Crawford believes that there should be an *exception* to Rule no. 2 in the specific context of national reconciliation governments. Thus, the basic principle under Rule no. 2 (i.e., that the acts committed by the rebels during the insurgency are attributed to the State) remains applicable in general (i.e. when the rebels have 'triumphed'),[428] but it 'should not be pressed too far' in the specific situation of governments of national reconciliation. This statement is rather ambiguous since 'it is not clear what the phrase "should not be pressed too far" means'.[429] As noted by Eatwell, 'the ILC did not make clear whether it intended for this exclusion to apply to all governments of national reconciliation in all their forms or whether this exclusion should be a matter of degree, dependent upon the extent to which the former insurrectional movement shares executive power with the pre-existing government'.[430] In any event, the reason explicitly mentioned by Crawford for not applying Rule no. 2 is that there is no 'real and substantial continuity' between the new government and the rebels.[431] This is presumably because the new government is formed with elements of the *former* government (and not just former rebels).[432] In the context of the ILC session discussing draft Article 15 (which later became Article

[427] Ibid., emphasis added. See also, Liesbeth Zegveld, *Accountability of Armed Opposition Groups in International Law* (Cambridge University Press, 2002), p. 157.

[428] ILC, Commentaries, 2001, p. 51, para. 7.

[429] Eatwell, *State Responsibility*, p. 184. See also, p. 208.

[430] Ibid., p. 208. She believes that the latter interpretation is more likely. For her, 'it appears to have been the intention of Special Rapporteur Crawford to qualify the ILC's early position', p. 185). In support, she quoted this passage from ILC, Crawford First Report, 1998, p. 52, fn. 347: '[i]t is doubtful how far this principle should be pressed in cases of governments of national reconciliation. A State should not be made responsible for the acts of a violent opposition movement merely because, in the interests of an overall peace settlement, elements of the opposition are drawn into a reconstructed government. *In this respect the commentary needs some qualification*' (emphasis added by the author).

[431] For a critical analysis of this position, see: ibid., p. 184.

[432] Ryngaert, 'State Responsibility and Non-State Actors', p. 175, agreeing with the 'sensible' approach adopted by Crawford and noting that national reconciliation governments

10), Crawford also stated that this provision should not apply if the insurrectional movement came to power through an election where a newly formed government would include representatives of the movement. This is because 'elections created a new situation with an interruption of the causal link with the earlier situation'.[433] The term used by Crawford suggests that the interrupted 'causal link' he is referring to is the continuity between the insurrectional movement and the new government. Indeed, Article 10(1) was *not* meant to apply to cases where an insurrection *ends* and is followed by an election.[434] This new situation breaks the 'causal link' of continuity between the rebels and the future elected government in which former rebels are taking part. The goal of Rule no. 2 is to cover situations where the actions of rebels during an insurgency *directly lead* to the establishment of a new government. The 1975 ILC Report also speaks of a new government 'established as a result of' the action of the movement.[435] In other words, the rebels gained power *because* they won their military struggle. In the context of a coalition government, it can be argued that the causal link still exists because any agreement with the government is a direct result of the rebels' success on the battlefield. In other words, it is the government's fear of the likelihood of a victory by the rebels that leads it to sit with them at the negotiation table. A government would logically never do that if their chances of victory were nil. In contrast, the success of former rebels at an election may be the result of many factors which are not necessarily connected to their actions on the battlefield.

In his subsequent book, Crawford put forward another justification in favour of his position: '[t]o apply Article 10(1) in such a case [of national

'only partly consist of representatives of (former) insurrectional movements, and the continuity is accordingly not complete'.

433 See also, comment by Crawford, ILC, 'Summary Records of the Meetings of the Fiftieth Session', 2556th meeting, 5 August 1998, UN Doc. A/CN.4/SER.A/1998, *ILC Yearbook* vol. I (1998), p. 249, p. 254, para. 41: 'what happened if the insurrectional movement ended with elections and the establishment of a Government which included representatives of the movement? When power was taken by force of arms it could be assumed that there would be at least continuity of the persons involved, but elections created a new situation with an interruption of the causal link with the earlier situation'.

434 *Contra*: d'Aspremont, 'Rebellion and State Responsibility', p. 428 ('The application of that rule is particularly problematic in the intricate situation of insurgents seizing power through democratic elections').

435 ILC, Report, 1975, p. 105, para. 21: '[f]or such an attribution, no condition is required other than the mere existence of that movement and the relationship of continuity between its organization and that of the new government or State established *as a result of its action*', emphasis added.

reconciliation governments] could act as a disincentive'.[436] In the ILC 1998 Report, he explained the argument as follows: 'If the Government of a State could only bring elements of an unlawful opposition movement into a new Government at the expense of assuming all the liabilities of the opposition movement, that would tend to discourage steps towards conflict resolution and national reconciliation.'[437] Eatwell has well-explained that the policy-based rationale behind the exclusion of governments of national reconciliation from the operation of Article 10 is based on 'two related presumptions: first, that attribution, and responsibility that results from it, is an obstacle to peace; and second, that peace outweighs interests in responsibility and accountability'.[438] The next section further examines Crawford's proposal to modify the scope of Rule no. 2 in order to include an exception concerning the specific situation of national reconciliation governments.

2.2.4.4.2 Crawford's Modification Proposal Provides an 'Incentive' for the Parties to Reach a Peace Settlement This section examines whether Crawford's proposal to modify the scope of application of Article 10(1) would give the opposing parties fighting each other an 'incentive' to reach a peace settlement and form a government of national reconciliation.

The first, rather obvious, point which should be highlighted is that the formation of a government of national reconciliation is *globally* a better outcome for *both* the rebels and the government in charge. For the government, sharing power with the rebels is certainly not the best ultimate solution; totally crushing the rebellion is. Yet, taking part in a coalition government is clearly better than losing power altogether. The same logic applies for the rebels. While they may hope for total victory, they are certainly better off sharing power with the government they are fighting against than facing the possibility of a defeat. Thus, at the end of the day, the creation of a coalition government may be deemed an acceptable compromise and middle ground solution when compared to the two extreme sides of the spectrum of possible outcomes (total victory and total defeat).

436 Crawford, *State Responsibility*, p. 176.

437 ILC, 'Report of the Commission to the General Assembly on the work of its fiftieth session', UN Doc. A/CN.4/SER.A/1998/Add.l (Part 2), *ILC Yearbook* vol. II(2) (1998), p. 85, para. 416.

438 Eatwell, 'State Responsibility, Successful, Insurrectional Movements', p. 394.

The interesting question is whether the 'normal' application of Rule no. 2 (i.e. without Crawford's modification proposal) actually provides any 'incentive' for the parties to the conflict to make any such compromise. The answer is in the negative.

Let's first consider the situation from the perspective of the government fighting the rebels. Under Article 10(1), the acts committed by the rebels during the insurgency would normally be attributable to the State (Rule no. 2). If the government in charge decides to form a coalition with the rebels, that new government would still have to provide reparation to the victims of the wrongful acts committed by the rebels. A government fighting a rebellion may not be very enthusiastic about such a scenario. Not only would that government have to share power with the rebels, but it would also have to pay for the wrongs they have committed while trying to overthrow it. For Crawford, in such a case the government 'would be too heavily penalized: they would in fact pay for their policy of reconciliation by being required to shoulder the full responsibility for the acts committed by the insurrectional movements during the insurrection'.[439] While this interpretation has been contested by some,[440] in my view, it seems difficult to deny that a government fighting rebels has limited 'incentive' to reach a peace settlement with them and form a government of national reconciliation.[441] In the words of Crawford mentioned in the ILC 1998 Report, the fact that under Article 10(1) the government will be 'assuming all the liabilities of the opposition movement' 'would tend to discourage steps towards conflict resolution and national reconciliation'.[442]

[439] See comment by Crawford in ILC, 'Summary Records of the Meetings of the Fiftieth Session', 2555th meeting, 4 August 1998, UN Doc. A/CN.4/SER.A/1998, *ILC Yearbook* (1998), p. 249, para. 55.

[440] Eatwell, *State Responsibility*, p. 193: 'the argument that to attribute the acts of an insurrectional movement to the state in the event of national reconciliation would be too heavy a penalty on the state is not convincing'.

[441] Kolb, *The International Law of State Responsibility*, p. 97: 'if the insurrection does not entirely succeed or entirely fail, but national reconciliation agreements are concluded, article 10 ASR could operate as a sort of dangerous disincentive. If that provision is applied because the insurrection is held to be "partially successful", the conclusion of such agreements could be hampered, since the State could then face important responsibility claims'. See also: Ryngaert, 'State Responsibility and Non-State Actors', p. 175.

[442] ILC, 'Report of the Commission to the General Assembly on the work of its fiftieth session', UN Doc. A/CN.4/SER.A/1998/Add.l (Part 2), *ILC Yearbook* vol. II(2) (1998), p. 85, para. 416. See also, the following comment made by Crawford, in ILC, 'Summary Records of the Meetings of the Fiftieth Session', 2556th meeting, 5 August 1998, UN Doc. A/CN.4/SER.A/1998, *ILC Yearbook* vol. I (1998), p. 249, p. 251, para. 8: 'a Government which had not been defeated by an insurrectional movement would hardly take the

Under Crawford's modification proposal, such wrongs would *not* be attributable to the coalition government. From the government's perspective, this is a much more appealing outcome when compared to the 'normal' application of Rule no. 2. But this scenario is nonetheless somewhat 'problematic'.[443] Thus, it should be recalled that, under this scenario, the government is still responsible for *its own* wrongs committed while fighting the rebels (Rule no. 1). Eatwell has rightly noted that this leads to a rather peculiar outcome which 'discriminates between the victims of the former government and victims of the insurrectional movement'.[444] Thus, only the former would get reparation for the damages suffered. She considers that this 'unequal treatment can only serve to undermine reconciliation rather than promote it'.[445]

What about the situation from the different perspective of the rebels? Crawford's modification proposal is a better scenario for them when compared to the 'normal' application of Rule no. 2. The rebels, once in power as part of the coalition government, would not have to be responsible for their past wrongs committed during the insurgency, whereas under the 'normal' application of Rule no. 2, they would. This may have an impact on the rebels' willingness to negotiate a peace settlement with the government. The reasons are explained by d'Aspremont as follows:

> [S]hould the rebels know that the violations of international law which they may have committed will not bind the State which they will control, they may prove more amenable to negotiated power-sharing solutions rather than resort to force to gain control of the State apparatus. In that sense, the exclusion of Article 10 in situations of national reconciliation or power-sharing agreements may serve as an incentive for the rebels to resort to negotiations rather than force to achieve their political agenda.[446]

trouble to initiate a process of reconciliation by welcoming members of the movement into the Government if, by so doing, it had to assume responsibility for the acts committed earlier by the insurrectional movement, which were very often illegal, even anti-constitutional, under internal law. It was thus better to keep to the current wording, so as to avoid discouraging reconciliation, which was in itself highly desirable.'

443 Eatwell, *State Responsibility*, p. 208.

444 Ibid., p. 208. This is because 'the state would only be under a legal obligation to provide reparation to the victims of the former government'. See also, p. 195.

445 Ibid., p. 194, adding: '[t]he legitimacy of the former government that continues to exist as part of the new government of national reconciliation may be damaged by claims of responsibility for violations of IHL and IHRL committed against members of the insurrectional movement and civilians during the conflict, while the former insurrectional movement, now transformed into a political party, may be untarnished by its previous conduct'.

446 d'Aspremont, 'Rebellion and State Responsibility', p. 436.

Yet, and importantly, d'Aspremont further noted that these theoretical aspects may not be so relevant in practice. This is because 'it is not certain that rebels are always mindful of the subtle technicalities of international law, especially in the field of State responsibility'.[447] Rebels may indeed ignore the 'positive' consequences resulting from the formation of a government of national reconciliation with their enemies.[448] D'Aspremont also indicates that if the rebels are actually aware of such technicalities, the possibility that they would not be accountable for their past wrongs if they were to join a coalition government may in fact have a negative impact of their actual behaviours on the battlefield during a rebellion.[449] As noted by Eatwell, the 'exclusion of governments of national reconciliation from the operation of Article 10(1) may legitimise the use of violence, criminality, war crimes and the abuse of human rights, to achieve political ends'.[450]

At the end of the day, one can agree with Crawford that the modification he has put forward for the scope of application of Article 10(1) would, at least in theory, give both fighting parties an 'incentive' to reach a peace settlement and form a government of national reconciliation.[451]

447 Ibid., p. 436.

448 Ibid.

449 d'Aspremont, 'Rebellion and State Responsibility', p. 436:

> [s]econd, even if we assume that rebels are aware of the main rules of inter-State responsibility, one could argue that excluding the application of Article 10 in case of negotiated agreements between rebels and the government could entice rebels to use political negotiations to purge and expunge their seizure of power from its most atrocious and monstrous deeds. It is true that the exclusion of Article 10 in case of national reconciliation or power-sharing agreement does not bring about an exclusion of the individual criminal responsibility of the insurgents. However, exclusion of attribution in that situation can be interpreted as meaning that the manner in which the insurgency is carried out (especially with respect to international humanitarian law) is of no importance and may give the impression that the rebels have a blank check as to means of warfare to which [they] can resort. In that sense, the exclusion of Article 10 in situations of national reconciliation or power-sharing agreements can backfire, as rebels may no longer feel deterred from resorting to inhuman means of warfare if negotiating an agreement with the government could ultimately bar accountability of the State in the international legal order.

450 Eatwell, *State Responsibility*, p. 196. See also: Verhoeven, 'International Responsibility', p. 292; Ryngaert, 'State Responsibility and Non-State Actors', p. 176.

451 d'Aspremont, 'Rebellion and State Responsibility', p. 436: '[i]ssues of responsibility can severely hinder the conclusion of such an agreement and prevent that peace be achieved through negotiations'. *Contra*: Eatwell, *State Responsibility*, p. 208: 'the ILC's concern that the attribution of responsibility in these circumstances would prevent the negotiation of a peace is not persuasive on a number of grounds'.

While the proposal may be considered problematic in many respects (as highlighted by the work of Eatwell),[452] it is at least logical from the perspective of the 'strategic' interests of both the rebels and the government.

In a detailed and comprehensive article on this question, d'Aspremont has put forward a *narrower* proposition based on Crawford's modification proposal regarding the scope of application of Article 10(1).[453] The proposal is based on his view that Rule no. 2 set out in Article 10(1) 'does not stem from any precise precedent or systemic logic but only from political motives', and that, therefore, 'there is no reason why one could not resort to a similar reasoning to define the currently hazy scope of application of that rule'.[454] D'Aspremont's proposition is discussed in the following paragraphs.

The 2001 ILC Commentaries make it clear that the question of the 'legitimacy' of a government or the illegality of its establishment is *not* relevant regarding the application of Article 10(1).[455] Yet, as noted by Eatwell, Crawford's position 'implies a value judgement based on the way in which power is achieved'.[456] On the one hand, 'if an insurrectional movement achieves power through "legitimate" means, i.e. the negotiation of a peace agreement, the state's responsibility will not be engaged for the acts of that movement committed during its struggle'.[457] On the other hand, 'if the insurrectional movement succeeds in usurping the pre-existing government by force, the state's responsibility will be engaged'.[458] There is obviously nothing wrong with the values behind

[452] Eatwell, ibid. See also, the comment by Verhoeven, 'International Responsibility', p. 291.
[453] For a critical analysis of his proposal, see: Eatwell, ibid., p. 196 ff.
[454] d'Aspremont, 'Rebellion and State Responsibility', p. 441.
[455] ILC, Commentaries, 2001, p. 51, para. 11:

> [n]o distinction should be made for the purposes of article 10 between different categories of movements on the basis of any international 'legitimacy' or of any illegality in respect of their establishment as a Government, despite the potential importance of such distinctions in other contexts. From the standpoint of the formulation of rules of law governing State responsibility, it is unnecessary and undesirable to exonerate a new Government or a new State from responsibility for the conduct of its personnel by reference to considerations of legitimacy or illegitimacy of its origin. Rather, the focus must be on the particular conduct in question, and on its lawfulness or otherwise under the applicable rules of international law.

[456] Eatwell, *State Responsibility*, p. 194.
[457] Ibid.
[458] Ibid.

this proposition. Everyone would agree that the world would be a better place if rebels were to drop their weapons and peacefully join coalition governments. In other words, 'rewarding' the rebels for their good behaviour can hardly be condemned. However, for Eatwell[459] this is somewhat of a paradox insofar as this is precisely the types of distinctions that the ILC wanted to avoid all along by refusing to distinguish between 'legitimate' and 'illegitimate' insurrectional movements.

In fact, d'Aspremont believes that legitimacy is indeed relevant here. For him, the 'sealing of a reconciliation or power-sharing agreement with the government bestows some sort of legitimacy upon the rebels – a legitimacy which may in turn strip the insurgency of its status of rebel'.[460] The very fact that Ago envisaged the specific situation of coalition governments under Article 10(1) 'demonstrates that arguments pertaining to the political context of the seizure of power cannot be entirely excluded when applying Article 10'.[461] Thus, 'nothing seems to theoretically exclude that questions of legitimacy, and especially democratic legitimacy, play a role for the sake of the responsibility of States for acts of insurgents'.[462] Yet, he believes that Crawford's modification does not go far enough. For d'Aspremont, a 'power-sharing or reconciliation agreement does not suffice to exclude the attribution of acts of victorious rebels to the State'.[463] For him, any such agreement must be 'immediately followed by *democratic elections*'.[464] Thus, 'the exclusion of that rule of attribution [set out in Article 10(1)] should be limited to hypotheses where such a national reconciliation or power-sharing agreement leads to national democratic elections which eventually bring the rebels to power'.[465]

459 Ibid.
460 d'Aspremont, 'Rebellion and State Responsibility', p. 436.
461 Ibid.
462 Ibid.
463 Ibid., p. 437.
464 Ibid., p. 437, emphasis added.
465 Ibid. He further explained (at p. 439) that this special rule should, however, 'not apply when rebels take the power through force and subsequently subject themselves to democratic elections to legitimize their power'. See also, this comment:

> [t]his means that if rebels resort to force to overthrow the government but subsequently organize democratic elections which they win, the rule of attribution of Article 10 should still apply. Indeed, it is the manner in which power was first seized that must be taken into account for the sake of the rule enshrined in Article 10. Drawing on the abovementioned political rationale supporting that rule, subsequent democratic elections of a government made of former rebels should not allow the State to

This approach certainly has the merit of putting the issue of legitimacy at centre stage. Yet, in my view, if an election takes place it will have the effect of breaking the 'causal link' of continuity between the rebels and the new government. As mentioned by Crawford[466] (and discussed above),[467] this was not a situation meant to be covered by Article 10(1). According to the general rules of State responsibility and attribution under the ILC Articles, it follows that a new government (led by former rebels) established after an election will not be responsible for acts committed by rebels during an insurgency.

2.2.4.4.3 How the Proposed Modification Results in an Unsatisfactory Outcome for the Injured Party While I favour the proposal put forward by Crawford, it is also undeniable that it comes with a (very high) price tag. The proposed modification to the scope of application of Rule no. 2 would mean, in practical terms, that illegal acts committed by the rebels during the insurgency would *not* be attributable to the new coalition government. Logically, these acts are attributable to the rebels themselves. Yet, at the end of the conflict, the rebels are no longer an independent entity since they are now part of the new coalition government. They no longer exist as 'rebels'. The wrongful acts they have committed in the past would therefore simply go unpunished. The victims of such wrongs (third States, foreigners) will get no reparation. This is clearly an unjust outcome for the victims.[468]

As mentioned above, d'Aspremont rightly noted that Rule no. 2 'undoubtedly was primarily designed to *fill an accountability gap*'.[469] He also noted that the idea of 'justice' was clearly underlying this exceptional rule of

> retroactively circumvent its responsibility for the former insurgent action of its government.

See also, the comment by Verhoeven, 'International Responsibility', p. 292: 'if the insurrectional movement through its struggle forced the government to share power and to hold elections it would only be justified to attribute the conduct to the State since without the armed struggle the rebel movement would not have obtained power'.

466 ILC, 'Summary Records of the Meetings of the Fiftieth Session', 2556th meeting, 5 August 1998, UN Doc. A/CN.4/SER.A/1998, *ILC Yearbook* vol. I (1998), p. 249, p. 254 (para. 41).

467 See Section 2.2.4.4.1.

468 Ryngaert, 'State Responsibility and Non-State Actors', p. 175–6.

469 d'Aspremont, 'Rebellion and State Responsibility', p. 432, emphasis added.

attribution.[470] In my view, the modification proposed by Crawford would, in fact, result in re-establishing this 'accountability gap' which Rule no. 2 was meant to resolve. It should be recalled that in his First Report, Crawford noted that the attribution rule under Article 10(1) 'strike[s] a fair balance *at the level of attribution* in terms of the conflicting interests involved'.[471] Yet, in my view, his modification proposal regarding coalition governments would no longer strike a fair balance between conflicting interests involved. The interests of the victims would not be protected. Cahin also noted that 'impunity and irresponsibility will go hand in hand'.[472] The proposed modification comes at the expense of protecting the interests of the victims of wrongs and results in impunity for the perpetrators.[473]

While Crawford's book is silent on this point, d'Aspremont addresses it head-on. He acknowledges that his proposal raises the 'question of the objectives that the institution of State responsibility ought to pursue' and that this debate 'echoes the choice that must ultimately be made between two conflicting objectives: *democracy* and *accountability*'.[474] In his view, his proposal is justified by the need to promote democracy: 'accountability should not always be the paramount political objective. It seems that the hypotheses of democratic elections of rebels constitute situations where accountability must yield to other considerations and, in particular, democracy'.[475] He further explains that such a proposal would 'provide an enticement for democratic settlement of civil wars'.[476] Specifically, he believes that 'considerations of democracy and peace can outstrip accountability-based arguments in situations of rebels seizing powers through democratic elections and justify that the State does not incur responsibility for acts of the victorious rebels'.[477]

[470] Ibid., p. 432.
[471] ILC, Crawford First Report, 1998, p. 53, para. 276, emphasis in the original.
[472] Cahin, 'Attribution of Conduct to the State', p. 250.
[473] Eatwell, *State Responsibility*, p. 195.
[474] d'Aspremont, 'Rebellion and State Responsibility', p. 441, emphasis in the original.
[475] Ibid., p. 438, further explaining that 'This is not to say that democracy and accountability cannot be reconciled.'
[476] Ibid., p. 439:

> [b]y excluding any attribution of the acts of rebels to the State in case of a seizure of power through democratic elections, international law would conversely provide an enticement for democratic settlement of civil wars. In other words, should it be made clear that the rule of Article 10 does not apply in case of accession to power through democratic elections, democracy would turn a more appealing as well as efficient means to settle conflicts.

[477] Ibid.

These considerations are indeed appealing. But whether or not 'accountability must yield to other considerations and, in particular, democracy'[478] really depends on who you ask. It may be that both the government in charge and the rebels would agree. However, this is not necessarily the case for the victims. In fact, in my view, the answer may very well depend on *who is actually the victim* of the wrongful acts being unpunished (a point examined in the next two paragraphs).

The reasoning put forward by d'Aspremont may be correct in the context of State-to-State relationship. A third *State* victim of a wrongful act committed by the rebels during an insurgency would naturally prefer to get some form of reparation for the damages suffered. Yet, there may be circumstances where a State victim could potentially consider that not getting any reparation is, on balance, a fair 'price to pay' for ending a civil war. That State may consider that the establishment of a peaceful coalition government is more important than getting reparation for its loss. The same may be true for other States. Thus, it may be that all States, as a community, will consider that, globally, ending a civil war is a much more important value to promote than making sure that rebels are held accountable for every single wrong they have committed in the past. Still, these considerations do not necessarily apply to the situation of a *foreign investor* victim of a wrong committed by the rebels during an insurgency. The fact that the rebels are now in power through a coalition government will provide little comfort to an investor whose property has been destroyed, seized or expropriated by the rebels. The world may very well be a better place for all as a result of the end of a civil war, but the investor will nevertheless get no reparation for the damages it suffered.

In my view, it is paramount to protect the interests of the victims of wrongful acts. While the rationale and the justification behind the modification proposal put forward by Crawford and d'Aspremont are sound and must be praised, it nevertheless has the undesirable effect of failing to adequately protect the interests of victims of wrongful acts. An important element that should be reminded here is that this book only deals with the responsibility of insurgents *as a group*. It may very well be that the *individuals* (former rebels) who have actually perpetrated wrongs could be held liable under the domestic law of the State where the incidents took place.[479] In such a case, a foreign investor may get some form of

[478] Ibid.

[479] Thus, as noted by Eatwell, *State Responsibility*, p. 208: '[a] state is not entirely absolved of responsibility in the event of a peace accord and establishment of a government of national reconciliation. The state remains responsible for the prosecution and

reparation before domestic courts. Another possibility is individual responsibility under relevant rules of international human rights law or international criminal law. The recognition of any such individual responsibility could also be part of a truth and national reconciliation effort.[480] This question of individual responsibility is beyond the scope of this book.[481] Further, the fact that an individual (a former member of an insurrectional movement) may face criminal prosecution and punishment for his/her crimes will generally provide little comfort to a foreign investor whose assets have been destroyed or expropriated by rebels. That foreign investor may still start court proceedings against individuals to get some form of monetary reparation for the damages it suffered. Yet, such a path is uncertain and unlikely to be successful in the end. In any event, what is clear is that a State should not block the possibility of such legal proceedings by granting an amnesty to former rebels.[482]

2.2.4.4.4 An Alternative Solution That Can Be Envisaged For all the reasons mentioned in the previous section, I believe that it is, on balance, preferable that the scope of application of Rule no. 2 remains intact, as it was first proposed by Ago in 1972. Article 10(1) should therefore, as a matter of principle, apply to *all* new governments established by rebels, including coalition governments.[483] Yet, the concrete application of this principle should take into account Eatwell's acute remarks. For Eatwell, 'it may be more realistic to consider the application of Article 10(1) to governments of national reconciliation dependant on the circumstances of each case and how power is allocated and shared'.[484] In other words, Article 10(1) should not necessarily apply in all cases where former rebels find themselves included in a government of national reconciliation. Two situations should be distinguished.

punishment of gross human rights violations, war'. Yet, she also noted that 'States are not always willing or able to do so, particularly in cases where the perpetrators or their allies hold government posts' (Eatwell, 'State Responsibility, Successful, Insurrectional Movements', p. 389).

480 See discussion in Eatwell, *State Responsibility*, p. 198.

481 Suffice it to note that any such individual responsibility 'does not have the gravitas of direct attribution of the unlawful acts of a movement that now governs the state, nor does it serve to deter insurrectional movements from violating international law in order to achieve their goals' (ibid., p. 208). See also, her analysis in Eatwell, 'State Responsibility, Successful, Insurrectional Movements', p. 398 ff.

482 This question is further examined below in Section 3.3.3.4.1.

483 See also, the comment by Verhoeven, 'International Responsibility', p. 291–2.

484 Eatwell, *State Responsibility*, p. 192.

First, the application of Article 10(1) would be limited to those coalition governments where the rebels end up achieving 'a substantial share of authority'[485] or where they are allocated the greatest number of cabinet position on a coalition government.[486] This is a situation where the rebels can be considered to have ultimately 'triumphed'. To paraphrase the reasoning of Ago, the 'State apparatus which results' from such a coalition government 'is in reality the *continuation of both the organizations* which confronted each other during the civil war'.[487] This is indeed a situation where it can be considered that there is a 'real and substantial continuity'[488] between the insurrection movement and the new government.[489] This is a situation where Rule no. 2 set out in Article 10(1) should therefore apply.[490]

Second, the 'real and substantial continuity' requirement would, however, 'not be satisfied if only a couple of key figures of a former insurrectional movement are absorbed into the government'.[491] In such a case, it could be argued that the rebels have not 'triumphed'[492] after all; they have not really established a 'new' government.[493] Thus, one should therefore consider this last situation as one where the rebels have ultimately been

485 Ibid., p. 173.

486 Ibid., p. 189, providing the example of the Maoist rebels (including the Communist Party of Nepal-Maoist: CPN-M) that succeeded in establishing a new government in 2006 in Nepal following ten years of armed conflict. The government of Nepal and the rebels agreed to the Kathmandu Comprehensive Peace Accord 2006 (CPA), under which an interim government was established by a coalition of the existing political parties. Following Constituent Assembly elections in Nepal, the CPN-M led a government securing 'the largest allocation of cabinet positions in multi-party coalition government, and largest allocation of seats in the legislature'. See also, p. 170. It should be noted that in her article she seems to have adopted a broader approach which include situations where the former rebels would detain only half of the positions in the coalition government: '[e]qually a government of national reconciliation that would meet the real and substantial continuity requirement is one in which each party enjoys an equal or significant share of power' (Eatwell, 'State Responsibility, Successful, Insurrectional Movements', p. 404).

487 ILC, Ago Report, 1972, p. 146, para. 199, emphasis added.

488 ILC, Commentaries, 2001, p. 51, para. 7.

489 Eatwell, *State Responsibility*, p. 191.

490 ILC, Ago Report, 1972, p. 146, para. 199: '[i]n that case, there is therefore nothing surprising in the attribution to the State of the acts not only of members of its preceding organization but also of members of the organization that grew up during the insurrection and is subsequently united with the preceding organization, which is thereby transformed to a greater or lesser extent'.

491 Eatwell, *State Responsibility*, p. 189. She provides this example as an illustration: the agreement between the government of Colombia and the FARC in the Peace Accord of 24 November 2016 whereby the FARC 'transformed into a political party, is guaranteed 10 congressional seats between 2018 and 2026'.

492 ILC, Commentaries, 2001, p. 51, para. 7.

493 Eatwell, *State Responsibility*, p. 188.

unsuccessful. This means, in turn, that it would *not* be covered by Rule no. 2. As further discussed below,[494] this situation is covered by Rule no. 3 (applicable when the insurgency has not been successful) whereby the acts committed by the rebels during the insurgency are not attributable to the State.[495] It could be argued that one possible negative effect of this proposal is that the victims of wrongs committed by rebels are still not protected in cases where a coalition government is made up of only a few former rebel members. This is true. Yet, if one considers this case as one where the rebels have not triumphed, the situation of the victims is not worse than that of other instances where the rebels are unsuccessful. They are treated alike and get no reparation.[496]

The approach put forward here has the undeniable benefit of following the logic of the 'real and substantial continuity' principle which has been the very reason why the ILC endorsed Rule no. 2 embodied in Article 10 of the ILC Articles.[497] Yet, the obvious drawback is that it does not offer a global solution which can be readily applied for all coalition government cases. Thus, whether or not a coalition government fulfils the continuity requirement will necessarily have to be determined on a case-by-case basis.[498]

494 See Section 3.1.

495 One question examined in Chapter 3 below is whether there is any exception to Rule no. 3.

496 As further examined below (Section 3.1.3), there is something unfair about the application of Rule no. 3. This is the reason why I have put forward two principles (Rules 4A and 4B) which can somewhat mitigate the hardship arising from its normal application. Another question examined below is the effect of granting an amnesty to former rebels.

497 ILC, Report, 1975, p. 105, para. 21: '[f]or such an attribution, no condition is required other than the mere existence of that movement and the *relationship of continuity* between its organization and that of the new government or State established as a result of its action', emphasis added.

498 Eatwell, 'State Responsibility, Successful, Insurrectional Movements', p. 405.

3

When the Rebels Are Not Successful at Establishing a New Government

Article 10(1) of the ILC Articles only deals with the situation (mentioned above in Chapter 2) where the rebels are *successful* at establishing a new government. Nothing is said about the opposite situation when the rebels are *not* successful. In subsequent writing, Crawford mentioned that the hypothesis of the insurgency *failing* at establishing a new government was in fact implicitly dealt with under Article 10.[499]

Chapter 3 examines the outcomes of the acts committed *by the rebels* during the insurgency and those committed *by the government* while fighting the rebels. In the next sections, I will examine the following guiding principles:

- As a matter of principle, the acts committed by the rebels during an insurgency are not attributable to the State once the rebellion has failed (this principle will hereinafter be referred to as 'Rule no. 3').
- I will examine whether there are any 'exceptions' to this general principle. In my view, even when the insurgency is ultimately unsuccessful, it remains that:
  - The State should nevertheless be bound by the governmental lawful 'routine activities' performed by rebels in situations where they have established a local de facto government (this principle will hereinafter be referred to as 'Rule no. 4A').
  - The State should also be responsible for the consequences arising from expropriation acts committed by rebels if they result in some benefits for the State (this principle will hereinafter be referred to as 'Rule no. 4B').
- The fact that, in general, the acts of *unsuccessful* rebels are not attributable to the State does not necessarily mean that such wrongs will go unpunished. Thus, the rebels are always responsible for their own wrongful acts (this principle will hereinafter be referred to as 'Rule no. 5').

[499] Crawford, *State Responsibility*, p. 174.

- Finally, even when an insurgency is ultimately unsuccessful, the State will always be responsible for *its own* failure to exercise its due diligence obligation to protect third States and foreigners during the rebellion (this principle will hereinafter be referred to as 'Rule no. 6').

3.1 Rule No. 3: The Acts Committed by the Rebels during the Insurgency Are Not Attributable to the State

The first section examines one of the most well-established principles: the acts committed by the rebels during the insurgency are not attributable to the State once the government has defeated the insurgency (Rule no. 3). However, as noted by Ago, nothing prevents a government to agree to 'a special convention' and 'to assume the responsibility which would have fallen on the insurrectional movement and which could not be invoked against the latter by the third State'.[500]

In the next sections, I will examine the following matters:

- Drafting history of Rule no. 3 (Section 3.1.1);
- The rationale behind the principle (Section 3.1.2);
- While the principle is logical and sound, it remains unfair for the victims of wrongs committed by the rebels (Section 3.1.3); and
- Case law and State practice support Rule no. 3 (Section 3.1.4).

3.1.1 Drafting History

Rule no. 3 was embodied in Article 12(2) of the 1972 version:

> 2. Similarly, the conduct of a person or group of persons acting in the territory of a State as organs of an insurrectional movement directed against that State and possessing separate international personality is not considered to be an act of that State in international law.

[500] ILC, Ago Report, 1972, p. 130, para. 156. But, according to the ILC, any such solution 'represents a clear departure from general international law' (ILC, Report, 1975, p. 93, para. 12, fn. 212). In any event, for the ILC, this not a question of attribution of responsibility, but one of 'succession' to responsibility between subjects of international law:

> [i]n this case it is obviously not a question of attribution to the State, as a source of responsibility, of acts committed earlier by another subject of international law, but a question of succession by a State to the *ex delicto* obligations which another subject of international law, having at one time exercised exclusive authority over a portion of State territory, incurred as a result of its actions.

The same basic principle was also contained in Article 14(1) of the 1975 Draft:

> 1. The conduct of an organ of an insurrectional movement, which is established in the territory of a State or in any other territory under its administration, shall not be considered as an act of that State under international law.

Four points should be highlighted about the changes between the 1972 and the 1975 drafts. First, the long phrase 'the conduct of a person or group of persons acting in the territory of a State as organs of an insurrectional movement' was thankfully condensed in the 1975 draft to what really matters: 'the conduct of an organ of an insurrectional movement'.[501] Moreover, the language of the last version of the 2001 draft (Article 10) was simplified to its bare minimum: 'the conduct of an insurrectional movement'. Second, the 1975 version no longer contains a reference to the insurrectional movement 'possessing separate international personality' (this issue will be specifically examined later).[502] Third, both versions explicitly mentioned that the movement is 'acting' or 'is established' in the territory of a State. The wording 'established in the territory of a State' was meant to cover situations where an insurrectional movement 'operates in, or from within, a third State'.[503] Fourth, the 1975 version no longer specifies the perhaps rather obvious fact that the relevant conduct of the insurrectional movement, for the purpose of this provision, is 'directed against' the State where it is 'acting' (or 'is established'). In other words, the provision only covers cases where the rebels are *fighting against* the State in which they are located.

In his First Report, Crawford noted (generally, in reference to both Rules no. 3 and no. 5) that 'the basic principle stated in article 14 [of the 1975 Draft] is well established, as the authorities cited in the [1975] commentary show'.[504] As he also pointed out, there was 'no need to state' 'specifically' the basic principle referred to in Article 14(2) (i.e. Rule no. 6: the State is responsible for its failure to exercise its due diligence obligation to protect foreigners and third States).[505] Yet, he also noted that deleting Article 14(2) would result in leaving Article 14(1) 'as

[501] ILC, Report, 1975, p. 99, para. 29, indicating that the case dealt with in this provision 'is clearly that in which the organ of the insurrectional movement acts *in that capacity*', emphasis added.

[502] See at the very end of Section 3.1.2.

[503] ILC, Report, 1975, p. 99, para. 29, emphasis added.

[504] Crawford First Report, 1998, p. 53, para. 273.

[505] Ibid.

an isolated negative attribution clause'.[506] He concluded that such 'negative attribution' was 'unnecessary and undesirable' in the ILC Draft Articles.[507] The content of Article 14(1) of the 1975 Draft was therefore deleted. New Article 15 put forward by Crawford still contained a 'negative attribution' clause 'to meet concerns expressed about the attribution to the State of unsuccessful insurrectional movements'.[508] The new Article 15 reads as follows:

> The conduct of an organ of an insurrectional movement, established in opposition to a State or to its government, shall not be considered an act of that State under international law unless:
>
> (a) The insurrectional movement succeeds in becoming the new Government of that State; or . . .

Ultimately, the Drafting Committee decided not to include such a 'negative attribution' clause and deleted the first paragraph.[509] It is important to note that the Drafting Committee also added this comment: '[t]he commentary to article 15 would, however, make reference to the principle that the conduct of an insurrectional movement established in the territory of a State should not be considered as such an act of that State under international law'.[510] In his subsequent writing, Crawford confirmed that 'although [Article 14(1)] was deleted during the second reading, this still reflects the default position under international law'.[511] In other words, deleting Article 14(1) had no effect on the undeniable existence of Rule no. 3, whereby, as a matter of principle, the acts committed by the rebels during an insurgency are *not* attributable to the State when the struggle ultimately fails.

3.1.2 The Rationale behind the Principle

As explained in the ILC Commentary, 'the acts of unsuccessful insurrectional movements are not attributable to the State'.[512] It is simply the application of the general rule of attribution under international

506 Ibid.

507 Ibid.

508 Ibid., note no. 4 to new Draft Article 15 (ibid. at p. 57).

509 ILC, 'Summary Records of the Meetings of the Fiftieth Session 20 April–12 June 1998 27 July–14 August 1998', UN Doc. A/CN.4/SER.A/1998, *ILC Yearbook* I (1998), p. 287, at p. 290, para. 86.

510 Ibid.

511 Crawford, *State Responsibility*, p. 179.

512 ILC, Commentaries, 2001, p. 50, para. 2.

law. In his book, Crawford puts it bluntly: '[a]s a general rule, a state is not held responsible for the acts of insurgents'.[513] A number of reasons explain this general rule. Three of these reasons are generally invoked and are summarized as follows by Umpire Ralston in the *Sambiaggio* case, decided by the Italy–Venezuela Claims Commission, which has been described as the 'most significant decision'[514] in this respect:

> The Government should not be held responsible for the acts of revolutionists because:
> 1. Revolutionists are not the agents of government, and a natural responsibility does not exist.
> 2. Their acts are committed to destroy the government, and no one should be held responsible for the acts of an enemy attempting his life.
> 3. The revolutionists were beyond governmental control, and the Government can not be held responsible for injuries committed by those who have escaped its restraint.[515]

In the following paragraphs, I will examine in detail the three reasons which have been highlighted in the *Sambiaggio* case. I will also mention two other justifications which were brought forward by Ago.

The first reason explaining the essence of Rule no. 3 is simple: the rebels and the government are *different entities* and, therefore, the acts of one cannot be attributable to the other. As explained in the ILC Commentary, 'the general principle that the conduct of an insurrectional or other movement is not attributable to the State is premised on the assumption that the structures and organization of the movement are and remain independent of those of the State'.[516] The independence of 'structure' and 'organization' explains why the acts of the former cannot be attributable to the latter.[517]

The point was well-explained by Umpire Ralston in the *Sambiaggio* Case. He first mentioned the most basic principle of State responsibility: '[t]he ordinary rule is that a government, like an individual, is only to be held responsible for the acts of its agents or for acts the responsibility for

513 Crawford, *State Responsibility*, p. 170.

514 ILC, Ago Report, 1972, p. 132, para. 161.

515 *Sambiaggio* case, 1903, p. 513.

516 ILC, Commentaries, 2001, p. 50, para. 4. See also, Cahin, 'Attribution of Conduct to the State', p. 253: 'this solution is justified by the impossibility of attributing to the State the unlawful conduct of an entity which is by definition structurally and functionally independent from it'.

517 Charles De Visscher, *Théories et réalités en droit international public* (2nd ed., Paris, Pedone, 1955), p. 347.

which is expressly assumed by it'.[518] He then asked the question of whether there could be an exception to the principle since the revolutionists are sometimes described as being 'related' to the government. He rejected this possibility because the rebels are fighting *against* the government with the aim of overthrowing it (a point further discussed below in the next section) and because they are 'not the agents of government, and a natural responsibility does not exist'.[519] In his book, Silvanie refers to many examples of awards based on the grounds that the 'State is not liable because unsuccessful insurgents are not the government or the "authorities" or agents of the State.'[520]

The second reason explaining the rationale behind Rule no. 3 is a direct consequence of the rebels and the government being different entities. As noted by Crawford, the insurgent movement 'is external to the formal structure of the state, exercises no constituted authority and cannot be considered to be under the state's "instruction, direction or control"'.[521] Thus, the acts of an insurrectional movement cannot be attributable to the government because it 'will not be in a position to exert effective control over its activities'.[522] This basic proposition is supported by writers.[523] The point was well-explained by Umpire Ralston in the *Sambiaggio* case:

518 *Sambiaggio* case, 1903, p. 512, also adding: '[t]o apply another doctrine, save under certain exceptional circumstances incident to the peculiar position occupied by a government toward those subject to its power, would be unnatural and illogical'.

519 Ibid., p. 512–51.

520 Silvanie, *Responsibility of States*, p. 145, 146 ff., citing *Salvador Prats* v. *United States*, United States–Mexico Mixed Commission, case no. 748, 4 July 1868, UNRIAA 29 [hereinafter referred to as '*Prats* case, 1868'], Mexican Commissioner, Mr Palacio; *McKenny* case, in Moore, *History and Digest of the International Arbitrations* (vol. III), p. 2881; *Jansen* case, ibid., p. 2902, 2930.

521 Crawford, *State Responsibility*, p. 170.

522 ILC, Commentaries, 2001, p. 50, para. 2. See also: ILC, Ago Report, 1972, p. 132, para. 161, referring to the 'the principle that as a general rule a Government was not responsible for injuries caused to aliens by the members of an armed insurrection which was beyond the control of the said Government'.

523 Silvanie, *Responsibility of States*, p. 149 ff., 151 ('the inability to control absolves a State from responsibility for tortuous acts of unsuccessful insurgents'); Daillier *et al.*, *Droit international public*, p. 870; Ganzory, 'International Claims and Insurgence', p. 81; Rousseau, *Droit international public*, p. 85; De Visscher, *Théories et réalités*, p. 347–8. See also: Hall, *International Law*, p. 274:

> [w]hen a government is temporarily unable to control the acts of private persons within the dominions owing to insurrection or civil commotion, it is not responsible for injury which may be received by foreign subjects in their person or property in the course of the struggle. Either through the measures

> Governments are responsible, as a general principle, for the acts of those they control. But the very existence of a flagrant revolution presupposes that a certain set of men have gone temporarily or permanently beyond the power of the authorities; and unless it clearly appear that the government has failed to use promptly and with appropriate force its constituted authority, it cannot reasonably be said that it should be responsible for a condition of affairs created without its volition. . . . We find ourselves therefore obliged to conclude, from the standpoint of general principle, that, save under . . . exceptional circumstances . . ., the Government should not be held responsible for the acts of revolutionists because . . . revolutionists were beyond governmental control, and the Government cannot be held responsible for injuries committed by those who have escaped its restraint.[524]

The same principle has been recognized in the *Henriquez* case, where Umpire Plumley stated that Venezuela could not be responsible 'for the acts of unsuccessful revolutionists' which caused damages to foreigners because it had no control over them.[525] Similarly, in the *Aroa Mines* case, Umpire Plumley of the British-Venezuelan Mixed Claims Commission referred to the 'position of all international law writers [which] was in substantial accord touching this matter of non responsibility of nations for the acts of unsuccessful revolutionists at the time this protocol was signed when those revolutionists had been *beyond their control*'.[526] He

> which it may be obliged to take for the recovery of its authority, or through acts done by the part of the population which has broken loose from control. (quoted in *Asian Agricultural Products ltd.* v. *Sri Lanka*, ICSID Case No ARB/87/3, Final Award, 27 June 1990 [hereinafter referred to as '*AAPL* case, 1990'], dissenting opinion of Asante)

524 *Sambiaggio* case, 1903, p. 513. On the contrary, the Italian Commissioner Agnoli, took the view that:

> responsibility [of the government] exists when, as in the case under consideration, the said authorities exercise a *de facto* power or when the said troops have a recognized military organization for the purpose of overthrowing the legal government, though the damage alleged may have been inflicted by detached bodies of troops (guerrillas), and that, on the contrary, such responsibility may be excluded when it is shown that such acts are committed by marauders who style themselves revolutionists solely that they may with impunity prosecute their nefarious calling.

525 *Henriquez* case, Netherlands–Venezuela Claims Commission, 1903, Opinion of the Umpire, UNRIAA 10, p. 713, 716: '[t]he umpire holds concerning the responsibility of Venezuela for the acts of unsuccessful revolutionists that the Government of Venezuela is responsible to aliens, commorant or resident, for injuries they receive in its territory from insurgents or revolutionists whom the Government *could control, and not otherwise*' (emphasis added).

526 *Aroa Mines* case, UK–Venezuela Claims Commission, UNRIAA 9, p. 439, emphasis added.

also made this remark: '[t]he sovereign is responsible to alien residents for injuries they receive in his territories from belligerent action, or from insurgents whom *he could control* or whom the claimant government has not recognized as belligerents'.[527] Several other awards have come to the same conclusion regarding the element of control, including the *Egerton and Barnett* case,[528] the *Salas* case[529] and others.[530]

One particularly relevant case is *Kummerow*, where Umpire Duffield made the following statement: '[i]n the opinion of the umpire, however, the modern doctrine, almost universally recognized, is that a nation is not liable for acts of revolutionists when the revolution has gone beyond the control of the titular government'.[531] Umpire Duffield succinctly summarized the point by stating that 'immunity follows inability'.[532] In other

[527] Ibid., emphasis added.

[528] *Egerton and Barnett* case, Chile and Great Britain arbitral tribunal, 25 September 1895, in Henri La Fontaine, *Pasicrisie Internationale: Histoire Documentaire des Arbitrages Internationaux (1794-1900)* (Berne, Imprimerie Stampelli & Cie, 1902), p. 455–6. The case involved the house of two British nationals burned as a result of acts of violence committed following the surrender of the city of Valparaiso to revolutionist forces during the 1891 Chilean revolution. The Tribunal concluded that the government of Chile was not responsible for the loss incurred by the Claimants and noted that 'when a Government is temporarily *incapable of controlling* within its territory a part of its population or persons who have escaped from its authority and risen against it, in cases of rebellion, civil war or local disturbance, it is not responsible for the losses suffered by foreigners', emphasis added.

[529] *Salas* cases, Netherlands–Venezuela Claims Commission, 1903, Opinion of the Umpire, UNRIAA 10, p. 714 ff., p. 720–1:

> while the attack upon Barquisimeto was successful and the revolutionary party for the time became the dominant force in that immediate vicinity, the revolution itself was unsuccessful. There can be no question that the injuries were received from the hands of revolutionary soldiers, who for the time being and within that city were *beyond the control* of the Government. The Government in fact was defeated and was driven out of the city, so that in no way can it be held that they could have prevented these acts, and they can not be charged with a neglect of duty in not having done what they could not do. (emphasis added).

[530] Opinion No. 8, US–Spain Claims Commission, instituted by the treaty of December 10, 1898, to settle claims of individuals of both Nations arising from the last Cuban insurrection: '[w]here an armed insurrection has gone *beyond the control* of the parent Government the general rule is that such Government is not responsible for damages caused to foreigners by the insurgents' (emphasis added, the Opinion is referred to in *Acquatella, Bianchi et al.* case, France–Venezuela Mixed Claims Commission, UNRIAA 10, p. 9).

[531] *Kummerow* v. *Venezuela*, German–Venezuela Mixed Commission, UNRIAA 9, p. 370, at p. 400, adding that 'It is not necessary that either a state of war, in an international sense, should exist or any recognition of belligerency'.

[532] Ibid., p. 400.

words, the acts of rebels are not attributable to the State ('immunity') *because* of its 'inability' to control them.[533] In applying the law to the facts of the case, he noted the 'condition of Venezuela during the present civil war' and the fact that 'there can be no doubt that from its outset it went beyond the power of the Government to control'.[534] Along these same lines, he indicated that 'during all this period considerable portions of the country and some of its principal cities have been held by revolutionary forces' and that 'large bodies of organized revolutionist troops have traversed the country, and in their train have followed the usual marauding and pillage by small bands of guerrillas and brigands'.[535] After mentioning that 'the supreme efforts of the Government were necessary and were directed to putting down the rebellion', he concluded that 'under such circumstances it would be contrary to established principles of international law and to justice and equity to hold the Government responsible' for the acts committed by the rebels.[536]

The element of control was also central to tribunals which have, through numerous decisions, examined claims arising from acts committed by the Confederate army in the context of the American Civil War,[537] including the *Hanna* case.[538] These cases involve an attempt by

[533] I will discuss below (see Section 3.3.3) the other question as to whether or not one can really speak of the State being 'responsible' for the acts of rebels, as Duffield expressly stated (ibid., p. 398: '[t]here is, therefore, a rule of international law under which Venezuela would be *held liable* in certain cases for acts of revolutionists', emphasis added).

[534] *Kummerow* v. *Venezuela*, German–Venezuela Mixed Commission, UNRIAA 9, p. 400.

[535] Ibid.

[536] Ibid.

[537] See, for instance, *Amelia de Brissot, Ralph Rawdon, Joseph Stackpole and Narcisa de Hammer* v. *Venezuela (the Steamer Apure case)*, US–Venezuela Claims Commission, UNRIAA 29, p. 240–60, at p. 258. The case dealt with claims by US nationals against Venezuela, but Commissioner Finlay made this relevant comment about the context of the secession of the Confederates States:

> it was urged in argument that the conditions were somewhat similar to those the United States was confronted with by the insurrection in the Southern States; but there is a wide difference between the cases. The South, as it was called, was a recognized belligerent *de facto* government, *beyond the jurisdiction and control of the United States for the time being*, and for this reason the United States could not be held responsible to foreign powers for acts done by the Confederates; but in this case Zamora occupied no such status. (emphasis added).

[538] *John H. Hanna* v. *United States*, US–Great Britain Mixed Claims Commission, case no. 2, award of 25 September 1873, discussed in Moore, *History and Digest of the International*

rebels to create a new State; they will be discussed in Part II. Suffice it to mention two specific extracts from the opinion of Mr Wadsworth, the United States Commissioner, in the *Prats* case:

> That Government was under no obligation, by treaty or the law of nations, to protect the property of aliens situated inside the enemy country against the enemy. The international duty of the United States or its engagements by treaty to extend protection to aliens, transient or dwelling, it its territories, ceased inside the territory held by the insurgents from the time such territory was *withdrawn by war from the control of that Government*, and until its authority and jurisdiction were again established over it.
>
> The principle of non-responsibility for acts of rebel enemies in time of civil war rests upon the ground that the latter have *withdrawn themselves by force of arms from the control and jurisdiction of the sovereign*, putting it out of his power, so long as they make their resistance effectual, to extend his protection within the hostile territory to either strangers or his own subjects, between whom, in this respect, no inequality of rights can justly be asserted.[539]

While everyone agrees with Silvanie that 'the inability to control absolves a State from responsibility for tortuous acts of unsuccessful insurgents', the difficult question is what does 'inability to control' actually mean.[540] In the past, one useful criterion was the fact that the rebels had been recognized the status of a belligerent power by the government they were fighting against or by third States.[541] As mentioned above,[542] the granting of such status to rebels was considered 'to release the State from responsibility for all acts of the insurgents subsequent to recognition'.[543] Yet, it was also noted that such recognition is not 'really essential to establish a proof of lack of governmental control over the insurgents'.[544] For Silvanie, what really matters is to show the existence of a civil war.[545] This is the 'real point of departure as to when the insurgents may be said to have gone beyond government control'[546]

Arbitrations (vol. III), p. 2984; UNRIAA 29, p. 144: '[t]he Commissioners are of opinion that the United States can not be held liable for injuries caused by the acts of rebels over whom *they could exercise no control*, and which acts they had no power to prevent', emphasis added.

539 *Prats* case, 1868, p. 192–3, emphasis added.
540 Silvanie, *Responsibility of States*, p. 149 ff., p. 151.
541 Ibid., p. 152.
542 See Introduction, Section 1.1.3.2.
543 Silvanie, *Responsibility of States*, p. 152.
544 Ibid., p. 154.
545 Ibid., p. 154–5.
546 Ibid., p. 158.

and, therefore, when the State should be released from responsibility for all insurgent actions.[547] The point was clearly made in the opinion of Mr Wadsworth, the United States Commissioner, in the *Prats* case (in the different context of a failed attempt to create a new State).[548]

There is a third reason that is often mentioned in support of Rule no. 3: the acts committed by the rebels cannot be attributable to the State because the government in charge was in fact fighting *against* the rebels. Thus, as noted by Crawford, 'by definition, such a [rebel] movement cannot be considered to be aligned to the interests of the state against which it is fighting'.[549] It would be rather 'illogical' to apply any attribution in such a case.[550] Indeed, the acts of the rebels were '*directed against* that State'.[551] In the words of Umpire Plumley in the *Henriquez* case, given that insurrections and revolutions 'are to be deplored' and are 'always against the will of the constituted government and originate without its ability in any way to prevent them', it follows that 'to hold the Government responsible for the means by which its life is sought would be destructive of all governmental conditions'.[552] Similarly, in the *Sambiaggio* case, decided by the Italy–Venezuela Claims

547 Ibid., p. 154–5.

548 *Prats* case, 1868, p. 191–2:

> Non-responsibility on the part of the United States for injuries by the Confederate enemy within the territories of that government to aliens did not result from the recognition of the belligerency of the rebel enemy by the strangers' sovereign. It resulted from *the fact of belligerency itself*, and whether recognized or not by other governments. ... These rights the United States exercised against Mexico and all other nations, and did it in virtue of the fact of war, and not because of the recognition of the belligerency of the insurgents. ... So far, therefore, as the responsibility of the United States to Mexico in this case is concerned, it is in nowise increased or diminished by the failure of the latter to accord belligerent rights to the Confederates. (emphasis added).

549 Crawford, *State Responsibility*, p. 170. See also: Ryngaert, 'State Responsibility and Non-State Actors', p. 175 ('given the hostilities between the state and the movement, the connection between them can hardly be more tenuous').

550 Daillier *et al.*, *Droit international public*, p. 870.

551 ILC, Ago Report, 1972, p. 132, para. 160. Ago asked this first question: '[t]he first [question] is obviously whether or not it is possible to attribute to a State, as a source of responsibility, acts committed by organs of an insurrectional movement *directed against that State*', emphasis added. He then referred to a 'second question, which presupposes a negative reply to the first'. This remark makes it clear that his answer to the first question must be in the negative. Later in the same paragraph, he affirmed this point very clearly: 'the acts committed by the organs of an insurrectional movement ... cannot be attributed to the State against which the movement is, or has been, directed'.

552 *Henriquez* case, Netherlands–Venezuela Claims Commission, 1903, Opinion of the Umpire, UNRIAA 10, p. 713, p. 716.

Commission, Umpire Ralston stated that the acts of insurgents 'are committed to destroy the government, and no one should be held responsible for the acts of an enemy attempting his life'.[553]

It is true that, under international law, a rebellion is considered as a factual situation. International law is 'neutral' with regard to such a phenomenon: it is not considered to be illegal, but neither is it encouraged.[554] However, from the domestic law perspective of the State fighting against the rebels, the situation is radically different. The rebels are considered by that government as outlaws acting illegally and, accordingly, their acts should be punished. Thus, as noted by Corten, 'le rebelle se définit par opposition au droit', adding that 'le droit semble ainsi avoir pour vocation à réprimer la rébellion'.[555] This explains why it would seem illogical that the State be held accountable for acts committed by outlaws whose aim is to seize power illegally by force.

In the next paragraphs, I will briefly examine two other justifications which have been put forward by Ago and others.

Another reason is sometimes mentioned by writers, including Atlam.[556] In his 1972 Report Ago mentioned that 'the acts committed by the organs of an insurrectional movement ... cannot be attributed to the State against which the movement is, or has been, directed',[557] because this is 'the situation of a State in relation to acts committed in its territory but emanating from organs of *other subjects* of international law'.[558] In other words, the acts

[553] *Sambiaggio* case, 1903, p. 513:

> The interest of a government, like that of an individual, lies in its preservation. The presumed interests of revolutionists lie in the destruction of the existing government and the substitution of another of different personnel or controlled by different principles. To say that a government is (as it naturally must be) responsible for the acts it commits in an attempt (for instance) to maintain its own existence, and to require it at the same moment to pay for the powder and ball expended and the soldiers engaged, in an attempt to destroy its life, is a proposition difficult to maintain, and yet it is to this point we arrive in the last analysis if governments are to compensate wrongs done by their would-be slayers when engaged in attempts to destroy them.

[554] Corten, *La rébellion et le droit international*, p. 21 ff.

[555] Ibid., p. 18–19 ('the rebel is defined in opposition to the law') and ('the law thus seems to be intended to suppress the rebellion').

[556] Atlam, *Succession d'États*, p. 425; Atlam, 'National Liberation Movements and International Responsibility', p. 36

[557] ILC, Ago Report, 1972, p. 132, para. 160.

[558] Ibid., emphasis added. See also, para. 193: '[o]ur conclusion was that the conduct of a person or group of persons acting in the territory of a State as organs of another State, or of an international organization, or of an insurrectional movement *possessing separate*

committed by the organ of an insurrectional movement are attributable to that entity only because the movement has *its own* international legal personality. This element was included in Article 12(2) of the 1972 version: it referred to the conduct of an insurrectional movement 'possessing separate international personality' not being considered as an act of the State. Interestingly, Article 14(1) of the 1975 draft dropped this reference to the 'separate international personality' of a movement. The 1975 commentary is also silent on that point. As mentioned above,[559] ILC Special Rapporteur Crawford completely abandoned this concept in the context of Article 10.

Finally, reference should be made to one comment made by Ago in his 1972 Report. As explained above,[560] Ago believes that the rationale behind Rule no. 2 (applicable when the rebels are successful) is 'the idea of continuity' which exists between one organization (the insurrectional movement) and another organization (the new government).[561] On the contrary, there is *no such continuity* when the rebels are defeated because their organization disappears. This is essentially why their acts are not attributable to the State. In other words, the State is only responsible for the acts of the government because it is the *only* organization that *continues to exist* after the rebels are defeated.[562]

3.1.3 *While the Principle Is Logical and Sound, It Remains Unfair for the Victims of Wrongs Committed by the Rebels*

As mentioned in the previous section, there are good and logical reasons for the existence of Rule no. 3 whereby the acts committed by the rebels during the insurgency are not attributable to the State. Yet, however

international personality, is not considered to be an act of that State in international law', emphasis added.

559 See Section 2.2.2.2.3.

560 See Section 2.2.2.2.

561 ILC, Ago Report, 1972, p. 145, para. 199.

562 Ibid., p. 145, para. 199:

> During a civil war, two organizations are opposed to each other and are fighting for final victory. Each of the two wishes to be the organization of the State; at the outset, one is so in fact and the other potentially. In the event of the struggle's ending in victory for the pre-existing power, the insurrectional organization is dissolved and only the established apparatus remains. It is logical that one should attribute to the State only the acts or omissions of the members of that apparatus, which *continues*, and not the acts of members of the organization which has *ceased to exist* without ever having succeeded in being the actual organization of the State or at least participating in it. (emphasis added).

logical Rule no. 3 may be, it remains that the solution of non-responsibility may be considered unfair from the perspective of the victims (third States, foreigners) of acts committed by the rebels during the insurgency. Since the State is not responsible for such acts, the victims can only turn to the rebels for reparation. As further discussed below,[563] there is no doubt that the rebels are, as a matter of principle, responsible for their own wrongful acts (Rule no. 5). Yet, any such claim against them can only be made during the insurgency while the rebels still exists as an autonomous entity before their defeat and their disintegration. For a number of reasons further explained below,[564] victims very rarely make such claims against the rebels and the actual likelihood of getting any reparation is limited. The only realistic option for the victim is to wait until the end of the insurgency to assess whether the damage it suffered can be compensated. If the government wins, any such claim will be rejected based on Rule no. 3. In practical terms, it means that the victims will almost certainly get no reparation for the damage suffered as a result of wrongful acts committed by the rebels (as a group).

One writer noted that while the solution adopted under Rule no. 3 is sound, it can nevertheless be 'criticized for sacrificing the interests of foreign victims of the conflict, leaving them to wish for the victory of the insurrection'.[565] The same remark was made by Rousseau: 'la règle ne vas pas sans danger, car on a fait remarquer qu'elle risquait d'encourager les étrangers à se départir de leur neutralité et à travailler au succès des insurgés – seule chance pour ceux-là d'être indemnisées par ceux-ci'.[566] This is indeed the case. Thus, the rebels' failure to establish a new government means, in practical terms, that the wrongs suffered by a foreigner or a third State will go unpunished. In such a context, the victims have good reasons to hope that the rebels are successful at establishing a new government. Whenever this is the case, Rule no. 2 applies and the acts committed by the rebels during the insurgency are attributable to the State. Ultimately, this is the only possibility for the victim to get reparation. In such a context, foreign investors and third States (victims of wrongs

[563] See Section 3.2.

[564] See Section 3.2.3.

[565] Cahin, 'Attribution of Conduct to the State', p. 253.

[566] Rousseau, *Droit international public*, p. 85 ('the rule is not without its dangers, as it has been pointed out that it might encourage foreigners to abandon their neutrality and work for the success of the insurgents – the only chance for foreigners to be compensated by them').

committed by the rebels during the insurgency) are unlikely to remain *neutral* with regard to the internal conflict. Indeed, their interests will only be protected if one outcome prevails (if the rebels ultimately win). This situation is problematic and goes against the principle of non-intervention in civil wars. Article 2 of the resolution on 'the Principle of Non-Intervention in Civil Wars' adopted by the Institute in 1975 provides that 'Third States shall refrain from giving assistance to parties to a civil war which is being fought in the territory of another State'.[567]

This is a point which was highlighted by the Italian Commissioner Agnoli in the *Sambiaggio* case. He believed that recognizing the existence of Rule no. 3 would

> furnish to foreigners a strong incentive for violating the laws of neutrality to make the distinction above mentioned, as in such a case it would be to their interest to side with one or the other faction, and to render more apparent the absurdity of the distinction [between cases where the rebels are successful and those where they are not] they would be inclined to side with their despoilers, since with the success of these latter would lie their own chance for securing future compensation for their losses.[568]

It is probably the idea that Umpire Ralston, in the *Sambiaggio* case, also had in mind when he stated: 'it is suggested that a decision holding Venezuela not responsible for the acts of revolutionists would tend to encourage them to seize the property of foreigners'.[569] He did not however elaborate on this point and denied it on the grounds that 'this appeal is of a political character and does not address itself to the umpire'.[570] In any event, it is not at all clear whether the remark made by Umpire Ralston is sound.[571] A similar argument was mentioned by Umpire Duffield, in the *Kummerow* case, before the German–Venezuela Mixed Commission: '[i]t is also suggested that if Venezuela is held liable for injuries caused by the acts of insurrectionists,

[567] Institute of International Law, 'The Principle of Non-Intervention in Civil Wars', Session of Wiesbaden, 1975.

[568] *Sambiaggio* case, 1903, p. 505.

[569] Ibid., p. 524.

[570] Ibid.

[571] The goal of the insurgents is obviously to take power. If they do so, they will be held responsible for the illegal acts (including seizing foreign properties) they have committed during the insurgency (Rule no. 2). It is hard to see why such an outcome could 'encourage' them to expropriate foreigners. They will anyway have to compensate that foreign investor once in power. Similarly, why would they be 'encouraged' to expropriate foreigners in the event where their struggle is ultimately *not* successful? Thus, the government is not going to be responsible for the acts (Rule no. 3). The rebels will also no longer exist as a group once they have been defeated.

it will tend to discourage future revolutions'.[572] He added that 'if the suggestion were pertinent, it might be possible to argue the opposite result; that, in the language of an eminent representative of the United States, "revolutions might then become a pastime for foreigners"'.[573] In any event, Umpire Duffield considered the matter to be 'not pertinent' given that the 'functions of the Commission are strictly judicial'.[574] In the end, it is clear that, under Rule no. 3, the victims of wrongs committed by the rebels during an insurgency are unlikely to remain neutral regarding the outcome of the fighting. They have good reasons for hoping that the rebels win.

Another point that needs to be highlighted is how the situation under Rule no. 3 is drastically different from the solution adopted when the rebels are *successful* at establishing a new government. As mentioned above,[575] there is also something asymmetrical about the outcome resulting from the application of Rule nos. 1 and 3.[576]

As noted by O'Connell, it is 'illogical' that the government 'as a whole escape liability for acts of violence on the part of the revolutionaries'.[577] While it may be rather 'illogical', it is not entirely clear what alternative solution would not be. Thus, it would be also quite illogical to consider a State 'responsible' for the acts committed by unsuccessful rebels. These acts are done by the rebels while *fighting the government* in charge. It would be absurd for these acts to be attributable to the government *during* the insurgency, while it is actually fighting these rebels at the same time. As mentioned in the previous section, there are several good reasons why a State should not be 'responsible' for such acts once the movement has been defeated. In this context, 'sacrificing the interests of foreign victims of the conflict'[578] may be considered, on balance, as probably the 'least illogical'

572 *Kummerow* v. *Venezuela*, German–Venezuela Mixed Commission, UNRIAA 9, p. 399.
573 Ibid.
574 Ibid., p. 399, adding that the functions of the Commission 'have nothing to do with questions of statecraft and diplomacy. Their simple duty is to determine the rights of the parties according to justice and equity. They must not be influenced in reaching their conclusions by theories or predictions as to the possible effect of their decisions upon the political future of Venezuela. It is none of their concern.'
575 See Section 2.1.3.
576 Thus, if the rebels win they *are* 'responsible' for the acts committed by the previous government while fighting against them, but if the government wins it is *not* 'responsible' for the acts committed by the rebels while fighting against it. This situation may, at first, seem rather 'unbalanced' from the perspective of the rebels. But then again the rules of international law are made *by States*, not rebels. The question is examined in Section 2.1.3.
577 O'Connell, *International Law*, p. 969.
578 Cahin, 'Attribution of Conduct to the State', p. 253.

solution when compared to others. It is indeed the conclusion reached by Umpire Ralston in the *Sambiaggio* case.[579]

It should be added that the 'unfairness' resulting from the application of Rule no. 3 is somewhat 'mitigated' by the existence of three rules which will be examined later.

First, as further explained below,[580] a State should, in my view, be bound by the consequences arising from one specific type of wrong committed by rebels during an insurgency. A State should provide proper reparation to a foreign investor to compensate any damages suffered as a result of an act of expropriation committed by the rebels whenever it resulted in some *benefits* for *the State* (not the rebels). In my view, this basic principle (Rule no. 4B) is a specific situation in which Rule no. 3 should not find application.

Second, I will also explain later[581] the existence of a well-known principle whereby whenever the rebels are unsuccessful in their attempt to establish a new government, the State remain responsible for its *own* failure to exercise its due diligence obligation to protect the rights of foreigners and third States in the context of wrongs committed by the rebels (Rule no. 6). There are therefore a number of circumstances where the victims may be able to get some form of reparation from the State if it can be shown that the State has not been vigilant enough in protecting their rights during the insurgency.

Finally, I will also show[582] the existence of another general principle whereby the State is bound by certain *legal* acts performed by the rebels during an insurgency. Thus, a State is bound by the governmental 'routine activities' performed by rebels when they have established a local de facto government in a part of a territory (Rule no. 4A).

3.1.4 *Case Law and State Practice Support Rule No. 3*

Rule no. 3, whereby the acts committed by the rebels during an (ultimately unsuccessful) insurgency are not attributable to the State, has been accepted by all writers.[583] This is also the conclusion reached by Ago who

[579] *Sambiaggio* case, 1903, p. 524: 'It is further urged that absolute equity should control the decisions of the Commission and that equitably sufferers from the acts of revolutionists should be recompensed. But this subject may be viewed from two standpoints. It is as inequitable to charge a government for wrongs it never committed as it would be to deny rights to a claimant for a technical reason.'

[580] See Section 3.1.6.

[581] See Section 3.3.

[582] See Section 3.1.5.

[583] Morris, 'Revolutionary Movements', p. 723, 753; Al-Rashid *et al.*, 'Investment Claims', p. 186–7; Daillier *et al.*, *Droit international public*, p. 870; Cahin, 'Attribution of Conduct

examined in detail the works of scholars.[584] I will show, in this section, that the principle has also been recognized by State practice and case law.

3.1.4.1 State Practice

Cahin refers to Rule no. 3 as a 'well-established principle of international law' which 'is based on a long and widely established practice'.[585] He refers to these examples:

> Developed during the 19th century, on the basis of such different situations as the American Civil War, the Commune of Paris, the revolt of Abi Pasha in Egypt, the Carlista movement in Spain, the insurrections for the independence of Cuba and against numerous Latin American governments, this rule was also applied by the arbitral case law mentioned earlier in relation to the victory of insurrectional movements and was also confirmed by States at the 1930 Hague Conference. After World War II and during the 1960s, the Indonesian rebellion at Celebes and the civil war in the Congo provided new precedents for the rule of non-responsibility of the State.[586]

Piguet also came to the same conclusion after having examined numerous examples of State practice.[587] In his First Report, Crawford also noted that 'the basic principle stated in article 14 is well established, as the authorities cited in the [1975] commentary show'.[588] In his book on the Mexican Claims Commissions, established with many European States after a series of revolutions in the early twentieth century, Feller mentioned that Rule no. 3 was indeed the position supported by Mexico and the one that was followed by the various commissions.[589] Silvanie referred to Rule no. 3 as 'a settled principle of international law'.[590] In his book, he mentioned several examples of State practice where the US and Great Britain took that position of non-responsibility regarding

to the State', p. 252–3; Piguet, *La Guerre civile en droit international*, p. 91–2; De Visscher, *Théories et réalités*, p. 347; Houghton, 'The Responsibility of the State', p. 255; Ryngaert, 'State Responsibility and Non-State Actors', p. 175.

584 A long list of writers is mentioned in ILC, Ago Report, 1972, p. 141, paras. 183–4. See also, para. 184, indicating that 'modern writers' 'agree almost unanimously that, under the rules now prevailing, injurious acts by the organs of an insurrectional movement are not attributed to the State and thus do not cause it to incur international responsibility'.

585 Cahin, 'Attribution of Conduct to the State', p. 253.

586 Ibid.

587 Piguet, *La Guerre civile en droit international*, p. 66–92. See his conclusion at p. 92.

588 ILC, Crawford First Report, 1998, p. 53, para. 273.

589 A.H. Feller, *The Mexican Claims Commissions, 1923-1934; A Study in the Law and Procedure of International Tribunals* (New York, Macmillan Co., 1935), p. 159–60.

590 Silvanie, *Responsibility of States*, p. 135.

damages suffered by their nationals during insurgencies abroad.[591] He also mentioned 'the practice of other European States as to the practically uniformed acceptance of the general rule [which] is evidence by numerous treaties between those States and certain Latin American republics'.[592] He speaks of a 'practically uniform acceptance and application by international arbitral tribunals and by foreign offices' of this principle.[593] One older relevant element of State practice is the 1930 Hague Conference. Having received comments from governments, the Preparatory Committee of the 1930 Hague Conference elaborated 'Basis of Discussion' no. 22: 'A State is, in principle, not responsible for damage caused to the person or property of a foreigner by persons taking part in an insurrection or riot or by mob violence.'[594]

3.1.4.2 Case Law

This section will first examine a number of older precedents supporting Rule no. 3 (Section 3.1.4.2.1). It will be followed by a detailed analysis of the recent *Cengiz* v. *Libya* case where the question was addressed by an investment tribunal in the context of the Libyan civil war (Section 3.1.4.2.2).

3.1.4.2.1 Older Precedents In his 1972 report, Ago noted that Rule no. 3 is a well-established principle of international law which has been recognized by international courts and tribunals.[595] Ago referred to various cases decided by the United States–Mexican Claims Commission established under the Convention of 4 July 1868,[596] including the *Solis* case[597] and the *Bond Coleman*

[591] Ibid., p. 136 ff.
[592] Ibid., p. 141.
[593] Ibid., p. 145.
[594] League of Nations, 1929, 'Basis of Discussion' no. 22 should be read together with 'Basis of Discussion' no. 22(a), dealing with the responsibility of the State for its own failure to fulfil its due diligence obligation (Rule no. 6, further discussed below in Section 3.3).
[595] ILC, Ago Report, 1972, p. 132, para. 161:

> [a]s far back as the nineteenth century, many mixed commissions affirmed on several occasions – on the basis, moreover, of explicit clauses in the treaties under which they had been established – the principle that as a general rule a Government was not responsible for injuries caused to aliens by the members of an armed insurrection which was beyond the control of the said Government.

[596] Ibid.
[597] *G.L. Solis (U.S.A.)* v. *United Mexican States*, Mexico–United States General Claims Commission, 3 October 1928, UNRIAA 4, p. 358 ff.

case.[598] The same conclusion has been reached by other writers.[599] The 2001 ILC Commentaries also stated that 'ample jurisprudence for this principle is found in arbitral jurisprudence'.[600] Silvanie also affirmed that Rule no. 3 'has been uniformly applied to a variety of claims by an impressive number of international arbitral commissions'.[601] In his article, he cited several cases.[602]

598 *Bond Coleman* case, Mexico–United States General Claims Commission, vol. 4, p. 364 ff.

599 Piguet, *La Guerre civile en droit international*, p. 92–104. See his conclusion at p. 92.

600 ILC, Commentaries, 2001, p. 50, para. 3:

> International arbitral bodies, including mixed claims commissions and arbitral tribunals have uniformly affirmed what Commissioner Nielsen in the Solis case described as a 'well-established principle of international law', that no Government can be held responsible for the conduct of rebellious groups committed in violation of its authority, where it is itself guilty of no breach of good faith, or of no negligence in suppressing insurrection. Diplomatic practice is remarkably consistent in recognizing that the conduct of an insurrectional movement cannot be attributed to the State.

601 Silvanie, *Responsibility of States*, p. 143. See also, Silvanie, 'Responsibility of States for Acts of Insurgent Governments', p. 90.

602 Silvanie, 'Responsibility of States for Acts of Insurgent Governments', p. 91:

> This principle has been applied in a variety of cases. For example, the United States and Mexican Claims Commission of 1849 disallowed a claim for pillage of goods of an American citizen by unsuccessful revolutionary forces in Mexico. . . . [O]n the other hand, claims against Mexico for damages for acts such as imprisonment and injury to persons of American nationality, and destruction and confiscation of American property caused by the Zuloaga, Miramon, and Maximilian governments, who were ultimately unsuccessful, and by other unsuccessful rebel forces. . . . The United States and Spanish Claims Commission of 1871 absolved Spain from any liability for damages caused as a result of an attack on an American plantation and for destruction of other property by Cuban insurgents in 1870. During the Venezuelan arbitrations of 1903 the umpires of practically all the various commissions assembled in Caracas were of the opinion that under international law there existed no responsibility on the part of the Venezuelan Government for the tortious acts of unsuccessful revolutionists, such as forced loans and requisitions, seizure of property, and damages to and destruction of property. During the arbitration between the United States and Great Britain under the convention of 1910, a claim for losses and damages sustained by an American religious society during a native rebellion in the British protectorate of Sierra Leone in 1898 was disallowed. And, lastly, during the recent arbitrations between the United States and Mexico, the General Claims Commission of 1923 rejected and disallowed a claim by the American Government to obtain compensation for cattle said to have been taken from the ranch of an American citizen in Mexico by the unsuccessful revolutionary forces of General de la Huerta in 1924.

For the present purposes, suffice it to mention just a few awards that have highlighted the principle:

- *Home Frontier* case, referring to 'the well-established principle of international law that no government can be held responsible for the act of rebellious bodies of men committed in violation of its authority, where it is itself guilty of no breach of good faith, or of no negligence in suppressing insurrection';[603]
- *Prats* case, Mexican Commissioner, Mr Palacio, indicating: '[t]he irresponsibility of the government for the mischiefs caused by the rebels in a civil war has in its favor the opinions and decisions of eminent statesmen';[604]
- *French Company of Venezuelan Railroads* case, Umpire Plumley stating: '[w]hen revolution laid waste both country and village, or seized the railroad and its material, or placed its hands upon the boats and wrought serious injury to all, it is regrettable, deplorable, but it is not chargeable upon the respondent Government, unless the revolution was successful';[605]
- *Aroa Mines* case, the Umpire noting that 'the position of all international law writers was in substantial accord touching this matter of non-responsibility of nations for the acts of unsuccessful revolutionists at the time this protocol was signed, as was well known to the parties to the protocols in question'.[606] Having quoted several awards, he added that 'the precedents form an unbroken line, so far as the umpire has been favored with a chance to study them, supporting the usual non-responsibility of governments for the acts of unsuccessful rebels';[607]

603 *Home Frontier and Foreign Missionary Society of the United Brethren in Christ (United States)* v. *Great Britain*, 18 December 1920, UNRIAA 6, p. 423–6.

604 *Prats* case, 1868, Mexican Commissioner, Mr Palacio, p. 194, p. 201 ff., citing several examples of State practice.

605 *French Company of Venezuelan Railroads* case, French–Venezuelan Mixed Claims Commission, Award of 31 July 1905, UNRIAA 10, p. 354. Yet, given that the revolution was in that case actually successful, the Tribunal held that the government was responsible.

606 *Aroa Mines* case, UK–Venezuela Claims Commission, UNRIAA 9, p. 439.

607 Ibid., p. 440. The same general principle is mentioned at the very end of the award, at p. 445:

> [t]he Government of Venezuela will not be held liable to the British Government for injuries to property or wrongful seizures thereof, or for damages, vexations, or exactions committed upon or suffered by British subjects in Venezuela during any unsuccessful insurrection or civil war

- *Padron* case, Spanish–Venezuelan Mixed Claims Commission, Umpire Gutierrez-Otero stating: '[i]t is an accepted principle of international law that States are not responsible to aliens resident in their territory for damages and injuries inflicted upon them by persons in revolt against the constituted authorities';[608]
- The same principle was also affirmed by Umpire Gutierrez-Otero of the Spanish–Venezuelan Mixed Claims Commission in the *Mena* case;[609]
- *Guastini case,* Umpire Ralston approving the *Sambiaggio* case and stating that 'it is worthy of note that, according to the opinions of nearly if not quite all the umpires now in Caracas in the various Commissions, there exists no legal responsibility on the part of Government for the acts of unsuccessful revolutionists';[610]
- *Pinson* case, indicating that 'si donc l'arbitrage actuel était un arbitrage basé sur les principes généraux du droit international, et que la Commission franco-mexicaine dût juger les réclamations à ce seul point de vue, il se pourrait très bien qu'il lui fallût rejeter en bloc toutes les réclamations qui se basent sur des actes illégaux commis par des

> which has occurred in that country unless there be proven fault or want of due diligence on the part of the Venezuelan authorities or their agents.

608 *Padron* case, Spanish–Venezuelan Mixed Claims Commission, UNRIAA 10, p. 742–3. This is the full quote:

> [t]his precise explanation having been made, it may be admitted as an established truth, that after a much debated discussion concerning the responsibility of states for damages which revolutionists cause to the persons and properties of foreigners residing in their territory, a negative solution has predominated and been accepted among the rules and principles, to which the umpire has heretofore alluded, that no right to demand indemnity for such damages exists; a principle, on the other hand, to which there have been pointed out various – we may say, numerous – exceptions which it is not necessary to state for the purposes of this decision.

609 *Mena* case, Spanish–Venezuelan Mixed Claims Commission, UNRIAA 10, p. 749: '[p]rimarily, the State is responsible only for the acts done by its agents, and not for damages which insurgents cause to foreigners, and therefore Gonzalez Mena has no right, from this point of view, to claim damages which the revolutionary forces may have caused him'. He also mentioned that this 'theory has undoubtedly prevailed concerning the irresponsibility of states for damages which insurgents cause to the persons or property of foreigners living in their territory, and such a principle is now considered as a rule properly called one of international law'. He however concluded that the rule did not 'govern a tribunal of the nature of this Mixed Commission, which, according to the protocol that created it, should, on the contrary, necessarily base its judgments upon absolute equity and not take into consideration objections of a technical nature which may be raised before it'.

610 *Guastini* case, Italy–Venezuela Claims Commission, UNRIAA 10, p. 578.

forces opposées à l'armée constitutionnaliste qui a fini par remporter la victoire dans la guerre civile';[611]

- *Puerto Cabello and Valencia Railroad Company* case, stating that 'It was settled for this Commission by the opinion of the umpire in the claim of the Bolivar Company that the respondent Government, subject to certain exceptions, was liable for the acts of successful revolutionists', but adding that this case involved acts of unsuccessful rebels for which the State could not be responsible.[612]

Finally, the question arose in the context of the establishment of the so-called Italian 'Social Republic' (the Republic of Salò), a fascist 'puppet government' which had been set up at the end of the Second World War in the German-occupied part of northern Italy. In the *Fubini* case, the US–Italian Conciliation Commission considered the situation of Italy, at the time, as one involving 'the co-existence of a legal Government and an insurrectional Government fighting one another over the possession of power in a State'.[613] Several Italian municipal courts considered the Italian 'Social Republic' to be a de facto government during the War. The 1963 ILC Digest of decisions explained that in the *Galatioto* v. *Ochoa* case, the Italian Court of Cassation 'held that enactments of a *de facto*

[611] *Pinson* case, 1928, p. 431 ('If, therefore, the present arbitration were an arbitration based on the general principles of international law, and the Franco-Mexican Commission had to judge the claims from that point of view alone, it might well be necessary to reject all claims that are based on illegal acts committed by forces opposed to the constitutionalist army that ended up winning the civil war'). The Commission however added that the case had to be decided based on equity principles. See also, p. 450: 'une responsabilité internationale du chef de dommages causés par des mouvements révolutionnaires, ne saurait être reconnue, à mon avis, pour ce qui concerne les actes juridiques ou délits de forces révolutionnaires qui ont échoué, le droit international ne grevant pas, ou pas encore, l'État des effets juridiques de pareils actes ou délits' ('international responsibility for damages caused by revolutionary movements, cannot be recognized, in my opinion, with regard to legal acts or offenses of revolutionary forces which have failed. Under international law, a State is not (at least yet) responsible for the legal effects of such acts or offenses').

[612] *Puerto Cabello and Valencia Railroad Company*, British–Venezuelan Commission, 1903, UNRIAA 9, p. 513: '[c]oncerning the sums charged of March 29 and of June 28, 1898, it is to be said that had these injuries been received at the hands of the Government, or of successful revolutionists, they might be allowed; but as the result of the *acts of unsuccessful revolutionists*, which is the character in which they appear before the umpire, they can not be allowed', emphasis added.

[613] *Fubini* case, Italian–United States Conciliation Commission, Decision No. 201, 12 December 1959, UNRIAA 14, p. 420–34, at p. 428, adding that (at p. 428): 'there did exist, during a period of nineteen months, two Governments in Italy, each of which denied the power of the other'.

government in enemy-occupied territory, such as the Italian Social Republic, retained their validity even after the legitimate government had recovered the territory, unless the enactments were of a purely political character or were annulled by the legitimate government'.[614] In other words, it considered that the legitimate Italian government after the War was bound by the 'routine' governmental activities performed by rebels which had established a local de facto government.[615] Italian tribunals also held that the legitimate Italian government after the War was responsible for the damage caused by a motor car of the fire brigade of the Italian army which was controlled at the time by the Italian 'Social Republic'.[616]

The question is generally considered to be one of succession of governments, not involving any matters of State succession. Thus, no new State was created. However, it should be noted that in some cases, Italian courts have viewed this example as one involving the establishment of a new State.[617] One relevant illustration is the *Rainoldi* case, in which a plaintiff had been run over during the War by a motorcar belonging to the army of the Italian 'Social Republic'.[618] The plaintiff's contention was that Italy, as the successor to the 'new State' (the Italian 'Social Republic', which had since then ceased to exist), should assume liabilities for such act. The Court concluded that the Italian 'Social Republic' had never been able to establish itself as a new State.[619] It considered that the 'Republic' was at most a group of insurgents with the status of belligerents; they had

614 *Galatioto* v. *Ochoa,* Italy, Court of Cassation, *Foro Italiano,* 69 (1944–6), 1,217, also in *Annual Digest* (1946) Case 18; ILC, 'Digest of Decisions of National Courts relating to Succession of States and Governments Study prepared by the Secretariat', UN Doc. A/CN.4/157, 18 April 1963, *ILC Yearbook* II (1963), p. 145.

615 This general rule (Rule no. 4A) will be further examined below, in Section 3.1.5.

616 *Costa* v. *Ministero della Guerra,* Court of First Instance of Genoa, judgment of 26 March 1946, in *Foro Italiano* 70 (1947) I, p. 256, mentioned in *Annual Digest* (1946), p. 9. Other cases decided by Italian courts are mentioned in *Annual Digest*, ibid.

617 In a decision of the Court of First Instance of Cremona dated 15 November 1945 (in *Foro Padano* (1946) I, 150) and in another decision of that same court dated 3 April 1946 (in *Giurisprudenza Italiana* (1946) I, p. 273) it was decided that the Italian 'Social Republic' had established itself as a *new State* during the War (and not merely as a new government). D. P. O'Connell, *State Succession in Municipal Law and International Law* (Cambridge University Press, 1967, vol. I), p. 492, also refers to the case of *Durchi* v. *The Commune of Genoa* (in *Foro Italiano* 70 (1947) I, p. 334) where Italy was found liable for the acts committed by the Italian 'Social Republic'.

618 *Rainoldi* v. *Ministero della Guerra,* Court of First Instance of Brescia (Italy), 20 February 1946, in *Foro Italiano* (1947) I, 151, in *Annual Digest* (1946), p. 6.

619 *Annual Digest* (1946), p. 6. However, in an *obiter dictum*, the Court indicated that had a new State been shortly established and had it later vanished, Italy would have been

only a de facto authority over a population which was effectively subject to the German military command. The Court held that Italy, which had never ceased to exist, should not be 'responsible' for the acts of the unsuccessful insurgents. In other words, the Court seems to have considered the Italian 'Social Republic' as a failed attempt by insurgents to establish a new government and, consequently, applied Rule no. 3.

3.1.4.2.2 The *Cengiz* v. *Libya* Case The case involved the Turkish Claimant's locally-created entity, Cengiz Libya, which entered into contracts with a Libyan State entity (Libyan Housing and Infrastructure Board, 'HIB') for the design and construction of housing and related infrastructure (roads, electricity distribution, water supply, etc.) in two remote regions in the south of the country: the Wadi Al Hayat (WAH) and Sebha zones. The Tribunal awarded some 50 US$ million to the investor on the grounds that Libya breached its FPS obligation under the Libya–Turkey BIT in the context of incidents which occurred during the civil war in 2011 and 2014.[620] In the following sections, I will examine two specific points relevant to the present analysis:

- Identification of the attackers and the government in charge at the time of the events (Section 3.1.4.2.2.1);
- The Tribunal's confusing reasoning on matters of attribution and responsibility in assessing whether Libya breached its duty to abstain under the FPS standard (Section 3.1.4.2.2.2); and
- The Tribunal could have avoided this confusion by interpreting the sequence of events differently (Section 3.1.4.2.2.3).

3.1.4.2.2.1 Identification of the Attackers and the Government in Charge at the Time of the Events One crucial point for the Tribunal was to determine who committed the attacks and who was in charge at the time

considered the successor State to that short-lived Republic and, consequently, that it would have had to assume liabilities for internationally wrongful acts committed by that Republic: '[w]e may admit, although this is not universally accepted, that international law imposed upon the successor State the duty to assume the liabilities of the predecessor State, both towards other States and private persons of foreign nationality. We may admit, further, that the successor State owes a corresponding duty towards its own citizens to recognise the succession in domestic law'. O'Connell, *State Succession*, p. 492, described this case as of 'doubtful merit'.

620 *Cengiz* case, 2018. The award has been challenged before French courts (the seat of arbitration). The application was dismissed by the Paris Court of Appeal in a decision rendered on 25 May 2021.

the events took place. The civil war started in early 2011. By March 2011, groups of insurgents formally established a transitional government: the Libyan National Transitional Council (NTC), which only had control over parts of the territory of Libya. By June 2011, several States had issued statements whereby they considered the NTC as the 'legitimate government' of Libya. It has been noted that some of the declarations recognizing the NTC as the 'legitimate authority' were mainly political in nature and did not have the effect of recognizing the NTC as the *new government*.[621] In any event, the Tribunal stated that 'on August 23, 2011, the rebels invaded Tripoli and thus, Libya fell under control of the opposition'.[622] This is important given that on the *very same day*, the Tribunal explained that 'a group of armed individuals of the Tarik Bin Ziyad Battalion, under the command of Battalion Commander Brigadier General Adbiilselam Ismail, violently restrained the site personnel at the WAH Main Camp and forcibly took equipment, motors and vehicles belonging to Cengiz Libya'.[623] Three days later, 'a group of citizens, supported by police vehicles and the Tank Battalion, again entered the WAH Main Camp and stole everything at hand'.[624] The award explained that the pillage in both cases was done by 'armed soldiers belonging to the Libyan army'[625] which were '*still* defending the *old* Gaddafi regime'.[626] The Tribunal also referred to other incidents that took place, at the same time, in the Sebha Main camp by other groups.[627] I will focus in the next paragraphs on the events that took place at the WAH Main Camp.

The Tribunal used the expression 'old' Gaddafi regime because it considered that at the time the attacks took place (23 August), the NTC

621 Akande, 'Which Entity Is the Government of Libya'. See also: Stefan Talmon, 'The Difference between Rhetoric and Reality', p. 5: 'Unlike recognition as the representative of a people or as a government, such recognition is without significance in international law.' He also referred to some declarations made by other States (Italy, France, UAE) which could be considered as recognitions of a new government. See also, analysis in G. Nesi, 'Recognition of The Libyan National Transitional Council: When, How and Why', *Italian YIL* 21(1) (2011), p. 46 ff. For a different perspective, See: Katie A. Johnston, 'Transformations of Conflict Status in Libya', *J. Conflict & Security L.* 17(1) (2012), p. 111, for whom 'by the middle of July, a significant number of States, including all those involved in the NATO intervention, had shown that, in their opinion, the legal status of the NTC was that of the sovereign government of Libya'.

622 *Cengiz* case, 2018, para. 174.

623 Ibid., para. 192. See also, para. 382.

624 Ibid., para. 194. See also, para. 385.

625 Ibid., para. 419.

626 Ibid., para. 421, emphasis added.

627 Ibid., paras. 389–90, 422.

had in fact already established itself as the *new government* and had in effect *replaced* the Gaddafi dictatorship. This is clear from several passages of the award. For instance, the Tribunal explicitly said that it 'agreed' with the Respondent's statement that the 'Libyan military units which attacked the WAH Main Camp were in fact loyal to the *previous* Government of Colonel Gaddafi and must be considered as unsuccessful insurrectional forces seeking to *displace the new government* of Libya'.[628] This passage can only be logically interpreted as meaning that on 23 August (the date of the first attack) the NTC already formed the *new government* and that the troops loyal to the Gaddafi regime were now considered as rebels fighting that new government. Yet, instead of focusing on this basic and crucial question, the Tribunal discussed another issue: who was the 'legitimate Government of Libya' at the time when the attack took place.[629] As discussed above,[630] this notion of 'legitimate' government is not useful at all in the context of insurgency. As noted by Talmon, recognition of an opposition group as the 'legitimate' representative of a people 'is a purely political act', which has 'only limited practical effect';[631] it must be distinguished from the legal act of formally recognizing a government. The Tribunal seemed to confuse this concept of 'legitimacy' with the other fundamental question of whether or not the NTC was forming the *new government* at the end of August 2011. In any event, the following passages show that the Tribunal believed that the NTC was indeed the new government at the time:

> Libya says that by the time when the first incidents occurred – end of August 2011 – the legitimate Government of Libya was that of the NTC
>
> The Tribunal tends to agree.
>
> Italy and France recognized the NTC government in April and June 2011, respectively, and on 15 July US Secretary of State Hillary Clinton stated that the US had decided to formally recognise the NTC as the country's 'legitimate authority'. The UK made a similar declaration on 27

[628] Ibid., para. 426, emphasis added.

[629] Ibid., para. 413.

[630] See Section 2.2.4.1.

[631] Talmon, 'Recognition of Opposition Groups', p. 231. See also, p. 243:

> [r]ecognition of an opposition group as the legitimate representative of a people leaves intact the international legal status of the incumbent government and does not establish any rights of representation on behalf of a people or State concerned. It is mainly of symbolic value, indicating political support for the opposition group recognized and implying that the recognizing State is ready to engage with the group, its institutions and representatives.

> July 2011. The evidence shows that by the end of August, international legitimacy had passed from the Gaddafi Government to the NTC Government, which had arisen out of the Libyan Revolution.
>
> And by that date, the NTC was also in control of the major part of Libyan territory. The exception may have been certain parts of the Southern Region, a traditional stronghold of Gaddafi supporters, which were still held by pro-Gaddafi forces. The battle of Sebha, which led to a defeat of such loyalist forces, was fought in September 2011 – leading to Coronel Gaddafi's demise in October 2011.[632]

The Tribunal therefore analysed the case as a failed attempt by the rebels (troops loyal to the Gaddafi regime) to overthrow the new NTC government.

3.1.4.2.2.2 The Tribunal's Confusing Reasoning on Matters of Attribution and Responsibility in Assessing Whether Libya Breached Its Duty to Abstain under the FPS Standard The Tribunal examined whether these attacks were in breach of the FPS standard and, specifically, of 'the negative obligation to refrain from directly harming the investment by acts of violence attributable to the State'.[633] The Tribunal mentioned the principle that a State 'is responsible for the acts carried out by its regular armed forces'.[634] However, it concluded that 'the attackers of the WAH Main Camp were members of the Libyan army, and consequently their acts are attributable to Libya'.[635] This is a rather strange conclusion given the Tribunal's earlier finding that by the time of the attack the NTC formed a new government and had, in effect, replaced the Gaddafi regime. In that context, the militia groups, which in the Tribunal's own words were '*still* defending the *old* Gaddafi regime',[636] could hardly be considered as Libya's 'regular armed forced'.[637] They were rebels. In fact, as mentioned above, the Tribunal expressly 'agreed'[638] with the respondent's position that 'Libyan military units which attacked the WAH Main Camp were in fact loyal to the *previous* Government of Colonel Gaddafi and must be considered as unsuccessful insurrectional forces seeking to displace the *new* government of Libya.'[639]

632 *Cengiz* case, 2018, paras. 414–17.
633 Ibid., para. 403.
634 Ibid., para. 425.
635 Ibid.
636 Ibid., para. 421, emphasis added.
637 Ibid., para. 425.
638 Ibid., para. 427.
639 Ibid., para. 426, emphasis added.

The Tribunal added that while it 'agreed' with this statement, it nevertheless 'disagrees with the conclusion' drawn by the Respondent, i.e. that the acts of Gaddafi-aligned forces 'cannot be attributable to Libya' because they were 'unsuccessful insurrectional forces'.[640] The conclusion reached by the Tribunal on this point is contrary to Rule no. 3. The acts of unsuccessful rebels cannot be attributable to the State. The Tribunal then made this surprising statement:

> It is likely that the Libyan military units which attacked the WAH Main Camp were at that time defending the Gaddafi regime. But that is irrelevant for the purposes of attribution: these units belonged to the regular Libyan army, as such they were an organ of the Libyan State, and their actions, under international law, were attributable to the State. Whether these units were loyal to the Gaddafi or the NTC Government does not affect the principle of attribution. The Libyan State, including its regular armed forces, never ceased to exist, even if one Government was toppled by the Libyan Revolution and a new Government was instated. The Libyan State must assume responsibility for the looting performed by its regular armed forces – independently of purpose or political affiliation.[641]

With respect to the attack on the WAH Main Camp, the statement can be criticized on many accounts. First, the Tribunal is incorrect when it affirms that the fact that the attacks were done by troops 'loyal to the Gaddafi or the NTC Government does not affect the principle of attribution'.[642] It matters a great deal under Article 4 of the ILC Articles. It is clearly not a question that is 'irrelevant for the purposes of attribution'. Second, given that the Tribunal expressly agreed with the Respondent's depiction of the attackers as 'unsuccessful insurrectional forces seeking to displace the new government of Libya',[643] it is difficult to understand how they can be qualified by the Tribunal as 'units belonged to the regular Libyan army'. They were not. An entity cannot be qualified as both rebels and the regular army *at the same time*. According to the Tribunal's very own interpretation of the sequence of events, the attackers were at that time members of the *old* army fighting *against* the *new* government (and its new army made up of militia groups which had successfully overthrown the Gaddafi regime). In other words, at the time of the attack these pro-Gaddafi soldiers were no longer 'belong[ing] to the regular Libyan army', they were now rebels. Third, it follows that

[640] Ibid., para. 412.
[641] Ibid., para. 428.
[642] Ibid., para. 428.
[643] Ibid., paras. 426–7.

these pro-Gaddafi rebels could not be considered as 'an organ of the Libyan State' under Article 4 of the ILC Articles. As such, the award is wrong to conclude that 'their actions, under international law, were attributable to the State'. According to the Tribunal's own interpretation of events, the only acts attributable to Libya at the time were those committed by militias loyal to the NTC government at the Sebha Main Camp.[644] Fourth, the actions of the pro-Gaddafi rebels would have been attributable to the State only if they were ultimately *successful* in their attempt to overthrow the new government of the NTC (Rule no. 2). But the pro-Gaddafi rebels were not successful and were defeated a few months later.[645]

In my view, considering the Tribunal's own interpretation of the sequence of events (and, most importantly, the fact that it viewed the NTC as having already formed a new government at the time the attacks took place), it should have reached a different conclusion regarding matters of attribution and responsibility. The Tribunal should have examined the issue as one involving attacks on the WAH Main Camp *by rebels* (not soldiers 'belong[ing] to the regular Libyan army')[646] who were ultimately *unsuccessful* in their struggle. Logically, the Tribunal should have applied Rule no. 3, whereby the acts committed by (unsuccessful) rebels during an insurgency are *not* attributable to the State.[647]

In this context, it is hard to understand why the Tribunal referred at all to Article 10 of the ILC Articles. The Tribunal said that 'the principle that a State also assumes responsibility for the acts of a successful insurrectional movement' was one of 'two principles of international law which

[644] The award mentioned that 'on August 26, 2011, the Sebha Main Camp was taken over by armed men and the remaining personnel on site were physically restrained and threatened, and machinery and equipment were taken away' (ibid., para. 389). Another incident took place in 2014: 'the 3rd Force of the Libya Shield took over the Sebha Main Camp and dispossessed Cengiz Libya' (para. 409). The Tribunal explained that the 'attackers belonged to militias controlled by the NTC Government: Free Martyrs Brigade of Sebha, a Military Brigade "in the service of Free Libya" and in 2014 the 3rd Force of the Libya Shield' (para. 422). Thus, these groups were 'loyal to the NTC government' (para. 390) and were 'a militia controlled by the Libyan government' (para. 409). In this context, the Tribunal was right to conclude that their actions were attributable to the State.

[645] Ibid., para. 417.

[646] Ibid., para. 428.

[647] It should be added that such a finding would not have changed much in terms of responsibility given that the Tribunal held that Libya was anyway responsible for the attacks committed at the Sebha Main Camp by 'a militia controlled by the Libyan government' (ibid., para. 409). Yet, such a finding could have had an effect on the amount of damages awarded.

are relevant for deciding this issue'.[648] The Tribunal correctly identified the basic principle behind Rule no. 2 as follows: '[t]he rule implies that acts committed by members of an insurrectional movement are attributable to the State, if such movement eventually is successful and takes over the Government of such State'.[649] Applying the rule to the facts of the case, the Tribunal said: 'the Libyan State must be deemed responsible for acts and omissions committed by . . . all insurrectional groups and militias, which defended the NTC Government and fought the Gaddafi regime, and which ultimately were successful'.[650] While this statement is undoubtedly true, it was not helpful at all given how the Tribunal interpreted the sequel of events.

The Tribunal did not refer to a *single act* which was committed by groups and militias *during* the insurgency in their struggle to establish the new NTC government. According to the Tribunal itself, all attacks mentioned in the award at WAH Main Camp were done *after* the new NTC government had *already* established itself as the new government. There was also no need at all to refer to Article 10 regarding the attacks which took place at the Sebha Main Camp, including those committed by the 'Force of the Libya Shield' in 2014, that is, a few years *after* the NTC government was established.[651] Article 10 would have been very relevant in relation to the attacks on the WAH Main Camp by pro-Gaddafi rebels, but the Tribunal (as mentioned in the previous paragraph) failed to apply Rule no. 3.

648 Ibid., para. 423.

649 Ibid., para. 430.

650 Ibid., para. 431.

651 The award mentioned that in 2014, 'the 3rd Force of the Libya Shield took over the Sebha Main Camp and dispossessed Cengiz Libya' (ibid., para. 409). The Tribunal noted that 'in its commencement the Libyan Shield was a group of militias, created to support the insurrection' and that 'since the Libyan Revolution eventually triumphed [in 2011], its actions are attributable to Libya under the principle set forth in Article 10 of the Draft ILC Articles' (para. 433). Yet, given that the attacks took place in 2014, i.e. a few years *after* the new NTC government had been established, the reference to Article 10 is irrelevant. This is clear from the award's next paragraph which explains that when the revolution was successful, 'the Libyan Shield became officially affiliated with the state security apparatus' and 'was transformed into an organ of the Libyan State, whose actions are directly attributable to Libya under Article 4 of the Draft ILC Articles' (para. 434). The Tribunal added that 'in this new capacity, the NTC Government sent the Libyan Shield to Sebha to enforce law and order – and eventually to take over Claimant's Sebha Main Camp' (para. 434). In other words, the Tribunal rightly concluded that these acts were attributable to Libya based on Article 4 of the ILC Articles. Article 10 was not relevant at all in this context.

3.1.4.2.2.3 The Tribunal Could Have Avoided This Confusion by Interpreting the Sequence of Events Differently This whole confusion regarding matters of attribution and responsibility could have been easily avoided by the Tribunal. Thus, the Tribunal could have simply considered that when the attacks took place the situation was still unclear on the ground. It could have reasonably assumed that at the end of August 2011, the Libyan army (loyal to the Gaddafi regime) had not yet been defeated and that the NTC had not yet firmly established itself as the new government. At the time, the situation was simply too fluid to draw any clear-cut conclusion on the matter. The factual timeline mentioned by the Tribunal would actually support such an approach. Thus, the Tribunal explicitly mentioned that the attack on the investor's property took place on the very same day (23 August 2011)[652] that 'the rebels [i.e. the militias supporting the NTC] invaded Tripoli and thus, Libya fell under control of the opposition'.[653] There is something very odd for the Tribunal to qualify the NTC as 'rebels' and as the 'opposition' to the government. This qualification cannot be reconciled with the fact that elsewhere in the award the Tribunal refers to the NTC as the 'legitimate government' of Libya.[654] The NTC cannot logically be considered as both the rebels and the new government *on the same day* (i.e. 23 August 2011). As mentioned by Talmon, 'the main criterion in international law for government status is that the individual or group of individuals claiming to be the government of a State exercise effective control over the State's territory' which means that 'it must be in possession of the machinery of State which, as a rule, requires control of the State's capital'.[655] Can it realistically be said that on 23 August 2011 (the day of the attack), the NTC had effective control of the territory and the capital, which it just invaded the very *same* day? It seems very doubtful if one considers the list of relevant factors mentioned by Morris.[656] On 23 August, it was clearly

652 Ibid., para. 192.

653 Ibid., para. 174.

654 Ibid., paras. 414–15: 'Libya says that by the time when the first incidents occurred [23 August 2011] the legitimate Government of Libya was that of the NTC' 'The Tribunal tends to agree'. See also, paras. 426–7, where the Tribunal 'agrees' with the following statement by the Respondent: 'Libyan military units which attacked the WAH Main Camp were in fact loyal to the previous Government of Colonel Gaddafi and must be considered as unsuccessful insurrectional forces seeking to displace the new government of Libya'.

655 Talmon, 'Recognition of Opposition Groups', p. 231.

656 Morris, 'Revolutionary Movements', p. 736, indicating the following factors necessary to assess whether or not effective control has been established by a government: 'these

too soon to assess whether the NTC was a 'stable government' which had a 'reasonable prospect' of remaining in power. The same conclusion seems inevitable if one takes into account the remark made by Bondu: 'momentary (or brief) effectiveness is not enough; it must be accompanied by at least a reasonable suspicion or a real likelihood that it will last'.[657] Given that there can only be *one* de jure government in a State at the same time,[658] it would have been perfectly reasonable for the Tribunal to assume that on 23 August 2011, the government was still represented by the Gaddafi regime.

In fact, the Tribunal acknowledged that at the end of August (when the attack on the WAH Main Camp took place) the NTC had no effective control over the entire territory and that the final battle where the pro-Gaddafi forces were ultimately defeated took place in September 2011.[659] It could be argued that any recognition of the NTC as the *new government* at the end of August was premature because the hostilities between the parties were still ongoing at this point.[660] At any rate, that was clearly

factors include the ability of the regime to control the State's territory (whether a portion of that territory in the case of a local de facto government or all or virtually all of the territory in the case of a general de facto government); the lack of significant resistance to the regime; the ability of the regime to govern effectively without the support or intervention of other States; whether the regime has succeeded in reviving the machinery of State or put in place a new structure, such as by appointing ministers and providing basic services for the populace; and whether the regime generally appears to be stable, with a reasonable prospect of remaining in control of the State'. The question was examined in Section 2.2.4.1.

657 Bundu, 'Recognition of Revolutionary Authorities', p. 43.

658 S. Talmon, *Recognition of Governments in International Law* (Oxford University Press, 1998), p. 105. See however the unique situation of Côte d'Ivoire after the 2010 election described in Yejoon Rim, 'Two Governments and One Legitimacy: International Responses to the Post-Election Crisis in Côte d'Ivoire', *Leiden JIL* 25 (2012), p. 692:

> the situation presented the extraordinary precedent of a state's having two competing entities claiming governmental authority, with one [incumbent president Laurent Gbagbo who refused to concede his defeat] only partially *de facto* in his actual control of the administration but nationally *de jure* based on the constitutionality granted by the Constitutional Council, while the other [Ouattara] was internationally *de facto* through the acceptance of his representation in the international community without having internal effectiveness, while remaining only potentially *de jure* via the theoretical democratic entitlement endowed by election victory.

659 *Cengiz* case, 2018, para. 417.

660 Nesi, 'Recognition of The Libyan National Transitional Council', p. 51–2, referring to a number of States which 'within a few months from the inception of the uprising had recognised the NTC as the only representative of Libya in international relation'. He

the case until the NTC took over the capital.[661] It is only on 16 September 2011, that the NTC was recognized by the UN General Assembly as the legitimate representative of Libya.[662] For Nesi, 'the UN system acted as a "catalyst" for the practice and took note of the position of the international community on the issue of recognition'.[663] According to him, 'as of 30 November 2011, more than one hundred United Nations Member States had announced their recognition of the NTC as the sole legitimate

concluded that 'since the hostilities between the incumbent government and the insurgents were at this point still ongoing, according to international law this position could amount to premature recognition and a violation of the principle of non-interference in internal affairs'. He refers to: R. Wolfrum and C. E. Philipp, 'The Status of the Taliban: Their Obligations and Rights under International Law', *Max Planck UNYB* (2002), p. 559 ff., p. 573, indicating (not in the context of the civil war in Libya):

> [a]s long as the lawful government offers resistance which is not ostensibly hopeless or purely nominal the recognition of the revolutionary party as a government would constitute a premature recognition which the government still in power is entitled to regard as an act of intervention, contrary to international law, simply because such recognition would amount to recognising the rebels either as the government of the entire state or as the government of a new state.

See also: Hersch Lauterpacht, *Recognition in International Law* (Cambridge University Press, 1947), p. 94; Daniella Dam-de Jong, 'Armed Opposition Groups and the Right to Exercise Control over Public Natural Resources: A Legal Analysis of the Cases of Libya and Syria', *Netherlands ILJ* 62(3) (2015), p. 24 ('as long as the outcomes of an armed conflict are undecided, any act recognising the opposition movement as the *de jure* government is unlawful and entails the responsibility of the recognizing state').

661 Stefan Talmon, 'Recognition of the Libyan National Transitional Council', *University of Oxford Legal Research Paper Series*, Paper no. 38/2011, June 2011, p. 5:

> [t]he main criterion in international law for the recognition of a rebel group as the government of a State is its exercise of effective control over the State's territory. As long as the NTC's control is limited to the eastern parts of Libya, with the capital Tripoli and western parts remaining under the control of Qadhafi forces, it may be recognized only as the local *de facto* government of the territory which it controls. Any recognition of the NTC as the *de jure* government of the State of Libya while Qadhafi forces are still in control of the capital seems premature and would constitute an illegal interference in the internal affairs of Libya.

See also: Akande, 'Recognition of Libyan National Transitional Council'; A. Schuit, 'Recognition of Governments in International Law and the Recent Conflict in Libya', *International Community Law Review* 14(4) (2012), p. 381–402.

662 See: www.un.org/press/en/2011/ga11137.doc.htm. The question is examined in Nesi, 'Recognition of The Libyan National Transitional Council', p. 53 ff.; Hamed Hasyemi Saugheh and Rohaida Nordin, 'Legitimacy as a Precondition for the Recognition of New Governments: A Case of Libya', *Sriwijaya Law Review* 2(1) (2018).

663 Nesi, 'Recognition of The Libyan National Transitional Council', p. 57.

representative body of Libya'.[664] On 23 October 2011, the NTC declared the 'liberation of Libya' and the official end of the war.

In sum, it would have been reasonable for the Tribunal to assume that on 23 August 2011, the attack on the WAH Main Camp had been executed by the Libyan army loyal to the Gaddafi regime still acting as the government. In that context, it would have been correct for the Tribunal to affirm that 'Libyan State must assume responsibility for the looting performed by its regular armed forces.'[665] The Tribunal could simply have applied Rule no. 1 at the time the award was rendered, whereby the new government of the NTC is responsible for the wrongs committed by the previous government while fighting the rebels. Had the Tribunal followed this approach, the attacks committed on the Sebha Main Camp on 26 August 2011 by militias loyal to the NTC would have been considered as acts by rebels who were (a month later) successful in establishing a new government. In this context, the Tribunal could have applied Article 10 of the ILC Articles and Rule no. 2 whereby the acts committed by the rebels are attributable to the State (Libya) once they have been successfully taken power as the new government. In my view, this approach would have been more logical. It would also have led to the same outcome in terms of responsibility as the one arrived at in the award. Thus, Libya would have been held liable for all attacks (at both the WAH and Sebha camps) which took place during the civil war against the investor's property.

3.1.5 Rule No. 4A: A State Is Bound by the Governmental 'Routine Activities' Performed by Rebels When They Have Established a Local De Facto Government

As mentioned above, a government in charge that has been successful at crushing a rebellion should, as a matter of principle, *not* be 'responsible' for acts committed by rebels during an insurgency. These acts are *not attributable* to the State (Rule no. 3). This section will examine whether there are any exceptions to Rule no. 3. I will demonstrate that a State should be bound by *lawful* 'governmental' 'routine activities' performed by rebels when they have established a local de facto government in a portion of a

[664] Ibid., p. 47. See also, p. 51: '[i]n all, some 130 States – more than two-thirds of the members of the General Assembly, i.e. the quorum required for the admission of a new State to the UN – directly or indirectly recognised the NTC as the authority governing Libya, even before the death of Gaddafi and the end of his regime'. See also, S. Talmon, 'Recognition of the Libyan National Transitional Council', *ASIL Insights*, 16 June 2011.

[665] *Cengiz* case, 2018, para. 428.

territory during an insurgency (Rule no. 4A). The following section will examine another very specific exception to Rule no. 3, according to which a State should be bound by the consequences arising from *wrongs* committed by rebels during an insurgency. In my view, a State should provide proper reparation to a foreign investor to compensate any damage suffered as a result of an act of expropriation committed by the rebels whenever it resulted in some *benefits* for *the State* (Rule no. 4B).[666]

Before examining the first question, a preliminary remark should be made. It has long been argued that the lawful 'governmental' 'routine activities' performed by the rebels during an insurgency are, in fact, *not attributable* to the State. Thus, for Ago this so-called 'exception' is, in fact, 'not an exception at all'.[667] He believes that it is simply a matter of a State being 'bound by certain obligations deriving from lawful routine acts of administration performed by the organs of an insurrectional government in territory formerly under its administration'.[668] Ago speaks of the situation where a State 'would be willing, or would be required, to assume *in proprio* certain obligations incurred by the insurrectional movement'.[669] For him, it is *not* a question of attribution: 'it seems clear that, in such cases, there can be no question of any *a posteriori* attribution to the State, as a source of international responsibility, of acts by organs of the insurrectional movement which no one thought of attributing to it when the movement was still active'.[670] Rather, he believes that it is a matter of *succession* of obligations between different subjects of international law.[671]

[666] The question is examined in Section 3.1.6.

[667] ILC, Ago Report, 1972, p. 142, para. 186:

> [i]t should also be recalled that, according to some of the writers cited above, such as Silvanie, Reuter, Schwarzenberger and O'Connell, an exception ought to be provided to the general rule that the acts of insurgents cannot be attributed to the State as a source of responsibility; the exception would apply to any routine administrative acts performed by the organs of the insurrectional movement in that part of the State territory which is under their control and administration. Actually, as has already been noted, this 'exception' is not an exception at all.

[668] Ibid.

[669] Ibid.

[670] Ibid., p. 130, para. 156.

[671] Ibid., p. 142, para. 186: '[e]ven if it agreed that in some cases the State would be willing, or would be required, to assume *in proprio* certain obligations incurred by the insurrectional movement, this would be done by virtue of the succession of one subject of international law to the obligations of another subject and not by virtue of the attribution to the former of the actions of the latter'. See also, ibid., p. 130, para. 156:

As mentioned above,[672] the ILC later rejected the relevance of the concept of rebels being a subject of international law for the purposes of Article 10.

In my view, the situations that will be discussed in the sections examining Rules no. 4A and 4B are examples where the State should be considered bound by the consequences arising from lawful acts (and one specific type of wrong)[673] performed by rebels during an insurgency, whenever certain specific conditions are met. The next section will first look at the distinction between 'personal' and 'impersonal' acts performed by rebels when acting as a local de facto government (Section 3.1.5.1). It will be followed by an analysis of whether taxes, customs duties, debts and loans as well as contracts and concession agreements should be considered as one or the other (Sections 3.1.5.2 and 3.1.5.3).

3.1.5.1 The Distinction between 'Personal' and 'Impersonal' Acts Performed by Rebels When Acting As a Local De Facto Government

Many writers have highlighted the need to distinguish between so-called 'personal' and 'impersonal' acts performed by rebels when acting as a local de facto government.[674] On the one hand, so-called 'personal' acts are those performed by the rebels for their own personal benefit or for the pursuit of the revolution itself.[675] It is generally recognized that these 'personal' acts *cannot* be attributable to the State after the rebels have been defeated. On the other hand, 'impersonal' acts are those performed by the rebels in the context of their 'normal' administration over the

> [a]ctually, the problem arising in such cases is the problem of possible 'succession' by the subject of international law constituted by the State to various obligations incurred by the subject constituted by the insurrectional movement. This is a problem that must be solved on the basis of the principles governing succession as between subjects of international law and not on the basis of the principles governing State responsibility.

[672] See Sections 2.2.2.2.3 and 3.1.2.

[673] See Section 3.1.6.

[674] Al-Rashid *et al.*, 'Investment Claims', p. 188 ff.; Morris, 'Revolutionary Movements', p. 732 ff.; Ganzory, 'International Claims and Insurgence', p. 84.

[675] K. Fortin, 'The Relevance of Article 9 of the Articles on State Responsibility for the Internationally Wrongful Acts of Armed Groups', in J. Summers and A. Gough (eds.), *Non-State Actors and International Obligations* (Leiden, Brill Nijhoff, 2018), p. 383: 'functions performed by an armed group which are intimately related to its military struggle with the government or their military or political agenda will never constitute acts of State. Examples of such activities would include actions relating to military campaigns, recruitment and training of troops, the conduct of hostilities and the purchase and supply of weapons.'

territory they de facto control.[676] These 'impersonal' acts are often referred to as 'routine activities' which are typically performed by governments.[677] In the context of the unsuccessful attempt at secession by the Confederate States, the US Supreme Court has indeed distinguished between acts which were in 'aid of the rebellion' and those which were 'done in the ordinary course of governmental routine'.[678] In the *Hopkins* case (further discussed below),[679] the Commission speaks of acts of 'purely government routine having no connection with or relation to the individuals administering the [insurgent] Government for the time being'.[680] These 'impersonal' acts are considered to have been performed by the rebels *on behalf* of the legitimate government as a result of their effective power and control over a portion of the territory.[681] It is generally recognized that these 'impersonal' acts performed by a local de facto government are binding on the State.[682]

The relevance of making a distinction between 'personal' and 'impersonal' acts performed by rebels is not supported by everyone.[683] As mentioned above, Ago (like others)[684] seems rather reluctant to recognize the existence of such an 'exception' to the general principle of non-attribution

[676] De Visscher, *Théories et réalités*, p. 348 (speaking of 'une gestion normale des services publics'); Morris, 'Revolutionary Movements', p. 732. See also: Fortin, 'The Relevance of Article 9', p. 383: '[e]xamples of such activities would include acts relating to the resolution of domestic disputes, the registration of births, deaths and marriages, the administration of basic policing and judicial functions, the provision of healthcare and education and the provision of telecommunication services in the territory'.

[677] For a detailed analysis, see: Silvanie, *Responsibility of States*, p. 84 ff.

[678] *Thorington* v. *Smith*, 75 US 1 (8 Wall.) 9, 1868, cited in Silvanie, *Responsibility of States*, p. 98.

[679] See Section 3.1.5.3.

[680] *Hopkins* case, 1926, p. 44.

[681] De Visscher, *Théories et réalités*, p. 349.

[682] Morris, 'Revolutionary Movements', p. 731 (citing Borchard, 'International Pecuniary Claims', p. 344: '[t]he temporary *de facto* government may legislate on all matters of local concern, and in so far as such legislation is not hostile to the subsequent de jure government which displaces it, its laws will be upheld'); Al-Rashid *et al.*, 'Investment Claims', p. 188; Ganzory, 'International Claims and Insurgence', p. 86; de Beus, *The Jurisprudence of the General Claims Commission*, p. 106 ('The Commission in the abovementioned Hopkins case did not content itself with drawing, in the paragraphs quoted, a line between the impersonal routine acts of an illegal government, for which the country is always liable, and the personal, particular acts of such government').

[683] See, for instance, Piguet, *La Guerre civile en droit international*, p. 144–5, for whom the principle that a State is bound by the governmental 'routine activities' performed by rebels when they have established a local de facto government is less well established by State practice and is not part of positive law.

[684] Atlam, *Succession d'États*, p. 395.

regarding so-called governmental 'routine activities' performed by insurgents.[685] He refers to the 'extreme vagueness of this description'.[686] In any event, he also makes it clear that a State can only be bound by '*lawful* routine acts of administration performed' by rebels and not *wrongful* acts.[687] Later in his Report,[688] Ago mentioned in a footnote that 'several arbitral decisions can be found which considered *lawful* acts committed during a civil war by successful insurgents, particularly *contracts*, to be acts of the State'.[689] However, he added that 'such decisions cannot generally be produced in support of the principle of State responsibility for the *wrongful* acts of the insurgents in question'.[690] Akehurst also supports the view that a distinction should be made between contracts and legislation, on the one hand, and delictual acts, on the other.[691] The distinction between lawful acts and wrongs is indeed relevant. All types of governmental 'routine activities' performed by insurgents which are examined in the following sections are lawful acts (the only exception analysed later is one specific example of unlawful expropriation resulting in a specific outcome).[692]

Likewise, O'Connell rejects this distinction between 'personal' and 'impersonal' acts by a local de facto government because it 'does not correspond with that between legitimate and illegitimate exercise of power'.[693] In other

[685] ILC, Ago Report, 1972, p. 130, para. 156.

[686] Ibid.

[687] Ibid., para. 186:

> while a State might conceivably acknowledge that it is bound by certain obligations deriving from *lawful* routine acts of administration performed by the organs of an insurrectional government in territory formerly under its administration, it is much harder to conceive that it would do likewise in the case of obligations arising out of *wrongful* acts by the same organs; it is not surprising that there is not a single case to be cited in practice. (emphasis added).

[688] The comment was made in a section dealing with the different question of rebels *successfully* establishing a new government.

[689] ILC, Ago Report, 1972, p. 146, para. 200, emphasis added.

[690] Ibid., p. 146, para. 200, emphasis added. Ago also noted (ibid., p. 142, para. 186) that 'it is not surprising that there is not a single case to be cited in practice' of a State declaring to be bound by wrongful acts committed by the rebels.

[691] Akehurst, 'State Responsibility', p. 49, fn. 3.

[692] See Section 3.1.6.

[693] O'Connell, *International Law* p. 970. See also: O'Connell, *International Law* (1970), p. 91:

> the distinction between 'personal' and 'impersonal' acts of government is not strictly between acts incidental to a legitimate exercise of sovereign power, and acts of a delictual character because, on the one hand, the State is liable for such wrongful actions on the part of the *de facto* governmental authorities as the cancellation of concessions, and, on the other, it is not

words, according to him, not all 'personal' acts of rebels are considered as an illegitimate exercise of power. He gives the example of a contract for the supply of weapons to the revolutionary government, for which a State should not be liable because it is considered as a 'personal' act by rebels.[694] Yet, in his view, 'this is no less legitimate an exercise of governmental authority than the purchase of school desks or stationery'.[695] He also believes that there is no perfect equation between 'impersonal' acts by rebels and a legitimate exercise of power. Thus, a 'State is liable for such wrongful actions on the part of the *de facto* governmental authorities as the cancellation of concessions.'[696] For him, 'the law should be indifferent towards the organisation which utilises the faculties of government, provided it is in fact a government'.[697] As a result, in his view, 'if the rebels constitute a *de facto* government at the relevant times and place the State would be liable for their acts, personal or otherwise'.[698]

Whether or not one agrees with the strict distinction between so-called 'personal' and 'impersonal' acts, it remains that there are solid reasons (and plenty of cases) supporting Rule no. 4A whereby a State is bound by the governmental 'routine activities' performed by the rebels when they are acting as a local de facto government.[699] Many writers support this general proposition.[700] The US Restatement highlights this point very clearly, to which I concur: '[A State] is responsible as well for the conduct of any revolutionary regime that has control over part of the state's territory as regards ordinary domestic legislation, administrative acts, or judicial decisions, but not for acts having as their principal objective furthering or maintaining that [revolutionary] regime's control.'[701]

> liable for contracts for the supply of arms to the revolutionary government, although this is no less legitimate an exercise of governmental authority than the purchase of school desks or stationery. (referred to in Morris, 'Revolutionary Movements', p. 732)

694 See also: O'Connell, *International Law* (1970), p. 91 (referred to in Morris, ibid.).

695 Ibid.

696 Ibid.

697 O'Connell, *International Law*, p. 969.

698 Ibid., p. 970.

699 For a detailed analysis, see: Silvanie, *Responsibility of States*, p. 84 ff.

700 Piguet, *La Guerre civile en droit international*, p. 94, 145; Ganzory, 'International Claims and Insurgence', p. 85–6; De Visscher, *Théories et réalités*, p. 348–9; Fortin, 'The Relevance of Article 9', p. 383 ('The case law reviewed above supports the idea that the "impersonal" governmental acts of an armed group may be considered acts of State').

701 *Restatement (Third), Foreign Relations Law of the United States* (Vol. I, St. Paul, American Law Institute Publ., 1987), § 207, comment (b), p. 97. See also: Houghton, 'The Responsibility of the State', p. 265: 'the laws enacted by a local *de facto* government

The next sections examine which types of acts performed by rebels can be considered as *lawful* 'routine activities'. I will first examine taxes, customs duties, debts and loans (Section 3.1.5.2) which will be followed by an assessment of State contracts and concession agreements (Section 3.1.5.3). Finally, while unlawful acts of expropriation done by the rebels cannot be considered as 'routine' governmental activities, I will examine whether the State should nevertheless be bound by such acts in some specific circumstances (Section 3.1.6).

Before turning to these issues, a few words should be said about the scope of Article 9 of the ILC Articles. The provision concerns the specific situation where 'a person or group of persons' is 'exercising elements of the governmental authority in the absence or default of the official authorities' in circumstances such as to call for the exercise of those elements of authority.[702] The ILC Commentaries emphasized the 'exceptional nature of the circumstances envisaged' under this provision, adding that 'such cases occur only rarely'.[703] One example mentioned in the ILC Commentaries is the *Yeager* case where the Iran–US Claims Tribunal held that the Revolutionary Guards 'exercised elements of governmental authority in the absence of official authorities, in operations of which the new Government must have had knowledge and to which it did not specifically object'.[704] In a very ambiguous passage (in the section dealing with Article 10), the ILC Commentaries refers to the acts of 'unsuccessful insurrectional movements' which may be

of ordinary domestic concern will usually be upheld by a subsequent *de jure* government, provided they are not hostile to the subsequent government'.

702 It reads as follows: '[t]he conduct of a person or group of persons shall be considered an act of a State under international law if the person or group of persons is in fact exercising elements of the governmental authority in the absence or default of the official authorities and in circumstances such as to call for the exercise of those elements of authority'. The scope of this provision is examined in Olivier de Frouville, 'Attribution of Conduct to the State: Private Individuals', in James Crawford, Alain Pellet, Simon Olleson and Kate Parlett (eds.), *The Law of International Responsibility* (Oxford University Press, 2010), p. 271 ff.

703 ILC, Commentaries, 2001, p. 49, para. 1. Reference is made to situations occurring 'during revolution, armed conflict or foreign occupation, where the regular authorities dissolve, are disintegrating, have been suppressed or are for the time being inoperative' (ibid.) The ILC also notes that this is a situation which does not involve a 'general' de facto government (the point is highlighted in Crawford, *State Responsibility*, p. 168) and that it 'presuppose[s] the existence of a Government in office and of State machinery whose place is taken by irregulars or whose action is supplemented in certain cases', adding that 'this may happen on part of the territory of a State which is for the time being out of control, or in other specific circumstances' (ibid., para. 4).

704 *Kenneth P. Yeager, a claim of less than US$250,000 presented by the United States of America* v. *The Islamic Republic of Iran*, Iran–US Claims Tribunal, Case No. 10199 (324-10199-l), Partial Award, 2 November 1987, para. 43.

attributed to a State 'in the special circumstances envisaged by Article 9'.[705] The question as to whether or not Article 9 can actually apply to armed groups in the context of civil wars is controversial.[706] It is noteworthy that the ILC Commentary on Article 9 contains no mention of the potential application of Article 9 to armed groups. While the question is beyond the scope of this book, I believe that the better view (expressed by Crawford himself in subsequent writing)[707] is that Article 9 does *not* apply to the specific case of an insurgent movement which is actually *fighting against* the general government to establish a new government.[708] In other words, the 'routine' activities' examined in the next sections are not those of 'a person or group of persons' covered by Article 9.

3.1.5.2 Taxes, Customs Duties, Debts and Loans

In a detailed analysis, Morris concluded that 'generally speaking, a local *de facto* government can bind future governments, but only to a limited extent; these limits are geographic, substantive, and temporal'.[709] Most

705 ILC, Commentaries, 2001, p. 50, para. 2.

706 For a detailed analysis, see: Fortin, 'The Relevance of Article 9', p. 383.

707 Crawford, *State Responsibility*, p. 168, examining Article 9: '[b]y contrast, if the governmental functions in question are exercised by an insurrectionist movement which has not established secure control of the state or which controls only some of its territory, responsibility will not attach to the state unless the insurrectionist movement succeeds in establishing a new government, a point discussed below in the context of ARSIWA Article 10'. The remark strongly suggests that Article 9 does not deal at all with insurrectionist movements.

708 Gérard Cahin, 'The Responsibility of Other Entities: Armed Bands and Criminal Groups', in James Crawford, Alain Pellet, Simon Olleson and Kate Parlett (eds.), *The Law of International Responsibility* (Oxford University Press, 2010), p. 335: '[Article 9 is] also apt to cover acts falling *outside* the hypothesis of attribution discussed in the previous paragraphs, where an insurrectional movement succeeds in its struggle and forms a new government or State' (emphasis added). See also: Veronika Bílková, 'Establishing Direct Responsibility of Armed Opposition Groups for Violations of International Humanitarian Law?', in N. Gal-Or, C. Ryngaert and M. Noortmann (eds.), *Responsibilities of the Non-State Actor in Armed Conflict and the Market Place* (Leiden, Brill Nijhoff, 2015), p. 269, indicating that the provision applies when 'the private actor exercises elements of the governmental authority solely or primarily because it seeks to replace, on a temporary basis, the absent or defaulted government, manifesting a bona fide attitude' and adding, however, that 'the substitution could not take place in the situation in which the [armed group] would have rendered the government absent or deficient in the first place – then, the bona fine attitude would be absent'. On the contrary, Fortin, 'The Relevance of Article 9', p. 378, argues that acts of insurrectional movements can, when some conditions are fulfilled, fall under Article 9 ('Article 9 could apply to the acts of a local *de facto* government set up by an insurgent group, existing contemporaneously with the legal government, and controlling territory in the absence of that government').

709 Morris, 'Revolutionary Movements', p. 729. She refers to the first limitation as meaning that 'the power of a local *de facto* government to bind the State is, unsurprisingly,

relevant for the present purpose is the 'ability of a local *de facto* government to collect taxes, customs duties, and other sums due to the State within the territory it controls during the period of its occupancy'.[710] This principle has been recognized by the *Socony Vacuum Oil Co. Claim*: '[a] local *de facto* government can, of course, perform valid acts pertaining to the civil administration of the occupied territory such as the collection of taxes, seize property belonging to the state, receive money owed the state, etc'.[711] As mentioned above, this is indeed the conclusion reached by Italian courts in the context of the establishment of the so-called Italian 'Social Republic' towards the end of the Second World War.[712] The State is considered bound by these 'impersonal' acts after the rebels have been defeated because these acts are deemed as a 'valid exercise of governmental power'[713] by a 'local *de facto* government'.[714] As a result, once it has regained control over the territory which used to be governed by the rebels, the government 'may not require aliens who have already satisfied these obligations to pay the new government a second time'.[715]

This basic proposition is supported by many writers with respect to taxes and customs duties imposed by rebels.[716] A number of tribunals have come

coextensive with the territory under its control' (citing *Central & South American Telegraph Co.* case, US–Chile Claims Commission, in Moore, *History and Digest of the International Arbitrations* (vol. III), p. 29). The third limitation (Morris, ibid., p. 733) is that the power of local *de facto* governments to create obligations binding on the State is temporal: 'a government may only bind successors while it exercises effective control'.

710 Morris, 'Revolutionary Movements', p. 730, referring to: *United States* v. *Rice*, US Supreme Court, 17 U.S. (4 Wheat.) 246 (1819).

711 *Socony Vacuum Oil Co. Claim*, US Foreign Claims Settlement Commission, Award, 1954, in *Settlements of Claims*, 1949–1955, p. 77; *ILR* (1954), p. 55, at p. 61. But in this case, the Commission was concerned 'only with invalid acts, such as the use of and damage to foreign owned property', for which it held that the State could not be held liable.

712 A number of cases are mentioned above in Section 3.1.4.2.1, in fine. One example is *Galatioto* v. *Ochoa* Italy, Court of Cassation (1945) *Foro Italiano*, 69 (1944–46), 1,217 *Annual Digest* (1946) Case 18.

713 O'Connell, *International Law*, p. 970, referring specifically to taxation.

714 Silvanie, 'Responsibility of States for Acts of Insurgent Governments', p. 95: '[f]or the purpose of taxes and customs duties such insurgents were regarded as local *de facto* governments, and hence taxpayers and merchants were protected in dealing with them on the spot'.

715 Morris, 'Revolutionary Movements', p. 730.

716 See inter alia: Borchard, 'International Pecuniary Claims against Mexico', p. 343–4:

> Foreigners must perforce submit to the power which thus exercises jurisdiction, and a subsequent *de jure* government cannot expose them to penalties for acts which were lawful and enforced by the *de facto* government when done. . . . The collection of taxes and customs duties within the territory and during the period of occupancy of the local *de facto* government relieves merchants and

to the same conclusion.[717] One relevant example is the *Guastini* case involving Mr Guastini, an Italian national, paying a tax enabling him to exercise a professional activity which he had paid to a temporary insurgent government controlling the town of El Pilar in Venezuela.[718] Once the central government regained control of the city its agents forced Mr Guastini to pay the license fee a second time. Mr Guastini brought a claim before the Italy-Venezuela Mixed Commission for a refund of the second payment. Umpire Ralston explained that at the time 'the revolutionary officials' of the region were undertaking the role of the 'displaced the legitimate authorities'.[719] Umpire Ralston also mentioned that 'money paid, therefore to the *de facto* authorities in the shape of public dues must be considered as lawfully paid, and receipts given by them regarded as sufficient to discharge the obligations to which they relate'.[720] He added that 'any other view would compel the

> tax-payers from a subsequent second payment upon the same goods to the succeeding *de jure* government.

See also, Ganzory, 'International Claims and Insurgence', p. 86 ff.; Silvanie, 'Responsibility of States for Acts of Insurgent Governments', p. 93:

> The rule that the state is not bound by acts and contracts of unsuccessful insurgents was, for the reasons stated above, generally applied by international tribunals until the recent Mexican arbitrations. To this rule only one important exception was recognized in these early decisions, and that exception dealt with taxes and customs duties collected by unsuccessful insurgents. The reported cases agree that taxes and duties paid by taxpayers and merchants to insurgent authorities in temporary control of a port or a section of the territory of the state cannot be collected for a second time by the restored government.

See also: O'Connell, *International Law*, p. 970, indicating that once the rebellion has been crashed, the central government is prevented 'from subsequently claiming the same taxes' in cases where 'the taxes collected are applied to ordinary governmental purposes'. For a detailed analysis, see: Silvanie, *Responsibility of States*, p. 104 ff.

717 Piguet, *La Guerre civile en droit international*, p. 118, 94 citing the case of *Sazerac de Forge et fils*, US–French Claims Commission, in Moore, *History and Digest of the International Arbitrations* (vol. III), p. 2781.

718 *Guastini* case, Italy–Venezuela Claims Commission, UNRIAA 10, p. 580.

719 Ibid., p. 580:

> During the period for which taxes were collected by the revolutionary government, the legitimate government ... performed no acts of government in El Pilar. It did not insure personal protection, carry on schools, attend to the needs of the poor, conduct courts, maintain streets and roads, look after the public health, etc. The revolutionary officials, whether they efficiently performed these duties or not during the time in question, displaced the legitimate authorities and undertook their performance.

720 Ibid.

taxpayer to determine at his own peril the validity of the acts of those exercising public functions in a regular manner'.[721] As a result, he concluded that 'the legitimate government cannot enforce a second payment of taxes once paid to revolutionary authorities when the latter were for the time being at the place in question the *de facto* government'.[722] The same principle has also been recognized in the *Santa Clara Estates Co* case decided by the UK–Venezuela Mixed Commission.[723]

Debts and loans are a different matter than taxes and customs duties imposed by rebels. Thus, according to Morris 'a succeeding government is not liable for debts contracted by a displaced local *de facto* government'.[724] As noted a while ago by Borchard, 'a person dealing with [a local *de facto* government] assumes the risk of his enterprise'.[725] In fact, a loan granted by a foreign investor to rebels is generally considered to be a 'personal' act for the benefits of the rebels and the pursuit of the revolution. It is not a 'routine activity' of government (one potential exception

[721] Ibid.

[722] Ibid., p. 561.

[723] *Santa Clara Estates Case (Supplementary Claim)*, UK–Venezuela Mixed Commission, UNRIAA 9, p. 455: '[t]he titular government has no right to collect taxes on property which have already been paid to a revolutionary government which had gained control over the portion of the national territory wherein the property is located, and taxes so collected must be returned'. See also, at p. 458:

> It is incontestably true that with the duty to pay public taxes flows the right of protection and the conscientious and careful discharge of all imposed public duties by the Government to which this tribute is made; that with the right to demand and exact revenue for the support of government stands the correlative duty to be competent and willing to discharge its public functions and conserve the welfare of the taxpayer, and that the one can not rightfully or lawfully exist in the absence of the other; but we have found it to be historically true that the Government of Venezuela was neither competent nor present to perform in any part its governmental functions at the place and within the period in question. They had wholly lost their sovereignty over this district and it was wholly out of their control and independent of the titular government, and the attempt to obtain or the obtaining of a second payment of public dues does not disturb the revolutionary status, while the original payment of taxes to the revolutionary government only makes more emphatic its complete control of the situation during the period in question.

The case is examined in Ganzory, 'International Claims and Insurgence', p. 87.

[724] Morris, 'Revolutionary Movements', p. 731. See also: Houghton, 'The Responsibility of the State', p. 257: '[a]s a general rule, a succeeding *de jure* government is not liable for debts contracted by a displaced local *de facto* government, and persons who deal with such a government assume the risk of the enterprise', citing many cases.

[725] Borchard, 'International Pecuniary Claims against Mexico', p. 345.

mentioned by Silvanie[726] is when that State 'received benefits' from a loan made to rebels).[727] Thus, Silvanie noted that 'a loan with an insurgent government which fails of success is a contract with a debtor which dies, leaving, in contemplation of international law, neither heirs nor assets'.[728] The same analogy has been made a long time ago by Moore for whom, 'those who lend money to insurgents take the risk of their failure', adding that 'whether prompted by the hope of gain or by sympathy with the cause is the nature of a bet that the insurrection will succeed' and 'if the cause is lost, equally so is the stake; and neither victor nor vanquished can be reproached'.[729]

Silvanie cited several cases supporting the basic principle that a government is not responsible for unpaid loans given by foreigners to (ultimately unsuccessful) rebels.[730] Relevant examples include the *Henriquez* case[731] and the *Jarvis* case.[732] In the *Acquatella, Bianchi et al.* case, Commissioner

726 Silvanie, 'Responsibility of States for Acts of Insurgent Governments', p. 100–1, giving this example: 'the state is bound if it derives benefits from a loan made to unsuccessful insurgents, that is, if the loan in question is used for a public purpose instead of for purposes of the civil war'. A number of other exceptions are mentioned in Silvanie, *Responsibility of States*, p. 19 ff.

727 *Hopkins* case, 1926, p. 47, referring to Mexico being bound by the acts of the rebels acting as the de facto government 'in the discharge of its usual and ordinary functions' as well as to 'the extent that it received benefits from transactions of an unusual nature'.

728 Silvanie, *Responsibility of States*, p. 12.

729 Letter of John Bassett Moore to the New York Times, 25 July 1932, dealing with Confederates debts, quoted in Silvanie, *Responsibility of States*, p. 11.

730 Silvanie, 'Responsibility of States for Acts of Insurgent Governments', p. 90 ff.:

> For example, the United States and Mexican Claims Commission of 1868 held in the Cuculla case, that Mexico was not bound by loans made by an American citizen to General Zuloaga and his partisans who were engaged in an unsuccessful civil war against the constitutional government in 1858; in the Barrett case the British-American Claims Commission of 1871 held that the United States was not bound by loans made by British subjects to the Confederate Government during the Civil War; and during the Venezuelan Arbitrations of 1903 the United States and Venezuelan Commission in the Jarvis case, and the Netherlands-Venezuelan Commission in the Henriquez case, held that Venezuela was not bound by loans made to unsuccessful insurgents by the citizens of the United States and The Netherlands.

He cited material from: Moore, *History and Digest of the International Arbitrations* (vol. III), p. 2873–81, 3477–83, 2900–1; Ralston, *Venezuelan Arbitrations of 1903*, p. 145, 896. These cases are examined in detail in his book (Silvanie, *Responsibility of States for Acts*, p. 11), noting that the situation is, of course, different in the event that the rebels are successful.

731 *Henriquez* case, Netherlands–Venezuela Claims Commission, 1903, Opinion of the Umpire, UNRIAA 10, p. 713, 714.

732 *Jarvis* case, US–Venezuela Claims Commission, in Ralston, *Venezuelan Arbitrations of 1903*, p. 150.

Paul explained that 'claims based on negotiations, loans contracted between revolutionary chiefs and private individuals, as well as those for forced requisitions and damages sustained at the hands of revolutionary troops by neutrals, do not entail the liability of the Government of Venezuela'.[733] He added that 'it would be absurd to assume that the Government of Venezuela is compelled to reimburse the money and supplies used by the revolutionary leaders to prolong the struggle, thus contributing to the resistance which cost the Republic 1,500 of her sons'.[734] Another good illustration of the principle is the *Barrett* case decided by the US–Great Britain Mixed Claims Commission of 1871 in the context of the failed attempt by the Confederate States to secede from the United States during the American Civil War (a case further discussed below in Part II).[735] The case involved Mr Barrett, a British citizen residing in England, who owned a cotton-loan bond issued by the Confederate States. During the war, the United States seized all the public assets of the Confederate States, which prevented them from paying Mr Barrett. The Commission held that loan agreements signed by the (ultimately unsuccessful) rebels with foreign nationals during the insurgency were not attributable to the State fighting them. The Commission explained that foreigners contracting with rebels should assume the risk of such ventures.[736]

3.1.5.3 Contracts and Concession Agreements

One controversial question that is especially relevant in the field of investment arbitration is whether so-called 'impersonal' acts by a local de facto government actually cover *contracts* signed by the insurgents during the period when they controlled part of the territory. In other words, once the rebels are defeated, what happens to the contracts signed by them with foreign investors?[737]

733 *Acquatella, Bianchi et al.* case, France–Venezuela Mixed Claims Commission, Commissioner Paul, UNRIAA 10, p. 5, at p. 7, referring to a quote taken from an article by M. Becker published in *Revue de Droit International* 7 (1875), p. 714.

734 Ibid., p. 9.

735 *Edward Alfred Barrett* v. *the United States*, American–British Commission under the treaty of 8 May 1871, Case No. 18, in Moore, *History and Digest of the International Arbitrations* (vol. III), p. 2900–1, UNRIAA 29, p. 137.

736 Ibid.: '[p]ersons contracting with the so-called Confederate States voluntarily assumed the risk of [their] failure, and accepted its obligations, subject to the paramount rights of the parent state by force to crush the rebel organization, and seize all its assets and property, whether hypothecated by it or not to its creditors'.

737 I have examined elsewhere the other question about the fate of *State contracts* in the different context of State succession where a new State is created. See: Dumberry, *A Guide to State Succession in International Investment Law*, p. 273 ff.; Patrick Dumberry,

At the outset, it is clear that *during* the period of insurrection and until the final outcome is known (i.e. whether the rebels are successful or not), such contracts are *not* binding on the central government. This is because the government no longer exercises control over the territory where the rebels have established a de facto government.[738] As mentioned above,[739] foreign investors may have good reasons for hoping that the insurgents do succeed in their efforts to establish a new government. Whenever the rebels are successful, their acts done during the insurgency, including contracts signed with foreign investors, are attributable to the State (Rule no. 2).[740] But, what if the rebels are *not* successful at establishing a new government? Some writers have suggested that the fate of contracts signed by rebels is rather unclear and that investors should therefore be cautious when contracting with them.[741]

In a detailed study of the question, Silvanie referred to a few cases where the State was held *not* responsible for 'concessions and alienations of state property made by unsuccessful insurgents' with foreign nationals during an insurgency.[742] Yet, he also pointed out that these tribunals

'State Succession to State Contracts: A New Framework of Analysis for an Unexplored Question', *J. World Invest. & Trade* 19 (2018), p. 1–32.

738 Al-Rashid *et al.*, 'Investment Claims', p. 188.

739 See Section 3.1.3.

740 The question was examined in Section 2.2.4.2.

741 Morris, 'Revolutionary Movements', p. 750: '[s]ome jurisprudence suggests that [the local *de facto* government] may also wield the authority of the State with respect to contracts concerning State property within their control, but this right is far from certain and investors should approach contract (re)negotiations with a local *de facto* government with great caution'. See also: Mohtashami, 'Protecting the Legitimacy of the Arbitral Process', p. 623; Al-Rashid *et al.*, 'Investment Claims', p. 188 ('Unless and until the movement emerges as a government, its actions are not likely to bind the nation. Accordingly, an investor that chooses to do business with insurgents assumes the risk of its enterprise – it cannot expect the nation to be responsible for its improvidence. It follows that contracts concluded with belligerents may not be binding on the nation's *de jure* government. In such circumstances, if after regaining control the government seizes the belligerents' property, it will be taking such property free of creditors' claims').

742 Silvanie, 'Responsibility of States of Insurgent Governments', p. 90. See also, Silvanie, *Responsibility of States*, p. 62 ff., referring (at ibid., p. 81 ff.) to the *Raborg* case, United States–Peruvian Claims Commission of 1863 (in Moore, *History and Digest of the International Arbitrations* (vol. II), p. 1613) involving a contract under which a US national advanced money to the rebels for the exportation of guano. The commission held that the contract was illegal because the Claimant had breached its obligation of neutrality in the conflict. In his book (p. 68 ff.) he also referred to the cases of the *Georgiana and the Lizzie Thompson* involving concessions and alienations of State-owned guano deposits by the unsuccessful insurgent government of General Vivanco to certain American citizens in 1857 (in Moore, *History and Digest of the International Arbitrations* (vol. II), p. 1593). Silvanie, ibid., p. 75–6 explained that the King of Belgium declined his appointment as sole arbitrator in this case, and explained to the American

reached such conclusions on the grounds that these contracts were made in violation of domestic laws.[743] Thus, he noted that the important question of whether 'unsuccessful insurgents could bind the State in the matter of concessions and alienations was discussed in a general way' in these awards and that, consequently, 'no definitive conclusions appear to have been reached on this point'.[744] Most importantly, Silvanie also referred to a number of other cases which have 'extended the rule of state liability for acts of unsuccessful insurgents' beyond taxes and customs duties and 'held the state liable for insurgent contracts benefiting the state and for insurgent acts of governmental routine'.[745] The first, and most important, of these cases is the *Hopkins* case.

The *Hopkins* case involved the Claimant purchasing postal money orders from the Mexican Government and later presented them to the Mexican Authorities for payment.[746] The payment was refused on the grounds that the postal money orders had been issued by the so-called 'Huerta Government'. The General Claims Commission considered the Huerta administration as *unsuccessful* insurgents because it was at no time in control of the State. The Government of Mexico therefore considered the acts of the Huerta administration to be illegal and, therefore, not binding on Mexico. At the outset of its analysis of the question, the Commission made this first important statement:

> Before considering the question of the validity or nullity of acts done by or contracts entered into with a government administration of this character it is necessary to state at once the impossibility of treating alike all acts done by such an administration or all transactions entered into by an individual with it. There seems to be a tendency both in jurisprudence and in literature to do so, to declare that all acts of a given administration, the

Minister to Belgium that he would have decided against the United States. The US ultimately accepted his view that Peru was not bound by the concessions. In his book (p. 62), he also mentions the case of *Beales, Nobles and Garrison*, US–Venezuelan Claims Commission of 1885, in Moore, *History and Digest of the International Arbitrations* (vol. IV), p. 3548–64, holding that Venezuela was not bound by contracts made by the (ultimately) unsuccessful insurgent government of General Paez in 1863 with American citizens for the purpose of granting concessions for a steamship service, and for a project of immigration and colonization which involved the alienation of extensive lands in Venezuela. The Commission held that the insurgents had not established themselves as a de facto government and did not control much of the country. In any event, the contracts were considered illegal under the constitution of Venezuela.

743 Silvanie, *Responsibility of States*, p. 61.

744 Ibid., p. 62.

745 Silvanie, 'Responsibility of States for Acts of Insurgent Governments', p. 95.

746 *Hopkins* case, 1926, p. 41 ff.

> legality of which is doubtful, must have been either valid or void. Facts and practice, however, point in a different direction.[747]

As noted by Silvanie,

> instead of following the precedents established by previous arbitral tribunals and holding the state not bound by contractual obligations and tortious acts of unsuccessful insurgents as a matter of general principle, the Commission declared that in order to establish state liability for acts and contracts of such insurgents 'the character of each transaction must be judged and determined by the facts of the particular case'.[748]

The Commission indicated that 'the greater part of governmental machinery of every modern country is not affected by changes in the higher administrative officers'.[749] Thus, many activities,[750] such as the acceptance of money orders, 'must go on, without being affected by new elections, government crises, dissolutions of parliament and even state strokes'.[751] Indeed, these activities do not have the 'personal character' that the 'voluntary undertaking to provide a revolutionary administration with money or arms or munitions' would have.[752] The Commission added that

[747] Ibid., p. 43.

[748] Silvanie, 'Responsibility of States for Acts of Insurgent Governments', p. 96.

[749] *Hopkins* case, 1926, p. 43.

[750] Ibid., referring to: '[t]he sale of postage stamps, the registration of letters, the acceptance of money orders and telegrams (where post and telegraph are government services), the sale of railroad tickets (where railroads are operated by the Government), the registration of births, deaths, and marriages, even many rulings by the police and the collection of several types of taxes'.

[751] Ibid., p. 43.

[752] Ibid.:

> The difficulty of distinguishing between the government itself and the administration of that government arises at the point where the voluntary dealings and relations between the individual and the government agencies assume a personal character in support of the particular agencies administering the government for the time being. To this class belong voluntary undertakings to provide a revolutionary administration with money or arms or munitions and the like. But the ordinary agencies, departments, and bureaus of the government must continue to function notwithstanding its principal administrative offices may be in the hands of usurpers, and in such a case the sale and delivery to these necessary and legitimate agencies of supplies, merchandise, and the like, to enable the government itself in its unpersonal aspect to function is a very different transaction from one having for its object the support of an individual or group of individuals seeking to maintain themselves in office. The character of each transaction must be judged and determined by the facts of the particular case.

> a resident in Mexico who cleans the government bureaus or pays his school fee to the administration does not and can not take into consideration the regularity or even legality of the present administration and the present congress; his business is not one with personal rulers, not one with a specific administration, but one with the Government itself in its unpersonal aspect.[753]

The application of the principle to the facts of the case led the Commission to the following conclusion: '[i]t is clear that the sale by the Mexican Government to and the purchase by the claimant Hopkins of postal money orders falls within the category of *purely government routine* having no connection with or relation to the individuals administering the Government for the time being'.[754] The contracts were 'unaffected by the character of the Huerta administration' and were therefore 'binding upon the United Mexican States as such'.[755] The same conclusion was reached by that Commission in a number of other cases involving money orders.[756]

Silvanie also referred to a number of other cases where the General Claims Commission (the same which rendered the *Hopkins* award) considered that 'ordinary commercial contracts for the purchase and sale of goods and merchandise between different departments and bureaus of the Huerta Administration' (the unsuccessful insurgent authorities) and foreign citizens were 'contracts of government routine and therefore binding on Mexico'.[757]

[753] Ibid.

[754] Ibid., p. 43–4, emphasis added.

[755] Ibid., p. 46.

[756] Silvanie, 'Responsibility of States for Acts of Insurgent Governments', p. 98, citing several cases. These cases are examined in Silvanie, *Responsibility of States*, p. 91 ff.

[757] Silvanie, 'Responsibility of States for Acts of Insurgent Governments', p. 98:

> [t]he Mexican Government was held liable, for instance, for certain automobile accessories purchased by and services relating to the repair of automobiles rendered to the Huerta government between the years of 1913 and 1914; for printing machinery, paper envelopes, and other goods sold to and purchased by various departments of the Mexican Government between 1912 and 1914, a part of the goods being sold and delivered during the period of the Huerta Administration; for certain linotype machine supplies, a book sewing machine, together with hooks and eye needles, and various kinds of press boards, sold and delivered to different departments of the Mexican Government in 1913; for a number of school benches ordered by and delivered to the Mexican Ministry of Public Instruction and Fine Arts during the period from December, 1913, to February, 1914; and for household furniture, fittings, fixtures, equipment, and utilities purchased during the same period by departments and bureaus of the Mexican Government.

See also, p. 99: '[t]he Commission held that these commercial contracts were contracts of government routine with the Mexican Government as an abstract entity and had nothing

Another noteworthy case is *Peerless Motor Car Co.* involving a contract for the purchase of two automobile ambulances from an American corporation by the Chief of the Military services of the Department of War and Navy of the Huerta government (the ultimately unsuccessful insurgents).[758] Commissioner Nielsen of the United States considered that the contract was a routine transaction of government by the Huerta Administration and, therefore, that it was binding on Mexico.[759] While the President Commissioner did not consider the purchase of ambulances as 'part of the ordinary routine of government business' per se, he nevertheless considered it 'much more akin to a transaction of government routine (the one extreme) than to any kind of voluntary undertaking "having for its object the support of an individual or group of individuals seeking to maintain themselves in office" (the other extreme)'.[760] This decision has been criticized for being 'too broad' in terms of the limits of the concept of act of government routine.[761] In fact, ambulances purchased by the army of an insurgent government 'may be considered as particularly useful from a military point of view' when fighting against the legitimate government and could, therefore, be regarded as 'war material' rather than an act of government routine.[762]

I believe, just like many other writers, that a State should be bound by 'all contractual obligations which can be considered as routine administrative transactions'.[763] This is also the position of O'Connell, for whom (citing

to do with the Huerta Administration in its personal aspect'. These cases are examined in Silvanie, *Responsibility of States*, p. 92 ff.

758 *Peerless Motor Car Co.* case, US–Mexico Claims Commission, 13 May 1927, in *Opinions*, 1927, p. 303–5 (also in *AJIL* 22 (1928), p. 180–1).

759 Ibid., Opinions of Commissioners, p. 303, 304:

> [i]n the view I take of this case it is unnecessary to consider the point as to the responsibility of Mexico grounded on the contention of the United States that it may be assumed from the record that Mexican authorities in power following the administration of General Huerta made use of the cars delivered by the company. Nor is it necessary to consider the Mexican Government's contention as to the character of the ambulances as war material. The United States contends, among other things, that the purchase of these motor ambulances was an unpersonal act, and that therefore, under the principles laid down in the Hopkins case … the Government of Mexico is liable for the purchase price of the ambulances. I am of the opinion that the contention is sound, and that an award should therefore be rendered in favor of the United States.

760 Ibid., Opinions of Commissioners, 1927, p. 304–5.

761 Silvanie, *Responsibility of States*, p. 96.

762 Ibid., p. 96.

763 de Beus, *The Jurisprudence of the General Claims Commission*, p. 113: '[i]n principle there exists no responsibility of a State under international law for damage caused by

the *Hopkins* case) 'all obligations perfunctorily incurred by the insurgents in the course of administration are binding' on the State.[764] Silvanie explained that a State should be bound by contracts signed by insurgents which are considered as 'governmental routine' since these acts are truly acts *of the State,* rather than that of a specific government.[765]

What about other contracts signed by an insurgent de facto government with foreign investors which *cannot* be considered as 'routine administrative transactions', such as concession contracts regarding the exploitation of natural resources? Whether rebels have any rights under international law to exploit such resources during an insurrection is controversial (and beyond the scope of this book).[766] The question is especially sensitive for third States. It has been noted that they do not

revolutionaries. However liability may be imposed for: A. all contractual obligations which can be considered as routine administrative transactions (as distinct from personal acts of a particular administration), whether undertaken by a local or by a general illegal government'.

764 O'Connell, *International Law*, p. 975, noting that the only exception would be for contracts 'for the purpose of overthrowing the central government'.

765 Silvanie, 'Responsibility of States for Acts of Insurgent Governments', p. 102:

> The result obtained in the recent Mexican cases is in many respects in contrast with that of previous decisions concerning the extent to which the state is bound by acts and contracts of unsuccessful insurgent governments. This difference is doubtless due chiefly to two conflicting views as to the relation of such governments to the state. As already stated, during the nineteenth century international courts of arbitration held as a rule that unsuccessful insurgents had no legal status in international law, that they were not agents or 'authorities' of the state, and that the state, therefore, was not bound by their acts, with the single exception of the collection of taxes and duties. For all intents and purposes unsuccessful insurgents were treated as being quite alien to the state. Apparently there was a failure to distinguish clearly between the state and government. Very often insurgent governments were spoken of as enemies of the state by virtue of the fact that they were enemies of the existing government. State responsibility was defined in the sense of government responsibility. In the Sambiaggio case, for instance, although the Commission was considering the relation of unsuccessful insurgents to the state, it nevertheless continued to speak of the government ... Thus, apparently the ultimate conclusion was reached that unsuccessful insurgents, being enemies of the government, were ipso facto enemies of the state, and hence the state was not bound by their acts. The decisions of the recent Mexican arbitrations, on the other hand, in effect maintain the distinction between the state and the government and speak of state responsibility for acts of unsuccessful insurgents and not of government responsibility. They proceed on the theory that an unsuccessful insurgent government is not alien to the state nor are its acts necessarily meant to destroy the state.

See also, the same position adopted by O'Connell, *International Law*, p. 975.

766 On this question, see: Dam-de Jong, 'Armed Opposition Groups', p. 24.

have the right to enter into contracts with rebels for the exploitation of natural resources unless they have recognized them as the new effective government.[767] The following paragraphs will examine the situation of contracts signed between rebels and private foreign investors.

For Silvanie, the answer depends on the nature of the contract. On the one hand, a State is *not* bound by a concession contract which 'is in some way detrimental to the interests of the State or is done by unsuccessful insurgents in pursuance and in aid of their political aims'.[768] An illustration of this view is the *Claim of Standard-Vacuum Oil Company* against the Soviet Government decided by the US Foreign Claims Settlement Commission. The case involved a contract for the sale of oil and kerosene by the Claimant's predecessor to the Ministry of Ways and Communications of the 'Kolchak government', an insurgent group which de facto controlled the Siberian part of the Russian Empire after the Bolshevik Revolution of 1917. The rebels were fighting against the newly established Soviet government. The award explained that this de facto government controlled the Trans-Siberian Railway, which at the time was 'the main, if not the sole, artery for the transport of troops and military supplies in Siberia'.[769] The Soviet government finally gained control over Siberia in 1919. The Commission thereof considered the claim as involving a contract with unsuccessful rebels and held that: 'in voluntary contractual dealings of a *personal nature*, the unsuccessful revolutionist government cannot bind the government which it sought to overthrow'.[770] The Commission considered that selling oil and kerosene to the rebels for the maintaining and functioning of the Trans-Siberian Railway, which was at that time a highly strategic assets for their military struggle, was a 'personal' act. It is the 'personal' nature of the contract that made it non-binding on the State.

For Silvanie, on the other hand, a State should be bound by a contract which is 'not detrimental to the State' and which may be 'regarded as "a

[767] Ibid., p. 10–11, also examining whether 'peoples' can be considered, in some circumstances, as subjects and beneficiaries of the right to sovereignty over public natural resources.

[768] Silvanie, *Responsibility of States*, p. 61, adding that a State is not bound by contracts made 'in aid of the rebellion'.

[769] *In the Matter of the Claim of Standard-Vacuum Oil Company*, US Foreign Claims Settlement Commission, Claim No. SOV-1789, Decision No. SOV-2977, Proposed Decision, 26 January 1959, Final Decision, 30 March 1959, MS. Department of State, in Whiteman, *Digest of International Law* (vol. 8), p. 824.

[770] Ibid. (emphasis added), citing this passage from the *Sambiaggio* case, 1903, p. 513: '[r] evolutionists are not the agents of government, and a natural responsibility does not exist. Their acts are committed to destroy the government (in power), and no one should be held responsible for the acts of any enemy attempting his life'.

fair and reasonable exercise of the authority under which it is made"'.[771] For instance, it would be the case 'when the other party to the contract acted in good faith and made expenditures for permanent improvement accruing to *the benefit of the State*'.[772] This is a sound distinction. Thus, acts of a 'personal character' performed by the rebels are not binding on the State precisely because they are not benefiting the State, but only the rebels. As explained by Silvanie,

> all insurgent acts of a discretionary character done in aid of rebellion, such as the purchase of arms and munitions, the borrowing of money for civil war purposes, and the granting of concessions and the forcible taking of property the proceeds of which were actually used to support the revolutionary movement, were held to fall in the category of acts not benefiting the state and therefore not binding on the state.[773]

In other words, the applicable test is whether a given contract can be considered to be of 'public utility' while resulting in some *benefits for the State* itself (not the rebels). Whenever this is the case, the State should be considered bound by the contract, even though it was signed by rebels during the insurgency.[774]

These findings, including the distinction put forward in the previous paragraph, are especially relevant in the context of foreign investments made in countries plagued by civil wars where several insurgent groups may de facto be controlling different parts of the country. Indeed, this situation prevailed in Syria from 2012 until very recently, and at the time

[771] Silvanie, *Responsibility of States*, p. 61.

[772] Ibid., p. 61, emphasis added. He also stated that whenever this is the case, 'the presumption is that the State may be exceptionally bound' by such a contract.

[773] Silvanie, 'Responsibility of States for Acts of Insurgent Governments', p. 103.

[774] Ibid., p. 102–3:

> It is true that unsuccessful insurgents do not become the government of the state; but during the period of the civil war they are, nevertheless, a government, one of two or more coexisting governments in the state. As a government in local control, such insurgents perform practically every function of government. Moreover, the performance of a variety of necessary acts of government by insurgents in time of civil conflict is very largely in the interest of the state. To this extent they should be considered as *de facto* authorities and agents of the state. The answer to the question whether the state is bound by their acts should therefore depend solely on the consideration whether such acts, or any of them, *accrue to the benefit of the state*. If a given insurgent act benefits the state, the state is bound by it; if certain other acts do not benefit the state, the state is not bound. (emphasis added).

of writing this book (end of 2020), it was also the situation existing in Libya and Yemen. Whether or not contracts signed between foreign investors and rebels (which are ultimately unsuccessful in their attempt to overthrow the government) will be binding on the State at the end of the civil war depends on whether such contracts result in some benefits for the State itself (and not the rebels). The concept of 'benefit to the State' will be further examined in the next section.

3.1.6 *Rule No. 4B: A State Is Responsible for the Consequences Arising from an Expropriation Act Committed by Rebels If It Results in Some Benefits for the State*

The previous sections have examined *lawful* acts performed by the rebels during an insurgency. This section examines the fate of one specific *unlawful* act.

As mentioned above, O'Connell takes the position that under Rule no. 3, it is 'illogical' that the government 'as a whole escape[s] liability for acts of violence on the part of the revolutionaries' when they are unsuccessful.[775] In his view, 'the correct position is that the delicts of rebels commit the State to liability, whether the rebels are successful or not, provided that at the relevant times, *they were a government*'.[776] For him, what matters is that the rebels are sometimes, in effect, the only government exercising de facto power over a certain territory. In his view, 'the law should be indifferent towards the organisation which utilises the faculties of government, provided it is in fact a government'.[777] However, in my view, O'Connell's position that the State should be bound by *all* wrongful acts committed by the rebels for the simple reason that they were the de facto government at the time is too broad. Yet, it should be noted that a passage from the *Pinson* award seems to be supporting such a wide-ranging proposition.[778]

[775] O'Connell, *International Law*, p. 969.

[776] Ibid., p. 970, emphasis added.

[777] Ibid.

[778] *Pinson* case, 1928, p. 450: 'Et quant aux *actes des Gouvernements de jure ou de facto*, ou des forces révolutionnaires qui l'ont emporté dans la guerre civile, il ne peut non plus être question de *responsabilité internationale de l'État* des dommages causés par les dits actes que dans les cas où il s'agit, soit d'actes de caractère purement contractuel tels que: prêts, achats, etc., soit de ceux qui appartiennent au domaine intermédiaire entre le droit privé et le droit public, ou d'actes juridiques émanant directement du pouvoir public de l'État, tels que: expropriations, réquisitions, prêts forcés, etc., soit d'actes qui rentrent dans la catégorie des *délits internationaux*, tels que: *pillages de propriétés étrangères, destructions de biens étrangers*

In my view, one important distinction should be made between different types of wrongs committed by rebels depending on their nature. The acts of rebels should not be attributable to the State when they are considered to have a 'personal character'. As noted by Silvanie (and already quoted above),

> all insurgent acts of a discretionary character done in aid of rebellion, such as the purchase of arms and munitions, the borrowing of money for civil war purposes, and the granting of concessions and the *forcible taking of property the proceeds of which were actually used to support the revolutionary movement,* were held to fall in the category of acts not benefiting the state and therefore not binding on the state.[779]

This is a sound proposition. Interestingly, illegal expropriation ('forcible taking of property') is listed as an example of an act having a 'personal character' which is considered not binding on the State. However, as Silvanie rightly noted, this is the case only when the proceeds of the expropriation were used by the rebels to support the revolutionary movement. It is sensible that a State should not be held liable for acts of expropriation taken by the rebels when the property, or the proceeds resulting from it, were actually used for revolutionary purposes. Logically, once the central government has regained control over the expropriated territory, it should not have to provide reparation to the foreign investor whose property had been expropriated by the rebels. It should simply return the property to its owner. It is true that this outcome may be 'unfair' for the injured victim which will get no reparation to cover the period of expropriation.[780] Yet, it would be equally unjust for the

sans nécessité militaire, confiscations de possessions étrangères, bombardements de villes non défendues, qui ont causé la mort d'étrangers, et *d'autres actes délictueux,* formellement qualifiés comme tels entre autres par le Règlement concernant les lois et coutumes de la guerre sur terre de 1907' ('And with regard to the acts of de jure or de facto Governments, or of the revolutionary forces which prevailed in the civil war, there can also be no question of international responsibility of the State for damage caused by such acts except in cases of cases where they are either acts of a purely contractual nature such as: loans, purchases, etc., or those which belong to the intermediary domain between private and public law, or legal acts emanating directly from the public power of the State, such as: expropriations, requisitions, forced loans, etc., *or acts that fall into the category of international crimes, such as: looting of foreign property, destruction of foreign property without military necessity, confiscation of foreign possessions,* bombardment of undefended towns, which caused death foreigners, and other criminal acts, formally qualified as such by, among others, the Regulations Concerning the Laws and Customs of War on Land from 1907') (emphasis added).

779 Silvanie, 'Responsibility of States for Acts of Insurgent Governments', p. 103, emphasis added.

780 It should be added that the question as to whether or not a foreign investor can file a claim for reparation against the insurgent group after its defeat, or any of its members individually, is a matter of domestic law. The question is beyond the scope of this book. In any event, as further examined below, the State has to fulfil its due diligence obligation in relation to the

State to be considered 'responsible' for wrongful acts which were committed by outlaw enemies with the specific aim of overthrowing its government.[781]

Nonetheless, the situation is different when the property or the infrastructure which belonged to a foreign investor (a factory, a road, a dam, a bridge, tunnel, etc.) is *not* used by the rebels for revolutionary purposes or their own personal interests. Thus, what if the infrastructures were actually used in a 'normal' way by the insurgents (acting as de facto government on a portion of the territory), just like any other 'government' would have used them in a situation of non-conflict? This would be the case if, for instance, the roads, dams, bridges, tunnels, were used by the population like in any other country. Thus, what if the proceeds resulting from a pay toll on a road, a bridge, or a tunnel were used by the rebels for public purposes, like education, health care or the building and repairing of infrastructures rather than for buying weapons? What if the factory or the land expropriated was used for legitimate public purposes, like schools and hospitals, instead of being used as a manufacture of weapons or training ground? In my view, these acts could hardly be qualified as having a 'personal character'. As a result, these are situations where the expropriation done by the rebels ultimately resulted in *some benefits* for the State, its territory and its population.

Silvanie mentioned that 'the doctrine that the state is exceptionally bound if it receives benefits from "transactions of an unusual nature" done by an unsuccessful insurgent government in its personal character *was applied also to tortious acts*'.[782] In his book, he refers to this situation (which he qualifies as 'responsibility for confiscated property used for public purposes')[783] as one of the few 'exceptions' to the 'general rule that the State is not liable for damages caused to foreign persons and property by wrongful acts of unsuccessful insurgents' (i.e. Rule no. 3).[784] As explained in the next paragraph, Silvanie cites one example supporting his position.

The *British Shareholders of the Mariposa Company* case,[785] decided by the British–Mexican Claims Commission under the convention of 1926, held that Mexico should be liable for forcible taking of British properties by the rebels. The case involved the federal army's troops taking horses and mules

conduct of rebels (Rule no. 6, see at Section 3.3), which includes an obligation to punish the wrongdoers and provide reparation (the question is examined in Section 3.3.3.2.3).

781 The question was examined in Sections 3.1.2 and 3.1.3.

782 Silvanie, 'Responsibility of States for Acts of Insurgent Governments', p. 101 (emphasis added), quoting *Hopkins* case, 1926, p. 43.

783 Silvanie, *Responsibility of States*, p. 197.

784 Ibid., p. 159.

785 *British Shareholders of the Mariposa Company* case, British–Mexican Claims Commission of 1926, Decisions and Opinions, 6 August 1931, UNRIAA 5, p. 272.

without any payment. The Commission held that Mexico was responsible for such actions. Around the same time, the rebels (the Villistra troops) also confiscated twenty heads of cattle from the Claimant company's ranch 'in order to supply the population of the town of Muzquiz with meat'.[786] The same rebels later 'took charge of the ranch' and left with several horses, three mules and other equipments (provisions, blankets and bedding).[787] Silvanie noted that there was apparently no established federal government at the time (1915) given that the Huerta government had been overthrown and that different groups of rebels (including Villistra troops) were fighting for power.[788] Interestingly, the Commission distinguished the confiscation of the cows from later wrongs. With respect to the former, the Commission seems to have considered that the rebels actually acted as the de facto government in the context of a political vacuum. Given that the cows were confiscated 'in order to supply meat to the population of the town',[789] the Commission concluded that 'it seems a postulate of equity, to award compensation for cattle thus exacted'.[790] Therefore, it held that Mexico should compensate the Claimant for some of the wrongful acts committed by the rebels (stealing cows) even if they were ultimately unsuccessful in their struggle. It did so on the grounds that the property confiscated was used for 'public purposes' by the rebels and that 'the people were benefited by it'.[791] No compensation was awarded for the damages resulting from the other subsequent incidents involving the rebels.

In my view, there should be one (rather limited in scope) 'exception' to Rule no. 3 in the specific context of acts of expropriation done by the rebels when their efforts to overthrow a government end up being unsuccessful.[792] The relevant test is whether an act of expropriation should be considered of 'public utility', and whether it resulted in some *benefits for the State* itself (not the rebels).[793] Whenever this is the case, the State should be considered

[786] Ibid., p. 274.

[787] Ibid., p. 273.

[788] Silvanie, *Responsibility of States*, p. 198.

[789] Ibid., p. 198.

[790] *British Shareholders of the Mariposa Company* case, British–Mexican Claims Commission of 1926, Decisions and Opinions, 6 August 1931, UNRIAA 5, p. 274.

[791] Silvanie, 'Responsibility of States for Acts of Insurgent Governments', p. 101.

[792] In fact, this idea is not truly an 'exception' to Rule no. 3. It is not suggested that the acts committed by the rebels during the insurgency should be *attributable* to the State nor is it argued that the State should be somehow *responsible* for the acts committed by *another entity* against which it was fighting. The idea is simply that in the circumstances described above, the State should take over the *consequences* arising from the commission of wrongful acts by the rebels.

[793] Silvanie, 'Responsibility of States for Acts of Insurgent Governments', p. 102–3.

responsible for the consequences arising from the commission of the wrongful acts by the rebels. The State should not only return the property to its owner, but also provide reparation to the foreign investor. The compensation should cover the period during which the property was used for 'public purposes' during the insurrection. In the examples listed above, the infrastructure will stay in place after the rebels are defeated and it may be that they will continue to be used by the government and the population once the rebels are gone. In such a case, the infrastructure will *continue to benefit* the State, its government, and the population living in that portion of the territory. This is a fortiori a situation where reparation should be provided to the foreign investor.[794]

In my view, this is a fair solution for all actors involved. It will also somewhat mitigate the hardship resulting from the strict application of Rule no. 3. My proposal would thus have the effect of providing some sort of reparation to some victims in the context of at least one type of wrongful acts committed by the rebels.

My proposal is also in line with a well-known 'general principle of law': the principle of unjust enrichment.[795] The concept of unjust enrichment (*enrichissement sans cause*) is intrinsically ambiguous and imprecise.[796] The obligation to compensate for any unjust enrichment does not arise directly from the commission of an act, but derives from a *state of fact*, which may be caused by a legal or an illegal act.[797] As one writer puts it, 'the basis of liability for unjust enrichment is not necessarily linked with any delictual responsibility as such, but is predicated on an injustice which must be remediated'.[798] According to another writer, the principle of unjust enrichment is a remedy used in judicial practice to 'reverse accretions of wealth under circumstances in which contractual or delictual principles would have been unable to reach this result'.[799] As O'Connell puts it, the function of the principle of unjust

794 The government should therefore provide reparation for not returning the property to its owner and continuing to use it for public purposes after the end of the conflict.

795 For an analysis showing that the principle of unjust enrichment is a 'general principle of law', see: Patrick Dumberry, *A Guide to General Principles of Law in International Investment Law* (Oxford University Press, 2020), p. 232.

796 D. P. O'Connell, *The Law of State Succession* (Cambridge University Press, 1956), p. 274.

797 G. C. Rodriguez Iglesias, 'El enriquecimiento sin causa comofundamento de responsabilidad internacional', *REDI* 34 (1982), p. 389.

798 Charles M. Fombad, 'The Principle of Unjustified Enrichment in International Law', *Comp. & Int'l L.J. S. Afr.* 30 (1997), p. 124.

799 Christoph H. Schreuer, 'Unjustified Enrichment in International Law', *Am. J. Comp. L.* 22 (1974), p. 289. See also: *Sea-Land Service, Inc.* v. *Iran, et al.*, Iran–US Claims Tribunal, Award No. 115-33-1, 22 June 1984, in 6 *Iran-US CTR* 149, at p. 169, which indicated that for the

enrichment 'is to mitigate the hardship which would result in certain cases from an application of strict law by applying principles of justice and equity'.[800] As noted above, the 'application of strict law' (Rule no. 3) would result in some clear hardship for the victims of acts of expropriation committed by the rebels. Thus, a wrong would go unpunished and a foreign investor would get no reparation. The concept of unjust enrichment is therefore relevant to the present analysis since it would, in the words of O'Connell, 'mitigate the hardship' resulting from the strict application of Rule no. 3.

In order for a State's action to qualify as an unjust enrichment, the consequence of such an act not only needs (i) to result in its enrichment, but the enrichment must also (ii) be 'unjust' and (iii) to be detrimental to another party.[801] I have examined elsewhere these three conditions in the application of the concept in the context of State succession to State contracts.[802] In my view, the facts mentioned above would fit the definition. Thus, the fact that a State benefited from some infrastructures 'for free' during an insurrection (i.e. without having to provide any compensation to the foreign investor owning the property) should undoubtedly be considered as an 'enrichment'. This is a fortiori the case if the State continues to benefit from the infrastructure 'for free' after the defeat of the rebels. Such an enrichment is also 'unjust'. International practice has considered specific situations to be 'unjust', such as the use of materials belonging to a foreign national by the army of a State,[803] and the use of property by the host State for which no compensation had been given to the foreign national.[804] Expropriation acts

concept of unjust enrichment to apply 'there must be no ... contractual or other remedy available to the injured party whereby he might seek compensation from the party enriched'.

800 D.P. O'Connell, 'Unjustified Enrichment', *Am. J. Comp. L.* 5(1) (1956), p. 16.

801 These different requirements were identified by the Iran–US Claims Tribunal in *Sea-Land Service, Inc.* v. *Iran, et al.*, Iran–US Claims Tribunal, Award No. 115-33-1, 22 June 1984, in 6 *Iran-US CTR* 149, at p. 168-169:

> [t]here are several instances of recourse to the principle of unjust enrichment before international tribunals. There must have been an enrichment of one party to the detriment of the other, and both must arise as a consequence of the same act or event. There must be no justification for the enrichment, and no contractual or other remedy available to the injured party whereby he might seek compensation from the party enriched.

802 Dumberry, *A Guide to State Succession in International Investment Law*, p. 382 ff.

803 *Thomas C. Baker Arbitration*, in Moore, *History and Digest of the International Arbitrations* (vol. II), p. 3668; *Sucrerie de Roustchouk* v. *État Hongrois*, Belgian–Hungarian Mixed Arbitral Tribunal, Award, 29 October 1925, in 5 *Recueil des décisions des tribunaux arbitraux mixtes*, p. 772.

804 *William A. Parker (United States)* v. *Mexico*, US–Mexico General Claims Commission, Award, 31 March 1926, UNRIAA 4, p. 35.

without compensation fall into this category. Finally, the expropriation is clearly detrimental to another party (the foreign investor), who will get no compensation for its confiscated property. This is a case where the enrichment is 'directly linked with and result in an impoverishment on the other side'.[805] Here the State has indeed 'benefited from [a] measure and the foreign interest involved has suffered a loss as a direct result'.[806] This is a case where the benefits gained by the State (having some infrastructure 'for free') are directly linked to the loss suffered by the investor (getting no compensation for its confiscated property).

After the defeat of the rebels, the State is likely to object to providing any compensation to the foreign investor on the simple grounds that the wrongful acts were committed by *another entity*, the rebels. Indeed, a State might rightly question why it should have to pay for the wrongs committed by others. Yet, at the same time, it should be recalled that the existence of an unjust enrichment is a *factual situation* which is not related to the commission of any breach of law. No wrongful act needs to be demonstrated for an unjust enrichment to exist.[807] The concept has often been used in instances involving the infringement of property rights of foreigners in cases where the actions *did not* amount to internationally wrongful acts.[808] What matters is that an enrichment 'has occurred and that it is without legal justification under international law'.[809] Thus, as noted by two writers, unjust enrichment is 'designed to redress undesirable shifts of control over assets which are not covered by other areas of the law', adding that 'typically, a situation giving rise to liability for unjust enrichment would therefore be covered neither by responsibility for a wrongful act nor by an underlying valid agreement'.[810]

805 Fombad, 'The Principle of Unjustified Enrichment', p. 123.

806 Ibid., p. 125.

807 *Sea-Land Service, Inc.* v. *Iran, et al.*, Iran–US Claims Tribunal, Award No. 115-33-1, 22 June 1984, in 6 *Iran-US CTR*, p. 149.

808 Christoph H. Schreuer, 'Unjustified Enrichment', in R. Bernhardt (ed.), *Encyclopedia of Public International Law* (Amsterdam, North Holland, vol. 9, 1986), p. 382. This situation was explained as follows by the Iran–US Claims Tribunal in *Sea-Land Service*, ibid., p. 169:

> [the concept of unjust enrichment] involves a duty to compensate, which is entirely reconcilable with the absence of any inherent unlawfulness of the acts in question. Thus the principle finds an obvious field of application in cases where a foreign investor has sustained a loss whereby another party has been enriched, but which does not arise out of an internationally unlawful act which would found a claim for damages.

809 Fombad, 'The Principle of Unjustified Enrichment', p. 123.

810 Christina Binder and Christophe Schreuer, 'Unjust Enrichment', in *Max Planck Encyclopedia of Public International Law* (Oxford University Press online ed. 2006), para. 2.

In fact, these two writers affirm that 'the remedies for an internationally wrongful act and for unjust enrichment are mutually exclusive' and that 'a remedy for unjust enrichment is available only where no other remedies, and in particular no claim to damages for a wrongful act, are available'.[811] In my view, the concept of unjust enrichment is relevant here precisely because 'no claim to damages for a wrongful act' would be available to the victim.[812] Accordingly, a State should provide proper reparation to the victim under these specific circumstances.[813] This is an exceptional situation where Rule no. 3 should not find application.

3.2 Rule No. 5: The Rebels Are Responsible for Their Own Wrongful Acts

As briefly mentioned above, the fact that the government is (in general)[814] not 'responsible' for the acts committed by the rebels during the (ultimately unsuccessful) insurgency (Rule no. 3) does not necessarily mean that such wrongs will go unpunished.[815] As the

811 Ibid., para. 30.

812 The possibility of redress against the rebels *as a group* after their defeat before domestic courts is unlikely to be successful given that they will no longer exist as an autonomous entity. Whether any claim can be filed against former rebel members *individually* is a matter of domestic law. As further examined below, the State has to fulfil its due diligence obligation in relation to the conduct of rebels (Rule no. 6, see at Section 3.3), which includes an obligation to punish the wrongdoers and provide reparation (the question is examined in Section 3.3.3.2.3). As further examined in the next section, in theory, the investor has the possibility *during* the insurrection to submit a claim against the rebels for the wrongs, but in reality, the chances of success of such an option are very limited.

813 It should be mentioned that the Iran–US Claims Tribunal in *Flexi-Van Leasing, Inc.* v. *Iran*, Iran–US Claims Tribunal, Award no. 259-36-1, 13 October 1986, 12 *Iran-US CTR* 335, at p. 353–5, stated that 'the damage for unjust enrichment should be measured in terms of the extent to which that State has been enriched'. Thus, what is sought as a remedy to unjust enrichment is the 'achievement of an acceptable economic equilibrium' between the two parties (Schreuer, 'Unjustified Enrichment', p. 381). Such a goal is reached by the reestablishment of the previous economic position of the enriched party. The amount of compensation 'will not exceed the amount by which the defendant's wealth has been increased or that by which the claimant has been impoverished' (Fombad, 'The Principle of Unjustified Enrichment', p. 125).

814 It should be recalled that even when the insurgency is ultimately unsuccessful, the State should nevertheless be bound by the governmental lawful 'routine activities' performed by rebels in situations where they have established a local de facto government in part of the territory (Rule no. 4A). Also, the State should be responsible for the consequences arising from expropriation acts committed by rebels when it resulted in some benefits for the State (Rule no. 4B).

815 Ryngaert, 'State Responsibility and Non-State Actors', p. 175–6, noting that 'the absence of any attribution to the state of acts of insurrectional movements that are not successful

ILC Commentaries explained, 'the insurrectional movement may itself be held responsible for its own conduct under international law, for example for a breach of international humanitarian law committed by its forces'.[816] Thus, as matter of principle, the rebels are responsible for *their own* wrongful acts (hereinafter referred to as Rule no. 5). This section will examine the following three points:

- The principle of responsibility under Rule no. 5 is well-established (Section 3.2.1);
- The rebels' responsibility arises only when they have an effective control over part of the territory of the State (Section 3.2.2); and
- Claims against rebels are rare and unlikely to be successful (Section 3.2.3).

3.2.1 *The Principle of Responsibility Is Well-Established*

It is now well-recognized that insurgents have an obligation under international law to respect basic principles existing, under, inter alia, humanitarian law and international human rights law (at least when they exercise de facto control over part of a territory).[817] The Security Council has, on many occasions, called upon armed groups to fulfil their obligations in those fields of law as well as under peace agreements to which they were parties.[818] Writers have recently examined the question as to how rebel groups can be *directly* held accountable for human rights abuses as well as violations of humanitarian law and international criminal law.[819] This question is beyond the scope of

in overthrowing the government . . . may necessitate contemplating the direct responsibility of nonstate actors'.

[816] ILC, Commentaries, 2001, p. 53, para. 15.

[817] For an overview: ILA, 'Non State Actors', 3rd Report prepared by Co-Rapporteurs, Cedric Ryngaert and Jean d'Aspremont, Washington Conference (2014), p. 5 ff. See also, p. 7 speaking also of 'possible obligations' of armed groups 'which could arise in connection to the peace agreements signed' with a government. See also: Katharine Fortin, *The Accountability of Armed Groups under Human Rights Law* (Oxford University Press, 2017); Daragh Murray, *Human Rights Obligations of Non-State Armed Groups* (West Sussex, Hart Publishing, 2016).

[818] Cahin, 'The Responsibility of Other Entities', p. 337–8; ILA, 'Non State Actors', p. 6, referring to several examples.

[819] See inter alia: A. Bellal, 'Establishing the Direct Responsibility of Non-State Armed Groups for Violations of International Norms: Issues of Attribution', in N. Gal-Or, C. Ryngaert and M. Noortmann (eds.), *Responsibilities of the Non-State Actor in Armed Conflict and the Market Place* (Leiden, Brill Nijhoff, 2015); V. Bílková,

this book. Suffice it to note that many writers support the view that rebels can be held responsible for *their own* wrongful acts under international law.[820] The question remains controversial.[821]

Importantly, in its 1975 Report, the ILC noted that the 'organs of an insurrectional movement . . . may engage in conduct liable to bring an international responsibility upon the insurrectional movement itself'.[822] In fact, Article 14(3) of the ILC 1975 draft expressly recognized this principle: 'Similarly, paragraph 1 is without prejudice to

'Establishing Direct Responsibility', in ibid.; A. Clapham, 'Extending International Criminal Responsibility beyond the Individual to Corporations and Armed Opposition Groups', *J. Int. Criminal Justice* 6 (2008), p. 899–926.

820 Kolb, *The International Law of State Responsibility*, p. 97; Cahin, 'Attribution of Conduct to the State', p. 253–4, referring the 'exceptional responsibility of the insurrectional movement' and noting that 'today the possibility of attaching responsibility to insurrectional movements is more easily obtained through other means' (including individual criminal responsibility).

821 Verhoeven, 'International Responsibility', p. 297, noting that: 'it is unclear that international law recognizes international accountability of insurrectional movements through the invocation of international responsibility of the movement, although there is some limited state practice in this respect, involving insurgents who have control over part of the State's territory'. See also, p. 299: '[t]he existence of international responsibility of armed opposition groups remains unclear, especially when the group does not have control over territory'. At the end of his article, he also made this comment: '[s]ince those movements have their own rights and obligations under international law and may conclude international agreements with other international subjects, the international responsibility of the movement for its violations of international law seems only logical', adding, however, that 'practice is too sparse to warrant the conclusion that such an international responsibility exists' (p. 303). The same position is taken in ILA, 'Non State Actors', speaking of the issue 'as very much a question of progressive development of international law' and adding that 'if it were someday established that [rebel groups] can incur direct responsibility under international law – which remains hypothetical in the present state of international law'. See also, K. Greenman, 'Re-Reading Vitoria: Re-Conceptualising the Responsibility of Rebel Movements', *Nordic JIL* 83 (2014), p. 378 ff., for a criticism of this narrative whereby the 'responsibility of rebel movements is presented as an essential next step in the history of the progressive development of international law' (p. 379) because 'rebel movements, a mounting threat to the liberal cosmopolitan values upon which modern international law is based, require an international law response' (p. 380). She noted that while 'it has simply proved impossible to find a convincing explanation for rebel movements being bound by international law by reference to its traditional sources', 'nevertheless, the majority of the literature . . . has simply moved on to consider enhancing compliance and ensuring accountability in case of violations' (p. 384). She is putting forward a completely different narrative.

822 ILC, Report, 1975, p. 92, para. 4: 'as soon as they begin their separate existence on the international scene, such movements may be capable within certain limits of committing internationally wrongful acts of their own'.

the attribution of the conduct of the organ of the insurrectional movement to that movement in any case in which such attribution may be made under international law.'[823] In his First Report, Crawford explained that Article 14(3) dealt with the 'international responsibility of liberation movements which are, ex hypothesi, not States' and that for that reason, this question 'falls outside the scope of the draft articles and should be omitted'.[824] This is essentially the reason why the 2001 Draft Articles do not contain a provision dealing specifically with this issue.[825] Yet, this omission does not undermine the existence of the principle. Thus, in his First Report, Crawford noted that 'the responsibility of such movements, for example, for breaches of international humanitarian law, can certainly be envisaged, but this can be dealt with in the commentary'.[826] As noted by one writer, 'the ILC has clearly accepted the existence of a principle of international responsibility of insurrectional movements, albeit without expressly including it in the text of the Articles'.[827] In his subsequent book, Crawford also noted that 'international law now apparently contemplates that the insurrectional movement may itself be held internationally responsible for its acts'.[828] As a result, the victim (third States, foreigners) of a wrong committed by the rebels can submit a claim to the insurrectional movement and request reparation for the damage it suffered.[829] The next section examines the conditions under which rebels' responsibility can arise.

823 See ibid., p. 99, para. 31, speaking of a 'safeguard clause'.

824 ILC, Crawford First Report, 1998, p. 53, para. 272.

825 See comment by Crawford in ILC, 'Summary Records of the Meetings of the Fiftieth Session', 2556th meeting, 5 August 1998, UN Doc. A/CN.4/SER.A/1998, *ILC Yearbook* I (1998), p. 249, at p. 254 (para. 38):

> [t]he Commission had to regulate only the question of the attribution of State responsibility. The question of the responsibility of insurrectional movements was not under consideration ... the Commission was only concerned with the responsibility of States and not with that of insurrectional movements. In the case in question it was impossible to say that the State was responsible for acts committed during the insurrection, unless there were other reasons for imputing them to the State. The situation seemed perfectly clear.

826 ILC, Crawford First Report, 1998, p. 53, para. 272.

827 Cahin, 'The Responsibility of Other Entities', p. 339.

828 Crawford, *State Responsibility*, p. 180.

829 Ibid., stating that 'a state may bring a distinct and quantified claim against an insurrectionist movement'.

3.2.2 Rebels' Responsibility Arises Only When They Have an Effective Control over Part of the Territory of the State

International responsibility of rebels arises only in cases where the insurgents have an effective control over part (but not all) of the territory of the State. The term 'local' de facto government (as opposed to 'general' de facto government) is used to describe this situation.[830] Kelsen mentioned that in such a case the insurgents 'resemble[] a state in the sense of international law'.[831] Accordingly, the rebels have the obligation to protect foreign investors and their properties in the territories they control.[832] This is simply because the government no longer has any effective control over that territory and cannot offer any protection and security to foreigners.[833]

Ago mentioned another explanation for the rebels' responsibility. In his 1972 Report, he noted that it was 'clearly established that actions emanating from organs of other subjects of international law, acting as such in the territory of a particular State, are not attributable to that State under international law and do not involve its international responsibility'.[834] He then asked the question as to whether the same could apply to an insurrectional movement. His answer suggests that any such attribution presupposes that the group has been recognized as a subject of international law.[835] In other words, for Ago, it is *because* an

830 Borchard, 'International Pecuniary Claims Against Mexico', p. 341–2. See also: Houghton, 'The Responsibility of the State', p. 254–5.

831 H. Kelsen, *Principles of International Law* (New York, Rinehart, 1952), p. 292, cited in ILC, Ago Report, 1972, p. 129, para. 153.

832 Mantilla Blanco, *Full Protection and Security*, p. 190–1.

833 Cahin, 'The Responsibility of Other Entities', p. 335–6, explains this point, albeit in the different context of 'armed bands' and 'criminal groups':

> [a]lthough it could, in theory, exist cumulatively with the international responsibility of the State, it is the lack of effectiveness of State responsibility in the situations in question which, above all, justifies the recognition of an international responsibility of armed bands and criminal groups. This lack of effectiveness results from the fact that these diverse entities enjoy, as regards both States and entities with aspirations to Statehood, a level of functional autonomy which makes it impossible to attribute their illicit behaviour to either one or the other.

834 ILC, Ago Report, 1972, p. 128, para. 151.

835 Ibid., p. 129, para. 152:

> It must also be borne in mind that such a question can only arise in our present line of inquiry if a particular condition is fulfilled. Let us suppose that an act injurious to a third State or to one of its nationals has been committed by a member of the organization of an insurrectional

insurrectional movement has been recognized as a subject of international law that it can be held accountable for its own wrongful acts.[836] As mentioned above,[837] the 1975 ILC Report no longer emphasized the insurrectional movement being a subject of international law.

Another relevant question is whether any importance should be given to the fact that the rebels have been recognized the status of 'belligerent power'. Such a status has long been reserved only to certain insurgent groups fulfilling a number of conditions.[838] Belligerents have the power to enter into agreements with other entities (States, companies) and are bound to

> movement, endowed as such with international personality: a problem of attribution or non-attribution to the State of an act by organs of another subject of international law could only arise if, at the time when the injured State presented a claim to the 'territorial' State in respect of the act committed, the insurrectional movement was still in existence as a separate subject of international law or possibly even if it had ceased to exist and its structures and organization had vanished with it.

The same position is adopted by Piguet, *La Guerre civile en droit international*, p. 143: the acts of the rebels 'engagent sa responsabilité durant la guerre civile dans la mesure où l'État qui a subi le dommage reconnait la personnalité du mouvement' ('Incur liability during the civil war insofar as the State which suffered the damage recognizes the personality of the movement').

836 ILC, Ago Report, 1972, p. 129, para. 153:

> What, in fact, characterizes the situation created by the emergence of an insurrectional movement as defined in international law is the very existence, parallel with the State and in a portion of the territory under its sovereignty of a separate subject of international law. To the extent allowed by its limited international capacity, this subject is perfectly capable of committing internationally wrongful acts. The actions of persons belonging to its organization, like those of the organs of another State or of an international organization acting within the State's territory are the actions of a subject of international law, which can involve the latter's responsibility where they constitute a violation of an international obligation assumed by that subject.

He also refers to 'the main responsibility falling on the insurrectional movement itself, that is, the subject of international law of which the perpetrators of the acts are organs'.

837 See Section 2.2.2.2.3.

838 Emily Crawford, 'Insurgency', in *Max Planck Encyclopedia of Public International Law* (Oxford University Press, 2012), para. 3:

> [o]nly if the insurgents fulfilled certain criteria, could they be officially, legally recognized as belligerents and be given the protections and rights granted to States under the law of armed conflict. These criteria were that an organized armed group must: a) possess control of some part of the territory in which they operate; b) exercise *de facto* administrative control over that territory; c) possess an armed force subject to military discipline; and d) conduct their armed activities in accordance with the laws of armed conflict.

respect the laws of war.[839] In the past, belligerent status was considered to be very important. Some writers believed that recognition of this status led to the creation of a new (partial and temporary) subject of international law with an international legal personality.[840] Recognition was also considered important on the battlefield. On the one hand, when a government fighting rebels recognized them the status of 'belligerent power' that meant that *both* parties were now considered bound to respect international humanitarian law. The insurgents would therefore have rights and obligations under the laws of war. On the other hand, recognition of the status of 'belligerent power' by a third State meant that it would observe neutrality in the conflict involving the rebels and the government.

Further, the recognition of the status of 'belligerent power' has traditionally been considered important in terms of responsibility. First, it has long been argued that the question of insurgents' responsibility for their *own* wrongful acts only arises in situations where they have been recognized the status of 'belligerent power' by other States.[841] In such a case, the victims of a breach of international law can claim reparation directly to the insurgents. This principle was, for instance, recognized by the Institute.[842] Second, recognition has an impact on the government fighting the rebels. For the government, recognition implies that the rebels have effective control over part of a territory and that, therefore, they are the *only* ones responsible for the activities conducted on that territory. As a result, recognition of the status of 'belligerent power' by a government sends the clear signal that it considers itself *no longer responsible* to protect the rights and interests of other States and foreigners in that specific territory.[843] The basic principle was recognized by the Institute[844] and the Harvard Draft of 1929.[845] In the words of Eagleton, 'if belligerent status is accorded to the rebels, it may be

[839] M. N. Shaw, *International Law* (6th ed. Cambridge University Press, 2008), p. 245.

[840] Atlam, *Succession d'États,* p. 306.

[841] Mantilla Blanco, *Full Protection and Security*, p. 194–5, citing many authorities.

[842] Institute of International Law, 'Responsabilité internationale des États à raison des dommages causés sur leur territoire à la personne et aux biens des étrangers', Resolution of 1927, Art. 2, in *Annuaire IDI* 18(1), p. 254 [hereinafter referred to as IIL, 'Responsabilité internationale des États' 1927].

[843] Ganzory, 'International Claims and Insurgence', p. 82–3; Atlam, *Succession d'États,* p. 309; Borchard, 'International Responsibility of the State for Injuries', p. 119; Houghton, 'The Responsibility of the State', p. 261.

[844] IIL, 'Responsabilité internationale des États' 1927, Art. 7.

[845] Harvard Draft Convention, 1929, Article 13(a): '[i]n the event of an unsuccessful revolution, a state is not responsible when an injury to an alien results from an act of the revolutionists committed *after their recognition as belligerents* either by itself or by the state of which the alien is a national', emphasis added.

taken as an admission of inability to control them; and, consequently, as a warning of non-liability for their actions'.[846] One principle mentioned by McNair is indeed that a State on whose territory an insurrection occurs 'is not responsible for loss or damage caused by the insurgents to a foreigner after that foreigner's State has recognized the belligerency of the insurgents'.[847] Third, recognition made by third States also has a considerable impact. When a third State does so, it admits that the legitimate government has no control over the rebels, and, therefore, cannot be responsible for what is taking place in that territory. According to Akehurst, 'such admissions will go a long way towards estopping the foreign State from claiming that the respondent State has failed to exercise due diligence in preventing injuries by the rebels to the foreign State's nationals'.[848]

The modern view, however, is that 'recognition of belligerency appears to be regarded as irrelevant'.[849] In practice, never has it happened that recognition of belligerency somehow had the effect of magically 'switching' responsibility.[850] Recognition was essentially used to show that a State

[846] Eagleton, *The Responsibility of States*, p. 147. See also: W.E. Hall, *A Treatise on International Law* (7th ed., Oxford University Press, 1917), p. 30, explaining that recognition of belligerency releases the parent government from responsibility for acts of insurgents:

> so soon as recognition takes place, the parent state ceases to be responsible to such states as have accorded recognition, and when it has itself granted recognition to all states, for the acts of the insurgents, and for losses or inconveniences suffered by a foreign power or its subjects in consequence of the inability of the state to perform its international obligations in such parts of its dominions as are not under its actual control.

[847] Lord McNair, *International Law Opinions* (Cambridge University Press, vol. 2, 1956), p. 245, referred to in Crawford, *Brownlie's Principles of Public International Law*, p. 553.

[848] Akehurst, 'State Responsibility', p. 45.

[849] James Crawford, *The Creation of States in International Law* (2nd ed., Oxford University Press, 2006), p. 659. In another book (Crawford, *State Responsibility*, p. 171), he goes so far as to say that 'recognition of insurgency' 'as an institution is virtually obsolete'. He also noted that (in ILC, Crawford First Report, 1998, p. 52, para. 270): 'the insurrectional movements considered in the earlier cases were by no means all at a level which might have entailed their having international personality as belligerents, and subsequent developments have done little to confirm the concept of the legal personality of belligerent forces in general. For example, recognition of belligerency in internal armed conflict is in virtual desuetude'. See also: Al-Rashid *et al.*, 'Investment Claims', p. 196 ('Recognition of belligerency – either by the state's *de jure* government or by a foreign government – does not seem to play a significant role in the analysis'); Piguet, *La Guerre civile en droit international*, p. 27 ff.

[850] *Prats* case, 1868, Commissioner Wadsworth in his Opinion, p. 191–2:

> [n]on responsibility on the part of the United States for injuries by the Confederate enemy within the territories of that government to aliens did not result from the recognition of the belligerency of the rebel enemy by the strangers' sovereign. It resulted from the fact of belligerency itself, and

believed that the insurgents were in control over a given territory. As mentioned by Blanco, recognition is 'a corollary of the change in the entity holding actual territorial control'.[851] The responsibility of insurgents for their own acts is therefore not based on their recognition by others as a 'belligerent power', but rather on 'effectivity'.[852] More generally, as noted by Piguet, 'la reconnaissance comme insurgés n'engendre que des effets très limités'.[853] The International Criminal Tribunal for the Former Yugoslavia has thus declared that crimes against humanity 'can be committed on behalf of entities exercising *de facto* control over a particular territory but without international recognition or formal status of a *de jure* state, or by a terrorist group or organization'.[854] At the end of the day, in terms of international responsibility, the fact that the insurgents have an effective control over part of the territory of the State is the relevant consideration. When this is the case, the rebels can be held responsible for their acts under international law.

3.2.3 Claims against Rebels Are Rare and Unlikely to Be Successful

Scholars have acknowledged that filing a claim against rebels remains a 'theoretical possibility' more than anything else.[855] In fact, Cahin goes so far as to say that 'in practice no injured State has ever brought claims against insurrectional movements'.[856] This statement may be slightly misleading. It

> whether recognized or not by other governments. But the proclaimed recognition of the fact by a government is conclusive evidence of the fact, and, so to speak, an estoppel as to that government.

He also noted that 'as the responsibility of the United States to Mexico in this case is concerned, it is in nowise increased or diminished by the failure of the latter to accord belligerent rights to the Confederates'.

851 Mantilla Blanco, *Full Protection and Security*, p. 196.

852 Atlam, *Succession d'États*, p. 311.

853 Piguet, *La Guerre civile en droit international*, p. 30 ('recognition as insurgents has very limited effects').

854 ICTY, *Prosecutor* v. *Tadić*, Case No IT-94-1-T, Judgment, Trial Chamber, 7 May 1997, in *ILR* 112, p. 220–2, paras. 654–7.

855 Cahin, 'Attribution of Conduct to the State', p. 252. See also: Kolb, *The International Law of State Responsibility*, p. 97 ('While there is no theoretical reason to refuse the responsibility of the movement, it is burdensome for the claiming governments to try to pursue claims against armed bands operating on foreign territories').

856 Cahin, 'Attribution of Conduct to the State', p. 252. He later (at p. 253–4) acknowledged the existence of 'claims addressed during the course of the hostilities to insurrectional movements by several States for damages caused to their nationals'.

is true that there may not be many situations where 'claims' have been formally filed against rebels before courts and tribunals. Yet, as noted by O'Connell, there are cases where States 'have protested and demanded compensation from [insurgents] for wrongs done to their nationals'.[857] Thus, in his 1972 Report, Ago noted that 'States have in fact sometimes presented claims to an insurrectional movement for injuries caused to them or their nationals by organs of that movement.'[858] He provides three concrete examples of such claims.[859] Clearly, the possibility for the injured party to submit a claim to the insurrectional movement is very much theoretical once the insurrection has *failed*. Thus, after their defeat, the insurgents simply no longer exist as an autonomous entity and it will be much harder to hold them responsible, as a group, for any past wrongs.[860]

What about *during* the insurgency (i.e. *before* the rebellion has failed)? It goes without saying that a State should *not* be responsible for any acts committed by the rebels during the period when it is actually fighting them.[861] In theory, nothing prevents an injured party from submitting a claim to the insurrectional movement during the insurgency. Yet, as explained by Atlam, 'there are many reasons why States make no claims from national Liberation Movements, or, for that matter, from other insurrectional movements, before the end of the fight'.[862] The same point is made by Cahin for whom, 'as evidenced by the rare and very old precedents cited by the ILC, the injured State will only exceptionally

[857] O'Connell, *International Law*, p. 972, referring to a number of examples.

[858] ILC, Ago Report, 1972, p. 139, para. 180.

[859] Ibid., p. 139, para. 181. The same examples are briefly mentioned in Crawford, *State Responsibility*, p. 180.

[860] ILC, Ago Report, 1972, p. 130, para. 155:

> Where the Government of the pre-existing State defeats the insurrectional movement, the ephemeral existence of this movement as a separate subject of international law will have come to an end, and there will no longer be a subject that can be considered, at the international level, to be the perpetrator of the acts injurious to foreign States or individuals committed by organs of the insurgents at the time of the conflict.

The *personal* responsibility of former individual members of such groups is a different issue which depends on each State's domestic law. This question is beyond the scope of this book.

[861] Ibid., p. 130, para. 156: '[e]ven at the time when it was fighting the insurrection, it seemed normal that the State should be held responsible *only* for any wrongful negligence on its part in preventing or punishing the wrongful acts of organs belonging to the insurgents', emphasis added. See also: ILC, Report, 1975, p. 93, para. 12: 'acts of the organs of the insurrectional movement cannot be attributed to the State as long as the struggle between that movement and constituted authority continues'.

[862] Atlam, 'National Liberation Movements and International Responsibility', p. 50.

assert the responsibility of the insurrectional movement'.[863] Indeed, it is not considered as a 'practical' solution for the injured party.[864] Atlam refers to the following three reasons: 'the extent of combat, the temporary nature of these movements', and 'the fear that presentations of international claims may be interpreted as implying recognition of those movements by the State which has suffered the injury'.[865] He added that he was aware of no instances where a claim was presented against a National Liberation Movement *during* the fighting. Ago (along with other writers)[866] has also argued that the presentation of a claim by the injured State 'could imply recognition' of the insurrectional movement.[867] It has been argued that this is, in fact, the reason why the ILC finally decided to eliminate any reference to the international responsibility of insurrectional movements in the Draft Articles.[868]

Ago mentioned another more practical reason behind the rare and ineffective character of asserting the responsibility of insurrectional movements. He explained that 'to establish the international responsibility incurred through an internationally wrongful act is an operation which often takes a relatively long time, perhaps a longer time than the insurrectional struggle lasts'.[869] This is because of the 'provisional' (or 'temporary') nature of insurgents as a subject of international law.[870] The 'temporary'

863 Cahin, 'Attribution of Conduct to the State', p. 254–5.

864 Eatwell, *State Responsibility*, p. 174.

865 Atlam, 'National Liberation Movements and International Responsibility', p. 50. See also: Verhoeven, 'International Responsibility', p. 294; Ezequiel Heffes, 'The Responsibility of Armed Opposition Groups for Violations of International Humanitarian Law: Challenging the State-Centric System of International Law', *J. Int. Humanitarian Legal Stud.* 4 (2013), p. 90.

866 Cahin, 'Attribution of Conduct to the State', p. 254–5: 'the injured State will not be very inclined, during an insurrection, to address to the movement a claim that is likely not to be accepted and that will be interpreted as a grant of an unwanted recognition to the movement'.

867 ILC, Ago Report, 1972, p. 129, para. 154:

> if the State which complains of injuries caused by wrongful acts of agents of an insurrectional movement does not recognize or intend to recognize the movement, with which it maintains no relations, presenting a claim and making responsibility effective could entail further difficulties, either in fact or in law, since there is a risk that the presentation of a claim could imply recognition.

868 Cahin, 'Attribution of Conduct to the State', p. 254–5.

869 ILC, Report, 1975, p. 93, para. 8.

870 ILC, Ago Report, 1972, p. 129, para. 154:

> At the same time we must concede that the international responsibility of an insurrectional movement is usually harder to make effective than that of a State or an international organization. The movement is essentially a 'provisional'

nature of insurgents is undeniable: either they succeed in their struggle or they don't.[871] Their existence as a group was always, by definition, not meant to be permanent.[872] Thus, as noted by one author, 'the movement either wins and then its international responsibility is absorbed into that of a state, or is defeated and then its international responsibility can hardly yield any results since the movement ceases its existence'.[873] Yet, however 'temporary' it may be, this period of insurgency can sometimes last decades (as seen, for instance, in the civil war in Sri Lanka).[874] An ILA Report noted that 'the long duration of many non-international armed conflicts and the ability of many [rebel movements] to survive the end of armed conflicts have however proved this assumption largely incorrect'.[875]

In any event, one has to agree with Ago for whom all of these reasons create 'uncertainty regarding the prospects of obtaining reparation from the movement, during the conflict, for an internationally wrongful act'.[876] For one thing, it is not at all clear whether during its armed struggle a rebel movement would have the financial means to provide any compensation to the victim.[877] Another question which remains to be fully explored is which rules of attribution would apply to rebel groups.[878] It has been argued that the rules applicable to conduct of State could apply, by analogy,

> subject of international law. The duration of its existence coincides with the duration of its fight against the pre-existing State or its Government. At the conclusion of that fight it must, in any event, cease to exist as such. If it is defeated, its existence comes to an end and its organization is dissolved. If it wins, it can as we have pointed out, either transfer its organizational structures to the pre-existing State or become a new State. Making the international responsibility engendered by an internationally wrongful act effective is an operation which often takes quite a long time, and frequently lasts longer than the temporary situation connected with the conflict.

See also: ILC, Report, 1975, p. 93, para. 8.

871 Eatwell, *State Responsibility*, p. 174: 'Insurrectional movements enjoy only a temporary existence – a movement will cease to exist either because it succeeds and becomes the new government or the government of a new state, or it fails and disintegrates.'

872 Cahin, 'Attribution of Conduct to the State', p. 247–8, noting that a movement's 'disappearance will occur in due course'.

873 E. David, *Principes de droit des conflits armés* (3rd ed., Brussels, Bruylant, 2002), p. 643, quoted (and translated) in ILA, 'Non State Actors', p. 9.

874 Verhoeven, 'International Responsibility', p. 296.

875 ILA, 'Non State Actors', p. 9.

876 ILC, Ago Report, 1972, p. 129, para. 154.

877 Ibid., noting that the rebel group 'may have no property which, when the need arises, could afford a means of compensation'. See also: Eatwell, *State Responsibility*, p. 174.

878 The question is examined in Heffes, 'The Responsibility of Armed Opposition Groups', p. 95–8.

at least in cases where 'organs' of a group can be identified.[879] It has also been suggested that the 'overall control test [proposed in *Tadić*] could be introduced to identify factual organs of the insurrectional movement'.[880] Other questions have also been raised about the type of reparation (if any) a movement should provide to the victim.[881] It is also not obvious in which jurisdiction such claims could eventually be filed.[882] Ago's conclusion is that 'the State which has suffered an injury itself or in the person of its nationals has very limited chances of obtaining from the insurrectional movement the satisfaction or reparation to which it considers itself entitled'.[883] This is the reason why 'States which are victims of internationally wrongful acts committed by organs of insurrectional movements sometimes find it expedient to wait until the situation becomes clearer before presenting claims'.[884]

There is indeed no doubt that the injured party may find it preferable to wait until the end of the conflict.[885] As mentioned above,[886] there are good reasons why the victim may hope that the rebels actually win. If they do, the victim may address its claim to the new government (now formed by the former rebels). Thus, the general principle is that the acts committed by the rebels during the insurgency are attributable to the State (Rule no. 2). On the contrary, in the event that the rebels are defeated, the opposite principle will prevail: the acts committed by the rebels during

[879] ILC, Report, 1975, p. 98, para. 28: 'there is a possibility of holding the movement itself responsible for the wrongful acts of its organs'. See Cahin, 'Attribution of Conduct to the State', p. 255, distinguishing between 'highly structured movements', such as one which 'has attained the authority of a *de facto* government' and 'more modest armed opposition groups which have only a rudimentary organization'.

[880] Verhoeven, 'International Responsibility', p. 299, adding that 'The test takes into account that insurrectional movements are organized armed groups wherein various units will have some degree of autonomy, but with a common goal, a common support and common military strategy' (at p. 301).

[881] The question is examined in Luke Moffett, 'Beyond Attribution: Responsibility of Armed Non-State Actors for Reparations in Northern Ireland, Colombia and Uganda', in N. Gal-Or, C. Ryngaert and M. Noortmann (eds.), *Responsibilities of the Non-State Actor in Armed Conflict and the Market Place. Theoretical Considerations and Empirical Findings* (Leiden, Brill, 2015); ILA, 'Non State Actors', p. 10.

[882] Verhoeven, 'International Responsibility', p. 294, noting that 'there is no international forum where claims against insurrectional movements can be settled'. A number of existing possibilities are examined in Heffes, 'The Responsibility of Armed Opposition Groups', p. 91–2.

[883] ILC, Ago Report, 1972, p. 129, para. 154.

[884] Ibid., p. 130, para. 155.

[885] Eatwell, *State Responsibility*, p. 175.

[886] See Section 3.1.3.

the insurgency are not attributable to the State (Rule no. 3). Under this scenario, and given that Rule no. 3 is well-established, it would be rather pointless for the injured party to address a claim to that State; that claim is very likely to be rejected.[887] Yet, the 1975 ILC Report seems to be suggesting, in one rather ambiguous passage, that it 'often happens that claims are addressed, at the end of the struggle' to the 'legitimate Government of the State' which has defeated the rebels.[888] The Report does not provide any illustration of such claims.

3.3 Rule No. 6: The State Is Responsible for Its Own Failure to Exercise Its Due Diligence Obligation to Protect Foreigners and Third States

As mentioned above,[889] the basic principle applicable when the rebels are *not* successful in their attempt to establish a new government is the following: the acts committed by the rebels during the insurgency are not attributable to the State (Rule no. 3).[890] The rebels are responsible for their own wrongful acts towards the victims (Rule no. 5). The victims can submit claims to the rebels requesting reparation for the damages they

887 As mentioned above (Section 3.1.5), the situation is different for governmental 'routine activities' performed by rebels in situations where they have established a local de facto government in part of the territory (Rule no. 4A). I have also examined (Section 3.1.6) the unique case of expropriation acts committed by rebels which result in some benefits for the State (Rule no. 4B).

888 ILC, Report, 1975, p. 93, para. 9:

> [t]hus it often happens that claims are addressed, at the end of the struggle, *either to the legitimate Government of the State, where that Government has put down the insurrection* and re-established its authority throughout the territory, or to the new government which has replaced the previous Government upon the victorious issue of the insurrection, or again to the government of a new State formed by the secession of part of the territory of the pre-existing State or by decolonization of a former dependent territory of that State. (emphasis added).

See also, this comment: ILC, Ago Report, 1972, p. 130, para. 155: '[d]epending on the outcome of the conflict, claims may be presented to the legitimate Government of the pre-existing State, where the latter has defeated the insurrectional movement and restored its authority over the entire territory'.

889 See Section 3.1.

890 As mentioned above (Section 3.1.5), even when the insurgency is ultimately unsuccessful, it remains that the State should nevertheless be bound by the governmental lawful 'routine activities' performed by rebels in situations where they have established a local de facto government in part of the territory (Rule no. 4A). Also, the State should be responsible for the consequences arising from any expropriation acts committed by rebels when it resulted in some benefits for the State (Rule no. 4B, examined in Section 3.1.6).

have suffered. Yet, as mentioned in the previous section, the likelihood of any such claims being successful is rather limited. The present section examines the different situation of acts (and omissions) committed *by the government* while fighting the rebels.

The only acts for which the government is truly *responsible* are those which it has *itself* committed during the insurgency.[891] Thus, in the context of its struggle against the rebels, the government in charge will take measures and commit acts (or omissions) which will have an impact on the rights and interests of *foreigners* (including foreign investors) and *third States*. The basic principle examined in this section is that the State is responsible for its own failure to exercise its due diligence obligation to protect foreigners and third States (hereinafter referred to as Rule no. 6). Rule no. 6 has therefore nothing to do with the issue of attribution to the State of acts committed *by the rebels*.

In the following sections, I will examine three issues:

- The drafting history of Article 10(3) of the ILC Articles (Section 3.3.1);
- The fact that a State is not responsible for damages resulting from its use of military force while fighting an insurgency unless its conduct breaches its international law obligations (Section 3.3.2); and
- Responsibility arises as a result of a State's failure to discharge its due diligence duty of vigilance, prevention and punishment regarding conduct of rebels (Section 3.3.3).

3.3.1 *Drafting History*

Rule no. 6 was embodied in Paragraph 3 of Article 12 of the 1972 draft:

> 3. However, the rules enunciated in paragraphs 1 and 2 are without prejudice to the attribution to the State of any omission on the part of its organs, where the latter ought to have acted to prevent or punish the conduct of the person or group of persons in question and failed to do so.[892]

The same basic principle can also be found in the 1975 draft in Article 14(2):

> 2. Paragraph 1 is without prejudice to the attribution to a State of any other conduct which is related to that of the organ of the insurrectional

[891] It should be mentioned at the outset that this section does not deal with the situation of a wrongful act committed by a successful government that caused damages *to the rebels*. Whenever this is the case, the government is theoretically responsible for such acts during and after the insurgency. Yet, after their defeat, the rebels will no longer exist as an autonomous entity. They will therefore not be able to claim (as a group) any reparation to the government.

[892] ILC, Ago Report, 1972, p. 143, para. 192.

movement and which is to be considered as an act of that State by virtue of articles 5 to 10.[893]

Interestingly, Article 12 of the 1972 draft explicitly defined the failure by a State to exercise its due diligence obligation (Rule no. 6) as the situation where a State had to act to 'prevent or punish' the conduct of the rebels and 'failed to do so'. The 1975 version no longer provides such an explicit definition of the concept. It simply refers to State 'conduct which is related to that of the organ of the insurrectional movement' and makes a general *renvoi* to other provisions of the ILC Draft Articles regarding its application.

The essence of Rule no. 6 can now be found in Article 10(3) of the 2001 ILC Articles.[894] This provision finds applications in two different types of situations: when the rebels are not successful at establishing a new government or when they have failed to create a new State. In terms of language, Article 10(3) is quite similar to that of Article 14(2) of the 1975 draft. One notable difference is that Article 10(3) no longer speaks of a 'conduct which *is related*' to the insurrectional movement but refers instead, more generally, to a 'conduct, *however related* to' the insurrectional movement. The 2001 ILC Commentaries indicates that the aim of this change was to give a 'broad meaning' to the application of Article 10(3).[895]

The following illustration is provided in the ILC Commentaries: 'the failure by a State to take available steps to protect the premises of diplomatic missions, threatened from attack by an insurrectional movement, is clearly conduct attributable to the State and is preserved by paragraph 3'.[896] This is an example where the State would be responsible for its own failure to protect a foreign State's embassy. The important point is that the only acts (and omissions) that are covered by Article 10(3) are those which are indeed 'related' (or 'connected')[897] to the conduct of the rebels during the insurgency. Article 10(3) does not cover other types of acts (and omissions) by the government which may affect third States and foreigners, but that have

[893] ILC, Report, 1975, p. 91, para. 1.

[894] Article 10(3) reads as follows: '[t]his article is without prejudice to the attribution to a State of any conduct, however related to that of the movement concerned, which is to be considered an act of that State by virtue of articles 4 to 9'.

[895] ILC, Commentaries, 2001, p. 51, para. 15; ILC, 'Summary records of the meetings of the fiftieth session', 2558th meeting 7 August 1998, UN Doc. A/CN.4/SER.A/1998, *ILC Yearbook* vol. I (1998), p. 287, at p. 291, para. 89.

[896] ILC, Commentaries, 2001, p. 51, para. 15.

[897] ILC, Ago Report, 1972, p. 137, para. 170: 'only conduct engaged in by organs of the State *in connexion with the injurious acts of the insurgents* could be attributed to the State and cause it to incur international responsibility if such conduct constituted a breach of an international obligation', emphasis added.

nothing to do with the rebellion. There must therefore exist some kind of *nexus* between the actions taken by the rebels and the measures (or failure to take any) adopted by the government in response. In the words of Ago, 'the lack of vigilance and failure to intervene on the part of the State authorities must obviously have occurred *in connexion* with the protection of the foreign States or individuals harmed by certain acts committed by the insurgents, and what is more, it must have occurred specifically *in relation* to those acts'.[898] Such measures are adopted and enforced in reaction to some types of actions by the rebels. To give a simple example, an act of expropriation committed by the government against a foreign investor in part of the territory, that is unaffected by any insurgency, is obviously not meant to be covered by Article 10(3).

The most important difference between the language contained in Article 10(3) of the 2001 Articles and Article 12 of the 1972 version is that the former no longer refers explicitly to the obligation to exercise due diligence. Article 10(3) simply makes a *renvoi* to other relevant provisions in Part II of the 2001 ILC Articles dealing with conduct considered as an act of State. Yet, that omission cannot, in any way, be considered as undermining Rule no. 6. In his First Report, Crawford noted that 'the basic principle stated in article 14 is well established, as the authorities cited in the [1975] commentary show'.[899] Crawford concluded that there was no need to explicitly mention the content of Rule no. 6 in Article 14 for the following reasons: '[i]t is true that the possibility of the State being held responsible independently for the acts of insurrectional movements remains, but this would of course be true in any event, since the "positive attribution" articles are cumulative in their effect; there is no need to state this specifically in article 14, paragraph 2'.[900] The ILC Drafting Committee on Second Reading agreed and deleted Article 14.[901] The 2001 Commentary also makes it clear that Rule no. 6 is covered by Article 10(3).[902] Crawford stresses the same view in his work: 'the state's

[898] Ibid., p. 139, para. 179, emphasis added.

[899] ILC, Crawford First Report, 1998, p. 53, para. 273.

[900] Ibid.

[901] ILC, 'Summary records of the meetings of the fiftieth session', 2558th meeting 7 August 1998, UN Doc. A/CN.4/SER.A/1998, *ILC Yearbook* vol. I (1998), p. 287, at p. 290, para. 86.

[902] ILC, Commentaries, 2001, para. 15:

> [e]xceptional cases may occur where the State was in a position to adopt measures of vigilance, prevention or punishment in respect of the movement's conduct but improperly failed to do so. This possibility is preserved by paragraph 3 of article 10, which provides that the attribution rules of paragraphs 1 and 2 are without prejudice to the attribution to a State of any

victory over an insurrectionist movement does not automatically excuse it from responsibility, a point made clear by ARSIWA Article 10(3), which preserves for application those grounds of attribution found in ARSIWA Articles 4–9'.[903]

3.3.2 *A State Is Not Responsible for Damages Resulting from Its Use of Military Force while Fighting an Insurgency Unless Its Conduct Breaches Its International Law Obligations*

In this section, I will examine two well-established principles.

After its victory against the rebels, the successful government is, as a matter of principle, *not* responsible for damages suffered by a third State or a foreigner as a result of its use of military force while fighting an insurgency.[904] Many awards and examples of State practice support this first basic principle.[905] For instance, the principle was laid out by the France–Mexico Commission in the *Pinson* case as follows: 'le simple fait que, pour supprimer des émeutes ou des révolutions, le Gouvernement légitime s'est trouvé dans la nécessité impérieuse de prendre des mesures militaires nuisibles à des ressortissants étrangers, n'engendre pas de responsabilité internationale de ce chef'.[906] The

> conduct, however related to that of the movement concerned, which is to be considered an act of that State by virtue of other provisions in Part II.

In this respect, the following remark by Greenman, 'The Secret History', p. 9, is misleading: 'unlike international investment law, the ARSIWA did not adopt the more controversial due diligence rule in respect of state responsibility for rebels'.

903 Crawford, *State Responsibility*, p. 179.

904 Piguet, *La Guerre civile en droit international*, p. 62 ('La pratique des États et la jurisprudence arbitrale nous permettent d'affirmer l'existence de la règle positive suivante: dans une guerre civile, les dommages directement causés par les opérations militaires [of the government] ne donne naissance à aucune responsabilité' ('State practice and arbitral jurisprudence allow us to affirm the existence of the following positive rule: in a civil war, damage directly caused by military operations [of the government] does not give rise to any liability'); de Beus, *The Jurisprudence of the General Claims Commission*, p. 112 ('the rule that a State cannot be held responsible for injury resulting from revolutions was upheld by the Commission on two occasions').

905 See analysis of Piguet, *La Guerre civile en droit international*, p. 49 ff. He examines several cases at p. 58 ff.

906 *Pinson* case, 1928, p. 450 ('the mere fact that, in order to suppress riots or revolutions, the legitimate Government has found itself in an imperative need to take military measures harmful to foreign nationals, does not give rise to international responsibility on this account').

same conclusion was reached by Huber in the *Biens britanniques au Maroc espagnol* case.[907]

This first principle is based on what Huber called in this case, 'the willingness of the State to achieve its primary goal: the maintenance of internal peace and social order'.[908] Indeed, a State has the right to defend itself against violent actions committed by rebels. They are considered outlaws under its own domestic law. It is legitimate for the State to use adequate, proportional and active military force to combat an insurrection. The fact that the use of force may sometimes cause damages to third States or foreigners is obviously regrettable. But that does not mean that the State is *necessarily* legally responsible for those damages.

A second principle has to be taken into account when dealing with such situations. Responsibility while fighting an insurrection will arise only if a State has 'failed in its duties'[909] under international law. In the words of Ago, a State will 'incur international responsibility' if its own conduct 'constituted a breach of an international obligation'.[910] There is nothing really surprising in this obvious statement. Thus, this is the situation prevailing in general international law under Article 3 of the ILC Articles. There are no logical reasons as to why any other solution should prevail in the specific context of rebellions. As noted by the American–Mexican Claims Commission in the *Simpson* case, examining claims for losses incurred during the 1929 'Escobar' revolution in Mexico, it is an 'established principal [sic] of international law that a government is responsible for the acts of its own forces, *even if they are*

907 *Affaire des biens britanniques au Maroc espagnol (Espagne* v. *Royaume-Uni),* 1 May 1925, UNRIAA 2 [hereinafter referred to as '*Affaire des biens britanniques au Maroc espagnol,* 1925'], p. 645: 'Il a été dit que l'État ne peut pas être rendu responsable du fait qu'une révolution éclate sur son territoire ou que le pays est entraîné dans une guerre. De cette thèse, il découle logiquement que l'État ne peut non plus être rendu responsable des conséquences de ce qu'il cherche à rétablir l'ordre ou à combattre l'ennemi par la force armée. En agissant ainsi, l'État n'accomplit qu'un devoir primordial. À ce sujet, il semble qu'une règle assez généralement reconnue existe: l'État n'est pas responsable des dommages causés même par les opérations militaires de ses propres troupes' ('It has been said that the state cannot be held responsible for the fact that a revolution breaks out in its territory or that the country is drawn into a war. From this thesis, it logically follows that the state can also not be held responsible for the consequences of its seeking to restore order or fight the enemy with armed force. In doing so, the state is fulfilling only a primary duty. In this regard, it seems that a fairly generally accepted rule exists: the state is not responsible for damage caused even by the military operations of its own troops').

908 Ibid.

909 Eagleton, *The Responsibility of States*, p. 147: '[a]cts of insurgents, like acts of individuals, are not primarily attributable to the state; and they can be imputed to the state only if the latter has failed in its duties'.

910 ILC, Ago Report, 1972, p. 137, para. 170.

engaged in suppressing a revolution'.[911] It must be highlighted that the use of military force by the government in order to suppress an insurgency does not, *in and of itself*, constitute a breach of international law. Something more needs to be demonstrated. It must be shown that the government has not fulfilled one of its obligations under international law. The obligations existing under the laws of war are especially relevant in this context.

The first basic principle (mentioned above) was recognized by the Preparatory Committee of the 1930 Hague Conference and its 'Basis of Discussion' no. 21: '[a] State is not responsible for damage caused to the person or property of a foreigner by its armed forces or authorities in the suppression of an insurrection, riot or other disturbance'.[912] Yet, there are several exceptions to this basic principle.[913] Thus, the Preparatory Committee has recognized, in its 'Basis of Discussion' no. 21, the existence of a second principle whereby a State fighting a rebellion has to respect a number of *specific obligations* under international law towards foreigners.[914] The *Pinson* award also mentioned a number of situations where a State should be held responsible for acts committed by its armed forces, including acts of expropriation.[915] The same position was adopted by the majority of

[911] *Claim of Jesse J. Simpson*, US–Mexico Claims Commission, Decision No. 63-E, p. 553, 554-555, in Whiteman, *Digest of International Law* (vol. 8), p. 824, emphasis added.

[912] League of Nations, 1929, 'Basis of Discussion' no. 21.

[913] Crawford, *Brownlie's Principles of Public International Law*, p. 552, referring to: McNair, *International Law Opinions*, vol. 2, p. 245: 'a State is not responsible for the damage resulting from military operations directed by its lawful government unless the damage was wanton or unnecessary, which appears to be substantially the same as the position of belligerent States in an international war'.

[914] League of Nations, 1929, 'Basis of Discussion' no. 21:

> The State must, however:
> (1) Make good damage caused to foreigners by the requisitioning or occupation of their property by its armed forces or authorities;
> (2) Make good damage caused to foreigners by destruction of property by its armed forces or authorities, or by their orders, unless such destruction is the direct consequence of combatant acts;
> (3) Make good damage caused to foreigners by acts of its armed forces or authorities where such acts manifestly went beyond the requirements of the situation or where its armed forces or authorities behaved in a manner manifestly incompatible with the rules generally observed by civilized States;
> (4) Accord to foreigners, to whom damage has been caused by its armed forces or authorities in the suppression of an insurrection, riot or other disturbance, the same indemnities as it accords to its own nationals in similar circumstances.

[915] *Pinson* case, 1928, p. 353: 'La thèse de l'irresponsabilité [supported by the Mexican government] est inacceptable, car il est incontestable qu'il peut se présenter bien des dommages révolutionnaires, dont l'État est sans aucun doute obligé d'assumer la responsabilité. . . . Par contre, si les dommages trouvent leur origine, par exemple dans des *réquisitions ou*

the Tribunal in the *Asian Agricultural Products* v. *Sri Lanka* case dealing with events taking place in the context of a rebellion of the Tamils Tiger, a group fighting for secession from Sri Lanka (and further discussed below in the Part dealing with failed attempt to create a new State).[916] The majority of the Tribunal made the following important statement which explicitly endorsed the two principles discussed in the previous paragraphs:

> It is a generally accepted rule of International Law, clearly stated in international arbitral awards and in the writings of the doctrinal authorities, that: (i) A State on whose territory an insurrection occurs is not responsible for the loss of damage sustained by foreign investors *unless it can be shown that the Government of that state failed to provide the standard of protection required, either by treaty, or under general customary law*, as the case may be; and (ii) Failure to provide the standard of protection required entails that state's international responsibility for losses suffered, regardless of whether the damages occurred during an insurgents' offensive act or resulting from governmental counter-insurgency activities.[917]

The award specifically mentioned that the obligation which the host State must observe is the standard of protection under international law and the BIT.[918] In this case, the applicable BIT between the UK and Sri Lanka includes a FPS clause which provides specific obligations for the host State regarding losses suffered by a foreign investor in the context of requisition and destruction of property by governmental forces arising in the situation of a civil war.[919] An analysis of such provisions, often found in BITs, is beyond the scope of this book. The same happens to be true regarding so-called 'war

contributions forcées réclamées par le Gouvernement légitime pendant sa lutte contre les insurgés, ou par les révolutionnaires avant leur triomphe final, ou qu'ils aient été causés par *des actes délictueux du Gouvernement légitime* ou de ses forces militaires, ou par des délits commis par les forces révolutionnaires victorieuses, la responsabilité de l'État ne saurait, à mon avis, être niée' ('The irresponsibility thesis [supported by the Mexican government] is unacceptable, for it is indisputable that there may well be revolutionary damage, for which the state is undoubtedly obliged to assume responsibility. … On the other hand, if the damage originates, for example in *requisitions or forced contributions demanded by the legitimate Government* during its struggle against the insurgents, or by the revolutionaries before their final triumph, or whether they were caused by *criminal acts of the legitimate Government or its military forces*, or by offenses committed by victorious revolutionary forces, the responsibility of the State cannot, in my opinion, be denied') (emphasis added).

916 See Part II, Section 5.2.2.1.

917 *AAPL* case, 1990, para. 72, emphasis added.

918 Ibid., para. 78.

919 The clause reads as follows:

> [w]ithout prejudice to paragraph (1) of this Article, nationals and companies of one Contracting Party who in any of the situations referred to in

clauses' found in some BITs and applicable in situations of wars, armed conflicts, revolutions, etc. These clauses (depending on their actual language) require the host State to provide (in a non-discriminatory way) compensation for war losses suffered by a foreign investor. The scope of 'war clauses' will not be addressed in this book.

The next sections examine in some detail one specific obligation for States under international law when fighting a rebellion: the obligation of due diligence towards foreigners and third States in relation to the conduct of rebels.

3.3.3 *Responsibility Arises As a Result of a State's Failure to Discharge Its Due Diligence Duty of Vigilance, Prevention and Punishment in Relation to the Conduct of Rebels*

States' obligations in the context of civil wars and insurrections are based on the general due diligence obligation under international law. As noted in a recent ILA Report on the question, the general due diligence principle has specific 'expressions' and 'manifestations'[920] in several subfields of international law,[921] including international human rights law, humanitarian law, and investment arbitration law.[922] This section will only examine the various aspects and impacts of this general due diligence obligation that are relevant in the narrower context of an insurgency. This general due diligence obligation is based on rules of State responsibility regarding the protection of foreigners.[923] It has long been recognized that the obligation of States towards foreigners includes two prime duties, namely a 'duty to abstain' and a 'duty to protect':

> that paragraph suffer losses in the territory of the other Contracting Party resulting from
> (a) requisitioning of their property by its forces or authorities, or
> (b) destruction of their property by its forces or authorities which was not caused in combat action or was not required by the necessity of the situation, shall be accorded restitution or adequate compensation.

920 ILA, 'Study Group on Due Diligence in International Law', Second Report by Duncan French (Chair) and Tim Stephens (Rapporteur), July 2016, p. 6.

921 See: ILA, 'Study Group on Due Diligence in International Law', First Report by Rapporteur Duncan French (Chair) and Tim Stephens (Rapporteur), 7 March 2014; ILA, ibid., providing an overview of all fields.

922 See ILA, 'Study Group on Due Diligence', First Report, p. 6 ff.

923 Ibid., p. 2 ff.; Eric de Brabandere, 'Host States' Due Diligence Obligations in International Investment Law', *Syracuse JIL & Commerce* 42(2) (2015), p. 324 ff.

> The first duty means that the State has the negative obligation to abstain from directly taking measures (through actions of its own organs) aimed at attacking the security of aliens. The second duty means instead that the territorial State has the positive obligation to protect aliens from harmful activities carried out by third persons (private individuals or the organs of other international entities) on its territory. This duty to protect includes, in turn, both an obligation to prevent harmful activities and an obligation, if such activities have occurred, to punish the persons responsible for the wrong suffered by the alien.[924]

In the context of investment arbitration, the FPS clause, which can be found in most, if not all investment treaties, requires the host State to provide both duties.[925]

924 Riccardo Pisillo-Mazzeschi, 'The Due Diligence Rule and the Nature of the International Responsibility of States', *German YIL* 35 (1992), p. 22. See also: Finnur Magnússon, *Full Protection and Security in International Law*, PhD Thesis, Vienna University (2012) p. 156:

> [t]herefore, a state's obligation is, on one hand, with regards to its own agents, negative which entails the absence of action. This means within the context of international investment law that a state is to refrain from taking action which could have adverse effects on the investor and his investment. On the other hand, the state's obligation is positive, i.e. the state is obliged to take action by exercising due diligence in the event that the investor and his investment is suffering from adverse effects stemming from the action or inaction of a third party or in the event that agencies of the state itself have taken action infringing upon the rights of the investor.

See also: Joanna Kulesza, *Due Diligence in International Law* (Leiden, Brill, 2016), p. 244–5.

925 *El Paso* v. *Argentina*, ICSID Case No. ARB/03/15, Award, 31 October 2011, paras. 522–3:

> [t]he BIT requires that Argentina provide 'full protection and security' to El Paso's investment. The Tribunal considers that the full protection and security standard is no more than the traditional obligation to protect aliens under international customary law . . . . A well-established aspect of the international standard of treatment is that States must use 'due diligence' to prevent wrongful injuries to the person or property of aliens caused by third parties within their territory, and, if they did not succeed, exercise at least 'due diligence' to punish such injuries.

See also: Magnússon, *Full Protection and Security*, p. 262:

> [t]he conclusion must be that the full protection and security standard is by its very nature a two-part standard founded on a treaty based standard with defined elements and a standard of due diligence which rests upon customary international law. These two foundations of the standard are different in nature – one entails an obligation to abstain from action whereas the other entails an obligation to take action.

Due diligence is a relevant concept regarding the 'duty to protect'.[926] It imposes an obligation on States in relation to the acts committed by *non-State actors* (such as individuals and insurgents) that are not attributable to the State. As noted by one writer, this 'duty to protect' includes two obligations of a differing nature: 'first, the obligation to try to prevent harmful acts of individuals and, second, the obligation, when a harmful act has occurred, to punish those responsible'.[927] De Brabandere has defined this 'duty to protect' as follows:

> The duty to protect the security of aliens and their property from acts of third parties in their territory has been accepted since long in international law. This obligation can be decomposed into three sub components:
> 1) the obligation of States to prevent acts of individuals that may harm the security of aliens and their property, by making use of their administrative and judicial apparatus to that effect;
> 2) the obligation of States to apprehend and bring to justice those responsible for injuries caused to aliens by making use of their administrative and judicial apparatus to that effect, and
> 3) the obligation for States to possess and make available to aliens a judicial and administrative system capable of preventing acts, and of punishing and apprehending those responsible for the acts.[928]

This section will focus on the concrete application of this 'duty to protect' in the specific context of rebellions.

What is the duty of States under international law towards third parties during an insurgency? Ago summarized this duty as follows: '[r]esponsibility can be attached to that State only because of some possible failure by its own organs to discharge the habitual obligations of *vigilance*, *prevention* and, in particular, *punishment*'.[929] The same assessment is made in the 2001 ILC Commentaries: '[e]xceptional cases may occur where the State

926 As noted by Pisillo-Mazzeschi, 'The Due Diligence Rule', p. 23, due diligence 'does not play any role' within the scope of the 'duty to abstain'.

927 Ibid., p. 26.

928 de Brabandere, 'Host States' Due Diligence Obligations', p. 324–5, referring to Pisillo-Mazzeschi, ibid.

929 ILC, Ago Report, 1972, p. 132, para. 160, emphasis added. See also, ibid., p. 130, para. 156:

> [i]t is hard to see how the acts committed in the course of the civil strife by insurgents fighting against it could be attributed, as a source of international responsibility, to the State which defeated the insurgents. Even at the time when it was fighting the insurrection, it seemed normal that the State should be held responsible only for any wrongful negligence on its part in *preventing or punishing* the wrongful acts of organs belonging to the insurgents. (emphasis added).

See also: Schwarzenberger, *International Law*, p. 629.

was in a position to adopt measures of *vigilance, prevention or punishment* in respect of the movement's conduct but improperly failed to do so'.[930] As noted by one writer, the due diligence obligation requires States 'to prevent, during the insurrection, and punish, especially after the insurrection, the unlawful acts of the movement'.[931] This principle has been accepted by many writers.[932] One classic example is the position of McNair:

> (i) A State on whose territory an insurrection occurs is not responsible for loss or damage sustained by a foreigner unless it can be shown that the Government of that State was negligent in the use of, or in the failure to use, the forces at its disposal for the prevention or suppression of the insurrection;
>
> (ii) this is a variable test, dependent on the circumstances of the insurrection; . . .[933]

Before examining in more detail the scope and content of this due diligence obligation, it must be highlighted that the State is responsible for *its own* failure to fulfil an obligation under international law.[934] It has *nothing* to do with the conduct of rebels being somewhat 'attributable' to the State. In the past, some tribunals have adopted some rather confusing language suggesting that the acts of the insurrectional movement were in fact 'attributable' to the State.[935] However, the most appropriate view to

930 ILC, Commentaries, 2001, p. 53, para. 16, emphasis added.

931 Cahin, 'Attribution of Conduct to the State', p. 253.

932 Morris, 'Revolutionary Movements', p. 723, 753; Shaw, *International Law*, p. 791; Cahin, 'Attribution of Conduct to the State', p. 253; Piguet, *La Guerre civile en droit international*, p. 91–2, 114 ff.; Rousseau, *Droit international public*, p. 85; Silvanie, *Responsibility of States*, p. 135 ff., 161 ff.; Schwarzenberger, *International Law*, p. 629; Borchard, *Diplomatic Protection*, p. 229 ('the state is not responsible for the injuries sustained by aliens at the hands of insurgents in civil war unless there is a proven fault or a want of due diligence on the part of the authorities in preventing or in suppressing the revolution'); Borchard, 'International Pecuniary Claims against Mexico', p. 339; Borchard, 'International Responsibility of the State', p. 118; Akehurst, 'State Responsibility', p. 49; Silvanie, 'Responsibility of States for Acts of Insurgent Governments', p. 91 ('it has been generally held by arbitral commissions and foreign offices that the state is not liable for wrongs and injuries inflicted upon foreign persons and property by unsuccessful insurgents who have gone beyond governmental control, unless it can be shown that the existing authorities were negligent either in preventing the injury or in suppressing the insurrection').

933 Crawford, *Brownlie's Principles of Public International Law*, p. 552, referring to: McNair, *International Law Opinions*, vol. 2, p. 245.

934 Piguet, *La Guerre civile en droit international*, p. 96.

935 One example is the reasoning of Umpire Duffield in the *Kwnmerov, Redles, Fulda, Fischback and Friedericy* case, German–Venezuelan Mixed Claims Commission, UNRIAA 10, p. 397–8:

adopt in such circumstances is that they clearly are not. This view was supported long ago by de Beus: 'the allowance of an indemnity is in reality always based upon a failure of the respondent government itself and not upon a responsibility for acts of the insurgents'.[936] Commenting on a statement made by Commissioner Nielsen in the *Solis* case (who said: 'in dealing with the question of *responsibility for acts of insurgents* two pertinent points have been stressed'),[937] de Beus rightly noted that 'it seems incorrect and confusing to speak, as the opinion quoted does, of

> all the authorities on international law agree that a nation *is responsible* for acts of revolutionists under certain conditions – such as lack of diligence, or negligence in failing to prevent such acts, when possible, or as far as possible to punish the wrongdoer and make reparation for the injury. *There is*, therefore, a rule of international law under which Venezuela would be held liable in certain cases for acts of revolutionists. (emphasis in the original).

Ago (ILC, Ago Report, 1972, p. 133, para. 162) rightly noted that 'the clarity of the language used [in that case] in defining the ruling principle in the matter left something to be desired'. Another confusing statement is made by the tribunal in *Home Frontier and Foreign Missionary Society of the United Brethren in Christ (United States)* v. *Great Britain*, 18 December 1920, UNRIAA 6, p. 42, referring to the 'well-established principle of international law that no government can be *held responsible for the act of rebellious bodies of men* committed in violation of its authority, *where it is itself guilty of no breach* of good faith, or of no *negligence in suppressing insurrection*' (emphasis added). The language suggests that if the government is 'guilty' of any 'negligence in suppressing insurrection', it will then be 'held responsible' for the act of rebels.

936 de Beus, *The Jurisprudence of the General Claims Commission*, p. 110. He also made other similar statements to the same effect:

> [w]ith regard to damage caused by the insurgent forces themselves, the principle stated means that a claim for compensation cannot be based merely upon the behaviour of such forces; the demand can only be admitted if it is based in last resort upon acts of the respondent government itself. Acts constituting a basis for an international award however may just as well be acts of omission as acts of commission. Accordingly, if aliens have suffered an injury at the hands of insurgents as a result of an omission of the government, e.g. a failure to provide sufficient protection, a claim may well be based upon such a failure. (ibid., p. 110)

See also, p. 113–14: '[i]n principle there exists no responsibility of a State under international law for damage caused by revolutionaries. However liability may be imposed for: … D. damage caused by wrongful acts of revolutionaries which were rendered possible by the government's own fault'. He added (p. 114) that 'never can liability be based merely upon illegal acts of revolutionists, nor upon behaviour of the government itself which would have been illegal if it had not been excused by the fact that it resulted from a revolution'.

937 *G.L. Solis (U.S.A.)* v. *United Mexican States*, Mexico–United States General Claims Commission, 3 October 1928, UNRIAA 4, p. 362, emphasis added.

"responsibility for acts of insurgents"; there is no such responsibility; the government can only be responsible for its own faults, although the damage sustained may but indirectly be caused by such faults'.[938] Indeed, a State is not 'responsible' for the acts of rebels. These two situations must be clearly distinguished, as highlighted by Huber in the *British Claims in the Spanish Zone of Morocco* case. Thus, responsibility for the action (or inaction) of the public authority 'is quite a different matter from responsibility for acts attributable to persons beyond the influence of the authorities or openly hostile to them'.[939] Huber also mentioned that 'while the State is not responsible for revolutionary events themselves, it may nevertheless be responsible [where] the authorities do not counter the consequences to the extent possible', adding that 'the State is bound to a certain vigilance'.[940] The point has also been well-explained by Ago.[941]

In the context of this passage, another question arises: what damages should be paid by the State for its failure to fulfil its due diligence obligation? It has been suggested by Ago that reparation should only cover the damages caused by the actions of the rebels.[942] For instance, in

938 de Beus, *The Jurisprudence of the General Claims Commission*, p. 111.

939 *Affaire des biens britanniques au Maroc espagnol*, 1925, p. 642, the original French text reads as follows: '[l]a responsabilité pour l'action ou l'inaction de la puissance publique est tout autre chose que la responsabilité pour des actes imputables à des personnes échappant à l'influence des autorités ou leur étant ouvertement hostiles'.

940 Ibid., p. 642: '[s]i l'État n'est pas responsable des événements révolutionnaires eux-mêmes, il peut être néanmoins responsable de ce que les autorités font ou ne font pas, pour parer, dans la mesure possible, aux suites'.

941 ILC, Ago Report, 1972, p. 139, para. 179:

> The fact that the State is said not to be responsible 'for the damage' caused by insurgents '*unless*' the State organs have in a specific case failed to provide protection *in no way means* that such negligence would suddenly make it possible to *attribute to the State the acts of the insurrectional movement*, in principle denied. The most that this could mean would be that in such cases the State, being responsible for the omission on the part of its organs, is required to compensate for the damage caused by the acts of the insurgents, in reparation for that omission. However, the internationally wrongful act of the State still remains nothing more than the omission itself. In relation to the conduct of the State, the act committed by the organs of the insurgents is nothing more than the external event which serves as a catalyst for the wrongfulness of that conduct. (emphasis added).

Other examples of State practice are mentioned in ibid., p. 135, paras. 167, 171 ff.

942 Ibid., p. 130, para. 156, fn. 331: 'there is no reason why, in the case we are now considering, the amount of reparation due as a result of a breach by the State of an

the event that the State failed to provide sufficient protection to the property of a foreign investor that was destroyed by the rebels, the amount of compensation to be paid by the State should cover the material damages suffered as a result of the destruction. Thus, while it is clear that a State is only responsible for *its own* failure to fulfil its due diligence obligation, it remains that it ultimately is bound to indemnify the victims of the damages *caused by others*.[943]

In the following sections, I will examine in detail how this due diligence obligation applies in the context of rebellions. I will address these questions:

- Is the due diligence obligation widely supported by State practice and case law? (Section 3.3.3.1);
- What is the scope and content of the obligation? (Section 3.3.3.2);
- What is the applicable test to determine whether any breach of the obligation has been committed? (Section 3.3.3.3); and
- Other related questions (Section 3.3.3.4).

3.3.3.1 The Due Diligence Obligation Is Widely Supported by State Practice and Case Law

The work of the ILC shows that the due diligence principle has been widely adopted in State practice in the context of rebellions.[944] Having received comments from governments, the Preparatory Committee of the 1930 Hague Conference came up with the following 'Basis of Discussion' no. 22 (a): 'Nevertheless, a State is responsible for damage caused to the person or property of a foreigner by persons taking part in an insurrection or riot or by mob violence if it failed to use such diligence as due in the circumstances in preventing the damage and punishing its authors.'[945] For Ago, 'it

obligation to prevent or punish should not be established on the basis of the material damage caused by the action of the individual serving as an organ of the insurrectional movement'. See also: ILC, Report, 1975, p. 97, para. 24.

943 This is indeed the position of Ago as shown in this passage (quoted above), indicating that the State is 'required to compensate for the damage caused by the acts of the insurgents, in reparation for [its own] omission' (ILC, Ago Report, 1972, p. 139, para. 179).

944 ILC, Ago Report, 1972, p. 135, para 167: 'It would thus appear that international arbitration bodies – whose precedents in the matter under discussion here were largely developed by the mid-1930s – show remarkable uniformity in their opinions. The same may be said of diplomatic practice.'

945 League of Nations publication (1929), p. 224.

is clear from the replies given by Governments to the request formulated by the Preparatory Committee that in 1930 there was substantial agreement among States' in favour of Rule no. 6 embodied in 'Basis of Discussion' no. 22 (a).[946] Ago provides several examples of State practice supporting Rule no. 6.[947]

Many international tribunals have explicitly mentioned this due diligence obligation. The relevant extracts of some of those awards referring to this obligation can be summarized as follows:

- *Sambiaggio* case, Italian–Venezuelan Commission, 'accept[ing] the rule that if in any case of reclamation submitted to him it is alleged and proved that Venezuelan authorities failed to exercise due diligence to prevent damages from being inflicted by revolutionists, that country should be held responsible';[948]
- *Kwnmerov, Redles, Fulda, Fischback and Friedericy* case, German–Venezuelan Mixed Claims Commission, Umpire Duffield referring to 'lack of diligence, or negligence in failing to prevent such acts, when possible, or as far as possible to punish the wrongdoer and make reparation for the injury';[949]
- *Batopilas Mining Co.* case, American–Mexican Claims Commission, denying the claim on the grounds that the 'revolution having terminated unsuccessfully, no claim for the loss alleged may be properly asserted against the Mexican Government without at the same time showing a want of due diligence on the part of the authorities in preventing the injury or in suppressing the revolution';[950]
- *Aroa Mines* case, UK–Venezuela Claims Commission, referring to the principle of 'non-responsibility of nations for the acts of unsuccessful revolutionists'[951] and later indicating that the 'claim is based wholly on the seizure of their property by revolutionary troops without proof of

[946] ILC, Ago Report, 1972, p. 137, para. 170.
[947] Ibid., p. 137, para. 170 ff.
[948] *Sambiaggio* case, 1903, p. 524.
[949] *Kwnmerov, Redles, Fulda, Fischback and Friedericy* case, German–Venezuelan Mixed Claims Commission, UNRIAA 10, p. 397–8.
[950] *Batopilas Mining Co.* case, US–Mexico Claims Commission, Decision No. 17-B, 1948, in V. Coussirat-Coustère and P. M. Eisemann, *Répertoire de la Jurisprudence Arbitrale Internationale* (Nijhoff, Dordrecht, vol. III, 1989), p. 1140–1 (see also, in Whiteman, *Digest of International Law* (vol. 8), p. 822). The case concerned the losses claimed by a US company due to forced loans, seizure of ores and equipment, and suspension of mining operations in its silver mines at Batopilas, Mexico, in 1871–2 by the unsuccessful rebellions of General Diaz.
[951] *Aroa Mines* case, UK–Venezuela Claims Commission, UNRIAA 9, p. 439.

any fault or lack of due diligence on the part of the titular and respondent Government';[952]

- *Russell* case, US–Mexico Special Claims Commission, stating that 'if it had been provided that responsibility should be fixed conformably to international law, liability would exist in cases revealing proof of negligence or of absence of good faith in preventing wrongful acts on the part of the insurgents', and adding that 'there would be no responsibility in cases in which the respondent government was not chargeable with negligence'.[953]

Finally, reference should be made to the work of Greenman, studying the actual doctrinal sources of Rule no. 6.[954] She cites Borchard's important work (*The Diplomatic Protection of Citizens Abroad, or, The Law of International Claims*, 1915) and his proposition that there was (at the time) 'general support' for a principle of non-responsibility for acts of rebels 'unless there is proven fault or a want of due diligence on the part of the authorities in preventing the injury or in suppressing the revolution'.[955] She pointed out that Borchard rejected in a long footnote 'the significance of a number of decisions making exception to his general principle' and that 'the only diplomatic practice cited is that of Britain and the US' which had denied responsibility for the wrongs committed by the failed attempt at secession by the Confederate rebels.[956] According to her, 'this footnote is typical of the way in which commentators manoeuvred the highly malleable materials to support their various positions, emphasizing particular sources over others and explaining contrary practice as exceptions to or breaches of their general principles'.[957] She goes further regarding the work of Eagleton and affirmed that the 'use of the arbitral practice takes matters beyond a manipulation of inherently malleable materials and into the realm of the sloppy and even the misleading – even his colleague Borchard apparently accused Eagleton of being "not intellectually honest"'.[958] In her view, the position adopted by these American scholars on Rule no. 6 (and Rule no. 2) must

[952] Ibid., p. 445.

[953] *Naomi Russell, In Her Own Right and As Administratrix and Guardian (U.S.A.)* v. *United Mexican States*, Mexico–US Special Claims Commission, Decision no. 5, 24 April 1931, opinion of Umpire Nielsen, UNRIAA 4, p. 824.

[954] Greenman, 'Aliens in Latin America', p. 631–2.

[955] Borchard, *The Diplomatic Protection*, p. 229.

[956] Greenman, 'Aliens in Latin America', p. 632.

[957] Ibid.

[958] Ibid.

be read 'in the context of decolonization, capitalist expansion and economic imperialism in Latin America'.[959] Thus, Western military interventions in Latin America 'produced the highly-contested doctrine of state responsibility for injuries to aliens caused by rebels' which 'was produced out of and used to manage the transition from old colonialism to new imperialism in the region so as to guarantee foreign trade and investment'.[960] The same conclusion was reached by Nissel.[961] One can hardly deny that the recognition by some scholars of the existence of a due diligence obligation was clearly influenced by political ideas prevalent at the time.[962] Yet, it is also undeniable that

959 Ibid., p. 617.

960 Ibid., p. 638–9.

961 Tzvika Alan Nissel, *A History of State Responsibility: The Struggle for International Standards (1870-1960)*, PhD Thesis, University of Helsinki (2016), p. 167: 'Prior to the U.S. turn to arbitration, international doctrine took a restrictive approach to the State responsibility. States were generally not considered responsible for injuries arising in the revolutionary context of political uprisings and military coups. In the New World, however, this changed. Arbitrators often imposed liability on newly formed governments for the acts of rebel forces.' See also at p. 171: 'The general expansion of the concept of attribution described above occurred largely in the context of the New World, where tribunals imposed international liability upon newly established Latin American governments for injuries resulting from the losing revolutionary forces in civil wars. Tribunals were less willing to hold Great Powers responsible in comparable circumstances' (citing the *Salvador Prats* case in support of the proposition mentioned in the last sentence). He also made this comment, p. 362:

> [a]rbitrators saw little problem with imposing State responsibility based on general principles of law. They believed they could resolve alien protection claims without the need for public codification. The resulting awards were predictably incoherent. For example, the intra-American practice of alien protection expanded the traditional doctrine of State responsibility to include the imposition of liability upon newly formed governments for the injurious acts of rebel forces. In contrast, the applicability of State responsibility to the wrongful omissions of States was narrowly construed, especially when the U.S. was a defendant, such as in claims arising out of its Civil War. It is likely that factors leading to arbitral results depended both on the facts of each case as well as on the identities of litigating parties and arbitrators.

962 Philip C. Jessup, 'Responsibility of States for Injuries to Individuals', *Columbia LR* 46 (1946), p. 906: '[t]he history of the development of the international law on the responsibility of states for injuries to aliens is thus an aspect of the history of "imperialism", of "dollar diplomacy"'. On this question, see: Frédéric Mégret, 'Mixed Claim Commissions and the Once Centrality of the Protection of Aliens', in Ignacio de la Rasilla and Jorge E. Viñuales, *Experiments in International Adjudication: Historical Accounts* (Cambridge University Press, 2019), p. 127 ff.

Rule no. 6 has been overwhelmingly recognized by international tribunals and scholars ever since. This point will be further examined in the next sections.

3.3.3.2 The Scope and Content of the Due Diligence Obligation

This section examines the scope and content of the due diligence obligation. I will first examine the *general* obligation imposed on governments to make all efforts within their capacity to suppress an insurrection (Section 3.3.3.2.1). I will then analyse two *specific* obligations that have long been recognized by Judge Huber in the *Spanish Zone of Morocco Claims* case:[963]

- The obligation to take reasonable measures to *prevent* injurious conduct by rebels and damages from occurring (Section 3.3.3.2.2); and
- The obligation to *punish* the wrongdoers and provide reparation (Section 3.3.3.2.3).

Finally, I will demonstrate that the claimant is subject to the burden of showing that the government has failed to fulfil its due diligence obligation (Section 3.3.3.2.4).

3.3.3.2.1 Obligation for a State to Make All Efforts within Its Capacity to Suppress an Insurrection At the outset, it must be mentioned that a State is not responsible under international law for the mere fact that a rebellion is taking place on its territory and that such events are causing damages to foreigners. As noted by Huber in the *Spanish Zone of Morocco Claims* case, '[i]l paraît incontestable que l'État n'est pas responsable pour le fait d'une émeute, révolte, guerre civile ou guerre internationale, ni pour le fait que ces événements provoquent des dommages sur son territoire'.[964] Yet, the fact that 'l'État n'est pas responsable des événements

[963] *Affaire des biens britanniques au Maroc espagnol*, 1925, p. 645: 'la responsabilité de l'État peut être engagée dans les situations en question, non seulement par un manque de vigilance dans la prévention des actes dommageables, mais aussi par un manque de diligence dans la poursuite pénale des fauteurs, ainsi que dans l'application des sanctions civiles voulues' ('State responsibility can be engaged in the situations in question, not only by a lack of vigilance in the prevention of harmful acts, but also by a lack of diligence in the criminal prosecution of the perpetrators, as well as in the application of desired civil sanctions').

[964] Ibid., p. 642 ('it seems indisputable that the state is not responsible for the fact of a riot, revolt, civil war or international war, nor for the fact that these events cause damage on its territory').

révolutionnaires eux-mêmes'[965] does not mean that the host State is never responsible.

The due diligence obligation requires a State to make all efforts, within the limits of its ability and capacity, to suppress an ongoing insurrection. This basic principle has been recognized by many awards.[966] As noted by Akehurst, the 'due diligence in suppressing a rebellion necessarily implies the use of force', adding that a government's failure 'to take any military action at all against the rebels would have been interpreted as negligence in suppressing the rebellion'.[967] Thus, a State must respond to an insurrection by using its military forces. A failure to do so may be considered as a breach of the due diligence obligation (depending on a number of circumstances).[968] In the *Prats* case, Mexican Commissioner, Mr Palacio, explained in some detail the course of action a State should take when it faces powerful and organized rebels who 'resist the legitimate authorities and oppose against them military forces enough to check their efforts and make impossible the capture and punishment they attempted'.[969] He asked 'what else can be done by the authorities for the perfect fulfillment of their duties?' He answered:

> It is clear that the only means the legitimate authorities possess to preserve order and maintain the empire of law consist *in raising the military forces required to subdue the rebels*, in obtaining from the national representative the pecuniary resources necessary to meet the expenses of the war, in calling around them all the good citizens and leading them to fight against the disobedient; in declaring, in fine, that these are rebels and enemies of

965 Ibid ('the State is not responsible for revolutionary events themselves').

966 *Claim of Jesse J. Simpson*, US–Mexico Claims Commission, Decision No. 63-E, p. 553, 554–5, in Whiteman, *Digest of International Law* (vol. 8), p. 824: '[i]t is an established principle of international law that the regularly constituted government of a country is not liable for the actions of unsuccessful revolutionists unless there is a showing that such government was *not diligent in its efforts to suppress the revolution*' (emphasis added). See also: *Batopilas Mining Co.* case, American–Mexican Claims Commission, Decision No. 17-B, 1948, in V. Coussirat-Coustère and P. M. Eisemann, *Répertoire de la Jurisprudence Arbitrale Internationale* (Nijhoff, Dordrecht, vol. III, 1989), p. 1140–1, speaking of the requirement of 'showing a want of due diligence on the part of the authorities in preventing the injury *or in suppressing the revolution*' (emphasis added).

967 Akehurst, 'State Responsibility', p. 53, referring to a number of cases: *Santa Clara Estates Case (Supplementary Claim)*, UK–Venezuela Mixed Commission, UNRIAA 9, p. 455, 456–8; *Venezuelan Steam Transportation Company* case, United States–Venezuelan Claims Commission, in Moore, *History and Digest of the International Arbitrations* (vol. II), p. 1693.

968 These circumstances are examined in Section 3.3.3.3.3.

969 *Prats* case, 1868, Mexican Commissioner, Mr Palacio, p. 194, p. 197.

the nation whose legal and moral existence they have attacked by their resistance.[970]

There exists, of course, no precise definition of how much (and what type of) military forces should be used by a government to suppress a rebellion. It has been argued that this duty is fulfilled when a State uses all available military resources at its disposal. Thus, as noted by one writer, 'if [a government] *uses all its armed forces and resources* to suppress the revolution and to cause the war to be short and exempt of disaster as possible, it fulfills its duty and cannot be blamed for omission or negligence, and consequently cannot have any responsibility'.[971] As noted by the Tribunal in the *Home Frontier and Foreign Missionary Society* case, what matters is that a State displays that it has taken 'every measure available'[972] to suppress the insurrection.[973] Similarly, the *Santa Clara* award refers to the standard according to which a government has to give 'the best resistance possible under all the existing circumstances to the revolutionary forces seeking its overthrow'.[974] In the *Sambiaggio* case, Umpire Ralston held that responsibility can only be possible when 'it clearly appear[s] that the government has failed to use *promptly and with appropriate force* its constituted authority'.[975] As further discussed below,[976] the applicable test is what a prudent, well-organized and diligent government would have done in similar circumstances. Some of the relevant circumstances pertain not only to the magnitude of the rebellion and the strength of the rebels, but also to the location where the wrong took place.[977] Another relevant criterion is the actual *capacity* (and willingness) of a government to suppress a revolution.[978] This basic principle has been recognized in several cases.

970 Ibid., p. 197, emphasis added.

971 Silvanie, *Responsibility of States*, p. 163, emphasis added.

972 *Home Frontier and Foreign Missionary Society of the United Brethren in Christ (United States)* v. *Great Britain*, 18 December 1920, UNRIAA 6, p. 44.

973 Ibid.

974 *Santa Clara Estates Case (Supplementary Claim)*, UK–Venezuela Mixed Commission, UNRIAA 9, p. 458.

975 *Sambiaggio* case, 1903, p. 513, emphasis added. See also: *Acquatella, Bianchi et al.* case, France–Venezuela Mixed Claims Commission, Commissioner Paul, UNRIAA 10, p. 5, p. 6: 'only when it appears that the Government has *failed to make prompt and efficient use of its authority* to cause a return of said dissatisfied party to obedience, and to protect, within the measure of its ability, the property and persons threatened by the revolutionary disturbance, may it be considered as liable for the consequences of such abnormal condition', emphasis added.

976 See Section 3.3.3.3.2.

977 These circumstances are examined below, see: Section 3.3.3.3.3.

978 See Section 3.3.3.3.3.2.

However, there is clearly no general obligation imposed on any government to completely and totally defeat an insurgency. It would be unrealistic to impose on a State such a compulsorily successful outcome against the rebels. In the *Gill* case, a British national working at a power plant was attacked in 1912 at his house by revolutionary forces opposing the Madero Government of Mexico and some of his property was stolen or destroyed. The British–Mexican Claims Commission stated that the governmental 'authorities cannot be blamed for omission or negligence, when the action taken by them *has not resulted in the entire suppression of the insurrections* . . . or has not led to the punishment of *all* the individuals responsible', adding that 'in those cases no responsibility will be admitted'.[979]

In any event, introducing any such requirement would be putting the threshold too high. It would mean, in practical terms, that any other type of governmental actions short of total victory would have to be considered as a breach of the due diligence obligation. But, as noted by the US Secretary of State Bayard in the context of an insurrection in Cuba, 'the mere fact that an insurrection occurred is not proof of negligence'.[980] Accordingly, a State does not incur any international responsibility from the simple fact that a rebellion is taking place in its territory. US Secretary of State Bayard further added that 'the fact that an insurrection maintains itself for any considerable length of time is prima facie proof of vis major which throws upon the party alleging particular negligence the burden of proving it'[981] (the possibility for States to invoke the defence of *force majeure* will be discussed below).[982] Ago well-explained why there is no such thing as a general obligation to completely 'suppress' an insurgency.[983]

979 *John Gill* case, British–Mexican Claims Commission, 19 May 1931, UNRIAA 5, p. 159, emphasis added.

980 Letter dated 6 January 1888, in Moore, *Digest of International Law* (vol. III), p. 961–4 (also in ILC, 'Force majeure and Fortuitous event as Circumstances Precluding Wrongfulness: Survey of State Practice, International Judicial Decisions and Doctrine', Study Prepared by the Secretariat, 1978, UN Doc. A/CN.4/315, in *ILC Yearbook* II(1) (1978) [hereinafter referred to as ILC, 'Force majeure and Fortuitous event', 1978] p. 116).

981 Ibid.

982 See Section 3.3.3.4.2.

983 ILC, Ago Report, 1972, p. 139, para. 179:

> The fact that reference is sometimes made to negligence on the part of public authorities 'in repressing insurrection' certainly does not mean that the State is regarded as responsible in the event of injuries caused by the organs of an insurrectional movement to a foreign State or to one of its nationals *on the grounds that the effort to crush the insurrection has not in general been conducted vigorously*. The lack of vigilance and failure

Some older cases seem to refer to the total 'suppression' of a rebellion as part of the due diligence obligation. One such instance is the *Home Frontier and Foreign Missionary Society* case.[984] Writers also often refer to such a duty.[985] In his book, Crawford indicates, however, that 'there is no modern example of a State being held responsible for negligent failure to suppress insurgents'.[986] He also added that 'whether, as suggested in the *Home Missionaries Society* case, a state could be responsible for "negligence in suppressing insurrection" is much more doubtful'.[987] Indeed, it is very doubtful since it would put the threshold of reasonable conduct too high. In this context, Crawford noted that 'decisions of tribunals and the other sources offer no definition of "due diligence"' and that 'if "due diligence" be taken to denote a fairly high standard of conduct the exception will overwhelm the rule [of non-responsibility]'.[988]

The issue arose in the *Oztas* v. *Libya* case involving a contract signed in 2008 by a Turkish company with a Libyan company which was mutually terminated by the parties in 2013 (as noted by the Tribunal, 'presumably as a result of the Libyan Civil War in 2011').[989] Alleging not having received due payment under the agreement, the Claimant started

> to intervene on the part of the State authorities must obviously have occurred in connexion with the protection of the foreign States or individuals harmed by certain acts committed by the insurgents, and what is more, it must have occurred specifically in relation to those acts. (emphasis added).

984 *Home Frontier and Foreign Missionary Society of the United Brethren in Christ (United States)* v. *Great Britain*, 18 December 1920, UNRIAA 6, p. 44: 'the well-established principle of international law that no government can be held responsible for the act of rebellious bodies of men committed in violation of its authority, where it is itself guilty of no breach of good faith, or of *no negligence in suppressing insurrection*', emphasis added.

985 See, for instance, McNair, *International Law Opinions*, vol. 2, p. 245: '[a] State on whose territory an insurrection occurs is not responsible for loss or damage sustained by a foreigner unless it can be shown that the Government of that State was negligent in the use of, or in the failure to use, the forces at its disposal for the prevention or *suppression of the insurrection*' (emphasis added) (quoted in Crawford, *Brownlie's Principles of Public International Law*, p. 552).

986 Crawford, *Brownlie's Principles of Public International Law*, p. 552. See also: Akehurst, 'State Responsibility', p. 51: '[n]ot surprisingly, no arbitral tribunal has ever found a State guilty of negligence in failing to prevent a rebellion'. He also added that awards show that States 'would have been liable if it had failed to take steps to prevent a rebellion that was reasonably foreseeable'.

987 Crawford, *State Responsibility*, p. 179.

988 Crawford, *Brownlie's Principles of Public International Law*, p. 552.

989 *Oztas Construction, Construction Materials Trading Inc.* v. *Libyan Investment Development Company and Libya*, ICC Arbitration No. 21603/ZF/AYZ, Final Award, 14 June 2018, para. 63.

arbitration proceedings under the Turkey–Libya BIT arguing that Libya had breached several provisions, including the FPS clause, and that it had failed to 'take necessary measures to avoid / block the Libyan Revolution /Libyan Civil War'.[990] The majority of the Tribunal rejected this allegation on the grounds that there exists no such obligation under international law: 'There is, so far as we are aware, no case in which an arbitral tribunal constituted pursuant to an investment treaty has found that an investment treaty was breached by *a failure to avoid a revolution or civil war.*'[991] At the end of the day, the government has the obligation to take all available reasonable measures to suppress the rebellion. As noted in a legal opinion of the UK Law Officers assessing whether the Venezuelan Government should be held responsible for injuries and losses suffered by foreigners in the context of a rebellion in 1858, responsibility only arises if a government 'having the power to do so, neglects or wilfully abstains from putting down insurgents'.[992]

[990] Ibid., para. 154.

[991] Ibid., para. 162. The Tribunal also added that: 'As a matter of international law, the condition of civil war or uprising, if existent, constitutes an extraordinary situation that negates any negligence or lack of due diligence against the State of Libya, and Claimant has not shown, let alone compellingly demonstrated, that the State of Libya has taken measures that directly aggravated or triggered the civil war and resulted in Claimant's alleged losses', emphasis added. This last statement (about the 'condition of civil war or uprising' somewhat 'negating' 'any negligence or lack of due diligence') is obviously incorrect. In contrast, in his dissenting opinion arbitrator Tolga Ayoglu, ibid., para. 28, refers to 'the passive attitude of the State of Libya, against this unstable political and economic situation [which] is not acceptable under the BIT'. He also noted that Libya had failed to 'maintain a stable framework for investments' in breach of the fair and equitable treatment standard and that it had not 'showed sufficient efforts to rebuild it, despite the fact that more than six years has passed following the Libyan Revolution and the break-out of the Libyan Civil War'.

[992] The Law Officers, Mr J.D. Harding *et al.*, opinion of 25 February 1861, in McNair, *International Law Opinions*, vol. 2, p. 260:

> As a matter, however, of international right, we do not think that the Venezuelan Government can be held responsible generally for injuries inflicted on the properties or persons of British subjects, or other foreigners, resident in the country, by insurgents engaged in open and armed hostility to the Government; and which injuries the Government had not the power to prevent. A foreigner cannot claim to be placed in a better situation than the natural-born subjects of the country. If the country be invaded by an enemy, and the foreigner's property is injured by the invading army, he has no title to claim compensation. Injury caused by insurgents or rebels is subject to the same rule. If, indeed, the Government, having the power to do so, *neglects or wilfully abstains from putting down insurgents, it may be regarded as an accomplice in the act complained* of, and there would be a right of the foreigner to demand compensation. In

The next section examines the first specific type of due diligence obligation imposed on host States in the context of rebellions.

3.3.3.2.2 Obligation to Take All Reasonable Measures to Prevent Injurious Conduct by Rebels and Damages from Occurring The due diligence obligation requires a State to take all reasonable measures to *prevent* the acts committed by rebels (that caused damages) from occurring in the first place. This duty to 'prevent' has been recognized by several arbitral tribunals.[993] One important point mentioned by Gardner, back in 1927, is that there exists no *general* obligation for States to actually *always* prevent the commission of *every possible wrong* against foreigners.[994] In the words of Gardner, 'where liability exists' for a State 'it is *not for failure to prevent wrongs*'.[995] Thus, the burden of any such all-encompassing obligation upon States would be both unrealistic and simply impossible to fulfil. Gardner explained that a State can only be held responsible for its '*failure to take reasonable measures to prevent*

> the case before us, we find no sufficient ground for alleging that the injuries complained of would not have occurred but for *gross neglect* on the part of the Venezuelan Government; and we do not think, therefore, that the facts, as far as we can ascertain them, would justify a demand for compensation. (emphasis added).

993 One example is Arbitrator Huber in *Affaire des biens britanniques au Maroc espagnol*, 1925, p. 642.

994 James W. Garner, 'Responsibility of States for Injuries Suffered by Foreigners within Their Territories on Account of Mob Violence, Riots and Insurrection', *ASIL Proc.*, 21 (1927), p. 51:

> It is, of course, an error to say, as has sometimes been said, that a state is bound by international law to *prevent* wrongs to aliens within its territories or to indemnify them in case it fails to do so. Such an obligation would make the state an insurance society obliged to guarantee them for all losses and injuries which it failed to prevent. No state, however well organized and however efficient and vigilant its peace officers and other functionaries may be, is capable of preventing wrongs from being committed at times against aliens, and international law imposes no such impossible obligation upon any state. What it does require, and this alone, is that the proper authorities of the state shall exercise due diligence to prevent the perpetration of such wrongs, that is, to do all that they can reasonably be expected to do, to prevent them. If they do that, the state cannot be held responsible, at least not to the extent of being liable for the payment of an indemnity to the victims or their surviving dependents. (emphasis in the original, see also, at p. 62).

995 Ibid., p. 51–2, emphasis added.

them [i.e. wrongs], or in case such measures are unsuccessful, for failure to adopt reasonable measures to apprehend and punish the guilty offenders'.[996]

The duty to 'prevent' requires a State to use all available military or police resources to ensure that foreigners are, as much as possible, not victims of illegal acts committed by rebels.[997] A State needs to 'employ all the means within its reach',[998] to have 'done everything in its power',[999] or, to use the words of the 1929 Harvard Draft Articles, 'a state has a duty to use the means at its disposal for the protection of aliens'.[1000] Similarly,

996 Ibid., p. 51–2, emphasis added. See also: Pisillo-Mazzeschi, 'The Due Diligence Rule', p. 26: 'the State is not obligated to absolutely prevent activities of private persons that are harmful to the security of aliens, but is bound only to exercise due diligence in order to prevent such activities'. The same position has been adopted by tribunals in the different context of mob violence (not involving rebels). See: *Walter A. Noyes (USA)* v. *Panama*, US–Panama Commission, 22 May 1933, UNRIAA 6, p. 311:

> [t]he mere fact that an alien has suffered at the hands of private persons an aggression, which could have been averted by the presence of a sufficient police force on the spot, does not make a government liable for damages under international law. There must be shown special circumstances from which the responsibility of the authorities arises: either their behavior in connection with the particular occurrence, or a general failure to comply with their duty to maintain order, to prevent crimes or to prosecute and punish criminals.

997 Piguet, *La Guerre civile en droit international*, p. 115, referring to De Visscher, *Théories et réalités*, p. 348.

998 Silvanie, *Responsibility of States*, p. 163.

999 ILC, Ago Report, 1972, p. 138, para. 174, referring to a note of 27 September 1938 from the Legal Department of the French Ministry of Foreign Affairs, which stated:

> [i]t is . . . generally accepted, particularly by arbitral tribunals which have dealt with questions of this kind, that in case of civil war a government is not responsible for damage sustained by aliens at the hands of insurgents. The only circumstances in which this would not apply would be where it was established that the regular government had committed a fault or had not *done everything in its power to prevent the damage or to put down the revolution.* (emphasis added, referred to in A.-Ch. Kiss, *Répertoire de la pratique française en matière de droit international public* (Paris, CNRS, vol. III, 1965), p. 637).

1000 See comments to Article 4, Harvard Draft Convention, 1929:

> [t]he failure to perform the duty, under normal conditions, may make it impossible for a state to avoid responsibility in certain cases where responsibility otherwise would not have existed. It is to be recognized, however, that in every state temporary abnormal conditions may result in the dislocation of the governmental organization, and such possibility is to be taken into account in determining whether responsibility exists in a given case. Even in abnormal times, however, a state has a duty to use the

the majority of the *AAPL* Tribunal held that Sri Lanka's 'inaction and omission violated its due diligence obligation which requires undertaking *all possible measures* that could be *reasonably expected* to prevent the eventual occurrence of killings and property destructions'.[1001] Responsibility therefore only arises when it can be shown that the government was 'in a position to prevent such injury', but has 'failed to use due diligence to do so'.[1002] I will explain below[1003] what is the appropriate test in order to determine concretely whether any breach of the obligation to 'prevent' has been committed. In the *Prats* case, decided by the United States–Mexico Mixed Commission (and further discussed in Part II dealing with rebels attempting to create a new State), Mexican Commissioner, Mr Palacio described the duty of States as follows:

> It is natural and proper that a nation carrying on a war, whether foreign or civil, should endeavor, for the sake of duty and convenience, to prevent her enemies from causing the mischiefs which they might attempt to commit. If, in this respect, *she does all in her power, and all that can be accomplished by means of her resources, it can be said that she fulfills the whole of her duties*, both toward her own citizens and the citizens of foreign countries. The evils which it *was not possible to avoid* constitute a calamity for which she can not be responsible; and there is not a shadow of reason in pretending that either a nation or an individual should be bound to do in behalf of others more than he has done in his own defense. If the nation herself could not avoid suffering incalculable losses, it is clear that she could not possibly avoid those sustained

> means at its disposal for the protection of aliens, and a failure to perform this duty may result in its becoming responsible to another state injured in consequence thereof. The term 'means at its disposal' is employed because it is desired to emphasize the instrumentalities of government that may be available for use.

1001 *AAPL* case, 1990, para 85(B), emphasis added.

1002 In the context of claims by US nationals for compensation arising from acts committed by insurgents in Cuba in 1895, US Acting Secretary of State, Mr Uhl, in a letter of 1 July 1895 (quoted in S.B. Crandall, 'Principles of international law applied by the Spanish Treaty Claims Commission', *AJIL* 4(4) (1910), p. 810) made this statement:

> [i]t is a generally accepted principle of international law that a sovereign government, is not ordinarily responsible to alien residents for injuries that they may receive within its territories from insurgents whose conduct it cannot control. ... In the event, however, of injury, a claim would necessarily have to be founded upon averment and reasonable proof that the responsible officers of the Spanish Government, *being in a position to position to prevent such injury, have failed to use due diligence to do so*. (emphasis added).

1003 See Section 3.3.3.3.

> by others. *Her only duty was to cause the war to be as short and exempt from disasters as possible;* and if she endeavored to do this and *employed all the means within her reach,* she can not be blamed for omission or neglect of duty and consequently can not have any responsibility. The United States fulfilled that duty nobly and worthily, and the immense magnitude of its efforts, which everybody knows, shows that the sufferings occasioned by the gigantic struggle could not be possibly avoided.[1004]

In any event, the obligation to prevent clearly only exists when it is *possible* and feasible for the government to take any such measure.[1005] In the *Prats* case, Mexican Commissioner, Mr Palacio, explained it very clearly.[1006] Mr Palacio explained that in a 'state of war' involving a rebellion 'the duty of the government must be measured in accordance with it, and its responsibility must be determined without losing sight of that important fact'.[1007] Thus, in such a 'state of war', 'it is not in the power of the nation to prevent or to avoid the injuries caused or intended

1004 *Prats* case, 1868, p. 199, emphasis added. He also indicated:

> [t]he same truth will be expressed in a more practical language by saying that the extent of the duties is to be commensurate with the extent of the means for performing [them] and that *he who has employed all the means within his reach has perfectly fulfilled his duty,* irrespective of the material result of his efforts. To ask of him some other thing would be the same as to [demand] an action *ultra posse,* which is positively an absurdity. (emphasis added).

1005 *Kwnmerov, Redles, Fulda, Fischback and Friedericy* case, German–Venezuelan Mixed Claims Commission, UNRIAA 10, p. 397–8, Umpire Duffield referring to 'lack of diligence, or negligence in failing to prevent such acts, *when possible,* or as far as possible to punish the wrongdoer and make reparation for the injury' (emphasis added). See also: *Affaire des biens britanniques au Maroc espagnol,* 1925, p. 615, 642, Huber mentioning that 'while the State is not responsible for revolutionary events themselves, it may nevertheless be responsible [where] the authorities do not counter the consequences *to the extent possible*' (emphasis added).

1006 *Prats* case, 1868, Mexican Commissioner, Mr Palacio, p. 194, at p. 196:

> It being thus ascertained that the duty of protection on the part of the Government, either by the general principles of international law or by the special agreements of the treaties, only goes as far as *permitted by possibility,* the following question arises: what is the degree of diligence required for the due performance of this duty? And the answer will be very obvious: that diligence must be such as to render impossible any other, better or more careful and attentive [performance], so as not to omit anything, practical or possible, which ought to have been done in the case. *Possibility is, indeed, the last limit of all the human obligations;* the most stringent and inviolable ones can not be extended to more. [To exceed] this limit would be equivalent to [attempting] an impossibility, and so the jurists and law writers, in establishing the maxim *ad impossibile nemo tenetur,* have merely been the interpreters of common sense. (emphasis added).

1007 Ibid., p. 197–8.

to be caused by the rebels, either to the foreign residents or to the native citizens of the country'.[1008] As explained by Mr Palacio, a government cannot have the obligation to do something that is simply *impossible* to accomplish: 'Under such a state of things it is not in the power of the nation to prevent or to avoid the injuries caused or intended to be caused by the rebels, either to the foreign residents or to the native citizens of the country; and as *nobody can be bound to do the impossible*, from that very moment the responsibility ceases to exist.'[1009]

The same observation has been made by Gardner: '[i]f the insurrectionary movement gets beyond the control of the State and a condition of *force majeure* comes into existence, so that it is physically *impossible* for the State to protect aliens against the acts of the insurgents, it is not liable to make reparation'.[1010] Other writers have also made reference to this point about 'impossibility'.[1011] Similarly, a number of tribunals

[1008] Ibid.

[1009] Ibid., emphasis added. See also this comment:

> There is no responsibility without fault (culpa), and it is too well known that there is no fault (culpa) in having failed to do what was impossible. The fault is essentially dependent upon the will, but as the will completely disappears before the force, whose action can not be resisted, it is a self-evident result that all the acts done by such force, without the possibility of being resisted by another equal or more powerful force, can neither involve a fault nor an injury nor a responsibility. (emphasis added).

[1010] Garner, 'Responsibility of States', p. 63, emphasis added.

[1011] C. De Visscher, *La responsabilité des États* (Leiden, Bibliotheca Visseriana, Brill, vol. II, 1924), p. 103–4:

> the circumstance that by reason of these disturbances themselves the local authorities may have found it *impossible* to take any really adequate preventive or repressive measures. International practice has, in effect, accepted here a case of *force majeure;* a Government cannot be held responsible for acts committed by insurgents when it has used such restricted authority as is available to it to repress a revolutionary movement directed against its own power. (cited and translated in ILC, 'Force majeure and Fortuitous event', 1978, p. 213, emphasis added).

See also, B. Cheng, *General Principles of Law as Applied by International Courts and Tribunals* (London, Stevens, 1953), p. 227: 'It cannot be doubted that *natural impossibility* extinguishes any obligation. With regard to the duty of a State to protect aliens within its territorial jurisdiction, it has frequently been recognized that, both in the prevention and in the repression of crimes, a State may be faced with natural limitations, and that the duty of the State does not extend beyond these limits', referred to in ILC, 'Force majeure and Fortuitous event', 1978, p. 214, para. 543, emphasis added.

(including the *Egerton and Barnett* case[1012] and the *Gill* case[1013]) have held that there exists no obligation for a government to prevent a rebellion, and by nature its adverse consequences, when it simply has *no power* to take any reasonable measures. One example is in the context of a rebellion taking place in Venezuela in 1858 where many foreigners suffered losses. In a legal opinion assessing whether the Venezuelan government could be held responsible for injuries inflicted on foreigners, the UK Law Officers stated that: 'As a matter, however, of international right, we do not think that the Venezuelan Government can be held responsible generally for injuries inflicted on the properties or persons of British subjects, or other foreigners, resident in the country, by insurgents engaged in open and armed hostility to the Government; and which injuries *the Government had not the power to prevent.*'[1014]

The question of the 'impossibility' to act was also found to be relevant in the *Strabag* case dealing with claims arising in the context of the Libyan civil war. In its analysis of the FPS clause contained in the Austria–Libya BIT regarding events that took place *after* the victory of the rebels of the NTC at the end of 2011, the Tribunal mentioned the position of Libya that 'it was *impossible* for the Libyan authorities *to guarantee full protection and security*, as they would normally do in peacetime'.[1015]

1012 *Egerton and Barnett* case, Chile and Great Britain arbitral tribunal, 25 September 1895, in Henri La Fontaine, *Pasicrisie Internationale: Histoire Documentaire des Arbitrages Internationaux (1794–1900)* (Berne, Imprimerie Stampelli & Cie, 1902), p. 455–6, where the Tribunal concluded that the Government of Chile was not responsible for the loss incurred by the Claimants and noted that 'international law requires the military authorities of a belligerent country *to do all in their power to ensure* respect by the persons subject to their orders for the property of peaceful inhabitants' (emphasis added).

1013 *John Gill* case, British–Mexican Claims Commission, 19 May 1931, UNRIAA 5, p. 152: '[t]he majority fully realize that there may be a number of cases, in which absence of action *is not due to negligence or omission but to the impossibility of taking immediate and decisive measures,* in which every Government may temporarily find [itself], when confronted with a situation of a very sudden nature', emphasis added.

1014 The Law Officers, Mr J. D. Harding, opinion of 25 February 1861, in McNair, *International Law Opinions*, vol. 2, p. 260, emphasis added.

1015 *Strabag* case, 2020, para. 233:

> Although the [National Transitional Council] proclaimed itself as the legitimate government of Libya on October 23, 2011, the situation in Libya remained unstable. Various armed groups claiming to be the legitimate government exercised control over different areas of the country since 2011. In such a situation, it was *impossible* for the Libyan authorities *to guarantee full protection and security,* as they would normally do in peacetime. The internationally recognized *government has not been in continuous direct control of much of the*

The Tribunal essentially agreed: '[i]n the circumstances prevailing in Libya during and since the Revolution' (i.e. 'widespread conflict, violence and disorder'), 'it was *not reasonably possible* for the Libyan authorities to take consistent and effective measures to protect Claimant's investment'.[1016] Under Claim 2, the Claimant argued that some of its equipment had disappeared in 2014 and that the government 'failed to act in response to the disappearance, showing a failure to provide constant protection and security in breach of Article 3(1) [of] the Treaty'.[1017] The Tribunal mentioned that 'the security situation in and around Tripoli in and after the summer of 2014 was unsettled and dangerous' and found that 'Claimant's evidence is not sufficient to establish a failure of due diligence by Respondent'.[1018] The Tribunal rejected the FPS claim 'with respect to the unexplained disappearance of Al Hani's property'.[1019] As mentioned above,[1020] it held however that Libya breached the war-losses clause contained in the Treaty regarding events that took place during the revolution.

Whether or not it is truly 'impossible' for a State to take any reasonable measures to prevent injurious rebels' actions cannot be assessed in the abstract. It will obviously depend on the specific circumstances of each case. These circumstances will be examined below.[1021]

Importantly, Ago stressed that international responsibility arising from a State's failure to exercise its duty of due diligence and to take preventive measures happens to be 'very rare'.[1022] The ILC 2001 Commentaries also refer to this situation as representing only 'exceptional cases'.[1023] In his comprehensive study, Silvanie noted that negli-

territory where the property in question was located, such as the areas of Tweisha and Tajura. (emphasis added).

1016 Ibid., para. 236, emphasis added.

1017 Ibid., para. 343.

1018 Ibid., paras. 344–5.

1019 Ibid., para. 345.

1020 See Section 2.1.2.2.3.2.

1021 See Section 3.3.3.3.3.

1022 ILC, Ago Report, 1972, p. 130, para. 156: 'the cases in which the "legitimate" Government was really in a position, during the civil war, to prevent or punish injurious acts committed by the person who is an organ of the insurrectional movement and failed to do so are very rare'. See also: Eagleton, *The Responsibility of States*, p. 148 ff.; Cahin, 'Attribution of Conduct to the State', p. 253.

1023 ILC, Commentaries, 2001, para. 15: '[e]*xceptional cases may occur* where the State was in a position to adopt measures of vigilance, prevention or punishment in respect of the movement's conduct but improperly failed to do so', emphasis added.

gence at preventing injuries is hard to prove. He refers solely to two cases where such claims have been allowed by tribunals.[1024] Yet, he also rightly noted[1025] that these cases 'involved issues other than that of negligence, and it is therefore practically impossible to say what degree of importance should be attached to the last issue'.[1026] Cases where a State has been found negligent for not taking reasonable preventive measures are rare and exceptional for a simple reason. A government will typically have *no control* over the activities of the rebels in the context of an insurrection of great magnitude.[1027] The importance of this notion of 'control' has been recognized by several arbitral tribunals.[1028] As further discussed below,[1029] the stronger the magnitude of an insurrection and the more powerful the strength of the rebels, the less likely it is that the government will be in control of the territory where the trouble is taking place. This lack of control naturally has a direct impact on what a government can realistically and effectively do regarding its duty to take preventive measures.[1030] In such a situation, a government will often not be able to adopt any measure of vigilance or prevention in relation to the conduct of rebels. Ago explained it as follows: 'The State against which the insurrectional movement has been fighting can only rarely be accused of having failed to fulfil its obligations to exercise vigilance and afford protection with respect to the activities of organs of that movement. More often than not, the activities in question are completely beyond

[1024] Silvanie, *Responsibility of States*, p. 168, referring to these two cases: *Baldwin* and *Montijo*.

[1025] As further examined below, these two cases involved matters of amnesty granted to the rebels by the successful government. The specific question of the effect of amnesty is examined in Section 3.3.3.4.1.

[1026] Silvanie, *Responsibility of States*, p. 168.

[1027] ILC, Commentaries, 2001, p. 50, para. 2. See also: Akehurst, 'State Responsibility', p. 63 ('it is submitted that a State is not liable for any of the acts of rebels whom it cannot control, and that the fact that some of the rebels may still hold official positions under the laws of the *de jure* regime makes no difference'); Silvanie, *Responsibility of States*, p. 149 ff., 151 ('the inability to control absolves a State from responsibility for tortuous acts of unsuccessful insurgents').

[1028] See analysis in Section 3.1.2.

[1029] See Section 3.3.3.3.3.

[1030] Cahin, 'Attribution of Conduct to the State', p. 253:

> [a]lthough this possibility is envisaged in article 10(3), the attribution of such a failure to the State is much more exceptional than in cases where the State is dealing with riots or mass demonstrations, for in the former case the attribution may be limited by various factors, such as the incapacity of the State to control the activities of a movement which has acquired and maintained control over a portion of its territory.

its control.'[1031] In this context, a State is likely to be able to show that, given the circumstances of the insurrection, it has taken all possible measures within its power to prevent wrongs committed against foreign investors or that it was simply impossible to take any such measures. That State may successfully argue that it has therefore fulfilled *this* specific element of its due diligence obligation. The next section examines another element of this obligation.

3.3.3.2.3 Obligation to Punish the Wrongdoers and Provide Reparation

As noted above, the due diligence obligation requires a State to take all reasonable and possible measures during an insurrection in order to *prevent* the commission of wrongs by rebels. This element of the obligation applies *during* the insurrection. In the aftermath of the unsuccessful insurrection, the government is subject to another obligation. It has the obligation of providing adequate *punishment* to the perpetrators (the former rebels) in light of the injurious acts they committed in the course of the civil war.[1032] The obligation is to 'punish the wrongdoer and make reparation for the injury'.[1033] Scholars have explained in some detail the scope and content of this obligation.[1034] A failure by the government to punish those individuals responsible would be contrary to its due diligence obligation.[1035] As pointed out by Ago, 'it makes no difference whether the negligence on the part of the State occurred before the insurrectional movement ceased active existence or afterwards'.[1036] This is because the obligation to punish happens to be aimed towards individuals (who are former rebels) and not the

[1031] ILC, Ago Report, 1972, p. 130, para. 154. See also: ILC, Report, 1975, p. 92, para. 4.

[1032] Cahin, 'Attribution of Conduct to the State', p. 253.

[1033] *Kwnmerov, Redles, Fulda, Fischback and Friedericy* case, German–Venezuelan Mixed Claims Commission, UNRIAA 10, p. 397-398.

[1034] Pisillo-Mazzeschi, 'The Due Diligence Rule', p. 28, indicating that the 'obligation to punish, like the obligation to prevent, contemplates two distinct obligations: that of possessing a minimum legal, administrative and judicial apparatus normally able to guarantee enforcement; and that of using such an apparatus'. He further mentioned the existence of a 'difference between the obligation, of the State's administrative authorities, to investigate events and to pursue and apprehend those responsible and the obligation, of the judiciary and/or administrative authorities, to try such persons, inflict an adequate penalty on them and see that the sentence is carried out' (p. 29).

[1035] ILC, Ago Report, 1972, p. 130, para. 156: 'it seemed normal that the State should be held responsible only for any wrongful negligence on its part in preventing or punishing the wrongful acts of organs belonging to the insurgents. This conclusion will be all the more valid when the perpetrators of the acts had reverted to the status of private individuals'.

[1036] Ibid., p. 130, para. 156.

insurrectional movement in itself, which is, in any event, likely to have been dismantled after its defeat.

An important point that should be noted is that this is an obligation that should be far easier to fulfil by any government than the obligation mentioned in the previous section.[1037] Thus, once the government has crushed the rebellion, it will regain control of its entire territory and will therefore be able to take appropriate measures to protect foreigners. The dynamic where the State cannot possibly and reasonably take measures to prevent injurious conduct has passed; it is now fully able to dictate a course of action. It will, normally, be in a position to adequately punish the perpetrators of wrongs committed during the insurrection.[1038] To paraphrase a passage from the ILC Commentary,[1039] after the defeat of the rebels, a State is much more likely to be 'in a position to adopt measures' of *punishment*, than it was 'in a position to adopt measures' of vigilance and prevention during the insurrection. Hence it is rather odd for the ILC Commentary to refer to *both* situations as 'exceptional cases'.[1040] There is nothing really 'exceptional' about a government taking appropriate measures to punish wrongdoers.

In any event, this is by no means an absolute obligation. Thus, as mentioned above in the *Gill* case, the British–Mexican Claims Commission stated that governmental authorities 'cannot be blamed for omission or negligence, when the action taken by them . . . has not led to the punishment of *all* the individuals responsible'.[1041] One can envisage several situations where a government will simply not have the power and/or be unable to adequately punish the perpetrators of wrongs in a satisfactory manner. In other cases, this failure will be based on a political decision. The capacity (and willingness) of a government to take such measures is indeed one of the relevant circumstances that needs to be taken into account when assessing whether a State has fulfilled its due diligence

[1037] ILC, Report, 1975, p. 93, para. 12, indicating that the failure 'to punish adequately the perpetrators of the injurious acts committed during the struggle' is one of those 'grounds that the responsibility of the State *will most often be invoked*, since cases in which the "legitimate" Government was materially able, during the struggle, to prevent or punish the injurious acts of a person acting as an organ of an insurrectional movement are rather rare' (emphasis added).

[1038] Pisillo-Mazzeschi, 'The Due Diligence Rule', p. 28.

[1039] ILC, Commentaries, 2001, p. 51, para. 15.

[1040] Id: '*[e]xceptional cases may occur* where the State was in a position to adopt measures of vigilance, prevention or *punishment* in respect of the movement's conduct but improperly failed to do so', emphasis added.

[1041] *John Gill* case, British–Mexican Claims Commission, 19 May 1931, UNRIAA 5, p. 159, emphasis added.

obligation.[1042] I will examine below the question as to whether a State should be considered to have breached its due diligence obligation if it decides to grant any kind of amnesty to individuals who are former rebels.[1043]

3.3.3.2.4 The Claimant Has the Burden to Show That the Government Has Failed to Fulfil Its Due Diligence Obligation In the context of arbitration proceedings, it is for the claimant to provide evidence that the government has failed to fulfil its due diligence obligation.[1044] This general principle has been mentioned by Umpire Ralston in the *Sambiagio* case,[1045] and in other cases,[1046] including recent investment arbitration awards.[1047] It is based on the grounds that, in the words of one writer, 'a legitimate government is supposed to have done its best, unless

1042 This question is further examined below. See Section 3.3.3.3.3.2.

1043 See Section 3.3.3.3.4.1.

1044 Piguet, *La Guerre civile en droit international*, p. 97; Ganzory, 'International Claims and Insurgence', p. 75 ff. (referring to a number of examples of State practice, see also, p. 80); Borchard, 'International Responsibility of the State for Injuries', p. 118 ('it is for the claimant to prove that 'at the time and place when and the where the injury was done the government authorities could, by due diligence, and should have prevented such injury'); Silvanie, *Responsibility of States*, p. 184 ff., citing many cases supporting this principle.

1045 *Sambiaggio* case, 1903, p. 524: '[t]he umpire therefore accepts the rule that if in any case of reclamation submitted to him it is alleged and proved that Venezuelan authorities failed to exercise due diligence to prevent damages from being inflicted by revolutionists, that country should be held responsible. In the present instance no such want of diligence is alleged and proved'.

1046 *Henriquez* case, Netherlands–Venezuela Claims Commission, 1903, Opinion of the Umpire, UNRIAA 10, p. 713, 716: '[t]hat the Government of Venezuela was negligent in a given case must be alleged and proved'. See also: *Aroa Mines case*, UK–Venezuela Claims Commission, UNRIAA 9, p. 442 ('It is also held that the want of due diligence must be made a part of the claimant's case and be established by competent evidence') and at p. 445:

> The Government of Venezuela will not be held liable to the British Government for injuries to property or wrongful seizures thereof, or for damages, vexations, or exactions committed upon or suffered by British subjects in Venezuela during any unsuccessful insurrection or civil war which has occurred in that country unless there be proven fault or want of due diligence on the part of the Venezuelan authorities or their agents.

1047 *Strabag* case, 2020, para. 335: '[c]laimant has the evidentiary burden of showing Respondent's failure to exercise due diligence in the circumstances'. See also: *Way2B ACE* v. *Libya*, ICC, Award, May 2018. The award is not available but it has been reported that the Tribunal rejected the due diligence argument raised by the Claimant because it did not present any evidence that Libya had failed to deploy sufficient resources to protect its investment from attacks by third parties (see: IAReporter 'Way2b v. Libya Tribunal Finds That Bit's War-Losses Clause Does Not Exclude Operation Of Other Bit Protections (Including Full Protection & Security), But Foreign Investor Fails To Meet Evidentiary Burdens', 8 January 2019).

there is evidence of neglect on its side'.[1048] This position has been endorsed by Asante in his dissenting opinion in the *AAPL* case, speaking of a presumption that the host State has complied with its due diligence obligation.[1049] ILC Special Rapporteur Garcia Amador has referred, in his 1957 report, to the requirement to show 'patent or manifest negligence'.[1050]

Many writers support the existence of such a presumption regarding the specific obligation to take measures to suppress an insurrection. For Eagleton, 'it may ordinarily be presumed, of course, since the government is fighting for its life, that due diligence has been employed to suppress an insurrection'.[1051] The Harvard Draft Convention has also stated that '[i]nasmuch as negligence on the part of the government in suppressing an insurrection against itself is improbable', as a result 'the claimant should be deemed to have the burden of showing negligence'.[1052] Akehurst has very well-explained this point.[1053]

1048 Ganzory, 'International Claims and Insurgence', p. 75, referring to a number of examples of State practice.

1049 *AAPL* case, 1990, dissenting opinion of Asante (in *ICSID Rev.* (1990), p. 590):

> [a]nother way of formulating this general rule of non-responsibility is that a host State's obligation to exercise due diligence with respect to the protection of alien property is easily discharged in the face of an insurrection or other civil commotion resulting in a temporary loss of control by the host country over the area of insurgency. In short, in these circumstances, there is a presumption that the due diligence rule has been complied with. (see Eagleton, *The Responsibility of States*, p. 150)

1050 ILC, 'International Responsibility', Second Report by F.V. Garcia Amador, Special Rapporteur, 15 February 1957, UN Doc. A/CN.4/106, *ILC Yearbook* vol. II (1957) [hereinafter referred to as 'ILC, Garcia Amador Report, 1957'], p. 122, para. 9:

> the basic principle apparent in previous codifications, in the decisions of international tribunals, and in the works of the learned authorities is that there is a presumption against responsibility. In other words, the State is not responsible unless it displayed, in the conduct of its organs or officials, patent or manifest negligence in taking the measures which are normally taken in the particular circumstances to prevent or punish the injurious acts.

1051 Eagleton, *The Responsibility of States*, p. 150.

1052 Crawford, *Brownlie's Principles of Public International Law*, p. 552, referring to Harvard Draft Convention, 1929. See also: Silvanie, *Responsibility of States*, p. 184; Garner, 'Responsibility of States', p. 57 ('The burden of proving the lack of such diligence is held to rest upon the injured state, a burden which is not always easy to discharge, even when lack of diligence is notorious').

1053 Akehurst, 'State Responsibility', p. 50:

> A State is only liable for the wrongful acts of rebels if it was at fault in failing to prevent those acts. The most extreme form of such failure is negligence in failing to prevent or suppress the rebellion as such. Normally it is very

It should be noted that there are few exceptional cases where the burden of proof rule mentioned above was not applied.[1054] For instance, the British–Mexican Claims Commission referred to 'the difficulty of imposing on the [Claimants] the duty of proving a negative fact such as omission on the part of the Mexican government to take reasonable measures'[1055] and instead relied on a prima facie test. In the *Mexico City Bombardment Claims* case, the Commission put forward the following two-conditions test:

> In a great many cases it will be extremely difficult to establish beyond any doubt the omission or the absence of suppressive or punitive measures. The Commission realizes that the evidence of negative facts can hardly ever be given in an absolutely convincing manner. But a strong *prima facie* evidence can be assumed to exist in these cases in which *first* the British Agent will be able to make it acceptable that the facts were known to the competent authorities, either because they were of public notoriety or because they were brought to their knowledge in due time, and *second* the Mexican Agent does not show any evidence as to action taken by the authorities.[1056]

One case where this test was applied is the *Gill* case, already mentioned above. In that case, the Commission stated that it was for the Respondent (Mexico) to show that it had taken appropriate measures to suppress the insurrection.[1057] Another relevant example is the *Willian E. Bowerman and Messrs. Burberry* case, involving 'the loss of a quantity of sample garments contained in a trunk' and personal items which were destroyed in a train attacked by rebels. The Commission referred to the test put forward in the *Mexico City*

> difficult to prove negligence in failing to prevent or suppress a rebellion. A very heavy onus of proof is placed on the claimant State, since it is assumed to be highly improbable that the *de jure* government of a State will be negligent in resisting its own overthrow.

1054 Silvanie, *Responsibility of States*, p. 186 ff., citing a number of cases.

1055 *John Gill* case, British–Mexican Claims Commission, 19 May 1931, UNRIAA 5, p. 159.

1056 *Mexico City Bombardment Claims* case, British–Mexican Claims Commission, 15 February 1930, UNRIAA 5, p. 80, emphasis in the original.

1057 *John Gill* case, British–Mexican Claims Commission, 19 May 1931, UNRIAA 5, p. 152:

> [t]hey are also aware that authorities cannot be blamed for omission or negligence when the action taken by them has not resulted in the *entire* suppression of the insurrections, risings, riots or acts of brigandage, or has not led to the punishment of *all* the individuals responsible. In those cases, no responsibility will be admitted. But in this case, nothing of the kind has been alleged. The highest authorities in the country were officially acquainted with what had occurred. They stated that they were touched by the account. They added that they had, as regarded compensation, to consider that the precedent might have grave consequences, but the Mexican agent has not shown a single proof that any action to inquire, suppress or prosecute was taken. (emphasis in the original).

Bombardment Claims and stated that 'an assault on, and the burning of, a train on the line from Mexico City to Veracruz was an occurrence of such importance that it cannot be supposed that the authorities were unaware of it, and the Mexican Agent has not shown that they took any action whatever in the matter'.[1058] The majority of the Commission held Mexico responsible for its failure to fulfil its due diligence obligation. This two-conditions test was challenged by the Mexican commissioners in a number of dissenting opinions in cases decided by the British–Mexican Claims Commission. They argued that the test was 'inverting the usual rule of evidence and shifting the burden of proof on the respondent State'.[1059] As noted by Silvanie, some of these decisions 'do not appear to be quite satisfactory' given that the claimant 'was not required to submit proof of negligence or of failure of the Mexican authorities to take action'.[1060] Ultimately, Silvanie believes that Mexico was held liable for acts of rebels over whom it had no control, and against which it could not have taken any action.[1061]

3.3.3.3 The Applicable Test to Determine Whether Any Breach of the Obligation Has Been Committed

In previous sections, I have examined the scope and content of the obligation for a State to fulfil its due diligence duty of vigilance, prevention and punishment in relation to the conduct of rebels. In this section, I will explain what the applicable test is in order to determine whether or not a State has breached any of the three components of this obligation. I will show that:

- States' conduct must be measured against an objective international minimum standard of treatment (Section 3.3.3.3.1); and
- The standard of analysis of such a conduct is what a prudent, well-organized and diligent government would have done in similar circumstances (Section 3.3.3.3.2).

Finally, I will examine specifically four circumstances that should be taken into account to assess whether any breach has been committed (Section 3.3.3.3.3).

1058 *Willian E. Bowerman and Messrs. Burberry* case, British–Mexican Claims Commission, 15 February 1930, UNRIAA 5, p. 106, 109.

1059 Silvanie, *Responsibility of States*, p. 190, citing several cases.

1060 Ibid., p. 190–1.

1061 Ibid., p. 191. He argued (at p. 191–2) that in such cases where Mexico was 'in no position to take action, it was obviously meaningless to inquire, as the Commission did, whether they did take action'.

3.3.3.3.1 States' Conduct Must Be Measured Against an Objective International Minimum Standard of Treatment The applicable test to determine whether a State has breached any of the three components of its due diligence obligation is based on an *objective* standard.[1062] A good illustration of the objective nature of the test has been put forward by Huber in the 1925 *Affaire des biens britanniques au Maroc espagnol*. He explained that States have an obligation to offer foreigners the level of protection and security that can *reasonably be expected* from them. He also refers to the existence of a threshold for the standard of vigilance below which a State would engage its responsibility.[1063] Around the same period, Eagleton (in 1927) indicated that the level of protection offered by States must be 'sufficient' and that, in any event, it must 'measure up to the international standard' or otherwise it will be considered contrary to international law.[1064] In other words, all States must provide protection

[1062] Piguet, *La Guerre civile en droit international*, p. 100: 'en droit international, le degrée de protection offert à un étranger se mesure *objectivement*', emphasis added. See also, p. 116.

[1063] *Affaire des biens britanniques au Maroc espagnol*, 1925, p. 644: 'La vigilance qu'au point de vue du droit international l'État est tenu de garantir, peut être caractérisée, en appliquant par analogie un terme du droit romain, comme une *diligentia quam in suis*. Cette règle, conforme au principe primordial de l'indépendance des États dans leurs affaires intérieures, offre en fait aux États, pour leurs ressortissants, *le degré de sécurité auquel ils peuvent raisonnablement s'attendre*. Du moment que la vigilance exercée tombe manifestement *au-dessous de ce niveau* par rapport aux ressortissants d'un État étranger déterminé, ce dernier est en droit de se considérer comme lésé dans des intérêts qui doivent jouir de la protection du droit international' ('The vigilance which from the point of view of international law the state is required to guarantee, can be characterized, by applying by analogy a term of Roman law, such as a diligentia quam in suis. This rule, consistent with the overarching principle of the independence of states in their internal affairs, in effect provides states with the *level of security for their nationals that they can reasonably expect*. As long as the vigilance exercised falls clearly *below this level* in relation to the nationals of a given foreign state, the latter is entitled to consider itself injured in interests which must enjoy the protection of international law') (emphasis added).

[1064] Eagleton, *The Responsibility of States*, p. 144:

> [w]hile, as has been repeatedly said, a state is left free to choose its own machinery, still, to quote Hall, 'it cannot avoid international responsibility on the plea of a deliberate preference for anarchy'. The duty of the state is usually to extend to the alien the same protection as its own citizens receive, provided this protection is sufficient. It is as true in the case of civil war injuries as elsewhere that, if the protection given to the alien *does not measure up to the international standard*, responsibility may be claimed *level of security for their nationals that they can reasonably expect*. (emphasis added, quoting Hall, *A Treatise on International Law*, p. 272).

Eagleton explained why claims for damages were often demanded to Latin American States:

at least in accordance with a *minimum threshold*, that is, an objective *international standard*. A State is therefore *not* 'bound *only* to exercise the degree of diligence it normally uses in its own internal affairs and with regard to its own citizens'.[1065] Gardner also spoke of the requirement for States to afford a degree of protection to foreigners which does not 'fall below the standard recognized among civilized states'.[1066] The same idea is found in 'Basis of Discussion' No. 10 drafted by the Preparatory Committee of The Hague Conference.[1067]

The reasons for establishing such a standard were explained by US Secretary of State, Mr Elihu Root, in an important article published in 1910.[1068] One important case, the 1926 *Neer* case, decided by the US–

> [i]t is a notorious fact, upon which one is free to put his own construction, that successful claims for damages due to civil war disturbances have rarely been prosecuted except against the Latin-American states, or occasionally against other weaker states. It is not necessary to conclude, however, that such action is always the bullying conduct of a more powerful against a weaker state unable to resist.

1065 Pisillo-Mazzeschi, 'The Due Diligence Rule', p. 41, emphasis added.

1066 Garner, 'Responsibility of States', p. 52:

> [i]t is often asserted that aliens are entitled under international law to no greater protection or different remedies than is accorded to nationals, and consequently the state is not liable except where it fails to accord equality of protection and means of redress. As a general principle this is a correct statement, but it is not true when the degree of protection or the efficacy of the means for obtaining redress fall below the standard recognized among civilized states. In that case foreign states expect a higher degree of protection for their nationals than is accorded citizens.

See also, p. 62:

> [t]here is a standard of treatment which states are bound to accord aliens residing within their territory, so generally recognized by civilized nations that it may be regarded as a principle of customary international law. It can no longer be admitted that each state is free to adopt its own standard of treatment if it falls short of the international standard.

1067 League of Nations, 1929, 'Basis of Discussion' no. 10, p. 67:

> [a] State is responsible for damage suffered by a foreigner as the result of failure on the part of the executive power to show such diligence in the protection of foreigners as, having regard to the circumstances and to the status of the person concerned, *could be expected from a civilized State*. The fact that a foreigner is invested with a recognized public status imposes upon the State a special duty of vigilance. (emphasis added).

1068 Elihu Root, 'The Basis of Protection to Citizens Residing Abroad', *AJIL* 4 (1910), p. 521:

Mexico Claims Commission,[1069] held that the 'propriety of governmental acts should be put to the test of *international standards*' and explained what that standard was: 'the treatment of an alien, in order to constitute an international delinquency, should amounts to an outrage, to bad faith, to wilful neglect of duty, or to an insufficiency of governmental action so far short of *international standards* that every reasonable and impartial man would readily recognize its insufficiency'.[1070] It should be added that at the time, Latin American diplomats and scholars have strongly disputed the very existence of any such standard under international law.[1071] It has been argued that this 'standard of civilisation' was 'an essential element of justification for the policies of expansionism and colonialism pursued by both the United States of America and the imperial States of Western Europe ... throughout the period [18th and 19th Century]'.[1072]

In the context of international investment law, this standard is known as the 'minimum standard of treatment' (MST). It is beyond the scope of this book to examine in detail the framework of this standard.[1073] Suffice

> [e]ach country is bound to give to the nationals of another country in its territory the benefit of the same laws, the same administration, the same protection, and the same redress for injury which it gives to its own citizens, and neither more nor less: *provided the protection which the country gives to its own citizens conforms to the established standard of civilization.* There is [however] a standard of justice very simple, very fundamental, and of such general acceptance by all civilized countries as to form a part of the international law of the world. The ... system of law and administration shall conform to this general standard. If any country's system of law and administration does not conform to that standard, although the people of the country may be content to live under it, no other country can be compelled to accept it as furnishing a satisfactory measure of treatment of its citizens. (emphasis added).

On this question, see: Martins Paparinskis, *The International Minimum Standard and Fair and Equitable Treatment* (Oxford University Press, 2013), p. 39–46.

1069 *USA (LF Neer)* v. *Mexico*, US–Mexico Claims Commission, Award, 15 October 1926, UNRIAA 4, p. 60, emphasis added.

1070 Ibid., p. 61–2, emphasis added.

1071 On this question, see: Santiago Montt, *State Liability in Investment Treaty Arbitration* (Oxford, Hart Publishing, 2009), p. 48 ff.; Nissel, *A History of State Responsibility*, p. 153.

1072 Todd Weiler, *The Interpretation of International Investment Law: Equality, Discrimination and Minimum Standards of Treatment in Historical Context* (Leiden, Martinus Nijhoff, 2013), p. 129.

1073 This question is examined in Patrick Dumberry, *The Fair and Equitable Treatment Standard: A Guide to NAFTA Case Law on Article 1105* (Alphen aan den Rijn, Wolters Kluwer, 2013).

it to mention that it has been consistently applied by investment tribunals.[1074] One example is the NAFTA *S.D. Myers* Tribunal explaining that the 'minimum standard' is a 'floor below which treatment of foreign investors must not fall' and that it is 'meant to serve as a floor, an absolute bottom, below which conduct is not accepted by the international community'.[1075] The *Glamis* Tribunal also noted that the standard 'cannot vary between nations as thus the protection afforded would have no minimum'.[1076] The MST is considered to be one of the few rules of customary international law applicable in the field of investment arbitration.[1077] The question of the interaction between the MST and the due diligence obligation is beyond the scope of this book.[1078]

3.3.3.3.2 The Standard Is What a Prudent, Well-Organized and Diligent Government Would Have Done in Similar Circumstances In its Report of 2016, the ILA explained (in the general context of international law) that the concept of 'reasonableness' 'is a golden thread in determining which measures States should take to act in a duly diligent manner' and that 'one might describe a due diligence obligation as an obligation for the State to take all measures it could *reasonably* be expected to take'.[1079]

As mentioned by Borchard, the doctrine according to which 'a state is not responsible for the injuries sustained by aliens at the hands of insurgents in civil war unless there is a proven fault or a want of due diligence on the part of the authorities in preventing or in suppressing the revolution' 'is predicated on the assumption that the *government is*

[1074] See cases examined in Patrick Dumberry, *The Formation and Identification of Rules of Customary International Law in International Investment Law* (Cambridge University Press, 2016).

[1075] *S.D. Myers Inc.* v. *Canada*, UNCITRAL, First Partial Award, 13 November 2000, para. 259.

[1076] *Glamis Gold Ltd* v. *United States*, UNCITRAL, Award, 14 May 2009, para. 615.

[1077] See analysis in Dumberry, *The Formation and Identification of Rules of Customary International Law*.

[1078] On this question, see: ILA, 'Study Group on Due Diligence', First Report, p. 9; de Brabandere, 'Host States' Due Diligence Obligations', p. 328 ff.

[1079] ILA, 'Study Group on Due Diligence', Second Report, p. 8, emphasis added, referring to: Jeswald W. Salacuse, *The Law of Investment Treaties* (Oxford University Press, 2010), p. 217. The Report also noted that 'in the history of international law, due diligence in the context of the protection of aliens was expressed as the need for States to take all measures it could "reasonably" be expected to take' (p. 8). See also: de Brabandere, 'Host States' Due Diligence Obligations', p. 352: '[r]easonableness indeed implies an evaluation of the measure taken by reference to what could be *expected* from a State' emphasis in the original. On this question, see: Mantilla Blanco, *Full Protection and Security*, p. 441 ff., examining investment awards.

reasonably well ordered, and that revolution and disorder are abnormal conditions'.[1080] While this last part of the quote has been criticized by some,[1081] it remains that this is a key point. There exists a general assumption in international law that a government is (or at least should be) reasonably well-ordered and well-organized. Piguet speaks of a 'négligence appréciée selon un critère *purement objectif*: quelle aurait été, dans les mêmes circonstances, la conduite d'un État *bien organisé* et *bien administré*'.[1082] This is indeed the standard against which any State conduct should be measured.[1083] Thus, the applicable test to assess whether a State has fulfilled any of the three components of its due diligence obligation,[1084] is the conduct of what a prudent, well-organized and diligent government would have done in similar circumstances.[1085]

1080 Borchard, 'International Responsibility of the State', p. 118, emphasis added.

1081 See Greenman, 'Aliens in Latin America', p. 634, pointing out that Borchard legitimized the right of intervention of States on behalf of their nationals in situations where (in the words of Borchard) 'a state has fallen into anarchy, or the administration of law has been nerveless or inefficient, or the government has failed to grant to a foreigner the protection afforded citizens, or measures within the power of the government have not been taken to protect those under its jurisdiction from the acts of revolutionists'.

1082 Piguet, *La Guerre civile en droit international*, p. 110, emphasis added ('negligence assessed on a *purely objective* basis: what would have been, in the same circumstances, the conduct of a *well-organized and well-administered* State'). See also, p. 117, 144.

1083 Mantilla Blanco, *Full Protection and Security*, p. 437; Pisillo-Mazzeschi, 'The Due Diligence Rule', p. 44 ('As a general rule, due diligence can be measured by the average general standard of behavior of the "civilized" or 'well-organized' State, just as, in some municipal legal systems, diligence is evaluated in relation to the behavior of a "bonus paterfamilias"'); Riccardo Pisillo Mazzeschi, *'Due diligence' e responsabilità internazionale degli stati* (Milan, Giuffrè Editore, 1989), p. 398–9; Alwyn V. Freeman, Responsibility of States for Unlawful Acts of Their Armed Forces, *Rec. des cours* 88 (1955), p. 277–8 ('The "due diligence" is nothing more nor less than the reasonable measures of prevention which a well-administered government could be expected to exercise under similar circumstances'). See also: Magnússon, *Full Protection and Security*, p. 165: '[w]hat this obligation entails in practical terms is that the state must take reasonable measures or appropriate measures within the context of prevention, restoration and investigation, prosecution and punishment as any well-administered government could be expected to take in similar circumstances', adding that 'under ordinary circumstances a state is to exercise active vigilance by providing police force, administrative tribunals and courts and other institutions necessary in order to fulfil its obligation'.

1084 See Section 3.3.3.2, referring to the obligation for a State (1) to make all efforts within its capacity to suppress an insurrection, (2) to take reasonable measures to prevent the conduct and the damages from occurring, and (3) to punish the wrongdoers and provide reparation.

1085 Ganzory, 'International Claims and Insurgence', p. 74; Piguet, *La Guerre civile en droit international*, p. 99 ('un gouvernement qui aurait agi raisonnablement dans les mêmes circonstances') ('a government that would have acted reasonably in the same circumstances').

The same idea is found in the resolution adopted by the Institute in 1927, speaking of the 'diligence qu'il convient d'apporter *normalement* dans les *mêmes circonstances*'.[1086] The ILA Report speaks of the 'expectation of "good government" as an element of duly diligent behaviour'.[1087]

The question as to whether due diligence is an objective or a subjective obligation is controversial.[1088] In *AAPL* v. *Sri Lanka*, the Tribunal supported the existence of an 'objective' standard of vigilance.[1089] The same formula has since been used by numerous investment tribunals.[1090] Others have opted for a subjective standard.[1091] While this question is beyond the scope of this book, a few words should be said on the matter. As a matter of principle, there exists an objective standard of behaviour which must be observed and respected by all States.[1092] They must act as a prudent, well-organized and diligent government.[1093] Additionally, their behaviour must be in accordance with the MST.[1094] Thus, the *AMT*

1086 IIL, 'Responsabilité internationale des États' 1927, Art. 7, emphasis added ('diligence that should *normally* be taken in the *same circumstances*').

1087 ILA, 'Study Group on Due Diligence', Second Report, p. 10.

1088 The issue is examined by de Brabandere, 'Host States' Due Diligence Obligations', p. 353 ff.; Mantilla Blanco, *Full Protection and Security*, p. 432.

1089 *AAPL* case, 1990, para. 77:

> A number of other contemporary international law authorities noticed the 'sliding scale', from the old 'subjective' criteria that takes into consideration the relatively limited existing possibilities of local authorities in a given context, towards an 'objective' standard of vigilance in assessing the required degree of protection and security with regard to what should be legitimately expected to be secured for foreign investors by a reasonably well organized modern State. (referring to Freeman, 'Responsibility of States for Unlawful Acts', p. 277–8).

1090 See analysis of Mantilla Blanco, *Full Protection and Security*, p. 437, referring to several awards.

1091 de Brabandere, 'Host States' Due Diligence Obligations', p. 356 ff., mentioning several cases, including *Pantechniki S.A. Contractors & Engineers* v. *Albania*, ICSID Case No. ARB/07/21, Award, 30 July 2009 [hereinafter referred to as '*Pantechniki* case, 2009'], para. 77.

1092 Pisillo-Mazzeschi, 'The Due Diligence Rule', p. 42: 'International practice confirms, in our view, that diligence has an objective content; that is, it must be seen as an objective standard of behaviour.'

1093 *AAPL* case, 1990, para. 77, mentioning the standard as a 'reasonably well organized modern State'.

1094 Mantilla Blanco, *Full Protection and Security*, p. 438, indicating in the context of FPS clauses that: 'adjudicators should compare the diligence displayed by local authorities with the conduct an average diligent state would exercise in the same situation. This approach has the obvious advantage of "objectivising", at least to some degree, the assessment of diligence. This seems consistent with the characterization of FPS as an element of the international minimum standard.'

Tribunal refers to 'an objective obligation which must not be inferior to the minimum standard of vigilance and care required by international law'.[1095] In the context of the FPS clause found in investment treaties, Blanco noted that the 'standard does not correspond with the conduct of an ideal and largely hypothetical "democratic state" or "well-administered government", but with the conduct that could be expected as a *minimum* from *any state* facing the same situation of fact as the host state'.[1096] In other words, the assessment 'does not require comparing the diligence displayed by the host state with the conduct that could be expected from an *ideal diligent state*, but against the *minimum* degree of diligence that can be expected from an *average state*'.[1097] Yet, it is also undeniable that the concrete application of what a prudent, well-organized and diligent government would do will necessarily depend on a number of circumstances (a point further examined below[1098]).[1099] Consequently, as noted by one writer, while there is no doubt that 'diligence is to be measured by an international standard and that it has an objective content', it is also clear that it 'has undoubtedly an elastic and relative nature'.[1100]

This duality has been recognized by State practice. In his decision to reject a claim made by a US national who lost his property as a result of acts committed by the rebels in the context of an insurrection in Cuba in 1887 (when Cuba was still a Spanish colony), US Secretary of State (Mr Bayard) referred to the concept of 'diligence good governments' that would be 'accustomed to exercise under the circumstances'.[1101] The next section examines what these relevant 'circumstances' are.

1095 *American Manufacturing & Trading Inc.* v. *Zaire*, ICSID Case No. ARB93/1, Award, 21 February 1997, para. 6.06.

1096 Mantilla Blanco, *Full Protection and Security*, p. 440, emphasis in the original.

1097 Ibid., p. 441, emphasis in the original.

1098 See Section 3.3.3.3.3.

1099 Pisillo-Mazzeschi, 'The Due Diligence Rule', p. 4: 'the degree of diligence that the State must observe depends, largely, on the particular circumstances of each specific case'.

1100 Ibid., p. 44.

1101 Letter dated 6 January 1888, in Moore, *Digest of International Law* (vol. III), p. 961–4:

> The measure of diligence to be exercised by a government in the repression of disorder is *not that of an insurer*, but such as *prudent governments* are, *under the circumstances of the case, accustomed to exercise.* To adopt the rule as stated in the Code of Justinian, and as imported from the Code into all modern jurisprudence, and accepted, therefore, by Spain, as well as by the United States, the law requires 'diligentiam qualem diligens paterfamilias suis rebus adhibere solet': remembering that 'paterfamilias', in the sense in which it is here used, represents one whose relations to his family under the old law

3.3.3.3.3 Relevant Circumstances That Should Be Taken into Account

What a well-organized and diligent government should have done cannot, of course, be determined in the abstract. It must be assessed by taking into account the *different circumstances* prevailing in each and every case.[1102] This basic proposition has been recognized by the *Ampal* Tribunal (which was recently endorsed by the *Strabag* Tribunal):[1103]

> The Tribunal is of the view that the duty imposed upon the host State by this standard [the FPS clause in the BIT] is not one of strict liability. Rather the State is obliged to exert due diligence in order to protect a claimant's investment – a standard that must be assessed *according to the particular circumstances in which the damage occurs.*[1104]

> served to illustrate the relations of the government to the State. The decisive word in this rule is 'solet'. It appeals to custom. The maxim is, that the *diligence good governments are accustomed to exercise under the circumstances* must be exercised in each case; and every government is liable to foreign Powers for injuries to them or their subjects from lack of such customary diligence in the preservation of order. emphasis added (also in ILC, 'Force majeure and Fortuitous event', 1978, p. 115).

In reference to this quote, Ian Brownlie, *System of the Law of Nations: State Responsibility* (Oxford, Clarendon Press, 1983), p. 170, indicated that '[t]here is good reason to believe that this exposition represents the law as it remains today'.

1102 Piguet, *La Guerre civile en droit international*, p. 117; De Visscher, *Théories et réalités*, p. 350 ('toute systématisation doit être évitée dans une matière où tout dépend, en définitive, d'une appréciation exacte et équitable de circonstances de fait qui comportent des nuances multiples et souvent fort délicates') ('any systematization must be avoided in a matter where everything ultimately depends on an accurate and fair assessment of factual circumstances which include multiple and often very delicate nuances'); Crawford, *Brownlie's Principles of Public International Law*, p. 552, referring to McNair, *International Law Opinions*, vol. 2., p. 245 ('this is a variable test, dependent on the circumstances of the insurrection'); Garner, 'Responsibility of States', p. 57 ('What is "due diligence" in a particular case must naturally depend upon the circumstances; what would be due diligence under a given set of conditions would not be under other conditions'); Eagleton, *The Responsibility of States*, p. 88 ('Whether the state has fulfilled its obligations in this regard is measured by the rule of due diligence; and it is impossible to state this rule with precision. No clear and definitive formula has ever been promulgated: it is necessary to study the cases, and to judge according to the circumstances in any particular situation'); ILC, Garcia Amador Report, 1957, p. 122, para. 7 ('The learned authorities are in almost unanimous agreement that the rule of "due diligence" cannot be reduced to a clear and accurate definition which might serve as an objective and automatic standard for deciding, regardless of the circumstances, whether a State was "diligent" in discharging its duty of vigilance and protection').

1103 *Strabag* case, 2020, paras. 234–5, 335: '[t]he Parties agree that Article 3(1) of the Treaty does not impose strict liability and that the applicable legal standard is instead one of due diligence'.

1104 *Ampal-American Israel Corp., Egi-Fund (08-10) Investors LLC, Egi-Series Investments LLC and BSS-EMG Investors LLC* v. *Egypt*, ICSID Case No. ARB/12/11, Decision on

What are the relevant circumstances that must be taken into account? In the *Solis* case, decided by the Mexico–United States General Claims Commission, Commissioner Nielsen stated that:

> In dealing with the question of responsibility for acts of insurgents two pertinent points have been stressed, namely, the *capacity to give protection*, and the disposition of authorities to employ proper, available measures to do so. Irrespective of the facts of any given case, *the character and extent* of an insurrectionary movement must be an important factor in relation to the question of power to give protection.[1105]

Taking into account the particular circumstances in which a damage has occurred is especially important to determine whether a State has breached *two* of the three components of its due diligence obligation, namely: (1) the obligation to make all efforts within its capacity to suppress an insurrection, and (2) the obligation to take all reasonable measures to prevent injurious conduct by rebels and damages from occurring. In the following sections, I will examine the following relevant circumstances:

- The strength of rebels and the magnitude of the insurrection (Section 3.3.3.3.3.1);
- The capacity and the willingness of the government to provide adequate protection (Section 3.3.3.3.3.2);
- The location where the wrong took place (Section 3.3.3.3.3.3); and
- Whether a State promptly responded to rebels' actions (Section 3.3.3.3.3.4).

In his award in the *Pantechniki* case (which did not involve an insurrection per se, but rather a wide-spread civil strife that shook Albania in 1997), Arbitrator Paulsson actually took into account these different factors when assessing whether Albania had breached the FPS clause contained in the BIT:

> A failure of protection and security is to the contrary likely to arise in an unpredictable instance of civic disorder which could have been readily controlled by a powerful state but which overwhelms the *limited capacities* of one which is poor and fragile. There is no issue of incentives or

Liability and Heads of Loss, 21 February 2017, para. 241, emphasis added. Article II(4) of the US-Egypt BIT provides that '[t]he treatment, protection and security of investments shall never be less than that required by international law and national legislation'.

1105 *G.L. Solis (U.S.A.)* v. *United Mexican States*, Mexico–United States General Claims Commission, 3 October 1928, UNRIAA 4, p. 362, emphasis added.

> disincentives with regard to unforeseen breakdowns of public order; it seems difficult to maintain that a government incurs international responsibility for failure to plan for *unprecedented trouble of unprecedented magnitude in unprecedented places.* The case for an element of *proportionality* in applying the international standard is stronger than with respect to claims of denial of justice.[1106]

Before examining these different circumstances in the following sections, four preliminary observations should be briefly made. First, it goes without saying that the due diligence obligation 'only applies when the State has knowledge of the situation, or should be aware of the risk of injury'.[1107] Thus, as noted by Blanco, States 'can only undertake positive action against a threat if they are aware of its existence'.[1108] It follows that, 'if state officials have knowledge that an attack will take place, the obligation arises to take active measures to prevent or provide protection'.[1109] This basic point was mentioned by the British–Mexican Claims Commission in the *Mexico City Bombardment Claims*,[1110] in State practice,[1111] as well as by many investment tribunals in the context of their analysis of FPS clauses.[1112] Second, one important element to consider in this respect is the foreseeability of the risk.[1113] Whether or not an attack

1106 *Pantechniki* case, 2009, para. 77, emphasis added.

1107 de Brabandere, 'Host States' Due Diligence Obligations', p. 352.

1108 Mantilla Blanco, *Full Protection and Security*, p. 459, adding that 'this does not however mean that ignorance about a threat necessarily excludes responsibility for lack of protection. States could be considered responsible if, in spite of being ignorant about the risk, they ought to have been aware of it'.

1109 Magnússon, *Full Protection and Security*, p. 166.

1110 *Mexico City Bombardment Claims* case, British–Mexican Claims Commission, 15 February 1930, UNRIAA 5, p. 79–80.

1111 ILC, Ago Report, 1972, p. 137, para. 172, referring to Acting US Secretary of State (Mr Castle) giving instructions to the American Ambassador to Cuba in 1932 explaining the position of the US as follows: 'the responsibility of an established Government for the acts of insurgents is engaged when the constituted authorities, *knowing of the imminence of the danger and being in a position to protect the property*, fail to exercise due diligence for its protection' (emphasis added) (in G.H. Hackworth, *Digest of International Law* (Washington, GPO, 1940), vol. V, p. 670).

1112 Mantilla Blanco, *Full Protection and Security*, examining the question at p. 459 ff. One important case is: *Wena Hotels Ltd. v. Republic of Egypt*, ICSID Case No. ARB/98/4, Award, 8 December 2000, paras. 82, 95.

1113 See, for instance, in the more general (and different) context of mob violence, Art. 13 of the Harvard Draft Convention on the International Responsibility of States for Injuries to Aliens, Draft No. 12, 15 April 1961 in Whiteman, *Digest of International Law* (vol. 8), p. 739:

> [a]mong the factors to be taken into account in determining whether the duty of due diligence has been discharged is that of the foreseeability of

can be considered as foreseeable will depend on many factors, including the important element of timing.[1114] Third, as noted by one writer, 'due diligence can only be exercised where there is a real possibility of adopting positive measures of protection'.[1115] As already noted above,[1116] one cannot require a State to take measures that are simply impossible to adopt (this question will be examined in more detail below when assessing the *force majeure* defence).[1117] Fourth, a government simply cannot be expected to react and take appropriate and reasonable measures regarding every situation involving a possible risk affecting the interests of foreign nationals.[1118] As Blanco noted, in the more specific context of FPS clauses, 'the diligence required from local authorities should be proportionate to the seriousness of the situation of risk' and, therefore, the 'higher probability of the harmful event, the higher the degree of diligence that can be expected from the state'.[1119] This is an important aspect to consider in the context of a rebellion or a civil war where the

> the risk. It can be easily assumed that a State should have anticipated the possibility of an injury to an alien if mobs are actually engaged in riotous activity or are expected shortly to do so or if bands of robbers and brigands are allowed to operate in certain portions of a country. A State may also be put on notice of a special duty to protect an alien if there has been violence against him or against groups of aliens or against nationals of a particular State or against aliens in general in the recent past or if there have been threats of violence and criminal conduct. A request for protection from an alien may also serve to give notice to the State that it ought to take special precautions regarding that alien.

1114 Magnússon, *Full Protection and Security*, p. 169:

> [h]ere, time is also of some importance as that can affect the due diligence principle, namely what measures could be considered reasonable taking into account the time the government has in order to prevent an occurrence that might have adverse effect on an investment. Again, Iran serves as an example where a government gradually loses control of a country. The revolution began with civil disturbances that later escalated into mass demonstrations, civil unrest in the form of general strikes and finally full-scale revolution. It is only logical that the culmination of individual occurrences over time affects the level of due diligence owed to an investor and in doing so influences the responsibility of a government to act on threats and intimidation shown towards an investor.

1115 Mantilla Blanco, *Full Protection and Security*, p. 457.

1116 See Section 3.3.3.2.2.

1117 See Section 3.3.3.4.2.

1118 Mantilla Blanco, *Full Protection and Security*, p. 469.

1119 Ibid. See also: Freeman, 'Responsibility of States for Unlawful Acts', p. 277–8 ('in international responsibility, the degree of danger measures the nature and amount of the diligence a Government must take to prevent injurious acts to another Government or its citizens').

seriousness of the situation regarding the interests of foreigners is rather obvious. Yet, as mentioned above, it would be truly unrealistic and unfair to impose such a higher degree of diligence on a State's shoulders, especially when it appears that it has completely lost control over key areas of its territory because of the strength of the rebels and the magnitude of the insurrection. This question is further examined in the next section.

3.3.3.3.3.1 The Strength of the Rebels and the Magnitude of the Insurrection
The first relevant circumstance that must be assessed to determine whether or not a State has fulfilled its due diligence obligation is the size and strength of the revolution or the insurrection.[1120] This principle has been recognized by many tribunals.[1121] In the *Home Insurance Co.*, case, the General Claims Commission concluded that the Mexican Government had not failed in its due diligence obligation of protection because of the strength of the insurrection: '[t]he sudden launching of this revolt against the constituted powers, the defection of a large proportion of the officers and men of the Federal Army, and the great personal and political following of the leader of the revolt, made it a *formidable uprising*'.[1122] Noting that one group of rebels had 'succeeded

[1120] Piguet, *La Guerre civile en droit international*, p. 99, 117; De Visscher, *Théories et réalités*, p. 348 ('le caractère et l'étendue du mouvement révolutionnaire sont un élément important dans l'appréciation du devoir de vigilance des autorités') ('the character and extent of the revolutionary movement is an important element in the appreciation of the duty of vigilance of the authorities'); Silvanie, *Responsibility of States*, p. 166 ('the capacity of the government to give protection depends not only upon the seriousness of the rebellions').

[1121] *G.L. Solis (U.S.A.)* v. *United Mexican States*, Mexico–United States General Claims Commission, 3 October 1928, UNRIAA 4, p. 362. See also: *Santa Clara Estates Case (Supplementary Claim)*, UK–Venezuela Mixed Commission, UNRIAA 9, p. 458: 'umpire is impressed with the fact that such control as the revolutionists obtained in certain portions of the country was owing rather to the financial aid which it received through its chief, Matos, who, *with the great body of men under his standard, made a combination for a time irresistible and overwhelming*, than to any weakness, inefficiency, or negligence on the part of the titular government . . . It is therefore the opinion of the umpire that there was no undue delay on the part of the Government in the restoration of its power in the district under consideration, and that it was not through the weakness, inefficiency, or passivity of the Government that the revolution of liberation remained in control for the time named, but rather through *its inherent strength in men, materials, and money, and in certain assisting circumstances*' (emphasis added).

[1122] *Home Insurance Co.* case, US–Mexico General Claims Commission, 31 March 1926, UNRIAA 4, p. 52, emphasis added. The case (described in ILC, 'Force majeure and Fortuitous event', 1978, p. 174, para. 426) involved a claim by the Home Insurance Co., an American corporation, to recover a sum it had paid to Westfeldt Brothers (a

in holding this territory on behalf of the revolutionists under de la Huerta and against the established authorities of the Obregon administration' and that communication with 'the outside world was cut off during a period of nearly five months', the Commission concluded that the Government of Mexico 'did not fail in the duty which in its sovereign capacity it owed to [foreigners] to protect their property'.[1123] The *Russell* case also referred to the 'magnitude' of the insurrection during the American Civil War and the fact that the Confederate States 'had some form of government, controlled an extensive area and possessed splendid armies' to explain why 'it is hardly to be expected that the Federal Government could often, if ever, be properly charged with negligence in preventing destruction or seizure of property or personal injuries by insurgents'.[1124]

Investment tribunals have also repeatedly mentioned this criterion. In *AAPL* v. *Sri Lanka*, the Tribunal took note of the magnitude of the insurrection to explain that the government had lost control over the area where the wrong took place.[1125] The most important case dealing with this matter is certainly the *Pantechniki* award. The case did not involve an insurrection per se, but rather a widespread civil strife that shook Albania in 1997. Sole Arbitrator Paulsson noted that 'the Albanian authorities were powerless in the face of social unrest of this magnitude' and (relying on the testimony of the project manager) that the police were unable to intervene to protect the investor.[1126] He also mentioned

company based in New Orleans) in compensation for the loss of two railroad car loads of coffee which had been seized in 1924 in Mexico by the forces of General Turruco, who was one of the supporters of the revolutionary movement launched by de la Huerta against the Government of President Obregon.

1123 Ibid.

1124 *Naomi Russell, In Her Own Right and As Administratrix and Guardian (U.S.A.)* v. *United Mexican States*, Mexico–US Special Claims Commission, Decision no. 5, 24 April 1931, opinion of Umpire Nielsen, UNRIAA 4, p. 824.

1125 *AAPL* case, 1990, para. 85(A): 'Both Parties are in agreement about one fact; that the infiltration by the rebels of the area in which Serendib's firm was located took *such magnitude that the entire district had been for several months before January 1987 practically out of the Government's control*' (emphasis added). The same remark is also found in ibid., dissenting opinion of Asante (in *ICSID Rev.* (1990), p. 592): '[i]n the case before the Tribunal, it is not disputed that the Claimant alleged loss of investments occurred during a *major insurrection* which resulted in a temporary *loss of control* by the Sri Lankan Government over the insurgent area, and that an armed conflict ensued from such insurrection' (emphasis added). See also, his reference to an 'insurrection that had been launched by *determined, formidable and well armed insurgents in inaccessible terrain*' (emphasis added).

1126 *Pantechniki* case, 2009, para. 82.

that 'it seems difficult to maintain that a government incurs international responsibility for failure to plan for *unprecedented trouble of unprecedented magnitude in unprecedented places*'.[1127] The size and strength of the unrest played a central part in the Arbitrator's conclusion that Albania had not violated its duty to provide full protection and security to the investor under the BIT.

Another relevant case is *Ampal* v. *Egypt*. In this case, the Claimant argued that Egypt had 'failed to take reasonable precautionary, preventive, and remedial measures to ensure the physical security of its pipeline network' from thirteen attacks by 'saboteurs' which took place in 2011–12 in the context of the Arab Spring Revolution.[1128] The Tribunal referred to a previous ICC award involving the same parties and events[1129] describing the general context as follows: 'With the eruption of the popular uprising that toppled President Mubarak in January 2011, Sinai's Bedouin seized the opportunity to shrug off Egypt's internal security yoke and push for communal empowerment. Militants grew strong and lawless, and their violence against the police led Egypt's State police to abandon the area. A security vacuum resulted.'[1130] The ICC award also noted that in the Sinai region, 'police took flight, while police stations and prisons were attacked', and that 'the Army, too preoccupied with events in Cairo and the Nile Valley, shied away from curbing the mayhem in the Sinai'.[1131] In this context, 'the Pipeline's security, which had mainly relied on police forces, literally disappeared overnight' and the 'insurgents soon took advantage of the vacuum and attacked the Pipeline'.[1132] The Tribunal referred to the attackers as 'saboteurs'[1133] and qualified the events as 'terrorist attacks'.[1134] It referred to (and approved) the findings of the ICC award which mentioned that three different Islamic terrorist groups claimed responsibility for the

1127 Ibid., para. 77, emphasis added.

1128 *Ampal-American Israel Corp., Egi-Fund (08-10) Investors LLC, Egi-Series Investments LLC and BSS-EMG Investors LLC* v. *Egypt*, ICSID Case No. ARB/12/11, Decision on Liability and Heads of Loss, 21 February 2017, para. 236.

1129 The Tribunal noted that the 'findings of fact in respect of the attacks of the pipeline' contained in a previous ICC award (*EMG* v. *EGPC, EGAS & IEC*, ICC Case No. 18215/GZ/MHM, Final Award, 4 December 2015) were 'res judicata between the parties in the present proceedings' (ibid., para. 274). It also indicated that it was 'satisfied that the findings of fact' contained in the ICC award were 'correct' (ibid., para. 282).

1130 Ibid., para. 254, referring to para. 603 of the ICC award.

1131 Ibid., para. 277, referring to other relevant passages from the ICC award.

1132 Ibid.

1133 Ibid., paras. 236, 288.

1134 Ibid., para. 254.

attacks on the Pipeline.[1135] Given that these jihadist groups have links with global terrorist organizations such as Al-Qaeda and ISIS, it can be fairly assumed that their ultimate objective was the overthrowing of the government of Egypt.

The *Ampal* Tribunal referred to (and approved) the *Pantechniki* award and noted that 'the adequacy of the State's response should be assessed in the light of the *scale of the disorder* and the extent of its resources'.[1136] Specifically, the Tribunal 'acknowledge[d] that the circumstances in the North Sinai Egypt were difficult in the wake of the Arab Spring Revolution' and that '[a]rmed militant groups took advantage of the political instability, security deterioration and general lawlessness that ensued in the North Sinai to [perpetrate] the attacks on the Trans-Sinai Pipeline'.[1137] In this context, the Tribunal considered that the first attack, which took place in February 2011, 'could not have been prevented by the Respondent and cannot amount to a breach of the full protection and security standard in itself'.[1138] As further discussed below,[1139] the Tribunal concluded that while the four first attacks could be excused considering the 'scale of the disorder' and the 'general lawlessness' which prevailed at the time, the same could not be said regarding the other attacks. The Tribunal concluded that Egypt's overall inaction regarding the thirteen attacks breached the FPS clause.

The findings of the *Ampal* award were recently endorsed by the *Strabag* Tribunal.[1140] The Tribunal mentioned that the 'Respondent's

[1135] Ibid., para. 278, referring to paras. 806–8 of the ICC award where one witness experts mentioned these groups: Ansar al-Hijad in the Sinai, Ansar Baytal-Maqdi and Al-Jabhahal-Salafiya fi Sinaa.

[1136] Ibid., para. 244, emphasis added.

[1137] Ibid., para. 284.

[1138] Ibid., para. 285, referring to this passage from *Pantechniki* case, 2009, para 77: 'it seems difficult to maintain that a government incurs international responsibility for failure to plan for *unprecedented trouble of unprecedented magnitude in unprecedented places*', emphasis added.

[1139] See Section 3.3.3.3.3.4.

[1140] *Strabag* case, 2020, paras. 234–5. As mentioned in a previous section (Section 2.1.2.2.3.2), the Tribunal applied the FPS clause only to damages arising from events that took place (in 2014) long *after* the rebels had been successful at establishing a new government (at the end of 2001). At the time, the new government (formally rebels) were themselves now fighting other insurgent groups. See claim 2, and analysis at paras. 334, 345. The Tribunal therefore correctly examined this specific claim (Claim 2) as one involving a situation where (at the time the award was rendered in June 2020) the rebels had *not* been successful at establishing a new government. The Tribunal concluded that the government was not responsible for any failure to exercise its due diligence obligation to protect foreigners and third States.

obligation under the Treaty to accord constant protection exists in a setting of weak and uncertain State authority, recurring armed conflict, and widespread breakdown of the law in wide areas of the country' and that 'the reality of these circumstances cannot be ignored in assessing Respondent's obligations'.[1141] The Tribunal essentially agreed with the Respondent's position that 'the situation in Libya, in terms of the gravity and the extent of the civil war, was equally bad and perhaps far worse than the situation of the civil unrest in *Pantechniki*'.[1142] It also agreed with the Respondent's position that as a result of 'various armed groups claiming to be the legitimate government' and 'exercis[ing] control over different areas of the country' it 'was *impossible* for the Libyan authorities *to guarantee full protection and security*, as they would normally do in peacetime'.[1143] For the Tribunal, 'in the circumstances prevailing in Libya during and since the Revolution' (i.e. 'widespread conflict, violence and disorder',[1144] elsewhere mentioning that 'the situation in Libya was chaotic, dangerous and unsettled'),[1145] 'it was *not reasonably possible* for the Libyan authorities to take consistent and effective measures to protect Claimant's investment'.[1146]

These awards show that the scale of a revolution matters when assessing whether a State has failed to respect its due diligence obligation to take appropriate measures to suppress an insurrection or to prevent attacks on foreigners. Fulfilling a State's due diligence obligation should not be problematic in cases of low intensity actions conducted by rather disorganized rebels. On the opposite end of the spectrum, even the most well-organized government may have great difficulty in protecting foreigners in cases of sudden, consistent and overwhelming attacks by rebels. The greater the magnitude of the rebellion, the likelier it is for a government to completely lose control over key parts of its territory. Whenever this is the case, a State could argue that it was very difficult (or simply impossible) to fulfil its due diligence obligation to prevent attacks in such circumstances. One relevant question examined below pertains to whether or not a State can invoke the *force majeure* defence in this context.[1147]

[1141] Ibid., para. 234.
[1142] Ibid., para. 232.
[1143] Ibid., para. 233, emphasis added.
[1144] Ibid., para. 236.
[1145] Ibid., para. 98.
[1146] Ibid., para. 236, emphasis added.
[1147] See Section 3.3.3.4.2.

3.3.3.3.3.2 The Capacity and the Willingness of the Government to Provide Adequate Protection The second relevant circumstance that should be taken into account to assess whether or not a State has fulfilled its due diligence obligation is the actual *capacity* of a government to suppress a revolution and prevent attacks by rebels. This basic principle has been recognized in the *Simpson* case where the Commission came to the conclusion that the Government of Mexico was 'not liable for the acts of rebel forces during the course of the "Escobar" revolution',[1148] based on the grounds that 'there has been no showing in this case that the Government of Mexico was in any way negligent or failed to assert *all the efforts within its capacity to suppress* the Escobar revolution'.[1149] Other tribunals have also referred to this notion of capacity, including the *Acquatella, Bianchi, et al.* case decided by the French–Venezuelan Mixed Claims Commission.[1150]

While there is no doubt that the capacity of a State to fulfil its obligation is relevant to the present analysis,[1151] one must nevertheless be

1148 As mentioned above, the Commission is wrong to use this terminology. Mexico cannot in any way be held 'liable for the acts of rebel forces'.

1149 *Claim of Jesse J. Simpson*, US–Mexico Claims Commission, Decision No. 63-E, p. 553, 554–5, in Whiteman, *Digest of International Law* (vol. 8), p. 824, emphasis added.

1150 *Acquatella, Bianchi et al.* case, France–Venezuela Mixed Claims Commission, Commissioner Paul, UNRIAA 10, p. 5, p. 6:

> This decision was not based on any exposition of principles invalidating the rules established by international law and by precedent decisions of other arbitral tribunals, from which has been derived the fixed doctrine of international law that governments, like individuals, are liable only for the acts of their agents, or of those who have directly assumed responsibility. These principles and precedents establish that the existence of a state of revolutionary struggle presupposes that a certain portion of the members composing the nation has temporarily withdrawn from its obedience to constituted authority, and that only when it appears that the *Government has failed to make prompt and efficient use of its authority to cause a return of said dissatisfied party to obedience, and to protect, within the measure of its ability, the property and persons threatened by the revolutionary disturbance,* may it be considered as liable for the consequences of such abnormal condition. Many decisions of international tribunals might be cited in support of this rule. (emphasis added).

1151 Mantilla Blanco, *Full Protection and Security*, p. 453: '[c]onsideration of the actual capacities of the host state in the assessment of diligence is therefore not only accepted under international law, but seems moreover to be justified from the standpoint of fairness and justice'. See also: C. H. Schreuer, 'The Protection of Investments in Armed Conflict', in Freya Baetens (ed.), *Investment Law Within International Law* (Cambridge University Press, 2013), p. 11, speaking of an obligation of due diligence that 'exists to the extent of the reasonable use of the host State's capacities'.

careful when trying to apply this criterion. It should be recalled that the question as to what a prudent, well-organized and diligent government would have done in similar circumstances is based on an international *objective* standard. The way a State acts cannot be situated below a certain threshold of acceptable behaviour. Thus, a State cannot argue its non-responsibility simply based on the grounds that it is *not* well-administered or organized and, therefore, does not have the military capacity and resources to suppress a rebellion or to prevent the commission of a wrongful act by the rebels. This sort of lack of capacity is no excuse for inaction. This is at least the case when the level of 'disorganization' of a government is *below* what the international standard requires.[1152]

I have found one older example of State practice which seems to have adopted the opposite solution. In response to a question asked about the rights of foreigners to obtain compensation from Congo (right after its independence in 1960), the Ministry of Foreign Affairs of Belgium (the former colonial power) noted that the criterion to assess whether a State has been vigilant in this context 'se modulent suivant le degré d'organisation des Nations' ('are modulated according to the degree of organization of Nations').[1153] He explained that one of the applicable principles was the following: 'l'État ne saurait être condamné pour une défaillance dans la répression de l'insurrection que s'il possède un appareil d'administration et de police qui corresponde à la situation générale du pays, notamment en relation avec son dégrée de peuplement et de civilisation'.[1154] The letter suggests that the obligation to exercise vigilance depends on each State's *degree of development.*[1155]

[1152] To give a simple illustration, Somalia is one of the clearest examples of a failed State that can be considered to have a governmental administration that is not well-organized. It can be reasonably argued that the level of organization of that government is below the international standard in this respect. In my view, Somalia should not be allowed to invoke its lack of capacity to suppress a rebellion or to prevent attacks by rebels simply based on its general 'disorganization'. This is because Somalia offers a level of protection to foreigners which is *below* the international minimum standard.

[1153] Letter of 10 December 1969, quoted in Jean Salmon and Michel Vincineau, 'La pratique du pouvoir exécutif et le contrôle des chambres législatives en matière de droit international', *RBDI* 8 (1969–70), p. 222–394, p. 372. The example is examined by Piguet, *La Guerre civile en droit international*, p. 81–2.

[1154] Ibid., ('the state can only be condemned for a failure in the repression of the insurgency if it possesses an administrative and police apparatus which corresponds to the general situation of the country, in particular in relation to its degree of population and civilization').

[1155] This also seems to be the position adopted by Piguet, *La Guerre civile en droit international*, p. 91–2: '[i]l parait exclu qu'une État réponde de la faiblesse de son

In my view, this element of capacity may only be possibly relevant to the extent that a government's degree of organization is *above* the minimum standard threshold required under international law.[1156] In the *Pantechniki* case, the sole Arbitrator asked the following questions: '[s]hould a state's international responsibility bear some proportion to its resources? Should a poor country be held accountable to a *minimum standard* which it could attain only at great sacrifice while a rich country would have little difficulty in doing so?'[1157] In my view, the second question must clearly be answered positively. The minimum standard of treatment *always* applies to *all States* (whether poor or rich, powerful or weak). A State cannot make an attempt to excuse its failure to fulfil its due diligence obligation in accordance with that standard based on its degree of development.[1158] In any event, what is clear is that the question (mentioned in the Belgian document mentioned above) as to whether a nation is 'civilized' or not is clearly outdated and inapplicable in contemporary international law. Some older cases have sometimes made reference to this dubious aspect.[1159]

The question of the 'capacity' of a State is therefore only relevant when the level of organization of a government is above this minimum standard threshold. Above that threshold, the capacity of a given State is, of course, a question of degree and gradation. One important element which can be taken into account, in this context, is a State's level of development. It has been noted by Newcombe and Paradell (who introduced the concept of 'modified objective standard') that 'due diligence is limited by a State's capacity to act' and that 'tribunals will likely consider

armée ou de son manque d'organisation interne si ces lacunes ne résultent pas de la négligence des autorités, mais de la nature du pays et de son degré de développement'.

1156 ILA, 'Study Group on Due Diligence', Second Report, p. 13, indicating that 'the level of a State's economic development can have a bearing on the operation of due diligence obligations in some circumstances'. Yet, the Report does not refer to the due diligence obligation of States in the context of insurrection as one such circumstances.

1157 *Pantechniki* case, 2009, para. 76, emphasis added.

1158 ILA, 'Study Group on Due Diligence', Second Report, p. 18. The Report states that 'there are some obligations of due diligence for which the same standard is required of all States and no account is taken of the economic resources of a State, its degree of control over its territory or other special characteristics'. The Report mentioned in the list 'certain aspects of the international minimum standards in international investment law' (p. 18).

1159 One example discussed below (at the end of Section 3.3.3.3.3.3) is *Home Frontier and Foreign Missionary Society of the United Brethren in Christ (United States)* v. *Great Britain*, 18 December 1920, UNRIAA 6, p. 43.

the state's level of development and stability as relevant circumstances in determining whether there has been due diligence'.[1160] Other investment arbitration scholars also support this position.[1161] The *Pantechniki* award adopted this position by making a distinction between the capacity of a 'powerful' and a 'poor and fragile' State: '[a] failure of protection and security is to the contrary likely to arise in an unpredictable instance of

[1160] Andrew Newcombe and Lluís Paradell, *Law and Practice of Investment Treaties: Standards of Treatment* (Alphen aan den Rijn, Kluwer Law International, 2009), p. 310:

> [t]he extent of due diligence an investor may expect will vary . . . according to local conditions. This means that due diligence is limited by a state's capacity to act – a state will not be responsible when action would have been impossible. Although the host state is required to exercise an objective minimum standard of due diligence, the standard of due diligence is that of a host state in the circumstances and with the resources of the state in question. This suggests that due diligence is *modified objective standard* – the host state must exercise the level of due diligence of a host state *in its particular circumstances.* In practice, tribunals will likely consider the state's *level of development and stability as relevant circumstances* in determining whether there has been due diligence. An investor investing in an area with endemic civil strife and poor governance cannot have the same expectation of physical security as one investing in London, New York or Tokyo. (emphasis added).

[1161] Ursula Kriebaum, 'The Relevance of Economic and Political Conditions for Protection under Investment Treaties', *LPICT* 10(3) (2011), p. 384:

> the due diligence obligation means that host States have to take measures which are reasonable under the circumstances to protect the investment. What is "reasonable" will be influenced by the circumstances prevailing in the host State, including the resources at its disposal. This would suggest that there is enough flexibility in the legal standards in investment law to take account of the different stages of development across nations.

See also: N. Gallus, 'The Influence of the Host State's Level of Development on International Investment Treaty Standards of Protection', *J. World Invest & Trade* 6 (2005), p. 711–29; Magnússon, *Full Protection and Security*, p. 197: '[a]rbitral practice supports the notion that the resources of the state should be taken into account when assessing the obligation of a state to provide protection'. He also identified the inherent risk associated with taking into account the level of development:

> [i]f the level of development of a host state is to play a role in determining its obligations within the context of absolute investment standards, such standards would face the risk of becoming too casuistic in practice. The end result would be that these standards, such as the full protection and security standard, would become diluted, as their application would depend on a case-by-case assessment of a country's level of development. Needless to say, such a scenario would not encourage states to increase their level of development as that might incur a stricter obligation to provide for investment protection. (p. 199).

civic disorder which could have been readily controlled by a *powerful state* but which overwhelms the limited *capacities* of one which *is poor and fragile*'.[1162] In *AMT* v. *Zaire*, the Tribunal took into account the country's level of development when deciding the amount of compensation to be awarded to the investor.[1163] In a detailed analysis, Kriebaum identified three different situations in which investment tribunals took into account economic and political circumstances: ex-communist countries in transition, host States confronted with economic and financial crises and host States having ongoing political disturbances.[1164] In the context of investment arbitration, these factors have been deemed to be crucial when assessing a foreign investor's legitimate expectations at the time when the investment is made.[1165]

While the level of development can be relevant in the context of assessing the capacity of a government to suppress a revolution or to prevent attacks, the same cannot be said about its obligation to punish wrongdoers. As noted in a 2016 ILA Report, 'the State's due diligence obligation to apprehend and punish those responsible for acts of violence committed towards aliens, whether one considers this as part of the FPS [full protection and security] standard or the international minimum standard of treatment, does not allow taking into consideration the means or economic development of the State'.[1166]

In the context of insurrections and civil wars, one relevant element of analysis will be a State's military resources and its capacity to respond to rebels' actions. It is undeniable that some States have better military resources and capacity than others. To give a simple illustration, the United States is certainly better equipped to face an insurrection than Costa Rica. It is therefore logically expected that it will be easier for the former to crush a rebellion than for the latter. In other words, while Costa

1162 *Pantechniki* case, 2009, para. 77, emphasis added.

1163 *AMT* v. *Zaire*, ICSID Case No. ARB/93/1, Award, 21 February 1997, paras. 7.14–7.15.

1164 Kriebaum, 'The Relevance of Economic and Political Conditions', p. 386.

1165 Magnússon, *Full Protection and Security*, p. 198 ('an investor who invests in a developing country cannot expect to enjoy the same level of protection as if the investment would be made in a developed country as the application of absolute investment standards, which are formulated in a relevant BIT, might be affected by the host state's development'); M. Gritsenko, 'Relevance of the Host State's Development Status in Investment Treaty Arbitration', in Freya Baetens (ed.), *Investment Law Within International Law* (Cambridge University Press, 2013), p. 344 ff.; Kriebaum, 'The Relevance of Economic and Political Conditions', p. 386 (also examining the impact of economic conditions on compensation awarded to investors, p. 399 ff.).

1166 ILA, 'Study Group on Due Diligence', Second Report, p. 18.

Rica could potentially argue for its non-responsibility for failing to take reasonable measures to suppress a rebellion or to prevent attacks by rebels based on its general lack of military capacity, the same argument could hardly be sustained regarding the United States. The United States' inaction faced with an insurrection could seldom be excused based on its lack of military capacity alone. It may simply be *unwilling* to take such reasonable measures. This is an important point further discussed in the next paragraphs.

Some tribunals (including *Solis*)[1167] have indicated that 'the test of liability' is to determine the '*capacity and willingness* on the part of the authorities to act'.[1168] In my view, both elements (capacity and willingness) must be part of the analysis in order to determine whether or not a government has fulfilled its due diligence obligation. As a matter of principle, 'a State cannot be considered to have acted diligently when the State has acted in bad faith or has knowingly refused to take any measures whatsoever'.[1169] Yet, a State's 'unwillingness' to take any appropriate action cannot be assessed in the abstract. It should be examined in combination with the question whether or not it has the capacity to act in the first place. In my view, the following propositions could serve as potential guidelines to assess the combination of both capacity *and* willingness:

- Logically, a government that has the military capacity and resources to take reasonable measures to suppress a rebellion or to prevent attacks *and* that is also willing to take appropriate action should not be facing any major obstacle in the course of crushing a rebellion. The question only arises when a government is either lacking capacity *and/or* willingness in doing so;

[1167] *G.L. Solis (U.S.A.)* v. *United Mexican States*, Mexico–United States General Claims Commission, 3 October 1928, UNRIAA 4, p. 362: 'in dealing with the question of responsibility for acts of insurgents two pertinent points have been stressed, namely, the capacity to give protection, *and the disposition of authorities* to employ proper, available measures to do so' (emphasis added).

[1168] *Naomi Russell, In Her Own Right and As Administratrix and Guardian (U.S.A.)* v. *United Mexican States*, Mexico–US Special Claims Commission, Decision no. 5, 24 April 1931, opinion of Umpire Nielsen, UNRIAA 4, p. 825: '[a]s a general rule, a government is responsible for the consequences of wrongdoing which it could have prevented by reasonably effective measures. And there is no good reason why that general rule of responsibility should not be applied in an appropriate case to acts of insurgents, *the test of liability* being *capacity and willingness* on the part of the authorities to act' (emphasis added).

[1169] De Brabandere, 'Host States' Due Diligence Obligations', p. 352.

- A government that *has* the military capacity and resources to take reasonable measures *cannot* excuse its failure to act based on its 'unwillingness' to take such appropriate action;
- On the contrary, a government that *does not* have the military capacity and resources to take reasonable measures to suppress a rebellion, may excuse its failure to do so if it can prove that it was willing to take such appropriate action (but simply could not). The argument is unlikely to be successful in the event that the government was not only *unable* but also *unwilling* to take any appropriate action.

A good illustration of the interplay between capacity and willingness is the recent *Cengiz* case (already discussed above)[1170] arising in the context of the Libyan civil war.[1171] In the context of its analysis as to whether Libya had breached the 'positive obligation to prevent that third parties cause physical damage to such investment',[1172] under the FPS clause contained in the BIT, the Tribunal affirmed that 'reasonableness must be measured taking into consideration the State's *means and resources* and the general situation of the country', a reference to the civil war plaguing Libya at the time when the attacks on the investor's property took place.[1173] The award mentioned two events:[1174] (1) 'on August 26, 2011, a group of citizens, supported by police vehicles and the Tank Battalion [a pro-Gaddafi groups], again entered the WAH Main Camp and stole everything at hand';[1175] (2) 'the Sebha campsite was raided by an armed mob' on November 5, 2013'.[1176] It should be added that these attacks took place *after* the NTC insurgents took over the capital and (at least, according to the Tribunal) replaced the Gaddafi regime to form the new government.[1177] The Tribunal held that 'Libya

1170 See Section 3.1.4.2.2.

1171 The Tribunal in *Way2B ACE* v. *Libya*, ICC, Award, May 2018, apparently took the same position and considered the host State's level of development and stability. The award is not available. See: IAReporter 'Way2b V. Libya Tribunal Finds That Bit's War-Losses Clause Does Not Exclude Operation of Other Bit Protections (Including Full Protection & Security), But Foreign Investor Fails to Meet Evidentiary Burdens', 8 January 2019.

1172 *Cengiz* case, 2018, para. 403.

1173 Ibid., para. 406, emphasis added.

1174 Ibid., para. 436.

1175 Ibid., para. 385.

1176 Ibid., para. 394.

1177 As mentioned above (see Section 3.1.4.2.2.1), the question as to whether the NTC can truly be considered to have had established a new government at the end of August 2011 is controversial.

totally failed to provide any security to the two Main Camps an investment worth almost USD 90 M, full of valuable machinery and equipment, located in the Southern region and subject to a heightened risk of attack.'[1178] The main reason for drawing such a conclusion was that 'Libya never deployed any unit of the regular Army, any police force nor Government controlled militia to protect such assets'[1179] and that, as a result, the investor 'was left on its own in the task of protecting the Main Camps'.[1180] The Tribunal concluded that Libya breached the FPS standard because 'it totally failed to provide any government-sponsored protection to the two Main Camps' and that such a failure 'facilitated that private mobs were repeatedly able to raid the Main Camps, looting equipment and destroying facilities'.[1181] The Tribunal also stated that it was 'unconvinced' by the Respondent's argument that 'in a situation of civil war and general unrest, it would be unreasonable to expect a government to use scarce resources to protect ancillary projects like the WAH and Sebha Project'.[1182] Thus, the Tribunal believed that Libya *had the capacity and resources* to take preventives measures and deploy counter action. The Tribunal explained what the due diligence obligation would have required in this context:

> First the Tribunal has concluded that due diligence required Libya to deploy means to protect Cengiz Libya's two Main Camps – not the ability to perform its construction activities and complete the WAH and Sebha Projects. … What Libya could reasonably have done is to provide basic static protection to the two Main Camps, as a deterrent against theft and plunder by violent mobs. Libya failed to provide such protection at all, and the result is that mobs repeatedly were able to enter the Main Camps and to loot and destroy the property. Second, *there is evidence that Libya, if it had wanted, would have been able to marshal the limited resources required to provide static protection to the two Main Camps.* … Third, there actually is a comparable example of a foreign investment which received this type of protection.[1183]

The extract is interesting because it shows that even in a situation of civil war and general unrest, such as the one prevailing in Libya at the time, and even taking into account a State's 'means and resources',[1184] it remains that the due diligence obligation imposes a duty to provide

[1178] *Cengiz* case, 2018, para. 438.
[1179] Ibid., para. 438.
[1180] Ibid., para. 441.
[1181] Ibid., para. 442.
[1182] Ibid., paras. 443–4.
[1183] Ibid., paras. 445–50, emphasis added.
[1184] Ibid., para. 406.

basic protection to an investor's property. In other words, a civil war is not a legitimate excuse for providing no protection at all. The award suggests that a State breaches its due diligence obligation whenever it fails to send *any* army or police forces to protect an investment. This is especially the case when the host *could have* reasonably provided such a protection. The case is an illustration of a situation where Libya (according to the Tribunal) had both the capacity and the resources to take preventive measures to protect foreigners, but was however *unwilling* (whatever the reasons may be) to do so.

One important point to mention here is that this element of capacity is compounded by the scale of the revolution (an issue examined in the previous section). Thus, the greater the magnitude of the insurgency and the strength of the rebels, the more likely the argument of non-responsibility based on lack of capacity will be appealing.[1185] This is indeed the reasoning which was adopted by Sole Arbitrator Paulsson in the *Pantechniki* case. Relying on the testimony of the project manager, he noted that the police 'were *unable* to intervene' to protect the investor, adding that this situation 'was crucially different from a *refusal* to intervene given the scale of the looting'.[1186] He concluded that 'the Albanian authorities were powerless in the face of social unrest of this magnitude'.[1187] In other words, it is *because* of the magnitude of the insurgency that Albania was *unable* to intervene.[1188]

It is noteworthy in this respect that the *Cengiz* Tribunal did not make any mention of the scale of the insurrection in its analysis of the two attacks mentioned above. The reasoning of the *Cengiz* Tribunal is therefore completely different from the position which was subsequently adopted by the *Strabag* Tribunal.[1189] The *Strabag* Tribunal acknowledged that Libya had 'weak and uncertain State authority' regarding the possibility

1185 Accordingly, as mentioned above, Costa Rica may reasonably argue that it should not be held responsible for its failure to take reasonable measures to suppress a rebellion or prevent attacks based on the grounds that it lacks military capacity and resources (and was willing to take action). This argument is likely to be *a fortiori* successful if it can further demonstrate the great magnitude of the rebellion it was facing.

1186 *Pantechniki* case, 2009, para. 82, emphasis in the original.

1187 Ibid., para. 82.

1188 On the contrary, in my view, the issue of the magnitude of the insurgency should not play a decisive role in a situation where a government does have the military capacity and resources to take reasonable measures to suppress a rebellion or prevent attacks, but is simply *unwilling* to take appropriate action.

1189 It should be highlighted that the *Strabag* Tribunal made its analysis of 'Claim 2' regarding damages which occurred in 2014, i.e. later than the events examined by the *Cengiz* Tribunal.

to take preventive measures to protect foreigners.[1190] However, as previously mentioned, the Tribunal essentially agreed with the Respondent's position that Libya was *unable* to provide protection under the FPS clause *because* of the magnitude of the insurgency.[1191]

3.3.3.3.3.3 The Location Where the Wrong Took Place The third relevant circumstance to assess whether or not a State has fulfilled its due diligence obligation is the geographical location where the wrong took place. As noted by the ILA in its 2016 Report, 'where a State does not have effective control over the entirety of its territory, the degree of diligence expected may also be mitigated accordingly'.[1192] Thus, as mentioned above, a State (as well-organized as it may be) cannot reasonably be expected to offer due diligence protection to aliens in areas of its territory where it has completely lost control at the hands of rebels. Another relevant aspect is whether the area where the wrong took place is sparsely populated or isolated.[1193] When events take place in isolated and remote areas, where policing and security are scarce and difficult, it is expected to be much harder for a State to take any measure to prevent attacks. A less stringent due diligence obligation should accordingly be imposed on that State in such circumstances.

This condition was expressly mentioned by US Secretary of State Bayard in the previously mentioned letter regarding the insurrection in Cuba.[1194]

[1190] *Strabag* case, 2020, para. 234: 'Respondent's [FPS] obligation under the Treaty to accord constant protection exists in a setting of weak and uncertain State authority, recurring armed conflict, and widespread breakdown of the law in wide areas of the country.'

[1191] Ibid., para. 236. The Tribunal noted that 'in the circumstances prevailing in Libya during and since the Revolution' (i.e., 'widespread conflict, violence and disorder'), 'it was *not reasonably possible* for the Libyan authorities to take consistent and effective measures to protect Claimant's investment' (emphasis added). One important point to mention is that the Tribunal held that Libya breached the war-losses clause contained in the treaty. In other words, the fact that Libya was anyway held liable under that specific clause may have had an impact on how the Tribunal assessed the FPS clause.

[1192] ILA, 'Study Group on Due Diligence', Second Report, p. 17. The Report also added that 'it is not clear, however, that this is truly a question of requiring less diligence or instead is a matter of force majeure as a (temporary) circumstance precluding wrongfulness'.

[1193] *AAPL* case, 1990, dissenting opinion of Asante (in *ICSID Rev.* (1990), p. 592), speaking of an 'insurrection that had been launched by determined, formidable and well armed insurgents in *inaccessible terrain*' (emphasis added).

[1194] Letter dated 6 January 1888, in Moore, *Digest of International Law* (vol. III), p. 961–4 (also in ILC, 'Force majeure and Fortuitous event', 1978, p. 112):

> the degree of diligence customary and reasonable in a newly and sparsely settled region of country where the police force is weak and scattered, where armed forces cannot be maintained and where custom throws, on

He noted that 'there are areas of revolt against which no government could protect itself'.[1195] He cited the example of the civil war in the United States (1861–5), when the government was found 'without the means of immediately suppressing the insurrection in which the property and persons of foreigners, as well as of citizens were involved'.[1196] He also cited the position of the US at the time: '[i]t is the duty of foreigners to withdraw from such risks and if they do not, or if they voluntarily expose themselves to such risk, they must take the consequences'.[1197] He explained that no State had 'the ability and duty . . . to have at all times a military force at hand . . . so large as to enable it to protect property wheresoever attacked by insurgents'.[1198] A State has therefore no obligation to 'have a military force stationed throughout its territories . . . sufficient to protect [foreign workers] at every remote point to which they might choose to resort'.[1199] US Secretary of State Bayard applied this principle to the facts of the case and rejected the claim of a US national who had invested in Cuba during a period of insurrection.[1200]

Authors support this finding.[1201] Thus, for Silvanie, a foreigner who stays in parts of a specific territory, infamously known to be plagued with a lawless dynamic and threatening disorder, therefore 'exposes himself to

> the individual, in a large degree, not merely the preservation of order but the vindication of supposed rights, is very different from the degree of diligence customary in a center of population under a well-organized police, and in which armed forces could be promptly summoned in support of the law.

1195 Ibid., p. 116.

1196 Ibid.

1197 Ibid.

1198 Ibid.

1199 Ibid.

1200 Ibid.:

> [i]t is a matter of notoriety that when Mr Negrete visited Cuba, and there purchased an estate, that island was in a state of insurrection. I have no information as to the price he paid for the property nor from whom he bought it, nor the conditions of the sale; nor what influence the existence of the insurrection had upon the price. It is, however, notorious that estates in the district exposed to insurrection were from that cause and naturally greatly depreciated in value. So far as the information before me goes, Mr Negrete voluntarily incurred the risks incidental to his purchase and naturally contemplated by him and all others who make investments in countries in an insurrectionary state [Cuba] and therefore has no right to call on this Government to demand from Spain indemnity for his losses so incurred.

1201 Piguet, *La Guerre civile en droit international*, p. 117; Borchard, 'International Responsibility of the State for Injuries', p. 119; Silvanie, *Responsibility of States*, p. 166.

danger and assumes the risk', which, in turn, results in 'relieving the government from its duty of protection and therefore of liability'.[1202] Foreigners must be aware of the degree of security that can be provided by the local authorities when they decide to invest.[1203] It goes without saying that no liability can exist in the particular situation where a foreigner decided to actively participate in an insurrection.[1204] The same principle of non-responsibility was also applied, more generally, in the broader context of a murder committed by armed bandits in a remote area controlled by rebels.[1205] Blanco further examined several investment cases involving FPS clauses where an investor knew (or

1202 Silvanie, ibid., p. 182, referring to State practice in support of this principle.

1203 This general principle has been followed by several tribunals. For instance, in the *Upton* case, US–Venezuela Mixed Claims Commission, UNRIAA 9, p. 113–318, Umpire Bainbridge, p. 234, at p. 236: the Claimant 'must be held, in going into a foreign country, to have voluntarily assumed the risks as well as the advantages of his residence there. Neither claimant nor his property can be exempted from the evils incident to a state or war to which all other persons and property within the same territory were exposed'. See also: Ralston, *Law and Procedure of International Tribunals*, p. 386, referring to the principle that 'the alien residing in a state exposed to war is compelled to accept, together with the citizens of the state, for himself and for his property, the dangers incident to surrounding conditions. and no more than they, poses a right to compensation therefore'.

1204 Silvanie, *Responsibility of States*, p. 183, citing a number of cases, including *Whitty*, in Moore, *History and Digest of the International Arbitrations* (vol. III), p. 2820.

1205 In the *Buckingham* case, British–Mexican Claims Commission, 3 August 1931, UNRIAA 5, p. 288, the Commission denied the existence of any failure on the part of the Mexican Government concerning the suppression of acts of violence or the punishment of their authors because the crimes were committed in a remote area which was controlled by rebel forces:

> [n]o Government of a country of the immense extent of the Mexican Republic, with scarce population, of a mountainous character and with great difficulty of communications, can be expected to furnish adequate military protection to all the isolated oil-fields, mines, haciendas and factories scattered over the territory. The oil camp where the murder was committed is in a very remote situation, and its connexions with the rest of the country are scarce and arduous. At the time of the events, the district was controlled by the rebel leader Castulo Perez, for whose protection against bandits and robbers a contribution was paid by the Aguila, as well as by other concerns. It was this leader who pursued the murderers and had them executed. It was outside the power of the Government forces to operate in the region, which was practically in the hands of others, who were superior in number, and therefore they cannot be blamed for not having punished the criminals'. It should be added that the Commission also considered that 'it is the duty of any Government to know the extent to which they can afford protection, and to warn subjects, as well as aliens, if they are unable to do so, leaving it to their judgment either to remain at their own risk or to withdraw from those isolated places, to where the hand of government does not reach.

should have been aware) of the risks involved prior to investing in certain areas, considering the security conditions prevailing at the time.[1206]

One relevant case in this respect is the *LESI* award involving the construction of a dam by Italian investors in a remote region of Algeria. The award explained that the work had been delayed because of security problems arising from an insurrection involving Islamic terrorists.[1207] Given that the project was taking place in a mountainous and partially remote area of the country, it was necessary to set up both 'active and 'passive' security measures before the work could actually begin.[1208] The parties disagreed on whether or not the host State took appropriate security measures and whether it had breached the FPS clause contained in the Italy–Algeria BIT.[1209]

An important aspect of this case is that Article 4 of the BIT contained both a FPS clause and a 'war clause', providing for the principle of non-discrimination regarding compensation for losses arising from an armed conflict, insurrection and revolution (Article 4.5). The Tribunal took a rather controversial stand on the question of the interaction between the two aspects. It held that, given the specific structure of the provision, it should be interpreted to mean that the host State did not have to provide FPS in a situation of insurrection.[1210] In one passage, the Tribunal seems to suggest that in any event in a situation of insurrection it would be simply *impossible* for the host State to provide such FPS.[1211] The Tribunal acknowledged that this interpretation had the effect of 'lowering

1206 Mantilla Blanco, *Full Protection and Security*, p. 471 ff.

1207 *LESI S.p.A. and ASTALDI S.p.A.* v. *Algeria*, ICSID Case No. ARB/05/3, Sentence, 12 November 2008, para. 11: 'Durant cette époque en effet, la situation politique était difficile en Algérie et spécialement dans la région, en raison de la lutte armée qui opposait depuis le début de l'année 1992 l'État algérien à des extrémistes islamistes' ('During this period, in fact, the political situation was difficult in Algeria and especially in the region, due to the armed struggle which, since the beginning of 1992, had opposed the Algerian state to Islamist extremists').

1208 Ibid., para. 11.

1209 Ibid., para. 165. Another alleged breached concerned the FET obligation. Noting that the 'security' aspect of the FET obligation was partially covered by the FPS clause, the Tribunal simply mentioned that a State is required to do *all it can do* (within its powers) to prevent foreigners suffering from a damage (para. 153: '[l]'obligation de sécurité implique dès lors que l'État d'accueil fasse tout ce qui est dans son pouvoir pour éviter qu'un dommage ne soit infligé aux investissements') ('the security obligation therefore implies that the host state does everything in its power to prevent damage from being inflicted on the investments'). It held that the host State had not breached its FET obligation.

1210 Ibid., para. 174.

1211 Ibid., para. 175.

substantially' the level of protection offered to the investor.[1212] Under the war clause, which was applied as *lex specialis*, the host State only had to provide a treatment to foreigners that was not less favourable than the one provided to its own nationals.

The award provides a detailed list of acts of violence which affected Algeria during the implementation of the contract,[1213] including terrorist attacks, destruction of infrastructures, and the kidnapping and killing of foreign workers in other projects. The Tribunal concluded that the situation prevailing at the time was one of a 'revolution' involving violent armed combats between governmental forces and terrorist groups which plagued all of Algeria (and in particular the region where the project was located).[1214] Given the 'gravity and persistence' of the violence, the Tribunal held that the war clause should indeed apply in these circumstances. Most importantly for present purposes, the award also referred to a series of security measures which were specifically taken by the government to protect the project, including setting up a security firm of some 250 men guarding the infrastructure. The Tribunal noted that such measures went beyond the level of security prevailing in the rest of the country at the time.[1215] One passage of the award explained the difficulty facing Algeria to take such measures given the isolated location of the project.[1216] The Tribunal concluded that Algeria had taken 'reasonable and proportionate' security measures considering the situation of the insurrection prevailing in the country at the time and, specifically, the remote location of the project. In any event, the level of protection offered by the government to the Claimant was not found to be below the one that existed for nationals, which were themselves faced with the same security concerns in the region.[1217] The Tribunal therefore concluded that Algeria had not breached the war clause contained in the BIT.

[1212] Ibid., para. 175.
[1213] Ibid., para. 176.
[1214] Ibid., para. 177.
[1215] Ibid., paras. 179–80.
[1216] Ibid., para. 180: '[a] cela s'ajoute que la région où le site est implanté présente des risques accrus, puisqu'il s'agit d'un *endroit très isolé* à proximité d'un petit hameau, *dont l'accès est très difficile* et pour lequel il faut créer des pistes. En d'autres termes, il s'agit d'un site vierge sur lequel il n'y a *aucune infrastructure*' ('In addition, the region where the site is located presents increased risks, since it is a *very isolated place* near a small hamlet, to which *access is very difficult* and requires creating roads. In other words, this is an empty site on which there is *no infrastructure*') (emphasis added).
[1217] Ibid., para. 182.

The *LESI* award is a relevant example since it describes the type of 'reasonable and proportionate' security measures which may be required. Such measures depend, inter alia, on the location where an alleged breach took place. A less stringent level of protection is expected from a State when an insurrection is taking place in an isolated region where the army and the police may have greater difficulties in applying law and order.[1218]

Finally, a few words should be said about one very dubious element (which clearly does not make any sense today) that the US–Great Britain Commission nevertheless took into account to assess whether a government had fulfilled its duty of protection: the degree of 'civilization' of the region where the troubles are taking place. The *Home Frontier and Foreign Missionary Society* case involved a local rebellion in the British Protectorate of Sierra Leone after the colonial British authorities had imposed a tax on the native people. Right at the outset, the award explained that 'as is common in the more uncivilized parts of Africa, it was marked by every circumstance of cruelty and by undiscriminating attacks on the persons and properties of all Europeans'.[1219] The Commission rejected the claim for loss and damages filed by a religious missionary organization on the grounds that the British colonial government had not been negligent in suppressing the insurrection and had not failed 'in its duty to afford adequate protection for life and property'.[1220] Thus, the authorities 'took every measure available for its repression'.[1221] One element taken into account by the Commission in its analysis of this duty was the fact that it considered Sierra Leone to be

1218 See explanatory note to Article 13(1), Harvard Draft Convention on the International Responsibility of States for Injures to Aliens, Draft No. 12, 15 April 1961, in Whiteman, *Digest of International law* (vol. 8), p. 739–40:

> [t]he means which a State has available to protect an alien must also be taken into account. In a thinly populated area, it cannot be expected that large police forces be mobilized in order to render safe those aliens who may wish to enter the area. It is, however, quite clear that a State must not stop at affording protection through police but must, if necessary, attempt to maintain order through the intervention of military forces as well. In sum, the duty of state to afford protection may vary with the character of the territory in question in the very same manner that the acts necessary for the exercise of sovereignty may vary with the nature of the terrain, the population and the degree of civilization of the area claimed.

1219 *Home Frontier and Foreign Missionary Society of the United Brethren in Christ (United States)* v. *Great Britain*, 18 December 1920, UNRIAA 6, p. 43.

1220 Ibid., p. 44.

1221 Ibid.

'a semi-barbarous and only partially colonized protectorate'.[1222] The Commission thus noted that: 'It is impossible to judge the system of police and protection of life and property in force in the savage regions of Africa by the standard of countries or cities which enjoy the social order, the respect for authority, and the settled administration of a high civilization.'[1223]

Finally, the Commission noted that the Claimants must have known of the difficult environment in which it was involved: 'it is obvious that the Missionary Society must have been aware of the difficulties and perils to which it exposes itself in its task of carrying Christianity to so remote and barbarous a people', adding that 'the contempt for difficulty and peril is one of the noblest sides of their missionary zeal. Indeed, it explains why they are able to succeed in fields which mere commercial enterprise can not be expected to enter'.[1224] It goes without saying that the degree of 'civilization' is no longer a relevant element to the due diligence analysis.

3.3.3.3.3.4 Whether a State Promptly Responded to Rebels' Actions
The fourth relevant circumstance to assess whether or not a State has fulfilled its due diligence obligation is the amount of time a government has taken to deal with a rebellion and specific rebels' actions. The question arose in the *Santa Clara Estates* Co case, decided by the UK–Venezuela Mixed Commission,[1225] involving a British Company doing business in the Orinoco district of Venezuela, which was then entirely taken at the hands of revolutionaries.[1226] The United Kingdom argued that Venezuela had not put down the rebellion within a reasonable

1222 Ibid., p. 43.

1223 Ibid., p. 44. It concluded: 'A Government can not be held liable as the insurer of lives and property under the circumstances presented in this case.'

1224 Ibid., p. 44.

1225 *Santa Clara Estates Case (Supplementary Claim)*, UK–Venezuela Mixed Commission, UNRIAA 9, p. 455. See the case examined in Al-Ganzory, 'International Claims and Insurgence', p. 87.

1226 ILC, 'Force majeure and Fortuitous event', 1978, p. 162, summarized the fact of the case as follows:

> [a] revolutionary body established itself as the government of that part of the country and to a certain extent entered upon the discharge of governmental functions. During that time, the livestock belonging to the Santa Clara Estates Company was taken for the use of the revolutionaries, thereby causing losses to the company. The British Government contended that there was negligence on the part of the titular Government in allowing its rebellious subjects to maintain an independent government

amount of time and that it had been tolerating an insurgent government for too long. As noted by Akehurst, Umpire Plumley stated that 'no arbitrary time-limit of a year or any other period could be set, pointing out that the war of American independence had lasted seven years and the American civil war four; and he found that the delay in repressing the rebels was due to the strength of the rebels, not to the passivity of the Government'.[1227] The reasoning of the Umpire shows that different factors need to be taken into account when assessing whether or not a State has promptly responded to rebels' actions.[1228] Other tribunals have come to the same conclusion.[1229] These factors include the military

for so long, and that there was a limit within which the Government should have been able to reduce the revolutionaries to subjection.

1227 Akehurst, 'State Responsibility', p. 53.

1228 *Santa Clara Estates Case (Supplementary Claim)*, UK–Venezuela Mixed Commission, UNRIAA 9, see at p. 358: 'Was the length of time during which this independent government existed the result of the inefficiency and negligence of the Government in its general efforts to put down the revolution and to regain its lost territory throughout the whole country of Venezuela, or was it due to the extent, strength, and force of the revolution itself?' See also at p. 358:

> A war in which there were, in a little over one year, twenty sanguinary battles, forty battles of considerable character, and more than one hundred lesser engagements between contending troops, with a resultant loss of 12,000 lives, can hardly suggest passivity or negligence on the part of the national Government towards the revolution; and the umpire is impressed with the fact that such control as the revolutionists obtained in certain portions of the country was owing rather to the financial aid which it received through its chief, Matos, who, with the great body of men under his standard, made a combination for a time irresistible and overwhelming, than to any weakness, inefficiency, or negligence on the part of the titular Government. In other words, history compels a belief that the Government did in fact what it has a right to have assumed it would do-made the best resistance possible under all the existing circumstances to the revolutionary forces seeking its overthrow. It is therefore the opinion of the umpire that there was no undue delay on the part of the Government in the restoration of its power in the district under consideration, and that it was not through the weakness, inefficiency, or passivity of the Government that the revolution of liberation remained in control for the time named, but rather through its inherent strength in men, materials and money, and in certain assisting circumstances.

1229 *Sambiaggio* case, 1903, p. 513: 'it clearly appear that the government has failed to use *promptly and with appropriate force* its constituted authority', emphasis added. See also: *Acquatella, Bianchi et al.* case, France–Venezuela Mixed Claims Commission, Commissioner Paul, UNRIAA 10, p. 5, p. 6: 'only when it appears that the Government has *failed to make prompt and efficient use of its authority* to cause a return of said dissatisfied party to obedience, and to protect, within the measure of its

means used by the government, the strength of the rebels, the scale of the rebellion and the resources available to the State.

In this context, the *Ampal* v. *Egypt* case is relevant. The Claimant argued that Egypt had 'failed to take reasonable precautionary, preventive, and remedial measures to ensure the physical security of its pipeline network' from thirteen attacks by 'saboteurs' (which the Tribunal later referred to as 'terrorist attacks')[1230] which took place in 2011–12 in the context of the Arab Spring Revolution.[1231] As mentioned above, the Tribunal referred to a previous ICC award[1232] which explained that in the context of the popular uprising that took place in January 2011, Sinai's Bedouin 'militants grew strong and lawless, and their violence against the police led Egypt's State police to abandon the area', adding that 'a security vacuum resulted'.[1233] The award described in some detail each of the thirteen attacks.[1234] The Tribunal held that the first four attacks were unforeseeable. It however considered that Egypt had failed to protect Ampal for the remaining nine attacks and breached its due diligence obligation under the FPS clause.[1235]

Thus, for the Tribunal Egypt's failure to take action regarding the first four attacks could be excused on the grounds that 'the circumstances in the North Sinai Egypt were difficult' at the time and that 'armed militant groups took advantage of the political instability, security deterioration

ability, the property and persons threatened by the revolutionary disturbance, may it be considered as liable for the consequences of such abnormal condition', emphasis added.

1230 *Ampal-American Israel Corp., Egi-Fund (08-10) Investors LLC, Egi-Series Investments LLC and BSS-EMG Investors LLC* v. *Egypt*, ICSID Case No. ARB/12/11, Decision on Liability and Heads of Loss, 21 February 2017, para. 254.

1231 Ibid., para. 236.

1232 The Tribunal noted that the 'findings of fact in respect of the attacks of the pipeline' contained in a previous ICC award were 'res judicata between the parties in the present proceedings' (ibid., para. 274, referring to: *EMG* v. *EGPC, EGAS & IEC*, ICC Case No. 18215/GZ/MHM, Final Award, 4 December 2015).

1233 Ibid., para. 254, referring to para. 603 of the ICC award.

1234 Ibid., para. 277, referring to para. 769 of the ICC award.

1235 Ibid., paras. 289–90:

> Clearly, these four first attacks should have been seen as a warning to the Egyptian State that further attacks might be carried out if security measures were not taken and implemented. It is thus clear to the Tribunal that the failure by the Egyptian authorities to take any concrete steps to protect the Claimants' investment from damage in reaction to third party attacks on the upstream pipeline system, as of the date of attack no. 5, to wit 12 July 2011, constitutes a breach of the obligation of due diligence that Egypt was required to exercise in ensuring the full protection and security of the Claimants' investment.

and general lawlessness'.[1236] In other words, these attacks were unforeseeable.[1237] However, there was no reasonable motive or justification that could account for Egypt's failure to act after these first four attacks. The award highlights the importance of the length of time a State takes in order to respond to actions by rebels when it knows about the risk. As noted by Huber in the *Spanish Zone of Morocco Claims* case, a State is responsible when 'des possibilités de secours sont, sans raison plausible, manifestement négligées, ou si les autorités, averties en temps utile, ne prennent aucune mesure de prévention'.[1238]

3.3.3.4 Other Related Questions

This section examines two specific questions in relation of the concrete application of the due diligence obligation:

- Does a State breach its due diligence obligation by granting an amnesty to former rebels? (Section 3.3.3.4.1); and
- Can a State invoke the defence of *force majeure* to justify its failure to fulfil its due diligence obligation? (Section 3.3.3.4.2).

3.3.3.4.1 Does a State Breach Its Due Diligence Obligation by Granting an Amnesty to Former Rebels? As noted above,[1239] the due diligence obligation requires a State, after an (unsuccessful) insurrection, to adequately punish the perpetrators (individuals, former members of insurgent groups) for the injurious acts committed during the civil war.[1240]

It has been argued by several writers that a State would breach its due diligence obligation if it were to fail to punish the unlawful acts committed by an unsuccessful insurrectional movement by granting the movement (or its members) an amnesty.[1241] Eatwell refers to several international human rights law cases where the principle was recognized

[1236] Ibid., para. 284.

[1237] This is an important point which will be examined in Section 3.3.3.4.2, dealing with the *force majeure* defence.

[1238] *Affaire des biens britanniques au Maroc espagnol*, 1925, p. 642 ('emergency possibilities are, without plausible reason, manifestly neglected, or if the authorities, warned in good time, do not take any preventive measures').

[1239] See Section 3.3.3.2.3.

[1240] Cahin, 'Attribution of Conduct to the State', p. 253.

[1241] Ibid., p. 253, arguing that 'the grant of a general amnesty to rebels constitute' a breach of the due diligence obligation of States. See also: Eatwell, *State Responsibility*, p. 201:

in the context of *individual* responsibility for human rights abuses.[1242] There are a number of older arbitration cases involving rebels which also support this position. They will be briefly examined in the next paragraphs.

The 1874 *Montijo* case involved a claim submitted to arbitration under the provisions of an agreement between the United States and Colombia.[1243] The Claimant requested compensation for a ship (the Montijo) seized in 1871 from its American owner by (ultimately unsuccessful) revolutionists in Panama (a federated State that was still part of Colombia at the time). The leaders of the unsuccessful rebels were granted amnesty under a peace treaty, whereby the government of Panama 'granted amnesty to the wrongdoers for all of their acts, and assumed the responsibility for all damages arising out of the revolution'.[1244] Based on this treaty, the revolutionaries were granted amnesty and the government therefore became responsible of their wrongdoing. The Umpire of the US–Colombian Commission held that 'even in the absence of any express stipulation to that effect, the grantor of an amnesty assumes as his own the liabilities previously incurred by the objects of his pardon toward persons or things over which the grantor has no control'.[1245] Columbia was ultimately considered liable for the

> the state that grants amnesty over international crimes may be responsible for its failure to investigate, prosecute and punish violations of international law, and for the expropriation of the right of action. This principle has developed from the law governing state responsibility for injuries to aliens, according to which a state that grants general or individual amnesty to persons responsible for the unlawful seizure of a foreigner's property will be responsible for its government's own action of depriving 'foreigners of the possibility of obtaining compensation.

1242 Eatwell, *State Responsibility*, p. 203, referring to cases before the InterAmerican Commission on Human Rights and adding that 'there is little reason to suggest that the principles advanced should not be applied to violations committed by insurrectional groups that also enjoy amnesty in situations of national reconciliation, or otherwise'.

1243 *Montijo Arbitration (U.S. v. Colombia)*, 1874, in Moore, *History and Digest of the International Arbitrations* (vol. II), p. 1421, 1438.

1244 Ibid., p. 1424.

1245 Ibid., p. 1438. The reasoning of the Umpire is as follows:

> If . . . before the captors had no right before the amnesty to take the Montijo, it is evident that the President of Panama could not by the terms of that document confer it on them. They, therefore, are liable to the owners for the expenses incurred and damages occasioned. If no amnesty had ever been granted . . . [there] would have been, at least, an open question whether their possible or even notorious inability to pay those damages would have rendered Colombia at large responsible for

damages due to the failure of the government of Panama to provide compensation to the American owners.

In the case of *Baldwin* v. *Mexico*, the Umpire of the Mexico–United States Claims Commission of 1839 held Mexico responsible for the confiscation of goods and the imprisonment of an American citizen, Mr Baldwin, residing in Mexico.[1246] The wrongs were committed by a revolutionary '*junta*' which controlled, as a local de facto government, the city of Tehauntepec. The Mexican government apparently made little to no effort in attempting to overthrow the junta and failed to protect Mr Baldwin in accordance with its due diligence obligation. Later, the government granted amnesty to the leaders of the *junta*, who stayed in office. The Umpire noted that instead of treating the leaders of the *junta* as 'lawless insurgents deserving punishment', the government had chosen to turn the other cheek and had 'bestowed on some of them high official station'.[1247] The Umpire awarded compensation to Mr Baldwin. Yet, it has been noted that the Umpire did not fully explain the reason for his decision, and that it was not clear whether the issue of amnesty was at all relevant to the outcome of his decision.[1248]

In the *Bovalins and Hudland* claim,[1249] an amnesty granted by the government was considered by the Tribunal as a tacit approval of rebels' acts. The case involved losses of personal effect of Swedish and Norwegian nationals by revolutionists who maintained a de facto government over part of the territory of Venezuela. The Swedish and Norwegian–Venezuelan Claims Commission of 1903 held Venezuela liable for compensation for the wrongs, on the grounds that 'at the time when the acts complained of were committed, and since then, the delinquents have not been chastised or prosecuted, but, on the contrary, their principal leaders have occupied for some time official positions,

> their acts. But the amnesty deprived the [claimants] of the power of trying the question. Therefore the President of Panama, having no right to dispose of interests which were not his property and which, on the contrary he was bound by a public treaty to protect, assumed the responsibility to the owners of those interests of the persons by whom they had been injured. It is an old saying that one must be just before one is generous. In Spanish the version is, *La bolsaajena es muy franca* – it is easy to pay one's debts out of another man's purse.

1246 *Baldwin's Tehuantepec* case *(U.S.* v. *Mexico)*, in Moore, *History and Digest of the International Arbitrations* (vol. III), p. 2859, 2862.

1247 Ibid., p. 2861.

1248 Silvanie, *Responsibility of States*, p. 200.

1249 *Bovallins and Hedlund (Sweden-Norway* v. *Venezuela)*, 1903, UNRIAA 10, p. 768.

having been appointed by the present Government of Venezuela, and that they are cloaked with authority in the very region where the events took place'.[1250] The Commission considered that by doing so, the Government of Venezuela 'tacitly approve[ed]' the conduct of the rebels and 'according to the principles recognized by public law makes itself responsible for all the acts done by them'.[1251]

Finally, the *Wenzel* case involved damages to the property of a German national, in Venezuela, caused by unsuccessful rebels (under the leadership of General Hernandez) in 1899–1900. After the events, President Castro of Venezuela granted a general amnesty to those involved in the troubles and even assigned General Hernandez as Venezuelan Minister to the United States. The Umpire noted that 'a general pardon of past offenses by a government is an amnesty' which 'is commonly defined to be an act of oblivion', adding that 'its effect is that the crimes and offenses named in the act are obliterated, and they can never again be charged against the guilty parties'.[1252] Although the effects of amnesty neutralized the potential for any prosecution, the Umpire however concluded that it had been granted illegally under the Venezuelan Constitution and that, therefore, Venezuela should not be held responsible for the acts.[1253]

Other cases have adopted a different position on the matter. One example is the *Divine* case involving a claim presented by the United States for compensation for property of American citizens seized and burned by unsuccessful revolutionists (under the leadership of General Carbajal) in Mexico in 1851.[1254] After his defeat, General Carbajal was pardoned by the government under a general amnesty law. He was subsequently appointed as military governor of one region and eventually sent to the United States in 1964 as a commissioner.[1255] For that reason, the United States argued that Mexico should be liable for the acts committed by the troops of General Carbajal. Sir Edward Thornton, Umpire of the Mexico–United States Claims Commission of 1868, dismissed the claim and held that granting an amnesty to revolutionists did *not* render the State liable for their acts. He thus noted that 'other

[1250] Ibid.

[1251] Ibid.

[1252] *Wenzel*, German–Venezuelan Commission, 1903, UNRIAA 10, p. 432.

[1253] Ibid., p. 428. The Report indicates that this case stands for the following proposition: 'amnesty granted by the Chief Executive of Venezuela, being in excess of his powers, does not make the State liable for damages inflicted by the persons pardoned'.

[1254] *Hugh Divine* v. *Mexico*, case no 553, 1875, in Moore, *History and Digest of the International Arbitrations* (vol. III), p. 2980, 2981.

[1255] Silvanie, *Responsibility of States*, p. 198.

governments, including that of the United States, have pardoned rebels, but they have not on this account engaged to reimburse to private individuals the losses caused by those rebels'.[1256] The specific contention of the appointment of rebel leaders to official governmental positions in the context of amnesty has been examined in detail by Akehurst.[1257]

It has been suggested by some scholars[1258] that an amnesty granted to rebels 'after their downfall may be viewed *as approval of their actions* by the state's government and therefore acceptance of responsibility for them'.[1259] Ago was rather sceptical of the position adopted by writers whom 'regard the granting of pardon to the insurgents as a kind of ratification of their acts'.[1260] For him, 'it seems rather strange to say that the mere fact of not punishing the acts of others when they ought to be punished constitutes endorsement of those acts'.[1261] In his book, Crawford also mentioned that 'there is older authority for the view that the granting of an amnesty to rebels constitutes a failure of duty and an acceptance of responsibility for the acts, but again this is doubtful absent conduct of the State amounting to complicity or adoption'.[1262] A similar position was adopted by Akehurst, in reference to cases which have regarded 'amnesties as making the State liable' on the grounds that 'by pardoning a criminal, a nation assumes the responsibility for his past acts'.[1263] One such case is the *Janes* case.[1264] For Akehurst, 'this rationale is totally unconvincing' because 'after all, in municipal law an amnesty is

1256 *Hugh Divine* v. *Mexico*, case no 553, 1875, in Moore, *History and Digest of the International Arbitrations* (vol. III), p. 2981.

1257 Akehurst, 'State Responsibility', p. 59–61.

1258 Rousseau, *Droit international public*, p. 85; Berlia, 'La guerre civile et la responsabilité internationale de l'État', p. 58–9.

1259 Al-Rashid *et al.*, 'Investment Claims', p. 192 (emphasis added). These authors cite two cases in support of this proposition, but they also admit that 'the cases are, however, not uniform in their treatment of amnesty' and that 'a number of other commissions have declined to find amnesty a ground for attribution of responsibility to the state' (p. 193). See also: Al-Ganzory, 'International Claims and Insurgence', p. 89–90.

1260 ILC, Ago Report, 1972, p. 142, para. 187.

1261 Ibid.

1262 Crawford, *Brownlie's Principles of Public International Law*, p. 552.

1263 Akehurst, 'State Responsibility', p. 57, citing *Cotesworth and Powell claim (UK* v. *Colombia)*, 1865, in Moore, *History and Digest of the International Arbitrations* (vol. III), p. 2050, 2079, 2085. The case did not involve acts by rebels but a denial of justice before Colombian courts.

1264 *Laura M.B. Janes et al. (U.S.A.)* v. *Mexico*, General Claims Commission, 16 November 1925, UNRIAA, p. 82. The case did not involve any acts committed by rebels, but the killing of a US national. The Commission made this remark, citing a number of cases which dealt with amnesties in the context of unsuccessful rebellions:

never treated as an assumption of responsibility for crimes, or as a tacit ratification of them'.[1265] However, he also noted that a State 'become liable for the acts of rebels when it *expressly* ratifies and approves those acts'.[1266]

These writers accurately point out that the mere fact of granting an amnesty to rebels *cannot* be considered per se as an 'acceptance of responsibility' for acts previously committed by the rebels. Something more is required in circumstances of this nature, such as, for instance, an express ratification of the acts by the government. In any event, what remains clear is that this is *not* a situation where the acts of the rebels are somewhat 'attributable' to the State. Ago explained very clearly that even if one were to consider the granting of amnesty as contrary to the due diligence obligation to punish, this is a case where the State is responsible for *its own acts*, not those of rebels: 'It may happen that the State, in granting amnesty, is contravening an international obligation to punish which it should have fulfilled; but, if so, it is that breach which will be attributed to it as a source of responsibility, and not the acts committed in the past by the organs of the insurrectional movement.'[1267]

> [a]t times international awards have held that, if a State shows serious lack of diligence in apprehending and/or punishing culprits, its liability is a derivative liability, assuming the character of some kind of complicity with the perpetrator himself and rendering the State responsible for the very consequences of the individual's misdemeanor. Opinions to this effect are to be found in the international awards in the Ruden & Company case (Moore 1655; under the Convention of December 4, 1868), in the Cotesworth & Powell case (Moore, 2053, 2082, 2085; under the Convention of December 14, 1872) and in the Bovallins and Hedlund cases (Ralston, Venezuelan Arbitrations of 1903, p. 953), separate opinions of seemingly the same tendency being expressed in the cases of De Brissot et al. (Moore, 2986, 2969; under the Convention of December 5, 1885). The reasons upon which such finding of complicity is usually based in cases in which a Government could not possibly have prevented the crime, is that the nonpunishment must be deemed to disclose some kind of approval of what has occurred, especially so if the Government has permitted the guilty parties to escape or has remitted the punishment by granting either pardon or amnesty. (at p. 86).

1265 Akehurst, 'State Responsibility', p. 57.

1266 Ibid., p. 61, emphasis in the original.

1267 ILC, Ago Report, 1972, p. 142, para. 187. See also, para. 209: 'the State can then be held responsible only for the acts of its own organs, and any amnesty which the latter may have granted to the insurgents may constitute a source of responsibility if it represents a failure in their duty to punish those guilty of acts injurious to foreigners'. See also: ILC, Report, 1975, p. 98, para. 26.

In the end, the effect of an amnesty on liability really depends on 'the nature and scope of the pardon given and its relation to different categories of insurgents acts in question'.[1268] The question whether or not an amnesty breaches a State's due diligence obligation cannot be determined in the abstract and must necessarily be investigated by taking into account the reasons behind the existence of such a policy.[1269] In fact, a number of distinctions need to be made to answer this question.

For instance, it has been suggested by Piguet that an amnesty granted to rebels with the aim of re-establishing peace in the aftermath of the conflict should be treated differently.[1270] It is clear that this is a situation which needs to be differentiated from other cases where the government grants an amnesty for purely opportunistic reasons unrelated to re-establishing peace. As noted by Akehurst, 'an amnesty must be limited to those acts which need to be pardoned in order to secure a political settlement'.[1271] In circumstances where the goal of the amnesty is to end a civil war and re-establishing peace, there may be good reasons to argue that granting such measures should *not* be considered as a failure by the State to punish those responsible for wrongful acts. In doing so, a State would therefore not breach its due diligence obligation. But one needs to be careful not to interpret the scope of this exception too broadly. To do so would result in many victims not being able to be awarded reparations for the damage they have suffered (a point further discussed in the following paragraphs).

In his insightful work, Akehurst elaborated a distinction between 'amnesties which extinguish rebels' civil liability and amnesties which extinguish their criminal liability'.[1272] This important distinction is examined in the next paragraphs.

On the one hand, an amnesty which extinguishes the rebels' *civil liability* 'makes the State granting the amnesty liable for the damage caused by the rebels'.[1273] He noted that 'it is perhaps better to regard the State as liable, not for the rebels' acts as such, but for expropriating the right of action which the alien had against the rebels'.[1274] Akehurst is indeed right on this aspect regarding civil

1268 Silvanie, *Responsibility of States*, p. 202.

1269 Al-Ganzory, 'International Claims and Insurgence', p. 91; Piguet, *La Guerre civile en droit international*, p. 118.

1270 Piguet, *La Guerre civile en droit international*, p. 103.

1271 Akehurst, 'State Responsibility', p. 59.

1272 Ibid., p. 56.

1273 Ibid.

1274 Ibid. For him:

liability. It should be recalled that the basic principle applicable when the rebels are not successful at establishing a new government is Rule no. 3, whereby the acts committed by the rebels during the insurgency are not attributable to the State. Therefore, as matter of principle (with one exception),[1275] the State is not responsible for the consequences arising from acts of destruction or expropriation committed by the rebels during the course of the insurrection against the property of foreigners. The foreign investor will therefore get no reparation *from the State*. Yet, and this is an important point, in the aftermath of the defeat of the rebels, the investor may still be able to seek reparation before domestic courts against the insurrectional movement itself or, most likely, against its individual members. While this is ultimately a matter of domestic law, it should be pointed out that this right has been recognized towards foreigners for more than a century regarding acts of expropriation. Thus, Conclusion no. 9 of the Report to the Council of the League of Nations issued in the 1920s mentioned that whenever the 'property belonging to strangers which has been seized or confiscated in time of war or revolution' by the insurgents, the State 'must place at the disposal of foreigners all necessary legal means to enable them to obtain effective compensation for the loss suffered and to enable them to take action against the offenders'.[1276] Most importantly for the present purpose, Conclusion no. 9 further added that 'the State would become directly responsible for such damage if, by a general or individual amnesty, it deprived foreigners of the possibility of obtaining compensation'.[1277] Thus, a

> [c]ompensation for the lost right of action should be equal to the amount which the alien would probably have recovered if the amnesty had not occurred; and this amount is likely to be small, since the only alternatives to an amnesty are either (i) continuation of the rebels in *de facto* local control (which will probably mean that no action can be brought against them), or (ii) a bloody war of repression, in the course of which the rebels may well lose all their possessions, so that they will not be worth suing afterwards.

1275 I mentioned above (Section 3.1.6) that there should be an 'exception' to this basic principle: a State is bound by the consequences arising from the commission of an act of expropriation by the rebels whenever it results in some benefits for the State (Rule no. 4B).

1276 League of Nations publication, V. Legal, 1927.V.1, doc. C.196.M.70.1927.V, p. 104 and 10, Conclusion 9, Report to the Council of the League of Nations on the Questions which Appear Ripe for International Regulation, Annex to Questionnaire 4, Report of the Sub-Committee, M. Guerrero, Rapporteur, 20 April 1927, quoted in ILC, Garcia Amador Report, 1957, p. 126.

1277 Ibid.

State cannot grant an amnesty which would result in depriving the foreign investor of its right to seek reparation before local courts regarding expropriation acts. To do so would be considered as a failure by the State to fulfil its due diligence obligation to punish the perpetrators of unlawful acts.[1278]

On the other hand, for Akehurst, the situation is different regarding *criminal* liability. He believes that, in general, 'an amnesty which merely extinguishes criminal liability does not make the State liable'.[1279] Yet, he also mentioned two exceptions where a State should nevertheless be held liable for its decision to grant an amnesty in the context of criminal liability during the unfolding of an insurrectional movement or regarding its individual members. These exceptions will be examined in the next paragraphs.

First, Akehurst mentioned the case where an amnesty regarding criminal liability is discriminatory towards foreigners.[1280] Clearly, a State breaches its due diligence obligation if its grants an amnesty to rebels (or its members) for acts committed against foreigners (or different groups of foreigners), but not for its own citizens. The principle of non-discrimination based on grounds of nationality regarding reparation for wrongs has long been recognized in international practice.[1281]

Second, Akehurst believes that a State should be liable for extinguishing criminal liability when the amnesty covers (quoting Hyde) 'essentially lawless conduct on the part of unsuccessful insurgents or bandits or other disaffected persons, such as acts not to be regarded as normal incidents of the public endeavour of the insurgents to attain their ends

1278 ILC, Ago Report, 1972, p. 142, para. 187, fn. 444.

1279 Akehurst, 'State Responsibility', p. 57–8.

1280 Ibid., p. 59:

> an amnesty extinguishing criminal liability will make the State liable if it is not a *bona fide* exercise of the State's discretion-for instance, if it is intended not to achieve a statesmanlike end to the rebellion, but to spite foreigners by pardoning crimes against them while maintaining criminal liability for similar crimes against the State's own nationals. Although there is no authority for this proposition, its justice is self-evident.

1281 League of Nations, 1929, 'Basis of Discussion' no. 22 (b): '[a] State must accord to foreigners to whom damage has been caused by persons taking part in an insurrection or riot or by mob violence the same indemnities as it accords to its own nationals in similar circumstances.

by force'.[1282] In other words, an amnesty should not cover acts of brigandage which are not 'incidental to revolution'. This specific distinction is also supported by other writers.[1283] Thus, Silvanie argued that a State should be liable 'if the scope of an amnesty is broad enough to pardon insurgent acts of brigandage and common law crimes, because in such case, the State voluntarily deprived itself of the possibility of prosecution and punishing the insurgent offenders and because claimants are thereby prevented from securing redress in local courts'.[1284] In contrast, according to Silvanie 'liability will not be incurred by the State if the scope of an amnesty is limited to insurrectionary acts or acts incidental to the conflict, presumably because such acts are to be regarded as proper objects of amnesty'.[1285] There are good and logical reasons to uphold this distinction. Thus, as a matter of principle, an amnesty should not cover common law crimes. That should *a fortiori* be the case for war crimes, genocide, crimes against humanity and gross human rights violations.[1286] An amnesty could potentially only cover criminal (but importantly, not civil) responsibility for 'insurrectionary acts' committed by rebels. Silvanie includes in that category all 'political and military acts' of insurgents, including 'acts in pursuance and in aid of rebellion' such as taking of property for the use of rebels, forced loans as well as other acts

1282 Akehurst, 'State Responsibility', p. 59, quoting Hyde, *International Law* (2nd ed., 1947), p. 983–4.

1283 Silvanie, *Responsibility of States*, p. 207–8. See also: Al-Ganzory, 'International Claims and Insurgence', p. 90, referring to Hyde, ibid., vol. I, p. 542–3, making a distinction between acts of insurgents committed having a 'public character' and those which have a 'private' end (such as common crimes). A government would be considered in breach of its due diligence obligation only when it grants an amnesty to rebels concerning the latter.

1284 Silvanie, *Responsibility of States*, p. 207–8, see also, p. 203. He includes (ibid., p. 208) in this category acts such as murders, imprisonment, torture, looting of property, and the destruction of property not incidental to the conflict. He refers at p. 204–6 to *West and Snapp* cases, US–Mexico General Claims Commission, 1923, in *Opinion*, 1927, p. 404.

1285 Silvanie, *Responsibility of States*, p. 207.

1286 On this question, see: Eatwell, *State Responsibility*, p. 200 ff. See also: Eatwell, 'State Responsibility, Successful, Insurrectional Movements', p. 397:

> [i]n practice, it is becoming more common for amnesties to exclude war crimes, genocide, crimes against humanity and gross human rights violations from their scope. Where they do not, the jurisprudence of both domestic and international criminal tribunals, and regional human rights courts and commissions generally support the principle that amnesties over international crimes and non-derogable human rights lack legal effect in international law. The United Nations has adopted the same approach. With specific regard to Croatia and Sierra Leone the UN Security Council, and generally, the United Nations have declared that amnesties should not cover international crimes.

incidental to the revolution.[1287] In any event, as noted above by Akehurst, 'an amnesty must be limited to those acts which need to be pardoned in order to secure a political settlement'.[1288] In other words, granting an amnesty to rebels for 'insurrectionary acts' (not for common law crimes) may be considered as legitimate (and not as a failure to punish those responsible for wrongful acts) only if this is part of a larger bargaining settlement at play in order to bring an end to the civil war and re-establish peace.

In sum, the circumstances where granting amnesty will not be considered as a failure to punish those responsible for wrongs are few and they must be interpreted restrictively. Granting an amnesty should be allowed only in a limited number of circumstances. The aim is to avoid, as much as possible, wrongs remaining unpunished.

Finally, Akehurst stated that 'the State may expressly assume liability for the rebels in the amnesty'.[1289] Silvanie provides several examples of State practice under protocols of arbitration.[1290] In such a case, it can be considered that a State has fulfilled its due diligence obligation.

3.3.3.4.2 Can a State Invoke the Defence of *Force Majeure* to Justify Its Failure to Fulfil Its Due Diligence Obligation? As mentioned above, Ago indicated that international responsibility arising from a State's failure to exercise its duty of due diligence to prevent attacks by rebels is 'very rare'.[1291] This is because a government will often have *no control* over the activities of rebels and will therefore simply not be able to adopt any effective measures of vigilance or protection in relation to their conduct.[1292] This is *a fortiori* the case when the actions of the rebels are very sudden and could not have been reasonably foreseen, even by the most well-organized government. In this specific context, there are good reasons to argue that a government should not be held accountable for its failure to adopt any measures to prevent the commission of wrongs by rebels.[1293]

1287 Silvanie, *Responsibility of States*, p. 208.

1288 Akehurst, 'State Responsibility', p. 59.

1289 Ibid.

1290 Silvanie, *Responsibility of States*, p. 211 ff., distinguishing these situations of admission of liability in three distinct categories.

1291 ILC, Ago Report, 1972, p. 130, para. 156 ('the cases in which the "legitimate" Government was really in a position, during the civil war, to prevent or punish injurious acts committed by the person who is an organ of the insurrectional movement and failed to do so are very rare'). See also: Eagleton, *The Responsibility of States*, p. 148 ff.

1292 ILC, Ago Report, 1972, p. 130, para. 154.

1293 Piguet, *La Guerre civile en droit international*, p. 98: 'l'État n'aura pas à réparer les conséquences d'actes de violence si soudains et inattendus qu'une prévision raisonnable

Writers support the view that a State may invoke the *force majeure* defence in the context of rebellions and civil war.[1294] In one comprehensive 1978 study conducted by the ILC on *force majeure*, reference is made to numerous writers who have made 'statements explaining the non-responsibility of the State for injuries caused to aliens by . . . unsuccessful insurgent forces, on the basis of the *force majeure* doctrine'.[1295] Yet, as noted by one writer, that does not mean that the mere existence of an insurrection should be considered to constitute *in itself* as a circumstance of *force majeure* 'and as such be able to automatically exempt the territorial State from responsibility for the related damage'.[1296] The defence of *force majeure* can only be successfully invoked when strict conditions are fulfilled.

In international law, the *force majeure* defence plays a role as a general exception for the non-performance of a treaty obligation.[1297] Therefore, it is firmly based on treaty law. It is also known as a means of defence in the context of secondary rules of State responsibility. Part V of the ILC Articles on State responsibility sets out six circumstances 'precluding the wrongfulness of conduct that would otherwise not be in conformity with the international obligations of the State concerned'.[1298] These six circumstances are: consent, self-defence, countermeasures, *force majeure*, distress and necessity. In other words, the existence of any of these circumstances in a given case 'provides a shield against an otherwise well-founded claim for the breach of an international obligation'.[1299] The principle of *force*

et l'emploi de précautions normales ne pouvaient les empêcher; sa responsabilité ne sera pas engagée' ('the state will not have to repair the consequences of acts of violence so sudden and unexpected that reasonable anticipation and the use of normal precautions could not prevent them; its responsibility will not be engaged').

1294 Ibid., p. 98 ff., 110 ff.; Rousseau, *Droit international public*, p. 85; Leonardo Carpentieri, 'The Invocation of State Defenses in Times of Conflict: Force Majeure, Necessity and the Libyan Example', *Int. J. Arab Arb.* 11(2) (2019), p. 20, 23 ('Force majeure is particularly suited to circumstances of civil unrest and revolution such as the recent civil wars taking place in Libya. Furthermore, force majeure is all the more likely to arise in circumstances where the events in question resulted in the State losing control over its territory and over its armed forces, as is often the case for revolutionary movements').

1295 ILC, 'Force majeure and Fortuitous event', 1978, p. 213, para. 543.

1296 Pisillo-Mazzeschi, 'The Due Diligence Rule', p. 45.

1297 *Vienna Convention on the Law of Treaties*, 1155 UNTS, p. 331, Art. 61.

1298 ILC, Commentaries, 2001, p. 71, para 1.

1299 Ibid.

majeure has been codified in Article 23 of the ILC Articles on State responsibility:

1. The wrongfulness of an act of a State not in conformity with an international obligation of that State is precluded if the act is due to force majeure, that is the occurrence of an irresistible force or of an unforeseen event, beyond the control of the State, making it materially impossible in the circumstances to perform the obligation.
2. Paragraph 1 does not apply if
   (a) the situation of force majeure is due, either alone or in combination with other factors, to the conduct of the State invoking it; or
   (b) the State has assumed the risk of that situation occurring.

Force majeure is a general principle of law.[1300] The ILC Commentary to Article 23 specifies that a situation of *force majeure* precluding wrongfulness only arises when three elements are met. The first two elements require that an action 'must be brought about by an irresistible force or an unforeseen event' which is 'beyond the control of the State concerned'.[1301] As noted by one author, the provision therefore refers to two types of events: 'uncontrollable, to the extent that either in view of their strength (irresistible events) or in view of their unexpected occurrence (unforeseen events) they leave no room for the state to react against them'.[1302] It has been noted that when a demand for protection against rebels' actions is made to the governmental authorities, the events cannot be considered unforeseeable.[1303] The question as to whether or not events such as riots[1304] and civil uprising[1305] can be considered as unforeseeable has been examined by a number of investment tribunals.[1306]

1300 See Dumberry, *A Guide to General Principles of Law*, p. 252 ff., providing a detailed analysis and mentioning numerous writers supporting this position as well as many others for whom it is, in fact, a rule of customary international law.

1301 ILC, Commentaries, 2001, p. 76, 170.

1302 Federica Paddeu, 'A Genealogy of Force Majeure in International Law', *British YIL* 82 (2011), p. 381, 394.

1303 Piguet, *La Guerre civile en droit international*, p. 98.

1304 *Autopista Concesionada De Venezuela, C.A.* v. *Venezuela*, ICSID Case No. ARB/00/5, Award, 23 Sept. 2003, para. 117.

1305 *RSM Production Corporation* v. *Central African Republic*, ICSID Case No. ARB/07/2, Sentence, 11 July 2011.

1306 On this question, see: Carpentieri, 'The Invocation of State Defenses', p. 23 ff.; A. M. Daza-Clark and D. Behn, 'Between War and Peace: Intermittent Armed Conflict and Investment Arbitration', in K. Fach Gómez, A. Gourgourinis and C. Titi (eds.)

The third element requires that the situation 'makes it materially impossible in the circumstances to perform the obligation'.[1307] Such a 'material impossibility' is a key constituent element of the *force majeure* defence. The event 'must be irresistible, so that the State concerned has no real possibility of escaping its effects'.[1308] Therefore, *force majeure* 'does not include circumstances in which performance of an obligation has become more difficult, for example due to some political or economic crisis'.[1309] Yet, one should not equate 'material impossibility' with the (different) concept of 'absolute impossibility' (as seems to be suggested by the *Rainbow Warrior* award[1310]).[1311] The ILC Commentary further specifies that such 'material impossibility of performance giving rise to *force majeure* may be due to a natural or physical event . . . or to human intervention'.[1312] Finally, under Article 23, a State may not invoke *force majeure* when the situation is attributable to the State invoking it or when the State has assumed the risk of the occurring situation.

Several awards have applied the *force majeure* defence in the context of rebellions.[1313] This is indeed the case in the context of the ongoing civil war in Libya.[1314] One older relevant example is the *Brissot et consorts* case.[1315] This case involved the presence of General Garcia (who was President of the State of Apure, one of the States forming the Republic of Venezuela) and a small military force, as passengers on board of a boat. During the course of its sail, it suddenly got attacked by a group of rebels fighting against the regime of General Garcia. In this case, the Claimants argued that Venezuela was responsible for the deaths and damage arising

International Investment Law and the Law of Armed Conflict (Cham, European Yearbook of International Economic Law, Springer, 2019), p. 63.

1307 ILC, Commentaries, 2001, p. 76, 170.

1308 Ibid., p. 76, para 3.

1309 Ibid.

1310 *Case concerning the difference between New Zealand and France concerning the interpretation or application of two agreements, concluded on 9 July 1986 between the two States and which related to the problems arising from the Rainbow Warrior Affair*, Decision of 30 April 1990, UNRIAA 20, p. 215, 253.

1311 Crawford, *State Responsibility*, p. 299.

1312 ILC, Commentaries, 2001, p. 76, para. 3.

1313 See case law examined in Piguet, *La Guerre civile en droit international*, p. 98 ff.

1314 On this question, see: Carpentieri, 'The Invocation of State Defenses', p. 23 ff. One relevant case is: *General Dynamics United Kingdom Ltd.* v. *State of Libya*, ICC Case No. 19222/EMT, Final Award, 5 January 2016, paras. 248 ff.

1315 *Amelia de Brissot, Ralph Rawdon, Joseph Stackpole and Narcisa de Hammer* v. *Venezuela* (the Steamer Apure case), US–Venezuela Claims Commission, UNRIAA 29, p. 240–60 (also in Moore, *History and Digest of the International Arbitrations* (vol. III), p. 2950). See Piguet, *La Guerre civile en droit international*, p. 98.

from the attack because it resulted from General Garcia boarding the boat and using it as a shelter during the attack.[1316] The majority of the commissioners of the US–Venezuela Claims Commission considered that Venezuela should not be held responsible for the damages because the attack was unforeseeable.[1317]

Another relevant example of State practice involved claims for compensation by British merchants in the context of an insurrection that took place in Brazil in 1835.[1318] Great Britain held that Brazil did not have to provide reparation for the damages suffered by British nationals. In one legal opinion, the British Law Officer stated that the government would have been justified to request Brazil to grant compensation to the British nationals only in this specific situation: 'if that Government had the power of preventing or suppressing the insurrection' and failed to take adequate steps for that purpose.[1319] In subsequent reports, he noted that, in the present case, the losses 'were occasioned by circumstances beyond the power of the Brazilian Government *either to foresee or to prevent*',[1320] and that the losses were not 'occasioned by the misconduct or wilful default of the Brazilian Government in not affording the requisite protection'.[1321] As

1316 ILC, 'Force majeure and Fortuitous event', 1978, p. 157.

1317 *Amelia de Brissot, Ralph Rawdon, Joseph Stackpole and Narcisa de Hammer* v. *Venezuela* (the Steamer Apure case), US–Venezuela Claims Commission, Opinion of Commissioner Findlay, UNRIAA 29, in Moore, *History and Digest of the International Arbitrations* (vol. III), p. 2969:

> After reading the record and carefully considering the arguments, which have been very full and exhaustive, on both sides, it does not seem to me that any case has been made out against Venezuela, except that it did not go as far as it ought in bringing the offenders to justice. It surely had no means of knowing of or anticipating such a murderous outbreak as that which occurred at Apurito. As I understand the testimony, General Garcia and his detachment of troops on board the *Apure* were entirely unprepared to meet the assault; and whatever may have been their expectations as to trouble somewhere on the route, certainly do not appear to have apprehended any difficulty at this particular point. The attack was in the nature of an ambuscade and a complete surprise. It would be wholly unwarranted, therefore, to hold Venezuela responsible for not anticipating and preventing an outbreak of which the persons most interested in knowing and the very actors on the spot had no knowledge.

1318 McNair, *International Law Opinions*, vol. 2, p. 247–50.

1319 Ibid., p. 247, citing an opinion dated 12 January 1836.

1320 Ibid., citing a report dated 29 September 1838, emphasis added.

1321 Ibid., p. 249, citing a report dated 3 April 1839. In another opinion dated 28 December 1841 (ibid., p. 250), he affirmed that the degree of protection which needs to be offered to foreigners is the same as that for nationals:

mentioned above,[1322] the *Ampal* Tribunal held that the first four attacks on the investor's infrastructures were unforeseeable, but not the other nine that followed shortly afterwards.[1323]

In the *Prats* case, Mexican Commissioner, Mr Palacio, explained that the applicable test of the duty of diligence requires States to do everything that is possible and feasible (but not what is *impossible*).[1324] Several writers support the application of the *force majeure* defence in situations where it is simply impossible for a State to take any reasonable measures of prevention or suppression.[1325]

> I apprehend it to be a general rule of the law of nations that the subjects of one State resident within the territory of another have a right to claim from the government of the country in which they reside the same degree of protection which that government affords to its own subjects, and that unless such protection is withheld from them, they cannot justly claim compensation for the losses sustained in consequence either of foreign or internal war. A British subject resident in a foreign country cannot stand in a more favourable situation than the native inhabitants.

1322 See Section 3.3.3.3.3.4.

1323 *Ampal-American Israel Corp., Egi-Fund (08-10) Investors LLC, Egi-Series Investments LLC and BSS-EMG Investors LLC* v. *Egypt*, ICSID Case No. ARB/12/11, Decision on Liability and Heads of Loss, 21 February 2017, para. 290.

1324 *Prats* case, 1868, Mexican Commissioner, Mr Palacio, p. 194, p. 196:

> [u]nder such a state of things [state of war], it is not in the power of the nation to prevent or to avoid the injuries caused or intended to be caused by the rebels, either to the foreign residents or to the native citizens of the country, and as *nobody can be bound to do the impossible*, from that very moment the responsibility ceases to exist. There is no responsibility without fault *(culpa)* and it is too well known that there is no fault *(culpa)* in having failed to do what was impossible. The fault is essentially dependent upon the will, but as the will completely disappears before the force, whose action can not be resisted, it is a self-evident result that all the acts done by such force, without the possibility of being resisted by another equal or more powerful force, can neither involve a fault nor an injury nor a responsibility. (emphasis added).

1325 De Visscher, 'La responsabilité des États', p. 103–4:

> the circumstance that by reason of these disturbances themselves the local authorities may have found it *impossible* to take any really adequate preventive or repressive measures. International practice has, in effect, accepted here a case of *force majeure;* a Government cannot be held responsible for acts committed by insurgents when it has used such restricted authority as is available to it to repress a revolutionary movement directed against its own power. (cited and translated in ILC, 'Force majeure and Fortuitous event', 1978, p. 213, emphasis added).

Finally, reference should be made to the Iran–US Claims Tribunal which accepted the *force majeure* defence in the *Gould* case arising in the context of the *successful* revolution in Iran in 1979. The case involved a US company that had entered into a contract with the Iranian Ministry of Defence to provide electronic equipment and services. The company stopped providing such services due to the civil unrest in Iran, resulting in a halt in the payment by the Ministry. Iran invoked *force majeure* to exclude its liability under the contract. The Tribunal essentially agreed that the *force majeure* conditions were fulfilled in that case.[1326] The question of the application of the *force majeure* defence is particularly relevant in the context of the on-going civil war in Libya and several claims that have been filed by foreign investors under BITs.[1327]

See also: Garner, 'Responsibility of States', p. 63:

> As regards acts committed by the insurgents or rebels themselves, the rules governing the responsibility of the State for the acts of private persons are applicable. If the insurrectionary movement gets beyond the control of the State and a condition of *force majeure* comes into existence, so that it is *physically impossible* for the State to protect aliens against the acts of the insurgents, it is not liable to make reparation. (referred to in ILC, 'Force majeure and Fortuitous event', 1978, p. 214, para. 543, emphasis added).

[1326] *Gould Marketing, Inc.* v. *Ministry of National Defence*, Iran–US Claims Tribunal, in 3 *Iran-US CTR*. See also: *Sylvania Technical Systems, Inc.* v. *Iran*, Iran–US Claims Tribunal, Award, Case No. 64 (180-64-1), 27 June 1985: 'The Islamic Revolution had created classic force majeure conditions at least in Iran's major cities. By "force majeure" we mean social and economic forces beyond the power of the state to control through the exercise of due diligence. Injuries caused by the operation at such forces are therefore not attributable to the state for purposes of its responding for damages'.

[1327] See Carpentieri, 'The Invocation of State Defenses'.

PART II

Acts Committed in the Context of the Creation of a New State

This Part will examine the following question: what happens to the acts committed by the rebels and the government when the rebellion is aimed at the creation of a *new State* (and not merely the establishment of a new government)?[1] Article 10(2) of the ILC Articles covers this scenario.

There are two possibilities that can be schematically envisaged when the insurrection ends. The applicable legal regime depends on whether or not the insurrectional movement (or any other types of rebel groups) succeeds in its struggle to establish a new State.[2] The following Chapters will focus on two situations:

- The insurrectional movement is *successful* in creating a new State (Chapter 4); and
- The insurrectional movement is *not successful* in creating a new State (Chapter 5).

[1] The determination of whether a new State has indeed been created is beyond the scope of this book. On this general question, see J. Crawford, *The Creation of States in International Law* (2nd ed., Oxford University Press, 2006).

[2] This Part is partially based on my early research: Patrick Dumberry, *State Succession to International Responsibility* (Leiden, Martinus Nijhoff Publishing, 2007) 224 ff.; Patrick Dumberry, 'New State Responsibility for Internationally Wrongful Acts by an Insurrectional Movement', *EJIL* 17(3) (2006), p. 605–21. The content has been substantially modified with the addition of several new examples of State practice, court decisions and awards as well as the inclusion of numerous scholarly works.

4

When the Insurrectional Movement Is Successful in Creating a New State

The first situation to be examined is when an insurrectional movement (or any other rebel group) *does succeed* in creating *a new State*. In such a case, a question arises as to whether or not the new State should be held responsible for obligations arising from internationally wrongful acts *committed by the insurrectional movement* against third States or other actors during the armed struggle for independence (Section 4.2). Another question is whether the new State should be held responsible for obligations arising from internationally wrongful acts *committed by the predecessor State* while fighting the rebels (which succeeded in creating that new State) (Section 4.3). In the following sections, two basic principles will be examined:

- The acts committed by the rebels during the insurgency are attributable to the new State (hereinafter referred to as Rule no. 7); and
- A new State is not responsible for the acts committed by the predecessor State while fighting the rebels during the insurgency (hereinafter referred to as Rule no. 8).

Before examining these two basic principles, a few words should be said (in the next section) about a hypothetical situation mentioned by Ago, but which will not be addressed in this book.

4.1 One Hypothetical Situation Not Addressed in This Book: The Creation of a New State in the Exact Same Territory As the Predecessor State

At the outset, it is important to note that this Part only focuses on the situation where the struggle of the insurrectional movement led to the creation of a new State *on part* of the territory of the predecessor State. Thus, Article 10(2) of the ILC Articles is concerned with cases where an insurrectional movement succeeds in establishing a new State 'in part of the territory of a pre-existing State' (such as in the case of secession) or in a territory under the 'administration' of the pre-existing state (for cases of

Newly Independent States). My book does not address the very exceptional (and rather hypothetical) cases where the insurrectional movement succeeds in creating a *new State* not only *in part* of the territory of the predecessor State but, in fact, on the *totality* of that territory. In my view, this situation is outside the scope of Article 10(2).[3] A number of writers (including Atlam)[4] have mentioned, in the past, the possibility that such a situation could occur.[5]

In his 1972 Report, ILC Special Rapporteur Ago referred to the following possible outcome: 'if an insurrectional movement were to be successful and if its structures were to become the structures of a new State constituted *within the same territorial boundaries as the pre-existing State*'.[6] In other words, 'the revolutionary change in the State structure might be so far-reaching as to affect the very continuity and identity of the State'.[7] Article 13(1) of the 1972 draft contained specific language dealing with this

[3] See T. J. Eatwell, *State Responsibility for the Unlawful Conduct of Armed Groups*, Doctoral Thesis, University of Cambridge (2019), two chapters on file with author, p. 217.

[4] The distinction is supported by Hazem M. Atlam, *Succession d'États et continuité en matière de responsabilité internationale*, Doctoral Thesis, Université de droit, d'économie et des sciences d'Aix-Marseille (France) (1986), p. 79–103, 258–67, 275–81, 289–93, suggesting (back in 1986, when the Apartheid regime still prevailed) that an eventual victory of the African National Congress (ANC) rebels, fighting South Africa's Apartheid regime, should be best analysed in the light of the creation of *a new State* rather than simply a change of government.

[5] R. Quadri, *Diritto internazionale pubblico* (4th ed., Milan, Priulla, 1963), p. 500–1; B. Conforti, *Lezioni di diritto internazionale* (2nd ed., Naples, Editoriale Scientifica, 1982), p. 97–9; Gaetano Arangio-Ruiz, *L'État dans le sens du droit des gens et la notion du droit international* (Bologna, Cooperativa libraria universitaria, 1975), p. 305. This question is discussed in International Law Commission, 'Report of the International Law Commission on the work of its twenty-seventh session', 5 May–25 July 1975, UN Doc. A/10010/Rev.l, *ILC Yearbook* vol. II (1975) [hereinafter referred to as ILC, Report, 1975], p. 47, p. 101, at para. 7. See also, more recently, the position adopted by Gérard Cahin, 'Attribution of Conduct to the State: Insurrectional Movements', in James Crawford, Alain Pellet, Simon Olleson and Kate Parlett (eds.), *The Law of International Responsibility* (Oxford University Press, 2010), p. 250:

> Nevertheless, according to the ILC, this distinction does not impede the possibility of taking into account exceptional cases, where the change in government in reality corresponds to a change in the identity of the State following a revolution or in a situation similar to the replacement of a racist regime like that of Ian Smith in Rhodesia by the national liberation movement which proclaimed the State of Zimbabwe.

[6] International Law Commission, 'Fourth Report on State Responsibility, by Mr. Roberto Ago, Special Rapporteur – The Internationally Wrongful Act of the State, Source of International Responsibility', 30 June 1972 and 9 April 1973, UN Doc. A/CN.4/264 and Add.l, *ILC Yearbook*, vol. II (1972) [hereinafter referred to as ILC, Ago Report, 1972], p. 144, para. 193, emphasis added.

[7] Ibid., p. 131, para. 157. See also, paras. 195, 199, 210.

situation.[8] Under the provision, the acts of the rebels are attributable to the 'new' State,[9] but not those of the 'organs of the pre-existing State'.[10] Interestingly, the ILC adopted a different position on the matter in its 1975 Report,[11] and, accordingly, the wording '*in all or part of the territory*' was no longer present in the 1975 draft.[12] For this reason, I will not examine this hypothetical scenario.

4.2 Rule No. 7: The Acts Committed by the Rebels during the Insurgency Are Attributable to the New State

This section examines the first basic rule applicable when an insurrection leads to the creation of a new State: the acts committed by the rebels during the insurgency are attributable to the new State (Rule no. 7). In the following section, I will examine these issues:

- The principle is recognized by the ILC and other organizations (Section 4.2.1);
- What is the scope of application of Rule no. 7 (Section 4.2.2);
- What is the rationale behind the principle (Section 4.2.3);
- The fact that there is limited case law and State practice, but it supports this principle (Section 4.2.4); and
- How does Rule no. 7 apply to different types of succession of States (Section 4.2.5).

4.2.1 *The Principle Is Recognized by the ILC and Other Organizations*

The conduct of an 'insurrectional movement', or, more generally, other types of 'movement' that subsequently succeed in creating a new State is referred to in Article 10(2) of the final ILC 2001 Articles, which stipulates that:

[8] Ibid., p. 151, para. 214:

> The conduct of a person or group of persons who, at the time when such conduct was engaged in, were organs of an insurrectional movement whose structures have subsequently become the structures of a new State constituted *in all or part of the territory* formerly under the sovereignty of the pre-existing State is retroactively considered to be an act of the newly constituted State. (emphasis added).

[9] ILC, Report, 1975, p. 101, para. 7; p. 146, para. 199.

[10] ILC, Ago Report, 1972, p. 131, para. 157. See also: ILC, Report, 1975, p. 146, para. 199; p. 101, para. 7.

[11] ILC, Report, 1975, p. 101, para. 7.

[12] Ibid., p. 100, para. 1.

> The conduct of a movement, insurrectional or other, which succeeds in establishing a new state in part of the territory of a pre-existing state or in a territory under its administration shall be considered an act of the new state under international law.[13]

The ILC Commentaries explain that by referring to both insurrectional movements and 'other' movements, the scope of Article 10(2) is broader than that of Article 10(1).[14] This was meant to 'reflect[] the existence of a greater variety of movements whose actions may result in the formation of a new State'.[15] The additional language is particularly relevant for Newly Independent States in the context of decolonization.[16] Under Article 10(2), the acts committed by the rebels during the insurgency are attributable to the new State. The new State is therefore considered 'responsible'[17] for the obligations arising from internationally wrongful acts committed by the 'movement' (whether 'insurrectional' or not) during the period of rebellion that led to its creation.

Perhaps surprisingly, Rule no. 7 set out in Article 10(2) has not been examined by many scholars.[18] The few writers who have tackled this specific question support Rule no. 7.[19] These writers are indeed

[13] The text of the provision of the 1996 draft adopted by the ILC ('Draft Articles on State Responsibility Adopted by the Commission on First Reading', 1996, Report of the ILC on the Work of its Forty-eighth Session, 6 May–26 July 1996, General Assembly Official Records, Fifty-first Session Supplement No. 10, UN Doc. A/51/10, chp. III, in *ILC Yearbook* vol. II(2) (1996)), was slightly different: '[t]he act of an insurrectional movement whose action results in the formation of a new state in part of the territory of a pre-existing state or in a territory under its administration shall be considered as an act of the new state'.

[14] The previous 1996 version of the Articles (ibid.) only made reference to 'insurrectional movements'.

[15] International Law Commission, 'Commentaries to the Draft Articles on Responsibility of States for Internationally Wrongful Acts Adopted by the ILC at its Fifty-Third Session', November 2001, UN Doc. A/56/10, *ILC Yearbook* vol. II (2) (2001) [hereinafter referred to as ILC, Commentaries, 2001], p. 51, para. 10.

[16] This question is discussed below in Section 4.2.5.2.1.

[17] The question as to whether this is actually an issue of 'responsibility' is further examined below in Section 4.2.2.

[18] ILC, Report, 1975, p. 104, para. 18:

> [writers] generally make no distinction between the situation where the insurgents have asserted their authority as a new government or new régime over the whole of the territory of the pre-existing State and the situation where they have, on the contrary, caused the formation of a new State in part of the territory of the pre-existing State, which is therefore detached from the latter.

See also, in ILC, Ago Report, 1972, p. 150, para. 210.

[19] Atlam, *Succession d'États*, p. 423 ff. (citing many writers); Brigitte Stern, 'Responsabilité internationale et succession d'États', in Laurence Boisson de Chazournes and

consistently referring to this principle as a well-established one.[20] I also came to the same conclusion in previous writing.[21] Rule no. 7 has been adopted by the Institute of International Law ('IIL') in its 2015 Resolution on State succession in matters of State Responsibility under Article 12(6) (applicable in the context of secession):

> The internationally wrongful act of an insurrectional or other movement which succeeds in establishing a new State on part of the territory of the predecessor State or in a territory under the administration of this latter State shall be considered an act of the new State under international law. Consequently, the predecessor State incurs no responsibility for the acts committed by the insurrectional or other movement.[22]

Vera Gowlland-Debbas (eds.), *The International Legal System in Quest of Equity and Universality / L'ordre juridique international, un système en quête d'équité et d'universalité. Liber amicorum Georges Abi-Saab* (Leiden, M. Nijhoff, 2001), p. 344; Liesbeth Zegveld, *Accountability of Armed Opposition Groups in International Law* (Cambridge University Press, 2002), p. 155–6; Patrick Daillier, Mathias Forteau and Alain Pellet, *Droit international public* (8th ed., Paris, LGDJ, 2009), p. 870; G. Balladore Pallieri, *Diritto internazionale pubblico* (8th ed., Milan, Giuffrè, 1962), p. 173; Manlio Udina, 'La succession des États quant aux obligations internationales autres que les dettes publiques', *Rec. des cours* 44 (1933-II), p. 768–9; Arangio-Ruiz, *L'État dans le sens du droit des gens*, p. 45; Gordon A. Christenson, 'The Doctrine of Attribution in State Responsibility', in R. B. Lillich, *International Law of State Responsibility of Injuries to Aliens* (Charlottesville, University of Virginia Press, 1983), p. 334; John Bassett Moore, *Digest of International Law* (Washington, GPO, vol. I, 1906), p. 44; John Quigley, 'State Responsibility for Ethnic Cleansing', *U.C. Davis L. Rev.* 32 (1999), p. 341, at p. 357; Sebastián Mantilla Blanco, *Full Protection and Security in International Investment Law* (Cham, Springer, 2019), p. 227; Haig Silvanie, 'Responsibility of States for Acts of Insurgent Governments', *AJIL* 33(1) (1939), p. 89, 90 (referring to 'the principle that a new state is bound by acts and contracts of insurgents who succeed in establishing its independence'); Michael Akehurst, 'State Responsibility for the Wrongful Acts of Rebels – An Aspect of the Southern Rhodesian Problem', *British YIL* 43 (1968–9), p. 55; Wladyslaw Czaplinski, 'State Succession and State Responsibility', *Canadian YIL* 28 (1990), p. 353; Michael John Volkovitsch, 'Righting Wrongs: Toward a New Theory of State Succession to Responsibility for International Delicts', *Colum. L. Rev.* 92(8) (1992), p. 2199; Eatwell, *State Responsibility*, p. 210–11.

20 Stern, 'Responsabilité internationale et succession d'États', p. 344 (describing this rule as a customary norm of international law); Atlam, *Succession d'États*, p. 422 (speaking of 'une règle bien établi en droit international', see also, his comments at p. 399, 410, 419 and 422); Czaplinski, 'State Succession and State Responsibility', p. 353 (speaking of a 'consistent' practice in this field). See also: Volkovitsch, 'Righting Wrongs', p. 2199.

21 Dumberry, *State Succession to International Responsibility*, p. 224 ff. See also: Dumberry, 'New State Responsibility'.

22 Institute of International Law, 'State Succession in Matters of State Responsibility', Rap. M.G. Kohen, Resolution of 2015, in *Annuaire IDI* 76 (2015), p. 703 [hereinafter referred to as IIL, 'State Succession in Matters of State Responsibility', 2015]. The same rule is also contained in Article 16(3) applicable in the context of Newly Independent States: '[t]he conduct, prior to the date of succession of States, of a national liberation movement which

Draft Article 7(4) (applicable in the context of secession) proposed by the ILC Special Rapporteur Šturma is along the same lines.[23]

4.2.2 *Scope of Application of Rule No. 7*

Before examining, in the next section, the rationale behind Article 10(2) of the ILC Articles, a number of observations should be made about the scope of this provision.

First, it is important to note that two types of acts are covered by Article 10(2). On the one hand, it covers internationally wrongful acts committed by an insurrectional movement which have caused damage to *a third party* (a third State or a foreigner). My book only focuses on such acts. On the other hand, it covers situations in which wrongs committed by the rebels before the date of succession have caused damage to the *predecessor* State. In cases where the predecessor State continues to exists following the creation of a new State, these acts are generally considered as 'war damages' between the predecessor State and the successor State.[24] Questions related to 'war damages' are usually excluded from the analysis of issues of State succession as they involve only matters of State responsibility.[25] However, although claims between the predecessor State and the successor State are not at the heart of this book, a few

succeeds in establishing a newly independent State shall be considered the act of the new State under international law'. For an analysis, see: Marcelo G. Kohen and Patrick Dumberry, *The Institute of International Law's Resolution on State Succession and State Responsibility: Introduction, Text and Commentaries* (Cambridge University Press, 2019).

[23] ILC, 'Second Report on Succession of States in Respect of State Responsibility', by Pavel Šturma, Special Rapporteur, 70th session, A/CN.4/719, 6 April 2018 [hereinafter referred to as 'ILC Second Report Šturma, 2018'], paras. 107 ff. Draft Article 7(4) reads as follows: '[t]he conduct of a movement, insurrectional or other, which succeeds in establishing a new State in part of the territory of a predecessor State or in a territory under its administration shall be considered an act of the new State under international law'. The same rule is also contained at Draft Article 8(3) applicable in the context of Newly Independent States: '[t]he conduct of a national liberation or other movement which succeeds in establishing a newly independent State shall be considered an act of the new State under international law'.

[24] On this question, see: Dumberry, *State Succession to International Responsibility*, p. 27–9.

[25] This is, for instance, the position of Stern, 'Responsabilité internationale et succession d'États', p. 342–3, as well as that of Udina, 'La succession des États', p. 751. See also: Arbitration Commission Opinion no. 13, 16 July 1993, *ILM* (1993), p. 1592: '[t]he rules applicable to State succession, on the one hand, and the rules of State responsibility, on which the question of war damages depends, on the other, fall within two distinct areas of international law'.

examples will be examined below (including in the context of the independence of Algeria).[26]

Second, another important aspect to consider is that the new State is responsible for the *contracts* that have been signed by the rebels during the insurgency.[27] As further explained in the next section, what matters is the element of organic and structural 'continuity' between the rebels and the new State. As mentioned above,[28] the word 'conduct' used in Article 10(2) is wide enough to cover acts other than wrongs.[29] Similarly, Article 18(1) of the 1961 *Harvard Draft Convention on International Responsibility* refers generally to 'acts' and 'omissions' of rebels.[30]

Third, it should be recalled (as noted by the ILC) that 'Article 10 deals with the *special case of attribution* to a State of conduct of an insurrectional or other movement which subsequently . . . succeeds in establishing a new State'.[31] The question of the 'special' nature of this rule of attribution was examined in detail when previously assessing Article

[26] See Sections 4.2.5.2.2 and 4.3.2.2.1.

[27] In Patrick Dumberry, *A Guide to State Succession in International Investment Law* (Cheltenham, Edward Elgar Publishing, 2018), p. 363, I examined the more general question of State succession to State contracts. I analysed several factors that may have an impact in assessing whether or not a successor State should be bound by a State contract signed by the predecessor State before the date of succession. One of those factors (at p. 376 ff.) is whether the contract was actually signed by an organ of a territorial unit of the predecessor State that has a structural continuity with the successor State. The rationale for such a rule is based on Article 10(2) of the ILC Articles and the existence of a continuity between the entity which signed the contract and the new State. In my view, the same principle should apply in cases where the rebels have signed a contract during the period of insurrection.

[28] See Part I, Section 2.1.2.2.2 dealing with rebellions resulting in the establishment of a new government.

[29] In his book, Haig Silvanie, *Responsibility of States for Acts of Unsuccessful Insurgent Governments* (New York, Columbia University Press, 1939), p. 11, 15 ff., refers to several cases where the new State was held responsible for *loans* made during an insurrection by foreign citizens to the (ultimately successful) insurgents.

[30] Harvard Draft Convention on the International Responsibility of States for Injuries to Aliens, 15 April 1961, by reporters Louis B. Sohn and Richard Baxter, in *AJIL* 55 (1961), p. 576 (emphasis added). See also: Article XIII (b), Harvard Draft Convention on the International Responsibility of States for Injuries to Aliens, *AJIL* Spec. Supp. 23 (1929), p. 131 ff.:

> In the event of a revolution or insurrection which brings about a change in the government of a State *or the establishment of a new State*, an act or omission of an organ, agency, official, or employee of a revolutionary or insurrectionary group is, for the purposes of this Convention, attributable to the State in which the group established itself as the government.

[31] ILC, Commentaries, 2001, p. 51, para. 1, emphasis added.

10(1).[32] Suffice it to note that Article 10(2) refers to the conduct of an *entity other than the new State* which shall nevertheless be 'considered an act of the new State'. This is because the new State *cannot* be held 'responsible' per se for acts that it did not commit itself. *A fortiori*, it is the case when that State *did not ever exist* when the acts were committed. Thus, as noted by Serbia in the *Genocide* case (further examined below)[33] 'within the framework of Part One, Chapter II of the ILC Articles on State Responsibility, the specific rule of attribution to be found in Article 10, para. 2, is *quite exceptional*'.[34] While all other provisions in the ILC Articles (including Article 10(1)) 'envisage attribution of conduct to an *existing* State',[35] 'in sharp contrast' Article 10(2) 'is the only provision in Chapter II that entails the attribution of conduct to a new State that only came into existence *after the conduct occurred*'.[36] This feature illustrates the truly *exceptional* nature of the special rule of attribution contained in Article 10(2). It should be added that Eatwell speaks of a rule of attribution of *responsibility* rather than a rule of attribution of conduct.[37]

Fourth, it is noteworthy that Article 10(2) is simply a (special) rule of attribution that has nothing do with the question of whether a certain conduct constitutes a breach of an international obligation.[38] In the words of the ILC Commentaries, the fact that a certain conduct is attributable to a State for the purposes of establishing responsibility 'says nothing, as such, about the legality or otherwise of that conduct'.[39] This point was emphasized by Serbia in the *Genocide* case.[40] In its judgment, the Court essentially

[32] See Part I, Section 2.2.2.1.
[33] See Section 4.2.5.3.2.
[34] *Application of the Convention on the Prevention and Punishment of the Crime of Genocide (Croatia* v. *Serbia),* ICJ, [hereinafter referred to as 'ICJ, *Genocide* case'], Serbia, Counter-Memorial, December 2009, para. 330, emphasis added.
[35] Ibid., para. 331, emphasis in the original.
[36] Ibid.
[37] Eatwell, *State Responsibility*, p. 210–11, for her, 'as much as it is desirable that a new state should be international[ly] responsible for the conduct of the insurrectional or other movement whose agitations led to that state's formation, it is questionable whether Article 10(2) can operate as a rule of attribution of conduct' (p. 228–9). See also, p. 229 ff. explaining that the rule would be 'narrow in its application' to cover violations of international humanitarian law committed by rebels.
[38] ILC, Second Report Šturma, 2018, para. 109. See also: Eatwell, *State Responsibility*, p. 222: '[a] rule of attribution of conduct of an insurrectional or other movement to a state is just that – it provides the circumstances in which the conduct of a person or entity is attributable to the state. A rule of attribution does not create international obligations of the state, retroactively or otherwise'.
[39] ILC, Commentaries, 2001, p. 39, para. 4.
[40] ICJ, *Genocide* case, Serbia, Counter-Memorial, December 2009, para. 333:

agreed with the position of Serbia and stated that Article 10(2) 'is concerned only with the attribution of acts to a new State; it does not create obligations binding upon either the new State or the movement that succeeded in establishing that new State'.[41] While this aspect of the reasoning of the Court has been praised by some scholars,[42] another has argued that it 'reveals a fundamental flaw in the operation of Article 10(2)'.[43]

Fifth, in the *Genocide* case, Serbia correctly mentioned that 'three essential elements' must be met for Article 10(2) to apply:

> It follows that there are three essential elements of this rule:
>
> a) the conduct in question has to be the conduct of a movement striving to establish a new State on part of the territory of a preexisting State or in a territory under its administration;
> b) this movement has to be an insurrectional or 'other' movement;
> c) this movement has to be successful.
>
> All three elements are necessary preconditions to the application of the norm formulated in Article 10, para. 2. The conduct of an insurrectional movement can only be ascribed to the new State if the situation matches *all* the elements of the scenario, specified in Article 10, para. 2.[44]

Sixth, Serbia mentioned an essential point in its pleading, that is, that the provision only applies if the rebels have *themselves* committed a violation

> While the scope of Article 10, para. 2 remains controversial in many respects, it is clear what the provision is not about. As a secondary rule of attribution, it does not affect the content of primary rules and therefore it cannot be relied upon to determine whether particular conduct 'constitutes a breach of an international obligation of [a] State' [Art. 2(b)]. That determination depends on the interpretation of applicable primary rules of international law.

41 Ibid., Judgment of 3 February 2015, ICJ Rep. 2015, para. 104.

42 Ines Gillich, 'Between Light and Shadow: The International Law Against Genocide in the International Court of Justice's Judgement in Croatia v. Serbia (2015)', *Pace ILR*, 28(1) (2016), p. 131.

43 Eatwell, *State Responsibility*, p. 226. See also, p. 231:

> the ICJ's conclusion that Article 10(2) cannot be applied to the question of Serbia's responsibility for acts of genocide committed before the state's proclamation as a new, independent state on 27 April 1992, reveals a fundamental flaw in the operation of Article 10(2). The effective operation of the rule relies upon the retroactive application of customary international law so as to bind a new state with respect to conduct committed before that state came into existence. However, there is no support in case law or doctrine for such a rule.

44 ICJ, *Genocide* case, Serbia, Counter-Memorial, December 2009, paras. 296–7, emphasis in the original.

of an applicable rule of international law during the insurgency. Croatia rejected this position.[45] The better view, as noted by Kolb, is indeed that the conduct of rebels 'represents an IWA [internationally wrongful act] only if at the time it was committed it breached some obligations of international law applicable to the armed group, e.g. under the law of armed conflicts or under agreements, armistice or other'.[46] To this list, Clapham adds general rules of international law (including rules protecting aliens and foreign investors) as well as international human rights law.[47] Serbia emphasized that the only role of Article 10(2) is to 'attribute' to the new State, after the date of succession, such a breach committed by the rebels.[48] Serbia also made this important remark: '[c]onversely, where a movement, insurrectional or other, does not violate its international obligations, Article 10, para. 2, cannot "create" responsibility of the subsequently-emerged State'.[49] Thus, as noted by Kolb, Article 10(2) does not 'create new IWAs that would not have existed at the time of the conduct for lack of an obligation binding upon the insurrectional

[45] Ibid., Verbatim Record, 7 March 2014, CR 2014/12, 21, Crawford (Croatia), para. 14:

> The rule reflected in Article 10 (2) is not concerned with the responsibility of a movement *qua* movement whether or not it succeeds. It is concerned with the conduct of a movement *qua* State in embryo – conduct by a movement that eventually attains statehood, which international law treats as conduct of the State and as subject to the international obligations of that State, from the beginning. . . . Article 10 (2) may apply even where the movement was *never* capable of attracting any international responsibility qua movement. It is international obligations of the State that apply to conduct attributable under Article 10 (2).

[46] R. Kolb, *The International Law of State Responsibility: An Introduction* (Cheltenham, Edward Elgar Publishing, 2018), p. 98. See also: Eatwell, *State Responsibility*, p. 210–11: '[i]t is accepted that the scope of application of such a rule will be limited to the conduct of an insurrectional or other movement that is itself bound by international humanitarian law'); S. I. Verhoeven, 'International Responsibility of Armed Opposition Groups. Lessons from State Responsibility for Actions of Armed Opposition Groups' in N. Gal-Or, C. Ryngaert and M. Noortmann (eds.), *Responsibilities of the Non-State Actor in Armed Conflict and the Market Place. Theoretical Considerations and Empirical Findings* (Leiden, Brill, 2015), p. 298–9 ('international responsibility of the armed opposition group will require that there is a breach of an international obligation, which can be attributed to that group').

[47] A. Clapham, 'Extending International Criminal Responsibility beyond the Individual to Corporations and Armed Opposition Groups', *J. Int. Criminal Justice* 6 (2008), p. 508–9.

[48] ICJ, *Genocide* case, Serbia, Counter-Memorial, December 2009, para. 346: 'the insurrectional or other movement must *itself* have committed a violation of an applicable rule of international law. Responsibility for this breach is then attributed to the newly created State by virtue of Article 10, para. 2, of the ILC Articles on State Responsibility' (emphasis in the original).

[49] Ibid., para. 346.

movement'.[50] The same position was adopted by the ILC in its 1975 Report.[51] This question will be further discussed below when assessing the *Genocide* case.[52]

Seventh, Serbia referring to the 2001 ILC Commentary[53] rightly noted that for Article 10 to apply, any such movement would have to be in 'continuing struggle with the constituted authority'.[54] Accordingly, 'an essential characteristic' is that these movements 'exist and operate *outside* and *against* the established structure of the State on whose territory they seek to establish a new State'.[55] The ILC Commentaries mentioned that the expression 'insurrectional or other' movements 'do not however extend to encompass the actions of a group of citizens advocating separation or revolution where these are carried out *within the framework of the predecessor State*'.[56] As Croatia noted, 'this was intended to exclude from the scope of Article 10 instances of constitutional advocacy for change'.[57] Therefore, Article 10(2) does not cover cases where a political party is advocating for secession by participating in democratic elections and holding a legal and peaceful referendum on independence.[58] Further, it is worth mentioning that Article 10(2) only applies when the rebels are fighting for statehood *against the predecessor State*. As further examined below, this important point was central to the arguments of both parties in the *Genocide* case.[59]

[50] Kolb, *The International Law of State Responsibility*, p. 98:

> [c]onversely, Article 10 ASR does not imply that all the obligations applicable to the territorial State are retroactively applied to the insurrectional movement so that a series of new IWAs could emerge retrospectively. It is true that this limits the number of breaches the movement can commit. But this is the true rationale of article 10: the IWAs of the insurrectional group are attributed to the State (and added to the IWAs of the State, if any); it is not to create new IWAs that would not have existed at the time of the conduct for lack of an obligation binding upon the insurrectional movement.

[51] ILC, Report, 1975, p. 91, para. 3: '[a]s organs of an insurrectional movement they may engage in conduct liable to bring an international responsibility upon the insurrectional movement itself if that conduct should constitute a breach of an international obligation recognized as incumbent on the insurrectional movement'.

[52] See Section 4.2.5.3.2.

[53] ILC, Commentaries, 2001, p. 50, para. 2.

[54] ICJ, *Genocide* case, Serbia, Counter-Memorial, December 2009, para. 301.

[55] Ibid., paras. 303–4, emphasis in the original.

[56] ILC, Commentaries, 2001, p. 51, para. 10, emphasis added. See also, Eatwell, *State Responsibility*, p. 212 ff.

[57] ICJ, *Genocide* case, Croatia, Reply, vol. 1, 20 December 2010, para. 7.60.

[58] See Eatwell, *State Responsibility*, p. 212.

[59] See Section 4.2.5.3.2.1.2.

4.2.3 *The Rationale behind the Principle*

This section examines the different theoretical foundations that have been put forward in doctrine to support the claim that 'responsibility' for internationally wrongful acts committed by the insurrectional movement should be taken over by the new State.[60]

4.2.3.1 The Two Doctrinal Approaches

In his doctoral thesis on the question, Atlam explains in some detail that there are two broad approaches to be distinguished. One approach focuses on the *discontinuity* between the movement and the new State (the 'succession theory'), while the other, on the contrary, explains the rationale behind Rule no. 7 based on the close *continuity* which exists between them (the 'continuity theory').[61]

According to the first approach (the 'succession theory'), the victory of the rebels results in the creation of a new subject of international law (the new State), which *is conceptually distinct* from the other subject (the insurrectional movement) that led to its creation.[62] Thus, the creation of the new State results in an extinction of the insurrectional movement and in a *break* in the chain of the continuity of legal personality between the movement and the new State.[63] The new State is also a different subject of international law than the predecessor State.[64] According to this approach, the devolution of responsibility to the new State is simply based on the existing 'ordinary' rules of State succession between *two distinct subjects* of international law.[65] In other words, this is a question of State succession to international responsibility. The work by Altam highlights the fact that this theory is only supported by a minority of writers.[66] Judge *ad hoc* Kreća

[60] Atlam, *Succession d'États*, p. 423 ff. providing a comprehensive analysis of these different theories.

[61] Ibid., p. 397, 424.

[62] Ibid., p. 424, 427–33.

[63] Ibid., p. 427–8.

[64] Ibid., p. 427.

[65] Ibid., p. 428.

[66] See, for instance: G. Cansacchi, 'Identité et continuité des sujets de droit international', *Rec. des cours,* 130 (1970-I), p. 42–3, for whom 'lorsque le gouvernement insurgé devient le seul gouvernement de l'État, on doit admettre que le sujet international particulier qu'il représentait s'est éteint, et qu'une succession internationale s'est ouverte entre lui et l'État dont il est devenu l'organe suprême' ('when the insurgent government becomes the sole government of the state, one must admit that the particular international subject it represented has died out, and that an international succession has opened up between it and the state from which it has become the supreme organ').

seems to have adopted this position in his separate opinion in the 2015 *Genocide* case.[67]

The second approach (the 'continuity theory') rejects the very foundation upon which the 'succession theory' is based.[68] Importantly, the 'continuity theory' is based on the application of rules of State responsibility rather than those existing in the field of State succession.[69] This is the position adopted by most writers.[70] It is also the one which has been followed by the Institute (and by ILC Special Rapporteur Šturma) [71] in its resolution on State succession to State responsibility.[72]

The work of the ILC has clearly adopted the 'continuity' theory.[73] ILC Special Rapporteur Ago envisaged the situation as one involving the

67 ICJ, *Genocide* case, 2015, Separate Opinion of Judge Kreća, para. 66.1:

> As regards 'a movement, insurrectional or other which succeeds in establishing a new State', the situation is entirely different. A new State is a new legal person in terms of international law, whose corpus of rights and obligations does not coincide with the rights and obligations of its parent State, but is determined on the basis of the rules of succession of States. From a legal point of view, responsibility of the new State is essentially an issue of the law of succession rather than an issue of State responsibility. Or, a combination of both. It is logical to presume that this is the reason why it is pointed out that 'Article 10 concerns the special case of responsibility'.

(referring to: J. Crawford, *The ILC Articles on State Responsibility: Introduction, Text and Commentaries* (Cambridge University Press, 2002), p. 93, para. 8)

68 See Atlam, *Succession d'États*, p. 434 ff.

69 Ibid., p. 433.

70 Stern, 'Responsabilité internationale et succession d'États', p. 344; Udina, 'La succession des États', p. 768–9; Jean d'Aspremont, 'Rebellion and State Responsibility: Wrongdoing by Democratically Elected Insurgents', *ICLQ* 58 (2009), p. 430 ('the responsibility of the State for the wrongful acts of victorious rebels has always been conceived as a *rule of attribution*', emphasis in the original). *Contra*: Czaplinski, 'State Succession and State Responsibility', p. 353, who seems to view this issue as one dealing with State succession. Thus, for him, this rule is 'the exception to the general rule of non-responsibility of the successor State for the acts of its predecessor'.

71 ILC, Second Report Šturma, 2018, para. 109, indicating that Article 10(1) 'is a rule of attribution rather than a rule of State succession to responsibility'.

72 Article 12(6), IIL, 'State Succession in Matters of State Responsibility', 2015. On this provision, see: Kohen and Dumberry, *The Institute of International Law's Resolution*, p. 106 ff. See also, IIL, 'Final Report' by Rapporteur Marcelo G. Kohen, 28 June 2015, in *Ann. IDI* 76 (2015), p. 511 ff. [hereinafter referred to as IIL, 'Final Report', 2015], para. 82.

73 ILC, Report, 1975, p. 101, para. 8: '[These wrongful] acts committed by agents of the insurrectional movement before the movement takes power are attributed to the state because there is continuity between the apparatus of the insurrectional movement and the new governmental apparatus of the state, *not a succession of the state as one*

same subject of international law which would have 'reached the final stage of its progressive evolution' from insurgents to a new State.[74] Ago thus speaks of the 'continuity' of the international legal personality between the insurrectional movement and the new State.[75] For Ago, 'an existing subject of international law would merely change category: from a mere embryo State it would become a State proper, without any interruption in its international personality resulting from the change'.[76] It is, in fact, the *same organization*.[77] Both have the *same structure*.[78] The question of attribution of responsibility is therefore not problematic if one considers it from the angle of the continuous

subject of international law to the insurrectional movement as another', emphasis added. A similar assessment is made in ILC, Ago Report, 1972, p. 131, para. 159: 'The attribution to the new State of the acts of organs of the insurrectional movement would therefore be only a normal application of the general rule providing for the attribution to any subject of international law of the conduct of its organs.' In International Law Commission, 'First Report on State Responsibility, by Mr. James Crawford, Special Rapporteur', 24 April, 1, 5, 11 and 26 May, 22 and 24 July, 12 August 1998, UN Doc. A/CN.4/490 and Add. 1–7*, *ILC Yearbook* vol. II(1) (1998) [hereinafter referred to as ILC, Crawford First Report, 1998], p. 51–2, para. 264, Crawford also made the same comment:

> [t]he commentary explains the two rules set out in article 15 on the basis of the organizational continuity of an insurrectional movement which succeeds in displacing the previous government of the State or even in forming a new State on part of its territory. This has nothing to do with State succession; in the former case there is no succession of States, and in the latter the rule of continuity applies whether or not the predecessor State was responsible for the conduct itself.

[74] ILC, Ago Report, 1972, p. 131, para. 157: 'It would not be a question of attributing to a subject of international law the conduct of organs of another subject, but merely of continuing to attribute to the same subject – which would only have reached the final stage of its progressive evolution the acts of its own organs.'

[75] Ibid., para. 159. See also, para. 194.

[76] Ibid., p. 131, para. 159. See also, para. 194.

[77] Ibid., p. 144, para. 195: 'The organization of the insurrectional movement is, prospectively, the organization of the new State which that movement sought to install. When that happens, the organization of the revolutionary movement automatically becomes the organization of the State, without any break in continuity between the two, even though changes, adjustments, and some integration necessarily ensue.'

[78] Ibid., p. 144, para. 194: 'the structures of the insurrectional movement become, after its victory, the structures of the newly independent State and that the organization of what was only an embryo State, a potential State, becomes the organization of a fully and definitively formed State'. See also, para. 194: '[i]t is in fact the same structural entity which formerly had the features of an insurrectional movement and now has the features of a State proper'.

evolution of the same subject of international law.[79] This is the result of the continuity between them.[80]

ILC Special Rapporteur Crawford focused on this idea of a structural 'continuity' between the rebels and the new State rather than on the fact that they could be considered as the *same subject* of international law. Crawford thus noted that 'at least outside the context of decolonization, there is strong resistance to admitting even the temporary legal personality of insurrectional movements'.[81] In any event, he believes that 'it is doubtful that tying responsibility to the legal personality of the insurgents as such is helpful'.[82] The same position has been adopted by ILC Special Rapporteur Šturma.[83] There is indeed one good reason for not focusing on the insurgents as a subject. The insurrectional movement is bound to disappear either because 'the insurrection fails or because it succeeds'.[84] The point of view is highlighted by Cahin: '[b]ut the movement is only a temporary entity, for its disappearance will occur in due course: either because of its defeat or because of its victory and consequent transformation into the government either of the pre-existing State or of a new State'.[85]

At least four different theories have been put forward by writers to explain the relationship of *continuity* between the insurrectional movement and the new State. These theories will be examined in the following

[79] Ibid., p. 131, para. 159: '[t]he attribution to the new State of the acts of organs of the insurrectional movement would therefore be only a normal application of the general rule providing for the attribution to any subject of international law of the conduct of its organs'.

[80] Ibid., p. 144, para. 194: 'Because of the continuity between the two, it is therefore normal to attribute to the new State, as a potential source of international responsibility, the acts of agents of the insurrectional movement'.

[81] James Crawford, *State Responsibility: The General Part* (Cambridge University Press, 2013), p. 171.

[82] Ibid. See also, Cahin, 'Attribution of Conduct to the State', p. 251–2, noting that

> the argument according to which these movements have the right to resort to armed force and apply the relevant rules of the law of armed conflicts contained in Additional Protocol I to the Geneva Conventions is without doubt pertinent for the purposes of determining the existence of violations of international law, but not for the purposes of determining the attributability of this conduct.

[83] ILC, Second Report Šturma, 2018, para. 112: 'it seems to be preferable, like the Commission several decades ago, not to enter into the issue of a potential legal personality of insurgents and to stick instead to the rationale expressed in the commentary to the final article 10 of the articles on State responsibility'.

[84] Crawford, *State Responsibility*, p. 171.

[85] Cahin, 'Attribution of Conduct to the State', p. 248.

sections. This will be followed by an analysis of another reason behind Rule no. 7: the need to prevent a gap in terms of responsibility.[86]

4.2.3.2 Theories Explaining the Relationship of Continuity between the Insurrectional Movement and the New State

4.2.3.2.1 Less Convincing Theories According to one theory, the continuity between the new State and the rebels arises from the fact that the latter were organized as a de facto government and acted as such throughout the hostilities.[87] From this *continuity of government*, it would result that the new State should be held responsible for the acts committed by the de facto rebel government prior to independence. I have already explained the weakness of this approach in the different context of the establishment of a *new government* by a rebellion[88] and the reasons why it has been rejected by the work of the ILC.[89]

To explain the theoretical foundation of continuity between the insurrectional movement and the new State, another theory supported by some in doctrine refers to the 'internal legitimacy' of the struggle of the former against the predecessor State.[90] The rebels' victory would thus truly represent the 'national will' of the people for whom they are fighting for. As explained above, this approach has been rejected by scholars[91] and by the ILC in the specific context of Article 10(2).[92]

In some cases, the 'new' State may actually be an 'ancient' State which ceased to exist as an independent entity only for a certain period of time.[93] The new State would thus be 'resurrected' through the struggle of the liberation movement.[94] Atlam cites a number of examples,

[86] See Section 4.2.3.3.
[87] Atlam, *Succession d'États*, p. 455–61.
[88] The question was examined in Part I, Section 2.2.2.2.1.
[89] ILC, Report, 1975, p. 100, para. 2. See also: ILC, Ago Report, 1972, p. 145, para. 198.
[90] Atlam, *Succession d'États*, p. 461.
[91] The question was examined in Part I, Section 2.2.2.2.1.
[92] This question is further examined below in Section 4.2.5.2.1.
[93] The general issue (unrelated to the specific question of insurrectional movements) is analysed in Vladimir D. Degan, 'Création et disparition de l'État (à la lumière du démembrement de trois fédérations multiethniques en Europe)', *Rec. des cours* 279 (1999), p. 293 ff.
[94] More recently, it has been argued that Montenegro's independence was simply 'restored' in 2006 because of its past status as an independent State from 1878 until 1918, when it joined the Kingdom of Serbs, Croats and Slovenes. This issue is discussed in J. Vidmar, 'Montenegro's Path to Independence: A Study of Self-Determination, Statehood and Recognition', *Hanse LR* 3(1) (2007), p. 73, p. 92, 99–100. He refers (at p. 89) to a declaration made by the Montenegrin Foreign Minister in December 1991 at the

including Poland (where the principle was adopted by its domestic courts[95]).[96] He also refers to the position adopted by several African and Asian States claiming this status after their independence and refusing to be qualified as 'new' States. This is, for instance, the position of Algeria.[97] A number of writers have supported this position in the past.[98] It has also been adopted by Judge Morena Quintana in his dissenting opinion in the *Right of Passage over Indian Territory* case.[99] According to this theory,[100] there would be a continuity of identity between the 'ancient' State, the insurrectional movement and the 'new' State. Consequently, the newly 'resuscitated' State would be responsible for obligations arising from internationally wrongful acts committed by the rebel movement prior to independence.

The 'resurrection' theory has been widely contested in doctrine. Indeed, whether a new State considers itself as the 'reincarnation' of an ancient entity is often based on political and moral justifications rather

Badinter Commission: '[w]hen Montenegro, upon unification became part of Yugoslavia, the sovereignty and international personality of Montenegro did not cease to exist, but became part of the sovereignty of the new state. In case Yugoslavia disunited and ceased to exist as an international entity, the independence and sovereignty of Montenegro continue their existence in their original form and substance'. Vidmar concludes that Montenegro simply ceased to exist as an independent State when it joined the Kingdom in 1918 and that its international legal personality could not be 'restored' in 2006.

95 Atlam, *Succession d'États*, p. 444, citing case law.

96 Ibid., p. 438–9.

97 See Mohammed Bedjaoui, *La révolution algérienne et le droit* (Brussels, Éditions de l'Association internationale des juristes démocrates, 1961), p. 18–39. The question is also examined in Atlam, ibid., p. 448 ff.

98 Atlam, ibid., p. 443, citing several authors. See also: Degan, 'Création et disparition de l'État', p. 293 ff. who indicates that the relevant factor is the lapse of time during which the State lost sovereignty. He is of the view that in situations where the lapse of time is short the issue should be best understood as one of continuity of State rather than one of succession.

99 *Case concerning Right of Passage over Indian Territory (Portugal* v. *India)* (Merits), Judgment of 12 April 1960, ICJ Rep. 1960, p. 6, Dissenting Opinion of Judge Morena Quintana, at p. 95:

> [w]hen it became independent, India made no fundamental change in the established system. We must not forget that India, as the territorial successor, was not acquiring the territory for the first time, but was recovering an independence lost long since. Its legal position at once reverted to what it had been more than a hundred years before, as though the British occupation had made no difference.

100 A summary of this thesis, as well as a list of writers supporting it, can be found in Atlam, *Succession d'États*, p. 437–55.

than legal facts.[101] The very concept of State 'resurrection' has been treated by authors as nothing more than a legal fiction without any foundation in international law.[102] In any event, States claiming to be identical to ancient States have often been regarded as new States.[103] It has also been noted that this theory could actually prevent, in some cases, the right to self-determination.[104] Moreover, this theory cannot be used to explain why new States should in general be responsible for obligations arising from internationally wrongful acts committed by rebels in their struggle to establish this new entity. For all of these reasons, this theory is not convincing.

4.2.3.2.2 The Organic or Structural Continuity Theory In my view, as well as that of many scholars[105] (including Atlam[106] and Crawford[107]), it is the *continuity of the structure* between the organization of the

[101] Ibid., p. 451.

[102] Cansacchi, 'Identité et continuité des sujets de droit international', p. 47–8. See also, Krystyna Marek, *Identity and Continuity of States in Public International Law* (Geneva, Librairie Droz, 1968), p. 6: 'It could, however, be asked whether . . . there might not be identity of a State without its continuity. Unless the possibility of legal miracle is admitted, the question must be answered emphatically in the negative: there is no legal resurrection in international law. Once a State has become extinct, it cannot resume a continued existence.'

[103] Atlam, *Succession d'États*, p. 451, referring to the work of Marek, ibid., p. 161–90.

[104] Ibid., p. 453.

[105] Arangio-Ruiz, *L'État dans le sens du droit des gens*, p. 304; Zegveld, *Accountability of Armed Opposition Groups*, p. 156; Cahin, 'Attribution of Conduct to the State', p. 279. A variation of this interpretation is provided by Schwarzenberger, *International Law*, p. 628 (in the context of rebels establishing a new *government*), for whom the concept of estoppel explains the retroactivity of the tortious liability for the acts of the rebels.

[106] Atlam, *Succession d'États*, p. 476, 79, speaking of 'les liens juridiques intrinsèques et substantiels existants entre le mouvement révolutionnaire et l'État issu de sa lutte' ('the intrinsic and substantial legal links existing between the revolutionary movement and the state that emerged from its struggle'). See also, p. 469: 'un telle identité trouve ici son fondement dans la permanence de la substance même de l'organe qui a simplement changé de catégorie en quittant définitivement sa qualité de mouvement pour rejoindre la stature originaire d'un gouvernement étatique' ('such an identity finds its foundation here in the permanence of the very substance of the organ which has simply changed category by definitively leaving its quality of movement to rejoin the original status of a state government'). He nevertheless adopts the theory with a slight variation for National Liberation Movements (ibid., p. 480 ff.). He refers to the international legal personality of the *people* entitled to self-determination rather than that of the National Liberation Movement. He thus speaks of the continuity between the people and the new State.

[107] Crawford, *State Responsibility*, p. 178–9. Yet, it should be added that in another book, Crawford, *The Creation of States in International Law*, p. 658, he noted that the fact that 'the legal rights and liabilities of the successful insurgents governments continue to bind the State so formed' 'may be an incident of the continuity *of legal personality* of the belligerent and the new State' (emphasis added).

insurrectional movement and that of the new State which is relevant in determining whether the latter should be liable for the acts committed by the former. As mentioned above in Part I, this theory has been endorsed by the ILC in the context of a rebellion leading to the establishment of a *new government*.[108] The same position was also adopted by the ILC regarding *new States*.[109]

This conception has, however, been rejected by Judge Kreća in his separate opinion in the *Genocide* case.[110] In my view, it seems hard to deny the existence of some elements of continuity in the context of

[108] See Part I, Section 2.2.2.2.4.

[109] ILC, Report, 1975, p. 101, para. 6:

> The attribution to the new state of the acts of the organs of the insurrectional movement which preceded it, and of such acts only, is then justified by virtue of the continuity between the organisation of the insurrectional movement and the organisation of the state to which it has given rise. From being only an embryo State, the insurrectional movement has become a State proper, without any break in the continuity between the two. It is in fact the same entity which previously had the characteristics of an insurrectional movement and which now has those of a State proper.

Very similar wording is used in ILC, Commentaries, 2001, p. 59 ff., para. 6. See also, in ILC, Ago Report, 1972, p. 131, paras. 159, 194.

[110] ICJ, *Genocide* case, 2015, Separate Opinion of Judge Kreća, paras. 65.3, 65.4:

> Or, in the elaborated concept of 'shared identity', which is, in fact, the negation of legal identity and continuity as usually understood, the crucial role is given to the notion of 'organic substitution', according to which, even in the case where succession took place, 'organic forces' or 'constitutive elements' of the predecessor State (its territory and its population) survive its disintegration, being only affected, but not extinguished (P. Dumberry, *State Succession to International Responsibility*, 2007, pp. 49–50). The concept implies that the successor State is equipped with an identity similar to that held by the predecessor State. Precisely 'shared identity' justifies the transfer of any responsibility that existed at the time of the succession. It appears that the concept of 'organic substitution' fails to take into account the element of legal identity and continuity as the very substance of international personality in the frame of territorial changes. It reduces the State to its physical attributes (territory, population), which are also possessed by territorial non-State entities devoid of the quality of subjects in terms of international law. 'Shared identity' as the product of the concept of 'organic substitution' portrays new States as a specific mix of the successor State and the continuator State expressed in percentage share, because each of them possesses a part of the territory and population of the predecessor State. It contains an element of legal absurdity, which is, perhaps, best illustrated in the case when, after separation of any part(s) of its territory, the predecessor State continues to exist, both States, the predecessor State and the newly emerged successor State

secession mentioned by Judge Kreća. Indeed, the population of the new State used to be that of the predecessor State; they are the same people. The same goes for the territory of the new State which used to be part of the territory of the predecessor State. In fact, it is difficult to envisage any situation of State succession where such elements of continuity would not exist. A good illustration is the history of the city of Lviv (mentioned in Philippe Sands' fascinating book).[111] The city used to belong to the Austrian-Hungarian Empire until the First World War, when it then became part of the independent State of Poland in 1918, which was followed by Soviet and German occupation during the Second World War. After the War, the city became part of the USSR and finally, in 1991, part of Ukraine. While sovereignty over the city changed four times in less than a hundred years, some of its people (and their families) remained the same, and they continued to live in the same place the whole time. One can hardly deny an element of continuity in that context.

Finally, it should be added that the application of the continuity theory is, however, not self-evident in cases where the efforts of not one, but many rebel groups have led to the creation of a new State.[112] In my book,[113] I noted that it had been suggested by Atlam that in such a case, the new State should be held responsible for obligations arising from the internationally wrongful acts of *all* revolutionary groups and not only for those which eventually became the new government of the new State.[114]

possess identity – the successor State with its predecessor State, whereas the predecessor State, retains its own.

[111] Philippe Sands, *East West Street: On the Origins of 'Genocide' and 'Crimes Against Humanity'* (New York, Weidenfeld Nicolson, 2016).

[112] One example of such a situation is in the context of Angola's independence from Portugal in 1975, where the new State was brought about through the actions of at least three anti-colonial movements: The União Nacional para a Independência Total de Angola (UNITA), Movimento Popular de Libertação de Angola (MPLA) and Frente Nacional de Libertação de Angola (FNLA).

[113] Dumberry, *State Succession to International Responsibility*, p. 246.

[114] Atlam, *Succession d'États*, p. 475, for whom the raison d'être of the continuity of the international legal personality between the new State and the other movements (other than the one now forming the new government) is based on the common goal of their struggle. For Atlam (p. 484–5), these questions simply do not arise in the case where the struggle involves a National Liberation Movement. Thus, since the international legal personality is vested *in the people* and not in the movement itself, it does not make any difference which of the competing groups actually succeeds in creating a new State. In all cases, the new State would be held responsible for the internationally wrongful acts committed by any of the groups which fought for independence.

While the ILC Commentaries are silent on this point, Crawford criticized this position in his subsequent book.[115] He is correct in emphasizing that the new State should *only* be responsible for the acts of the insurgent group(s) with which it has an 'organic' or 'structural' continuity.[116] If the government of the new State is a coalition representing different rebel groups that fought for independence, such continuity may exist between the State and one or several groups. It has been suggested by Eatwell that whether or not there exists any such continuity 'will depend upon the extent to which each group secures a foothold in government'.[117] In any event, it is clear that one should reject the possibility that *none* of the acts committed by these groups be attributable to the new State in the context of a coalition government.[118]

4.2.3.3 The Rule Prevents a Gap in Terms of Responsibility

After having mentioned this idea of continuity (as explained in the previous section), the ILC Commentaries seem to be adding another reason. The Commentaries noted that '[t]he predecessor State will not be responsible for those acts [i.e. acts committed by an insurrectional movement]'[119] and added that '[*t*]*he only possibility* is that the new State be *required* to assume responsibility for conduct committed with a view to its own establishment'.[120] A similar comment (and, most notably, the use of the word 'required') is also found in the ILC Commentaries regarding Article 10(1) of the ILC Articles dealing with the situation where the rebels establish a *new government* (not a new

[115] Crawford, *State Responsibility*, p. 179.

[116] See also: Kolb, *The International Law of State Responsibility*, p. 97: 'if a series of insurrectional movements succeed together in the creation of a new State (e.g. Angola) or seize governmental power (e.g. Libya after 2011), the attribution to the State is made for all the acts of each one of the successful movements'.

[117] On this question, see: Eatwell, *State Responsibility*, p. 191 (making her comment in the context of rebels establishing a new government, not a new State):

> [i]n these circumstances it may be possible to identify real and substantial continuity from the organisational structure of each movement to that of the government. On the other hand, the majority of the new government may be formed out of one dominating insurrectional movement, whilst others may have some representation in the form of one or two representatives. In the latter case, only the majority party would pass the 'real and substantial continuity' test.

See also, p. 208–9.

[118] For the same view: Verhoeven, 'International Responsibility', p. 290.

[119] ILC, Commentaries, 2001, p. 51, para. 6.

[120] Ibid., emphasis added.

State). It should be recalled (as examined above)[121] that under that provision, the conduct *of an insurrectional movement* during the insurgency is attributable to the State (Rule no. 2). In this context, the ILC Commentaries explained that the State was the 'only subject of international law to which responsibility can be attributed' and that such a 'situation *requires* that acts committed during the struggle for power by the apparatus of the insurrectional movement should be attributable to the State, alongside acts of the then established Government'.[122] D'Aspremont rightly noted that Rule no. 2 concerning 'attribution of the acts of the rebels to the State following their triumph undoubtedly was primarily designed to *fill an accountability gap*'.[123]

The same remarks apply to the two above-mentioned sentences used by the ILC Commentaries in the context of Article 10(2). Thus, they suggest that a new State is *required* 'to assume responsibility' precisely *because* the predecessor State will not be responsible for those acts. In other words, if the new State does not assume such responsibility, no other State will. This was noted by Serbia in the *Genocide* case: '[t]he ILC accepted the need for a transfer of attribution, from a movement to a subsequently-emerging State, because this was the only way of avoiding a problematic *gap in the attribution of responsibility*'.[124] Article 10(2) is therefore based not only on the idea of continuity between the movement and the new State, but also on the need to prevent any responsibility gap.[125] As such, it has been qualified as being 'the product of a notion of fairness, justice, and equity'.[126]

It should be added that in the *Genocide* case, Serbia argued that there was 'no "responsibility gap" to be filled, and there [was] therefore no need to apply an exceptional rule such as Article 10, para. 2, that seeks to close such a gap'.[127] For Serbia, Article 10(2) does *not* apply in situations where there is no gap to be filled.[128] Consequently, it mentioned that 'Article 10,

121 See Part I, Section 2.2.

122 ILC, Commentaries, 2001, p. 50, para. 5, emphasis added.

123 d'Aspremont, 'Rebellion and State Responsibility', p. 432, emphasis added.

124 ICJ, *Genocide* case, Serbia, Counter-Memorial, December 2009, para. 354, emphasis added.

125 See also: Eatwell, *State Responsibility,* p. 226: '[t]here should be no gap in the law of responsibility that would allow a new state to avoid responsibility, and therefore the obligation to provide reparation, for internationally wrongful acts committed by its founders'.

126 Ibid.

127 ICJ, *Genocide* case, Serbia, Counter-Memorial, December 2009, para. 359.

128 Ibid., para. 360: '[t]he rationale requiring, in view of the ILC, an exceptional transfer of attribution from a movement to a new State therefore does not apply in the present case'. See also, at para. 361: 'Article 10, para. 2 of the ILC Articles on State Responsibility, provided it forms part of customary law and further provided it matches the facts of

para. 2, does not apply to situations in which a predecessor State is responsible for the alleged acts'.[129] As further examined below (when examining Rule no. 8),[130] the rationale behind the view that Article 10(2) should not apply in such a case is simply that the predecessor State continues to exist after the date of succession and should therefore, quite logically, *remain* responsible for *its own* wrongs committed in the past. However, in the context of State dissolution, the predecessor State does *not* continue to exist. This is a clear case where a 'responsibility gap' exists.[131] While admitting that the break-up of the SFRY was a case of *dissolution* of State, Serbia nevertheless argued that no gap existed in the instant case because the FRY had 'succeeded' to the rights and obligations of the SFRY (the predecessor State).[132] Thus, for Serbia, 'unlike in the scenario envisaged in Article 10, para. 2, at all relevant times, there existed a State for the purposes of State responsibility, and at all relevant times this State could be held responsible for internationally wrongful acts'.[133] In other words, given that the FRY had succeeded to the responsibility of the SFRY, there existed no 'responsibility gap' in that case. As a result, there was no break in the chain of responsibility between the SFRY and the FRY.[134]

Finally, it is noteworthy that nothing prevents a new successor State from freely accepting (after the date of succession) obligations arising from an internationally wrongful act committed by the predecessor State. This possibility is recognized by the Institute in Article 6(3) of its 2015 resolution[135] and by ILC Special Rapporteur

a given case, quod non, might justify the exceptional transfer of attribution in cases where there might otherwise be a gap in responsibility.'

129 Ibid., para. 365, in fine. See also, at p. 123, point (d).

130 See Section 4.3.2.

131 See Section 4.3.3.

132 ICJ, *Genocide* case, Serbia, Counter-Memorial, December 2009, para. 358:

> *First*, unlike in the scenario envisaged in Article 10, para. 2, the Court has to deal with a case of State succession. There existed a predecessor State, the SFRY. There emerged several new successor States, including the FRY/Serbia. As the Court clarified in its judgment of 18 November 2008, on 27 April 1992, the FRY *succeeded* to the rights and obligations of the former SFRY with respect to the Genocide Convention. This is therefore 'essentially a case of succession', which Article 10, para. 2, does not attempt to deal with. (emphasis in the original).

133 Ibid., para. 359.

134 The case is further examined below in Section 4.2.5.3.2.

135 Art. 6(3), IIL, 'State Succession in Matters of State Responsibility', 2015. The question is examined in Kohen and Dumberry, *The Institute of International Law's Resolution*, p. 47 ff.

Šturma.[136] Moreover, the fact that a successor State can decide to succeed to the consequences arising from the commission of an internationally wrongful act by the predecessor State has been recognized by scholars.[137] In previous writing, I have examined several examples of State practice of successor States accepting to take over the consequences of responsibility.[138] Whenever this is the case, there is simply no need to rely on Article 10(2). This is indeed a situation where there exists no 'responsibility gap' that needs to be filed.

4.2.4 *There Is Limited Case Law and State Practice, But It Supports This Principle*

An analysis of State practice and case law (which will be undertaken in the next section) leads to the conclusion that Rule no. 7 embodied in Article 10(2) does not rest on grounds as solid as is often expressed in doctrine. One cannot, therefore, fully agree with the statement made by the ILC Special Rapporteur Crawford that 'the earlier jurisprudence and doctrine, at least, *firmly support* the two rules set out in article 15 [now Article 10]'.[139] As a matter of fact, the ILC Commentaries to the Draft Articles adopted on First Reading by the Commission (in 1996) only mentions a single case of State practice and no judicial decisions.[140] Crawford's First Report on State Responsibility (addendum no. 5), refers to one judicial decision, which is however not relevant in this context (as rightly highlighted by Crawford himself[141]).[142] The rarity of State practice is also apparent in the comprehensive work of Atlam, who considers this

[136] ILC, Second Report Šturma, 2018, Draft Article 4.

[137] Stern, 'Responsabilité internationale et succession d'États', p. 350; P. Šturma, 'State Succession in Respect of International Responsibility,' *George Washington ILR* 48 (2016), p. 669. See also: Dumberry, *State Succession to International Responsibility*, p. 215, referring several writers.

[138] Dumberry, *State Succession to International Responsibility*, p. 215 ff.; Kohen and Dumberry, *The Institute of International Law's Resolution*, p. 48 ff.

[139] ILC, Crawford First Report, 1998, para. 267, emphasis added.

[140] This is the case of the (unsuccessful) struggle of the Confederate Army to secede from the United States during the American Civil War (1861–5). This example is examined in Section 5.1.2.1.

[141] ILC, Crawford First Report, 1998, para. 274.

[142] ILC, 'First Report on State Responsibility (Addendum no. 5)', by James Crawford, Special Rapporteur, 22 July 1998, UN Doc. A/CN.4/490/Add.-17., para. 274, referring to a case decided by the High Court of Namibia: *Minister of Defence, Namibia* v. *Mwandinghi*, in 1992 (2) *SA* 355 p. 359–60, in *ILR* 91, p. 341, at p. 361. However, this case (examined below in Section 4.3.2.2.2) deals with the *different question* of the devolution of acts committed not by the rebels, but *by the predecessor State*.

principle to be well established,[143] but does not mention a single case of judicial decisions or State practice where the rule was referred to, let alone applied.[144]

In fact, as I have noted in previous writing (in 2007),[145] the principle seems to be more of a doctrinal construction than one based on actual State practice.[146] My own investigation in earlier writing has led to the discovery of a number of examples of case law dealing with the issue. As further discussed in the next section, these examples support the principle expressed in Article 10(2) of the ILC Articles.[147]

143 Atlam, *Succession d'États*, p. 422.

144 Atlam, ibid., acknowledging (see at p. 410 ff.) the rarity of State practice in support of the principle. In fact, the only international judicial decision he mentions in support of the principle (*Case Concerning Certain German Interests in Upper-Silesia (Merits)*, Judgment of 25 May 1926, PCIJ, *Serie A*, no. 7) is not relevant. Thus, this case does not deal specifically with the question of succession to responsibility for acts committed by rebels but with the issue of State succession to treaties. Atlam also makes reference (at p. 410, 448–50) to the fact that there is apparently evidence that insurrectional movements (such as the *Front de Libération Nationale* (FLN) of Algeria) had themselves taken the view that the new State, which they wanted to create, should be responsible for their acts committed during their struggle for independence. However, the many references he used from the work of Bedjaoui, *La révolution algérienne et le droit*, do not deal with the acceptance by Algeria of any responsibility for internationally wrongful acts committed by the FLN during the national liberation war prior to independence.

145 See analysis in Dumberry, 'New State Responsibility', p. 612 ff.; Dumberry, *State Succession to International Responsibility*, p. 234.

146 See also: Eatwell, *State Responsibility*, p. 219, noting that 'there is a distinct lack of case law or examples of state practice supporting the existence of the rule provided by Article 10(2)' and that 'The scarcity of judicial precedent and state practice is evident in the ILC Commentary on Article 10', adding that 'no authority is cited in direct support of Article 10(2)'. See also: Verhoeven, 'International Responsibility', p. 287.

147 On the contrary, Eatwell, *State Responsibility*, p. 221, believes that State practice only supports the different *statu nascendi* principle:

> [t]here is support for the principle that a new state should be responsible for the conduct of its organs from the date that state in fact came to exist, rather than from the date of a state's recognition as a state. However, this principle has been expressed in terms of the 'retroactive validation of the legal order' of a state in statu nascendi, rather than in terms of the attribution of conduct of the insurrectional or other movement that succeeded in forming a state to that new state.

See also, p. 228:

> the authorities that appear to support the rule provided by Article 10(2) are at most expressions of the principle that once a new state has been recognised the retroactive validation of its legal order, and of the rights and obligations created by the acts of that state before its recognition, is justified. However, the authorities only support retroactive validation to

In a recent book I have published with Professor Kohen, which examines the Resolution adopted by the Institute in 2015, we also noted that while the principle expressed in Article 10(2) is certainly necessary and justified in contemporary international law, it remains that an analysis of State practice shows that it does not rest on grounds as solid as it is often believed in doctrine. The Final Report by Rapporteur Kohen also mentioned that 'the ILC position is based on a logical inference rather than on established practice' and that 'the relevant case law only referred to situations of an insurrectional movement becoming the government of the State or cases of State succession in which the person concerned had acquired the nationality of the same State having caused the injury, not cases of secession or decolonisation'.[148] ILC Special Rapporteur Šturma also noted the limited practice.[149] The same assessment was made by Judge Kreća in his separate opinion in the 2015 *Genocide* case. He noted that the explanation given in the ILC Commentaries to the effect that 'more recent decisions and practice do not, on the whole, give any reason to doubt the propositions contained in Article 10'[150] is, according to him, a characterization which 'is, in terms of law, wishful thinking rather than a respectable argument'.[151] It seems that Crawford may have taken into account these remarks when he wrote, in his subsequent book, that while 'the rule stated within Article 10(2) is again relatively uncontroversial', it remains that 'state and judicial practice is relatively sparse'.[152]

In this context, the question arises as to whether or not Article 10(2) can be considered as a customary rule. In the *Genocide* case,[153] Serbia argued

> the date the new state was proclaimed or established in fact, not the date at which the movement whose struggles led to the formation of that state came into being.

[148] IIL, 'Final Report', 2015, para. 82, referring to examples cited in ILC, Commentaries, 2001, p. 51, paras. 12–14. The question is also examined in Crawford, *The Creation of States in International Law*, p. 658–64. See also, Kohen and Dumberry, *The Institute of International Law's Resolution*, p. 109.

[149] ILC, Second Report Šturma, 2018, para. 116: '[h]owever, the Institute of International Law in its travaux préparatoires of 2015 and some authors point to a relative scarcity of practice'.

[150] ILC, Commentaries, 2001, p. 51, para. 14.

[151] ICJ, *Genocide* case, 2015, Separate Opinion of Judge Kreća, paras. 66.2, 67 ff. (referring to: Dumberry, *State Succession to International Responsibility*). He cites one recent study conducted to provide 'a portrayal of the impact and influence' of the ILC articles since their adoption in 2001 which came to the conclusion that 'there appears to have been no international judicial reference to Article 10' (referring to: Simon Olleson, 'The Impact of the ILC's Articles on Responsibility of States for Internationally Wrongful Acts; Preliminary Draft', *British IICL* (2007), p. 95).

[152] Crawford, *State Responsibility*, p. 176, referring to Dumberry, 'New State Responsibility'.

[153] The case is further examined below in Section 4.2.5.3.2.

that the rule 'does not reflect customary international law'.[154] Specifically, it argued that 'the content of Article 10, para. 2, of the ILC Articles on State Responsibility did not, as of 1992, represent customary international law'.[155] The argument is essentially based on the lack of State practice necessary for any customary rule to crystallize.[156] Croatia acknowledged that it was 'true that much of the practice relates to insurrectional governments rather than movements to create a new State', but added that the ILC 'was clear that there were good reasons to cover both situations',[157] and that 'Government comments . . . were generally favourable as well, and in the end Article 10 proved uncontroversial.'[158] Croatia did not directly address the issue of whether or not the rule should be considered as custom. It simply argued that it should apply because it was supported by State practice and doctrine.[159] In its oral pleadings, Croatia mentioned that 'the rule has been recognized in the literature since at least the early twentieth century',[160] and that Serbia did not 'identify a single commentator who can provide support for the assertion that it is a new rule'.[161]

In my view, Serbia is right to point out that examples of State practice are rare. In this context, the rule contained in Article 10(2) can hardly be considered as a rule of custom.[162] In its 2008 preliminary objections judgment in the *Genocide* case, the Court used the following expression: '[i]n so far as Article 10, paragraph 2, of the ILC Articles on State Responsibility reflects customary international law on the subject'.[163]

[154] ICJ, *Genocide* case, Serbia, Counter-Memorial, December 2009, para. 284, point (a), para. 286. See also: ibid., Serbia, Rejoinder, November 2011, paras. 161 ff.

[155] Ibid., Serbia, Rejoinder, para. 161 ff.

[156] ICJ, *Genocide* case, Serbia, Counter-Memorial, December 2009, paras. 289–93.

[157] Ibid., Croatia, Reply, vol. 1, 20 December 2010, para. 7.54.

[158] Ibid., para. 7.55.

[159] Ibid., para. 7.57: 'The Respondent relies on a single academic article [my article published in the EJIL], focusing on 19th century authority, to counteract this substantial and consistent record. It is submitted that the ILC's conclusions on Article 10, supported by contemporary and subsequent responses of States and by the preponderance of modern practice and doctrine, should stand.'

[160] Ibid., Verbatim Record, 6 March 2014, CR 2014/10, Crawford (Croatia), para. 20, referring to several authorities.

[161] Ibid.

[162] For the same position: Gillich, 'Between Light and Shadow', p. 131; Eatwell, *State Responsibility*, p. 226 ('The limited examples of case law and state practice supporting the existence of Article 10(2) lead one to suspect that had the ICJ considered the question whether Article 10(2) is an expression of customary international law, it is likely that the Court would have answered the question in the negative'). *Contra*: Mantilla Blanco, *Full Protection and Security*, p. 227.

[163] ICJ, *Genocide* case, Preliminary Objections, ICJ Rep. 2008, p. 459, paras. 126–7.

Serbia correctly stated that 'the court's cautious choice of words is telling and, this caution was justified'.[164] The wording suggests that the Court considered Article 10(2) not to be a rule of custom. As further explained below,[165] in its 2015 decision on the merits, the Court did not have to take a stance on the customary nature of Article 10(2).[166] Yet, the wording used again suggests that it was not convinced at all about the customary status of Article 10(2).[167]

Finally, it should be added that the fact that the rule contained in Article 10(2) is not customary law does not mean that it simply *cannot be applied* by the Court. Perhaps surprisingly, this is precisely what has been asserted by Serbia.[168] In my view, the Court can apply the rule contained in Article 10(2) even if it is not considered to be a rule of custom nor a general principle of law. In any event, as mentioned above, the rule is logical and sound as a matter of policy. One has to agree with Crawford (counsel for Croatia) in his statement that 'Serbia argued that State practice on Article 10 (2) is sparse, as if sparseness in itself could justify the Court in departing from the principle', adding that 'Yet Serbia has still not pointed to any authority credibly denying the existence of the principle.'[169] To the best of my knowledge, no one is denying the existence of Rule no. 7, even if State practice supporting it is not as solid as one could have expected.[170]

164 Ibid., Serbia, Counter-Memorial, December 2009, para. 288.

165 See Section 4.2.5.3.2.

166 ICJ, *Genocide* case, 2015, para. 105:

> Article 10 (2) cannot, therefore, serve to bring the dispute regarding those acts within the scope of Article IX of the Convention. That conclusion makes it unnecessary for the Court to consider whether Article 10 (2) expresses a principle that formed part of customary international law in 1991–1992 (or, indeed, at any time thereafter), or whether, if it did so, the conditions for its application are satisfied in the present case.

167 Ibid., para. 104: 'even if Article 10 (2) of the ILC Articles on State Responsibility could be regarded as declaratory of customary international law at the relevant time'.

168 Ibid., Serbia, Counter-Memorial, December 2009, para. 293:

> [i]t is therefore submitted that said rule does not reflect international custom. Also, there is no evidence that this rule is a general principle of law. Accordingly, it cannot be applied by the Court in the resolution of the present dispute. Finally, it should be emphasized that, as a matter of principle, the onus is on Croatia to demonstrate that the rule contained in Article 10, para.2, reflects an international custom binding on the Respondent.

169 Ibid., Verbatim Record, 21 March 2014, CR 2014/21, Crawford (Croatia), para. 52.

170 Eatwell, *State Responsibility*, p. 229, has argued that there is no State practice supporting Article 10(2) and that, consequently, 'as much as it is desirable that a new State should be international responsible for the conduct of the insurrectional or other movement whose agitations led to that state's formation, it is questionable whether Article 10(2) can

State practice and case law will be examined separately in the following sections for each type of State succession. I will refer to a number of examples already mentioned in my 2007 book,[171] as well as those reported in Crawford's recent book[172] and in the Second Report by ILC Special Rapporteur Šturma.[173] I will also analyse a number of new cases, including a detailed analysis of the parties' arguments and the judges' reasoning in the 2015 *Genocide* case (which was rendered after my book was published). I will show in the following sections that case law and State practice generally support Rule no. 7.

4.2.5 *The Application of Rule No. 7 to Different Types of Succession of States*

The question examined in this section is whether Rule no. 7 should find application for all types of State succession.[174] Before addressing this question, a few words should be said about the classification of different types of succession of States and their definition. I have adopted elsewhere a typology of six types of State succession[175] which can be grouped in two broad categories based on the consequences that an event may have on the existence of the predecessor State(s).

First, there are cases where the predecessor State will *cease* to exist following the events affecting its territorial integrity. When it is the case, three different scenarios must be differentiated:

- Unification of States, whereby at least two States will cease to exist and will merge to form a new State;
- Dissolution of a State, whereby the extinction of the predecessor State results in the creation of many new States on its original territory; and

operate as a rule of attribution of conduct'. Yet, she does not go as far as to dismiss altogether the existence and relevance of Rule no. 7, which she considers to be fair and just (Ibid., p. 226 ff.). She believes that it 'is better to regard Article 10(2) as a rule of attribution of responsibility and not a rule of attribution of conduct'.

171 Dumberry, *State Succession to International Responsibility*, p. 234 ff.

172 Crawford, *State Responsibility*, p. 176–7.

173 ILC, Second Report Šturma, 2018, paras. 116 ff.

174 It should be added that this is a question which has, perhaps surprisingly, never been systematically addressed by scholars. I have very briefly mentioned the issue in Dumberry, *State Succession to International Responsibility*, p. 246–9.

175 Ibid., p. 61 ff.; Dumberry, *A Guide to State Succession in International Investment Law*, p. 25 ff.

- Incorporation (or 'integration', 'absorption') of a State, whereby the extinction of the predecessor State results not in the creation of a new State but in the enlargement of the territory of another existing State.

Second, in other cases the predecessor State will *continue* to exist following the events affecting its territorial integrity. Three different scenarios must also be differentiated in such cases:

- Separation (or secession), whereby a new State will emerge from the break-up of an already existing State which will nevertheless continue its existence after the loss of part of its territory;
- Newly Independent States, involving the same pattern as separation, but (and this is important) in the specific context of decolonization; and
- Cession or transfer of territory from one existing State to another existing State, whereby the events affecting the territorial integrity of the predecessor State results not in its extinction, nor in the creation of a new State, but rather in the enlargement of the territory of another existing State.

ILC Special Rapporteur Šturma mentioned that the rule set out in Article 10(2) of the ILC Articles 'is fully applicable to *certain* categories of succession, namely secession and creation of a newly independent State'.[176] The emphasis on the word 'certain' and the express mention of two types of succession shows that Šturma considers that Rule no. 7 does *not* apply to other types of succession.[177] The ILC Commentaries on the 2001 Articles also indicate that Article 10(2) does not cover a 'situation where an insurrectional movement within a territory succeeds in its agitation for *union with another State*'.[178] This comment suggests that the provision would not find application in the context of incorporation of State, unification of States and in situations of transfer of territory from one State to another. A few passages in the ILC 1975 Report also suggests that the provision only applies to cases of secession and Newly Independent States.[179]

[176] ILC, Second Report Šturma, 2018, para. 108, emphasis in the original.

[177] See also, this comment, ibid., para. 76: 'the rule seems to be relevant only to certain (and not all) situations of succession, namely separation of parts of a State (secession) and creation of newly independent States'.

[178] ILC, Commentaries, 2001, p. 51, para. 10, emphasis added.

[179] ILC, Report, 1975, p. 105, para. 22, indicating that this provision 'concerns the case of the formation of a new State by means of secession or decolonization'. See also, p. 100, para. 1.

In the following sections, I will examine whether or not Article 10(2) should apply to different types of State succession. Most importantly, I will focus on the likely consequences of *not* applying the provision in these situations. Finally, I will discuss whether any alternative solution could be contemplated in these cases.

4.2.5.1 Secession

The events affecting the territorial integrity of the predecessor State may sometimes result in the creation of a *new State* (or even more than one new States). The predecessor State (often described as the 'continuing' or 'continuator'[180] State) will continue its existence after losing a part of its territory. Recent cases of secession include those of Montenegro (2006) and South Sudan (2009). There is some controversy as to the proper terminology that should be used to make reference to this phenomenon and whether the term 'separation' should be used instead of 'secession'.[181] For example, the work of the ILC used the term 'separation'.[182] Yet, for some writers, the term 'secession' should be reserved more specifically to describe instances where the removal of one part of the territory is made *without the consent* of the predecessor State.[183] As the examples examined in this section involve rebels fighting

[180] ICJ, *Application of the Convention on the Prevention and Punishment of the Crime of Genocide (Bosnia and Herzegovina v. Serbia and Montenegro)*, Judgment 26 February 2007, ICJ Rep. 2007, using that term, paras. 71, 75, 80, 81, 106, 130, 131.

[181] Some writers use the term 'separation' in the context of a unitary State and 'secession' for federal States. For instance: Jacques Brossard and Daniel Turp, *L'accession à la souveraineté et le cas du Québec* (2nd ed., Montreal, PUM, 1995), p. 94; Daniel Turp, *Le droit de choisir: Essais sur le droit du Québec à disposer de lui-même/ The Right to Choose: Essays on Québec's Right of Self-Determination* (Montreal, Thémis, 2001), p. 22.

[182] Both the *1978 Vienna Convention on Succession of States in Respect of Treaties*, UN Doc. ST/LEG/SER.E/10, in *ILM* 17 (1978), p. 1488 (in Article 34) and the *1983 Vienna Convention on Succession of States in Respect of State Property, Archives and Debts*, in *ILM* 22 (1983), p. 306 (not yet entered into force) (Article 17) use the term 'separation'. This is also the case of the ILC, 'Draft Articles on Nationality of Natural Persons in Relation to the Succession of States', adopted by the ILC on second reading in 1999, ILC Report, UN Doc. A/54/10, 1999, chp. IV, annexed to UN GA Resolution 55/153, 12 December 2000, *ILC Yearbook* vol. II(2) (1999), p. 13. See, however, ILC, Second Report Šturma, 2018, paras. 78 ff., using both expressions at Draft Article 7.

[183] See: Marcelo G. Kohen, 'Le problème des frontières en cas de dissolution et de séparation d'États: quelles alternatives?', in Olivier Corten, Barbara Delcourt, Pierre Klein and Nicolas Levrat (eds.), *Démembrement d'États et délimitations territoriales: L'uti possidetis en question(s)* (Brussels, Bruylant, 1999), p. 368–9; Marcelo G. Kohen, 'Introduction', in Marcelo G. Kohen (ed.), *Secession: International Law Perspectives* (Cambridge University Press, 2006), p. 2–3; Crawford, *The Creation of States in International Law*, p. 247; James Crawford, 'State Practice and International Law in Relation to Secession',

against the predecessor State for independence, I will therefore use the term 'secession'.

In the following sections, I will first examine the rationale for applying Rule no. 7 in the context of secession, which will be followed by an analysis of State practice and case law.

4.2.5.1.1 The Rationale for Applying Rule No. 7 The principle established in Article 10(2) (Rule no. 7) seems perfectly applicable to cases of secession. The new State should be held 'responsible' for the consequences of obligations arising from internationally wrongful acts committed by the secessionist rebels against third States or foreign investors. This is indeed the position adopted by scholars.[184] The ILC 1975 Report leaves no doubt as to the application of Article 10(2) (then Article 15(2)) to situations arising from secession.[185] Accordingly, the continuing State should *not* be held accountable for the internationally wrongful acts committed by successful secessionist rebels.[186] Any other solution would be unjust. Thus, why should the continuing State be held liable for wrongs committed by another entity whose successful armed struggle

British YIL (1998), p. 85. Similarly, D. P. O'Connell, *State Succession in Municipal Law and International Law* (Cambridge University Press, vol. II, 1967), p. 88, speaks of 'revolutionary secession' and 'evolutionary secession'.

[184] ILC, Second Report Šturma, 2018, para. 108; Crawford, *The Creation of States in International Law*, p. 656 (referring to 'the well established rule that a seceding State will be held internationally responsible for acts performed by it in the process of its formation'). See also, Silvanie, 'Responsibility of States for Acts of Insurgent Governments', p. 89:

> [i]n the case of a secession no question arises as to the liability of the old state for the acts and contracts of the successfully seceding government. The problem is one chiefly of state succession and not of succession of governments. A seceding government does not pretend to act in the name and on behalf of the old state; its acts and contracts are normally intended to bind the new state. In such a case the sole question is: How far is the new state bound by the acts and contracts of insurgents who created it?

[185] ILC, Report, 1975, p. 100, para. 1. See also, para. 6:

> [Article 15(2)] should therefore be understood that the questions of attribution contemplated in the present article arise solely in the case where the insurrectional movement, having triumphed, has substituted its structures for those of the previous government of the State in question, or in the case where the structures of the insurrectional movement have become those of a new State, constituted *by secession* or decolonization in part of the territory which was previously subject to the sovereignty or administration of the pre-existing State. (emphasis added).

[186] ILC, Commentaries, 2001, p. 51, para. 6.

ultimately led to the dismemberment of its territorial integrity and the loss of part of its territory? After all, the State that continues to exist is the first 'victim' of a successful secession by the rebels. It would therefore clearly be unfair if that State had to pay for the rebels' wrongs.

4.2.5.1.2 State Practice and Case Law Support That Principle In this section, I will examine a number of examples of State practice and case law which occurred in the context of secession. While a number of them are clearly not the strongest precedents, they generally support Rule no. 7.

The first example concerns the *unsuccessful* struggle of the Confederate Army for the secession of the Southern States from the United States during the American Civil War (1861–5). Several examples arising from this important event will be examined below.[187] One relevant example (for the purpose of the present discussion) is a legal opinion given by the Law Officers of the British Crown during the War (on 16 February 1863).[188] The Opinion of Phillimore stated that if the rebels were to *succeed* in their secession efforts, the new State would be held 'responsible' for its acts committed before independence: 'In the event of the war having ceased, and the authority of the Confederate State being *de jure* as well as *de facto* established, it will be competent to Her Majesty's Government to urge the payment of a compensation for the losses inflicted on Her Majesty's subjects by the Confederate Authorities during the War.' This is obviously not the strongest element of State practice given the hypothetical nature of the point of law discussed in the legal opinion. Thus, as noted by Serbia in the *Genocide* case, the example 'dealt with a hypothetical situation in which the confederate insurgents would succeed, and stated that compensation for the losses inflicted to British subjects by the insurgents during the war could be claimed if the Confederate States were *de jure* and *de facto* established'.[189] Yet, the example nevertheless shows the writer's belief about the state of the law at the time.

A few years later, in 1877 (after the War), the US Supreme Court endorsed Rule no. 7. In the *Williams* v. *Bruffy* case, the Court mentioned that had the Confederacy Army succeeded in their struggle and had been

[187] See Section 5.1.2.1.

[188] Legal Opinion of the Law Officers of the British Crown, 16 February 1863, in Lord McNair, *International Law Opinions* (Cambridge University Press, vol. II, 1956), p. 257. This example is reported in ILC, Report, 1975, p. 103, para. 12, and also discussed in Crawford, *State Responsibility*, p. 176–7.

[189] ICJ, *Genocide* case, Serbia, Counter-Memorial, December 2009, para. 290.

'recognized' by other States, 'its acts from the commencement of its existence' would have been 'upheld as those of an independent nation'. The US Supreme Court referred to the successful rebellion of the United States seceding from Great Britain as an example supporting Rule no. 7.[190] One passage indicates that if an attempt at secession is successful and its claim to statehood is recognized by other States, that new State should be held responsible for the acts committed starting from its *declaration of independence.* Eatwell refers to the example as one supporting the 'retroactive validation of the legal order of a State *in statu nascendi*', that is, 'the principle that a new state should be responsible for the conduct of its organs from the date that state in fact came to exist, rather than from the date of a state's recognition as a state'.[191] This is an important point. The *Williams* v. *Bruffy* case does not say anything about the fate of the acts which were committed by rebels during the insurgency but *before* any formal declaration of independence was made. The judgement does not stipulate that such acts committed by the insurgents should be attributable to the new State.[192] The case is therefore not the strongest precedent in support of Rule no. 7.

[190] *Williams* v. *Bruffy*, 96 US 176, 186 (1877):

> The other kind of *de facto* government . . . is such as exists where a portion of the inhabitants of a country have separated themselves from the parent State and established an independent government. The validity of its acts, both against the parent State and its citizens or subjects, depends entirely upon its ultimate success. If it fails to establish itself permanently, all such acts perish with it. If it succeeds and becomes recognized, *its acts from the commencement of its existence are upheld as those of an independent nation.* Such was the case of the state governments under the old confederation on their separation from the British Crown. Having made good their *declaration of independence*, everything they [i.e., the American insurgents] did *from that date* was as valid as if their independence had been at once acknowledged. Confiscations, therefore, of enemy's property made by them [i.e., the American insurgents] were sustained as if made by an independent nation. But if they had failed in securing their independence, and the authority of the King [of Great Britain] had been re-established in this country, no one would contend that their acts against him, or his loyal subjects, could have been upheld as resting upon any legal foundation. No case has been cited in argument, and we think none can be found, in which the acts of a portion of a State unsuccessfully attempting to establish a separate revolutionary government have been sustained as a matter of legal right. (emphasis added).

[191] Eatwell, *State Responsibility*, p. 221.

[192] Ibid., p. 224.

Second, a number of cases arose in the context of the secession of Mexico from Spain in 1821. These claims were decided by the claims commissions established by the United States and Mexico between 1839 and 1849. Silvanie examined these awards which were rendered 'in favor of certain persons, citizens of the United States, who had furnished money and various military supplies to the leaders of the revolutionary government in Mexico while it was engaged in its revolt against Spain and before its independence had been recognized by any foreign Power'.[193] In other words, the claims involved contracts signed during the insurgency between US nationals and the rebels.[194] According to Silvanie, these claims all involved US nationals who had 'furnished goods and military supplies for "the promotion of the general object" of the independence and self-government of Mexico and by express contract with agents duly appointed and sent by the leaders of the Mexican revolution to the United States to procure aid, with a promise that all obligations contracted by such agents should be ratified by the revolutionary government'.[195] These awards held that the new State was responsible for the contracts entered into by the rebels.[196] The Mexican Commissioner agreed with such findings. In fact, this outcome was not

[193] Silvanie, 'Responsibility of States for Acts of Insurgent Governments', p. 89.

[194] Ibid. He summarized these claims as follows:

> The Commission of 1839 rendered awards in the Hunter case for gunpowder purchased from an American citizen by an authorized agent of the so-called independent government in Mexico in 1816; in the Duncan case for 'moneys, vessels, and munitions of war' furnished by an American citizen to 'diverse Mexican patriots engaged in the years 1815, 1816, and 1817 in the struggle of Mexico against Spain for the independence and self-government of the former'; in the Oliver case for arms, vessels, munitions of war, goods, and money furnished by citizens of the United States to General Mina for the use of Mexico in the years 1816 and 1817; in the Hepburn and Welman case for the equipment and sale of a ship to General Mina in 1817; in the Tenant case for military supplies furnished to a Mexican schooner in 1817; and in the Wheeler and Murray case for the sale of muskets in 1816 to General Victoria, an agent of the insurgent government in Mexico. Similarly, the Commission of 1849 rendered awards in the Cox and Elkins case for supplies furnished and moneys advanced to General Herrera, an agent of the Mexican insurgents; and in the Meade case for expenses incurred and 'for commissions charged by Meade for receiving and delivering to the Mexican Government certain vessels of war which were fitted out in the United States for that government about 1825'.

[195] Ibid., p. 90, citing: J.B. Moore, *History and Digest of the International Arbitrations to which the United States Has Been a Party* (Washington, GPO, vol. 4, 1898), at p. 3427.

[196] The awards are examined in Moore, ibid., p. 3426–7, 3427, 3427–8, 3430–2.

surprising given that Mexico after its independence 'recognized and sanctioned the acts of these agents and assumed liability for their contracts'.[197] These cases therefore support Rule no. 7 whereby the acts of rebels (including signing contracts with foreigners) made during an insurgency are attributable to the new State once the rebellion has been successfully completed.

Third, a few cases were decided by the US–Venezuela Claims Commission of 1885 in the context of the independence of Venezuela from Spain which took place in 1821.[198] The *Idler* case involved an American citizen who had furnished large quantities of arms and army stores to authorized agents of Simon Bolivar's revolutionaries in 1817, during Venezuela's war of independence against Spain. The Commission ruled in favour of the Claimant.[199] Silvanie considered this case as an application of the 'principle that a new state is bound by acts and contracts of insurgents who succeed in establishing its independence'.[200]

Fourth, the *Socony Vacuum* case involved the *failed attempt* by rebels during the Second World War to create a new independent State in Croatia and secede from Yugoslavia.[201] After the War, the United States set up a domestic tribunal (the International Claims Commission) to deal with claims of US nationals, including those arising from events which took place in Yugoslavia during the War.[202] The *Socony* case concerns the taking of property belonging to the Claimant (a US company) by the puppet 'independent' State of Croatia during the War. The Claimant requested a payment of US$ 11.325 million by Yugoslavia on the grounds that the latter should be held responsible for the internationally wrongful acts committed by the 'independent' State of Croatia. The Commission clearly indicated that Yugoslavia should *not* be held responsible for the internationally wrongful acts committed by an *unsuccessful* insurrectional

[197] Silvanie, ibid., p. 90. See also, the conclusion reached by the Commission in the *Parrott* case and the *Cox and Elkins* case, cited in Moore, *History and Digest of the International Arbitrations* (vol. IV), at p. 3429–30.

[198] Moore, ibid., p. 3491–544.

[199] Silvanie, 'Responsibility of States for Acts of Insurgent Governments', p. 90.

[200] Ibid.

[201] *Socony Vacuum Oil Company*, US International Claims Commission, in *Settlements of Claims* (1949–55), p. 77; *ILR* (1954), p. 55.

[202] On 19 July 1948, the United States and Yugoslavia entered into an agreement for the settlement of claims of nationals of the United States against Yugoslavia for taking of property and other measures of confiscation which occurred during and after the Second World War (i.e. from 1 September 1939 to the date of the agreement). Yugoslavia paid the amount of US$ 17 million to the United States which established the International Claims Commission to adjudicate the claims of US nationals.

movement (the 'independent' State of Croatia). This case will be examined later when assessing Rule no. 9.[203] What is relevant for the present discussion is the reference made by the Claims Commission, in one *obiter dictum*, to the *successful* secession of the United States from the British Crown in 1776. The Commission indicated that in such a case of a successful attempt to create a new State, that State was responsible for the acts of the rebels. The Commission quoted, in approval, the above-mentioned passage from the US Supreme Court in the *Williams* v. *Bruffy* case.[204] Yet, as noted above, the *Williams* v. *Bruffy* case is silent on the fate of acts committed by rebels *before* any formal declaration of independence. It does not stipulate that such acts committed by the insurgents should be attributable to the new State.[205]

Fifth, the case of *Irish Free State* v. *Guaranty Safe Deposit Co.* involved the creation of the new State of Ireland. In 1916 an uprising against the British government took place and was suppressed. A few years later, in 1918, the Republican Party (Sinn Fein) was successful in getting its candidates elected to the British Parliament, but instead decided to constitute its own parliament (the Dail Eireann) and declared in 1919 the independence of Ireland (the 'Irish Republic' or 'Republic of Ireland'). Although the question is controversial,[206] the Party never quite succeeded at establishing a de facto government and the new State was not recognized by any foreign government. At the time, the republican 'government' authorized loans from sympathizers of

[203] See Section 5.1.2.2.

[204] As noted by Crawford, *State Responsibility*, p. 177, the Commission misattributed this quote to Moore, *Digest of International Law* (vol. I), p. 44, instead of to the *Williams* v. *Bruffy* case decided by the US Supreme Court.

[205] Eatwell, *State Responsibility*, p. 224.

[206] On this question, see Charles Keith Uren, 'The Succession of the Irish Free State', *Michigan LR* 28(2) (1929), p. 149–62, p. 158:

> [t]he facts probably are that the Dail Eireann never did have complete *de facto* control over all of Ireland. Even the Irish court before whom no doubt the best evidence of the true state of affairs could be presented nowhere says that the Dail had established a *de facto* government completely. On the other hand it did achieve some status as the governing body of Ireland. The Dail was a National Assembly even though it may have been 'on the run'. It did maintain armed resistance to the *de jure* government quite embarrassing to the latter. The facts that it had no school system, nor railroad control, nor stamps, nor post offices, nor currency, even that it raised no taxes, are no more than evidence of the character of the organization and are by no means conclusive on its status. The Dail did put the British local boards out of control, it did appoint consular officers, and carried out in all the outward forms a regular governmental machinery.

independence in the United States.[207] Some of the money was used by the republican 'government', but part of it was left in a New York bank account. A few years later, in 1921–2, an agreement was finally reached between the separatists and the United Kingdom for the establishment of the 'Irish Free State' (on the territory of today's Ireland, without Northern Ireland which remains part of the United Kingdom), having a Dominion status with the British Empire.

The government of the new State filed a claim before a New York Court to recover the rest of the money which had been collected by the republicans (some US$ 2.5 million). It argued that it was entitled to the funds as the 'successor' to the de facto republican 'government' (the so-called 'Republic of Ireland') which had raised the money in favour of independence. The New York Court rejected the claim. It concluded that 'the so-called Irish Republic never existed as a *de facto* government' and that it was 'simply an organization fostering a rebellion or revolt against the British government in Ireland'.[208] It held that the new State (the Irish Free State) actually succeeded to the predecessor de jure government of the United Kingdom in Ireland. It did not succeed to the 'Irish Republic', which was considered as an unsuccessful rebel movement.[209] This conclusion has been praised by some[210] and contested by others.[211]

Even though the judgment does not use these words, it is clear that the decision was based on the fact that there was no structural *continuity*

[207] See Edwin D. Dickinson, 'The Case of the Irish Republic's Funds', *AJIL* 21(4) (1927), p. 747–53.

[208] *Irish Free State* v. *Guaranty Safe Deposit Co.*, 215 N.Y.S. 255 (1927). It should be noted that an Irish Court (1926 Irish Rep. 531, 574) had come to the opposite conclusion that the Irish Free State was the successor to the de facto revolutionary government and that it was therefore entitled to the property of that government.

[209] Ibid., p. 182, 194, 188. The Court stated: '[a]s the Dail Eireann did not succeed in establishing a *de facto* government. It follows, therefore, that the Irish Free State succeeded to the only government in existence in Ireland at the time it came into being, to wit, the *de jure* government of Great Britain'.

[210] Dickinson, 'The Case of the Irish Republic's Funds'; J.W. Garner, 'A Question of State Succession,' *AJIL* 21(4) (1927).

[211] Uren, 'The Succession of the Irish Free State', p. 159:

> [i]t was not, therefore, the impaired *de jure* [British] government alone to which the Irish Free State succeeded, but it succeeded also by agreement of the Dail itself to the revolutionary organization and whatever status *de facto* it may have possessed. The nearest approach to the actual facts seems to be that it succeeded to both the *de jure* and the revolutionary governments, both of which were exercising a divided *de facto* control over the territory.

between the republican 'rebels' (who had not succeeded in creating a new State, the so-called 'Irish Republic', to which the money belonged), and the new State (Irish Free State) that subsequently emerged in 1921–2.[212] Thus, the Court considered that the new State had *not* been created as a direct result of the successful struggle of the rebels. While not everyone will agree with the findings of the Court on this specific point, this case is nevertheless relevant to the present discussion. It shows that in order for Rule no. 7 to apply in the context of secession there should be no gap in the chain of continuity between the armed struggle by the rebels and the creation of the new State.

4.2.5.2 Newly Independent States

There is another type of succession of States that is similar to cases of secession insofar as the events affecting the territorial integrity of the predecessor State results in the creation of a new State while the predecessor State continues to exist. This is the case of the creation of 'Newly Independent States' in the context of decolonization. It is generally admitted that the territory of a colony should not be considered as a part of the territory of the colonial State administrating it.[213] In this regard, a Newly Independent State is a new State that cannot be said to have 'seceded' from the colonial power to the extent that its territory was never formally a part of it.[214] There is some controversy in doctrine as to whether Newly Independent States should be considered as a distinct type of succession of States.[215] Supporters of the distinction rely on the specific circumstances

[212] As Garner, 'A Question of State Succession', p. 755, noted in a comment about the case:

> The government which was finally established in 1922 was not that of the Independent Republic of Ireland for which the funds were raised, but a totally different government, that of the Irish Free State; it was set up by the British Government with the consent of the people of Southern Ireland, and it was the successor, not of the Dail organization of the so-called Irish Republic, but of the government established in Ireland under the Act of 1800, as modified by the Government of Ireland Act of 1920. How, [the judge] asked, can a new government be said to have succeeded an unsuccessful revolt against the existing government or a rebellious organization which never became a *de facto* government.

[213] Declaration of Principles of International Law Concerning Friendly Relations and Co-Operation Among States in Accordance with the Charter of the United Nations, adopted by GA Res. 2625 (XXV), 24 October 1970.

[214] Zidane Meriboute, *La codification de la succession d'États aux traités: décolonisation, sécession, unification* (Paris, PUF, 1984), p. 174.

[215] Some writers do not view this type as a distinct category: Degan, 'Création et disparition de l'État', p. 298–9. See also: *Restatement (Third), Foreign Relations Law of the United*

of decolonization and on the fact that different rules of State succession apply to these States in order for them to freely exercise their right to self-determination and to break the vicious circle of economic domination.[216] The work of the ILC on State succession has recognized the specificity of this category.[217] Both Vienna Conventions on matters of State succession have thus adopted different rules applicable to Newly Independent States to adequately manage this distinction.[218] However, the ILC Draft Articles on nationality in relation to State Succession did not.[219] The recent work of the Institute on State succession also adopted a specific regime for Newly Independent States in the context of decolonization.[220] In his Final Report, Rapporteur Kohen explained several reasons why he considered it 'indispensable' to include Newly Independent States as a specific category of State succession of its own.[221] ILC Special Rapporteur Šturma has also adopted the same position.[222]

States (Vol. I, St. Paul, American Law Institute Publ., 1987), § 210, Reporters' notes no. 4 (at p. 113).

216 See, for instance, the position held by Yilma Makonnen, 'State Succession in Africa: Selected Problems', *Rec. des cours* 200 (1986-V), p. 130–1, for whom 'the guiding principles governing the consequences of State succession are the complete elimination of "colonialism" in all form and manifestation and creating the conditions for the realization of the right to self-determination by the newly independent States'. See also, Mohammed Bedjaoui, 'Problèmes récents de succession d'États dans les États nouveaux', *Rec. des cours* 130 (1970-II), p. 468–9, 530.

217 This is discussed in Meriboute, *La codification de la succession d'États aux traités*, p. 29–30, 49, 56, 63.

218 Thus, Article 16 of the *Vienna Convention on Succession of States in Respect of Treaties* indicates that treaties entered into by the predecessor State are not binding on a Newly Independent State, while other new States emerging from a dissolution of State or separation/secession are bound by such treaties (Article 34). Similarly, Article 38 of the *Vienna Convention on Succession of States in Respect of State Property, Archives and Debts* indicates that, in principle, and without any agreement to the contrary, debts of the predecessor State do not pass to the Newly Independent State. A different regime applies to cases of unification of States (where debts pass to the successor State, Article 39) and cases of separation and dissolution of State (where an 'equitable share' of the predecessor State's debts pass to the new State(s), Articles 40 and 41).

219 'Draft Articles on Nationality of Natural Persons', p. 41, paras. 1, 3 (dealing with Article 26). The Commentary to the Articles recognizes the theoretical distinction between Newly Independent States and 'separation of part or parts of the territory' (i.e. secession). However, it also indicates that the 'substantive rules' established for cases of secession (i.e. Articles 24 to 26) would be applicable mutatis mutandis to any remaining cases of decolonization in the future. Therefore, no separate section was included in the Draft Articles to deal specifically with Newly Independent States.

220 IIL, 'State Succession in Matters of State Responsibility', 2015, Article 16.

221 Institute of International Law, 'Final Report', 2015, p. 12.

222 ILC, Second Report Šturma, 2018.

In the following sections, I will first examine the rationale for applying Rule no. 7, which will be followed by an analysis of State practice and case law.

4.2.5.2.1 The Rationale for Applying Rule No. 7 The principle established in Article 10(2) is clearly applicable to Newly Independent States. In its 2001 Commentaries the ILC mentioned that 'the expression "or in a territory under its administration" is included in order to take account of the differing legal status of different dependent territories'.[223] Such wording was clearly meant to cover national liberation movements in the context of decolonization.[224] The expression was indeed introduced in the 1975 draft 'in order to take into account of the legal status of dependent territories'.[225] Thus, the Report noted that 'it is now incorrect to describe' dependent territories 'as the "territory of a State"'.[226]

The fact that Article 10(2) covers Newly Independent States is also clear from its use of the words 'movement, insurrectional or other'.[227] The words 'or other' were added by the Drafting Committee; they were not present in the earlier draft until the 2001 final version.[228] The Drafting Committee explained that it 'felt that the concept of "insurrectional movement" might be too restrictive, as there was a greater variety of movements whose action might result in the formation of a new State'.[229] The word 'other' was meant to include National Liberation Movements struggling in

223 ILC, Commentaries, 2001, p. 51, para. 8.

224 The same position has been adopted by ILC, Second Report Šturma, 2018, para. 131: '[t]he broad term of an insurrectional or other movement clearly encompasses the case of liberation movements too'. See also: Eatwell, *State Responsibility*, p. 215 ff.; Verhoeven, 'International Responsibility', p. 293.

225 ILC, Report, 1975, p. 105–6, para. 22. See also, p. 100, para. 1:

> [Article 15(2)] should therefore be understood that the questions of attribution contemplated in the present article arise solely in the case where the insurrectional movement, having triumphed, has substituted its structures for those of the previous government of the State in question, or in the case where the structures of the insurrectional movement have become those of a new State, constituted by secession *or decolonization in part of the territory which was previously subject to the sovereignty or administration of the pre-existing State.* (emphasis added).

226 Ibid., p. 99, para. 29.

227 Cahin, 'Attribution of Conduct to the State', p. 252.

228 For a detailed analysis of the origin of the words 'or other', see: ICJ, *Genocide* case, Verbatim Record, 11 March 2014, CR 2014/14, 21, Tams (Serbia), paras. 70 ff.

229 International Law Commission, 'Summary Records of the Meetings of the Fiftieth Session 20 April–12 June 1998 27 July–14 August 1998', UN Doc. A/CN.4/SER.A/ 1998, *ILC Yearbook* vol. I (1998), p. 287, at p. 290, para. 88, adding that 'It had thus

the particular context of decolonization. The ILC thus rejected the distinction between National Liberation Movements and other movements in the context of this provision.[230]

The ILC 1975 Report goes further and indicates that 'it would be extremely dangerous to introduce' the concept of 'legitimacy'.[231] Crawford is clear on that point in his subsequent writing: 'Article 10 treats all insurrections generally and makes no attempt to distinguish between a struggle for national liberation on the one hand and a simple rebellion on the other.'[232] This is because, in the words of the ILC, it was 'not the Commission's business to establish when an insurrectional movement was or was not legitimate, or when, how, or with respect to whom, it acquired international personality'.[233] Crawford has subsequently made the same observation that 'no distinction should be made' under Article 10 'between different categories of insurrectional movements on the basis of any international "legitimacy" or any illegality in respect of their establishment of government'.[234] This

been decided to use the phrase "movement, insurrectional or other" to indicate that the intention was to cover ejusdem generis movements.'

230 ILC, Report, 1975, p. 105, at para. 20: '[t]he Commission considered that no distinction should be made, for the purposes of this article, between different categories of insurrectional movements on the basis of any international "legitimacy" or any illegality in respect of their establishment as the government, despite the possible importance of such distinctions in other contexts'. The same comments were made in ILC, Commentaries, 2001, p. 51, para. 11: '[f]rom the standpoint of the formulation of rules of law governing State responsibility, it is unnecessary and undesirable to exonerate a new government or a new State from responsibility for the conduct of its personnel by reference to considerations of legitimacy or illegitimacy of its origin'.

231 ILC, Report, 1975, p. 105, para. 20.

232 Crawford, *State Responsibility*, p. 172. See also: Meriam Al-Rashid, Ulyana Bardyn and Levon Golendukhin, 'Investment Claims amid Civil Unrest: Questions of Attribution and Responsibility,' *BCDR Int. Arb. Rev.* 3(2) (2016), p. 190: 'the legitimacy of a *de facto* government under international law is not determinative of that government's ability to create binding obligations for the nation'.

233 Crawford, *State Responsibility*, p. 173, quoting from the work of the ILC in *ILC Yearbook* I (1975), p. 60. See also: ILC, Report, 1975, p. 91, para. 7:

> In formulating . . . the present article, the Commission . . . is not required to say anything about the various forms which insurrection may take according to whether there is a relatively limited internal struggle, a genuine civil war situation, an anti-colonial struggle, the action of a national liberation front, revolutionary or counter-revolutionary movement and so on, or about the questions which may arise in connexion with the problem of the international legitimacy of some of these forms.

234 Crawford, *State Responsibility*, p. 172.

position has been praised by many[235] and endorsed by ILC Special Rapporteur Šturma.[236]

The assimilation of the two concepts has been criticized in doctrine,[237] as well as by several members of the Commission.[238] It was also contested by some States on the grounds that this assimilation would not take into account the legitimacy of the struggle for independence of National Liberation Movements.[239] It was suggested by some States that a new State resulting from the struggle of a National Liberation Movement *should not* be held accountable for the internationally wrongful acts committed by the Movement against third States.[240] Others have argued that the specific situation of national liberation movements in the context of decolonization is *not* covered by Article 10 and that the regime of responsibility applicable is that of the laws of war.[241] While Atlam generally supports the principle of attribution set out under Article 10(2), he is also critical of assimilating the specific situation of national liberation movements with other instances of insurgents in terms of responsibility.[242]

235 Cahin, 'Attribution of Conduct to the State', p. 252.

236 ILC, Second Report Šturma, 2018, para. 108: '[i]t is important to stress that article 10 treats all insurrections generally and makes no attempt to distinguish between a struggle for national liberation on the one hand and a simple rebellion on the other'.

237 Atlam, *Succession d'États*, p. 258, 419–21. See also: Atlam, 'National Liberation Movements and International Responsibility', p. 55.

238 ILC, 'Report of the International Law Commission on the Work of its Twenty-Seventh Session', 5 May to 25 July 1975, Discussion in Plenary: 1303rd to 1317th meetings (6 to 27 May 1975), and 1345th meeting (7 July 1975), ILC Report, A/10010/Rev.1 (A/30/10), 1975, chp. II, paras. 9–52, in *ILC Yearbook* vol. I (1975), p. 3–72, 213–20. See the comments by: Mohamed Bedjaoui (ibid., p. 48–9), Taslim Olawale Elias (ibid., p. 50, at para. 30), Paul Reuter (ibid., p. 45–6, 58), Nikolai A. Ushakov (ibid., p. 47, para. 7; p. 64, para. 20; p. 70, para. 26), and Abdul Hakim Tabibi (ibid., p. 59, para. 34).

239 See the discussion held during the Sixth Committee of the General Assembly in 1975 on the ILC's Report: 'Documents officiels de l'Assemblée générale des Nations unies, 30e session, sixième Commission. Questions juridiques'. See the full reference in Dumberry, *State Succession to International Responsibility*, p. 247–8.

240 See the discussion held during the Sixth Committee of the General Assembly in 1975 on the ILC's Report, ibid, and Dumberry, ibid. A balanced position is taken by Atlam, 'National Liberation Movements and International Responsibility', p. 49.

241 Dallier *et al.*, *Droit international public*, p. 870–1.

242 Atlam, *Succession d'États*, p. 419 ff., p. 425; Atlam, 'National Liberation Movements and International Responsibility', p. 55:

> the international responsibility of liberation movements is not and cannot be the same as the international responsibility of insurrectional movement' because of the legitimacy of the cause that the former are pursuing and the legality of their fight for self-determination.

In my view, the principle established in Article 10(2) should apply to Newly Independent States in the same way as for cases of secession. The colonial continuing State should *not* be 'responsible' for internationally wrongful acts committed by successful rebels in their efforts to establish a new State in the context of decolonization. The same position is adopted by the Institute.[243] Article 16(3) of the Resolution adopted by the Institute provides that the conduct of a national liberation movement, representing the people entitled to self-determination, which succeeds in establishing a Newly Independent State will be considered as an act of that State under international law.[244] The solution is supported by scholars,[245] and has recently been adopted by ILC Special Rapporteur Šturma.[246]

4.2.5.2.2 The Principle Has Been Applied by French Municipal Court Decisions in the Context of the Independence of Algeria Rule no. 7 was applied in the context of the independence of Algeria in 1962.[247] This is a case where there was a 'structural' continuity between the rebel group (the FLN) and the new government which took office upon independence.

He has argued that 'certain actions may constitute the violation of an international obligation when committed by an insurrectional movement, yet may be lawful when committed by national liberation movement' (ibid., p. 425). He is of the view that the ILC 'minimized the impact of the international legality of national liberation movements' in dealing with insurrectional movements 'on an equal footing' (ibid.). He noted that national liberation movements have an international legal personality as a result of the 'international legality of their struggle and in their specific effectiveness' (ibid.). In terms of responsibility towards *third* States (i.e. not the colonial power) affected by acts committed by national liberation movements, he distinguished the military operations from the non-military activities. In his view, the new State should not be held responsible for *military* operations carried out by the movement in its struggle for self-determination which injured a third State (see Atlam, 'National Liberation Movements and International Responsibility', p. 49).

243 On this question, see: Kohen and Dumberry, *The Institute of International Law's Resolution*, p. 128 ff.

244 IIL, 'State Succession in Matters of State Responsibility', 2015, Article 16(3) reads as follows: '[t]he conduct, prior to the date of succession of States, of a national liberation movement which succeeds in establishing a newly independent State shall be considered the act of the new State under international law'.

245 Dumberry, *State Succession to International Responsibility*, p. 171–2, 247, referring to a long list of writers.

246 ILC, Second Report Šturma, 2018, paras. 108, 115. See: Draft Article 8(3).

247 See analysis in Dumberry, *State Succession to International Responsibility*, p. 235 ff. Even Eatwell, *State Responsibility*, p. 220–1, who believes that State practice does not support the principle set out in Article 10(2) admits that this example provides 'some limited support for the rule'.

In his pleading in the *Genocide* case, Crawford (counsel for Croatia) referred to this example as one of a few illustrations of Rule no. 7 whereby the acts committed by the rebels during the insurgency are attributable to the new State.[248] For him, this is an example of 'the *statu nascendi* rule' which is a 'necessary construction dealing with the fact that States do not come into existence in situations of belligerency at a single moment in time'.[249]

French municipal courts applied Article 18 of the *Déclaration de principes relative à la cooperation économique et financière* by holding that France should remain responsible for the internationally wrongful acts *it had* committed before the independence of Algeria.[250] However, they took a different position regarding the acts committed *by the FLN*, the national liberation movement. French courts have consistently held that the new State of Algeria should in principle provide compensation to French nationals victims of internationally wrongful acts committed by the *FLN* in its war efforts to achieve independence.[251] This is an example where the acts were committed by the insurrectional movement *against the predecessor State* and its nationals (and not against a third State).[252] In any event, as Algeria was not a party in any of the proceedings before these French municipal courts, these court decisions did not formally hold Algeria responsible for the obligations arising from internationally wrongful acts committed by the FLN. These decisions simply held that France could not be responsible for such acts, which only 'concerned' ('intéressent') Algeria.

4.2.5.3 Dissolution of State

The extinction of the predecessor State may result in the creation of many new States on its original territory. This is the case of the dissolution of a State. Classic examples of State dissolution are those of Czechoslovakia and Yugoslavia. In the next sections, I will first examine the rationale behind the application of Rule no. 7, which will be followed by an analysis of State practice and case law.

248 ICJ, *Genocide* case, Verbatim Record, 21 March 2014, CR 2014/21, 21, Crawford (Croatia), para. 53.

249 Ibid., para. 54.

250 This question is further examined below, in Section 4.3.2.2.1.

251 See Dumberry, *State Succession to International Responsibility*, p. 236–7, examining several cases, including: *Perriquet*, Conseil d'État, case no. 119737, 15 March 1995, in *Recueil Lebon*; *Hespel*, Conseil d'État, 2/6 SSR, case no. 11092, 5 December 1980, in *Tables du Recueil Lebon*.

252 As mentioned above, these acts are generally considered as 'war damages' between the predecessor State and the successor State.

4.2.5.3.1 The Rationale for Applying Rule No. 7 As mentioned above, ILC Special Rapporteur Šturma has made it clear that Article 10(2) was 'fully applicable to *certain* categories of succession, namely secession and creation of a newly independent State'.[253] He did not mention anything about dissolution of State. ILC Draft Article 11, dealing with dissolution of State, does not refer to the conduct of rebels as a ground for succession to responsibility (unlike Draft Articles 7(4) and 8(3) which specifically refers to such conduct in the different context of secession and Newly Independent States).[254] This omission suggests that ILC Special Rapporteur Šturma does not consider that cases of dissolution are covered by Article 10(2).

The ILC Commentaries are silent on the matter. The remark mentioned above indicating that Article 10(2) does not cover a 'situation where an insurrectional movement within a territory succeeds in its agitation for union with another State'[255] is not relevant in the context of dissolution. Thus, dissolution involves a situation where there is an extinction of the predecessor State and the creation of *several new States* on its original territory. The ILC Commentaries also indicate that Article 10(2) 'focuses on the continuity of the movement concerned and the eventual new Government or State, as the case may be'.[256] This remark does not seem to prevent the application of Article 10(2) in the specific context of dissolution.[257] One can indeed foresee a scenario where the break-up of a State (and its dissolution) is the result of the successful struggle of *several* insurrectional movements, each fighting at the same time for the creation of *their own* States. The example of the dissolution of Yugoslavia (further discussed in the next paragraphs) is a good illustration of that situation. In this context, there may be a structural and organizational continuity between *each* rebel group and the respective new States they have created. Another possible scenario is the struggle of *only one* insurrectional movement which becomes ultimately successful at creating its own State, which in turn, leads to the subsequent disintegration of the rest of the State from which the new State is detached.[258] In

253 ILC, Second Report Šturma, 2018, para. 108, emphasis in the original.
254 Ibid.
255 ILC, Commentaries, 2001, p. 51, para. 10.
256 Ibid.
257 For the same view, Verhoeven, 'International Responsibility', p. 292.
258 This is a scenario which could potentially occur in Iraq in the future. Thus, the military actions of Kurdish insurgents in Iraq may eventually be successful and lead to the secession of Iraqi Kurdistan. If this happens, it is far from certain that the rest of Iraq, which has been plagued with sectarian violence for years, will remain united. It may very

sum, there seems to be no theoretical obstacle preventing the application of Article 10(2) to cases of dissolution.[259]

One reason why Article 10(2) should apply to cases of dissolution is to prevent any potential situation resulting in a 'responsibility gap'.[260] The point can be explained by reference to the *Genocide* case (which will be fully examined in the next section). Serbia argued that Article 10(2) 'does not apply to situations in which the responsibility of the predecessor State can be established'.[261] This is because in such a case, the predecessor State remains responsible for the wrongs it has itself committed. As mentioned above, this is indeed the case when the predecessor State *continues to exist* after the date of succession. Serbia further explained the rationale behind Article 10(2) as follows:

> The ILC accepted the need for a transfer of attribution, from a movement to a subsequently-emerging State, because this was the only way of avoiding a problematic gap in the attribution of responsibility. Hence the ILC noted that, '[t]he predecessor State will not be responsible for those acts [i.e. acts committed by an insurrectional movement]'. As a consequence, '[t]he only possibility is that the new State be required to assume responsibility for conduct committed with a view to its own establishment'.[262]

Serbia argued that there was in the present case, 'no "responsibility gap" to be filled, and there is therefore no need to apply an exceptional rule such as Article 10, para. 2, that seeks to close such a gap'.[263] Thus, 'unlike

well be that the Sunni and Shia populations will each create their own State and that Iraq, as a sovereign State, will simply disappear. Another (very much fictional and unlikely) scenario could involve the successful insurrection of a rebel group in Catalonia which would lead to the creation of a new independent State of Catalonia. The secession of such an important region could potentially lead (but this is very unlikely) to the total collapse of Spain with several other autonomous regions becoming independent States (Galicia, Andalusia, Basque country, etc.). This could potentially be an example where the insurrection of *only one* rebel group could eventually result in a dissolution of State and the emergence of *several* new States.

259 See also: Eatwell, *State Responsibility*, p. 216: 'it is arguable that Article 10(2) would apply to the dissolution of a state that results in the creation of a number of new states on the territory of the predecessor state, and the extinction of the latter'.

260 IIL, 'Final Report', 2015, p. 534, indicating that one of the most fundamental goals guiding the Resolution adopted by the Institute was to 'prevent situations of State succession from leading to an avoidance of the consequences of internationally wrongful acts, particularly in the form of the extinction or disappearance of the obligation to repair, by virtue of the mere fact of the State succession'.

261 ICJ, *Genocide* case, Serbia, Counter-Memorial, December 2009, para. 351.

262 Ibid., para. 354.

263 Ibid., para. 359.

in the scenario envisaged in Article 10, para. 2, at all relevant times, there existed a State for the purposes of State responsibility, and at all relevant times this State could be held responsible for internationally wrongful acts'.[264] Serbia's argument is that the SFRY is in fact that predecessor State.[265] In its Rejoinder, Serbia clarified its position, according to which it believed that: 'in the case at hand where the SFRY still existed until its dissolution in April 1992 and where the relevant acts (such as the alleged acts of genocide Croatia claims have been committed by JNA units) are attributable to the predecessor State, such required responsibility gap does not exist'.[266] It is true that there was no 'responsibility gap' *before* the dissolution of State. At that time, the SFRY (as the predecessor State) was indeed responsible for its own acts. The question, however, is what happens *after* the date of dissolution of the SFRY (in April 1992)? At that date, the predecessor State (SFRY) no longer existed. Serbia argued that on 27 April 1992, the FRY took over any responsibility from the former SFRY with respect to the Genocide Convention.[267] Given that this was 'essentially a case of succession', Serbia added that 'Article 10, para. 2, does not attempt to deal with' such case.[268] Thus, since the FRY *succeeded* to the obligations of the former SFRY, there was no 'responsibility gap' *after* the dissolution. In other words, Serbia's argument was that Article 10(2) did not apply in this case because there was simply no 'responsibility gap' (either before or after the dissolution).

The situation is entirely different in the event where *none* of the successor States decide to take over the obligations arising from the commission of wrongful acts by the rebels. This is a case where there is indeed a 'responsibility gap'. In fact, there is such a gap if Article 10(2) does *not* apply to cases of dissolution. Thus, an internationally wrongful act committed by rebels during the insurgency would simply remain unpunished. The injured State or the foreign investor victim of such an act would be left without any debtor against whom it can file a claim for reparation. This is an outcome that can certainly be considered unfair for the victims of a wrongful act. In my view, this is the reason why Rule no. 7

264 Ibid., para. 359.

265 Ibid., para. 358: '[t]here existed a predecessor State, the SFRY. There emerged several new successor States, including the FRY/Serbia'.

266 Ibid., para. 186.

267 Ibid., para. 358: '[a]s the Court clarified in its judgment of 18 November 2008, on 27 April 1992, the FRY *succeeded* to the rights and obligations of the former SFRY with respect to the Genocide Convention', emphasis in the original.

268 Ibid., para. 358.

should apply: the acts committed by the rebels during the insurgency are attributable to the new State. In the context of dissolution, the only remaining question is *which one* of the many successor States should be responsible for the acts of the rebels?

The answer should be based on the existence of a relationship of *continuity* between the insurrectional movement that committed the wrong and *one* new State. As further discussed in the next section, this is indeed the main argument that was developed by Croatia in the *Genocide* case. For reasons explained below, the Court did not address the argument raised by Croatia about Article 10(2). Yet, what is also noticeable is that the Court did not reject the possibility of applying Article 10(2) in the context of dissolution.

In this context, the solution adopted by the Institute's Resolution on State succession to responsibility could be used *by analogy*. Article 15 applies to cases of dissolution in general (i.e. not involving insurrectional movements per se).[269] Under that provision, the obligations arising from an internationally wrongful act committed by the predecessor State against another State (or a foreign investor) are transferred to one successor State when the author of the act was an *organ* of the predecessor State that later became an organ of that new State.[270] One example would be the wrongful act committed by the authorities of a province, a federated State or an autonomous region which later becomes an independent State. The same general approach has been adopted by the ILC Special Rapporteur Šturma.[271] In fact, this argument about 'organ' continuity was invoked by Croatia in the *Genocide* case as a second 'alternative' argument.[272]

4.2.5.3.2 The 2015 *Genocide* Case (*Croatia* v. *Serbia*) In the *Genocide* case, Article 10(2) of the ILC Articles was expressly brought up by Croatia.[273] Before examining two of the arguments developed by the parties, as well as the reasoning of the Court, a few words should be said about the turbulent history marking the end of Yugoslavia.

[269] IIL, 'State Succession in Matters of State Responsibility', 2015, Article 15.

[270] See analysis in Kohen and Dumberry, *The Institute of International Law's Resolution*, p. 126 ff.

[271] ILC, Second Report Šturma, 2018, paras. 147, 167, 185, 188. See Draft Article 11.

[272] See Kohen and Dumberry, *The Institute of International Law's Resolution*, p. 127, referring to the *Genocide* case as one example of the concrete application of Article 15 in cases of dissolution.

[273] ICJ, *Genocide* case, 2015, p. 51–3, paras. 82, 102. The example is examined in ILC, Second Report Šturma, 2018, para. 119.

As a result of the different declarations of independence by Croatia, Slovenia, Macedonia, and Bosnia and Herzegovina in 1991–2, what remained of the former Socialist Federal Republic of Yugoslavia (SFRY) were the two former republics of Serbia and Montenegro. In April 1992, both republics reorganized the old federation in the form of the smaller two-member federation now called the 'Federal Republic of Yugoslavia' (FRY). The new Constitution proclaimed it to be the 'continuator' of the former SFRY.[274] This claim of continuity was however rejected by other States and even the FRY ultimately abandoned this position (in 2000). On 14 March 2002, Serbia and Montenegro once again reorganized their constitutional framework with the creation of the 'State Union of Serbia and Montenegro'.[275] In accordance with the Constitution, a referendum on independence was held in Montenegro on 21 May 2006. On 3 June 2006, the National Assembly of Montenegro made a formal declaration of independence.[276] The independence of the new State was soon recognized by several members of the international community, including Serbia, and on 28 June 2006 Montenegro was admitted to the United Nations.[277] Kosovo also made a unilateral declaration of independence in 2009 and its claim to statehood has been recognized by many States. Finally, it should be added that at the time of the proceedings on the merits in the *Genocide* case, all parties agreed to consider the break-up of the SFRY as an example of dissolution of State.

4.2.5.3.2.1 The Arguments of the Parties This section will focus on the main arguments put forward by the parties at the merits stage of the proceedings in relation to Article 10(2).

4.2.5.3.2.1.1 Croatia's Description of the Emergence of the FRY As a State *in Statu Nascendi*

Croatia explained that 'the process of dissolution of the SFRY and the emergence of the constituent Republics which were eventually

[274] Declaration on the Formation of the Federal Republic of Yugoslavia, joint session of the Yugoslavia Assembly, the National Assembly of the Republic of Serbia and the Assembly of the Republic of Montenegro, 27 April 1992, annexed to UN Doc S/23877, 5 May 1992. See also, Letter of the interim Chargé d'Affaires at the Permanent Mission of Yugoslavia at the United Nations to the UN Secretary-General, 6 May 1993, UN Doc. A/46/915, 7 May 1992.

[275] Agreement on Principles of Relations Between Serbia and Montenegro within the Framework of a Union of States, signed in Belgrade on 14 March 2002 (see in particular Articles 1.2, 1.5 and 5.1).

[276] Decision on Proclamation of Independence of the Republic of Montenegro, Article 1.

[277] UN SC Res 1691 (2006); GA Res A/60/264 (2006).

recognised as new states occurred contemporaneously'.[278] As a result, 'the newly emergent states in the former SFRY assumed responsibility, in respect of the conduct of their organs and officials and of others under their direction and control, in the period from spring 1991 to April 1992'.[279] During that time, the newly emergent States (including the FRY) assumed responsibility for the application of the Genocide Convention.

Croatia considered that in the period between the start of the break-up of the SFRY (spring 1991) and the official proclamation of the FRY as a State (27 April 1992), the FRY emerged as a State *in statu nascendi.* It argued that the acts carried out by the officials and organs of the emerging State of the FRY (taking place *before* 27 April 1992) should be attributable to the FRY.[280] For Croatia, 'the principle that a state *in statu nascendi* is responsible for conduct carried out by its officials and organs or otherwise under its direction and control is well-established, and is recognised in Article 10(2)'.[281] The relevance of this concept in the present context has been contested by writers.[282]

[278] ICJ, *Genocide* case, Croatia, Memorial, 1 March 2001, para. 8.43.

[279] Ibid., para. 8.44.

[280] Ibid., para. 8.40, stating that the fact that the FRY 'only formally proclaimed itself on 27 April 1992 does not mean that acts occurring prior to that date cannot be attributed to it'.

[281] Ibid., para. 8.42, referring to I. Brownlie, *Principles of Public International Law* (5th ed., Oxford, Clarendon Press, 1998), p. 77–8. In its Written Statement (29 April 2003, p. 18, point (i)), Croatia further explained that it is 'well established that a State may be responsible for conduct prior to the establishment of the State' and explained the rationale behind this principle (ibid., para. 3.24).

[282] It has been noted by Eatwell, *State Responsibility*, p. 224, that the concept of a State *in statu nascendi* deals with a 'retroactive validation' of the legal status of an entity once statehood is achieved through recognition. This is relevant for acts committed by that entity *after* a formal declaration of independence and *before* its claim to statehood has been recognized. As such, the concept of a State *in statu nascendi* does not seem to be directly related to the question of attribution of acts of insurgents that are committed during a rebellion *before* the establishment of a new State. It appears that Crawford, *The Creation of States in International Law*, p. 659, has adopted a different approach. Thus, in a section of his book dealing with the concept of a State *in statu nascendi* he stated that it is 'well established that legal rights and liabilities of successful insurgent governments continue to bind the State so formed', and that 'the rule was affirmed as one of attribution by the ILC in Article 10 (…)'. On this specific point, Eatwell, ibid., p. 224, stated: 'however, Crawford apparently misinterprets Article 10(2) ARS' since 'the doctrine of retroactive validation of a legal order of a recognised state is different from the attribution of conduct of the insurrectional or other movement, before it succeeded in forming a new state in fact, to that state'.

In Croatia's view, the proclamation of April 1992 formally creating the FRY 'did not create a State out of thin air', it only 'formalised a set of social, economic and political arrangement which were, at that time, already largely in place'.[283] Thus, the proclamation simply 'formalised a preexistent situation'[284] 'which had arisen with the dissolution of the SFRY, namely the emergence of FRY (comprising the Republics of Serbia and Montenegro) as a State *in statu nascendi*, under the control of President Milošević and the rest of the Serbian leadership'.[285] For Croatia, 'international responsibility could be engaged and attributable to the FRY' before 27 April 1992, starting from the 'moment at which the organs of what was later become the FRY had cemented their separate existence from the rest of the SFRY'.[286] Croatia emphasized on the existence of 'sufficient continuity in terms of personnel and organization between the movement itself and the subsequent government'[287] and the existence of a 'factual connection between the movement and the subsequent formation of a new State'.[288]

283 ICJ, *Genocide* case, Croatia, Written Statement, 29 April 2003, para. 3.25.
284 Ibid., para. 3.25.
285 Ibid., Croatia, Memorial, 1 March 2001, para. 8.40. Croatia explained that 'from October 1991, the relevant organs of government and other federal authorities of the SFRY ceased to function as such and became *de facto* organs and authorities of the emerging FRY acting under the direct control of the Serbian leadership, embodied in particular in the President of Serbia but extending also to relevant officials in Ministries of Defence and Interior' (Ibid., para. 8.40). Moreover, before April 1992, the so-called 'Serbian leadership' also 'controlled the relevant political apparatus and the military, in the form of the JNA and the Serb paramilitary groups' (ibid., para. 8.40: 'the JNA ceased to be the army of the SFRY and became, initially, a *de facto* organ of the emerging FRY (comprised of the Republics of Serbia and Montenegro) taking instructions directly from, and acting in the service of, the Serbian leadership').
286 Ibid., Croatia, Written Statement, 29 April 2003, para. 3.25.
287 Ibid., paras. 3.36, 3.37.
288 Ibid., para. 3.38. See also, para. 3.40, referring to the 'considerable *de facto* continuity in personnel and policies between a number of significant organs of the SFRY once they had fallen into the hands of the Serbian leadership and those of the FRY following its formal creation in April 1992'. See also: ibid., Croatia, Memorial, 1 March 2001, para. 8.45:

> [m]oreover, by virtue of its insistence (at the time and until the year 2000) on its constitutional and political continuity with the former SFRY, the FRY explicitly recognised the links between the former SFRY's state administration and officials of the Socialist Republic of Serbia and Socialist Republic of Montenegro. These were the same people, carrying out the same policies, policies which, it has been shown, were genocidal in character.

4.2.5.3.2.1.2 Serbia's Argument That Article 10(2) Does Not Apply Because the Instant Case Did Not Involve a Movement Struggling to Create a New State

Serbia's main argument[289] was that 'the context' of Article 10(2) was 'completely different from the pattern of events that led to the creation of the FRY'.[290] Serbia and Montenegro 'did not want to secede' and create a new State.[291] In any event, the instant case did not involve any 'movement' that was actually 'successful' in establishing a *new State*.[292] The fact patterns of the events leading to the total dissolution of the SFRY actually support this position. Thus, when the Republic of Serbia and the Republic of Montenegro proclaimed the formation of the FRY on 27 April 1992, the declaration mentioned expressly that the FRY was '*continuing* the State, international legal and political personality' of the SFRY and that it would 'strictly abide by all the commitments that the [SFRY] assumed internationally'.[293] The Constitution of the FRY, which was adopted on 27 April 1992, also referred in its preamble to the '*unbroken continuity* of Yugoslavia'.[294] Therefore, the specific situation of the FRY does not seem to fit well within the scope of application of Article 10. The following paragraphs examine different aspects of Serbia's main argument.

The first point raised by Serbia was regarding the existence of a 'movement'. Croatia focused on the application of Article 10(2) to 'any movement', regardless of whether it can be considered as 'insurrectional' or not.[295] For Serbia, the identity of that 'movement' was rather

[289] Ibid., Serbia, Counter-Memorial, December 2009, paras. 295 ff.

[290] Ibid., FRY, Preliminary Objection, September 2002, p. 96, para. 4.8.

[291] Ibid. See also, para. 4.12: '[t]he independence of a State which would have encompassed the present territory of the FRY was neither the stated goal nor the secret aim of any of the participants of the conflict. The creation of the FRY was not on the banner of any "insurrectional or other" movement; there was no party to the conflict which would have adopted this objective'.

[292] Ibid., Serbia, Counter-Memorial, December 2009, para. 311, quoting Croatia indicating that 'the Serbian nationalist movement ultimately succeeded in establishing the FRY' and making the following statement: '[h]owever, this "success" does not correspond to any stated or hidden aim or purpose. Indeed, there was no need to have an "insurrection or other movement" in order to establish the FRY as a State, since no one opposed this'.

[293] UN Doc. A/46/915, emphasis added.

[294] The document is mentioned in ICJ, *Genocide* case, Croatia, Memorial, 1 March 2001, para. 2.139, emphasis added.

[295] Ibid., para. 8.33. Serbia noted (Ibid., Serbia, Rejoinder, November 2011, para. 168) that 'even if one were to agree that the term "movement" ought to be broadly construed it must, at the very least, possess *some* contours and structures since otherwise ... any action by a group of *private* individuals could be attributable under Article 10, para. 2, to the State to be created which certainly is not the case', emphasis added.

'unclear', 'elusive and unspecified'.[296] The second and most important point raised by Serbia was that 'there was no movement during the Yugoslav crisis (insurrectional or similar), which endeavoured to establish a new state on the territory of the FRY'.[297] Thus, there was no movement 'which aimed at, and succeeded in, establishing the FRY'.[298]

Serbia referred to the ILC 2001 Commentary,[299] and rightly noted that in order for Article 10 to apply, any such a movement would have to be in 'continuing struggle with the constituted authority'.[300] Thus, 'an essential characteristic of the movements that fall within the scope of Article 10, para. 2 is that they exist and operate *outside* and *against* the established structure of the State on whose territory they seek to establish a new State'.[301] Citing Ago's 1972 Report, Serbia emphasized that it has to be shown that the movement was 'working against the territorial State'.[302]

[296] Ibid., Serbia, Counter-Memorial, December 2009, para. 299. Croatia described the nature of that 'movement' as follows: '[t]he ICTY found in Martić that from at least August 1991, the Serbian leadership had a common political objective to unite Serb areas in Croatia and Bosnia-Herzegovina with Serbia in order to establish a unified Serb State' (ibid., Verbatim Record, 6 March 2014, CR 2014/10, Crawford (Croatia), para. 21).

[297] Ibid., FRY, Preliminary Objections, September 2002, p. 96, para. 4.8. See also, at para. 4.9, and in ibid., Serbia, Counter-Memorial, para. 298.

[298] Ibid., Serbia, Counter-Memorial, December 2009, para. 300. See also: ibid., Serbia, Rejoinder, November 2011, paras. 169–70:

> In the case at hand this means that the alleged 'Serbian movement' must have *aimed at* either the separation of the FRY from the SFRY or at the dissolution of the SFRY. Yet, as the Respondent has already demonstrated, if ever there was such a movement, *quod non*, its political aim was not to provide for the dissolution of the SFRY or to create a rump State consisting of Serbia and Montenegro only, but rather to preserve the overall predecessor State, i.e. the SFRY in which, obviously, all Serbs could continue to live together in one single State. (emphasis in the original).

See also, at para. 171:

> [c]ontrary to all plausibility and publicly available facts, Croatia indeed claims that it was not Slovenia, Croatia (and later Bosnia and Herzegovina and finally Macedonia) that seceded from the SFRY aiming at the dissolution of the SFRY leaving the rump territory (consisting of Serbia and Montenegro) with no other choice but to create the FRY, but rather that it was the aim of the alleged 'Serbian movement' to expel the other constituent republics of the SFRY so as to be able to create the FRY (and later Serbia proper).

[299] ILC, Commentaries, 2001, p. 50, para. 2.

[300] ICJ, *Genocide* case, Serbia, Counter-Memorial, December 2009, para. 301.

[301] Ibid., para. 303, emphasis in the original.

[302] Ibid., Verbatim Record, 11 March 2014, CR 2014/14, 21, Tams (Serbia), para. 76.

Croatia had a hard time responding to this argument during the proceedings.[303] While this point remains controversial,[304] in my view, Serbia was correct in outlining that the specific circumstances related to this case did 'not fall within' the scope of Article 10(2).[305]

Serbia argued that 'clearly, there was no movement that acted outside the framework of the predecessor State (i.e. the SFRY) that resulted in the creation of the FRY'.[306] Thus, 'the "movement" in question was in fact in control of the established authority (i.e. the SFRY) rather than in a struggle with it, and in control of the JNA rather than challenging it'.[307] On this point, Croatia responded that while 'those responsible for the conduct of Serbia's

303 Ibid., Verbatim Record, 6 March 2014, CR 2014/10, p. 42, Crawford (Croatia), para. 23:

> Serbia turns to the ILC's comment that Article 10 (2) does not 'encompass the actions of a group of citizens advocating separation or revolution where these are carried out within the framework of the predecessor state'. But that formula was simply intended to exclude instances of constitutional advocacy, within the predecessor State, for change. The reference to 'revolution' – a reference in a comment about what Article 10 (2) excludes – from that reference Serbia manufactures a requirement that the movement must constitute a 'revolutionary force'. It even puts the phrase 'revolutionary force' in quotation marks, although without any citation. Similarly, it quotes a reference by the ILC to movements in a 'continuing struggle with the constituted structure'190. But, again, this is totally out of context: the ILC here is distinguishing such movements generally from the circumstances covered by Article 10 – including the circumstances covered here by Article 10 (2).

304 See the position of Eatwell, *State Responsibility*, p. 214:

> [i]t would not be desirable for a political authority such as that led by President Milosevic to escape the reach of Article 10(2) simply because it managed to subsume the organs of the predecessor state by political machination. The underlying purpose of Article 10(2) is to ensure that responsibility for violations of international law committed by the organs or agents of a movement is not evaded merely because that movement has transformed into the organisation of a new state and therefore the movement as such no longer exists. In order to ensure responsibility, the definition of 'other movement' for the purposes of Article 10(2) should be broad, and not restricted so as to exclude movements that achieve control over the organs of the predecessor state through political means if that movement, through those organs, commits violations of international law before the formal establishment of the new state.

Yet, it should be pointed out (as mentioned above) that in that case, Serbia (as a new State) had in fact *succeeded* to the obligations (including wrongful acts) of the former SFRY. There was therefore no responsibility 'gap' resulting from the non-application of Article 10(2).

305 ICJ, *Genocide* case, Serbia, Counter-Memorial, December 2009, para. 318.

306 Ibid., para. 304.

307 Ibid., para. 302. Thus, the JNA 'was an organ of the SFRY and acted in that capacity during the relevant period'; it was 'neither an insurrectional nor revolutionary force' (Ibid., para. 305). In other words, the JNA 'was trying to uphold the continued existence

affairs proclaimed their continuity with SFRY', it remains that 'the reality' was that 'they were acting against the principle of Yugoslavia as a whole and not at all "within the framework of the predecessor State"'.[308] Consequently, before April 1992, 'the FRY was indeed a State *in statu nascendi*' and the perpetrators of wrongs 'acted with the aim of creating a Serbian State'.[309]

Finally, Serbia argued that in order for Article 10(2) to apply, it would have to be shown that the 'movement' actually *succeeded* in establishing a new State. It argued that if its 'goal' (according to Croatia) was to establish a 'larger Serbia, including dominantly ethnically Serb-populated areas of Croatia and Bosnia (Republika Srpska)', it had not been successful.[310] Croatia rejected that argument.[311] In its pleadings, Croatia never quite answered the issue raised by Serbia that the aim of the 'movement' was *not* to create a *new* State.[312] Instead (as mentioned in the previous section), it focused on this concept of State *in statu nascendi*.

4.2.5.3.2.2 The Reasoning of the Court In this section, I will examine the Court's conclusion regarding the arguments based on Article 10(2).[313]

of the SFRY rather than ... aiming at the creation of the FRY consisting of Serbia and Montenegro only' (ibid., Serbia, Rejoinder, November 2011, para. 176).

308 Ibid., Croatia, Reply, vol. 1, 20 December 2010, para. 7.61.

309 Ibid., para. 7.63.

310 Ibid., Serbia, Rejoinder, November 2011, paras. 178 ff. See also: ibid., Verbatim Record, 11 March 2014, CR 2014/14, 21, Tams (Serbia), para. 83:

> [a]gainst that background, Mr. President, we may be permitted to ask: where is that 'triumph'? Where is this triumphant movement that had fought the SFRY with a view to breaking away from it? Again, Croatia is curiously quiet on this: perhaps it thinks of the Serbian leaders who, for a decade, claimed identity with the SFRY. But can you succeed in establishing a new State, as Article 10 requires, without desiring to do so? Can you triumph over a predecessor State while claiming to be identical with it? Or, if we focus on the alleged Greater Serbia movement: where is its triumph? Where is the new State that that movement had successfully established, fighting the predecessor State? A quick glance at the map is sufficient to see that the alleged Greater Serbia movement has not been successful in creating a new State.

311 Ibid., Verbatim Record, 6 March 2014, CR 2014/10, Crawford (Croatia), para. 24: '[t]he fact that Serbia did not achieve the full extent of its territorial ambitions cannot relieve it of responsibility for what it actually did'.

312 See, however, these remarks: ibid., Croatia, Memorial, 1 March 2001, para. 8.33 (referring to 'the conduct of [a] movement which succeeds in establishing a new state on certain territory'), para. 3.33 ('the Serbian nationalist movement ultimately succeeded in establishing the FRY').

313 I have examined the Court's conclusion on the issue of State succession to international responsibility, in Kohen and Dumberry, *The Institute of International Law's Resolution*, p. 11–13, 127.

Serbia noted that the Court had already ruled, in its 2008 judgment, that Serbia had become a party to the Genocide Convention on 27 April 1992 by virtue of its Declaration which the Court considered as a declaration of succession. Therefore, Serbia was not a party to the Genocide Convention prior to 27 April 1992. Even if one were to assume that prior to that date, Serbia was (as alleged by Croatia) a State *in statu nascendi*,[314] it remains that Serbia, at that time, 'did not yet exist and thus *was not* yet and *could not have been* a contracting party of the Genocide Convention'.[315] Only a State can become party to the Convention. As a result, Serbia argued that it could not be held responsible for any breach of the Genocide Convention regarding conduct that took place before 27 April 1992. Thus, 'as a secondary rule of attribution, [Article 10(2)] does not and cannot affect the scope of the primary rules, and it cannot therefore turn conduct occurring prior to 27 April 1992 into a breach of the Genocide Convention that only became binding on Serbia on that date by way of succession'.[316] In the words of the Court, the argument was that 'Article 10 (2) of the ILC Articles is no more than a principle of attribution; it has no bearing on the question of what obligations bind the new State or the earlier "movement", nor does it make treaty obligations accepted by the new State after its emergence retroactively applicable to acts of the pre-State "movement", even if it treats those acts as attributable to the new State.'[317]

On the contrary, Croatia argued that 'Article IX does not exclude disputes concerning succession to or assumption of responsibility or disputes concerning the application of principles of attribution such as that embodied in Article 10(2) of the ILC's Articles on State Responsibility.'[318] It asserted that 'a dispute over State A's succession to or assumption of responsibility for genocide allegedly committed by its personnel while it was *in statu nascendi* would fall within Article IX of the Convention'.[319]

The Court explained that 'the FRY was not bound by the obligations contained in the Genocide Convention until it became party to that Convention', that is, on 27 April 1992 (the date of the notification of succession by the FRY and the date when the new State came into

[314] Ibid., Serbia, Counter-Memorial, December 2009, para. 342.
[315] Ibid., para. 321, emphasis in the original.
[316] Ibid., para. 322.
[317] Ibid., Judgment of 3 February 2015, ICJ Rep. 2015, para. 103.
[318] Ibid., Croatia, Reply, vol. 1, 20 December 2010, para. 7.71.
[319] Ibid., para. 7.72.

existence).[320] Hence, the Court concluded that even if any acts alleged by Croatia that took place before that date could be attributable to a 'movement', 'they cannot have involved a violation of the provisions of the Genocide Convention but, at most, only of the customary international law prohibition of genocide'.[321] Therefore, the Court did not take position on whether the acts committed prior to 27 April 1992 'were attributable to a "movement", within the meaning of Article 10 (2) of the ILC Articles'.[322] It also did not examine whether these acts 'became attributable to the FRY by operation of the principle' set out in Article 10(2).[323] At the end of the day, the Court's decision does not provide many insights as to the nature and scope of application of Article 10(2).

A few judges have examined the scope of Article 10(2) in their individual opinions. The most vehement critic of the position adopted by Croatia came from Judge *ad hoc* Kreća in his dissenting opinion in the 2008 judgement on Preliminary Objections. He said that the assertion that the FRY 'came into being as a consequence of a successful insurrectional movement, hardly deserves another qualification' than being 'manifestly absurd, in serious conflict with common sense and cogent legal considerations'.[324] It should be added that although Judge Tomka rejected the Court's jurisdiction over the events that have taken place before 27 April 1992, he nevertheless recognized that nothing should prevent the Court from considering these acts, adding that 'there was undoubtedly a certain factual continuation and identity between those who were actors in the period of armed conflict which raged in Croatia both before and after 27 April 1992'.[325] The same conclusion was also reached by Judge Cançado Trindade in his dissenting opinion.[326]

4.2.5.4 Transfer of Territory

The events affecting the territorial integrity of the predecessor State may sometimes *not* result in the creation of a new State, but rather in the *enlargement* of the territory of an *existing* State. This is the case of a 'cession' or 'transfer' of territory from one existing State to another.

320 Ibid., Judgment of 3 February 2015, ICJ Rep. 2015, paras. 104–5.
321 Ibid., para. 105.
322 Ibid.
323 Ibid.
324 Ibid., Judgment on Preliminary Objections, 18 November 2008, ICJ Rep. 2008, p. 633, para. 192.
325 Ibid., Judgment of 3 February 2015, ICJ Rep. 2015, Separate Opinion of Judge Tomka, para. 26.
326 Ibid., Dissenting Opinion of Judge Cançado Trindade, paras. 24–5.

In the context of a rebellion by an insurrectional movement, the term 'transfer' should be used.[327] This type of territorial transformation is somewhat different compared to other mechanisms of State succession insofar as it results in neither the extinction of a State nor in the creation of a new State.[328] Nevertheless, it remains a distinct type of State succession.[329] This conclusion was adopted by the ILC in the different instruments regarding matters of State succession,[330] as well as in the recent work of the Institute.[331] A classic example of cession of territory is that of Alsace-Lorraine from Germany to France in 1919. Other examples include the transfers of Hong Kong from Great Britain to China (1999) and that of Macao from Portugal to China (1997).

The question as to whether Article 10(2) of the ILC Articles can be applied to transfers of territory is controversial. As mentioned above, ILC Special Rapporteur Šturma made it clear that Article 10(2) was 'fully applicable to *certain* categories of succession, namely secession and creation of a newly independent State',[332] but he did not mention transfers of territory. ILC Draft Article 9, dealing specifically with transfers of territory, does not refer to the conduct of rebels as a ground for succession to responsibility.[333] This omission suggests that ILC Special Rapporteur Šturma did not consider Article 10(2) to cover cases of transfers of territory. The ILC, in its Commentaries, indicates that this

[327] The term 'cession' is used only to refer to cases where the territorial change is made pursuant to a treaty to which the predecessor State is a party. On the contrary, a 'transfer' of territory applies to situations where there is no agreement between the predecessor State and the successor State. See: O. Dörr, 'Cession', in *Max Planck Encyclopedia of Public International Law* (Oxford University Press, online ed., 2006), paras. 1, 8.

[328] There is one main difference between cases of 'cession' of territory and cases of 'incorporation'. Cases of cession of territory only deal with *part of a territory* of a State which passes to another State, while cases of incorporation involve the *whole territory* of the State which is integrated into another State. Another difference is that in the context of cession of territory, the predecessor State is not extinguished as a result of the loss of part of its territory.

[329] This is emphasized by Brigitte Stern, 'La succession d'États', *Rec. des cours* 262 (1996), p. 105; Dörr, 'Cession', para. 1.

[330] Article 15 of the *Vienna Convention on Succession of States in Respect of Treaties* does not use the concept of 'cession' but refers instead to the situation '[w]hen part of the territory of a State, or when any territory for the international relations of which a State is responsible, not being part of the territory of that State, becomes part of the territory of another State'. See also: Article 14, *Vienna Convention on Succession of States in Respect of State Property, Archives and Debts*; Article 20, 'Draft Articles on Nationality'. See also: ILC, Second Report Šturma, 2018, Draft Article 9.

[331] IIL, 'State Succession in Matters of State Responsibility', 2015, Article 11.

[332] ILC, Second Report Šturma, 2018, para. 108, emphasis in the original.

[333] Ibid., ILC Draft Article 9.

provision does not cover a 'situation where an insurrectional movement within a territory succeeds in its agitation *for union* with another State'.[334] Article 10(2) would therefore not cover transfers of territory. The ILC Commentaries further added: '[t]his is essentially a case of succession, and outside the scope of the articles, whereas article 10 focuses on the *continuity of the movement* concerned and the eventual *new* Government or *State*, as the case may be'.[335] These two remarks suggest that the application of Article 10(2) requires the existence of two elements: (1) the fact that a new State is created, and (2) the idea of a '*continuity*' between the movement and that new State. The following paragraphs examine how these two conditions apply in the context of transfer of territory.

Given that *no new State* is created as a result of a transfer of territory, it would appear that Article 10(2) does not apply to this specific type of State succession.[336] Yet, it should be added that when the Drafting Committee adopted Article 10(2), it made a remark suggesting that the provision should *not only* apply to the 'new' State, but also to 'the case where an entity of a State seceded and became part of another State'.[337] While this expression is not entirely clear, it is probably a reference to the situation of a transfer of territory from one State to another. Interestingly enough, the Drafting Committee specifically stated that 'the commentary would explain that' aspect. It did not. In fact, the ILC, in its Commentaries, indicates the opposite.[338]

Another problem related to the application of Article 10(2) is the requirement of a '*continuity*' between the rebels and the governing entity.[339] In the context of a transfer of territory, it is not enough for the rebels to have won their struggle and successfully achieved their goal of removing part of the territory of the predecessor State and transferred it to that of the successor State. For the 'continuity' requirement to be

[334] ILC, Commentaries, 2001, p. 51, p. 115, para. 10, emphasis added.
[335] Ibid., emphasis added.
[336] Eatwell, *State Responsibility*, p. 218–19. See also, p. 216.
[337] ILC 'Summary Records of the Meetings of the Fiftieth Session 20 April-12 June 1998 27 July–14 August 1998', UN Doc. A/CN.4/SER.A/1998, *ILC Yearbook* vol. I (1998), p. 287, p. 291, para. 89: '[t]he commentary would explain that, while paragraph 2 envisaged only the case of the formation of a new State, it would apply, mutatis mutandis, to the case where an entity of a State seceded and became part of another State'.
[338] ILC, Commentaries, 2001, p. 51, para. 10, indicating that this provision does not cover a 'situation where an insurrectional movement within a territory succeeds in its agitation *for union* with another State', emphasis added.
[339] This important aspect is overlooked by Verhoeven, 'International Responsibility', p. 293.

fulfilled under Article 10(2), the rebels would probably have to gain power and *become the new government* of the already existing successor State. This is indeed the only scenario where there can truly be some sort of organic and structural continuity between the rebels and the government in power in the enlarged successor State.[340] While such a scenario is actually possible,[341] it remains that it is rather unlikely to occur in practical terms.[342] Thus, rebels are seldom *that* 'successful' in their efforts to transfer territory. In the event that there is an absence of continuity between the rebel movement and the government in charge, it seems that Article 10(2) would not apply to specific cases of transfer of territory.

Yet, in my view, the preliminary conclusion reached in the previous paragraph is only part of the analysis. One also needs to consider what would be the practical consequences resulting from the *non-application* of Article 10(2) in the context of transfers of territory. The answer is quite straightforward: the internationally wrongful acts committed by the rebels before the date of succession would simply go unpunished. That result seems unfair for the victims of the acts (third States, foreign investors) who will be unable to get any reparation for the damages suffered.[343] For the injured party who has suffered a damage, it matters little whether the actions of the rebels led to the creation of a 'new' State (secession) or to a transfer of territory.[344]

It begs the question as to what would be the alternative solution. Could the *predecessor* State be held responsible for the wrongs committed by the rebels before the date of succession? This solution seems unfair for the predecessor State (which continues to exist, albeit with a reduced territory). Indeed, why would it have to pay for the damages done by rebels who were successful at dismembering its own territory? Given that the predecessor

340 Another possibility that could be envisaged is for the rebels to take a substantial part in a coalition government with the government in power in the successor State. The question of national coalition governments has been examined above, see Part I, Section 2.2.4.4.

341 Kohen and Dumberry, *The Institute of International Law's Resolution*, p. 87 ff., p. 88 (para. 244) envisaging the application of Article 11(3) in the specific context of a struggle by an insurrectional movement.

342 Eatwell, *State Responsibility*, p. 218, also noting that in the context of transfers of territory, 'there will be a break in continuity between the organisational structure of the movement and the other state as the former are either absorbed into or dissolved by the organisational structure of latter'.

343 The same position is adopted by Verhoeven, 'International Responsibility', p. 294.

344 Yet, in terms of the application of Article 10(2), the difference is important. Thus, as mentioned above, an investor would get some reparation if a successful insurrection is considered a secession, but that would not be the case if a transfer of territory is the ultimate outcome of the struggle.

State lost part of its territory as a result of the successful actions taken by the rebels, it seems particularly unjust for it to have to pay any reparation to the victim of such action.[345] This is because the predecessor State is, after all, the first obvious victim of the success of the rebels.

It seems that there is only one option left if the aim is to prevent (as much as possible) wrongs committed by rebels to simply go unpunished. In my view, there may be good reasons to recognize that the successor State (which now has an enlarged territory as a result of the successful actions of the rebels) should provide reparation to the injured party when specific circumstances are present. First, Article 10(2) can only apply to situations of transfers of territory if there is truly an organic and structural continuity between the rebels and the government of the successor State.[346] Second, I have previously explained that in the different context of rebels being *unsuccessful* at establishing *a new government*, the basic principle applied should be that the acts committed by the rebels during the insurgency are *not* attributable to the State (Rule no. 3).[347] Yet, I also noted that there should exist one exception to that basic principle.[348] A State is bound by the consequences arising from the commission of an act of expropriation by the rebels whenever it resulted in some benefits for the State (Rule no. 4B). I believe that the same principle should be applied for successful rebels in the context of transfer of territory. This is an exceptional case where Rule no. 7 should apply.[349]

345 The same position is adopted by Verhoeven, ibid., p. 294.

346 My position addresses the concern raised by Verhoeven, ibid., p. 293:

> it would be equally unfair to attribute the conduct of the insurrectional movement to the State which acquires the territory. It would lead to the unjust result that a State would for instance be held responsible for violations of human rights law and international humanitarian law committed by rebel movements, whereas the State that acquired the territory did not act through its organs or did not have control over the rebel movement. *Since there is no continuation between the movement and the State* acquiring the territory, the acts of the rebels would only become attributable because the State has acquired territory for which there is no support in international law. (emphasis added).

347 See Part I, Section 3.1.

348 See Part I, Section 3.1.6.

349 One illustration would be an expropriation (without any compensation) done by the rebels of some infrastructures (road, bridge, dam, mining facility, airport, etc.) which belonged to a foreign investor. In the event that the successor State does not return the property to its owner and that the infrastructures are used for public purposes after the transfer, the population and the authorities of that territory will likely continue benefiting from them. This is a situation where the successor State ultimately benefits from the actions taken by the rebels.

In sum, the fact that, in general, Article 10(2) does not find application per se in the context of transfers of a territory does not necessarily mean that the conduct of rebels should never be attributable to the successor State. There are some exceptional circumstances where that should be the case.

4.2.5.5 Incorporation and Unification of States

As mentioned above, the ILC, in its Commentaries, indicates that Article 10(2) does not cover a 'situation where an insurrectional movement within a territory succeeds in its agitation *for union* with another State'.[350] Two other remarks made in the ILC Commentaries suggest that what matters for the application of Article 10(2) is that two conditions must be fulfilled: (1) a *new* State is created, and (2) there is a '*continuity*' between the movement and that new State.[351]

One can theoretically envisage a situation where the rebels are fighting the governmental forces of a State with the aim of completely integrating the entire territory of that State within another already existing State.[352] Yet, and importantly, cases of 'incorporation' do not involve the creation of any 'new State', but rather the *enlargement* of the territory of an *existing* State.[353] The absence of the creation of a new State suggests that Article 10(2) does not apply to cases of incorporation. Another reason for not applying Article 10(2) is the possible lack of 'continuity' between the rebel movement and the government in charge in the enlarged successor State.[354] In any event, Article 10(2) only covers situations where the rebels establish a new State '*in part* of the territory of the pre-existing State'. That condition simply cannot be fulfilled in the context of incorporation. Here, the rebels established a new State in the *entire* territory of the pre-existing State.

350 ILC, Commentaries, 2001, p. 51, para. 10, emphasis added.

351 Ibid., emphasis added.

352 One hypothetical case could be, for instance, a rebellion in Moldova against the central government aiming at the total absorption by Romania of the entire territory of Moldova.

353 The territory of a State (the successor State) is thus enlarged as a result of the integration of the *entirety* of the territory of the predecessor State. The most recent example of a incorporation of State is in 1990 when the German Democratic Republic ceased to exist as an independent State and its territory, comprised of five *Länder*, was integrated into the already existing Federal Republic of Germany.

354 Thus, in the example mentioned above, the rebels would need not only to have totally 'incorporated' the territory of Moldova into Romania, but they would also need to have successfully taken power and formed the new government of Romania in Bucharest.

The same comment mentioned in the previous paragraph also applies to cases of *unification* of States.[355] Given that unification cases involve the creation of a new State, it would seem, at first, that Article 10(2) could apply in such a situation.[356] Yet, Article 10(2) only covers situations where the rebels establish a new State '*in part* of the territory of the pre-existing State'. That condition simply cannot be fulfilled in the context of an unification. Here, the rebels establish a new State in the *entire* territory of *two* (not one) pre-existing States. In any event, it is also difficult to consider how the 'continuity' requirement could be fulfilled.[357]

The practical consequences resulting from the *non-application* of Article 10(2) in the context of incorporation and unification are simple: the internationally wrongful acts committed by the rebels before the date of succession will simply go unpunished. This seems unfair for the victims of the acts (third States, foreign investors) who will be unable to get any reparation for the damages suffered. But what would be the alternative solution? In the context of unification and integration, the predecessor State no longer exists; it therefore cannot be held responsible for any acts committed by the rebels. Could the successor State be responsible? In my view, the exceptional situation mentioned in the previous section dealing with transfers of territory could possibly also apply in the context of incorporation and unification.

[355] This situation involves (at least) *two* existing States which will merge to form a new State. Here, the extinction of the predecessor State results in the creation of *one* new State (the successor State). The most recent case of unification is that of Yemen in 1990.

[356] This is the position of Eatwell, *State Responsibility*, p. 215–16.

[357] Thus, it would firstly require *two distinct groups* of rebels, each fighting in parallel against their own central government and each being ultimately successful at creating a new unified State. Moreover, it would secondly require for them to share power together in the government of that new State. Such a possibility cannot be completely excluded. See Verhoeven, 'International Responsibility', p. 292, for whom Article 10(2) applies to unification: '[i]f armed opposition groups in different States succeed in ousting the government and decide to unify these States a new State is created through the actions of the successful insurrectional movements'. One potential hypothetical scenario could involve the terrorist group ISIS (Islamic State of Iraq and Syria), which in June 2014 proclaimed a worldwide 'Caliphate' and is currently fighting the central governments of both Iraq and Syria. It would appear that one of the aims of the group is to erase the border between the two States and effectively unite the two States together. Under that scenario, both predecessor States (Iraq and Syria) would disappear and a new State would potentially emerge. This is a scenario where there could potentially be a structural continuity between the rebels and the new government of the unified State.

4.3 Rule No. 8: A New State Is Not Responsible for the Acts Committed by the Predecessor State while Fighting the Rebels during an Insurgency

The previous section examined the situation where an insurrectional movement succeeds in establishing a new State and the question as to whether or not the acts committed *by the rebels* during the insurgency are attributable to that new State. The present section addresses another issue: what happens to the wrongful acts committed *by the predecessor State* during the armed struggle against the rebels which caused a damage to *a third party* (a State or a foreign investor)? Another type of wrong, which is not specifically covered in this book, involves acts of the predecessor State that were committed *against the insurrectional movement* during the fighting.[358]

This section will show that, as a matter of principle, a new State is not responsible for the acts committed by the predecessor State when fighting the rebels during an insurgency (Rule no. 8). As a matter of principle, the predecessor State remains responsible for its own wrongs. In the following sections, I will examine the following issues:

- What is the rationale behind the principle? (Section 4.3.1); and
- Rule no. 8 applies in situations where the predecessor State continues to exist (Section 4.3.2), but its application is problematic when the predecessor State ceases to exist (Section 4.3.3).

4.3.1 *The Rationale behind the Principle*

Article 10(3) of the ILC Articles applies to *both* situations where the rebels establish either a new government or a new State. Article 10(3) reads as follows: 'This article [i.e. Articles 10(1) and (2)] is without prejudice to the attribution to a State of any conduct, however related to that of the movement concerned, which is to be considered an act of that State by virtue of articles 4 to 9.' Importantly, the rationale behind this provision and its concrete application are completely different depending on whether a given situation concerns rebels establishing a new *government* (Article 10(1)) or creating a new *State* (Article

[358] Once the rebels have been successful in their struggle to create a new State, this situation could result in that new State claiming reparation to the predecessor State (if it continues to exist) for damages suffered by rebels during the insurgency. This question of so-called 'war damages' is, however, beyond the scope of this book.

10(2)). Thus, the reference in Article 10(3) to 'an act of that State' actually refers to acts of *different States* depending on whether paragraph 1 or 2 of Article 10 applies.

On the one hand, as mentioned above,[359] in the context of Article 10(1), the rule set out in Article 10(3) is based on one of the most well-established principles of international law: a change of government does not affect the identity of a State. The new government (established by successful rebels) will therefore continue to be responsible for the State's international obligations, including the wrongful acts committed by the previous government while fighting the rebels (Rule no. 1). This is because there is State *continuity*. It is the same State (with the same international legal personality) before and after the changes affecting the government. There is simply no reason why *that same* State should not continue to be responsible for *its own* wrongful acts after a change of government.

On the other hand, in the context of Article 10(2) there is no such State continuity. The struggle by successful rebels leads to the creation of a *new* State. The rationale mentioned in the previous paragraph for Rule no. 1 embodied in Article 10(3) simply cannot be applied in the context of Article 10(2). The situation does not involve the *same State*; it concerns two different States (the new State and the predecessor State). In fact, the reference in Article 10(3) to the conduct of a 'State' that can be attributable to that 'State' does not concern the new State, but rather another State: the *predecessor State*. As a result, in the context of the application of Article 10(2) (involving a new State), the meaning to be given to Article 10(3) is as follows: the fact that the acts committed by the rebels during the insurgency are attributable to the new State (Rule no. 7) 'is without prejudice to the attribution to' the *predecessor State* 'of any conduct, however related to that of the [rebel] movement concerned, which is to be considered an act of that [predecessor] State by virtue of articles 4 to 9'. In other words, the existence of Rule no. 7 *does not* mean that the predecessor State should not continue to be responsible for *its own* wrongful acts committed before the date of succession. This is indeed how Croatia, in the 2015 *Genocide* case,[360] explained the rationale behind Article 10(3): 'the possibility that the predecessor State may *also* be responsible for the conduct on some basis is expressly preserved by Article 10(3), which the ILC decided to retain even though questions had been raised as to its utility'.[361]

[359] See Part I, Section 2.1.2.

[360] See Section 4.2.5.3.2.

[361] ICJ, *Genocide* case, Croatia, Reply, vol. 1, 20 December 2010, para. 7.69, emphasis added. In his pleading, Crawford (counsel for Croatia) mentioned that the situation was

Therefore, after the date of succession, two different issues of State responsibility could arise *at the same time*:

- On the one hand, the new State can be 'responsible' for the obligations arising from the consequences of wrongful acts committed *by the rebels* during the insurgency (Rule no. 7); and
- On the other hand, the predecessor State can continue to be responsible for its *own acts* committed during the insurgency, including its failure to exercise its due diligence obligation in relation to the conduct of the rebels (Rule no. 8).[362]

One important point which must be highlighted at this stage is that the rationale behind the principle set out in Article 10(3) in the specific context of the application of Article 10(2) only makes sense in cases where *there exists* a predecessor State. In other words, after the date of succession the predecessor State can, quite logically, only continue to be responsible for its own acts committed during the insurgency *if it still exists* following the events affecting its territorial integrity. Yet, *not all* types of State succession involve situations where the predecessor State continues to exist. In the following sections, I will distinguish cases where the predecessor State continues its existence following the events affecting its territorial integrity (Section 4.3.2) from other examples where it ceases to exist (Section 4.3.3).

4.3.2 Rule No. 8 Applies in Situations Where the Predecessor State Continues to Exist

As mentioned in the previous section, Article 10(3) only makes sense in situations where the predecessor State continues its existence following the events affecting its territorial integrity. The term 'continuing' State is often used by scholars to refer to the predecessor State in the situation just described.[363] In its 2007 final judgment in the *Bosnia and Herzegovina Genocide Convention* Case, the ICJ, however, used the

addressed by Article 10 (3), and further explained that: 'The possibility that the predecessor State might also be notionally responsible for the conduct on some basis does not mean that a State in statu nascendi can escape responsibility. It is possible for two States to be responsible for the same conduct on different grounds. The ILC commentary confirms this, I would say, self-evident, point' (Verbatim Record, 6 March 2014, CR 2014/10, Crawford (Croatia), paras. 26–7).

362 I have already examined above the different types of acts of the predecessor States that are covered by this Rule. See Part I, Section 2.1.2.2.2.

363 See, for instance: Dumberry, *State Succession to International Responsibility*, p. 16–17.

expression 'continuator' State.[364] Both terms can be used and have the same meaning.

The following sections will first examine the principle (Section 4.3.2.1), and then analyse applicable State practice and case law (Section 4.3.2.2).

4.3.2.1 The Principle Is Well-Established

To the extent that the predecessor State continues to exist after the emergence of a new State on what used to be part of its territory,[365] there is no reason for it not to be held responsible for *its own* internationally wrongful acts committed during the period of uprising. As explained in previous writing,[366] this provision reflects Article 1 of the ILC's Articles whereby 'each State is responsible for its own wrongful conduct'.[367] In other words, only the State that has actually committed an internationally wrongful act should engage its responsibility for it. In these situations, the predecessor State should *remain* responsible for *its own* internationally wrongful acts, including those committed *before* the date of succession. This general principle is followed by the Institute,[368] ILC Special Rapporteur Šturma[369] and is widely supported amongst scholars.[370]

As a matter of principle, in such cases, the new State should *not* be held 'responsible' for obligations arising from internationally wrongful acts committed by the predecessor State before the date of succession. This basic principle is recognized by scholars[371] and by ILC Special Rapporteur

364 *Application of the Convention on the Prevention and Punishment of the Crime of Genocide (Bosnia and Herzegovina v. Serbia and Montenegro),* Judgment 26 February 2007, ICJ Rep. 2007, paras. 71, 75, 80, 81, 106, 130, 131.

365 Such as in situations of transfers of territory, secession and Newly Independent States.

366 Kohen and Dumberry, *The Institute of International Law's Resolution*, p. 32 ff.

367 ILC, 'First Report on State Responsibility (Addendum no. 4)', Mr. James Crawford, Special Rapporteur, 26 May 1998, UN Doc. A/CN.4/490/Add.4, para. 110.

368 IIL, 'State Succession in Matters of State Responsibility', 2015, Article 4. See also, the same principle applied for specific types of State succession: Article 11 (transfer of territory), Article 12 (separation) and Article 16 (Newly Independent States).

369 ILC, Second Report Šturma, 2018, paras. 45–7.

370 See several writers mentioned in Dumberry, *State Succession to International Responsibility*, p. 143–4.

371 This is, for instance, the position of D.P. O'Connell, 'Recent Problems of State Succession in Relation to New States', *Rec. des cours* 130 (1970-II), p. 164: '[t]here is common sense in the view that successor States should not be required to foot the bill for such acts of their predecessors as wrongful arrest or damage in war or revolution'. See also: Atlam, *Succession d'États*, p. 255, 258, 420; Cahin, 'Attribution of Conduct to the State', p. 250 ('In the second hypothesis, the only acts attributable to the State created by secession or

Šturma.[372] It is also implicitly recognized in Article 10(2) of the ILC Articles which indicates that *only* the conduct of the 'movement, insurrectional or other' (and not that of the predecessor State) is considered that of the new State.[373]

In my view, the application of Rule no. 8 in the context where the predecessor State continues to exist is not only logical, but also reasonable and fair. Indeed, it protects the rights of victims of wrongful acts. The concrete application of the rule (in combination with Rule no. 7) means that all wrongs committed by the belligerents during a successful rebellion to create a new State will get punished. Those who have suffered damages as a result of a wrongful act committed by either the government or the rebels will get reparation.

4.3.2.2 Case Law and State Practice Support This Principle

I have found a number of relevant examples of State practice and case law illustrating how Rule no. 8 has been applied in situations where the predecessor State continues to exist. The first three examples (examined in the next sections) involve cases of Newly Independent States, and the fourth one, an instance of secession. As mentioned above,[374] my book does not intend to specifically examine wrongful acts committed by the predecessor State *against the local population* of the territory where the

decolonization are those of the insurrectional movement at its origin, while the State from which the new State broke away without affecting its identity continues to assume responsibility for the conduct of its organs engaged in the fight against the insurrectional movement'); Crawford, *State Responsibility*, p. 176 ('In contrast to ARSIWA Article 10(1), any acts undertaken by the predecessor state in attempting to suppress the insurgency will not be attributed to the new state'). See also: Atlam, 'National Liberation Movements and International Responsibility', p. 49, endorsing this position in the specific context of National Liberation Movements creating Newly Independent States.

372 ILC, 'First Report on Succession of States in Respect of State Responsibility', by P. Šturma, Special Rapporteur, 69th session, 2017, UN Doc. A/CN.4/708, 31 May 2017, para. 17: '[t]he common point in those two articles [Art. 4 and 5] is the continuing existence of the predecessor State. It reflects a general rule of non-succession if the predecessor State continues to exist.'

373 The principle has also been recognized by the ILC elsewhere: ILC, Report, 1975, p. 101, para. 6: '[t]he acts of the organs of the pre-existing State are in no way attributable to the new State, which has separated from the pre-existing State by secession or decolonization. These are and remain exclusively the acts of the pre-existing State, which as a general rule, moreover, will continue to exist after the constitution of the new State by the insurrectional movement.' See also, ibid., p. 105, para. 22: '[i]t goes without saying that, since the pre-existing State will continue to exist, although with a reduced territory, it will still be responsible for its own acts carried out before the creation of the new State'.

374 See Introduction, Section 1.1.3.3.

insurgency took place. Yet, the first three examples analysed involve such wrongs. I have decided to examine them nonetheless because they are often referred to by writers when addressing Article 10(2). They are also important for the present discussion because the reasoning contained in these decisions is applicable, more broadly, in the different context where the victim of a wrong is a third party (such as a foreigner).

4.3.2.2.1 The Official Position Taken by France and French Municipal Court Decisions in the Context of the Independence of Algeria The principle of non-succession was applied in the context of the independence of Algeria in 1962.[375] The former French colony of Algeria became an independent State in July 1962 after a national liberation war that lasted eight years. Many issues of succession of States have arisen in the years that followed independence.[376] Article 18 of the *Déclaration de principes relative à la coopération économique et financière* (dated 19 March 1962), entered into between France and Algeria as part of the *Evian Accords* that ended the war, indicates that Algeria (the successor State) took over the obligations arising from internationally wrongful acts committed before the date of succession.[377] The new State of Algeria did not fully implement its obligations under Article 18 of the *Déclaration*.[378] Faced with such a refusal by the Algerian authorities, France decided to compensate *French nationals* who had suffered damages during the national liberation war.

The official position taken by France was that the new State of Algeria *should not* be held accountable for acts committed *by the French colonial authorities* 'not in the name' of Algeria.[379] In reply to a request by the Conseil d'État for an interpretation of Article 18 of the *Déclaration*, the Ministry of Foreign Affairs of France took the view that the new State of

[375] This example is discussed in Dumberry, *State Succession to International Responsibility*, p. 250.

[376] These issues are discussed in Maurice Flory, Bruno Etienne, Gérard Fouilloux and Jean-Pierre Santucci, *La succession d'États en Afrique du Nord* (Paris, Coll. Etudes de l'Annuaire de l'Afrique du Nord, CNRS, 1968), p. 104; Ch. Rousseau, 'Chronique des faits internationaux', *RGDIP* (1963), p. 118–31.

[377] The text of the Agreement is found in *JORF*, 20 March 1962, p. 3019–32: 'Algeria shall assume the obligations and enjoy the rights contracted on behalf of itself or of Algerian public establishments by the competent French authorities.'

[378] This is the conclusion reached by M. Charpentier, 'Pratique française du droit international', *AFDI* (1963), p. 1015–16, 1021–3.

[379] Statement of the French State Secretary for Algerian Affairs, in *JORF Assemblée nationale*, no. 3814, 28 September 1963, at p. 4919, quoted in Charpentier, 'Pratique française', p. 1021.

Algeria should not be held responsible for the acts and measures taken by France (the predecessor State) against French nationals that were *specifically directed against the rebellion of the FLN.*[380] This principle has received support in doctrine.[381]

This principle of non-succession has been consistently applied by French municipal courts.[382] These cases support Rule no. 8 whereby a new State is *not* responsible for the acts committed by the predecessor State while fighting the rebels during the insurgency. It is true that these cases involved wrongful acts which had been committed by the predecessor State *against the local population* (in fact, French nationals living in Algeria at the time). None of these claims involved wrongs committed

[380] The official position of the Ministry is expressed in 'Conclusions de M. le Commissaire du Gouvernement Fournier', extract of which can be found in an analysis by R. Pinto, in *JDI* (1967), p. 387. This position was delivered to the Conseil d'État in letters dated 13 February 1963 and 30 July 1963 in the *Union régionale d'Algérie de la C.F.T.C.* case, decided by the Conseil d'État, 5 March 1965 (in Ch. Rousseau, 'Jurisprudence française en matière de droit international public', *RGDIP* (1965), p. 846–7; *ILR* 44, p. 43). The Conseil d'État speaks of 'mesures prises spécialement et directement en vue de faire échec aux mouvements insurrectionnels' ('measures taken specifically and directly to crush the insurgency movements'). In reference to acts committed by France while fighting the rebels of the FLN, the letters indicates:

> [f]irst of all, this country's (Algeria's) accession to independence was preceded by a prolonged conflict during which a certain number of measures were taken by the French government in order, specifically, to prevent such accession to independence. It could not be envisaged, regardless of what the two countries' relationship might be in the future, that the Algerian authorities would agree to take over the obligations contracted in this way by the French state. Consequently, it is normal to consider that the litigation arising out of these measures, taken in order to quell the insurgency movements, does not involve the Algerian state pursuant to the Protocol. This is in line with a distinction made long ago by international law theorists who, whilst they accept that the successor State must take over part of its predecessor's liabilities, always exclude debts known as war or regime debts, that is to say debts that were incurred in order to prevent annexation or to oppose emancipation.

(English translation in *Mutua et al.* v. *The Foreign and Commonwealth Office*, 21 July 2011, [2011] EWHC 1913 (QB) and of 5 October 2012, [2012] EWHC 2678 (QB), Judgment, para. 91)

[381] In reference to the *Kaddour* case, Conseil d'État, case no. 04642, 10 May 1968, in *Recueil Lebon*, Jean-François Lachaume, 'Jurisprudence française relative au droit international (1984)', *AFDI* (1985), p. 930, indicates that this position is in conformity with traditional rules of international law.

[382] See Dumberry, *State Succession to International Responsibility*, p. 252 ff., examining several cases, including: *État français* v. *Consorts Caldumbide*, Cass. Civ. 3e, 7 November 1969; *Kaddour*, Conseil d'État, case no. 04642, 10 May 1968, in *Recueil Lebon*.

against foreigners or other States. Yet, what matters is that the official position adopted by France on this question is in line with Rule no. 8. In other words, had French courts been faced with claims by foreigners, they would have certainly applied Rule no. 8.

4.3.2.2.2 The *Mutua et al.* v. *The Foreign and Commonwealth Office* Case in the Context of the Mau-Mau Rebellion in Kenya The case involves allegations of 'torts of assault and battery and negligence' committed by the Colonial British Government in Kenya during the so-called 'Mau-Mau' uprising in the 1950s. The revolt against British colonial rule in Kenya led to the proclamation of a formal state of emergency (which lasted from 1952 until 1960).[383] The claim was filed by five Claimants who were veterans of the Mau Mau movement.[384] The claim was filed before an English Court on the grounds that the defendant (the United Kingdom) was liable for acts committed by the colonial authority, or, in the alternative, owed a duty of care which it negligently failed to discharge.[385] The defendant argued that no claim could be brought against the UK government, since the Colonial Administration had acted on its own. It filed an application for orders to strike out the claims and/or for summary judgment dismissing it.[386] Accordingly, this case involves a wrongful act committed by the predecessor State (the British colonial authorities) *against the local population* of Kenya during the period of insurrection before independence.

Justice McCombe of the High Court considered that 'the liability for present claims (in so far as available against the Colonial Government) would have passed to/remained with the new independent monarchy in December 1963' (i.e. when Kenya became an independent State).[387] Justice McCombe added that 'it was for Kenya, as an independent State, to decide whether or not it was willing to assume the liabilities of the British Colonial Administration'.[388] Yet, as mentioned by the Claimants, 'neither the Kenya

[383] *Mutua et al.* v. *The Foreign and Commonwealth Office*, High Court of Justice (Justice McCombe), judgments of 21 July 2011, [2011] EWHC 1913 (QB) and of 5 October 2012, [2012] EWHC 2678 (QB).

[384] *Mutua et al.*, Judgment of 21 July 2011, ibid., para. 1.

[385] Ibid., Summary of Judgment, para. 5.

[386] Ibid., Summary of Judgment, para. 3.

[387] Ibid., para. 79.

[388] Ibid., para. 79. See also, para. 83:

> [i]n this case, there was no express transfer of rights and liabilities to the new Kenyan state by the Independence Act. However, the mechanism of the Act and related instruments was to leave the rights and liabilities of the

Independence Act 1963, nor any other UK statute or instrument, addresses the question of the succession of liabilities of the Colonial Administration for assaults against the Claimants'.[389] Therefore, for the Judge, the matter had to be 'resolved under the Common Law', adding that 'one source of the common law is customary international law, including principles on state succession'.[390] It is in this context that the High Court examined issues of State succession to responsibility.

The Claimants argued that under a principle of 'customary international law', after the independence of a former colony, the predecessor State remains responsible for its own wrongful acts committed against the population of that colony.[391] Specifically, the Claimants stated (referring to French cases mentioned above in the context of the independence of Algeria)[392] that 'in the context of decolonisation it has been accepted by predecessor states that liabilities for tortious acts of their colonial administrations in respect of the suppression of an insurrectional movement should be opposable to the predecessor state upon independence'.[393] Justice McCombe was however not persuaded by that position: 'I agree with the defendant, however, that the Claimants have not been able to establish with any clarity a sufficiently "extensive and virtually uniform" rule of customary international law to constitute it as the basis of a claim under the common law of England.'[394] As a result, the High Court was hesitant to recognize the principle which had been adopted by France in the context of the independence of Algeria whereby a new State should not be held responsible for the actions of the

> old Kenyan administration with the new Kenyan administration. As I have said, it was for the independent Kenya to determine the extent to which it wished to exclude its government from such liabilities before its own courts for the future.

389 Ibid., para. 81(a).

390 Ibid., para. 81(a)(b).

391 Ibid., para. 81(d):

> In accordance with the principles of customary international law relating to the creation of a new state in the context of decolonisation (the successor state), a liability of the colonial administration of the predecessor state in respect of tortious acts committed against the native population devolves to the predecessor state upon independence. Therefore, under the common law, the liability to compensate the Claimants for injuries inflicted by the Colonial Administration of the Crown in right of Kenya devolved to the Crown in right of the United Kingdom upon the independence of Kenya.

392 See Section 4.3.2.2.1.

393 *Mutua et al.*, Judgment of 21 July 2011, para. 90.

394 Ibid., para. 95.

predecessor State (i.e., the colonial authorities) while fighting secessionist rebels which later established a new independent State (Rule no. 8).[395]

The High Court rejected the Defendant's request to dismiss the case before it would come to a trial. This first judgment then opened the way for an examination of the responsibility of the British Government for the alleged acts at the merits stage of the trial. A settlement was eventually reached between the Claimants and the United Kingdom in 2013 for the 'payment of a settlement sum in respect of 5,228 claimants, as well as a gross costs sum, to the total value of £19.9 million'.[396] In his declaration to the House of Commons, Foreign Secretary Hague stated that while the United Kingdom 'continue[s] to deny liability . . . for the actions of the colonial administration in respect of the claims' and that 'the courts have made no finding of liability against the Government in this case', it nevertheless 'recognises that Kenyans were subject to torture and other forms of ill treatment at the hands of the colonial administration' and 'sincerely regrets that these abuses took place, and that they marred Kenya's progress towards independence'.[397]

At the end of the day, the judgment remains somewhat neutral regarding Rule no. 8. However, it is evident that Justice McCombe *did not* endorse the opposite view. He never said that Kenya was, as a matter of principle, *responsible* for obligations arising from wrongful acts committed by the British colonial authorities (the predecessor State) during the armed struggle led by an 'insurrectional movement' to establish that new State. Thus, he made it clear that, upon independence in 1963, 'it was a matter for the Kenyan parliament to decide whether it wished to exclude such claims by separate legislation'.[398] The Kenyan parliament was free 'to enact legislation to prevent the Kenyan government being

[395] Ibid., para. 93:

> [a]gain, however, I think that there is force in the defendant's submission that the French cases (to which I was not taken individually or in any detail) seem to have turned upon the agreements known as the Evian Accords and Protocols and were, in effect, decisions on specific treaties made on the creation of the independent Algeria. It is argued that this series of cases cannot, therefore, simply be transposed onto the circumstances of the Mau Mau uprising and the subsequent independence of Kenya.

[396] 'Statement to Parliament on settlement of Mau Mau claims', Foreign & Commonwealth Office and The Rt Hon William Hague, 6 June 2013, www.gov.uk/government/news/statement-to-parliament-on-settlement-of-mau-mau-claims.

[397] Ibid.

[398] *Mutua et al.*, Judgment of 21 July 2011, para. 79.

sued in the Kenyan courts in respect of such pre-December 1963 government liabilities as it chose', adding that 'the remedy lay in the hands of an independent Kenya – a result which is hardly repugnant to the concept of a free and independent state'.[399] In other words, the Judge recognized the basic principle whereby a new State is always free to accept responsibility for wrongs committed before the date of succession.[400]

4.3.2.2.3 The Bombardment of the City of Antwerp in the Context of the Secession of Belgium from the Kingdom of the Netherlands (1830) This example arose in the context of the secession of Belgium from the Kingdom of the Netherlands (1830).[401] During an armed revolt, and prior to the independence of Belgium, the city of Antwerp (situated in the Belgian provinces of the Netherlands) was bombarded in October 1830 by the Dutch forces. This bombardment resulted in the destruction of a public warehouse in which were stored the goods of several foreigners. This is therefore an example where the victims were a third party to the conflict.

After Belgium became an independent State, Great Britain took the view that the Kingdom of the Netherlands (the predecessor and continuing State) 'was not liable for the disasters occasioned by the bombardment' of October 1830.[402] Apparently, Austria, Brazil, France and Prussia also adopted the same position.[403] France, Great Britain, Prussia and the United States made a joint application to Belgium requesting compensation for the damages 'solely [based] upon the ground that the obligation to indemnify for such losses rested upon the country within which the injury was inflicted'.[404]

More information is available with respect to the claims filed by the United States against *both* Belgium and the Kingdom of the Netherlands in the hope that they would come up with a satisfactory

[399] Ibid., para. 78.

[400] See Dumberry, *State Succession to International Responsibility*, p. 215 ff.

[401] The example is mentioned in Dumberry, ibid., p. 161 ff., 257–8.

[402] This is apparently what the Attorney General of England concluded following a request made by the British Minister of Foreign Affairs. This information is found in a letter (dated 26 February 1857) of US Secretary of State, Mr Marcy, to French Minister, Count Sartiges, concerning the claims of French subjects as a result of the US bombardment of Greytown in 1854, in MS. Notes to French Leg. VI. 301; S. Ex. Doc. 9, 35 Cong. 1 sess. 3, in Moore, *Digest of International Law* (vol. VI), p. 929.

[403] This is the conclusion reached by US Secretary of State, Mr Marcy, in a correspondence dated 26 February 1857, ibid.

[404] Ibid., p. 929.

and voluntary arrangement regarding the proportion of responsibility that each one would bear for the damages suffered by US nationals as a result of the bombardment of October 1830.[405] The United States submitted its claim against the Kingdom of the Netherlands as the actual perpetrator of the act. Apparently, the Dutch government excused its bombardment of the city on the grounds that the Belgian insurgents had breached an agreement to suspend hostilities for the protection of the city.[406] It is not clear from the information available whether or not the Kingdom of the Netherlands ended up paying any compensation to the United States.

For the United States, there was no doubt as to the responsibility of the new State of Belgium for the internationally wrongful act committed by the Netherlands against the Belgian city.[407] One of the legal grounds invoked by the United States was the 'territorial link' between the act and Belgium. Since the acts took place in the territory of what would later become Belgium, the United States took the view that the new State should therefore be held responsible for it.[408] Another legal argument invoked by the United States was that Belgium should be held responsible based on the well-recognized principle of international law according to which a new government established by successful rebels is responsible for the acts committed by the previous government (Rule

[405] Message of US President Jackson of 5 December 1836, in *Messages and Papers of the Presidents*, vol. 3, p. 237, in Moore, *Digest of International Law* (vol. VI), p. 947 ff. The issue is also mentioned in this internal US diplomatic communication: Letter of US Secretary of State, Mr Forsyth, to Mr Davezac, US Chargé d'Affaires to the Netherlands, 10 September 1836, in MS. Inst. Netherlands, XIV. 24, in Moore, ibid., p. 943.

[406] Moore, ibid., p. 947.

[407] Letter of US Secretary of State, Mr Forsyth, to Mr Marcy, US Chargé d'affaires to Belgium, 12 June 1837, in MS. Inst. Belgium, I. 24, in Moore, ibid., p. 945.

[408] This assessment of the position taken by the United States concerning the Antwerp bombardment is made in Letter of US Secretary of State, Mr Marcy, to French Minister, Count Sartiges, concerning the claims of French subjects as a result of the US bombardment of Greytown in 1854, 26 February 1857, in MS. Notes to French Leg. VI. 301; S. Ex. Doc. 9, 35 Cong. 1 sess. 3, in Moore, ibid., p. 929–30:

> The governments of the respective merchants whose property was destroyed by the bombardment claimed indemnity for these losses from the Kingdom of Belgium. The ground of the claims was, that the injury was inflicted on a territory which, at the time the reclamation was made, had become a part of Belgium; but Belgium attempted to evade it by alleging that the Dutch government received the property, had it in possession, and destroyed it; and from Holland, and not Belgium, indemnity must be sought.

no. 1).[409] The position adopted by the United States seems to be based on a fundamental mischaracterization of the events of 1830. These events should not be analysed as mere change of government but, rather, as the emergence of a new State. Belgium initially denied its responsibility on the grounds that the acts had been committed by the Dutch forces.[410] Yet, it apparently subsequently changed its view on the matter and finally agreed to pay compensation to the owners of the merchandise destroyed during the incident.[411]

Verzijl described this example as a 'clear case of asserted responsibility of a territorial successor to injuries inflicted by its predecessor'.[412] This case is indeed one rare example of State practice contrary to Rule no. 8.[413] Thus, the new State (created by successful rebels) was held accountable for the consequences of internationally wrongful acts committed by the predecessor State during the insurgency. This case is also an illustration of the well-established principle that a new State is always free to take over responsibilities for wrongs committed by the predecessor State.[414] In any event, little is known about the reason why Belgium accepted such

[409] Letter of US Secretary of State, Mr Webster, to Mr Marcy, US Chargé d'Affaires to Belgium, 26 February 1842, in MS. Inst. Belgium, I. 34, in Moore, ibid., p. 945–7:

> [t]here is no doubt that the duty or obligation of indemnity, whatever it is, for the losses at Antwerp, falls upon Belgium. The Belgians, as a civilized people, must be considered at all times under some form of civil government, and however often they may see fit to change this form, these changes cannot affect their just responsibility to any foreign state, its citizens or subjects. *Succeeding governments necessarily take upon themselves, so far at least as foreign nations are concerned, the obligations of the governments which preceded them*, whether those obligations were created by treaty or by the general principles of national law. It is on this ground that the restored governments of Europe have made indemnities to foreign states for excesses committed on the property of citizens or subjects of these states by the revolutionary governments ... The Belgians saw fit to change their government which, so far as foreign nations are concerned, they had a right to do. But in doing this they shook off no national responsibility. The moment the authority of the King of the Netherlands ceased over the Belgians, that moment every one of his obligations towards foreign nations, so far as that part of his Kingdom was concerned, devolved on the new government that succeeded him. (emphasis added).

[410] Moore, ibid., p. 947.

[411] J. H. W. Verzijl, *International Law in Historical Perspective, t. VII (State Succession)* (Leiden, A.W. Sijthoff, 1974), p. 226–7.

[412] Ibid., p. 226–7.

[413] Dumberry, *State Succession to International Responsibility*, p. 257–8.

[414] See analysis in ibid., p. 215 ff.

responsibility. Its position may have been guided by political reasons more than anything else. At the time of its independence, Belgium was probably not in a position to refuse to provide reparation to the much more powerful claimant States. In fact, I have argued in previous writing,[415] that this case is an illustration of the importance to be given to the existence of a *direct territorial link* between a wrongful act committed by the predecessor and the new State. In such a situation, the obligations arising from such an act can be assumed by *both* the predecessor State and the successor State.[416]

4.3.2.2.4 Other Cases This section will briefly examine three other examples of State practice.

First, reference should be made to a little known, and rather marginal, case of State practice. During the American Revolution for independence, British troops apparently caused damages to a church in the State of Pennsylvania (a fence burned).[417] Some 183 years later, a Philadelphia clergyman presented a claim to Great Britain (the predecessor State) for compensation for the damage. In response, the Office of the Chancellor of the Exchequer wrote: 'The convention is that claims by a citizen of colonial territories against the Government, which have not been settled by the date of independence, lie against the successor Government unless a special arrangement is made to the

[415] Kohen and Dumberry, *The Institute of International Law's Resolution*, p. 101. See also the position taken in ILC, Second Report Šturma, 2018, para. 101.

[416] Kohen and Dumberry, Ibid. See Article 12 of the IIL, 'State Succession in Matters of State Responsibility', 2015. See also: Draft Article 7(3), ILC, Second Report Šturma, 2018, para. 103.

[417] The case is referred to in M. M. Whiteman, *Digest of International Law* (Washington, Dept. of State, vol. II, 1973), p. 875–6, indicating the source of the information as: *New York Times*, Sept. 12, 1961, p. 1, 13. Whiteman also made this other comment about the background of this case:

> [t]he Reverend Joseph Koci's claim was based on vestry minutes which showed that a British Commander, Major Edward Williams, Royal Artillery, had written that the British Commander would pay a 'reasonable allowance' for the broken fence. The Chancellor of the Exchequer, Selwyn Lloyd, paid $18 asked by the minister out of his own pocket 'as a token of deep regard for the American people'. Reportedly, with reference to the $760,000 asked by the minister for 183 years of compound interest at 6 percent, he added that he hoped that it would not be considered prejudicial 'to your claim against the United States or Pennsylvania Governments'.

contrary.'[418] The letter ended as follows: 'I am asked to advise that you should refer your claim either to the Federal Government of the U.S.A. or to the State Government of Pennsylvania.' The quote suggests that, contrary to Rule no. 8, the new successor State (the United States) may be held responsible for obligations arising from internationally wrongful acts committed by the predecessor State during the insurrection. Yet, this outcome may be explained by the fact that almost 200 years had elapsed between the moment when the wrong took place and the request for reparation was finally made.

The second example is the *Mwandinghi* case. The ILC Commentaries noted that 'more recent decisions and practice do not, on the whole, give any reason to doubt the propositions contained in Article 10',[419] adding that 'in one case, the Supreme Court of Namibia went even further in accepting responsibility for "anything done" by the predecessor administration of South Africa'.[420] While this case clearly involved the creation of *a new State*, the Supreme Court made a number of confusing statements whereby it considered it as one involving the establishment of a *new government*.[421] It is also noteworthy that this case did *not* directly involve acts committed in relation to the conduct of rebels. The case is therefore more relevant in the context of analysing another question concerning State succession to responsibility: whether the new successor State (Namibia) could be held accountable for the consequences of wrongful acts committed *by the predecessor State* (South Africa).[422] Suffice it to note that the Court was wrong to state that the work of the ILC supports in any way the proposition that 'when a national liberation movement becomes the new government of a State, as was the case in Namibia, the new State will be attributed with the conduct which would have been previously considered as an act of the pre-existing state, that is, the new government inherits responsibility for the acts committed by the previous organs of the State'.[423] As noted by ILC Special Rapporteur

418 Ibid.

419 ILC, Commentaries, 2001, p. 51, para. 14.

420 Ibid. The footnote further mentioned: '[g]uided in particular by a constitutional provision, the Supreme Court of Namibia held that "the new government inherits responsibility for the acts committed by the previous organs of the State"'.

421 The case and these statements are examined in Dumberry, *State Succession to International Responsibility*, p. 194 ff.

422 Ibid. This important point was highlighted in ICJ, *Genocide* case, 2015, Separate Opinion of Judge Kreća, para. 66.2.

423 *Minister of Defence, Namibia* v. *Mwandinghi*, Supreme Court, 25 October 1991, in 1992 (2) *SA* 355 (NmS), in *ILR* 91, p. 358, p. 360–1.

Crawford, Namibia had no obligation *under Article 10(2)* of the ILC Articles to take over the liability for the internationally wrongful acts committed by South Africa (the predecessor State) before its independence.[424] Yet, nothing prevents a new State from deciding, based on policy grounds, to do so.[425]

The third case is *Van der Have*, decided by the District Court of The Hague in the context of the independence of Indonesia.[426] The case dealt with the death of an Indonesian native who was unlawfully killed by a soldier of the Royal Netherlands Indies Army during the repression by the Dutch Army of the rebellion of native Indonesian secessionist groups in Java (these events are known as the 'second military action' of 18 December 1948).[427] After the Second World War, the widow sought to recover compensation before Dutch Courts for the loss she had suffered from the death of her husband. The Netherlands argued that, according to Article 4 of the 1949 *Draft Agreement on Transitional Measures* entered into between the Kingdom of the Netherlands and the Republic of Indonesia, liabilities for the 'Asian part' of the Kingdom of the Netherlands were transferred to the new Republic of Indonesia.[428]

[424] ILC, 'First Report on State Responsibility (addendum no. 5)', Mr. James Crawford, Special Rapporteur, 22 July 1998, UN Doc. A/CN.4/490/Add.1-7, p. 53, at para. 274:

> Namibia, as a new State created as the result, *inter alia*, of the actions of the South West Africa People's Organization, a recognized national liberation movement, was not responsible for the conduct of South Africa in respect of its territory. That it assumed such a responsibility attests to its concern for individual rights, but it was not required by the principles of article 15 [now Article 10].

[425] See analysis at the end of Section 4.2.3.3. The rule was codified in IIL, 'State Succession in Matters of State Responsibility', 2015, Article 6(3). See analysis in Kohen and Dumberry, *The Institute of International Law's Resolution*, p. 47 ff. See also: ILC, Second Report Šturma, 2018, 2018, Draft Article 4.

[426] Dumberry, *State Succession to International Responsibility*, p. 186, 258.

[427] *Van der Have* v. *State of the Netherlands*, District Court of The Hague, 12 January 1953, in *N.J.*, 1953, no. 133, in *ILR* (1953), p. 80.

[428] *Draft Agreement on Transitional Measures*, which is part of the *Round-Table Conference Agreement* between the Kingdom of the Netherlands and the Government of the Republic of Indonesia of 2 November 1949, in *UNTS* 69, p. 200, at p. 267. Article 4 reads as follows: '[t]he Kingdom of the Netherlands and the Republic of the United States of Indonesia recognize and accept that all rights and obligations of Indonesia, under private and public law, are ipso jure transferred to the Republic of the United States of Indonesia, unless otherwise provided for in the special agreements included in the Union Statute'. The Netherlands stated that it was only the 'European part' of the Kingdom of the Netherlands and that the military forces which operated during the second military action on Java were in fact doing so

The District Court of The Hague rendered its judgment in 1953, and held that it was, in principle, the Republic of Indonesia (as the successor State) who should be responsible for the unlawful acts committed by the Dutch Army during its military campaign combating secessionist rebel groups. The Court further indicated that this did not, however, exclude the possible responsibility of the State of the Netherlands for the internationally wrongful act. It seems that the Court found the new State and the continuing State both responsible for the internationally wrongful act. In any event, the outcome of the case is not clear, and writers disagree on the actual finding of the Court.[429] The fact that the Court decided that the new State of Indonesia should be held accountable for the internationally wrongful acts committed by the predecessor State was criticized in doctrine.[430] This surprising conclusion, contrary to Rule no. 8, may be explained by the existence of an express provision contained in a treaty between Indonesia and the Netherlands, whereby the new State was held responsible for the acts committed by the Netherlands before the date of succession.[431] Thus, in another case the Supreme Court interpreted Article 4 of the *Draft Agreement on Transitional Measures* between the Netherlands and Indonesia as reflecting 'the accepted rules of international law, that the Republic [of Indonesia] – which succeeded to all the rights of the former Netherlands Indies – should also have to bear all

in the service of the other 'Asian part' of the Kingdom. The State of the Netherlands therefore contended that liability for internationally wrongful acts committed by soldiers rested on the 'Asian part' of the Kingdom.

429 Some in doctrine have indicated that the Court finally decided that the Netherlands should also compensate the plaintiff based on internal constitutional grounds. See the analysis of H. Lauterpacht, in *ILR* (1953), p. 80. This is also the position of Volkovitsch, 'Righting Wrongs', p. 2182, 2201, for whom both Indonesia and the Netherlands were held responsible by the Court. For him, the Court 'strongly urged the recognition of a principle of joint liability by which the former power would not escape responsibility'. Others writers (such as Verzijl, *International Law*, p. 226) have concluded that only Indonesia was found liable by the Court.

430 For instance, Verzijl, ibid., p. 226, concluding that the Court was entirely wrong to hold the Republic of Indonesia responsible for the unlawful acts committed by the Dutch Army. Similarly, Lauterpacht, ibid., p. 80, stating that 'from the perspective of international law the judgment seems to depart drastically from the accepted practice in respect of the liability of the successor State for torts'.

431 This is the view of Czaplinski, 'State Succession and State Responsibility', p. 348, for whom the findings of the Court were solely based upon the application of Article 4 of the Treaty between Indonesia and the Netherlands and did not express any rule of international law.

its obligations'.[432] These cases are therefore an illustration of the well-established principle that a new State is always free to decide to take over responsibility for wrongs committed by the predecessor State.[433]

4.3.3 *The Application of Rule No. 8 Is Problematic in Situations Where the Predecessor State Ceases to Exist*

As mentioned in the previous section, in the context of the creation of a new State Article 10(3) is only sensible in cases where the predecessor State *continues its existence* following the events affecting its territorial integrity. The basic principle applicable in such cases is not controversial: the predecessor State continues to be held responsible for *its own* internationally wrongful acts committed during the period of uprising (Rule no. 8).[434] However, what happens in the different context where the predecessor State *ceases to exist*, such as, for instance, in a situation of State dissolution?[435] It is evident that a State which no longer exists cannot be held accountable for wrongs committed in the past. In such cases, the predecessor State simply cannot be held responsible for such wrongs. As a result, the internationally wrongful acts committed *by the predecessor State* against a third State or a foreign investor during the period of uprising will go unpunished. The victim is left with no creditor for the damages it suffered, and it will not be able to recover any reparation. This outcome is certainly unfair for the victim.

432 *Poldermans* v. *State of the Netherlands*, Netherlands, Court of Appeal of The Hague (First Chamber), 8 December 1955, in *N.J.* (1959), no. 7 (with an analysis by Boltjes), reported in *ILR* (1957), p. 69; *Poldermans* v. *State of the Netherlands*, Netherlands, Supreme Court, 15 June 1956, in ibid. The Court added that 'since no specification of those obligations was given at the time, the provision must be construed as covering all debts which at the time of the transfer of sovereignty existed according to the Indonesian law then in force'. The case arose from the internment by the Japanese occupation authorities of a Dutch civil servant (from 1942 to 1945). During the period of internment, the plaintiff received no salary while his contract of service had not been terminated or cancelled. After the War, he sued the Netherlands for payment of that salary.

433 See analysis in Dumberry, *State Succession to International Responsibility*, p. 215 ff.

434 Thus, as noted in ILC, Report, 1975, p. 105, para. 22: 'it goes without saying that, since the pre-existing State will continue to exist, although with a reduced territory, it will still be responsible for its own acts carried out before the creation of the new State'.

435 The predecessor State also ceases to exist in situations of integration (or incorporation) of State and in instances of unification of States. I will not examine these situations because they are unlikely to arise in the specific context of wrongful acts committed *by* the predecessor State (and not by the rebels).

In my view, the solution to this problem should be based, *by analogy*, on the analysis developed by the Institute in its Resolution on State succession to responsibility.[436] Under Article 15, the obligations arising from the commission of an internationally wrongful act by the predecessor State pass to one of the successor States depending on a number of circumstances referred to under that provision.[437]

[436] IIL, 'State Succession in Matters of State Responsibility', 2015. See analysis in Kohen and Dumberry, *The Institute of International Law's Resolution*, p. 118 ff.

[437] One factor is whether the author of the internationally wrongful act was an organ of the predecessor State that later became an organ of the successor State. Another one is the existence of a 'direct link' between the consequences of a wrongful act and the territory or population of one of the successor States. See also, Article 7.

5

When the Insurrectional Movement Is Unsuccessful in Creating a New State

In the previous section, I have examined the situation where an insurrectional movement is successful in creating a new State. I will now analyse the opposite case where an insurrectional movement is *unsuccessful* in its struggle for power. Two principles will be examined in the next sections:

- The acts committed by the rebels during the insurgency are not attributable to the State (hereinafter referred to as Rule no. 9, Section 5.1); and
- The State is responsible for its own failure to exercise its due diligence obligation in order to protect foreigners and third States (hereinafter referred to as Rule no. 10, Section 5.2).

5.1 Rule No. 9: The Acts Committed by the Rebels during the Insurgency Are Not Attributable to the State

This section examines the well-recognized principle in State practice and case law whereby, as a matter of principle, a State should not be held responsible for internationally wrongful acts that have been committed by an *unsuccessful* insurrectional movement in its failed struggle to create a new State (Rule no. 9). I will first examine the rationale behind Rule no. 9 (Section 5.1.1), which will then be followed by an analysis of State practice and case law supporting this principle (Section 5.1.2).

5.1.1 The Rationale behind the Principle

Rule no. 9 has long been recognized by scholars.[438] In fact, this rule was the object of a separate provision in the 1975 draft Articles.[439] The

[438] See, writers mentioned in Atlam, *Succession d'États*, p. 296–300, 394–5.

[439] Article 14(1), ILC, 'Draft Articles on State Responsibility Adopted by the Commission on First Reading', 1996, Report of the ILC on the Work of its Forty-eighth Session, 6 May–26 July 1996, General Assembly Official Records, Fifty-first Session Supplement No. 10,

specific provision was, however, not kept in later drafts.[440] Yet, as noted by Crawford, 'although [this rule] was deleted during the second reading, this still reflects the default position under international law'.[441] In his book, the very first line he devoted to the question of 'responsibility for the acts of insurgents' indicates what the fundamental principle is: '[a]s a general rule, a State is not held responsible for the acts of insurgents'.[442] This is the same principle as Rule no. 3 (which applies, however, in the different context of a rebellion aiming at establishing a new government).[443]

It should be noted that the work of the ILC only discussed the rule in the context of situations where the insurgents aimed at establishing a *new government*.[444] In my view, there is no reason why this basic principle (Rule no. 3) should not apply in the different context where the rebels tried and failed to create a *new State*. My analysis of Rule no. 3, above, led me to the conclusion that there were at least three good reasons that justify the existence of this basic principle whereby the acts committed by the rebels in the course of an insurgency are not attributable to the State.[445] These reasons also find application when the rebels are unsuccessful in their attempt to create a new State. The conclusion, reached by Commissioner Wadsworth in his Opinion in the *Prats* case (discussed below in Section 5.1.2.1), is indeed based, inter alia, on the fact that the acts of the rebels could not be attributable to the United States because it had no control over them. The same conclusion was reached by the US–Great Britain Mixed Claims Commission in the *Hanna* case.[446] Similarly, Commissioner Palacio, in his Opinion in the *Prats* case, also mentioned that it would seem absurd to impose on the United States a duty to

UN Doc. A/51/10, chp. III, in *ILC Yearbook* vol. II(2) (1996), p. 58–65. The provision reads as follows: '[t]he conduct of an organ of an insurrectional movement which is established in the territory of a State or in any other territory under its administration shall not be considered as an act of that State under international law'.

440 The drafting history of this provision was examined above in Part I, Section 3.1.1 dealing with Rule no. 3.

441 Crawford, *State Responsibility*, p. 179.

442 Ibid., p. 170.

443 See Part I, Section 3.1.

444 Thus, Ago does not discuss in his 1972 Report the rule in the context of the (failed) attempt by rebels to create a new State. Crawford is also silent on this point.

445 See Part I, Section 3.1.2, explaining the rationale behind Rule no. 3.

446 *John H. Hanna* v. *United States*, US–Great Britain Mixed Claims Commission, case no. 2, award of 25 September 1873, discussed in Moore, *History and Digest of the International Arbitrations* (vol. III), p. 2982; UNRIAA 29, p. 144.

provide reparation to the victims of wrongful acts committed by the rebels who are the enemies against whom that State was fighting.[447]

I have noted above,[448] that while Rule no. 3 is logical and sound, it remains unfair for the victims (third States and foreigners) of wrongs committed by the rebels during the insurgency. In Part I, I explained that the existence of Rule no. 3 does not necessarily mean that such wrongs will go unpunished. Thus, the rebels are always responsible of their own wrongful acts (Rule no. 5).[449] The same rationale applies in the context of the failed attempt by rebels to create a new State. I have also noted, however, that claims against rebels were actually very rare and unlikely to be successful.[450] For that reason, I explained that there should be two 'exceptions' to Rule no. 3:

- The State should be bound by the governmental lawful 'routine activities' performed by rebels in situations where they have established a local de facto government in part of the territory (Rule no. 4A)[451]; and
- The State should also be held responsible for the consequences arising from expropriation acts committed by rebels when it resulted in some benefits for the State (Rule no. 4B).[452]

In my view, there is no reason why these two 'exceptions'[453] to Rule no. 3 should not also apply in the different context where the rebels are unsuccessful in their struggle to create a *new State*. From the perspective of the injured party, which has suffered a damage, it matters very little whether or not the insurgency led by the rebels was ultimately aimed at establishing a new government or creating a new State. In fact, in the *Socony* case (already

447 *Salvador Prats* v. *United States*, United States–Mexico Mixed Commission, case no. 748, in Moore, ibid., p. 2886; UNRIAA 29 [hereinafter referred to as '*Prats* case, 1868'], p. 187, Mexican Commissioner, Mr Palacio, p. 194, p. 198:

> [n]obody has thus far believed that the duty of governments was to indemnify their citizens for the losses and injuries sustained by cause of war; and it is not easy to perceive the reason why an alien might be entitled to claim what is refused to the citizen. Nations can and must afford protection, and prevent and punish the offenses, by all the means they have within their reach; but none has had the temerity to maintain as a principle of public law the duty of indemnifying for losses and injuries caused by *the enemy*. (emphasis in the original).

448 Part I, Section 3.1.3.

449 Part I, Section 3.2.

450 Part I, Section 3.2.3.

451 See Part I, Section 3.1.5.

452 See Part I, Section 3.1.6.

453 In fact, I believe that Rule no. 4B is not really an 'exception' to Rule no. 3. This point is examined in Part I, Section 3.1.6.

mentioned above and further discussed in the next section),[454] the Commission indicated that Yugoslavia was not responsible for the expropriation acts committed by unsuccessful rebels, who failed to create a new State in Croatia.[455] The Commission also noted that 'it further seems clear that neither the government of Yugoslavia nor its peoples *received benefits* from the takings' of property by the 'puppet' government of Croatia.[456] This passage is interesting for it shows that the question as to whether or not the government (successful at defeating the rebels) had 'benefited' from the acts of expropriation was part of the Commission's analysis. This example illustrates the relevance of Rule no. 4B in the context of the application of Rule no. 9.

5.1.2 *Case Law and State Practice Support This Principle*

The basic principle according to which the acts of *unsuccessful* rebels are not attributable to the government that defeated the insurgency has been applied in case law.[457]

5.1.2.1 The Failed Attempt by the Confederate States to Secede during the American Civil War (1861–1865)

Numerous examples of State practice and case law support Rule no. 9 in the context of the failed attempt by the Confederate forces to secede from the United States during the American Civil War (1861–5).

[454] See Section 5.1.2.2.

[455] *Socony Vacuum Oil Company*, US International Claims Commission, in *Settlements of Claims* (1949–1955), p. 77; *ILR* (1954), p. 59.

[456] Ibid., p. 59, emphasis added. The full quote is as follows:

> [t]he Kingdom of Croatia came into being as a creation of the war. It was unwanted by, and never became a part of, the permanent Government of Yugoslavia. It was not established through any dereliction on the part of the Government of Yugoslavia and that government had no control over the acts of Croatia. It further seems clear that neither the Government of Yugoslavia nor its peoples received benefits from the takings alleged by claimant. We are persuaded that the present Government of Yugoslavia has not been impressed with international responsibility for 'takings by Croatia' and, as a result, there is no reason for treating the words 'by Yugoslavia' and 'by Croatia' as synonymous. Neither do we believe that there is basis for believing that the negotiators of the Agreement intended to settle claims for takings by Croatia of the sort for which compensation is sought by claimant.

[457] It should be noted that this question was not examined by the work of the ILC. Therefore, none of the cases discussed in this section were examined by ILC Special Rapporteurs Ago or Crawford in their reports. The cases examined in this section were analysed in my book, Dumberry, *State Succession to International Responsibility*, p. 225.

First, the principle is recognized in the domestic law of the United States. Under Section 4 of the Fourteenth Amendment to the US Constitution, enacted on 28 July 1868, the United States does not assume any obligations or debts incurred by anyone 'in aid of insurrection or rebellion' of the Confederate forces.[458] The US Supreme Court also recognized the principle in *Williams* v. *Bruffy*. The Court mentioned that in the context of secession (described as 'where a portion of the inhabitants of a country have separated themselves from the parent State and established an independent government'), 'the validity of its acts, both against the parent State and its citizens or subjects, depends entirely upon its ultimate success'.[459] Thus, on the one hand, 'if [the rebels] fails to establish itself permanently [as a new State], all such acts perish with it'.[460] On the other hand, if the insurgency 'succeeds and becomes recognized, its acts from the commencement of its existence are upheld as those of an independent nation'. The Court added that: '[n]o case has been cited in argument, and we think none can be found, in which the acts of a portion of a State unsuccessfully attempting to establish a separate revolutionary government have been sustained as a matter of legal right'.[461]

Second, as a matter of State practice, the position of the United States has consistently been that it cannot be held responsible for the acts of the rebels who have been unsuccessful in their attempt to secede. US Secretary of State Seward expressed that position clearly in letters to Prussia in response to its claim for compensation for damages suffered by its nationals during the Civil War.[462]

Third, Rule no. 9 has been consistently applied by arbitral tribunals dealing with claims arising from acts committed by the Confederate armed forces in the context of the Civil War.

The principle was recognized by the US–Great Britain Mixed Claims Commission established under Articles XII–XVII of the Treaty of Washington of 8 May 1871 between the United States and Great Britain. The Treaty rejected any responsibility on behalf of the United States for the acts committed by the Confederate armed forces and, in

[458] US Const. amend. XIV, sect. 4: 'neither the United States nor any State shall assume or pay any debt or obligation incurred in aid of insurrection or rebellion against the United States, or any claims for the loss or emancipation of any slave; but all such debts, obligations, and claims shall be held illegal and void'.

[459] *Williams* v. *Bruffy*, 96 US 176, 186 (1877).

[460] Ibid.

[461] Ibid.

[462] Mr Seward, US Secretary of State to Baron Gerolt, Prussian Minister, 9 January 1866, in Moore, *Digest of International Law* (vol. VI), p. 957.

particular, 'injuries inflicted by the Confederate authorities or by private citizens of the Confederacy'.[463]

For instance, the rule has been applied in the *John H. Hanna, No. 2* case. It involved a claim filed by Mr Hanna, an English national, against the United States regarding 819 bales of cotton which had been 'destroyed by orders of the authorities of the Confederate States and of the rebel State of Louisiana, for the purpose of preventing the same from falling into the hands of the Federal forces'.[464] Great Britain, acting on behalf of the Claimant, argued that the 'so-called secession of the State of Louisiana and the other States forming the so-called Confederate States did not extinguish or suspend the liability of the United States for internationally wrongful acts committed by said States'.[465] The United States refuted this argument and maintained, on the contrary, that 'no responsibility can attach to the United States for the destruction of the claimant's property under colour of the authority of the State of Louisiana, because its destruction was not authorised by any officials representing or authorised to represent or act for the State of Louisiana under the Constitution and laws of the United States'.[466]

The Commission rejected the claim and came to the conclusion that 'the United States can not be held liable for injuries caused by the acts of rebels over whom they could exercise no control, and over which acts they had no power to prevent'.[467] In his separate opinion, US Commissioner Fraser mentioned that 'the Confederate forces were engaged at the time in a formidable rebellion against the Government of the United States'. He described the 'State of Louisiana' which had 'concurred and participated in the destruction of the claimant's property' as a 'a rebel organization, existing and acting as much in hostility to the Government of the United States as was the Confederate States, so called'.[468] He further described the 'State of Louisiana' as 'in form and fact a creature unknown to the Constitution of the United States, and acting in hostility to it'.[469] This entity 'was an instrumentality of the

[463] Moore, *History and Digest of the International Arbitrations* (vol. III), p. 684. These cases are also referred to in Moore, *Digest of International Law* (vol. I), p. 60.

[464] *John H. Hanna* v. *United States*, US–Great Britain Mixed Claims Commission, case no. 2, award of 25 September 1873, UNRIAA 29, p. 143–5; Moore, *History and Digest of the International Arbitrations* (vol. III), p. 2983.

[465] Ibid., p. 2983.

[466] Ibid., p. 2984–5.

[467] Ibid., p. 2985.

[468] Ibid., p. 2986–7.

[469] Ibid.

rebellion' and 'its agency, in the spoliation of this cotton can not be likened to the act of a State of the American Union claiming to exist under the Constitution'.[470] He concluded that the United States government could not be held responsible for the acts committed by unsuccessful rebels.[471] The issue also arose in cases decided by the US–Great Britain Mixed Claims Commission in the *Stewart* case[472] and in the *A. E. Campbell & Co.* case.[473]

In his book, Silvanie cited several cases where the United States was held not responsible for *loans* made by foreign citizens to the (ultimately unsuccessful) insurgents during the war.[474] One relevant example is the *Barrett* case decided by the US–Great Britain Mixed Claims Commission of 1871.[475] The case involved Mr Barrett, a British citizen and business owner residing in England, who had in his possession a cotton-loan bond issued by the Confederate States (whereby the Confederate States paid

[470] Ibid.

[471] Ibid.

[472] *Stewart* v. *United States*, US–Great Britain Mixed Claims Commission, case no. 339, in Moore, *History and Digest of the International Arbitrations* (vol. III), p. 2989. The case involved the purchase of cotton by Mr Stewart in Mississippi. He proceeded to send a steamboat to bring back that same cotton, but was prevented to do so by the captain of a gunboat. Soon after, his cotton was burned by the Confederate rebels. The Commission concluded that the captain committed no wrong. It also held that 'the subsequent destruction of the property by the rebels was not necessary or natural consequence of any wrongful act of the United States or any officer of the United States, and that no liability existed against the United States in respect of the transaction'.

[473] *A.E. Campbell & Co.* v. *United States*, US–Great Britain Mixed Claims Commission, case no. 290, in Moore, *History and Digest of the International Arbitrations* (vol. III), p. 2990. During the Civil War, a ship belonging to British merchants residing in England, which was transporting a cargo of sugar from Trinidad de Cuba to England, was captured by the Confederate Army and sent to Charleston, South Carolina. The Confederate States recognized the neutrality of the ship. As a result, when the content of the cargo was sold, the Confederates agreed to hold the proceedings of the sale and to refund the England merchants. When the United States Army conquered the city of Charleston, it seized the Confederates treasury, including the proceeds of the cargo of sugar belonging to the British national. The United States argued, inter alia, that it could not be responsible for any action committed by the Confederates. The Commission did not discuss this argument because the claim was rejected on the grounds that no evidence had been provided showing that the cargo was the property of the British Merchants. Another relevant case is *Laurie and others*, in Moore, *History and Digest of the International Arbitrations* (vol. III), p. 2987, involving the destruction of property (tobacco) by the rebels. The Commission rejected the claims without providing much reasoning on the question of State responsibility under international law.

[474] Silvanie, *Responsibility of States*, p. 11, 15 ff.

[475] *Edward Alfred Barrett* v. *United States*, American–British Commission, 14 December 1871, No. 18, in *Hale's Report*, p. 154; Moore, *History and Digest of the International Arbitrations* (vol. III), p. 2901.

200£ sterling with interest of 7 per cent per annum, until redemption of the principal at par). In 1865, the United States seized all the public assets of the Confederate States. This seizure of such property prevented the Confederate States from paying their cotton-loan bond holders to Mr Barrett, effectively denying him of the securities he was entitled to. The Commission held that the United States 'was not liable for the payment of debts contracted by the rebel authorities' because 'the rebellion was a struggle against the United States for the establishment in a portion of the country belonging to the United States of a new state in the family of nations, and it failed'.[476] The Commission therefore endorsed Rule no. 9 whereby loan agreements signed by (ultimately unsuccessful) rebels with foreign nationals during the insurgency are not attributable to the State fighting them. The Commission explained that foreigners contracting with rebels should assume the risk related to the nature of such a venture.[477]

Another Mixed Commission established under a treaty enacted between the United States and Mexico on 4 July 1868 also reached the same conclusion of non-responsibility.[478] The *Prats* case dealt with the claim of a Mexican national who had stocked 213 bales of cotton on board of a British vessel in the port of New Orleans. After the capture of New Orleans by the United States forces, men, which were acting under the authority of the Confederate Army, boarded the British ship and burned the vessel and its content.[479] At the outset, Commissioner Wadsworth in his Opinion referred to the conflict as a 'war' involving the United States against 'a portion of its citizens styling themselves "the Confederate States of America"'.[480] He asked the following question: 'is the United States responsible for injuries committed during the late civil war within the arena of the struggle by the armed forces of the so-called Confederate States to the property of aliens, "transient or dwelling?"'[481] He answered the question in the negative. He explained that the main reason which justifies the absence of responsibility for the United States

[476] Ibid., Moore, ibid., p. 2901.

[477] Ibid., UNRIAA 29, p. 137, 138: '[p]ersons contracting with the so-called Confederate States voluntarily assumed the risk of [its] failure, and accepted its obligations, subject to the paramount rights of the parent state by force to crush the rebel organization, and seize all its assets and property, whether hypothecated by it or not to its creditors'.

[478] The work of the commission is discussed in Moore, *History and Digest of the International Arbitrations* (vol. III), p. 2144–67.

[479] *Prats* case, 1868, p. 187.

[480] Ibid., Commissioner Wadsworth in his Opinion, p. 190.

[481] Ibid., p. 192.

had nothing to do with the question as to whether or not the rebels had been recognized the status of belligerent by other States.[482] In fact, non-responsibility resulted from the United States having *no control* over the territory conquered by the Confederate States.[483] Commissioner Wadsworth also mentioned that 'aliens residing and trading inside the rebel territory acted at their peril'.[484] He concluded that the Claimant, conducting business in New Orleans in 1862, was indeed 'engaged in commerce injurious to the United States'.[485] The Mexican Commissioner, Mr Palacio, agreed that the claim should be rejected on the grounds that the United States had fulfilled its due diligence obligation towards foreigners in the context of the Civil War.[486] His reasoning on this important point will be examined below.[487]

Finally, it should be added that similar findings, dealing with 'tortious' acts committed by the Confederate Army, were made by the Mexican–US Mixed Commission in the *Nieves Olirares* case[488] and in the *Baltimore Insurance Co.* case.[489] The *Alleghanian* case, decided by the Peruvian–US Claims Commission, will be examined below.[490]

[482] Ibid., p. 191: '[n]on responsibility on the part of the United States for injuries by the Confederate enemy within the territories of that government to aliens did not result from the recognition of the belligerency of the rebel enemy by the strangers' sovereign. It resulted from the fact of belligerency itself, and whether recognized or not by other governments'.

[483] Ibid., p. 192:

> The principle of non-responsibility for acts of rebel enemies in time of civil war rests upon the ground that the latter have withdrawn themselves by force of arms from the control and jurisdiction of the sovereign, putting it out of his power, so long as they make their resistance effectual, to extend his protection within the hostile territory to either strangers or his own subjects, between whom, in this respect, no inequality of rights can justly be asserted.

[484] Ibid., p. 193. He added that 'the fact of residence and trade constituted them enemies of the United States, in common with the rest of the inhabitants whose "spirit and industry" contributed to the resources of the enemy'.

[485] Ibid., p. 193. On this point, he added: '[w]e are at a loss, therefore, to perceive on what ground aliens resident in the hostile territory could claim the protection of a power lawfully exercising the rights of war against that territory and all its inhabitants'.

[486] Ibid., p. 196.

[487] See Section 5.2.2.2.

[488] *Nieves Olirares* v. *United States*, US–Mexico Mixed Commission, case no. 749, in MS. Op. VI. p. 160; Moore, *History and Digest of the International Arbitrations* (vol. III), p. 2900.

[489] *Baltimore Insurance Co.* v. *United States*, US–Mexico Mixed Commission, case no. 756, in MS. Op. V. p. 446; Moore, ibid.

[490] See Section 5.2.2.2.

5.1.2.2 *Socony Vacuum Oil Company* Case

The *Socony Vacuum Oil Company* case decided by the US International Claims Commission has already been mentioned above.[491] The case involved the taking of property of the Claimant (a US company) by the 'independent' State of Croatia during the Second World War. The Claims Commission concluded that this so-called 'independent' State was actually a 'puppet' State which had been created and controlled by Italy and Germany.[492] Thus, at no point in time did the government of this 'puppet' State had partial nor complete control over its territory and population; it simply disappeared upon the retreat of these foreign troops.[493] In other words, the Claims Commission considered the 'independent' State of Croatia as an *unsuccessful* attempt by an insurrectional group (backed by foreign troops) to secede from Yugoslavia. This is therefore an example where the rebellion had failed at creating a new State. Yugoslavia had never ceased to exist. The Claims Commission ultimately rejected the claim on the grounds that the taking of property which occurred under the authority of the 'puppet' State of Croatia was not covered by the 1948 bilateral agreement entered into by the United States and Yugoslavia, which only covered the 'taking by Yugoslavia of property'. Yugoslavia was therefore not held responsible for such acts.

The case supports Rule no. 9 whereby a State should not be held responsible for internationally wrongful acts committed by an *unsuccessful* insurrectional movement in its struggle for secession. Thus, the decision explicitly stated that it was 'settled that a state has no international legal responsibility to compensate for damage to or confiscation of property by a "puppet state" or local *de facto* government' like Croatia, which, the Commission importantly added, 'also possesses

[491] *Socony Vacuum Oil Company*, US International Claims Commission, in *Settlements of Claims* (1949–1955), p. 77; *ILR* (1954), p. 55. See Section 4.2.5.1.2.

[492] Ibid., p. 60:

> Croatia is defined by contemporary writers as a 'puppet state' or 'puppet government', terms which appear to be of comparatively recent adoption in the field of international law. We have found no decisions of international arbitral tribunals which have decided whether a 'parent' state is responsible for takings of property by a 'puppet state' or 'puppet government' which was established and maintained within its borders while a war was in progress and claimant has brought none to our attention.

[493] Ibid., p. 59: '[i]t appears well established that the Kingdom of Croatia was created by German and Italian forces and threat of force; that during its entire 4-year life it was subject to the will of Germany or Italy, or both, in varying degrees, except as to civil administration matters; and that it ceased to exist upon the retreat of the German forces'.

characteristics of '*unsuccessful revolutionists*".[494] While the case has been analysed on a few occasions by writers as one involving insurgents unsuccessfully attempting to establish a new *government*,[495] it is, in my view, more appropriate to consider it as one involving a (failed) attempt at secession.[496] Finally, it should be added that the Claims Commission came to the exact same conclusion in two other cases dealing with damage caused by the 'puppet' State of Croatia: the *Popp* case[497] involving the taking of a motor car, and the *Versic* case concerning personal injuries suffered in a camp.[498]

5.1.2.3 Other Cases

In his article,[499] Silvanie refers to the case of *Emma McGrady & Augustus Wilson* v. *Spain* as one where the US–Spain Claims Commission of 1871 'absolved Spain from any liability for damages caused as a result of an attack on an American plantation and for destruction of other property by Cuban insurgents in 1870'.[500] The events took place during one of several liberation wars conducted by insurgents fighting for the independence of Cuba against Spain (until the Island was ceded by Spain to the United States in 1898). Not much information is available about this case aside from the fact that Spain argued that its soldiers had protected the plantation against the attacks led by insurgents, while stating that it could not be held responsible for the wrongs committed by them. In his book, Moore simply noted that the arbitrator agreed with Spain's position in the matter and rejected the claim.[501]

[494] Ibid., p. 61, emphasis added.

[495] Danielle Morris, 'Revolutionary Movements and De Facto Governments – Implications of the "Arab Spring" for International Investors,' *Arb. Int.* 28(4) (2012), p. 738; Rousseau, *Droit international public* (vol. III), p. 510.

[496] Crawford, *State Responsibility*, p. 177.

[497] *Popp Claim*, US International Claims Commission, in *Settlements of Claims, 1949–1955*, p. 76; *ILR* (1954), p. 63.

[498] *Versic Claim*, US International Claims Commission, in *Settlements of Claims, 1949–1955*, p. 58; *ILR* (1954), p. 63.

[499] Silvanie, 'Responsibility of States for Acts of Insurgent Governments', p. 91.

[500] *Emma McGrady & Augustus Wilson* v. *Spain*, 25 April 1874, no. 59, *Span Com.* (1871); Moore, *History and Digest of the International Arbitrations* (vol. III), p. 2981–2.

[501] Moore, ibid., p. 2982. Moore also referred (p. 2982) to the *Zaldivar* case decided by the same Commission which involved the destruction of property: *Miguel Zaldivar* v. *Spain*, 26 Dec. 1882, no. 127, *Span Com.* (1871). The evidence was not conclusive as to whether the destruction was the result of the actions of either the rebels or the Spanish soldiers. Moore simple noted that 'in this conflict of testimony the arbitrators held that they must act upon the presumption that exist in favour of the party who defends'.

5.2 Rule No. 10: The State Is Responsible for Its Own Failure to Exercise Its Due Diligence Obligation to Protect Foreigners and Third States

This section investigates the consequences of the acts committed *by the government* while fighting rebels during the insurrection once their attempt to create a new State has failed. In the following sections, I will first examine the rationale behind Rule no. 10, whereby the State is responsible for its own failure to exercise its due diligence obligation to protect foreigners and third States in relation to the conduct of rebels (Section 5.2.1). This analysis will then be followed by a survey of State practice and case law supporting this principle (Section 5.2.2).

5.2.1 The Rationale behind the Principle

As mentioned above,[502] when dealing with unsuccessful attempts of rebels to establish new *governments*, the ILC Commentaries stated that there was 'ample jurisprudence for th[e] principle', mentioned in the *Home Frontier and Foreign Missionary Society* case,[503] that 'no Government can be held responsible for the conduct of rebellious groups committed in violation of its authority, where it is itself guilty of no breach of good faith, or of no negligence in suppressing insurrection'.[504] Thus, as a matter of principle, a State is not responsible for damages resulting from its *own use* of proportionate and reasonable military force while fighting an insurgency, unless its conduct is in violation of one of its international law obligations.[505] Responsibility arises as a result of a State's own failure to discharge its due diligence duty of vigilance, prevention and punishment in relation to the conduct of rebels.[506] This is the basic principle applicable in the context where the rebels fail in their attempt to establish a *new government* (Rule no. 6).[507] There is no reason for not applying the same principle in a situation where the rebels are crushed in their attempt to create a *new State*.[508] Thus, as noted by

502 See Part I, Section 3.1.

503 *Home Frontier and Foreign Missionary Society of the United Brethren in Christ (United States)* v. *Great Britain*, 18 December 1920, UNRIAA 6.

504 ILC, Commentaries, 2001, p. 50, para. 3.

505 This principle has already been examined above. See Part I, Section 3.3.2.

506 See Part I, Section 3.3.3.

507 See Part I, Section 3.3.

508 Akehurst, 'State Responsibility for the Wrongful Acts of Rebels', p. 49, indicating that 'the defendant State must not have been negligent in permitting foreign subjects to suffer

Crawford in his book, 'the state's victory over an insurrectionist movement does not automatically excuse it from responsibility, a point made clear by ARSIWA Article 10(3), which preserves for application those grounds of attribution found in ARSIWA Articles 4–9'.[509] The 2001 ILC Commentaries made it clear that the exception mentioned in Article 10(3) applies in the specific context of the creation of a *new State* (dealt with in Article 10(2)).[510]

5.2.2 *Case Law and State Practice Support This Principle*

The findings of awards examined in Part I on the scope and content of this due diligence obligation are perfectly applicable to the situation analysed in this section.[511] I have found only a few cases dealing with the question of a State's due diligence obligation in the specific context where the rebels have been defeated in their attempt to create a new State. These cases are discussed in the next sections.

5.2.2.1 *AAPL* v. *Sri Lanka* Case

The *AAPL* case concerned the destruction in 1987 of shrimp farming facilities partially owned by a Hong Kong company and the killing of several civilian staff members of that farm. The Sri Lankan Security Forces launched an attack that led to damages in the context of their counterinsurgency operation against the Liberation Fighters of Tamil Elaam (the 'Tamil Tigers'). At the time of the events, the rebels were in control of the key areas where the farm was located. The rebels were fighting for the self-determination of the Tamil nation and its secession from Sri Lanka. The

injuries at the hands of the rebels' and that 'the rule may now be regarded as firmly established, and applies to all rebellions, whether the object of the rebellion is the overthrow of the central government or the secession of a portion of the State's territory to form a new State'.

509 Crawford, *State Responsibility*, p. 179.

510 ILC, Commentaries, 2001, p. 53, para. 16:

> [e]xceptional cases may occur where the State was in a position to adopt measures of vigilance, prevention or punishment in respect of the movement's conduct but improperly failed to do so. This possibility is preserved by paragraph 3 of article 10, which provides that the attribution rules of *paragraphs 1 and 2* are without prejudice to the attribution to a State of any conduct, however related to that of the movement concerned, which is to be considered an act of that State by virtue of other provisions in Part II. (emphasis added).

511 See Part I, Sections 3.3.3.2 and 3.3.3.3.

award was rendered in 1990 when the insurrection was still an on-going struggle for power. The events could therefore be considered at the time as a (so far) failed attempt at secession. It is only many years later (in 2009) that the central government finally crushed the rebellion.

The majority of the Tribunal explained that 'it is a generally accepted rule of International Law, clearly stated in international arbitral awards and in the writings of the doctrinal authorities' that 'a State on whose territory an insurrection occurs is not responsible for the loss of damage sustained by foreign investors *unless it can be shown that the Government of that state failed to provide the standard of protection required, either by treaty, or under general customary law*' and that 'failure to provide the standard of protection required entails that state's international responsibility for losses suffered'.[512] While it has been contested by Asante in his dissenting opinion,[513] this statement is in accordance with the previously mentioned general principle embodied in Rule no. 6.[514] One important point which should be highlighted here, is that the destruction of the facility were *not* accomplished by the rebels.[515] Thus, the majority of the Tribunal noted that 'all the events in question [i.e. the destruction of the facility] took place during the two weeks period when the farm was under the exclusive control of the security forces'.[516] The majority of the Tribunal was, however, unable to establish with certainty whether such wrongs had been committed by the governmental forces.[517]

512 *Asian Agricultural Products ltd.* v. *Sri Lanka*, ICSID Case No ARB/87/3, Final Award, 27 June 1990 [hereinafter referred to as '*AAPL* case, 1990'], para. 72, emphasis added.

513 Ibid., Dissenting Opinion of Asante, in *ICSID Rev.* (1990), p. 589:

> [t]he majority opinion goes to great lengths to stress only the exceptional situations in which a host country may be held liable for loss or damage sustained by aliens in armed conflict or other civil commotion, but pays scant attention to the general rule of customary international law that a host State is not liable for such losses or damage. Numerous publicists and decisions of international tribunals overwhelmingly support the position that, as a general rule, a host State is not liable under customary international law for losses or damage sustained by a foreigner due to war, armed conflict, insurrection, revolt, riot, a national emergency or other civil disturbances.

514 See Part I, Section 3.3.

515 *AAPL* case, 1990, para. 85(d): 'no conclusive evidence sustains the Respondent's allegation that the destruction were "caused directly by the terrorist action"'.

516 Ibid., para. 85(d).

517 Ibid., para. 85(d):

> [n]ether Party succeeded in providing the Tribunal with convincing evidence about: (i) the circumstances under which the destruction of the premises took place after they came under the control of the governmental

As noted by one writer, 'faced with the impossibility of establishing who was directly responsible for the acts, the Tribunal thus engaged in an analysis of whether the governmental forces were capable of providing protection to prevent the destruction of the farm, which indeed was assessed through application of the due diligence standard'.[518] Thus, as explained by the majority of the Tribunal, 'the adjudication of the State's responsibility has to be undertaken by determining whether the governmental forces were capable, under the prevailing circumstances, to provide adequate protection that could have prevented the destructions from taking place totally or partially'.[519] The analysis of whether or not the due diligence obligation had been breached focused on the 'inaction and omission'[520] by the State to take precautionary measures to protect the foreign investor. The majority of the Tribunal considered that Sri Lanka had failed to take reasonable and appropriate precautionary measures to remove suspected staff members from the farm through peaceful means before launching its counter-insurgency attack against the rebels.[521] It considered that Sri Lanka 'violated its due diligence obligation which requires undertaking all possible measures that could be reasonably expected to prevent the eventual occurrence of killings and property destruction'.[522] As one writer rightly pointed out, the majority of the Tribunal in this case 'did not apply the due diligence standard to the acts of State organs which had caused harm'.[523] The reasoning of the majority of the Tribunal is rather curious. For example, it applied the standard of due diligence to the government's *omissions*.[524] As rightly noted by Blanco, 'a possible self-reference problem becomes apparent' since it

forces, (ii) who are the persons responsible for the effective destruction of the farm premises (iii) how war the destruction committed; and (iv) how the subsequent acts causing the loss of the prawns in ponds took place.

518 Eric de Brabandere, 'Host States' Due Diligence Obligations in International Investment Law', *Syracuse JIL & Commerce* 42(2) (2015), p. 335.

519 *AAPL* case, 1990, para. 85(d).

520 Ibid., para. 85(b).

521 Ibid., para. 85(d).

522 Ibid., para. 85(b). It held that the 'Respondent's responsibility is established under international law' (para. 86) and ordered it to pay the Claimant some US $ 460,000 in compensation.

523 de Brabandere, 'Host States' Due Diligence Obligations', p. 335. This position is critically assessed by Mantilla Blanco, *Full Protection and Security*, p. 261–2.

524 On this point, see: Stephen C. Vasciannie, 'Bilateral Investment Treaties and Civil Strife: The AAPL v. Sri Lanka Arbitration', *Netherlands ILR* (1992), p. 335: 'in the end, the majority found the Government liable not because of acts of commission on the part of its agents, but rather on grounds pertaining to the Government's failure to provide adequate protection for the claimant's property'.

would 'require the state to exercise due diligence in respect of *its own conduct*, as opposed to some *external* phenomenon'.[525]

Asante in his dissenting opinion came to the conclusion that the Government had not been 'negligent in the use or failure to use the forces at its disposal for the prevention or suppression of the insurrection' and that it 'applied itself energetically in employing its forces for the suppression of the insurrection that had been launched by determined, formidable and well armed insurgents in inaccessible terrain'.[526] According to him, the Government's security forces could not be considered guilty of wanton destruction of property since the majority of the Tribunal could not establish that such forces had actually destroyed the farm.[527] He is also very critical of the findings of the majority of the Tribunal on the question of the failure by the government to take precautionary measures in breach of its due diligence obligation.[528] There is some merit to the observation made by Asante. The element of precautionary measures, referred to by the majority of the Tribunal, seems to put a very high threshold of conduct on the Respondent. It has also been noted that the award's test imposed, in effect, a strict or absolute standard of liability on the Government.[529] Finally, another

525 Mantilla Blanco, *Full Protection and Security*, p. 261, emphasis in the original.

526 *AAPL* case, 1990, Dissenting Opinion of Asante, in *ICSID Rev.* (1990), p. 592.

527 Ibid.

528 Ibid., p. 593–4:

> The Tribunal's enunciation and application of due diligence rule fails to take into account the national emergency and extraordinary conditions under which the Government mounted a strategic and highly sensitive security operation to regain its sovereign control of the area of insurgency. The Government was confronted with essentially a force majeure situation. Once it is conceded that the Government had a compelling sovereign duty to undertake a military operation to regain control, the timing and modalities of the security operation must surely fall within its exclusive discretion. In this regard the Tribunal should be slow to second-guess the tactics and strategies of military commanders on the ground.

529 John Baloro, 'Aspects of the Law on the Responsibility of a Host State for Injuries to Foreign Investment During Internal Armed Conflicts: The ICSID Award in Asian Agricultural Products Limited (AAPL) v. Republic of Sri Lanka', *South African YIL* 18 (1992–3), p. 125–6, noting that the imposition of such an absolute standard 'rendered the government of Sri Lanka an all-weather insurer or guarantor of foreign investors operating in its territory'. See also, Mantilla Blanco, *Full Protection and Security*, p. 261–2, highlighting what the award stands for in terms of the level of due diligence required from States:

> This holding provides a clear indication that responsibility was established for an *omission* in the exercise of due diligence in the *mitigation* of

relevant point that should be highlighted is that it may not have been at all possible and feasible for the Government to actually take any of the precautionary measures envisaged by the majority.[530]

5.2.2.2 Other Cases

The first relevant example is the *Alleghanian* case involving an American ship transporting guano, which belonged to the government of Peru, from Baltimore to the United Kingdom.[531] The ship was attacked in 1862 in Virginia during the American Civil War by men belonging to the Confederate Navy. The ship was sunk and part of the cargo of guano was lost (some of the guano was recovered). The Government of Peru filed a claim for compensation to the Peruvian–US Claims Commission for the damage sustained.[532] The United States rejected the claim on the grounds that the damage had been caused by the rebels. This position is clearly expressed in a diplomatic note dated 9 January 1863 from Mr Seward, US Secretary of State, to Mr Barreda, the Peruvian Minister to

> damages, including public damages, that could *eventually* occur in connection with the military maneuver planned by the Sri Lankan army. It could hence be said that the state was held liable not only for failing to prevent injuries by the rebels but, most importantly, at least for present purposes, *for failing to mitigate collateral damages* associated to its *own actions*. (emphasis in the original).

530 *AAPL* case, 1990, Dissenting Opinion of Asante, in *ICSID Rev.* (1990), p. 593–4:

> [t]he precautionary measure envisaged by the majority opinion would have been a reasonable police measure if the situation to be addressed was no more than an ordinary case of civil disorder. However, in the face of a major insurrection launched by well-armed insurgents engaged in a sophisticated guerrilla warfare against Government forces, it seems unrealistic to expect a major counter-insurgency operation to be preceded by routine police warnings. It does not seem feasible or reasonable to expect the Government to take such a step when launching a sensitive security operation against powered insurgents who had infiltrated the entire Batticaloa area. . . . The majority opinion hardly adverts to the fact that the insurrection had developed into a full-scale civil war with tragic loss of life on both sides. . . . These conditions of civil war, in my opinion, constituted an extraordinary situation which did not admit of reliance on the type of leisurely police precautionary measures envisaged by the Tribunal. In the circumstances I would reject any finding of negligence or lack of due diligence against the Respondent.

On this point, see: Vasciannie, 'Bilateral Investment Treaties', p. 353.

531 *Alleghanian* case, in Moore, *History and Digest of the International Arbitrations* (vol. II), p. 1621 ff.

532 The work of the commission is discussed in Moore, ibid., p. 1615 ff.

the United States.[533] The letter was sent *during* the Civil War and the events are described as 'act of treasons and piracy' committed by 'revolutionary insurgents' for which the United States should not be responsible.[534] Mr Seward also emphasized that the United States had, in any event, fulfilled its due diligence obligation to prevent the commission of wrongful acts and to repress and punish the wrongdoers.[535] The Commission held that it did not have jurisdiction over the claim on the grounds that the claim had not been filed by an individual (but by the Government of Peru).[536] This case is nevertheless relevant for it provides a concrete example of where the Respondent State recognized the existence of Rule no. 10.

Another relevant instance is the *Socony* award (mentioned above)[537] where the Commission stated that it had been 'settled that a state has no international legal responsibility to compensate for damage to or confiscation of property' committed by 'unsuccessful revolutionists' who

533 Note of US Secretary of State Mr Seward to Mr Barreda, the Peruvian Minister to the United States, 9 January 1863, in Moore, ibid., p. 1622 ff.: '[t]he United States Government is not liable for loss to Peruvian citizens caused by the destruction of their property on board a ship in Chesapeake Bay, in 1862, such destruction being effected by a sudden attack of insurgents, which could not by due diligence have been averted by the Government of the United States'.

534 Moore, ibid., p. 1623.

535 Ibid., p. 1623–4:

> [The Reports and papers from the US Navy Department] clearly show that the government was in no wise informed or cognizant of the crime before its commission, although it was extraordinarily vigilant and active in military and naval operations on the waters and shores of the Chesapeake; that its agents hastened to arrest and defeat the criminal enterprise as soon as it came to their knowledge, and that those agents adopted the most energetic and effective measures to prevent the destruction of the ship and cargo, and to bring the offenders to punishment, and to compel them to make restitution to the parties aggrieved. . . . This government regrets as sincerely as the Peruvian Government can that its efforts to accomplish these objects have been thus far unsuccessful. What has happened, however, in the case of the *Alleghanian* has occurred without any fault whatever on the part of this government, has been committed by disloyal citizens over whom, through the operations of civil war, it has temporarily lost its control. The government, moreover, has spared no reasonable effort to redress the injuries which have been committed and to repair the losses which have been incurred.

536 Subsequently to this correspondence, the guano aboard the ship was recovered in a damage condition and was sold in Baltimore in 1863. The Peruvian government in fact received half of the proceeds (i.e. US$ 12,981.20): Moore, ibid., p. 1624.

537 See Section 5.1.2.2.

wanted to create the new State of Croatia during the Second World War.[538] The award also noted that there were 'exceptions to the general principle as for instance where there is fault or lack of diligence on the part of the State in suppression of the revolution'.[539] Therefore, the award endorsed Rule no. 10.

In the *Prats* case (mentioned above),[540] Commissioner Wadsworth recognized, in his opinion, the basic principle that after its victory the government is *not* responsible for any damage suffered by a third State or a foreigner as a result of its use of military force while fighting an insurgency.[541] He also acknowledged the possibility that the United States could be held 'liable for neglect of' its due diligence duty to protect foreigners under international law.[542] He, however, believed that it 'would be difficult to show such neglect, in view of the history of the late civil war, and particularly of the capture of New Orleans'. Importantly, as mentioned above, for him, 'no such duty, in fact, rested on the United States after the commencement of the war' because the United States had effectively no control over the territory of the Confederate States.[543] In his Opinion, the Mexican Commissioner, Mr Palacio, focused on defining the applicable test of the due diligence obligation required from State. As mentioned above in Part I,[544] he explained in some detail that this duty of protection requires

538 *Socony Vacuum Oil Company*, US International Claims Commission, in *Settlements of Claims* (1949–1955), p. 77; *ILR* (1954), p. 61.

539 Ibid., p. 61.

540 See Section 5.1.2.1.

541 *Prats* case, 1868, p. 193–4: 'We are at a loss, therefore, to perceive on what ground aliens resident in the hostile territory could claim the protection of a power lawfully exercising the rights of war against that territory and all its inhabitants. It is certain, if the forces of the United States, in the course of their operations to reduce the forts of the enemy below New Orleans and to capture the city, had destroyed the vessel and cotton, that government would not thereby have incurred any responsibility to claimant's government . . . If, therefore, persons residing within the arena of the struggle have no right to demand compensation from either of the belligerents, much less can such persons rightly demand indemnity from one belligerent for losses inflicted by the other'.

542 Ibid., Opinion of Commissioner Wadsworth, p. 192.

543 Ibid.:

> [t]hat government was under no obligation, by treaty or the law of nations, to protect the property of aliens situate inside the enemy country against the enemy. The international duty of the United States or its engagements by treaty to extend protection to aliens, transient or dwelling, in its territories, ceased inside the territory held by the insurgents from the time such territory was withdrawn by war from the control of that government, and until her authority and jurisdiction were again established over it.

544 See Part I, Sections 3.3.3.2.1 and 3.3.3.2.2.

a State to do everything that is possible and feasible (but not what is impossible).[545] He concluded that the United States had not failed in its duty of protection towards foreigners and rejected the claim.

Finally, the last relevant example is the *Iloilo Claims* case arising from the internationally wrongful acts committed by Filipino insurgents against British nationals in the context of a rebellion in the Philippines.[546] Under a treaty signed in December 1898, Spain ceded sovereignty over the Philippines to the United States, but the treaty was only ratified in April 1899. In the meantime, after the Spanish army evacuated the Iloilo islands in December 1898, Filipino insurgents took over and an insurrection started. About two months later, the US Army arrived on the Islands to put down the revolt. During this period of turmoil, some property belonging to British nationals were destroyed. They claimed compensation before the British-United States Claims Commission. This claim therefore involved wrongful acts committed by unsuccessful Filipino insurgents in their failed attempt at secession from the United States (to which the Islands had just been ceded a few months before the events).[547] Great Britain essentially argued that the United States had been negligent in its response to the actions taken by the insurgents. The Commission came to the conclusion that the United States had adequately fulfilled its due diligence obligation.[548]

545 *Prats* case, 1868, Mexican Commissioner, Mr Palacio, p. 194, p. 196.

546 *Several British Subjects (Great Britain)* v. *United States [the Iloilo Claims]*, British–United States Claims Commission, 19 November 1925, in *AJIL* 20 (1926), p. 382–4; UNRIAA 6, p. 158.

547 The so-called Filipino Republic made a Declaration of war against United States on 4 February 1899.

548 *Several British Subjects*, p. 160:

> [t]here was no wanton or intentional destruction of property by the vessels or troops of the United States. Indeed, there is evidence that the troops exerted themselves vigorously to put out the fires and to stop looting. The most that is claimed is that, if the operations of landing and taking the town had been carried out in a different way, the burning by the insurgents might have been prevented. But the circumstances were difficult and the general situation was trying. The operations were in charge of experienced officers and we do not feel competent to criticize their judgment as to the conduct of military operations. Considering all the circumstances, we do not think that any culpable disregard of the interests of the claimants has been shown.

Conclusion

Summary of Findings

In this final chapter, I will summarize my findings and briefly identify the ten basic 'rules' set out in this book:

- Rule no. 1: When a rebel group is successful at establishing a new government, that new government remains responsible for the acts committed by the previous government while fighting the rebels.
- Rule no. 2: When a rebel group is successful at establishing a new government, the acts committed by the rebels during the insurgency are attributable to the State after their victory.
- Rule no. 3: When the rebels are not successful in their attempt to establish a new government, as a matter of principle, the acts committed by them during the insurgency are not attributable to the State once the insurgency has failed.
- Rule no. 4A: When the rebels are not successful in their attempt to establish a new government, the State should be bound by the 'governmental' lawful 'routine activities' performed by the rebels in situations where they have established a local de facto government in part of the territory.
- Rule no. 4B: When the rebels are not successful in their attempt to establish a new government, the State should also be held responsible for the consequences arising from an expropriation act committed by the rebels when it results in some benefits for the State.
- Rule no. 5: The fact that the acts of unsuccessful rebels (to establish a new government) are not attributable to the State does not necessarily mean that such wrongs will go unpunished: the rebels are always responsible for their own wrongful acts.
- Rule no. 6: When the rebels are not successful in their attempt to establish a new government, a State is generally not responsible for damages resulting from the use of its own military force in the course of fighting an insurgency, unless its conduct breaches one of its

international law obligations. Yet, it remains that a State is always responsible for its own failure to exercise its due diligence obligation to protect foreigners and third States. Thus, responsibility arises as a result of a State's failure to discharge its due diligence obligation of vigilance, prevention and punishment in relation to the conduct of rebels.

- Rule no. 7: When a rebel group is successful in creating a new State, the acts committed by the rebels during the insurgency are attributable to the new State.
- Rule no. 8: When a rebel group is successful in creating a new State, that State is not responsible for acts committed by the predecessor State while fighting the rebels during the insurgency. The predecessor State (if it continues to exists) remains responsible for its own wrongs.
- Rule no. 9: When the rebels are not successful in their attempt to create a new State, the acts committed by them during the insurgency are not attributable to the State.
- Rule no. 10: When the rebels are not successful in their attempt to create a new State, the State remains responsible for its own failure to exercise its due diligence obligation to protect foreigners and third States in relation to the conduct of rebels.

INDEX

CAMBRIDGE STUDIES IN INTERNATIONAL AND COMPARATIVE LAW

Books in the Series

165 *Rebellions and Civil Wars: State Responsibility for the Conduct of Insurgents*
Patrick Dumberry

164 *The International Law of Energy*
Jorge Viñuales

163 *The Three Ages of International Commercial Arbitration*
Mikaël Schinazi

162 *Repetition and International Law*
Wouter Werner

161 *State Responsibility and Rebels: The History and Legacy of Protecting Investment Against Revolution*
Kathryn Greenman

160 *Rewriting Histories of the Use of Force: The Narrative of 'Indifference'*
Agatha Verdebout

159 *The League of Nations and the Protection of the Environment*
Omer Aloni

158 *International Investment Law and Legal Theory: Expropriation and the Fragmentation of Sources*
Jörg Kammerhofer

157 *Legal Barbarians: Identity, Modern Comparative Law and the Global South*
Daniel Bonilla Maldonado

156 *International Human Rights Law Beyond State Territorial Control*
Antal Berkes

155 *The Crime of Aggression under the Rome Statute of the International Criminal Court*
Carrie McDougall

154 *Minorities and the Making of Postcolonial States in International Law*
Mohammad Shahabuddin

153 *Preclassical Conflict of Laws*
Nikitas E. Hatzimihail

152 *International Law and History: Modern Interfaces*
Ignacio de la Rasilla

151 *Marketing Global Justice: The Political Economy of International Criminal Law*
Christine Schwöbel-Patel

150 *International Status in the Shadow of Empire*
Cait Storr

149 *Treaties in Motion: The Evolution of Treaties from Formation to Termination*
Edited by Malgosia Fitzmaurice and Panos Merkouris

148 *Humanitarian Disarmament: An Historical Enquiry*
Treasa Dunworth

147 *Complementarity, Catalysts, Compliance: The International Criminal Court in Uganda, Kenya, and the Democratic Republic of Congo*
Christian M. De Vos

146 *Cyber Operations and International Law*
François Delerue

145 *Comparative Reasoning in International Courts and Tribunals*
Daniel Peat

144 *Maritime Delimitation as a Judicial Process*
Massimo Lando

143 *Prosecuting Sexual and Gender-Based Crimes at the International Criminal Court: Practice, Progress and Potential*
Rosemary Grey

142 *Capitalism As Civilisation: A History of International Law*
Ntina Tzouvala

141 *Sovereignty in China: A Genealogy of a Concept Since 1840*
Adele Carrai

140 *Narratives of Hunger in International Law: Feeding the World in Times of Climate Change*
Anne Saab

139 *Victim Reparation under the Ius Post Bellum: An Historical and Normative Perspective*
Shavana Musa

138 *The Analogy between States and International Organizations*
Fernando Lusa Bordin

137 *The Process of International Legal Reproduction: Inequality, Historiography, Resistance*
Rose Parfitt

136 *State Responsibility for Breaches of Investment Contracts*
Jean Ho

135 *Coalitions of the Willing and International Law: The Interplay between Formality and Informality*
Alejandro Rodiles

134 *Self-Determination in Disputed Colonial Territories*
Jamie Trinidad

133 *International Law as a Belief System*
Jean d'Aspremont

132 *Legal Consequences of Peremptory Norms in International Law*
Daniel Costelloe

131 *Third-Party Countermeasures in International Law*
Martin Dawidowicz

130 *Justification and Excuse in International Law: Concept and Theory of General Defences*
Federica Paddeu

129 *Exclusion from Public Space: A Comparative Constitutional Analysis*
Daniel Moeckli

128 *Provisional Measures before International Courts and Tribunals*
Cameron A. Miles

127 *Humanity at Sea: Maritime Migration and the Foundations of International Law*
Itamar Mann

126 *Beyond Human Rights: The Legal Status of the Individual in International Law*
Anne Peters

125 *The Doctrine of Odious Debt in International Law: A Restatement*
Jeff King

124 *Static and Evolutive Treaty Interpretation: A Functional Reconstruction*
Christian Djeffal

123 *Civil Liability in Europe for Terrorism-Related Risk*
Lucas Bergkamp, Michael Faure, Monika Hinteregger and Niels Philipsen

122 *Proportionality and Deference in Investor-State Arbitration: Balancing Investment Protection and Regulatory Autonomy*
Caroline Henckels

121 *International Law and Governance of Natural Resources in Conflict and Post-Conflict Situations*
Daniëlla Dam-de Jong

120 *Proof of Causation in Tort Law*
Sandy Steel

119 *The Formation and Identification of Rules of Customary International Law in International Investment Law*
Patrick Dumberry

118 *Religious Hatred and International Law: The Prohibition of Incitement to Violence or Discrimination*
Jeroen Temperman

117 *Taking Economic, Social and Cultural Rights Seriously in International Criminal Law*
Evelyne Schmid

116 *Climate Change Litigation: Regulatory Pathways to Cleaner Energy*
Jacqueline Peel and Hari M. Osofsky

115 *Mestizo International Law: A Global Intellectual History 1842–1933*
Arnulf Becker Lorca

114 *Sugar and the Making of International Trade Law*
Michael Fakhri

113 *Strategically Created Treaty Conflicts and the Politics of International Law*
Surabhi Ranganathan

112 *Investment Treaty Arbitration As Public International Law: Procedural Aspects and Implications*
Eric De Brabandere

111 *The New Entrants Problem in International Fisheries Law*
Andrew Serdy

110 *Substantive Protection under Investment Treaties: A Legal and Economic Analysis*
Jonathan Bonnitcha

109 *Popular Governance of Post-Conflict Reconstruction: The Role of International Law*
Matthew Saul

108 *Evolution of International Environmental Regimes: The Case of Climate Change*
Simone Schiele

107 *Judges, Law and War: The Judicial Development of International Humanitarian Law*
Shane Darcy

106 *Religious Offence and Human Rights: The Implications of Defamation of Religions*
Lorenz Langer

105 *Forum Shopping in International Adjudication: The Role of Preliminary Objections*
Luiz Eduardo Salles

104 *Domestic Politics and International Human Rights Tribunals: The Problem of Compliance*
Courtney Hillebrecht

103 *International Law and the Arctic*
Michael Byers

102 *Cooperation in the Law of Transboundary Water Resources*
Christina Leb

101 *Underwater Cultural Heritage and International Law*
Sarah Dromgoole

100 *State Responsibility: The General Part*
James Crawford

99 *The Origins of International Investment Law: Empire, Environment and the Safeguarding of Capital*
Kate Miles

98 *The Crime of Aggression under the Rome Statute of the International Criminal Court*
Carrie McDougall

97 *'Crimes against Peace' and International Law*
Kirsten Sellars

96 *Non-Legality in International Law: Unruly Law*
Fleur Johns

95 *Armed Conflict and Displacement: The Protection of Refugees and Displaced Persons under International Humanitarian Law*
Mélanie Jacques

94 *Foreign Investment and the Environment in International Law*
Jorge E. Viñuales

93 *The Human Rights Treaty Obligations of Peacekeepers*
Kjetil Mujezinović Larsen

92 *Cyber Warfare and the Laws of War*
Heather Harrison Dinniss

91 *The Right to Reparation in International Law for Victims of Armed Conflict*
Christine Evans

90 *Global Public Interest in International Investment Law*
Andreas Kulick

89 *State Immunity in International Law*
Xiaodong Yang

88 *Reparations and Victim Support in the International Criminal Court*
Conor McCarthy

87 *Reducing Genocide to Law: Definition, Meaning, and the Ultimate Crime*
Payam Akhavan

86 *Decolonising International Law: Development, Economic Growth and the Politics of Universality*
Sundhya Pahuja

85 *Complicity and the Law of State Responsibility*
Helmut Philipp Aust

84 *State Control over Private Military and Security Companies in Armed Conflict*
Hannah Tonkin

83 *'Fair and Equitable Treatment' in International Investment Law*
Roland Kläger

82 *The UN and Human Rights: Who Guards the Guardians?*
Guglielmo Verdirame

81 *Sovereign Defaults before International Courts and Tribunals*
Michael Waibel

80 *Making the Law of the Sea: A Study in the Development of International Law*
James Harrison

79 *Science and the Precautionary Principle in International Courts and Tribunals: Expert Evidence, Burden of Proof and Finality*
Caroline E. Foster

78 *Transition from Illegal Regimes under International Law*
Yaël Ronen

77 *Access to Asylum: International Refugee Law and the Globalisation of Migration Control*
Thomas Gammeltoft-Hansen

76 *Trading Fish, Saving Fish: The Interaction between Regimes in International Law*
Margaret A. Young

75 *The Individual in the International Legal System: Continuity and Change in International Law*
Kate Parlett

74 *'Armed Attack' and Article 51 of the UN Charter: Evolutions in Customary Law and Practice*
Tom Ruys

73 *Theatre of the Rule of Law: Transnational Legal Intervention in Theory and Practice*
Stephen Humphreys

72 *Science and Risk Regulation in International Law*
Jacqueline Peel

71 *The Participation of States in International Organisations: The Role of Human Rights and Democracy*
Alison Duxbury

70 *Legal Personality in International Law*
Roland Portmann

69 *Vicarious Liability in Tort: A Comparative Perspective*
Paula Giliker

68 *The Public International Law Theory of Hans Kelsen: Believing in Universal Law*
Jochen von Bernstorff

67 *Legitimacy and Legality in International Law: An Interactional Account*
Jutta Brunnée and Stephen J. Toope

66 *The Concept of Non-International Armed Conflict in International Humanitarian Law*
Anthony Cullen

65 *The Principle of Legality in International and Comparative Criminal Law*
Kenneth S. Gallant

64 *The Challenge of Child Labour in International Law*
Franziska Humbert

63 *Shipping Interdiction and the Law of the Sea*
Douglas Guilfoyle

62 *International Courts and Environmental Protection*
Tim Stephens

61 *Legal Principles in WTO Disputes*
Andrew D. Mitchell

60 *War Crimes in Internal Armed Conflicts*
Eve La Haye

59 *Humanitarian Occupation*
Gregory H. Fox

58 *The International Law of Environmental Impact Assessment: Process, Substance and Integration*
Neil Craik

57 *The Law and Practice of International Territorial Administration: Versailles to Iraq and Beyond*
Carsten Stahn

56 *United Nations Sanctions and the Rule of Law*
Jeremy Matam Farrall

55 *National Law in WTO Law: Effectiveness and Good Governance in the World Trading System*
Sharif Bhuiyan

54 *Cultural Products and the World Trade Organization*
Tania Voon

53 *The Threat of Force in International Law*
Nikolas Stürchler

52 *Indigenous Rights and United Nations Standards: Self-Determination, Culture and Land*
Alexandra Xanthaki

51 *International Refugee Law and Socio-Economic Rights: Refuge from Deprivation*
Michelle Foster

50 *The Protection of Cultural Property in Armed Conflict*
Roger O'Keefe

49 *Interpretation and Revision of International Boundary Decisions*
Kaiyan Homi Kaikobad

48 *Multinationals and Corporate Social Responsibility: Limitations and Opportunities in International Law*
Jennifer A. Zerk

47 *Judiciaries within Europe: A Comparative Review*
John Bell

46 *Law in Times of Crisis: Emergency Powers in Theory and Practice*
Oren Gross and Fionnuala Ní Aoláin

45 *Vessel-Source Marine Pollution: The Law and Politics of International Regulation*
Alan Khee-Jin Tan

44 *Enforcing Obligations Erga Omnes in International Law*
Christian J. Tams

43 *Non-Governmental Organisations in International Law*
Anna-Karin Lindblom

42 *Democracy, Minorities and International Law*
Steven Wheatley

41 *Prosecuting International Crimes: Selectivity and the International Criminal Law Regime*
Robert Cryer

40 *Compensation for Personal Injury in English, German and Italian Law: A Comparative Outline*
Basil Markesinis, Michael Coester, Guido Alpa and Augustus Ullstein

39 *Dispute Settlement in the UN Convention on the Law of the Sea*
Natalie Klein

38 *The International Protection of Internally Displaced Persons*
Catherine Phuong

37 *Imperialism, Sovereignty and the Making of International Law*
Antony Anghie

36 *Principles of the Institutional Law of International Organizations*
C. F. Amerasinghe

35 *Necessity, Proportionality and the Use of Force by States*
Judith Gardam

34 *International Legal Argument in the Permanent Court of International Justice: The Rise of the International Judiciary*
Ole Spiermann

33 –

32 *Great Powers and Outlaw States: Unequal Sovereigns in the International Legal Order*
Gerry Simpson

31 *Local Remedies in International Law (second edition)*
Chittharanjan Felix Amerasinghe

30 *Reading Humanitarian Intervention: Human Rights and the Use of Force in International Law*
Anne Orford

29 *Conflict of Norms in Public International Law: How WTO Law Relates to Other Rules of International Law*
Joost Pauwelyn

28 –

27 *Transboundary Damage in International Law*
Hanqin Xue

26 –

25 *European Criminal Procedures*
Edited by Mireille Delmas-Marty and J. R. Spencer

24 *Accountability of Armed Opposition Groups in International Law*
Liesbeth Zegveld

23 *Sharing Transboundary Resources: International Law and Optimal Resource Use*
Eyal Benvenisti

22 *International Human Rights and Humanitarian Law*
René Provost

21 *Remedies against International Organisations*
Karel Wellens

20 *Diversity and Self-Determination in International Law*
Karen Knop

19 *The Law of Internal Armed Conflict*
Lindsay Moir

18 *International Commercial Arbitration and African States: Practice, Participation and Institutional Development*
Amazu A. Asouzu

17 *The Enforceability of Promises in European Contract Law*
James Gordley

16 *International Law in Antiquity*
David J. Bederman

15 *Money Laundering: A New International Law Enforcement Model*
Guy Stessens

14 *Good Faith in European Contract Law*
Reinhard Zimmermann and Simon Whittaker

13 *On Civil Procedure*
J. A. Jolowicz

12 *Trusts: A Comparative Study*
Maurizio Lupoi and Simon Dix

11 *The Right to Property in Commonwealth Constitutions*
Tom Allen

10 *International Organizations before National Courts*
August Reinisch

9 *The Changing International Law of High Seas Fisheries*
Francisco Orrego Vicuña

8 *Trade and the Environment: A Comparative Study of EC and US Law*
Damien Geradin

7 *Unjust Enrichment: A Study of Private Law and Public Values*
Hanoch Dagan

6 *Religious Liberty and International Law in Europe*
Malcolm D. Evans

5 *Ethics and Authority in International Law*
Alfred P. Rubin

4 *Sovereignty over Natural Resources: Balancing Rights and Duties*
Nico Schrijver

3 *The Polar Regions and the Development of International Law*
Donald R. Rothwell

2 *Fragmentation and the International Relations of Micro-States: Self-Determination and Statehood*
Jorri C. Duursma

1 *Principles of the Institutional Law of International Organizations*
C. F. Amerasinghe

For EU product safety concerns, contact us at Calle de José Abascal, 56–1°,
28003 Madrid, Spain or eugpsr@cambridge.org.

www.ingramcontent.com/pod-product-compliance
Lightning Source LLC
LaVergne TN
LVHW011658200926
848484LV00004B/984